European Constitutional Law

The European Union has existed for over half a century. Having started as the 'Europe of the Six' in a specific industrial sector, the Union today has twenty-seven Member States and acts within almost all areas of social life. The Union's constitutional structures have evolved in parallel with this immense growth. Born as an international organisation, the Union has developed into a constitutional Union of States. This new textbook analyses the constitutional law of the European Union after Lisbon in a clear and structured way. Examining the EU in a classic constitutional perspective, it explores the central themes of the subject: the history and structure of the Union, the powers and procedures of its branches of government, and the rights and remedies of European citizens. A clear three-part structure and numerous illustrations will facilitate understanding. Critical and comprehensive, this is required reading for all students of European constitutional law.

Robert Schütze is a Reader in Law at Durham University.

European Constitutional Law

ROBERT SCHÜTZE

CAMBRIDGE
UNIVERSITY PRESS

CAMBRIDGE UNIVERSITY PRESS
Cambridge, New York, Melbourne, Madrid, Cape Town,
Singapore, São Paulo, Delhi, Mexico City

Cambridge University Press
The Edinburgh Building, Cambridge CB2 8RU, UK

Published in the United States of America by Cambridge University Press, New York

www.cambridge.org
Information on this title: www.cambridge.org/9780521504904

First published 2012

Printed in the United Kingdom at the University Press, Cambridge

A catalogue record for this publication is available from the British Library

Library of Congress Cataloging in Publication data
Schütze, Robert.
European constitutional law / Robert Schütze.
   p.   cm.
ISBN 978-0-521-50490-4 (hardback)
1. Constitutional law – European Union countries.   I. Title.
KJE4445.S348   2012
342.24–dc23

                                                              2011039144

ISBN 978-0-521-50490-4 Hardback
ISBN 978-0-521-73275-8 Paperback

In Memory of Pierre Pescatore (1919–2010)

Summary Contents

Introduction: European Constitutional Law   *page* 1

Part I: History and Structure

1. Constitutional History: From Paris to Lisbon   9
2. Constitutional Nature: A Federation of States   47
3. Governmental Structure: Union Institutions I   80
4. Governmental Structure: Union Institutions II   116

Part II: Powers and Procedures

5. Legislative Powers: Competences and Procedures   151
6. External Powers: Competences and Procedures   187
7. Executive Powers: Competences and Procedures   223
8. Judicial Powers: Competences and Procedures   258

Part III: Rights and Remedies

9. European Law: Direct and Indirect Effect   305
10. European Law: Supremacy and Preemption   347
11. European Law: Remedies and Liabilities   380
12. In Particular: European Human Rights   409

Contents

List of Illustrations   xviii
List of Tables   xix
Preface   xxi
Acknowledgements   xxii
Table of Cases   xxiii
Table of Equivalences   xxxvi
List of Abbreviations   lii

Introduction: European Constitutional Law   1

Part I: History and Structure

1 Constitutional History: From Paris to Lisbon   9
   Introduction   9
   1. From Paris to Rome: the European Coal and Steel Community   12
      (a) The (supranational) structure of the ECSC   13
      (b) The (failed) European Defence Community   16
   2. From Rome to Maastricht: the European (Economic) Community   18
      (a) Normative supranationalism: the nature of European law   19
      (b) Decisional supranationalism: the governmental structure   20
      (c) Intergovernmental developments outside the EEC   23
      (d) Supranational and intergovernmental reforms through the
            Single European Act   26
   3. From Maastricht to Nice: the (old) European Union   27
      (a) The Temple Structure: the Three Pillars of the
            (Maastricht) Union   29
          (i)   The First Pillar: the European Communities   29
          (ii)   The Second Pillar: Common Foreign and Security Policy   32
          (iii) The Third Pillar: Justice and Home Affairs   33
      (b) A decade of 'constitutional bricolage': Amsterdam and Nice   33
          (i)   The Amsterdam Treaty: dividing the Third Pillar   33
          (ii)   The Nice Treaty: limited institutional reform   35

4. From Nice to Lisbon: the (new) European Union   37
    (a) The (failed) Constitutional Treaty: formal 'total revision'   38
    (b) The Lisbon Treaty: substantive 'total revision'   41
    Conclusion   45

2 Constitutional Nature: A Federation of States   47
    Introduction   47
1. The American constitutional tradition: federalism as
    (inter)national law   49
2. The European constitutional tradition: international versus
    national law   53
    (a) Conceptual polarisation: 'Confederation' versus 'Federation'   54
    (b) Early criticism: the European tradition and the (missing)
         federal genus   56
3. The European Union in light of the American constitutional
    tradition   59
    (a) The foundational dimension: Europe's 'Constitutional
         Treaty'   60
    (b) The institutional dimension: a European Union of States and
         people(s)   62
    (c) The functional dimension: the division of powers in Europe   64
    (d) Overall classification: the European Union on federal
         'middle ground'   65
4. The European Union in light of the European constitutional
    tradition   66
    (a) The *sui generis* 'theory': the 'incomparable' European Union   67
    (b) The international law theory: the 'Maastricht Decision'   68
    (c) Europe's statist tradition unearthed: three constitutional
         denials   71
    (d) *Excursus*: Europe's democratic 'deficit' as a 'false problem'?   74
    Conclusion   77

3 Governmental Structure: Union Institutions I   80
    Introduction   81
1. The 'separation-of-powers' principle and the European Union   83
2. The European Parliament   87
    (a) Formation: electing Parliament   87
         (i)   Parliament's size and composition   88
         (ii) Members of the European Parliament and
               political parties   91
    (b) Internal structure: parliamentary organs   93
    (c) The plenary: decision-making and voting   94

	(d)	Parliamentary powers	96
		(i) Legislative powers	96
		(ii) Budgetary powers	97
		(iii) Supervisory powers	98
		(iv) Elective powers	99
3.	The European Council	100
	(a)	The President of the European Council	102
	(b)	The European Council: functions and powers	103
4.	The Council	104
	(a)	The Council: composition and configuration	105
	(b)	Internal structure and organs	106
		(i) The Presidency of the Council	106
		(ii) 'Coreper' and specialised committees	107
		(iii) *Excursus*: the High Representative of Foreign Affairs	
		and Security Policy	110
	(c)	Decision-making and voting	111
	(d)	Functions and powers	114

4 Governmental Structure: Union Institutions II   **116**

1.	The Commission	116
	(a)	Composition and structure	117
		(i) The President and 'his' college	118
		(ii) The Commission's administrative organs	119
	(b)	Decision-making within the Commission	122
	(c)	Functions and powers of the Commission	123
	(d)	*Excursus*: European Agencies and the Commission	125
2.	The Court of Justice of the European Union	128
	(a)	Judicial architecture: the European court system	129
		(i) The Court of Justice: composition and structure	130
		(ii) The General Court: composition and structure	131
		(iii) *Excursus*: the Advocates General	132
		(iv) The 'specialised court(s)': the Civil Service Tribunal	134
	(b)	The judicial procedure(s)	135
	(c)	Judicial reasoning: methods of interpretation	136
	(d)	Jurisdiction and judicial powers	138
3.	The European Central Bank	139
	(a)	The special status of the ECB	140
	(b)	Organs and administrative structure	142
	(c)	Internal divisions and decision-making	143
	(d)	Functions and powers	144
4.	The Court of Auditors	145
	Conclusion	147

Part II: Powers and Procedures

5   Legislative Powers: Competences and Procedures   151

Introduction   151

1.   The scope of Union competences   152

   (a)   Teleological interpretation   153

   (b)   The general competences of the Union   157

      (i)   The harmonisation competence: Article 114 TFEU   157

      (ii)   The residual competence: Article 352 TFEU   160

2.   The categories of Union competences   162

   (a)   Exclusive competences: Article 3 TFEU   164

   (b)   Shared competences: Article 4 TFEU   166

   (c)   Coordinating competences: Article 5 TFEU   167

   (d)   Complementary competences: Article 6 TFEU   168

3.   Legislative procedures: ordinary and special   169

   (a)   The 'ordinary' legislative procedure   171

      (i)   Constitutional theory: formal text   171

      (ii)   Constitutional practice: informal trilogues   174

   (b)   The 'special' legislative procedures   176

4.   The principle of subsidiarity   177

   (a)   Procedural standard: subsidiarity as a political safeguard
of federalism   178

   (b)   Substantive standard: subsidiarity as a judicial safeguard
of federalism   181

Conclusion   184

6   External Powers: Competences and Procedures   187

Introduction   188

1.   The external competences of the Union   190

   (a)   The Common Foreign and Security Policy   192

   (b)   The Union's special external powers   192

   (c)   The residual treaty power: Article 216 TFEU   194

   (d)   The relationship between the CFSP and the special
external competences   197

2.   The nature of external competences   199

   (a)   The *sui generis* nature of the CFSP competence   200

   (b)   Article 3 (2) TFEU: subsequent exclusive treaty powers   201

      (i)   Three lines of exclusivity: codifying constitutional
practice?   201

      (ii)   Subsequent exclusivity: criticising constitutional
theory   203

3.   External decision-making procedures   204
     (a)   The 'specificity' of CFSP decision-making procedures   205
           (i)   Institutional actors and institutional balance   205
           (ii)   Voting arrangements in the Council   206
     (b)   The Union's (ordinary) treaty-making procedure   207
           (i)   Initiation and negotiation   208
           (ii)   Signing and conclusion   210
           (iii) Modification, suspension (and termination)   211
           (iv)   Union succession to international agreements of the
                  Member States   212
4.   Sharing external power: constitutional safeguards of unitarianism   213
     (a)   Mixed agreements: an international and political safeguard   214
     (b)   The duty of cooperation: an internal and judicial safeguard   216
           (i)   Member States as 'trustees of the Union'   217
           (ii)   'Reversed' subsidiarity: restrictions on the exercise of
                  shared State power   218
     Conclusion   220

7   Executive Powers: Competences and Procedures   223
     Introduction   223
1.   Governmental powers: the Union's dual executive   225
     (a)   The legal instruments of political leadership   226
     (b)   The informal procedure(s) of government   228
2.   Law-making powers: delegated and implementing acts   230
     (a)   The delegation of 'legislative' power: Article 290 TFEU   231
           (i)   Judicial safeguards: constitutional limits to
                  delegated acts   233
           (ii)   Political safeguards: control rights of the Union
                  legislator   236
     (b)   The 'conferral' of executive power: Article 291 TFEU   238
           (i)   The scope of Article 291 TFEU   238
           (ii)   Constitutional safeguards for implementing
                  legislation   240
3.   Administrative powers I: centralised enforcement   243
     (a)   The scope of the Union's administrative powers   244
     (b)   Administrative powers and the subsidiarity principle   248
4.   Administrative powers II: decentralised enforcement   250
     (a)   The effects of national administrative acts   251
     (b)   National administrative autonomy and its limits   253
     Conclusion   256

8 Judicial Powers: Competences and Procedures   258

    Introduction   259

    1. Annulment powers: judicial review   262

       (a) The existence of a 'reviewable' act   263

       (b) Legitimate grounds for review   264

           (i) 'Formal' and 'substantive' grounds   265

           (ii) In particular: the proportionality principle   267

       (c) Legal standing before the European Court   268

           (i) The Rome formulation and its judicial interpretation   270

           (ii) The Lisbon formulation and its interpretative
problems   273

       (d) The indirect review of European law   275

           (i) Collateral review: the plea of illegality   275

           (ii) Indirect review through preliminary rulings   276

    2. Remedial powers: liability actions   278

       (a) Procedural conditions: from dependent to independent
action   279

       (b) Substantive conditions: from *Schöppenstedt* to *Bergaderm*   280

    3. Adjudicatory powers I: enforcement actions   283

       (a) Enforcement actions against Member States   283

           (i) The procedural conditions under Article 258 TFEU   283

           (ii) Judicial enforcement through financial sanctions   286

       (b) Enforcement actions against the Union: failure to act   287

    4. Adjudicatory powers II: preliminary rulings   289

       (a) Paragraph 1: the jurisdiction of the European Court   291

       (b) Paragraph 2: the conditions for a preliminary ruling   292

           (i) 'Who': national courts and tribunals   293

           (ii) 'What': necessary questions   295

       (c) Paragraph 3: the obligation to refer and '*acte clair*'   296

       (d) The legal nature of preliminary rulings   299

    Conclusion   301

Part III: Rights and Remedies

9 European Law: Direct and Indirect Effect   305

    Introduction   306

    1. Constitutional law: the effect of European primary law   310

       (a) Direct effect: from strict to lenient test   312

       (b) The dimensions of direct effect: vertical and horizontal
direct effect   315

2. Direct Union law: regulations and decisions   317
    (a) Regulations: the 'legislative' instrument   317
         (i)   General application in all Member States   317
         (ii) Direct application and direct effect   318
    (b) Decisions: the executive instrument   320
         (i)   Specifically addressed decisions   321
         (ii) Non-addressed decisions   322
3. Indirect Union law: directives   323
    (a) Direct effect and directives: conditions and limits   323
         (i)   The no-horizontal-direct-effect rule   326
         (ii) The limitation to the rule: the wide definition of
               State (actions)   327
         (iii) The exception to the rule: incidental horizontal
               direct effect   329
    (b) Indirect effects through national and (primary) European law 331
         (i)   The doctrine of consistent interpretation of national law 331
         (ii) Indirect effects through the medium of European law 334
4. External Union law: international agreements   337
    (a) Direct effects of Union agreements   338
         (i)   The conditions for direct effect   339
         (ii) The dimensions of direct effect   341
    (b) Indirect effects: the interpretation and implementation
         principles   342
    Conclusion   344

10 **European Law: Supremacy and Preemption**   347
    Introduction   347
1. The European perspective: absolute supremacy   349
    (a) The absolute scope of the supremacy principle   350
         (i)   Supremacy over internal laws of the Member States   350
         (ii) Supremacy over international treaties of the
               Member States   352
    (b) The 'executive' nature of supremacy: disapplication, not
         invalidation   355
2. The national perspective: relative supremacy   358
    (a) Fundamental rights limits: the 'so-long' jurisprudence   359
    (b) Competences limits: from '*Maastricht*' to '*Mangold*'   361
3. Legislative preemption: nature and effect   363
    (a) Preemption categories: the relative effects of preemption 364
         (i)   Field preemption   365
         (ii) Obstacle preemption   366
         (iii) Rule preemption   366
    (b) Modes of preemption: express and implied preemption   367

4.   Constitutional limits to legislative preemption   368
     (a) Union instruments and their preemptive capacity   369
          (i)   The preemptive capacity of regulations   369
          (ii) The preemptive capacity of directives   371
          (iii) The preemptive capacity of international agreements 372
     (b) Competence limits to preemption   374
          (i)   Competences for minimum harmonisation   375
          (ii) Complementary competences excluding
                harmonisation   376
     Conclusion   378

11 European Law: Remedies and Liabilities   380
     Introduction   380
1.   The (consistent) interpretation principle   383
2.   The equivalence principle   384
     (a) Non-discrimination: extending national remedies to European
          actions   385
     (b) 'Similar' actions: the equivalence test   386
3.   The effectiveness principle   387
     (a) The historical evolution of the effectiveness standard   388
     (b) Procedural limits to the invocability of European law   393
4.   The liability principle   396
     (a) State liability: the *Francovich* doctrine   397
          (i)   The three conditions for State liability   399
          (ii) State liability for judicial breaches of European law 402
     (b) Private liability: the *Courage* doctrine   405
     Conclusion   407

12 In Particular: European Human Rights   409
     Introduction   410
1.   The 'unwritten' bill of rights: human rights as 'general principles' 411
     (a) The birth of European fundamental rights   412
          (i)   The European standard – an 'autonomous' standard   414
          (ii) Limitations, and 'limitations on limitations'   418
     (b) United Nations law: external limits to European
          human rights?   419
2.   The 'written' bill of rights: the Charter of Fundamental Rights 422
     (a) The Charter: structure and content   423
          (i)   (Hard) rights and (soft) principles   425
          (ii) Limitations, and 'limitations on limitations'   426
     (b) Relations with the European Treaties (and the European
          Convention)   427

3.   The 'external' bill of rights: the European Convention of
     Human Rights   429
     (a)   The Convention standard for Union acts   430
           (i)   Before accession: (limited) indirect review of Union acts   431
           (ii)   After accession: (full) direct review of Union acts   433
     (b)   Union accession to the European Convention: constitutional
           preconditions   434
4.   The 'incorporation doctrine': European rights and national law   435
     (a)   Incorporation and general principles: implementation and
           derogation   436
     (b)   Incorporation and the Charter of Fundamental Rights   439
           (i)   General rules for all Member States   439
           (ii)   Special rules for Poland and the United Kingdom   441
     (c)   Incorporation and the European Convention of
           Human Rights?   443
     (d)   *Excursus*: incorporation and individuals – human rights and
           private actions   444
     Conclusion   445

Appendices

1.   European Treaties (Chronology)   448
2.   Territorial Evolution of the European Union   450
3.   Extracts from the 'Luxembourg Compromise'   453
4.   Extracts from James Madison's 'Federalist No. 39'   457
5.   Extracts from the 1976 'European Parliament Direct Election Act'   460
6.   Extracts from Decision 2009/908 on the Council Presidency   464
7.   Directorate-General Home Affairs (Organigramme)   466
8.   Extracts from the 'Comitology' Regulation   467

Index   473

Illustrations

1.	Structure of the Book	5
2.	Historical Evolution of the Union	11
3.	Pillar Structure of the 'old' (Maastricht) Union	30
4.	Dual Treaty basis before and after Lisbon	42
5.	Distribution of Seats in the European Parliament (Political Parties)	92
6.	Preparatory Committees to the Council	109
7.	Internal Commission Structure	121
8.	Structure of the Court of Justice of the European Union	130
9.	Structure of the European Central Bank	142
9a.	General and Special Competences	158
9b.	Competence Types	164
10.	Structure of the Union Legislator	170
11.	Ordinary Legislative Procedure under Article 294 TFEU	172
12.	Declining Democratic Representation	175
13.	Structure of the Social Policy Competence	185
14.	Relationship among Union External Competences	199
15.	Dual Executive of the Union	226
16.	'Comitology' as defined by Regulation 182/2011	243
17.	Judicial Federalism in Comparative Perspective	290
18.	Preliminary Rulings under Article 267 TFEU	295
19.	Monism and Dualism	307
20.	Direct Applicability, Direct Effect and Private Party Actions	316
21.	Preemption Types: Field, Obstacle, Rule Preemption	365
22.	Limits on National Procedural Autonomy	383
23.	Standards of Effectiveness	388
24.	Inspiration Theory versus Incorporation Theory	417
25.	Principles and Rights within the Charter	426
26.	Relationship between the Union's three 'Bills of Rights'	445
27.	Territory of the European Union	452
28.	Directorate-General Home Affairs (Organigramme)	466

Tables

1. Structure of the TEU and TFEU   43
2. Treaty provisions on the institutions   82
3. Union institutions correlating to governmental functions   86
4. Distribution of seats in the European Parliament (Member States)   89
5. Standing Committees of the European Parliament   94
6. Council Configurations   105
7. Weighted Votes System within the Council   112
8. Commission College: President and Portfolios   120
9. (Selected) European Agencies and Decentralised Bodies   126
10. Union Policies and Internal Actions   154
11. Union External Policies   191
12. Judicial Competences and Procedures   261
13. Structure of the Charter of Fundamental Rights   424
14. European Treaties (Chronology)   448
15. Member States of the European Union (Evolution)   451

Preface

The European Union has existed for over half a century. Having started in 1952 as 'the Europe of the Six' in a specific industrial sector, the Union today has twenty-seven Member States and acts within almost all areas of social life. The Union's constitutional structures have evolved in parallel with its vivid growth. Born as an international organisation, the Union has developed into a mature federation of States. The European Union thereby underwent its greatest 'transformation' in the first decade of the twenty-first century. This fundamental reform started in 2001 with the Laeken Declaration on the Future of the European Union and would – despite the failure of the 2004 'Treaty establishing a Constitution for Europe' – find its way into the 2007 Reform (Lisbon) Treaty. And the Union after Lisbon is not the Union that it was before. This book presents the structures and powers of this 'renewed' Union in 'renewed' constitutional terms. It is the fruit of my lectures and writings during the – tumultuous – last decade. Thanks go to many a colleague and friend, and especially to Antonis Antoniadis, Amandine Garde, Konrad Lachmayer, as well as Dieter and Isolde Schütze. On the editorial side, I profoundly thank Sinéad Moloney of Cambridge University Press for her boundless patience and professionalism. The book is dedicated to Pierre Pescatore – the greatest twentieth century 'painter' of the European Union.

Acknowledgements

Grateful acknowledgements are made to Hart Publishing, Kluwer Law International, Oxford University Press, Sweet & Maxwell, as well as Wiley for their kind permission to incorporate sections from previously published material. In particular, Chapter 2 represents a shortened and amended version of a chapter published in *From Dual to Cooperative Federalism: The Changing Structure of European Law* (Oxford University Press, 2009). Thanks also go to Cambridge University Press for allowing me to reproduce parts of the *Federalist No. 39* from the series on 'Texts in the History of Political Thought'. For illustrations 2 and 5, 27 and 28 acknowledgements go – respectively – to Wikipedia and the European Union's website(s).

Table of Cases

Contents

1. Court of Justice of the European Union   xxiii
   - (a) European Court of Justice: Cases (numerical)   xxiii
   - (b) European Court of Justice: Opinions (numerical)   xxxiv
   - (c) General Court: Cases (numerical)   xxxiv
2. Other jurisdictions   xxxv
   - (a) European Court of Human Rights: Cases (chronological)   xxxv
   - (b) German Constitutional Court: Cases (chronological)   xxxv
   - (c) United States Supreme Court: Cases (chronological)   xxxv

1. Court of Justice of the European Union

(a) European Court of Justice: Cases (numerical)

Case 8/55, *Fédération Charbonnière de Belgique* v. *High Authority of the European Coal and Steel Community*, [1955] ECR 245   155, 267

Case 9/56, *Meroni & Co, Industrie Metallurgische, SpA* v. *High Authority of the European Coal and Steel Community*, [1958] ECR 133   234, 235

Case 1/58, *Stork & Cie* v. *High Authority of the European Coal and Steel Community*, [1958] ECR 17   412

Case 20/59, *Italy* v. *High Authority*, [1960] ECR 325   283

Case 30/59, *De Gezamenlijke Steenkolenmijnen in Limburg* v. *High Authority of the European Coal and Steel Community*, [1961] ECR 1   163

Joined Cases 36, 37, 38/59 and 40/59, *Geitling Ruhrkohlen-Verkaufsgesellschaft mbH, Mausegatt Ruhrkohlen-Verkaufsgesellschaft mbH and I. Nold KG* v. *High Authority of the European Coal and Steel Community*, [1959] ECR 423   413

Case 6/60, *Humblet* v. *Belgium*, [1960] ECR 559   397

Case 10/61, *Commission* v. *Italy*, [1962] ECR 1   353

Joined Cases 16–17/62, *Confédération Nationale des Producteurs de Fruits et Légumes and others* v. *Council*, [1962] ECR 471   270, 317, 318

Case 25/62, *Plaumann v. Commission*, [1963] ECR 95   272, 279

Case 26/62, *Van Gend en Loos v. Netherlands Inland Revenue Administration*, [1963] ECR (Special English Edition) 1   19, 133, 296, 307, 308, 310, 312, 315

Joined Cases 28–30/62, *Da Costa et al. v. Netherlands Inland Revenue Administration*, [1963] ECR 31   292, 296, 299

Joined Cases 31/62 and 33/62, *Lütticke et al. v. Commission*, [1962] ECR 501   279

Case 75/63, *Hoekstra (née Unger)*, [1964] ECR 177   291

Joined Cases 90–91/63, *Commission v. Luxemburg and Belgium*, [1964] ECR 625   60, 287

Case 6/64, *Costa v. ENEL*, [1964] ECR 585   20, 60, 59, 162, 291, 295, 297, 350

Joined Cases 18 and 35/65, *Gutmann v. Commission*, [1965] ECR 103   266

Case 34/67, *Firma Gebrüder Luck v. Hauptzollamt Köln-Rheinau*, [1968] ECR 245   355, 357

Case 6/68, *Zuckerfabrik Watenstedt GmbH v. Council*, [1968] ECR 409   317

Case 13/68, *Salgoil v. Italian Ministry of Foreign Trade*, [1968] ECR 453   314

Case 9/69, *Sayag et al. v. Leduc et al.*, [1969] ECR 329   280

Case 29/69, *Stauder v. City of Ulm*, [1969] ECR 419   413, 415

Case 40/69, *Hauptzollamt Hamburg Oberelbe v. Bollmann*, [1970] ECR 69   370

Case 64/69, *Compagnie Française commerciale et financière v. Commission*, [1970] ECR 221   318

Case 74/69, *Hauptzollamt Bremen-Freihafen v. Waren-Import-Gesellschaft Krohn & Co.*, [1970] ECR 451   253

Case 9/70, *Grad v. Finanzamt Traunstein*, [1970] ECR 825   321

Case 11/70, *Internationale Handelsgesellschaft mbH v. Einfuhr- und Vorratsstelle für Getreide und Futtermittel*, [1970] ECR 1125   61, 352, 359, 413

Case 15/70, *Chevallery v. Commission*, [1970] ECR 975   288

Case 22/70, *Commission v. Council (ERTA)*, [1971] ECR 263   195, 202, 264, 266

Case 25/70, *Einfuhr- und Vorratsstelle für Getreide und Futtermittel v. Köster et Berodt & Co*, [1970] ECR 1161   233, 241

Case 39/70, *Norddeutsches Vieh- und Fleischkontor GmbH v. Hauptzollamt Hamburg-St. Annen*, [1971] ECR 49   253, 381

Joined Cases 41–44/70, *International Fruit Company and others v. Commission*, [1971] ECR 411   270, 318

Case 5/71, *Schöppenstedt v. Council*, [1971] ECR 975   279, 281, 282

Case 48/71, *Commission v. Italy*, [1978] ECR 629   355

Joined Cases 51 to 54/71, *International Fruit Company NV and others v. Produktschap voor groenten en fruit*, [1971] ECR 1107   253

Case 18/72, *Granaria v. Produktschap voor Veevoeder*, [1972] ECR 1163   370

Joined Cases 21–24/72, *International Fruit Company NV v. Produktschap voor Groenten en Fruit*, [1972] ECR 1219   213, 339, 340

Case 30/72, *Commission v. Italy*, [1973] ECR 161   285

Case 39/72, *Commission v. Italy*, [1973] ECR 101   371

Cases 63–69/72, *Werhahn Hansamühle and others v. Council*, [1973] ECR 1229   280

Case 4/73, *Nold* v. *Commission*, [1974] ECR 491   413, 415–6, 418–9

Case 34/73, *Fratelli Variola Spa* v. *Amministrazione delle finanze dello Stato*, [1973] ECR 981   318

Case 166/73, *Rheinmühlen-Düsseldorf*, [1974] ECR 33   294

Case 167/73, *Commission* v. *France*, [1974] ECR 359   357

Case 169/73, *Compagnie Continentale France* v. *Council*, [1975] ECR 117   280

Case 181/73, *Haegemann* v. *Belgium*, [1974] ECR 449   338

Case 2/74, *Reyners* v. *Belgian State*, [1974] ECR 631   313

Case 9/74, *Casagrande* v. *Landeshauptstadt München*, [1974] ECR 773   156

Case 36/74, *Walrave et al.* v. *Association Union cycliste internationale et al.*, [1974] ECR 1405   316

Case 41/74, *van Duyn* v. *Home Office*, [1974] ECR 1337   314, 323, 324

Case 100/74, *CAM* v. *Commission*, [1975] ECR 1393   272

Case 23/75, *Rey Soda* v. *Cassa Conguaglio Zucchero*, [1975] ECR 1279   233

Case 36/75, *Rutili* v. *Ministre de l'intérieur*, [1975] ECR 1219   414, 436

Case 43/75, *Defrenne* v. *Sabena*, [1976] ECR 455   301, 313, 316, 444

Case 60/75, *Russo* v. *Azienda di Stato per gli interventi sul mercato agricolo*, [1976] ECR 45   397

Joined Cases 15 and 16/76, *France* v. *Commission*, [1979] ECR 32   286

Case 26/76, *Metro-SB-Großmärkte* v. *Commission*, [1977] ECR 1875   272

Case 27/76R, *United Brands* v. *Commission*, [1976] ECR 425   136

Case 27/76, *United Brands* v. *Commission*, [1978] ECR 207   136

Case 33/76, *Rewe-Zentralfinanz eG and Rewe-Zentral AG* v. *Landwirtschafts-kammer für das Saarlan*, [1976] ECR 1989   381–2, 384, 388–9

Case 45/76, *Comet BV* v. *Produktschap voor Siergewassen*, [1976] ECR 2043   382, 389

Case 52/76, *Benedetti* v. *Munari*, [1977] ECR 163   299

Case 74/76, *Iannelli & Volpi SpA* v. *Ditta Paolo Meroni*, [1977] ECR 557   312, 315

Joined Cases 83 and 94/76, 4, 15 and 40/77, *Bayerische HNL Vermehrungsbetriebe and others* v. *Council and Commission*, [1978] ECR 1209   281

Case 38/77, *Enka BV* v. *Inspecteur der invoerrechten en accijnzen*, [1977] ECR 2203   371

Case 55/77, *M. Maris, wife of R. Reboulet* v. *Rijksdienst voor Werknemers-pensioenen*, [1977] ECR 2327   370

Case 106/77, *Amministrazione delle Finanze dello Stato* v. *Simmenthal*, [1978] ECR 629   289, 318, 355, 356

Case 31/78, *Bussone* v. *Italian Ministry of Agriculture*, [1978] ECR 2429   368, 370

Case 92/78, *Simmenthal* v. *Commission*, [1979] ECR 777   276

Case 120/78, *Rewe-Zentral* v. *Bundesmonopolverwaltung für Branntwein (Cassis de Dijon)*, [1979] ECR 649   23

Case 148/78, *Ratti*, [1979] ECR 1629   325, 356, 365, 372

Case 230/78, *SpA Eridania-Zuccherifici nazionali and SpA Societa Italiana per l'Industria degli Zuccheri* v. *Minister of Agriculture and Forestry, Minister for*

Industry, Trade and Craft Trades and SpA Zuccherifici Meridionali, [1979] ECR 2749   319

Case 44/79, *Hauer v. Land Rheinland-Pfalz*, [1979] ECR 3727   416, 418

Case 61/79, *Amministrazione delle finanze dello Stato v. Denkavit*, [1980] ECR 1205   300

Case 102/79, *Commission v. Belgium*, [1980] ECR 1473   344

Case 104/79, *Foglia v. Novello*, [1980] ECR 745   295

Case 130/79, *Express Dairy Foods Limited v. Intervention Board for Agricultural Produce* [1980] ECR 1887   389

Case 133/79, *Sucrimex SA and Westzucker GmbH v. Commission*, [1980] ECR 1299   253

Case 138/79, *Roquette Frères v. Council (Isoglucose)*, [1980] ECR 3333   23, 85, 96, 176

Case 155/79, *AM & S Europe Limited v. Commission*, [1982] ECR 1575   415

Case 790/79, *Calpak v. Commission*, [1980] ECR 1949   271

Case 804/79, *Commission v. United Kingdom*, [1981] ECR 1045   165

Case 812/79, *Attorney General v. Juan C. Burgoa*, [1980] ECR 2787   353

Case 66/80, *International Chemical Corporation v. Amministrazione delle finanze dello Stato*, [1981] ECR 1191   277, 298

Case 98/80, *Romano v. Institut national d'assurance maladie-invalidité*, [1981] ECR 1241   235

Case 137/80, *Commission v. Belgium*, [1981] ECR 653   319

Case 158/80, *Rewe-Handelsgesellschaft Nord mbH and Rewe-Markt Steffen v. Hauptzollamt Kiel (Butter-Cruises)*, [1981] ECR 1805   392–3, 396

Case 244/80, *Folgia v. Novello (No. 2)*, [1981] ECR 3045   296

Case 246/80, *Broekmeulen v. Huisarts Registratie Commissie*, [1981] ECR 2311   293

Case 270/80, *Polydor and others v. Harlequin and others*, [1982] ECR 329   341, 372

Case 8/81, *Becker v. Finanzamt Münster-Innenstadt*, [1982] ECR 53   344

Case 17/81, *Pabst & Richarz KG v. Hauptzollamt Oldenburg*, [1982] ECR 1331   373

Case 60/81, *International Business Machines (IBM) v. Commission*, [1981] ECR 2639   264

Case 104/81, *Hauptzollamt Mainz v. Kupferberg & Cie.*, [1982] ECR 3641   338, 339

Case 249/81, *Commission v. Ireland (Buy Irish)*, [1982] ECR 4005   285

Case 283/81, *CILFIT and others v. Ministry of Health*, [1982] ECR 3415   298

Case 11/82, *Piraiki-Patraiki and others v. Commission*, [1985] ECR 207   272

Case 199/82, *Amministrazione delle Finanze dello Stato v. SpA San Giorgio*, [1983] ECR 3595   392

Joined Cases 205–215/82, *Deutsche Milchkontor GmbH and others v. Federal Republic of Germany*, [1983] ECR 2633   253

Case 13/83, *Parliament v. Council*, [1985] ECR 1513   288

Case 14/83, *Von Colson and Elisabeth Kamann* v. *Land Nordrhein-Westfalen*, [1984] ECR 1891   331, 333, 384, 388–9

Case 118/83, *CMC Cooperativa muratori e cementisti and others* v. *Commission*, [1985] ECR 2325   280

Case 145/83, *Adams* v. *Commission*, [1985] ECR 3539   281

Case 294/83, *Parti écologiste 'Les Verts'* v. *European Parliament*, [1986] ECR 1339   61, 260, 271, 276, 410, 419

Joined Cases 60 and 61/84, *Cinéthèque SA and others* v. *Fédération nationale des cinémas français*, [1985] ECR 2605   438–9

Case 152/84, *Marshall* v. *Southampton and South-West Hampshire Area Health Authority*, [1986] ECR 723   326, 328, 356

Case 222/84, *Johnston* v. *Chief Constable of the Royal Ulster Constabulary*, [1986] ECR 1651   328, 336

Case 5/85, *AKZO Chemie* v. *Commission*, [1986] ECR 2585   123

Case 69/85 (Order), *Wünsche Handelsgesellschaft* v. *Germany*, [1986] ECR 947   300

Case 72/85, *Commission* v. *The Netherlands*, [1986] ECR 1219   319

Case 149/85, *Wybot* v. *Faure*, [1986] ECR 2391   84

Case 218/85, *Association comite économique agricole régional fruits et légumes de Bretagne* v. *A Le Campion (CERAFEL)*, [1986] ECR 3513   365

Case 293/85, *Commission* v. *Belgium*, [1988] ECR 305   284

Case 314/85, *Foto-Frost* v. *Hauptzollamt Lübeck-Ost*, [1987] ECR 4199   277

Case 12/86, *Demirel* v. *Stadt Schwäbisch Gmünd*, [1987] ECR 3719   193, 339

Case 60/86, *Commission* v. *United Kingdom (Dim-dip)*, [1988] ECR 3921   367

Case 68/86, *United Kingdom* v. *Council*, [1988] ECR 855   266

Case 74/86, *Commission* v. *Germany*, [1988] ECR 2139   357

Case 80/86, *Kolpinghuis Nijmegen BV*, [1987] ECR 3969   325, 333, 344

Joined Cases 89 and 91/86, *L'Étoile Commerciale et Comptoir National Technique Agricole (CNTA)* v. *Commission*, [1987] ECR 3005   251

Case 104/86, *Commission* v. *Italy*, [1988] ECR 1799   357

Case 22/87, *Commission* v. *Italian Republic*, [1989] ECR 143   398

Joined Cases 46/87 and 227/88, *Höchst* v. *Commission*, [1989] ECR 2859   414, 416

Case 70/87, *FEDIOL* v. *Commission*, [1989] ECR 1781   343

Case 165/87, *Commission* v. *Council*, [1988] ECR 5545   266

Case 247/87, *Star Fruit Co.* v. *Commission*, [1989] ECR 291   287, 288

Case 302/87, *Parliament* v. *Council*, [1988] ECR 5615   288

Case 377/87, *Parliament* v. *Council*, [1988] ECR 4017   288

Case 5/88, *Wachauf* v. *Bundesamt für Ernährung und Forstwirtschaft*, [1989] ECR 2609   419, 436–7

Case 16/88, *Commission* v. *Council*, [1989] ECR 3457   233

Case C-39/88, *Commission* v. *Ireland*, [1990] ECR I-4271   285

Case C-70/88, *Parliament* v. *Council (Chernobyl)*, [1990] ECR I-2041   84–5, 87, 269

Case 103/88, *Costanzo SpA* v. *Comune di Milano*, [1989] ECR 1839   328, 345

Case C-145/88, *Torfaen Borough Council*, [1989] ECR I-3851   292

Case C-177/88, *Dekker v. Stichting Vormingscentrum voor Jong Volwassenen (VJV-Centrum) Plus*, [1990] ECR 3941   390

Case 322/88, *Grimaldi v. Fonds des maladies professionnelles*, [1989] ECR 4407   277, 309

Case C-331/88, *The Queen v. Minister of Agriculture, Fisheries and Food and Secretary of State for Health, ex parte Fedesa and others*, [1990] ECR I-4023   267–8

Case C-69/89, *Nakajima All Precision v. Council*, [1991] ECR I-2069   343

Case C-106/89, *Marleasing v. La Comercial Internacional de Alimentacion*, [1990] ECR I-4135   331–2, 384

Case C-188/89, *Foster and others v. British Gas*, [1990] ECR I-3313   328

Case C-192/89, *Sevince v. Staatssecretaris van Justitie*, [1990] ECR I-3461   338, 341

Case C-213/89, *The Queen v. Secretary of State for Transport, ex parte Factortame Ltd and others*, [1990] ECR I-2433   388, 390

Case C-260/89, *Elliniki Radiophonia Tiléorassi (ERT) et al. v. Dimotiki Etairia Pliroforissis and Sotirios Kouvelas and Nicolaos Avdellas et al.*, [1991] ECR I-2925   437–8

Case C-298/89, *Gibraltar v. Council*, [1993] ECR I-3605   344

Case C-300/89, *Commission v. Council*, [1991] ECR I-2867   266

Case C-309/89, *Codorniu v. Council*, [1994] ECR I-1853   271

Case C-368/89, *Crispoltoni v. Fattoria autonoma tabacchi di Città di Castello*, [1991] ECR I-3695   268

Case C-370/89, *SGEEM & Etroy v. European Investment Bank*, [1993] ECR I-2583   280

Joined Cases C-6/90 and C-9/90, *Francovich and Bonifaci et al. v. Italy*, [1991] ECR I-5357   396, 408

Case C-31/90, *Johnson v. Chief Adjudication Officer*, [1991] ECR I-3723   392

Case C-159/90, *Society for the Protection of Unborn Children Ireland Ltd v. Stephen Grogan and others*, [1991] ECR I-4685   415

Case C-208/90, *Emmott v. Minister for Social Welfare and Attorney General*, [1991] ECR I-4269   391

Case C-240/90, *Germany v. Commission*, [1992] ECR I-5383   234

Case C-282/90, *Vreugdenhil BV v. Commission*, [1992] ECR I-1937   281

Case C-25/91, *Pesqueras Echebastar v. Commission*, [1993] ECR I-1719   288

Case C-158/91, *Criminal Proceedings against Jean-Claude Levy*, [1993] ECR I-4287   353

Case C-169/91, *Stoke-on-Trent v. B&Q*, [1992] ECR I-6635   292

Joined Cases C-267/91 and C-268/91, *Criminal proceedings against Keck and Mithouard*, [1993] ECR I-6097   272

Case C-271/91, *Marshall v. Southampton and South-West Hampshire Area Health Authority*, [1993] ECR I-4367   390

Case C-316/91, *Parliament v. Council* [1994] ECR I-625   215, 269

Case C-338/91, *Steenhorst-Neerings* v. *Bestuur van de Bedrijfsvereniging voor Detailhandel, Ambachten en Huisvrouwen*, [1993] ECR I-5475   392

Case C-2/92, *The Queen* v. *Ministry of Agriculture, Fisheries and Food, ex parte Dennis Clifford Bostock*, [1994] ECR I-955   437, 440

Case C-11/92, *The Queen* v. *Secretary of State for Health, ex parte Gallaher Ltd, Imperial Tobacco Ltd and Rothmans International Tobacco (UK) Ltd*, [1993] ECR I-3545   367

Case C-91/92, *Faccini Dori* v. *Recreb*, [1994] ECR I-3325   326, 369, 408

Case C-128/92, *Banks & Co. Ltd* v. *British Coal Corporation*, [1994] ECR I-1209   405

Case C-137/92P, *Commission* v. *BASF et al.*, [1994] ECR I-2555   123

Case C-188/92, *TWD* v. *Germany*, [1994] ECR I-833   277

Case C-350/92, *Spain* v. *Council*, [1995] ECR I-1985   157, 159, 168, 377

Case C-359/92, *Germany* v. *Council*, [1994] ECR I-3681   245

Case C-410/92, *Johnson* v. *Chief Adjudication Officer*, [1994] ECR I-5483   391

Case C-431/92, *Commission* v. *Germany*, [1995] ECR I-2189   284

Case C-32/93, *Webb* v. *EMO Air Cargo*, [1994] ECR I-3567   332

Joined Cases C-46/93 and C-48/93, *Brasserie du Pêcheur SA* v. *Bundesrepublik Deutschland* and *The Queen* v. *Secretary of State for Transport, ex parte Factortame Ltd and others*, [1996] ECR I-1029   135, 399

Case C-65/93, *Parliament* v. *Council*, [1995] ECR I-643   177

Case C-187/93, *Parliament* v. *Council*, [1994] ECR I-2857   269, 370

Case C-280/93, *Germany* v. *Council*, [1993] ECR I-4973   339

Case C-312/93, *Peterbroeck, Van Campenhout & Cie* v. *Belgian State*, [1995] ECR I-4599   382, 392

Case C-316/93, *Vaneetveld* v. *Le Foyer*, [1994] ECR I-763   330

Case C-324/93, *The Queen* v. *Secretary of State for Home Department, ex parte Evans Medical Ltd and Macfarlan Smith Ltd*, [1995] ECR I-563   353

Case C-392/93, *The Queen* v. *HM Treasury, ex parte British Telecommunications*, [1996] ECR I-10631   401

Case C-415/93, *Union Royale Belge des Sociétés de Football Association ASBL* v. *Jean-Marc Bosman*, [1995] ECR I-4921   316

Case C-417/93, *Parliament* v. *Council*, [1995] ECR I-1185   177

Joined Cases C-430/93 and C-431/93, *Van Schijndel and Johannes Nicolaas Cornelis van Veen* v. *Stichting Pensioenfonds voor Fysiotherapeuten*, [1995] ECR I-4705   394

Case C-466/93, *Atlanta Fruchthandelsgesellschaft mbH and others* v. *Bundesamt für Ernährung und Forstwirtschaft* [1995] ECR I-3799   277

Case C-476/93P, *Nutral* v. *Commission*, [1995] ECR I-4125   251

Case C-5/94, *The Queen* v. *Ministry of Agriculture, Fisheries and Food, ex parte Hedley Lomas*, [1996] ECR I-2553   401

Case C-61/94, *Commission* v. *Germany (IDA)*, [1996] ECR I-3989   4, 285, 342, 372

Case C-84/94, *United Kingdom of Great Britain and Northern Ireland* v. *Council*, [1996] ECR I-5755   155

Case C-178/94, *Dillenkofer* v. *Germany*, [1996] ECR I-4845   402

Case C-194/94, *CIA Security* v. *Signalson and Securitel*, [1996] ECR I-2201   329

Case C-233/94, *Germany* v. *Parliament and Council (Deposit Guarantee Scheme)*, [1997] ECR I-2405   182

Joined Cases C-283 and 291–2/94, *Denkavit et al.* v. *Bundesamt für Finanzen*, [1996] ECR I-4845   402

Case C-68/95, *T. Port GmbH & Co. KG* v. *Bundesanstalt für Landwirtschaft und Ernährung*, [1996] ECR I-6065   287

Case C-84/95, *Bosphorus Hava Yollari Turizm ve Ticaret AS* v. *Minister for Transport, Energy and Communications and others*, [1996] ECR I-3953   420

Case C-122/95, *Germany* v. *Council (Bananas)*, [1998] ECR I-973   268

Case C-168/95, *Arcaro*, [1996] ECR I-4705   333

Case C-177/95, *Ebony Maritime et al.* v. *Prefetto della Provincia di Brindisi et al.*, [1997] ECR I-1111   320

Case C-299/95, *Kremzow* v. *Austria*, [1997] ECR I-2629   438

Case C-367/95P, *Commission* v. *Sytraval and Brink's*, [1998] ECR I-1719   267

Case C-368/95, *Vereinigte Familiapress Zeitungsverlags- und vertriebs GmbH* v. *Bauer Verlag*, [1997] ECR I-3689   315

Case C-408/95, *Eurotunnel SA* v. *Sea France*, [1997] ECR I-6315   277

Case C-54/96, *Dorsch Consult Ingenieugesellschaft* v. *Bundesbaugesellschaft Berlin*, [1997] ECR I-4961   293

Case C-85/96, *Martínez Sala* v. *Freistaat Bayern*, [1998] ECR I-2691   313

Case C-129/96, *Inter-Environnement Wallonie ASBL* v. *Region Wallonne*, [1997] ECR I-7411   331

Case C-149/96, *Portuguese Republic* v. *Council of the European Union*, [1999] ECR I-8395   340, 343

Case C-170/96, *Commission* v. *Council (Airport Transit Visa)* [1998] ECR I-2763   197

Case C-185/96, *Commission* v. *Hellenic Republic*, [1998] ECR I-6601   357

Case C-231/96, *Edilizia Industriale Siderurgica Srl (Edis)* v. *Ministero delle Finanze*, [1998] ECR I-4951   386

Case C-264/96, *Imperial Chemical Industries (ICI)* v. *Kenneth Hall Colmer (Her Majesty's Inspector of Taxes)*, [1998] ECR I-4695   296

Case C-309/96, *Annibaldi* v. *Sindaco del Comune di Guidonia and Presidente Regione Lazio*, [1997] ECR I-7493   438

Case C-319/96, *Brinkmann Tabakfabriken GmbH* v. *Skatteministeriet*, [1998] ECR I-5255   400

Case C-326/96, *Levez* v. *Jennings (Harlow Pools) Ltd*, [1998] ECR I-7835   386

Case C-2/97, *Società italiana petroli SPA (IP)* v. *Borsana* [1998] ECR I-8597   437

Joined Cases C-10–22/97, *Ministero delle Finanze* v. *IN.CO.GE.'90 Srl and others*, [1998] ECR I-6307   356

Case C-126/97, *Eco Swiss China Time Ltd* v. *Benetton International NV*, [1999] ECR 3055   395

Joined Cases C-176 and 177/97, *Commission* v. *Belgium & Luxembourg*, [1998] ECR I-3557   354

Case C-189/97, *Parliament* v. *Council (Mauritania Fisheries Agreement)*, [1999] ECR I-4741   210

Case C-292/97, *Karlsson*, [2000] ECR I-2737   440

Case C-424/97, *Haim* v. *Kassenzahnärztliche Vereinigung Nordrhein*, [2000] ECR I-5123   401

Case C-78/98, *Preston et al.* v. *Wolverhampton Healthcare NHS Trust and Others*, [2000] ECR I-3201   387, 392

Case C-164/98P, *DIR International Film Srl et al.* v. *Commission*, [2000] ECR I-447   235

Case C-240/98, *Océano Grupo Editorial* v. *Rocío Murciano Quintero*, [2000] ECR I-4941   395

Case C-318/98, *Fornasar et al.* v. *Sante Chiarcosso*, [2000] ECR I-4785   376

Case C-352/98P, *Bergaderm et al.* v. *Commission*, [2000] ECR I-5291   281

Case C-376/98, *Germany* v. *Parliament and Council (Tobacco Advertising)*, [2000] ECR I-8419   156, 255, 377

Case C-377/98, *Netherlands* v. *Council and Parliament*, [2001] ECR I-7079   159, 373

Joined Cases C-397/98 and C-410/98, *Metallgesellschaft et al.* v. *Commissioners of Inland Revenue et al.*, [2001] ECR I-1727   395

Case C-403/98, *Azienda Agricola Monte Arcosa Srl*, [2001] ECR I-103   319

Case C-443/98, *Unilever Italia* v. *Central Food*, [2000] ECR I-7535   329

Case C-476/98, *Commission* v. *Germany (Open Skies)* [2002] ECR I-9855   202

Case C-150/99, *Sweden* v. *Stockhold Lindöpark*, [2001] ECR I-493   408

Case C-239/99, *Nachi Europe*, [2001], ECR I-1197   276

Case C-453/99, *Courage* v. *Crehan*, [2001] ECR I-6297   405

Case C-11/00, *Commission* v. *European Central Bank*, [2003] ECR I-7147   140

Case C-50/00, *Unión de Pequeños Agricultores (UPA)* v. *Council*, [2002] ECR I-6677   133, 272

Case C-62/00, *Marks & Spencer* v. *Commissioners of Customs & Excise*, [2002] ECR I-6325   344

Case C-99/00, *Lyckeskog*, [2002] ECR I-4839   297

Case C-112/00, *Schmidberger, Internationale Transporte und Planzüge* v. *Austria*, [2003] ECR I–5659   417

Case C-118/00, *Larsy* v. *Institut national d'assurances sociales pour travailleurs indépendants*, [2001] ECR I-5063   401

Case C-129/00, *Commission* v. *Italy*, [2003] ECR I-14637   285

Case C-253/00, *Muñoz & Superior Fruiticola* v. *Frumar & Redbridge Produce Marketing*, [2002] ECR I-7289   393

Case C-378/00, *Commission* v. *Parliament and Council*, [2003] ECR I-937   267

Case C-383/00, *Commission* v. *Germany*, [2002] ECR I-4219   285

Case C-438/00, *Deutscher Handballbund eV* v. *Maros Kolpak*, [2003] ECR I-4135   341

Case 453/00, *Kühne & Heitz v. Productschap voor Pluimvee en Eieren*, [2004] ECR I-837   300–1

Case 76/01P, *Eurocoton et al. v. Council*, [2003] ECR I-10091   271

Case C-103/01 *Commission v. Germany*, [2003] ECR I-5369   183

Case C-218/01, *Henkel v. Deutsches Patent- und Markenamt*, [2004] ECR I-1725   331, 384

Case C-224/01, *Köbler v. Austria*, [2003] ECR I-10239   403

Joined Cases C-397/01 to C-403/01, *Pfeiffer et al. v. Deutsches Rotes Kreuz, Kreisverband Waldshut*, [2004] ECR I-8835   330, 384

Case C-491/01, *The Queen v. Secretary of State for Health, ex parte British American Tobacco et al.*, [2002] ECR I-11453   159

Case C-494/01, *Commission v. Ireland (Irish Waste)*, [2005] ECR I-3331   286

Case C-60/02, *Criminal proceedings against X*, [2004] ECR I-651   320

Case C-201/02, *The Queen v. Secretary of State for Transport, Local Government and the Regions, ex parte Wells*, [2004] ECR I-723   254, 327, 381

Case C-222/02, *Paul et al. v. Germany*, [2004] ECR I-9425   400

Case C-263/02 P, *Commission v. Jégo-Quéré*, [2004] ECR I-3425   275

Case C-304/02, *Commission v. France (French Fisheries II)*, [2005] ECR I-6262   286

Case 377/02, *Van Parys*, [2005] ECR I-1465   340

Case C-6/03, *Deponiezweckverband Eiterköpfe v. Land Rheinland-Pfalz*, [2005] ECR I-2753   376, 437

Case C-53/03, *Syfait et al. v. GlaxoSmithKline*, [2005] ECR I-4609   293

Case C-105/03, *Pupine*, [2005] ECR I-5285   33

Case C-110/03 *Belgium v. Commission*, [2005] ECR I-2801   183

Case C-173/03, *Traghetti del Mediterraneo v. Italy*, [2006] ECR I-5177   404

Case C-176/03, *Commission v. Council (Environmental Criminal Penalties)*, [2005] ECR I-7879   197

Case C-210/03, *Swedish Match*, [2004] ECR I-11893   159

Case C-265/03, *Simutenkov v. Ministerio de Educacion y Cultura and Real Federacion Espanola de Futbol*, [2005] ECR I-2579   342

Case C-266/03, *Commission v. Luxembourg*, [2005] ECR I-4805   217, 219

Case C-380/03, *Germany v. Parliament and Council (Tobacco Advertising II)*, [2006] ECR I-11573   159

Case C-436/03, *European Parliament v. Council of the EU*, [2006] ECR I-3733   159

Case C-459/03, *Commission v. Ireland (Mox Plant)*, [2006] ECR I-4657   216

Case C-461/03, *Schul Douane-expediteur*, [2005] ECR I-10513   277

Case C-470/03, *A.G.M.-COS.MET et al. v. Suomen Valtio et al.* [2007] ECR I-2749   401

Case C-540/03, *Parliament v. Council*, [2006] ECR I-5769   423

Case C-66/04, *United Kingdom v. Parliament and Council*, [2005] ECR I-10553   246

Case C-144/04, *Mangold v. Helm*, [2005] ECR I-9981   334

Case C-145/04, *Spain v. United Kingdom*, [2006] ECR I-7917   284, 430

Joined Cases C-154 and 155/04, *The Queen, ex parte National Association of Health Stores and others v. Secretary of State for Health*, [2005] ECR I-6451   183, 235

Case C-180/04, *Vassallo v. Azienda Ospedaliera Ospedale San Martino di Genova et al.*, [2006] ECR I-7251   328

Case C-212/04, *Adeneler and Others v. Ellinikos Organismos Galaktos (ELOG)*, [2006] ECR I-6057   331

Case C-217/04, *United Kingdom v. Parliament and Council (ENISA)*, [2006] ECR I-3771   246

Joined Cases C-295/04 to C-298/04, *Manfredi et al. v. Lloyd Adriatico Assicurazioni et al.*, [2006] ECR I-6619   406

Case C-344/04, *The Queen on the application of International Air Transport Association et al. v. Department of Transport*, [2006] ECR I-403   173, 277, 297

Joined Cases C-392/04 and C-422/04, *i-21 Germany & Arcor v. Germany*, [2006] ECR I-8559   381

Case C-417/04P, *Regione Siciliana v. Commission*, [2006] ECR I-3881   273

Case C-91/05, *Commission v. Council (ECOWAS)* [2008] ECR I-3651   197

Case C-120/05, *Schulze v. Hauptzollamt Hamburg-Jonas*, [2006] ECR I-10745   382

Case C-222/05, *Van der Weerd et al. v. Minister van Landbouw, Natuur en Voedselkwaliteit*, [2007] ECR I-4233   395

Case C-282/05P, *Holcim v. Commission*, [2007] ECR I-2941   282

Case C-402/05P, *Kadi and Al Barakaat International Foundation v. Council and Commission*, [2008] ECR I-6351   161, 198, 268, 353, 421

Case C-411/05, *Palacios de la Villa*, [2007] ECR I-8531   335

Case C-432/05, *Unibet v. Justitiekanslern*, [2007] ECR I-2271   393

Case C-440/05, *Commission v. Council (Ship-Source Pollution)* [2007] ECR I-9097   197

Case C-2/06, *Kempter v. Hauptzollamt Hamburg-Jonas*, [2008] ECR I-411   299, 301, 395

Case C-55/06, *Arcor v. Germany*, [2008] ECR I-2931   184

Joined Cases C-37/06 and C-58/06, *Viamex Agrar Handels GmbH & Zuchtvieh-Kontor GmbH, v. Hauptzollant Hamburg-Jonas*, [2008] ECR I-69   334

Case C-80/06, *Carp v. Ecorad*, [2007] ECR I-4473   322

Case C-120/06P, *FIAMM et al. v. Council and Commission*, [2008] ECR I-6513   282

Case C-210/06, *Cartesio*, [2008] ECR I-9641   293

Case C-275/06, *Promusicae v. Telefónica de España*, [2008] ECR I-271   437, 440

Case C-308/06, *Intertanko and others v. Secretary of State for Transport*, [2008] ECR I-4057   212, 340

Joined Cases C-55 and C-56/07, *Michaeler et al. v. Amt für sozialen Arbeitsschutz Bozen*, [2008] ECR I-3135   336

Case C-188/07, *Commune de Mesquer v. Total*, [2008] ECR I-4501   212

Case C-246/07, *Commission v. Sweden*, (nyr)   219, 220, 222

Case C-550/07P, *Akzo Nobel Chemicals et al. v. Commission* (nyr)   165

Case C-555/07, *Kücükdeveci v. Swedex*, (nyr)   333, 336, 439

Case C-40/08, *Asturcom Telecomunicaciones v. Rodríguez Nogueira*, (nyr)   395

Case C-58/08, *The Queen, ex parte Vodafone et al. v. Secretary of State*, (nyr)   159

Case C-301/08, *Bogiatzi v. Deutscher Luftpool and others*, (nyr)   213

Case C-314/08, *Filipiak v. Dyrektor Izby Skarbowej w Poznaniu*, (nyr)   357

Case C-323/08, *Rodríguez Mayor v. Herencia Yacente de Rafael de las Heras Dávila*, (nyr)   439

Case C-34/09, *Zambrano v. Office national de l'emploi*, (nyr)   419

Case C-109/09, *Deutsche Lufthansa*, (nyr)   384

Case C-173/09, *Elchinov v. Natsionalna zdravnoosiguritelna kasa*, (nyr)   294

Case C-279/09, *Deutsche Energiehandels- und Beratungsgesellschaft mbH*, (nyr)   428

(b) European Court of Justice: Opinions (numerical)

Opinion 1/75 (*Local Cost Standard*), [1975] ECR 1355   165, 209

Opinion 1/76 (*Laying-Up Fund*), [1977] ECR 741   196, 202, 209, 215, 331

Opinion 1/78 (*Natural Rubber Agreement*), [1979] ECR 2871   209

Opinion 1/91 (*EEA Draft Agreement*), [1991] ECR I-6079   3, 61, 209, 373

Opinion 2/91 (*ILO Convention 170*), [1993] ECR I-1061   203, 209, 218

Opinion 1/92 (*EFTA Agreement II*), [1992] ECR I-2821   209

Opinion 2/92 (*Third Revised Decision of the OECD on national treatment*), [1995] ECR I-521   202, 209

Opinion 1/94 (*WTO Agreement*), [1994] ECR I-5267   202, 209, 218

Opinion 2/94 (*Accession to ECHR*), [1996] ECR I-1759   161, 190, 209, 434

Opinion 3/94 (*Banana Framework Agreement*), [1995] ECR I-4577   209

Opinion 1/00 (*European Common Aviation Area*), [2002] ECR I-3493   209

Opinion 2/00 (*Cartagena Protocol*) [2002] ECR I-9713   209

Opinion 1/03 (*Lugano Convention*), [2006] ECR I-1145   202, 209

Opinion 1/08 (*GATS*), (nyr)   209

Opinion 1/09 (*European Patent Court*), (nyr)   209, 289

(c) General Court: Cases (numerical)

Case T-115/94, *Opel Austria GmbH v. Council*, [1997] ECR II-39   373

Case T-184/95, *Dorsch Consult v. Council & Commission*, [1998] ECR II-667   282

Case T-135/96, *Union Européenne de l'artisanat et des petites et moyennes entreprises (UEAPME) v. Council*, [1998] ECR II-02335   273

Case T-315/01, *Kadi v. Council and Commission*, [2005] ECR II-3649   420

Case T-339/04, *France Télécom SA v. Commission*, [2007] ECR II-521   250

2. Other jurisdictions

(a) European Court of Human Rights: Cases (chronological)

Confédération Française Démocratique Du Travail v. European Communities (alternatively, their Member States), (1978) 13 DR 231 431
M & Co v. Federal Republic of Germany, (1990) 64 DR 138 431
Matthews v. the United Kingdom, (1999) 28 EHRR 361 430–31
Bosphorus Hava Yollari Turizm ve Ticaret Anonim Sirketi v. Ireland, (2006) 42 EHRR 1 432

(b) German Constitutional Court: Cases (chronological)

BVerfGE 7, 198 (*Lüth*) 444
BVerfGE 11, 6 (*Dampfkessel*) 251
BVerfGE 22, 293 (*EWG Verordnungen*) 73
BVerfGE 37, 271 (*Solange I*) 359
BVerfGE 73, 339 (*Solange II*) 360
BVerfGE 89, 155 (*Maastricht*) 69, 361
2 BvR 1481/04 (*Görgülü*) 444
BVerfGE 123, 267 (*Lisbon*) 160, 362
2 BvR 2661/06 (*Honeywell*) 362

(c) United States Supreme Court: Cases (chronological)

Marbury v. Madison, 5 US 137 (1803) 259
McCulloch v. Maryland, 17 US 316 (1819) 50, 139
Foster v. Neilson, 27 US (2 Pet.) 253 (1829) 338
Barron v. Mayor of Baltimore, 32 US (7 Pet.) 243 (1833) 435
Texas v. White, 74 US 700 (1868) 56, 189
Field v. Clark, 143 US 649 (1892) 55, 67, 85, 224
Gitlow v. New York 268 US 652 (1925) 436
Rice v. Santa Fe Elevator Corp, 331 US 218 (1947) 368
Pacific Gas & Electric Co. v. State Energy Resources Conservation & Development Commission, 461 US 190 (1983) 364
Hillsborough County v. Automated Medical Laboratories, 471 US 707 (1985) 368
Boyle v. United Technologies, 487 US 500 (1988) 368
Alden v. Maine, 527 US 706 (1999) 396

Table of Equivalences[1]

1. Treaty on European Union

Rome (1958 – 1999)	Amsterdam (1999 – 2009)	Lisbon (2009 – today)
Article A	Article 1	Article 1
		Article 2
Article B	Article 2	Article 3
Article C	Article 3 (repealed)[1]	
		Article 4
		Article 5[2]
Article D	Article 4 (repealed)[3]	
Article E	Article 5 (repealed)[4]	
Article F	Article 6	Article 6
Article F.1 (*)	Article 7	Article 7
		Article 8
Article G	Article 8 (repealed)[5]	Article 9
		Article 10[6]
		Article 11
		Article 12
Article H	Article 9 (repealed)[7]	Article 13
		Article 14[8]
		Article 15[9]
		Article 16[10]
		Article 17[11]
		Article 18
		Article 19[12]

[1] This comparative Table was produced on the basis of the two official 'Tables of Equivalences' respectively attached to the Amsterdam Treaty ([1997] OJ C340/85) and the Lisbon Treaty ([2007] OJ C306/202). However, it is important to keep in mind that they are not always correct. For example, ex-Article 12 EEC was *not* renumbered into ex-Article 25 EC, which in turn became Article 30 TFEU. Article 30 resulted from a consolidation of ex-Articles 13 and 16 EEC. And, to provide a second note of caution: ex-Article 118a EEC did not become Article 138 EC and subsequently Article 154 TFEU. The lineage here is: Article 118a EEC – Article 137 EC – Article 153 TFEU. While not corrected within the Tables of Equivalences themselves, the book has taken account of these editorial mistakes.

Rome (1958 – 1999)	Amsterdam (1999 – 2009)	Lisbon (2009 – today)
Article I	Article 10 (repealed)[13]	Article 20[14]
	[Articles 27 A – E (replaced)]	
	[Article 40 – 40 B (replaced)]	
	[Article 43 – 45 (replaced)]	
		Article 21
		Article 22
		Article 23
Article J.1	Article 11	Article 24
Article J.2	Article 12	Article 25
Article J.3	Article 13	Article 26
		Article 27
Article J.4	Article 14	Article 28
Article J.5	Article 15	Article 29
	[Article 22]	Article 30
	[Article 23]	Article 31
Article J.6	Article 16	Article 32
Article J.7	Article 17 (moved)	[Article 42]
Article J.8	Article 18	Article 33
Article J.9	Article 19	Article 34
Article J.10	Article 20	Article 35
Article J.11	Article 21	Article 36
Article J.12	Article 22 (moved)	[Article 30]
Article J.13	Article 23 (moved)	[Article 31]
Article J.14	Article 24	Article 37
Article J.15	Article 25	Article 38
		Article 39
	[Article 47]	Article 40
Article J.16	Article 26 (repealed)	
Article J.17	Article 27 (repealed)	
	Article 27 A–E (replaced)[15]	[Article 20]
Article J.18	Article 28	Article 41
	[Article 17]	Article 42
		Article 43
		Article 44
		Article 45
		Article 46
Article K.1	Article 29 (replaced)[16], [17]	
Article K.2	Article 30 (replaced)[18]	
Article K.3	Article 31 (replaced)[19]	
Article K.4	Article 32 (replaced)[20]	
Article K.5	Article 33 (replaced)[21]	
Article K.6	Article 34 (repealed)	
Article K.7	Article 35 (repealed)	
Article K.8	Article 36 (replaced)[22]	

Rome (1958 – 1999)	Amsterdam (1999 – 2009)	Lisbon (2009 – today)
Article K.9	Article 37 (repealed))	
Article K.10	Article 38 (repealed)	
Article K.11	Article 39 (repealed)	
Article K.12	Article 40 (replaced)[23]	[Article 20]
	Article 40 A (replaced)[23]	[Article 20]
	Article 40 B (replaced)[23]	[Article 20]
Article K.13	Article 41 (repealed)	
Article K.14	Article 42 (repealed)	
Article K.15 (*)	Article 43 (replaced)[24]	[Article 20]
	Article 43 A (replaced)[24]	[Article 20]
	Article 43 B (replaced)[24]	[Article 20]
Article K.16 (*)	Article 44 (replaced)[24]	[Article 20]
	Article 44 A (replaced)[24]	[Article 20]
Article K.17 (*)	Article 45 (replaced)[24]	[Article 20]
Article L	Article 46 (repealed)	
Article M	Article 47 (moved)	[Article 40]
Article N	Article 48	Article 48
Article O	Article 49	Article 49
		Article 50
		Article 51
		Article 52
Article P	Article 50 (repealed)	
Article Q	Article 51	Article 53
Article R	Article 52	Article 54
Article S	Article 53	Article 55

(*) New Article introduced by the Treaty of Amsterdam

[1] Replaced, in substance, by Article 2 F (renumbered 7) of the Treaty on the Functioning of the European Union ('TFEU') and by Articles 9 (1) and 10 A, paragraph 3, second subparagraph (renumbered 13 and 21) of the Treaty on European Union ('TEU').

[2] Replaces Article 5 of the Treaty establishing the European Community ('TEC').

[3] Replaced, in substance, by Article 9 B (renumbered 15).

[4] Replaced, in substance, by Article 9, paragraph 2 (renumbered 13).

[5] Article 8 TEU, which was in force until the entry into force of the Treaty of Lisbon (hereinafter 'current'), amended the TEC. Those amendments are incorporated into the latter Treaty and Article 8 is repealed. Its number is used to insert a new provision.

[6] Paragraph 4 replaces, in substance, the first subparagraph of Article 191 TEC.

[7] The current Article 9 TEU amended the Treaty establishing the European Coal and Steel Community. This latter expired on 23 July 2002. Article 9 is repealed and the number thereof is used to insert another provision.

[8] – Paragraphs 1 and 2 replace, in substance, Article 189 TEC;
  – Paragraphs 1 to 3 replace, in substance, paragraphs 1 to 3 of Article 190 TEC;
  – Paragraph 1 replaces, in substance, the first subparagraph of Article 192 TEC;
  – Paragraph 4 replaces, in substance, the first subparagraph of Article 197 TEC.

[9] Replaces, in substance, Article 4.

[10] – Paragraph 1 replaces, in substance, the first and second indents of Article 202 TEC;
  – Paragraphs 2 and 9 replace, in substance, Article 203 TEC;
  – Paragraphs 4 and 5 replace, in substance, paragraphs 2 and 4 of Article 205 TEC.

[11] – Paragraph 1 replaces, in substance, Article 211 TEC;
  – Paragraphs 3 and 7 replace, in substance, Article 214 TEC;
  – Paragraph 6 replaces, in substance, paragraphs 1, 3 and 4 of Article 217 TEC.

[12] Replaces, in substance, Article 220 TEC.
  – The second subparagraph of paragraph 2 replaces, in substance, the first subparagraph of Article 221 TEC.

[13] The current Article 10 TEU amended the Treaty establishing the European Atomic Energy Community. Those amendments are incorporated into the Treaty of Lisbon. Article 10 is repealed and the number thereof is used to insert another provision.

[14] Also replaces Articles 11 and 11a TEC.

[15] The current Articles 27 A to 27 E, on enhanced cooperation, are also replaced by Articles 280 A to 280 I TFEU (renumbered 326 to 334).

[16] The current provisions of Title VI of the TEU, on police and judicial cooperation in criminal matters, are replaced by the provisions of Chapters 1, 5 and 5 of Title IV of Part Three of the TFEU.

[17] Replaced by Article 61 TFEU (renumbered 67).

[18] Replaced by Articles 69 F and 69 G TFEU (renumbered 87 and 88).

[19] Replaced by Articles 69 A, 69 B and 69 D TFEU (renumbered 82, 83 and 85).

[20] Replaced by Article 69 H TFEU (renumbered 89).

[21] Replaced by Article 61 E TFEU (renumbered 72).

[22] Replaced by Article 61 D TFEU (renumbered 71).

[23] The current Articles 40 to 40 B, on enhanced cooperation, are also replaced by Articles 280 A to 280 I TFEU (renumbered 326 to 334).

[24] The current Articles 43 to 45 and Title VII of the TEU, on enhanced cooperation, are also replaced by Articles 280 A to 280 I TFEU (renumbered 326 to 334).

2. Treaty establishing the European Community

Rome (1958 – 1999)	Amsterdam (1999 – 2009)	Lisbon (2009 – today)
Article 1	Article 1 (repealed)	
		Article 1
Article 2	Article 2 (repealed)[1]	
		Article 2
		Article 3
		Article 4
		Article 5
		Article 6
		Article 7

Rome (1958 – 1999)	Amsterdam (1999 – 2009)	Lisbon (2009 – today)
Article 3	Article 3$^{(2)}$	Article 8
Article 3a	Article 4 (moved)	[Article 119]
Article 3b	Article 5 (replaced)$^{(3)}$	
		Article 9
		Article 10
Article 3c (*)	Article 6	Article 11
	[Article 153 (2)]	Article 12
		Article 13$^{(4)}$
Article 4	Article 7 (repealed)$^{(5)}$	
Article 4a	Article 8 (repealed)$^{(6)}$	
Article 4b	Article 9 (repealed)	
Article 5	Article 10 (repealed)$^{(7)}$	
Article 5a (*)	Article 11 (replaced)$^{(8)}$	[Articles 326–334]
	Article 11 a (replaced)$^{(8)}$	[Articles 326–334]
Article 6	Article 12 (repealed)	Article 18
Article 6a (*)	Article 13 (moved)	[Article 19]
Article 7 (repealed)		
Article 7a	Article 14 (moved)	[Article 26]
Article 7b (repealed)		
Article 7c	Article 15 (moved)	[Article 27]
Article 7d (*)	Article 16	Article 14
	[Article 255]	Article 15
	[Article 286]	Article 16
		Article 17
	[Article 12]	Article 18
	[Article 13]	Article 19
Article 8	Article 17	Article 20
Article 8a	Article 18	Article 21
Article 8b	Article 19	Article 22
Article 8c	Article 20	Article 23
Article 8d	Article 21	Article 24
Article 8e	Article 22	Article 25
	[Article 14]	Article 26
	[Article 15]	Article 27
Article 9	Article 23	Article 28
Article 10	Article 24	Article 29
Article 11 (repealed)		
Article 12	Article 25	Article 30
Article 13 (repealed)		
Article 14 (repealed)		
Article 15 (repealed)		
Article 16 (repealed		
Article 17 (repealed)		

Rome (1958 – 1999)	Amsterdam (1999 – 2009)	Lisbon (2009 – today)
Section 2 (deleted)		
Article 18 (repealed)		
Article 19 (repealed)		
Article 20 (repealed)		
Article 21 (repealed)		
Article 22 (repealed)		
Article 23 (repealed)		
Article 24 (repealed)		
Article 25 (repealed)		
Article 26 (repealed)		
Article 27 (repealed)		
Article 28	Article 26	Article 31
Article 29	Article 27	Article 32
	[Article 135]	Article 33
Article 30	Article 28	Article 34
Article 31 (repealed)		
Article 32 (repealed)		
Article 33 (repealed)		
Article 34	Article 29	Article 35
Article 35 (repealed)		
Article 36	Article 30	Article 36
Article 37	Article 31	Article 37
Article 38	Article 32	Article 38
Article 39	Article 33	Article 39
Article 40	Article 34	Article 40
Article 41	Article 35	Article 41
Article 42	Article 36	Article 42
Article 43	Article 37	Article 43
Article 44 (repealed)		
Article 45 (repealed)		
Article 46	Article 38	Article 44
Article 47 (repealed)		
Article 48	Article 39	Article 45
Article 49	Article 40	Article 46
Article 50	Article 41	Article 47
Article 51	Article 42	Article 48
Article 52	Article 43	Article 49
Article 53 (repealed)		
Article 54	Article 44	Article 50
Article 55	Article 45	Article 51
Article 56	Article 46	Article 52
Article 57	Article 47	Article 53
Article 58	Article 48	Article 54
	[Article 294]	Article 55
Article 59	Article 49	Article 56

Rome (1958 – 1999)	Amsterdam (1999 – 2009)	Lisbon (2009 – today)
Article 60	Article 50	Article 57
Article 61	Article 51	Article 58
Article 62 (repealed)		
Article 63	Article 52	Article 59
Article 64	Article 53	Article 60
Article 65	Article 54	Article 61
Article 66	Article 55	Article 62
Article 67 (repealed)		
Article 68 (repealed)		
Article 69 (repealed)		
Article 70 (repealed)		
Article 71 (repealed)		
Article 72 (repealed)		
Article 73 (repealed)		
Article 73a (repealed)		
Article 73b	Article 56	Article 63
Article 73c	Article 57	Article 64
Article 73d	Article 58	Article 65
Article 73e (repealed)		
Article 73f	Article 59	Article 66
Article 73g	Article 60 (moved)	[Article 75]
Article 73h (repealed)		
Article 73i (*)	Article 61	Article 67[9]
		Article 68
		Article 69
		Article 70
		Article 71[10]
	[Article 64 (1) replaced]	Article 72[11]
		Article 73
	[Article 66 replaced]	Article 74
	Article 60 (moved)	Article 75
		Article 76
Article 73j (*)	Article 62	Article 77
Article 73k (*)	Article 63[12]	Articles 78–80
Article 73l (*)	Article 64 (replaced)	[Article 72]
Article 73m (*)	Article 65	Article 81
Article 73n (*)	Article 66 (replaced)	[Article 74]
Article 73o (*)	Article 67 (repealed)	
Article 73p (*)	Article 68 (repealed)	
Article 73q (*)	Article 69 (repealed)	
		Article 82[13]
		Article 83[13]
		Article 84
		Article 85[13]

Rome (1958 – 1999)	Amsterdam (1999 – 2009)	Lisbon (2009 – today)
		Article 86
		Article 87[14]
		Article 88[14]
		Article 89[15]
Article 74	Article 70	Article 90
Article 75	Article 71	Article 91
Article 76	Article 72	Article 92
Article 77	Article 73	Article 93
Article 78	Article 74	Article 94
Article 79	Article 75	Article 95
Article 80	Article 76	Article 96
Article 81	Article 77	Article 97
Article 82	Article 78	Article 98
Article 83	Article 79	Article 99
Article 84	Article 80	Article 100
Article 85	Article 81	Article 101
Article 86	Article 82	Article 102
Article 87	Article 83	Article 103
Article 88	Article 84	Article 104
Article 89	Article 85	Article 105
Article 90	Article 86	Article 106
Article 91 (repealed)		
Article 92	Article 87	Article 107
Article 93	Article 88	Article 108
Article 94	Article 89	Article 109
Article 95	Article 90	Article 110
Article 96	Article 91	Article 111
Article 97 (repealed)		
Article 98	Article 92	Article 112
Article 99	Article 93	Article 113
Article 100	Article 94	[Article 115]
Article 100a	Article 95	Article 114
	[Article 94]	Article 115
Article 100b (repealed)		
Article 100c (repealed)		
Article 100d (repealed)		
Article 101	Article 96	Article 116
Article 102	Article 97	Article 117
		Article 118
	[Article 4]	Article 119
Article 102a	Article 98	Article 120
Article 103	Article 99	Article 121
Article 103a	Article 100	Article 122
Article 104	Article 101	Article 123

Rome (1958 – 1999)	Amsterdam (1999 – 2009)	Lisbon (2009 – today)
Article 104a	Article 102	Article 124
Article 104b	Article 103	Article 125
Article 104c	Article 104	Article 126
Article 105	Article 105	Article 127
Article 105a	Article 106	Article 128
Article 106	Article 107	Article 129
Article 107	Article 108	Article 130
Article 108	Article 109	Article 131
Article 108a	Article 110	Article 132
Article 109	Article 111 (1), (3), (5)	[Article 219]
	Article 111 (4)	[Article 138]
		Article 133
Article 109a	Article 112 (moved)	[Article 283]
Article 109b	Article 113 (moved)	[Article 284]
Article 109c	Article 114	Article 134
Article 109d	Article 115	Article 135
		Article 136
		Article 137
	[Article 111(4)]	Article 138
Article 109e	Article 116 (repealed)	
		Article 139
Article 109f	Article 117 (moved)	[Article 141(2)]
	[Article 121–3]	Article 140[16], [17], [18]
	[Articles 123 & 117]	Article 141[19], [20]
	[Article 124(1)]	Article 142
Article 109g	Article 118 (repealed)	
Article 109h	Article 119	Article 143
Article 109i	Article 120	Article 144
Article 109j	Article 121 (moved)	[Article 140 (1)]
Article 109k	Article 122 (moved)	[Article 140 (2)]
Article 109l	Article 123 (moved)	[Article 140 (3) and 141 (1)]
Article 109m	Article 124 (moved)	[Article 142]
Article 109n (*)	Article 125	Article 145
Article 109o (*)	Article 126	Article 146
Article 109p (*)	Article 127	Article 147
Article 109q (*)	Article 128	Article 148
Article 109r (*)	Article 129	Article 149
Article 109s (*)	Article 130	Article 150
Article 110	Article 131 (moved)	[Article 206]
Article 111 (repealed)		
Article 112	Article 132 (repealed)	
Article 113	Article 133 (moved)	[Article 207]
Article 114 (repealed)		
Article 115	Article 134 (repealed)	

Rome (1958 – 1999)	Amsterdam (1999 – 2009)	Lisbon (2009 – today)
Article 116 (*)	Article 135 (moved)	[Article 33]
Article 117	Article 136	Article 151
		Article 152
Article 118	Article 137	Article 153
Article 118a	Article 138	Article 154
Article 118b	Article 139	Article 155
Article 118c	Article 140	Article 156
Article 119	Article 141	Article 157
Article 119a	Article 142	Article 158
Article 120	Article 143	Article 159
Article 121	Article 144	Article 160
Article 122	Article 145	Article 161
Article 123	Article 146	Article 162
Article 124	Article 147	Article 163
Article 125	Article 148	Article 164
Article 126	Article 149	Article 165
Article 127	Article 150	Article 166
Article 128	Article 151	Article 167
Article 129	Article 152	Article 168
Article 129a	Article 153	Article 169 & [Article 12]
Article 129b	Article 154	Article 170
Article 129c	Article 155	Article 171
Article 129d	Article 156	Article 172
Article 130	Article 157	Article 173
Article 130a	Article 158	Article 174
Article 130b	Article 159	Article 175
Article 130c	Article 160	Article 176
Article 130d	Article 161	Article 177
Article 130e	Article 162	Article 178
Article 130f	Article 163	Article 179
Article 130g	Article 164	Article 180
Article 130h	Article 165	Article 181
Article 130i	Article 166	Article 182
Article 130j	Article 167	Article 183
Article 130k	Article 168	Article 184
Article 130l	Article 169	Article 185
Article 130m	Article 170	Article 186
Article 130n	Article 171	Article 187
Article 130o	Article 172	Article 188
		Article 189
Article 130p	Article 173	Article 190
Article 130q (repealed)		
Article 130r	Article 174	Article 191
Article 130s	Article 175	Article 192

Rome (1958 – 1999)	Amsterdam (1999 – 2009)	Lisbon (2009 – today)
Article 130t	Article 176	Article 193
		Article 194
		Article 195
		Article 196
		Article 197
Article 130u	Article 177 (moved)	[Article 208]
Article 130v	Article 178 (repealed)[21]	
Article 130w	Article 179 (moved)	[Article 209]
Article 130x	Article 180 (moved)	[Article 210]
Article 130y	Article 181 (moved)	[Article 211]
	Article 181a (moved)	[Article 212]
Article 131	Article 182	Article 198
Article 132	Article 183	Article 199
Article 133	Article 184	Article 200
Article 134	Article 185	Article 202
Article 135	Article 186	Article 202
Article 136	Article 187	Article 203
Article 136a	Article 188	Article 204
		Article 205
	[Article 131]	Article 206
	[Article 133]	Article 207
	[Article 177]	Article 208[22]
	[Article 179]	Article 209
	[Article 180]	Article 210
	[Article 181]	Article 211
	[Article 181a]	Article 212
		Article 213
		Article 214
	[Article 301]	Article 215
		Article 216
	[Article 310]	Article 217
	[Article 300]	Article 218
	[Article 111]	Article 219
	[Articles 302–304]	Article 220
		Article 221
		Article 222
Article 137	Article 189[23]	
Article 138	Article 190[24]	Article 223
Article 138a	Article 191[25]	Article 224
Article 138b	Article 192[26]	Article 225
Article 138c	Article 193	Article 226
Article 138d	Article 194	Article 227
Article 138e	Article 195	Article 228
Article 139	Article 196	Article 229

Rome (1958 – 1999)	Amsterdam (1999 – 2009)	Lisbon (2009 – today)
Article 140	Article 197[27]	Article 230
Article 141	Article 198	Article 231
Article 142	Article 199	Article 232
Article 143	Article 200	Article 233
Article 144	Article 201	Article 234
Article 145	Article 202 (repealed)[28]	
Article 146	Article 203 (repealed)[29]	
Article 147	Article 204	Article 237
Article 148	Article 205[30]	Article 238
Article 149 (repealed)		
Article 150	Article 206	Article 239
Article 151	Article 207	Article 240
Article 152	Article 208	Article 241
Article 153	Article 209	Article 242
Article 154	Article 210	Article 243
Article 155	Article 211 (repealed)[31]	
		Article 244
Article 156	Article 212 (moved)	[Article 249 (2)]
Article 157	Article 213	Article 245
Article 158	Article 214 (repealed)[32]	
Article 159	Article 215	Article 246
Article 160	Article 216	Article 247
Article 161	Article 217[33]	Article 248
Article 162	Article 218[34]	Article 249
Article 163	Article 219	Article 250
Article 164	Article 220 (repealed)[35]	
Article 165	Article 221[36]	Article 251
Article 166	Article 222	Article 252
Article 167	Article 223	Article 253
Article 168	Article 224[37]	Article 254
		Article 255
Article 168a	Article 225	Article 256
	Article 225a	Article 257
Article 169	Article 226	Article 258
Article 170	Article 227	Article 259
Article 171	Article 228	Article 260
Article 172	Article 229	Article 261
	Article 229a	Article 262
Article 173	Article 230	Article 263
Article 174	Article 231	Article 264
Article 175	Article 232	Article 265
Article 176	Article 233	Article 266
Article 177	Article 234	Article 267
Article 178	Article 235	Article 268

Rome (1958 – 1999)	Amsterdam (1999 – 2009)	Lisbon (2009 – today)
		Article 269
Article 179	Article 236	Article 270
Article 180	Article 237	Article 271
Article 181	Article 238	Article 272
Article 182	Article 239	Article 273
Article 183	Article 240	Article 274
		Article 275
		Article 276
Article 184	Article 241	Article 277
Article 185	Article 242	Article 278
Article 186	Article 243	Article 279
Article 187	Article 244	Article 280
Article 188	Article 245	Article 281
		Article 282
	[Article 112]	Article 283
	[Article 113]	Article 284
Article 188a	Article 246	Article 285
Article 188b	Article 247	Article 286
Article 188c	Article 248	Article 287
Article 189	Article 249	Article 288
		Article 289
		Article 290$^{(38)}$
		Article 291$^{(38)}$
		Article 292
Article 189a	Article 250	Article 293
Article 189b	Article 251	Article 294
Article 189c	Article 252 (repealed)	
		Article 295
Article 190	Article 253	Article 296
Article 191	Article 254	Article 297
		Article 298
Article 191a (*)	Article 255 (moved)	[Article 15]
Article 192	Article 256	Article 299
		Article 300
Article 193	Article 257$^{(39)}$	
Article 194	Article 258$^{(40)}$	Article 301
Article 195	Article 259	Article 302
Article 196	Article 260	Article 303
Article 197	Article 261 (repealed)	
Article 198	Article 262	Article 304
Article 198a	Article 263$^{(41)}$	Article 305
Article 198b	Article 264	Article 306
Article 198c	Article 265	Article 307
Article 198d	Article 266	Article 308

Rome (1958 – 1999)	Amsterdam (1999 – 2009)	Lisbon (2009 – today)
Article 198e	Article 267	Article 309
Article 199	Article 268	Article 310
Article 200 (repealed)		
Article 201	Article 269	Article 311
Article 201a	Article 270 (repealed)[42]	
		Article 312
	[Article 272 (1)]	Article 313
Article 202	Article 271 (moved)	[Article 316]
Article 203	Article 272	[Article 313 &] Article 314
Article 204	Article 273	Article 315
	[Article 271]	Article 316
Article 205	Article 274	Article 317
Article 205a	Article 275	Article 318
Article 206	Article 276	Article 319
Article 206a (repealed)		
Article 207	Article 277	Article 320
Article 208	Article 278	Article 321
Article 209	Article 279	Article 322
		Article 323
		Article 324
Article 209a	Article 280	Article 325
	[Articles 11 and 11 A]	Article 326[43]
	[Articles 11 and 11 A]	Article 327[43]
	[Articles 11 and 11 A]	Article 328[43]
	[Articles 11 and 11 A]	Article 329[43]
	[Articles 11 and 11 A]	Article 330[43]
	[Articles 11 and 11 A]	Article 331[43]
	[Articles 11 and 11 A]	Article 332[43]
	[Articles 11 and 11 A]	Article 333[43]
	[Articles 11 and 11 A]	Article 334[43]
Article 210	Article 281 (repealed)[44]	
Article 211	Article 282	Article 335
Article 212 (*)	Article 283	Article 336
Article 213	Article 284	Article 337
Article 213a (*)	Article 285	Article 338
Article 213b (*)	Article 286 (moved)	[Article 16]
Article 214	Article 287	Article 339
Article 215	Article 288	Article 340
Article 216	Article 289	Article 341
Article 217	Article 290	Article 342
Article 218 (*)	Article 291	Article 343
Article 219	Article 292	Article 344
Article 220	Article 293	
Article 221	Article 294 (moved)	[Article 55]

Rome (1958 – 1999)	Amsterdam (1999 – 2009)	Lisbon (2009 – today)
Article 222	Article 295	Article 345
Article 223	Article 296	Article 346
Article 224	Article 297	Article 347
Article 225	Article 298	Article 348
Article 226 (repealed)		
Article 227	Article 299[45]	Article 349 [& Article 355]
Article 228	Article 300	[Article 218]
Article 228a	Article 301	[Article 215]
Article 229	Article 302	[Article 220]
Article 230	Article 303	[Article 220]
Article 231	Article 304	[Article 220]
Article 232	Article 305	
Article 233	Article 306	Article 350
Article 234	Article 307	Article 351
Article 235	Article 308	Article 352
		Article 353
Article 236 (*)	Article 309	Article 354
Article 237 (repealed)		
Article 238	Article 310 (moved)	[Article 217]
Article 239	Article 311 (repealed)[46]	
	[Article 299]	Article 355
Article 240	Article 312	Article 356
Article 241 (repealed)		
Article 242 (repealed)		
Article 243 (repealed)		
Article 244 (repealed)		
Article 245 (repealed)		
Article 246 (repealed)		
Article 247	Article 313	Article 357
		Article 358
Article 248	Article 314 (repealed)[47]	

(*) New Article introduced by the Treaty of Amsterdam.

[1] Replaced, in substance, by Article 2 TEU (renumbered 3).

[2] Replaced, in substance, by Articles 2 B to 2 E TFEU (renumbered 3 to 6).

[3] Replaced, in substance, by Article 3b TEU (renumbered 5).

[4] Insertion of the operative part of the Protocol on protection and welfare of animals.

[5] Replaced, in substance, by Article 9 TEU (renumbered 13).

[6] Replaced, in substance, by Article 9 TEU (renumbered 13) and Article 245a, paragraph 1, TFEU (renumbered 282).

[7] Replaced, in substance, by Article 3a, paragraph 3, TEU (renumbered 4).

[8] Also replaced by Article 10 TEU (renumbered 20).

[9] Also replaces the current Article 29 TEU.

[10] Also replaces the current Article 36 TEU.

[11] Also replaces the current Article 33 TEU.

⁽¹²⁾ Points 1 and 2 of Article 63 EC are replaced by paragraphs 1 and 2 of Article 63 TFEU, and paragraph 2 of Article 64 is replaced by paragraph 3 of Article 63 TFEU.

⁽¹³⁾ Replaces the current Article 31 TEU.

⁽¹⁴⁾ Replaces the current Article 30 TEU.

⁽¹⁵⁾ Replaces the current Article 32 TEU.

⁽¹⁶⁾ Article 117a, paragraph 1, (renumbered 140) takes over the wording of paragraph 1 of Article 121.

⁽¹⁷⁾ Article 117a, paragraph 2, (renumbered 140) takes over the second sentence of paragraph 2 of Article 122.

⁽¹⁸⁾ Article 117a, paragraph 3, (renumbered 140) takes over paragraph 5 of Article 123.

⁽¹⁹⁾ Article 118a, paragraph 1, (renumbered 140) takes over paragraph 3 of Article 123.

⁽²⁰⁾ Article 118a, paragraph 2, (renumbered 141) takes over the first five indents of paragraph 2 of Article 117.

⁽²¹⁾ Replaced, in substance, by the second sentence of the second subparagraph of paragraph 1 of Article 188 D TFEU.

⁽²²⁾ The second sentence of the second subparagraph of paragraph 1 replaces, in substance, Article 178 TEC.

⁽²³⁾ Replaced, in substance, by Article 9 A, paragraphs 1 and 2, TEU (renumbered 14).

⁽²⁴⁾ Replaced, in substance, by Article 9 A, paragraphs 1 to 3, TEU (renumbered 14).

⁽²⁵⁾ Replaced, in substance, by Article 8 A, paragraph 4, TEU (renumbered 11).

⁽²⁶⁾ Replaced, in substance, by Article 9 A, paragraph 1, TEU (renumbered 14).

⁽²⁷⁾ Replaced, in substance, by Article 9 A, paragraph 4, TEU (renumbered 14).

⁽²⁸⁾ Replaced, in substance, by Article 9 C, paragraph 1, TEU (renumbered 16) and Articles 249 B and 249 C TFEU (renumbered 290 and 291).

⁽²⁹⁾ Replaced, in substance, by Article 9 C, paragraphs 2 and 9 TEU (renumbered 16).

⁽³⁰⁾ Replaced, in substance, by Article 9 C, paragraphs 4 and 5 TEU (renumbered 16).

⁽³¹⁾ Replaced, in substance, by Article 9 D, paragraph 1 TEU (renumbered 17).

⁽³²⁾ Replaced, in substance, by Article 9 D, paragraphs 3 and 7 TEU (renumbered 17).

⁽³³⁾ Replaced, in substance, by Article 9 D, paragraph 6, TEU (renumbered 17).

⁽³⁴⁾ Replaced, in substance, by Article 252a TFEU (renumbered 295).

⁽³⁵⁾ Replaced, in substance, by Article 9 F TEU (renumbered 19).

⁽³⁶⁾ Replaced, in substance, by Article 9 F, paragraph 2, first subparagraph, of the TEU (renumbered 19).

⁽³⁷⁾ The first sentence of the first subparagraph is replaced, in substance, by Article 9 F, paragraph 2, second subparagraph of the TEU (renumbered 19).

⁽³⁸⁾ Replaces, in substance, the third indent of Article 202 TEC.

⁽³⁹⁾ Replaced, in substance, by Article 256a, paragraph 2 of the TFEU (renumbered 300).

⁽⁴⁰⁾ Replaced, in substance, by Article 256a, paragraph 4 of the TFEU (renumbered 300).

⁽⁴¹⁾ Replaced, in substance, by Article 256a, paragraphs 3 and 4, TFEU (renumbered 300).

⁽⁴²⁾ Replaced, in substance, by Article 268, paragraph 4, TFEU (renumbered 310).

⁽⁴³⁾ Also replaces the current Articles 27 A to 27 E, 40 to 40 B, and 43 to 45 TEU.

⁽⁴⁴⁾ Replaced, in substance, by Article 49 C TEU (renumbered 52).

⁽⁴⁵⁾ Replaced, in substance by Article 49 C TEU (renumbered 52).

⁽⁴⁶⁾ Replaced, in substance by Article 49 B TEU (renumbered 51).

⁽⁴⁷⁾ Replaced, in substance by Article 53 TEU (renumbered 55).

Abbreviations

AFSJ	Area of Freedom, Security and Justice
CAP	Common Agricultural Policy
CCP	Common Commercial Policy
CDE	Cahiers de Droit Européen
CFSP	Common Foreign and Security Policy
CMO	Common Market Organisation
CoA	Court of Auditors
CML Rev	Common Market Law Review
Coreper	Committee of the Permanent Representatives
COSI	Standing Committee on Operational Cooperation on Internal Security
CSDP	Common Security and Defence Policy
CST	Civil Service Tribunal
CT	Constitutional Treaty
EC	European Community (Treaty)
ECB	European Central Bank
ECHR	European Convention on Human Rights
ECJ	European Court of Justice
ECOFIN	Council of Ministers for Economics and Finance
ECR	European Court Reports
ECSC	European Coal and Steel Community
ECtHR	European Court of Human Rights
EDC	European Defence Community
EEA	European Economic Area
EEAS	European External Action Service
EEC	European Economic Community (Treaty)
EFTA	European Free Trade Association
EHRR	European Human Rights Report
EL Rev	European Law Review
EMU	European Monetary Union
ENP	European Neighbourhood Policy
EPC	European Political Cooperation
ESCB	European System of Central Banks

ESDP	European Security and Defence Policy
EU (old)	European Union (Maastricht Treaty)
EuR	Europarecht
Euratom	European Atomic Energy Community
FYRM	Former Yugoslav Republic of Macedonia
GATS	General Agreement on Trade in Services
GATT	General Agreement on Tariffs and Trade
GC	General Court
HA	Humanitarian Aid
ICJ	International Court of Justice
IGC	Intergovernmental Conference
ILO	International Labour Organisation
JHA	Justice and Home Affairs
MEEQR	Measures having an Equivalent Effect to Quantitative Restrictions
MEP	Member of the European Parliament
MLR	Modern Law Review
NATO	North Atlantic Treaty Association
OECD	Organisation for Economic Cooperation and Development
OEEC	Organisation for European Economic Cooperation
OJ	Official Journal of the European Union
OMC	Open Method of Coordination
PJCC	Police and Judicial Cooperation in Criminal Matters
QMV	Qualified Majority Voting
SEA	Single European Act
SGP	Stability and Growth Pact
TA	Treaty of Amsterdam
TC	Technical Cooperation
TEU	Treaty on European Union (post Lisbon)
TFEU	Treaty on the Functioning of the European Union
TN	Treaty of Nice
TRIPS	Agreement on Trade-Related Aspects of Intellectual Property Rights
UN	United Nations
US	United States
WEU	Western European Union
WTO	World Trade Organization
YEL	Yearbook of European Law

Introduction: European Constitutional Law

'The life of the law has not been logic; it has been experience.'[1] But if it is the fate of the common law to 'stumbl[e] into wisdom',[2] this should be less true of the civil law.[3] For it is the task of legal codes to order experiences into a logical system of norms. Constitutional law is – more often than not – codified law.[4] Most constitutional orders are based on a written constitution; and this written constitution is designed to establish a logical system of rules that provide the 'grammar of politics'.[5] Learning constitutional law is thus like learning a language. One cannot solely learn the words expressing different experiences, one also needs to study the grammatical system that binds these words together. Yet surely, constitutional law is not all about logical rules. As in a language, there may exist exceptions next to the rules, and next to the exceptions may exist absurdities. These exceptions and absurdities are not the result of logic, but of historical experience. Constitutional law will therefore always be about logic *and* experience. It is that part of the law where political theory meets historical reality.

The object of constitutional law is the 'constitution'. But what is a 'constitution'? From a purely 'descriptive' point of view, constitutions simply reflect the institutions and powers of government.[6] From a 'normative' perspective, on the

---

[1] O. W. Holmes, *The Common Law* (Echo Library, 2007), 3.

[2] Cf. G. Radbruch, *Der Geist des Englischen Rechts und die Anglo-Amerikanische Jurisprudenz* (LIT, 2006), 97. Thanks go to my colleague and friend M. Bohlander for pointing me to this treasure.

[3] For the 'civil law' tradition, see: J. H. Merryman, *The Civil Law Tradition: An Introduction to the Legal Systems of Europe and Latin America* (Stanford University Press, 2007).

[4] The 'unwritten' constitution of the United Kingdom is indeed an exception. On its 'exceptional' nature, see: S. E. Finer (et al.), *Comparing Constitutions* (Clarendon Press, 1995), Chapter 3.

[5] H. Laski, *A Grammar of Politics* (HarperCollins, 1967); and see also: T. Paine, *Rights of Man* (Kessinger, 1998), 44: 'The American constitutions were to liberty what a grammar is to language: they define its parts of speech, and practically construct them into syntax.'

[6] This 'descriptive' sense of 'constitution' can be found in Aristotle, *Politics* (translated: E. Baker (OUP, 1998)), Book III, §6–7, 97: 'A constitution may be defined as the organization of the city, in respect of its offices generally, but especially in respect of that particular office which is sovereign in all issues. The civic body is everywhere the sovereign of the city; in fact the civic body is the constitution itself.' In this 'descriptive' sense, there is indeed no distinction between the 'government' and the 'constitution' (cf. E. Zoller, *Droit Constitutionnel* (Presses Universitaires de France, 1998), 10). For the British tradition of the 'descriptive' or 'political' constitution, see: C. Turpin and A. Tomkins, *British Government and the Constitution* (Cambridge University Press, 2011), esp. Chapters 1 and 2.

other hand, constitutions are to 'order' societies according to particular political principles. Normative constitutions thus do not merely reflect the existing 'government', but prescribe its composition and actions. Yet in order to be able to set normative limits to a government, the constitution must be 'above' the government.[7] The normative definition of 'constitution' therefore defines it as the 'highest' law within a society. The constitution has an elevated position above the ordinary law governing a society. (Its higher status is thereby achieved by prohibiting constitutional changes through simple legislation. Constitutions can only be amended by 'constitutional' amendment.[8]) Formally, then, a constitution is best defined as the collection of those norms that 'constitute' a society's highest laws. Within the last two hundred years, this formal definition has competed with a material understanding of what a constitution ought to be. This second definition links the concept of constitution to particular political principles. Following the 'liberal' principle, a constitution should thus establish the rule of law and a separation of powers.[9] And according to the 'democratic' principle, a constitution should set up a 'government of the people, by the people, for the people'.[10]

Is there a European constitution? This question has plagued European law ever since its birth.[11] If we define a constitution as those foundational laws ordering society, then Europe undoubtedly has a constitution.[12] But if we – formally – limit the concept of 'constitution' by reference to the concept of the 'State',[13] then Europe cannot have a constitution. For the European Union is not a State, it is a union of *States*. The state-centred definition of 'constitution' became fashionable in the nineteenth century; and it was partly the result of the state-centred structure of international law.[14] The problem with this reductionist

---

[7] Cf. Paine, *Rights of Man* (supra n. 5), 29: 'A Constitution is a thing antecedent to a government, and a government is only the creature of a constitution.'

[8] The procedural requirements for constitutional amendments are more demanding than for legislative amendments of existing laws. On the amendment power in the United States and the European Union, see: Chapters 1 and 2 below.

[9] Cf. 1789 Declaration of the Rights of Man and of the Citizen, whose Article 16 states: 'A society in which the observance of the law is not assured, nor the separation of powers defined, has no constitution at all.' On the connection between this constitutional 'ideal' and the rise of (bourgeois) liberalism, see: C. Schmitt, *Verfassungslehre* (Duncker & Humblot, 1993), 36.

[10] A. Lincoln, 'Gettysburg Address, 1863' in H. S. Commager and M. Cantor (eds.), *Documents of American History* (Prentice Hall, 1988), vol. I, 428 at 429.

[11] The European legal order is not the only one suffering from this doubt. For the question whether the United Kingdom has a legal constitution, see: E. Barendt, 'Is there a United Kingdom Constitution?' [1997] 12 OJLS 137.

[12] The European Union not only has a 'government' in a descriptive sense. From a normative perspective, it is generally accepted that the Union institutions are the creation of the European Treaties, and that the European Treaties stand above European legislation. And since the European Treaties establish a democratic system in which the 'rule of law' is assured and a separation powers effected, it also has a material constitution. On all these aspects, see: Chapter 2 below.

[13] On this traditional mistake of 'European' constitutionalism, see: Chapter 2 below.

[14] M. Koskenniemi, *From Apology to Utopia: The Structure of International Legal Argument* (Cambridge University Press, 2006).

definition of constitutional law is that it ignores most of the 'constitutional' experiences of humankind in the last two millennia.[15] For did ancient Athens not have a 'constitution'?[16] And what about the 'constitution' of the Roman Republic?[17] And did the 'colonials' who created the 'United *States* of America' not think that the document they had drafted was a 'constitution'?[18] When viewed in light of the broader historical tradition, the European Union has a constitution. And this view corresponds to the self-understanding of the European legal order. In the words of the Court of Justice of the European Union:

> [T]he [EU] Treaty, albeit concluded in the form of an international agreement, none the less constitutes the constitutional charter of a [Union] based on the rule of law. As the Court of Justice has consistently held, the [European] Treaties established a new legal order for the benefit of which the States have limited their sovereign rights, in ever wider fields, and the subjects of which comprise not only Member States but also their nationals. The essential characteristics of the [Union] legal order which has thus been established are in particular its primacy over the law of the Member States and the direct effect of a whole series of provisions which are applicable to their nationals and to the Member States themselves.[19]

The European legal order thus insists that there 'is' a European constitution. Indeed, the 'real' problem of the European Union is not whether there is a European constitution, but that there is '[t]oo much constitutional law'.[20] For in comparison to the 34 articles and amendments that make up the written constitution of the United States, the European Treaties alone contain 413 articles.[21] The European Treaties are thus – with regard to their length – 'bad' constitutional law. For it is the task of constitutions to define the very *principles* on which societies are based. Constitutions should be the 'condensed' – poetic – expression of a legal order.[22] A constitution – as well as the constitutional lawyer – must aspire to be a 'painter of modern life' for they must be able 'to extract from fashion whatever element it may contain of poetry within history,

---

[15] Cf. C. McIlwain, *Constitutionalism: Ancient and Modern* (Liberty Fund, 2008).

[16] Cf. Aristotle, *Constitution of Athens* (translated: K. von Fritz & E. Kapp (Hafner Press, 1974)).

[17] C. A. Lintott, *The Constitution of the Roman Republic* (Oxford University Press, 2003).

[18] On this point, see: Chapter 2 below.

[19] Opinion 1/91 (European Economic Area), [1991] ECR I-6079, para. 21.

[20] For this excellent point – albeit in a specific context – see: B. de Witte, 'Too Much Constitutional Law in the European Union's Foreign Relations?' in M. Cremona and B. de Witte (eds.), *EU Foreign Relations Law – Constitutional Fundamentals* (Hart, 2008), 3.

[21] And this number is – dramatically – increased by the existence of numerous 'Protocols', which enjoy constitutional status. Why was this 'Protocology' (cf. Editorial Comments [2009] CML Rev 1785) necessary? Was there truly a need for a constitutional provision 'concerning imports into the European Union of petroleum products refined in the Netherlands Antilles' (Protocol No. 31)? Here we encounter the historical peculiarities – if not absurdities – of the European Constitution.

[22] On poetry as the most concentrated form of verbal expression, see E. Pound, *ABC of Reading* (New Directions, 1960), 36: 'Dichten = condensare'.

to distil the eternal from the transitory'.[23] Constitutional law must explain how transient governmental experiences 'fit' the constitutional logic of a society.

Length is – unfortunately – not the sole problem of the European constitution. For unlike other constitutional orders, the European constitutional order still struggles with its 'vocabulary'. This not only concerns the difference between 'Union' and 'Community',[24] but such elementary linguistic conventions as what constitutes 'European law'[25] and, within this body of law, 'secondary legislation'.[26] This terminological turmoil is the result of the constant evolution of the European Union. In the past fifty years, the Union hardly ever sat still. For the constitutional 'painter' it has not been a patient 'sitter'. For if constitutional law is about describing fixed – 'constituted' – structures and principles, the Union had often outgrown them before the portrait was finished. The European Union has indeed a *changing* constitution.[27] This constitutional change has come close to being 'revolutionary' with the Lisbon Treaty. The Lisbon Treaty – unlike any

---

[23] C. Baudelaire, *The Painter of Modern Life (and other Essays)* (translated and edited: J. Mayne (Phaidon Press, 1995)), 12.

[24] Students of the European Union will indeed first have to come to terms with the – confusing – terminology. Words and numbers seem in a process of constant change. The Merger Treaty had changed the terminology of the first European Community; the Maastricht Treaty changed the name of the European Economic Community into European Community and created the European Union; the Amsterdam Treaty renumbered all Treaty articles; and, with the Lisbon Treaty, the European Community has been re-baptised into the European Union and all Treaty articles have been renumbered again. The following study will use the term 'European Union' in its broadest sense, that is: as the all-embracing entity within which all European integration has taken place. Thus, even if much of the constitutional consolidation of Europe has historically taken place within the European Community, the book will refer to the constitutional evolution of the European Union. This is the official position after the Lisbon Treaty. For according to Article 1 TEU – third indent: 'The Union shall replace and succeed the European Community'. With the exception of Chapter 1, the book indeed avoids all references to the 'Community', and has tried to 'Lisbonise' all Treaty articles.

[25] The term 'European law' for European Union law still encounters criticism from purist quarters. But was not the 2004 Constitutional Treaty called 'Treaty establishing a Constitution *for Europe*'? And has the Council of Europe a better claim to be 'European law' in light of a membership that stretches beyond Europe? In the following study, European Union law will thus be referred to as 'European law'.

[26] The lack of a common vocabulary within the European legal order is, indeed, most striking with regard to what is meant by 'secondary legislation'. Even the most seasoned European lawyers – including the Court – continue to refer to acts adopted on the basis of the Treaties as 'secondary legislation', or worse: use 'primary' and 'secondary' legislation interchangeably. But this is – especially after the Lisbon Treaty – a serious mistake. For the European Treaties are not primary *Union legislation*. The Treaties are not acts that can be attributed to the Union, nor are they unilateral acts. The European Treaties are authored by the Member States; and, as such, they constitute multilateral treaties – albeit with 'constitutional' effects. For examples of the – wrong – use of 'secondary legislation', see: S. Douglas-Scott, *Constitutional Law of the European Union* (Longman, 2002), 208 and passim; D. Chalmers (et al.), *European Union Law* (Cambridge University Press, 2010), 98 and passim; P. Craig and G. de Búrca, *EU Law* (Oxford University Press, 2011), 180 and passim; A. Dashwood (et al.), *European Union Law* (Hart, 2011), 558 and passim. For the Court's linguistic insensitivity, see: Case C-61/94, *Commission* v. *Germany (IDA)*, [1996] ECR I-3989, para. 52.

[27] On the British *changing* constitution, see: J. Jowell and D. Oliver, *The Changing Constitution* (Oxford University Press, 2011).

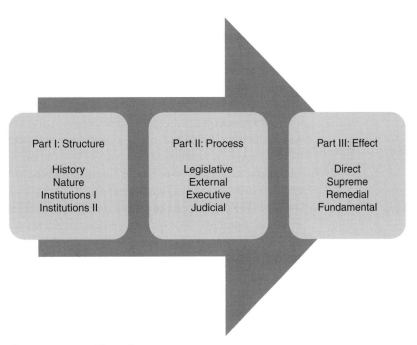

Figure 1 Structure of the Book

other amendment preceding it – has radically altered the constitutional structure of the Union. And it is hard to predict how this structure will be set in motion in the future. To that extent, any constitutional portrait of the Union requires more than a sober analytical eye; it helps to be a 'clairvoyant' or 'seer' to foresee the permanent in the transient.

What then is the structure of this book on European constitutional law? Its structure – significantly – departs from the way in which the European Union is commonly described.[28] It treats the Union as a 'mature' constitutional entity that follows 'classic' constitutional parameters. The book is thereby divided into three parts, which – roughly – correspond to the three ideas of 'structure', 'process', and 'effect'.

Part I analyses the 'structure' of the Union. Chapter 1 here starts by looking at the historical evolution of this structure. The European Treaties are the result of 60 years of constitutional creation and amendment. Is the European Union a federal union; or, is the Union an 'unidentified' *sui generis* object? Chapter 2 attempts to describe the present constitutional structure of the European Union in comparative constitutional terms. It identifies the European Union as a federal union of States. Chapters 3 and 4 zoom in on the governmental structure

---

[28] It is striking that many good textbooks have hardly changed their essential structure – despite the fact that the European Union has significantly changed its structure in the last decades. For an illustration of this – detached – 'traditionalism', see: T. Hartley, *The Foundations of European Union Law* (Oxford University Press, 2010).

of the Union. They analyse each of the Union's 'institutions' as set up by the European Treaties.

The Union will typically discharge its governmental functions by combining various institutions in a 'process'. The 'joint' exercise of governmental powers thereby creates a system of checks and balances. Part II looks at this system by analysing the Union's governmental functions. Chapter 5 starts with the Union's legislative powers and procedures, while Chapter 6 specifically concentrates on its external powers. Chapters 7 and 8 examine – respectively – the executive and judicial branch of the Union.

The results of these processes will lead to European (secondary) law. The effects of this law will be discussed in Part III. We shall see there that European law establishes rights and obligations that directly affect individuals. The direct effects of European law in the national legal orders will be discussed in Chapter 9. Where a European norm is directly effective, it will also be 'supreme' over national law. The 'supremacy' of European law is the subject of Chapter 10. Yet in addition to demanding that conflicting national law be disapplied, how can individuals enforce their European rights? Chapter 11 looks at the availability of remedies that prevent or sanction violations of European law. And the last chapter, Chapter 12, looks – finally – at one particular category of European rights: fundamental rights as guaranteed by the European Constitution.

The book thus moves from the most 'abstract' to the most 'concrete' aspect of European constitutional law. And for those who think from the concrete to the abstract, it might – at first sight – be tempting to read the book from the end to the beginning. The perspective would be as follows: what are the *remedies* in a court examining the *compatibility of national legislation* with an *executive* Union act implementing European *legislation* adopted by the Union *institutions* whose *nature* has been shaped by the *history* of European integration? This perspective is nonetheless not recommended. For each of the chapters builds on its predecessors and for that reason one has to start at the beginning – even if that beginning is farther removed from the everyday experiences of the European citizen. But this 'remoteness' from the private experiences of citizens results from the nature of constitutional rules. For much constitutional law is not about 'primary rules', that is: rules directing individual conduct. It generally deals with 'secondary rules', that is: rules that determine the creation and use of primary rules.[29] In this respect constitutional rules indeed come close to establishing the 'grammar of politics'. For they establish the fundamental rules, which all legal rules within a society must obey.

---

[29] On the distinction between 'primary' and 'secondary' rules in a legal system, see: H. Hart, *The Concept of Law* (Clarendon Press, 1997).

Part I
History and Structure

The European Union has existed for more than half a century. It was originally created between six European States wishing to cooperate closer in the area of coal and steel. Since 1952, the European Union has grown both geographically and thematically. The Union today not only has twenty-seven Member States, it also acts within almost all areas of modern life. Its constitutional and institutional structures have thereby changed in parallel in the past six decades. This first Part looks at this – remarkable – constitutional evolution in Chapter 1. What type of legal 'animal' is the European Union? Can it be described as a 'federal' union? Chapter 2 analyses this question from a comparative constitutional perspective. Chapters 3 and 4 look at the governmental *architecture* of the European Union. Each Union institution will be – individually – presented. By contrast, the interplay between the institutions in discharging the Union's governmental *functions* will be examined in Part II.

Chapter 1 – Constitutional History: From Paris to Lisbon

Chapter 2 – Constitutional Nature: A Federation of States

Chapter 3 – Governmental Structure: Institutions I

Chapter 4 – Governmental Structure: Institutions II

1

Constitutional History: From Paris to Lisbon

Contents

Introduction		9
1.	From Paris to Rome: the European Coal and Steel Community	12
	(a) The (supranational) structure of the ECSC	13
	(b) The (failed) European Defence Community	16
2.	From Rome to Maastricht: the European (Economic) Community	18
	(a) Normative supranationalism: the nature of European law	19
	(b) Decisional supranationalism: the governmental structure	20
	(c) Intergovernmental developments outside the EEC	23
	(d) Supranational and intergovernmental reforms through the Single European Act	26
3.	From Maastricht to Nice: the (old) European Union	27
	(a) The Temple Structure: the Three Pillars of the (Maastricht) Union	29
	(i) The First Pillar: the European Communities	29
	(ii) The Second Pillar: Common Foreign and Security Policy	32
	(iii) The Third Pillar: Justice and Home Affairs	33
	(b) A decade of 'constitutional bricolage': Amsterdam and Nice	33
	(i) The Amsterdam Treaty: dividing the Third Pillar	33
	(ii) The Nice Treaty: limited institutional reform	35
4.	From Nice to Lisbon: the (new) European Union	37
	(a) The (failed) Constitutional Treaty: formal 'total revision'	38
	(b) The Lisbon Treaty: substantive 'total revision'	41
Conclusion		45

Introduction

The idea of European unification is as old as the European idea of the sovereign State.[1] Yet the spectacular rise of the latter overshadowed the idea of European

---

[1] R. H. Foerster, *Die Idee Europa 1300–1946, Quellen zur Geschichte der politischen Einigung* (Deutscher Taschenbuchverlag, 1963).

union for centuries. Within the twentieth century, two ruinous world wars and the social forces of globalisation have discredited the idea of the *sovereign* State. The decline of the monadic State found expression in the spread of inter-state cooperation.[2] And the rise of international cooperation caused a fundamental transformation in the substance and structure of international law. The changed reality of international relations necessitated a change in the theory of international law.[3] The various efforts at European cooperation after the Second World War indeed formed part of this general transition from an international law of coexistence to an international law of cooperation.[4] 'Europe was beginning to get organised.'[5] This development began with three international organisations. First: the Organisation for European Economic Cooperation (1948), which had been created after the Second World War by sixteen European States to administer the international aid offered by the United States for European reconstruction.[6] Second: the Western European Union (1948, 1954) that established a security alliance to prevent another war in Europe.[7] Third: the Council of Europe (1949), which had inter alia been founded to protect human rights and fundamental freedoms in Europe.[8]

None of these grand international organisations was to lead to the European Union. The birth of the latter was to take place in a much humbler sector. The 1951 Treaty of Paris set up the European Coal and Steel Community (ECSC).[9]

---

[2] G. Schwarzenberger, *The Frontiers of International Law* (Stevens, 1962).

[3] C. de Visscher, *Theory and Reality in Public International Law* (Princeton University Press, 1968).

[4] W. G. Friedmann, *The Changing Structure of International Law* (Stevens, 1964).

[5] A. H. Robertson, *European Institutions: Co-Operation, Integration, Unification* (Stevens & Sons, 1973), 17.

[6] The 'European Recovery Programme', also known as the 'Marshall Plan', was named after the (then) Secretary of State of the United States, George C. Marshall. Article 1 of the OEEC Treaty stated: 'The Contracting Parties agree to work in close cooperation in their economic relations with one another. As their immediate task, they will undertake the elaboration and execution of a joint recovery programme.' In 1960, the OEEC was transformed into the thematically broader Organisation for Economic Cooperation and Development (OECD) with the United States and Canada becoming full members of that organisation.

[7] Article IV of the 1948 Brussels Treaty stated: 'If any of the High Contracting Parties should be the object of an armed attack in Europe, the other High Contracting Parties will, in accordance with the provisions of Article 51 of the Charter of the United Nations, afford the party so attacked all the military and other aid and assistance in their power.'

[8] According to Article 1 of the Statute of the Council of Europe, its aim 'is to achieve a greater unity between its Members for the purpose of safeguarding and realising the ideals and principles which are their common heritage and facilitating their economic and social progress' (*ibid.*, paragraph a). This aim was to be pursued through common organs 'by discussion of questions of common concern and by agreements and common action in economic, social, cultural, scientific, legal and admin-istrative matters and in the maintenance and further realisation of human rights and fundamental freedoms' (*ibid.*, paragraph b). The most important expression of this second aim was the development of a common standard of human rights in the form of the European Convention on Human Rights (ECHR). The Convention was signed in 1950 and entered into force in 1953. The Convention established a European Court of Human Rights in Strasbourg (1959).

[9] For a detailed discussion of the negotiations leading up to the signature of the ECSC Treaty, see: H. Mosler, 'Der Vertrag über die Europäische Gemeinschaft für Kohle und Stahl' [1951/2] 14 *Zeitschrift für ausländisches öffentliches Recht und Völkerrecht* 1.

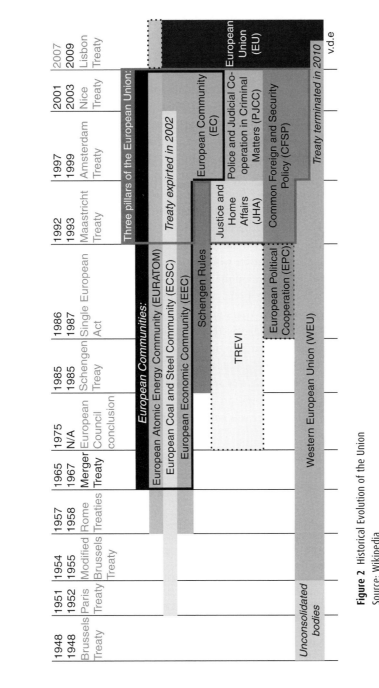

Figure 2 Historical Evolution of the Union

Source: Wikipedia

Its original members were six European States: Belgium, France, Germany, Italy, Luxembourg and the Netherlands. The Community had been created to *integrate* one industrial sector; and the very concept of *integration* indicated the wish of the contracting States 'to break with the ordinary forms of international treaties and organisations'.[10] The Treaty of Paris led to the 1957 Treaties of Rome. The latter created two additional Communities: the European Atomic Energy Community and the European (Economic) Community. The 'three Communities' were partly 'merged' in 1967,[11] but continued to exist in relative independence. A major organisational leap was taken in 1993, when the Maastricht Treaty integrated the three Communities into the European Union. But for a decade, the Treaty on European Union was under constant constitutional construction. And in an attempt to prepare the Union for the twenty-first century, a European Convention was charged to draft a Constitutional Treaty in 2001. Yet the latter failed; and it took almost another decade to rescue the reform as the 2007 Reform (Lisbon) Treaty. The latter replaced the 'old' European Union with the 'new' European Union.

This chapter surveys the historical evolution of the European Union in four sections. Section 1 starts with the humble origins of the Union: the European Coal and Steel Community (ECSC). While limited in its scope, the ECSC introduced a supranational formula that was to become the trademark of the European Economic Community (EEC). The European Economic Community having been analysed in Section 2, Section 3 investigates the development of the (old) European Union founded through the Treaty of Maastricht. Finally, Section 4 reviews the reform efforts of the last decade, and analyses the structure of the – substantively – new European Union as established by the Treaty of Lisbon. Concentrating on the constitutional evolution of the European Union,[12] this chapter will *not* present its geographic development.[13]

1. From Paris to Rome: the European Coal and Steel Community

The initiative to integrate the coal and steel sector came – after an American suggestion – from France.[14] The French Foreign Minister, Robert Schuman,

---

[10] *Ibid.*, 24 (translated: R. Schütze).

[11] This was achieved through the 1965 'Merger Treaty' (see Treaty establishing a Single Council and a Single Commission of the European Communities).

[12] For an overview of the Union's constitutional amendments, see: Annex 1 of this book.

[13] For an overview of the Union's geographic development, see: Annex 2 of this book.

[14] This is how the (then) US Secretary of State, Dean Acheson, wrote to the French Foreign Minister, Robert Schuman: 'Whether Germany will in the future be a benefit or a curse to the free world will be determined, not only by Germany, but by the occupying powers. No country has a greater stake than France in the answer. Our own stake and responsibility is also great. Now is the time for French initiative and leadership of the type required to integrate the German Federal Republic promptly and decisively into Western Europe ... We here in America, with all the will in the world to help and support, cannot give the lead. That, if we are to succeed in this joint endeavour, must come from France.' (US Department of State, Foreign Relations of the United States (Government Printing Office, 1974), vol. III (1949), 623 and 625.)

revealed the plan to build a European Community for Coal and Steel on 9 May 1950:

> Europe will not be made all at once, nor according to a single, general plan. It will be formed by taking measures which work primarily to bring about real solidarity. The gathering of the European nations requires the elimination of the age-old opposition of France and Germany. The action to be taken must first of all concern these two countries. With this aim in view, the French Government proposes to take immediate action on one limited but decisive point. The French Government proposes that Franco-German production of coal and steel be placed under a common [Commission], within an organisation open to the participation of the other European nations. *The pooling of coal and steel production will immediately ensure the establishment of common bases for economic development as a first step in the federation of Europe, and will change the destinies of those regions which have long been devoted to the manufacture of arms, to which they themselves were the constant victims.*[15]

The 'Schuman Plan' was behind the Treaty of Paris (1951) establishing the European Coal and Steel Community. Six European States would create this Community for a period of fifty years.[16] The Treaty of Paris was no grand international peace treaty. It was designed to 'remove the main obstacle to an economic partnership'.[17] This small but decisive first step towards a federal or *supranational* Europe will be discussed first. The 'supranational' idea would soon be exported into wider fields. However, the attempt to establish a supranational European Defence Community, and with it a European Political Community, would fail. Until the Rome Treaties, the European Coal and Steel Community would thus remain the sole supranational Community in Europe.

(a) The (supranational) structure of the ECSC

The structure of the ECSC differed from that of ordinary intergovernmental organisations. It was endowed with a 'Commission',[18] a Parliament,[19] a

---

[15] Schuman Declaration (Paris, 9 May 1950), reproduced in: A. G. Harryvan and J. van der Harst (eds.), *Documents on European Union* (St. Martin's Press, 1997), 61 (emphasis added).

[16] Article 97 ECSC: 'This Treaty is concluded for a period of fifty years from its entry into force.' The Paris Treaty entered into force on 23 July 1952 and expired fifty years later.

[17] J. Gillingham, *Coal, Steel, and the Rebirth of Europe, 1945–1955: The Germans and French from Ruhr Conflict to Economic Community* (Cambridge University Press, 1991), 298.

[18] The original name in the ECSC Treaty was 'High Authority'. In the wake of the 1965 Merger Treaty (cf. Treaty establishing a Single Council and a Single Commission of the European Communities), this name was changed to 'Commission' (*ibid.*, Article 9).

[19] Originally, the ECSC Treaty used the name 'Assembly'. However, in order to simplify the terminology and to allow for horizontal comparisons between the various Communities, I have chosen to refer to the 'Assembly' throughout as 'Parliament'. This is partly justified by the 1957 Convention on Certain Institutions Common to the European Communities (signed on the same day as the Rome Treaties) that established that all three Communities would be served by a single 'Assembly' and a single 'Court'. Early on, the Assembly renamed itself 'Parliament', a change that was only formally recognised by the 1986 SEA.

'Council', and a 'Court'.[20] The ECSC Treaty had placed the Commission at its centre. It was its duty to ensure that the objectives of the Community would be attained.[21] To carry out this task, the Commission would adopt decisions, recommendations and opinions.[22] The Commission would thereby be composed in the following way:

> The [Commission] shall consist of nine members appointed for six years and chosen on the grounds of their general competence ... The members of the [Commission] shall, in the general interest of the Community, be completely independent in the performance of these duties, they shall neither seek nor take instructions from any Government or from any other body. They shall refrain from any action incompatible with the *supranational character of their duties*. Each Member State undertakes to respect this *supranational character* and not to seek to influence the members of the [Commission] in the performance of their tasks.[23]

The Commission constituted the supranational heart of the new Community, while the three remaining institutions were peripheral to its functioning. The Parliament, consisting of delegates who would 'be designated by the respective Parliaments from among their members',[24] had purely advisory functions.[25] The Council,[26] composed of representatives of the national governments,[27] was charged to 'harmonise the action of the [Commission] and that of the Governments, which are responsible for the general economic policies of their countries'.[28] Finally, a Court – formed by seven independent judges – was to 'ensure that in the interpretation and application of this Treaty, and of rules laid down for the implementation thereof, the law is observed'.[29]

In what ways was the European Coal and Steel Community a 'supranational' phenomenon?[30] It could carry out its tasks through the adoption of 'decisions',

---

[20] Article 7 ECSC.   [21] Article 8 ECSC.

[22] Article 14 ECSC. Community acts were thus considered to be acts of the Commission, even if other Community organs had been involved in the decision-making process.

[23] Article 9 ECSC (emphasis added).   [24] Article 21 ECSC.

[25] Article 22 ECSC. The provision envisaged a single annual session for the second Tuesday of March. (Extraordinary sessions could only be held at the request of the Council or the Commission.) The Parliament's powers were defined in Article 24 ECSC and consisted of discussing the general report submitted by the Commission, and a motion of censure on the activities of the Commission.

[26] During the drafting of the ECSC Treaty, the Council had been – reluctantly – added by Jean Monnet to please the Netherlands. The Netherlands had argued that coal and steel issues could not be separated from broader economic issues (see D. Dinan, *Europe Recast: A History of European Union* (Palgrave, 2004) 51). Under the Paris Treaty, the Council's task was primarily that of 'harmonising the action of the [Commission] and that of the governments, which are responsible for the general economic policy of their countries' (Article 26 ECSC). It was seen as a 'political safeguard' to coordinate activities that fell into the scope of the ECSC with those economic sectors that had not been brought into the Community sphere, see: Mosler (supra n. 9), 41.

[27] Article 27 ECSC.   [28] Article 26 ECSC.   [29] Article 31 ECSC.

[30] On the birth of the term 'supranational', see in particular: P. Reuter, 'Le Plan Schuman' [1952] 81 *Recueil des Cours de l'Académie de la Haye* 519, 543 : 'Au cours des négociations sur le Traité on vit apparaître spontanément comme une chose allant de soi le terme de « supranational ». Le succès de cette expression, plutôt nouvelle dans la langue française, fut considérable.'

which would be 'binding in their entirety'.[31] And the directly effective nature of ECSC law led early commentators to presume an 'inherent supremacy of Community law'.[32] The novel character of the Community – its 'break' with the ordinary forms of international organisations – thus lay in the normative quality of its secondary law. Piercing the dualist veil of classic international law, Community law did not require a 'validating' national act before it could become binding on individuals. The Member States were thus deprived of their 'normative veto' at the borders of their national legal orders. The transfer of decision-making powers to the Community indeed represented a transfer of 'sovereign' powers.[33] While the Community still lacked *physical* powers,[34] it was its *normative* powers that would become identified with its 'supranational' character.[35]

However, this was only one dimension of the Community's 'supranationalism'. Under the Treaty of Paris, the organ endowed with supranational powers was itself 'supranational', that is independent of the will of the Member States. The Commission was composed of independent 'bureaucrats' and could act by a majority of its members.[36] While the Commission was admittedly not the only organ of the European Coal and Steel Community, it was its *central* decision-maker. This ability of the Community to bind Member States against their will departed from the 'international' ideal of sovereign equality through unanimity voting. And indeed, it was *this* decisional dimension that had inspired the very notion of supranationalism.[37] Early analysis consequently linked the concept of supranationality to the decision-making mode of the

---

[31] Article 14 (2) ECSC.

[32] Cf. G. Bebr, 'The Relation of the European Coal and Steel Community Law to the Law of the Member States: A Peculiar Legal Symbiosis' [1958] 58 *Columbia Law Review* 767, 788 (emphasis added): 'The supremacy of the Community law is sometimes asserted on the traditional ground of the supremacy of international law. Undeniably the European Coal and Steel Community Treaty is an international Treaty concluded among the several member states. However, any attempt to assimilate the Treaty with traditional international treaties beclouds the true nature of the Treaty. *The fact that Community law can be enforced directly demonstrates the inherent supremacy of the Community law better than any analogy to traditional international treaties which do not penetrate so deeply into national legal systems.*'

[33] Reuter, supra n. 30 at 543.

[34] According to Article 86 ECSC, the Member States undertook 'to take all appropriate measures, whether general or particular, to ensure fulfilment of the obligations resulting from decisions or recommendations of the institutions of the Community and to facilitate the performance of the Community's tasks'. For pecuniary decisions adopted by the Commission, Article 92 (2) ECSC expressly stipulated as follows: 'Enforcement in the territory of Member States shall be carried out by means of the legal procedure in force in each State, after the order for enforcement in the form in use in the State in whose territory the decision is to be enforced has been appended to the decision, without other formality than verification of the authenticity of the decision. This formality shall be carried out at the instance of a Minister designated for this purpose by each of the Governments.' The same was true for judgments of the Court of Justice, cf. Article 44 ECSC.

[35] Cf. A. H. Robertson, 'Legal Problems of European Integration' [1957] 91 *Recueil des Cours de l'Académie de la Haye* 105 at 143–145.

[36] Article 13 ECSC (repealed by the Merger Treaty and replaced by Article 17 ECSC).

[37] On the composition of the Commission, see above.

Community.[38] But the legal formula behind the European Coal and Steel Community was dual: the absence of a normative veto in the national legal orders was complemented by the absence of a decisional veto in the Community legal order.[39]

This dual nature of supranationalism was to become the trademark of the European Union and attempts were soon made to export it into wider fields.

(b) The (failed) European Defence Community

The European Coal and Steel Community had only been 'a first step in the federation of Europe';[40] and the six Member States soon tried to expand the supranational sphere to the area of defence. The idea came from the (then) French Prime Minister, René Pléven. The 'Pléven Plan' suggested 'the creation, for our common defence, of a European army under the political institutions of a united Europe'.[41] For that '[a] minister of defence would be nominated by the participating governments and would be responsible, under conditions to be determined, to those appointing him and to a European [Parliament]'.[42] The plan was translated into a second Treaty signed in Paris that was to establish a second European Community: the European Defence Community (EDC).

The 1952 Paris Treaty was to 'ensure the security of the Member States against aggression' through 'the *integration* of the defence forces of the Member States'.[43] The Treaty thus envisaged the creation of a European army under the command of a supranational institution.[44] Due to disagreement between the Member States, the exact nature of the supranational *political* institution to command the European army had, however, been deliberately left open. The Treaty postponed the problem until six months *after* its coming into force by charging the future Parliament of the EDC to produce an institutional solution:

---

[38] G. Bebr, 'The European Coal and Steel Community: A Political and Legal Innovation' [1953–4] 63 *Yale Law Journal* 1 at 20–4 defining 'supranational powers' as those 'exercised by the [Commission]' alone, 'limited supranational powers' as those acts for which 'the [Commission] needs the concurrence of the Council of Ministers' – qualified or unanimous. Powers reserved to the States were identified with the Council's exclusive competences, that is, where the Treaty required a unanimous decision of the Council without any involvement of the Commission.

[39] Cf. H. L. Mason, *The European Coal and Steel Community: Experiment in Supranationalism* (Martinus Nijhoff, 1955), 34–5.

[40] Cf. 'Schuman Declaration' (supra n. 15).

[41] For the 'Pléven Plan', see: Harryvan and van der Harst (eds.), *Documents on European Union* (supra n. 15), 67.

[42] *Ibid.*   [43] Article 2 (2) EDC.

[44] Article 9 EDC states: 'The Armed Forces of the Community, hereinafter called "European Defence Forces" shall be composed of contingents placed at the disposal of the Community by the Member States with a view to their fusion under the conditions provided for in the present Treaty. No Member State shall recruit or maintain national armed forces aside from those provided for in Article 10 below.' On the history and structure of the European Defence Community (EDC), see: G. Bebr, 'The European Defence Community and the Western European Union: An Agonizing Dilemma' [1954–5] 7 *Stanford Law Review* 169.

Within the period provided for in Section 2 of this Article, the [Parliament] shall study:

(a) the creation of a [Parliament] of the European Defence Community elected on a democratic basis;

(b) the powers which might be granted to such an [Parliament]; and

(c) the modifications which should be made in the provisions of the present Treaty relating to other institutions of the Community, particularly with a view to safeguarding an appropriate representation of the States.

In its work, the [Parliament] will particularly bear in mind the following principles:

The definitive organisation which will take the place of the present transitional organisation should be conceived so as to be capable of constituting one of the elements of an ultimately federal or confederal structure, based upon the principle of the separation of powers and including, particularly, a bicameral representative system.

The [Parliament] shall also study the problems to which the coexistence of different organisations for European cooperation, now in being or to be created in the future, give rise, in order to ensure that these organisations are coordinated within the framework of the federal or confederal structure.[45]

The problem with this postponement strategy was that it did not work. The exact nature of the political authority behind a European army came to be seen as part and parcel of the European Defence Community. And in order to obtain French ratification of the EDC Treaty, the Council of the European Coal and Steel Community decided to create an ad hoc Parliament that would anticipate the work of the future Parliament of the European Defence Community.[46]

The fruit of this anticipatory effort was a proposal for a European Political Community.[47] The Draft Treaty establishing the European Political Community suggested the establishment of a 'European Community of a supranational character', which was to be 'founded upon a union of peoples and States'.[48] The European Political Community was thereby aimed at merging the European Coal and Steel Community and the European Defence Community into a new overall institutional structure.[49] Its central institution was a 'Parliament' that would have consisted of two Houses – the House of

---

[45] Article 38 EDC.

[46] G. Clemens et al., *Geschichte der europäischen Integration* (UTB, 2008), 114.

[47] Draft Treaty embodying the Statute of the European Community (Secretariat of the Constitutional Committee, 1953).

[48] Article 1 Draft Treaty.

[49] Article 5 Draft Treaty: 'The Community, together with the European Coal and Steel Community, and the European Defence Community, shall constitute a single legal entity, within which certain organs may retain such administrative and financial autonomy as is necessary to the accomplishment of the tasks assigned by the treaties instituting the European Coal and Steel Community and the European Defence Community.' See also: Article 56 Draft Treaty: 'The Community shall, with due regard to the provisions of Article 5, exercise the powers and competence of the European Coal and Steel Community and those of the European Defence Community.'

the Peoples and the Senate. This bicameral parliament would have been the principal law-making organ of the European (Political) Community.[50] The novel constitutional structure thus promised to establish a democratic and responsible political authority behind the European Defence Community. Yet despite all efforts and assurances, the European Defence Community – and with it the European Political Community – was a failure. The French Parliament rejected the ratification of the second Paris Treaty in 1954.

The failure of the EDC discredited the idea of *political* integration for decades. European integration consequently returned to the philosophy of *economic* integration.[51] A first suggestion for a 'European revival' concerned the integration of an economic sector adjacent to coal: nuclear energy. This French proposal for further sectoral integration met the criticism of those Member States favouring the creation of a common market for *all* economic sectors.[52] In the end, a compromise solution was chosen that proposed the creation of *two* additional European Communities: the European Atomic Energy Community and the European Economic Community. Each Community was based on a separate international Treaty signed in Rome in 1957. Thanks to its non-sectoral approach, the second Rome Treaty would become the foundation and yardstick for all future European projects.[53] For by establishing a common market, the European Economic Community was to 'lay the foundations of an ever closer union among the peoples of Europe'.[54]

2. From Rome to Maastricht: the European (Economic) Community

The idea of a European Economic Community had first been discussed in 1955 in the Italian city of Messina. The Messina Conference had charged Paul-Henry Spaak to produce a report on the advantages of a common market. On the basis of the 'Spaak Report', the 1957 Rome Treaty establishing the European Economic Community decided to create a common market – both in industrial and agricultural products.

---

[50] Article 10 Draft Treaty: 'Parliament shall enact legislation and make recommendations and proposals. It shall also approve the budget and pass a bill approving the accounts of the Community. It shall exercise such powers of supervision as are conferred upon it by the present Statute.' For an analysis of the European Political Community, see: A. H. Robertson, 'The European Political Community' [1952] 29 *British Yearbook of International Law* 383.

[51] In the words of Paul H. Spaak: 'After the [EDC] venture it was not reasonable to repeat exactly the same experiment a few months later. A means must be found of reaching the same goal – that distant goal of an integrated Europe – by other methods and through other channels. We then considered that, having failed on the political plane, we should take up the question on the economic plane and use the so-called functional method, availing ourselves to some extent – although, of course, without drawing any strict parallels – of the admittedly successful experiment already made with the European Coal and Steel Community.' Cf. Address to the Parliament, 21 October 1955 – quoted in Robertson, *supra* n. 5, at 26.

[52] Clemens (supra n. 46), 126.

[53] According to Dinan (supra n. 26), 76: 'most member states regarded Euratom as irrelevant'.

[54] Article 2 EEC.

The inner core of the European common market was the creation of a customs union. A customs union is an economic union with *no* customs duties and *one* external customs tariff.[55] But the idea behind the EEC Treaty went beyond a customs union. It aimed at the establishment of a common market in goods as well as 'the abolition, as between Member States, of obstacles to freedom of movement for persons, services and capital'.[56] The European Economic Community was equally charged with, inter alia, the adoption of a common transport policy and 'the institution of a system ensuring that competition in the common market is not distorted'.[57] The Rome Treaty was thus – much more than the Treaty of Paris – a framework treaty. It provided a basic constitutional framework and charged the European institutions to adopt legislation to fulfil the objectives of the Treaty. What would this mean for the character of the European Economic Community?

(a) Normative supranationalism: the nature of European law

Like the ECSC, the European Economic Community would enjoy autonomous powers. The EEC Treaty indeed acknowledged two 'supranational' instruments in Article 189 EEC. The Community could directly act upon individuals through legislative 'regulations' or executive 'decisions'. These acts were designed to be directly applicable within the national legal orders. But the Court soon showed its eagerness to go beyond the drafter's design by declaring that, since 'the Community constitutes a new legal order of international law', individuals' rights 'arise not only where they are expressly granted by the Treaty, but also by reason of obligations which the Treaty imposes in a clearly defined way upon individuals as well as upon the Member States'.[58] The direct effect of Community law – its ability to be applied by national courts – would indeed become the 'ordinary' state of European law.[59] The normative quality of European law contrasted with the 'ordinary' state of international law:

> By contrast with ordinary international treaties, the EEC Treaty has created its own legal system which, on the entry into force of the Treaty, became an integral part of the legal systems of the Member States and which their courts are bound to apply . . . The integration into the laws of each Member State of provisions which derive from the Community, and more generally the terms and the spirit of the Treaty, make it impossible for the States, as a corollary, to accord precedence to a unilateral and subsequent measure over a legal system accepted by them on a basis of reciprocity. Such a measure cannot therefore be inconsistent with that

---

[55] The existence of a single external custom distinguishes a customs union from a free trade area. Within the 'European' context, such a free trade area existed in the 'European Free Trade Association' (EFTA) established in 1960. EFTA had originally been suggested by Great Britain to create a counterweight to the EEC's common market project. The original seven EFTA members were: Austria, Denmark, Norway, Portugal, Sweden, Switzerland, and the United Kingdom.

[56] Article 3 (c) EEC.   [57] Article 3 (e) and (f) EEC.

[58] Case 26/62, *Van Gend en Loos*, [1963] ECR 1 at 12.   [59] On this point, see: Chapter 9 below.

legal system. The executive force of Community law cannot vary from one State to another in deference to subsequent domestic laws, without jeopardizing the attainment of the objectives of the Treaty[.][60]

This famous passage announced the supremacy of Community law over national law. Where two equally applicable norms of European and national law would come into conflict, the former would prevail over the latter. The law stemming from the EEC Treaty was 'an independent source of law' that 'could not, because of its special and original nature, be overridden by domestic legal provisions, however framed, without being deprived of its character as Community law and without the legal basis of the Community itself being called into question'.[61] European law would thus not only enjoy direct effect, it would also be a supreme law in the Member States. The Court thus confirmed and developed the supranational quality of European law anticipated by the European Coal and Steel Community.

(b) Decisional supranationalism: the governmental structure

The Rome Treaty had established a number of institutions, which were modelled on those of the Paris Treaty.[62] Yet underneath semantic similarities, the institutional balance within the European Economic Community differed significantly from that of the European Coal and Steel Community. Indeed, the EEC Treaty carefully avoided all references to the concept of 'supranationalism'.[63]

Had this decline in decisional supranationalism been designed? Early doubts about the supranational nature of the EEC were not confined to semantics. The enormously enlarged scope for European integration had required a price: the return to a more international format of decision-making. Emblematically, the EEC Treaty now charged the Council – not the Commission – with the task '[t]o ensure that the objectives set out in this Treaty are attained'.[64] Instead of the 'supranational' Commission, it was the 'international' Council that operated as the central decision-maker.[65] The Council was composed of 'representatives of the Member States';[66] and it would, when deciding by unanimous agreement, follow traditional international law logic.[67] However, the

---

[60] Case 6/64, *Costa* v. *ENEL*, [1964] ECR 585 at 593–4.   [61] *Ibid.*, at 594.

[62] Article 4 EEC. The Rome Treaty had been drafted on the understanding that the Parliament and the Court of the European Coal and Steel Community would be the same for the European Economic Community. However, the executive organs of both Communities still differed. This institutional 'separatism' changed with the 1965 Merger Treaty that 'merged' the executive organs of all three Communities.

[63] R. Efron and A. S. Nanes, 'The Common Market and Euratom Treaties: Supranationality and the Integration of Europe' [1957] 6 *International & Comparative Law Quarterly* 670 at 682.

[64] Article 145 EEC.

[65] Cf. Robertson (supra n. 35), 159–60: 'Indeed, it was the reluctance of governments in subsequent years to accept anything in the nature of the supranational which produced the result that the powers of the Commission of the EEC were less extensive than those of the [ECSC Commission].'

[66] Article 146 EEC.   [67] Efron and Nanes, supra n. 63, 675.

Rome Treaty avoided a pure intergovernmental solution by insisting on the prerogative of the (supranational) Commission to initiate Community bills.

Decisional supranationalism could be seen at work once the Council acted by (qualified) majority. Following a transitional period,[68] the Rome Treaty indeed envisaged a range of legal bases allowing for qualified majority voting in the Council. Yet famously, the supranational machinery received – early on – an intergovernmental spanner. The political interruption stemmed again from France, but this time it was not the French Parliament which rocked the European boat. Behind the first constitutional crisis of the EEC stood the (then) French President: General Charles de Gaulle. What was the General's problem? The Community was about to start using qualified majority voting when it passed into the third transitional phase on 1 January 1966.[69] In March 1965, the Commission had made a – daring – proposal for the financing of the Community budget. The Council stormily discussed the proposal in June of that year; and after an inconclusive debate, the French Foreign Minister declared the discussions to have failed. The Commission made a new proposal, but the French government boycotted the Council. This boycott became famous as France's 'empty chair' policy. France would not take its chair within the Council unless a 'compromise' was found that balanced the (imminent) move to majority voting with France's national interests. To solve this constitutional conflict, the Community organised two extraordinary Council sessions in Luxembourg. The compromise between the supranational interests of the Community and the national interests of its Member States became known as the 'Luxembourg Compromise'.[70] The latter declared:

> Where, in the case of decisions which may be taken by majority vote on a proposal of the Commission, very important interests of one or more partners are at stake, the Members of the Council will endeavour, within a reasonable time, to reach solutions which can be adopted by all the Members of the Council while respecting their mutual interests and those of the Community, in accordance with Article 2 of the Treaty. With regard to the preceding paragraph, the French delegation considers that where very important interests are at stake, the discussion must be continued until unanimous agreement is reached. The six delegations note that there is a divergence of views on what should be done in

[68] The Rome Treaty had established a transitional period of twelve years, divided into three stages of four years. The procedure for this transitional period was set out in Article 8 EEC. During the first two stages of the transitional period unanimous decisions would remain the rule; e.g., Article 43 (2) EEC: 'The Council shall, on a proposal from the Commission and after consulting the [Parliament], acting unanimously during the first two stages and by a qualified majority thereafter, make regulations, issue directives, or take decisions, without prejudice to any recommendations it may also make.'

[69] While Article 8 EEC had envisaged a political decision to pass from the first to the second stage (paragraph 3), the passage from the second to the third stage was to be automatic. France would thus not have been able to block the transition by 'legal' means established in the EEC Treaty.

[70] 'Final Communiqué of the Extraordinary Session of the Council' [1966] 3 *Bulletin of the European Communities* 5. For an extensive extract from the 'Luxembourg Compromise', see: Appendix 3 of this book.

the event of a failure to reach complete agreement. The six delegations never-theless consider that this divergence does not prevent the Community's work being resumed in accordance with the normal procedure.[71]

The formal status of the Luxembourg Compromise, as well as its substantive content, was ambiguous. Textually, its wording did not grant each Member State a constitutional right to veto Community decisions. Nonetheless, decision-making in the Council would henceforth take place under the 'shadow of the veto'.[72] The Damoclean sword of the Luxembourg Compromise led to consen-sual decision-making within the Council even for legal bases that allowed for (qualified) majority voting.[73] This 'constitutional convention' would influence the decisional practice of the Community for almost two decades.[74]

But the young European Economic Community (partly) balanced this decline of decisional supranationalism *in the Council* by a rise of decisional supranationalism in two other Community institutions. A small but significant step towards decisional supranationalism was achieved in the European Parliament, when the Community chose to replace the financial contributions of the Member States with its own resources.[75] To compensate for this decline of *national* parliamentary control over State contributions, it was felt necessary to increase the *supranational* controlling powers of the European Parliament.[76] And to increase the democratic credentials of that Parliament, the latter was 'transformed' from an 'assembly' of national parliamentarians into a directly elected Parliament.[77] Sadly, this rise in the Parliament's democratic credentials was not immediately matched by a rise in its powers beyond the budgetary

---

[71] *Ibid.*

[72] For this nice metaphor, see: J. Weiler, 'The Transformation of Europe' [1990–1] 100 *Yale Law Journal* 2403 at 2450.

[73] There is not yet much historical evidence on the politico-constitutional impact of the Luxembourg Compromise. Suffice to say here that the 1974 Paris Communiqué (infra n. 95, paragraph 6) noted that the Heads of State 'consider that it is necessary to renounce the practice which consists of making agreement on all questions conditional on the unanimous consent of the Member States, whatever their respective position may be regarding the conclusions reached in Luxembourg on 28 January 1966'.

[74] On the gradual decline of the Luxembourg Compromise, see: L. Van Middelaar, 'Spanning the River : the Constitutional Crisis of 1965–1966 as the Genesis of Europe's Political Order' [2008] 4 *European Constitutional Law Review* 98 at 119–23.

[75] Cf. 'First Budget Treaty' ('Treaty amending Certain Budgetary Provisions', 1970), 1971 OJ L2/1 and 'Second Budget Treaty' ('Treaty amending Certain Financial Provisions', 1975), 1977 OJ L359/1.

[76] The First Budget Treaty distinguished between compulsory and non-compulsory expenditure and gave Parliament the power to control the latter (cf. Article 4 of the 1970 Budget Treaty). The 1975 Treaty increased the budgetary power of Parliament to reject the Community budget as a whole (cf. Article 12 of the 1975 Budget Treaty), and would create the Court of Auditors (cf. Article 15 of the 1975 Budget Treaty).

[77] This transformation had been envisaged, from the very beginning, by Article 138 (3) EEC: 'The [Parliament] shall draw up proposals for elections by direct universal suffrage in accordance with a uniform procedure in all Member States. The Council shall, acting unanimously, lay down the appropriate provisions, which it shall recommend to Member States for adoption in accordance with their respective constitutional requirements.' The Council decision was taken on 20 September 1976 and the Member States ratified it in 1977. On 8 April 1978, the Council decided

process. Parliamentary involvement in the exercise of the Community's legislative powers would have to wait until the Single European Act.[78]

Until this time, it was a third institution that came to rescue the 'deficient
Community legislator' – the Court of Justice.[79] In the late 1970s, the Court
decided to take decision-making into its own hands. Instead of waiting for
positive integration through European legislation, the Court chose to integrate
the common market *negatively*. This strategy of 'negative integration' would not
depend on political agreement within the Council.[80] It pressed for market
integration by judicial means. The famous illustration of this shift *within*
decisional supranationalism from positive integration to negative integration
is *Cassis de Dijon*.[81] The case concerned a sale prohibition for a French fruit
liqueur in Germany. The importer had applied for a marketing authorisation,
which had been refused by the German authorities on the ground that, in the
absence of European harmonisation, the national rules on consumer protection
applied. Despite a proposal for the harmonisation of the relevant national
rules,[82] no action had been forthcoming as a result of the decisional intergovernmentalism in the Council. This would originally have been the end of
the story. But after a decade of judicial patience, the Court had none of it. It
declared that – even in the absence of positive harmonisation – the Member
States could not impose their national legislation on imports, unless this
was justified by *European* mandatory requirements of public interest.[83] The
judgment elevated the principle of mutual recognition to a general constitutional principle of the common market. The constitutional idea behind *Cassis de
Dijon* was that the decline of decisional supranationalism in the Council would,
if need be, be compensated for by the rise of judicial supranationalism.

(c) Intergovernmental developments outside the EEC

The analysis of the second period in the evolution of the European Union
would be incomplete if we concentrated solely on the supranational developments *within* the European Economic Community. For there were important
developments *outside* the Community, which would – with time – shape the

---

to hold the Parliament's first elections on 7–10 June 1979. On today's election procedure for the
European Parliament, see: Chapter 3 – Section 2(a) below.

[78] Beyond its budgetary powers, Parliament remained primarily an 'advisory' institution – even if
its advice was to be a compulsory procedural requirement. Cf. Case 138/79, *Roquette Frères* v.
Council (Isoglucose), [1980] ECR 3333.

[79] P. Pescatore, 'La Carence du Législateur Communautaire et le Devoir du Juge' in G. Lüke,
G. Ress, and M. R. Will (eds.), *Rechtsvergleichung, Europarecht und Staatenintegration:
Gedächtnisschrift für Léontin-Jean Constantinesco* (Heymanns, 1983), 559.

[80] The distinction between 'positive' and 'negative' integration is said to stem from J. Pinder,
'Positive Integration and Negative Integration: Some Problems of Economic Union in the EEC'
[1968] 24 *The World Today* 88.

[81] Case 120/78, *Rewe-Zentral* v. *Bundesmonopolverwaltung für Branntwein (Cassis de Dijon)*,
[1979] ECR 649.

[82] *Ibid.*, paragraph 8.   [83] *Ibid.*

structure and content of the future European Union. These intergovernmental developments began when the transitional period of the EEC came to a close by the end of the 1960s. Far from constituting the 'dark ages' of the Community, this period saw '[t]he revival of ambition'.[84] The search for a 'Europe of the second generation' began in 1969 with the Hague Summit.[85] Its Final Communiqué called inter alia for the promotion of 'economic and monetary union', and 'progress in the matter of political unification'.[86]

The possibility of economic and monetary union was explored in the Werner Report.[87] The report called for the realisation of monetary union 'to ensure growth and stability within the Community and reinforce the contribution it can make to economic and monetary equilibrium in the world and make it a pillar of stability'.[88] However, disagreement existed on how to achieve this aim. Should economic union precede monetary union; or should monetary union precede and precipitate economic union?[89] The dispute was never resolved; but a compromise would – after years of debate and delay – lead to the establishment of the European Monetary System in 1979.

The possibility of political union was explored in the Davignon Report, which laid the foundations for a 'European Political Cooperation'. The report linked political unification with cooperation in the field of foreign policy. This cooperation was to 'ensure greater mutual understanding with respect to the major issues of international politics, by exchanging information and consulting regularly' and to 'increase their solidarity by working for a harmonisation of views, concertation of attitudes and joint action when it appears feasible and desirable'.[90] To achieve these objectives, the Member States decided to have their foreign Ministers regularly meet at the initiative of the President-in-office-of the Council. But importantly, this was not the creation of a supranational foreign policy: European Political Cooperation was a strictly intergovernmental mechanism outside the European Communities. In this way, old French wounds from the (failed) European Defence and Political Communities would not be re-opened.[91]

A third intergovernmental development concerned the area of justice and home affairs. Following discussions on European Political Cooperation, the

---

[84] This is the title of Chapter 11 of D. Urwin, *The Community of Europe: A History of European Integration Since 1945* (Longman, 1994).

[85] Cf. R. Bieber (ed.), *Das Europa der Zweiten Generation: Gedächtnisschrift für Christoph Sasse* (Engel, 1981).

[86] 'Final Communiqué of the Meeting of the Heads of State or Government of the EEC (The Hague, 1969)' in Harryvan and van der Harst (eds.), *Documents* (supra n. 15), 168–9, paragraphs 8 and 15.

[87] For the 'Werner Report', see also: *ibid.*, 169.   [88] *Ibid.*, 170.

[89] The former option was advocated by Germany and is known as the 'coronation theory', and its advocates were referred to as the 'economists'. The second option was argued by France and is known as the 'locomotive theory', and its advocates were known as the 'monetarists'.

[90] Harryvan and van der Harst (eds.), *Documents* (supra n. 15), 173 at 174.

[91] Urwin (supra n. 84), 147.

Member States decided to set up the 'TREVI' mechanism.[92] Originally designed as a political instrument to fight international terrorism, its scope was subsequently enlarged to the coordination of police and judicial efforts to combat organised crime. In light of this development, some Member States were increasingly willing to abolish border controls; and an international treaty between five Member States was signed in 1985 near Schengen.[93] The Schengen Agreement and its implementing convention aimed at establishing an area without border controls, with common rules on visas, and police and judicial cooperation.[94] This 'Schengen Area' would constitute an independent intergovernmental regime outside the European Communities until it was integrated into the European Union structure a decade later.

Finally, there is a fourth intergovernmental development that emerges in this period of European integration: the birth of the 'European Council'. The 1969 Hague Summit had shown the potential for impulse that the Heads of State or Government could give to the evolution of the European Communities. And when the Community traversed the global recession in the 1970s, the Heads of State or Government decided to realise this potential and began to meet regularly. The Final Communiqué of the 1974 Paris Summit thus 'institutionalised' these summit meetings in the following terms:

> Recognizing the need for an overall approach to the internal problems involved in achieving European unity and the external problems facing Europe, the Heads of Government consider it essential to ensure progress and overall consistency in the activities of the Communities and in the work on political cooperation. The Heads of Government have therefore decided to meet, accompanied by the Ministers of Foreign Affairs, three times a year and whenever necessary, in the Council of the Communities in the context of political cooperation. The administrative secretariat will be provided for in an appropriate manner with due regard to existing practices and procedures. In order to ensure consistency in Community activities and continuity of work, the Ministers of Foreign Affairs, meeting in the Council of the Community, will act as initiators and coordinators. They may hold political cooperation meetings at the same time.[95]

---

[92] The mechanism was established following the Rome European Council of 1 December 1975. In French, the French acronym 'TREVI' came to stand for 'terrorism', 'radicalism', 'extremism' and 'international' 'violence'. However, 'Trevi' is also the name of a famous fountain in Rome.

[93] Agreement between the Governments of the States of the Benelux Economic Union, the Federal Republic of Germany and the French Republic on the gradual abolition of checks at their common borders ('Schengen Agreement'), [2000] OJ L 239, 13–18. The original 'Schengen States' were: Belgium, France, Germany, Luxembourg and the Netherlands. These Member States signed the 1990 'Convention implementing the Schengen Agreements', [2000] OJ L 239/19–62.

[94] The Schengen Agreement and the Schengen Convention contained provisions dealing with police cooperation, cf. Articles 39–47 of the Schengen Convention. For an early analysis of 'Schengen', see: J. Schutte, 'Schengen: its meaning for the free movement of persons in Europe' [1991] 28 CML Rev 549.

[95] 'Communiqué of the Meeting of the Heads of State or Government (Paris, 1974)' reproduced in: Harryvan and van der Harst (eds.), *Documents on European Union* (supra n. 15), 181.

The establishment of the European Council as a semi-permanent 'government' of the European Communities was a momentous development.[96] While formally created 'outside' the Rome Treaty, it would evolve into a powerful political motor of European integration and thereby complement the task of the supranational engine of the Commission.

(d) Supranational and intergovernmental reforms through the Single European Act

Despite important supranational and intergovernmental developments within and without the European Communities in thirty years, the first major Treaty reform would only take place in 1986 through the Single European Act (SEA). The Act received its name from the fact that it combined two reforms in a *single* document. On the one hand, the SEA represented a constitutional reform of the European Economic Community.[97] On the other hand, it reformed the European Political Cooperation as an intergovernmental mechanism outside the formal structure of the European Communities.[98]

The core of the constitutional reform within the European Communities lay in the idea of completing the internal market by '1992'.[99] The project had been devised in the 1985 White Paper 'Completing the Internal Market',[100] which would become the centrepiece of the newly invested Delors Commission. Leaving the legislative failures of the past behind, it sought to revamp the idea of positive integration. A fresh term – the internal market – reflected the desire to break with the past and to realise this fundamental aim of the original Rome Treaty. In order to achieve this aim, the SEA not only expanded the Community's competences significantly, but it equally reformed its institutional

---

[96] This was confirmed in the 'Solemn Declaration on European Union' (Stuttgart, 1983), reproduced in: Harryvan and van der Harst (eds.), *Documents on European Union* (supra n. 15), 214 at 215 (paragraph 2.1.2): 'In the perspective of the European Union, the European Council provides a general political impetus to the construction of Europe; defines approaches to further the construction of Europe and issues general political guidelines for the European Communities and European Political Cooperation; deliberates upon matters concerning European Union in its different aspects with due regard to consistency among them; initiates cooperation in new areas of activity; solemnly expresses the common position in questions of external relations.'

[97] Title II of the SEA deals with 'Provisions amending the Treaties establishing the European Communities'.

[98] Article 1 SEA: 'Political Cooperation shall be governed by Title III. The provisions of that Title shall confirm and supplement the procedures agreed in the reports of Luxembourg (1970), Copenhagen (1973), London (1981), the Solemn Declaration on European Union (1983) and the practices gradually established among the Member States.'

[99] Article 13 SEA was to introduce the following provision into the EEC Treaty: 'The Community shall adopt measures with the aims of progressively establishing the internal market over a period expiring on 31 December 1992 . . . The internal market shall comprise an area without internal frontiers in which the free movement of goods, persons, services and capital is ensured in accordance with the provisions of this Treaty.'

[100] 'Completing the Internal Market: White Paper from the Commission to the European Council', COM (85) 310.

structure in three ways. First, the Single European Act expanded supranational decision-making in the Council by adding legal bases allowing for (qualified) majority voting.[101] Second, the legislative powers of the European Parliament were significantly enhanced by means of a new law-making procedure: the cooperation procedure.[102] Third, the Court of Justice would be assisted by another court. Due to its jurisdiction 'to hear and determine at first instance', the Court would become known as the 'Court of First Instance'.[103]

However, the constitutional reforms of the Single European Act also had left important aspects outside the supranational structure of the European Communities. Indeed, all four intergovernmental developments discussed in the previous subsection continued to be outside the European Treaties. The Single European Act indeed did *not* bring the 'European Monetary System' under a supranational roof.[104] The SEA did *not* integrate foreign affairs – even if it placed EPC on a more formal legal footing. The SEA did *not* bring justice and home affairs within the scope of the European Treaties. And while formally recognising the European Council,[105] the SEA had *not* elevated it to the status of a Community institution. It would take two more decades before all four issues were finally resolved.

These future developments took place in a third historical period. They will be discussed in the next section.

3. From Maastricht to Nice: the (old) European Union

Thanks to its thematic proximity to the internal market, economic and monetary union soon came to be seen as the next stage in the process of European integration. Following the 'Delors Report',[106] the 1989 European Council decided to push the matter by calling for an Intergovernmental Conference.[107] The decision provoked an inspired response from the European Parliament, which argued that it was 'increasingly necessary rapidly to transform the European Community into a European Union of federal type'.[108] Pointing to the Single

---

[101]   The most famous additional legal basis to put this constitutional mandate into effect was – what is today – Article 114 TFEU allowing the Community to adopt harmonisation measures by qualified majority.

[102]   Cf. Articles 6 and 7 SEA.   [103]   Article 11 SEA.

[104]   However, in order to ensure the convergence of economic and monetary policies, Article 20 SEA imposed a duty on the Member States to 'take account of the experience acquired in cooperation within the framework of the European Monetary System (EMS) and in developing the ECU'.

[105]   Article 2 SEA.

[106]   European Communities, 'Report of the Committee for the Study of Economic and Monetary Union' [1989] 4 *Bulletin of the European Communities*, 8. For an early analysis of the report, see: N. Thygesen, 'The Delors Report and European Economic and Monetary Union' [1989] 65 *International Affairs* 637.

[107]   European Council (Madrid, 26 and 27 June 1989), 'Conclusions of the Presidency' [1989] 6 *Bulletin of the European Communities* 8 at 11.

[108]   European Parliament, Resolution of 14 March 1990 on the Intergovernmental Conference in the context of Parliament's strategy for European Union ([1990] OJ C 96/114), Preamble B.

European Act,[109] Parliament insisted: 'the agenda of the Intergovernmental Conference must be enlarged beyond economic and monetary union'.[110] Having received eminent support,[111] this request for a link between *monetary* and *political* union was heard by the European Council.[112] The European Council thus called for *two* parallel intergovernmental conferences. They would result in the 'Treaty on European Union' signed in Maastricht in 1992, which entered into force a year later.[113]

The Treaty on European Union represented 'a new stage in the process of European integration'.[114] Yet it was a constitutional compromise: the Member States had been unable to agree on placing all new policies into the supranational structure of the European Communities. From the four Single European Act 'leftovers', solely economic and monetary union would become a supranational policy – and that at the price of differential integration.[115] By contrast, the European Council as well as the two remaining intergovernmental policies – Foreign and Security Policy and Justice and Home Affairs – would retain their intergovernmental character. However, it was agreed to strengthen their institutional links with the Community system. This was achieved by placing the European Council, the two intergovernmental policies *as well as the European Communities* under a common legal roof: the European Union. The overall constitutional structure was defined by the first article of the (old) Treaty on European Union:

> By this Treaty, the High Contracting Parties establish among themselves a European Union, hereinafter called 'the Union'. This Treaty marks a new stage in the process of creating an ever closer union among the peoples of Europe, in

---

[109] The commitment to review the procedures on European Political Cooperation had been made in Article 30 (12) SEA: 'Five years after the entry into force of this Act the High Contracting Parties shall examine whether any revision of Title III is required.'

[110] European Parliament (supra n. 108), paragraph 1.

[111] Cf. letter by the German Chancellor Kohl and the French President Mitterrand to the Irish Presidency (19 April 1990), in: Harryvan and van der Harst (eds.), *Documents on European Union* (supra n. 15), 252: 'In the light of far-reaching changes in Europe and in view of the completion of the single market and the realisation of economic and monetary union, we consider it necessary to accelerate the political construction of the Europe of the Twelve.'

[112] European Council (Rome, 14 and 15 December 1990), 'Presidency Conclusions' [1990] 12 *Bulletin of the European Communities* 7.

[113] The Treaty on European Union was, at first, rejected by Denmark. It was eventually ratified after concessions made to Denmark by the Edinburgh European Council (cf. 'Denmark and the Treaty on European Union', [1992] OJ C 348/1). The German Constitutional Court posed a second ratification challenge. On the famous 'Maastricht Decision' of the German Constitutional Court, see: Chapter 2 Section 4(b).

[114] Preamble of the TEU.

[115] 'Differential integration' means that not all Member States take part in the integration project. The decision to establish a differential constitutional regime for economic and monetary union had been taken early on in the negotiations of the Maastricht Treaty. Only those States fulfilling the 'convergence criteria' would be allowed to participate. In addition, the Member States agreed to allow for opt-outs to those Member States that, while entitled to participate, would not wish to do so (infra n. 128).

which decisions are taken as closely as possible to the citizens. The Union shall be founded on the European Communities, supplemented by the policies and forms of cooperation established by this Treaty. Its task shall be to organise, in a manner demonstrating consistency and solidarity, relations between the Member States and between their peoples.[116]

The provision established a separate international organisation – the European Union – that was different from the European Communities. What was the relationship between the two organisations? Due to the textual structure of the Maastricht Treaty, the relationship came to be compared – somewhat misleadingly – to a Greek temple. This temple architecture became the defining characteristic of the 'old' (Maastricht) European Union and will be discussed first. Subsequent treaty amendments within this third period kept the Union's pillar structure intact, but strengthened and widened the supranational elements of the First Pillar significantly.

(a) The Temple Structure: the Three Pillars of the (Maastricht) Union

The legal structure of the Maastricht *Treaty* led the European Union to be identified with a Greek temple. The 'common provisions' would form the roof of the Union 'temple'. They laid down common objectives,[117] and established that the Union was to 'be served by a single institutional framework'.[118] Underneath this common roof were the three pillars of the Union: the European Communities (First Pillar), the Common Foreign and Security Policy (Second Pillar), and Justice and Home Affairs (Third Pillar). The base of the temple was formed by a second set of provisions common to all three pillars: the 'final provisions' of the Maastricht Treaty. These final provisions not only determined the relationship between the pillars,[119] but also contained common rules for their amendment.[120] Importantly, apart from the common and final provisions, each of the three pillars was subject to its own rules. The constitutional fragmentation caused by the Maastricht Treaty was consequently criticised as having created a 'Europe of bits and pieces'.[121]

(i) The First Pillar: the European Communities
At the heart of the Maastricht Treaty lay a fundamental reform of the European Communities and, in particular: the European Economic Community. And due to the substantially enlarged scope, the latter would henceforth be renamed the European Community.[122]

---

[116] Article A EU (old).   [117] Article B EU (old).
[118] Article C EU (old). Remarkably, no common legal personality was established for the Union.
[119] Article M EU (old).   [120] Article N EU (old).
[121] D. Curtin, 'The constitutional structure of the Union: a Europe of bits and pieces' [1993] 30 CML Rev 17.
[122] Article G (A) (1) EU (old): 'The term "European Economic Community" shall be replaced by the term "European Community".'

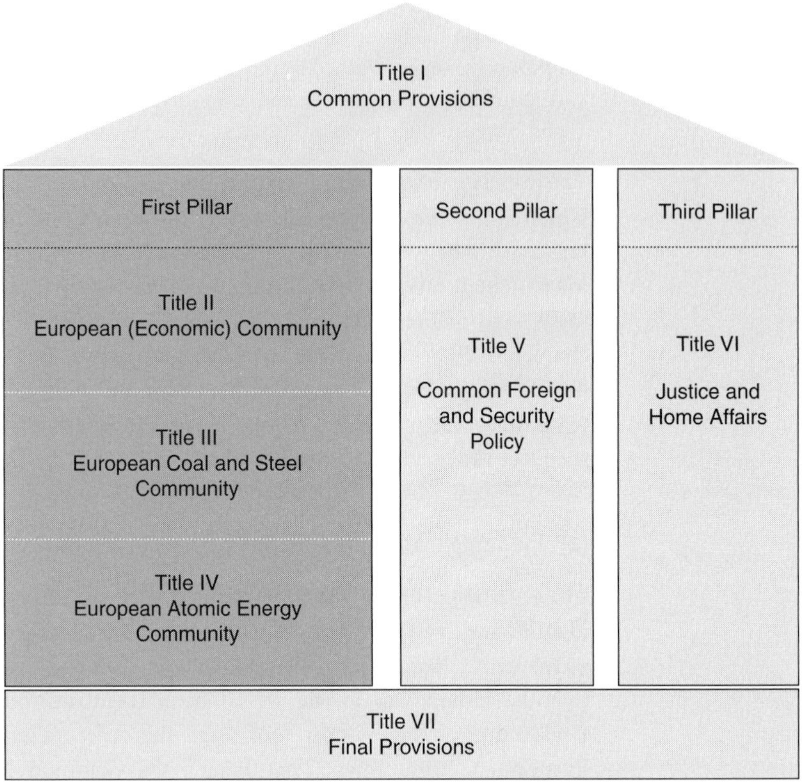

Figure 3 Pillar Structure of the 'old' (Maastricht) Union

The Maastricht Treaty significantly enlarged the competences of the European Community. Most importantly, it introduced a supranational monetary policy and thereby established the 'European System of Central Banks' (ESCB) and the 'European Central Bank' (ECB).[123] The primary objective of the latter was to maintain price stability and its basic tasks would include 'to define and implement the monetary policy of the Community' and 'to conduct foreign exchange operations'.[124] The ECB would eventually have the exclusive right to authorise the issue of bank notes ('euros') within the Community.[125] The process leading to monetary union was thereby divided into three stages. Participation in the

---

[123] Article G (B) (7) EU (old).   [124] Article G (D) (25) EU (old).

[125] *Ibid*. The timetable was set by what was to become the future Article 100j EC. The Council was called to decide 'not later than 31 December 1996' 'whether it is appropriate for the Community to enter the third stage; and if so, set the date for the beginning of the third stage' (*ibid*., paragraph 3). And if that had not been done by the end of 1997, it was provided that 'the third stage shall start on 1 January 1999' (*ibid*., paragraph 4). The decision to introduce the euro was eventually taken by (Council) Regulation 974/98 on the Introduction of the Euro ([1998] OJ L 139/1), cf. Article 2: 'As from 1 January 1999 the currency of the participating Member States shall be the euro. The currency unit shall be one euro. One euro shall be divided into one hundred cents.'; and Article 10 determined the date for the introduction of the euro notes: 'As from 1 January 2002, the ECB and the central banks of the participating Member States shall put into circulation banknotes denominated in euro. Without prejudice to Article 15, these

third stage would depend on the fulfilment of certain economic criteria.[126] Member States were obliged to avoid excessive government deficits and the Commission would be entitled to monitor budgetary discipline.[127] For two Member States, this was too much supranationalism and they decided to 'opt out' of economic and monetary union.[128]

What institutional changes were brought by the Maastricht reform? With regard to political union, the Maastricht Treaty created a number of important innovations. First, it introduced the political status of a 'citizenship of the Union'.[129] Apart from free movement rights, Union citizens would henceforth enjoy a number of political rights. These would include 'the right to vote and to stand as a candidate at municipal elections' in another Member State, 'the right to vote and to stand as a candidate in elections to the European Parliament' in another Member State, as well as the right to protection by the diplomatic or consular authorities of any Member State.[130] Second, the constitutional prerogatives of the European Parliament were significantly expanded.[131] The most striking aspect of the rising *democratic* supranationalism within the Union was the introduction of a new legislative procedure: the co-decision procedure. Going beyond the cooperation procedure of the Single European Act, the

banknotes denominated in euro shall be the only banknotes which have the status of legal tender in all these Member States.'

[126] Article G (D) (25) EU (old) – inserting Article 109j EC. The convergence criteria were further defined in the 'Protocol on the Convergence Criteria referred to in Article 109j of the TEU' that was attached to the Maastricht Treaty.

[127] Article G (D) (25) EU (old) – inserting Article 104c EC. The details of the excessive deficit procedure referred to in Article 104c EC Treaty were spelled out in the 'Protocol on the excessive deficit procedure' attached to the Maastricht Treaty. The Protocol would subsequently be complemented by the 'Stability and Growth Pact', which was to be created by the (Amsterdam) European Council in 1997 (cf. Resolution of the European Council on the Stability and Growth Pact, Amsterdam, 17 June 1997 [1997] OJ C 236/01). The Resolution defined the Pact as follows (*ibid.*, Preamble III): 'The Stability and Growth Pact, which provides both for prevention and deterrence, consists of this Resolution and two Council Regulations, one on the strengthening of the surveillance of budgetary positions and the surveillance and coordination of economic policies and another on speeding up and clarifying the implementation of the excessive deficit procedure.' The two regulations subsequently adopted were soon referred to as the 'preventive arm' (cf. Regulation 1466/97 on the strengthening of the surveillance of budgetary positions and the surveillance and coordination of economic policies, [1997] OJ L 209/1), and the 'corrective arm' (cf. Regulation 1467/97 on speeding up and clarifying the implementation of the excessive deficit procedure [1997] OJ L 209/6) of the Stability and Growth Pact.

[128] Cf. Protocol on Certain Provisions relating to the United Kingdom, which recognised 'that the United Kingdom shall not be obliged or committed to move to the third stage of Economic and Monetary Union without a separate decision to do so by its government and Parliament' (recital 1). For the similar position of Denmark, see: Protocol on certain Provisions relating to Denmark.

[129] Article G (C) EU (old) – introducing Article 8 (1) EC: 'Citizenship of the Union is hereby established. Every person holding the nationality of a Member State shall be a citizen of the Union.'

[130] Article G (C) EU (old) – introducing Articles 8a to 8c EC.

[131] Article G (D) (53) EU (old) – amending Article 173 EC that now allowed for actions by the European Parliament for the purpose of protecting its prerogatives.

co-decision procedure would allow the European Parliament to 'co-decide' European legislation on a par with the Council.[132] Finally, the Maastricht Treaty continued the expansion of qualified majority voting in the Council.

(ii) The Second Pillar: Common Foreign and Security Policy

Under the Single European Act, the cooperation of national foreign affairs within the 'European Political Cooperation' had still been conducted *outside* the European Treaties. This changed with the Maastricht Treaty which brought foreign and security affairs *inside* the European Union. A 'Common Foreign and Security Policy' (CFSP) would henceforth constitute the Union's Second Pillar.[133] The latter could potentially cover the area of defence;[134] yet the exact legal relationship between a future European Security and Defence Policy (ESDP) and the 'Western European Union' was left for another day.[135]

Importantly, the integration of foreign and security policy into the Union did not mean that it had become a supranational policy. On the contrary, the Maastricht compromise determined that the CFSP could retain its intergovernmental character. The dominant Union actors were thus the European Council and the Council – two intergovernmental institutions. The role of the supranational institutions was, by contrast, minimalist. The Parliament only enjoyed the right to be consulted and to make recommendations,[136] while the Commission was only entitled to be 'fully associated' with the CFSP.[137] The decisional intergovernmentalism within the CFSP was matched by its normative intergovernmentalism. Indeed, the objectives of the CFSP were not to be pursued by the Community's ordinary legal acts – such as regulations and decisions. On the contrary, the Second Pillar had established a number of specific instruments such as 'common positions' and 'joint actions'.[138] And since the Court of Justice was not to have any jurisdiction within this area,[139] the direct effect and supremacy of these instruments was in serious doubt.

---

[132] For a discussion of this procedure, see: Chapter 5 Section 3(a).

[133] Article J EU (old): 'A common foreign and security policy is hereby established[.]'

[134] Article J.4 (1) EU (old): 'The common foreign and security policy shall include all questions relating to the security of the Union, including the eventual framing of a common defence policy, which might in time lead to a common defence.'

[135] Article J.4 (6) EU (old): 'With a view to furthering the objective of this Treaty and having in view the date of 1998 in the context of Article XII of the Brussels Treaty, the provisions of this Article may be revised as provided for in Article N(2) on the basis of a report to be presented in 1996 by the Council to the European Council, which shall include an evaluation of the progress made and the experience gained until then.' The relationship between the EU and the WEU was further clarified by a 'Declaration relating to Western European Union'. This declared that the 'WEU will be developed as the defence component of the European Union and as a means to strengthen the European pillar of the Atlantic Alliance' (paragraph 2). And according to paragraph 3: 'The objective is to build up WEU in stages as the defence component of the European Union. To this end, WEU is prepared, at the request of the European Union, to elaborate and implement decisions and actions of the Union which have defence implications.'

[136] Article J.7 EU (old).   [137] Article J.9 EU (old).

[138] Articles J.1 (3) as well as J.2 and J.3 EU (old).   [139] Article L EU (old).

(iii) The Third Pillar: Justice and Home Affairs

The Third Pillar expanded the competences of the European Union into the field of 'Justice and Home Affairs' so as to better achieve the free movement of persons. For this purpose, it was given the power to act, inter alia, in the areas of asylum, immigration, judicial cooperation in civil and criminal matters, and police cooperation.[140] The 'Justice and Home Affairs' pillar would thus incorporate and replace the TREVI mechanism. However, the Union would not (yet) integrate the 'Schengen Area' and its *acquis*.

The nature of the Third Pillar was as intergovernmental as that of the Second Pillar. Its decision-making processes as well as the normative quality of its law lacked a supranational character.[141]

(b) A decade of 'constitutional bricolage': Amsterdam and Nice

The decade following the Maastricht Treaty was an accelerated decade: Treaty amendment followed Treaty amendment. The increased demand for constitutional change was partly caused by a changed geo-political context. With the fall of the Berlin Wall, Eastern Europe wished to join Western Europe under the legal roof of the European Union. Eastern enlargement however posed formidable constitutional problems. For how could an institutional system that worked for twelve States be made to work for twice that number? But *widening* was only one aspect of the demand for constitutional change. For the Union equally wished to *deepen* its evolution towards political union by establishing more democratic and transparent institutions.

The search for institutional solutions to these questions began with the 1997 Treaty of Amsterdam and continued with the 2001 Treaty of Nice. While both treaties introduced *minor* changes, none succeeded in offering the much-needed *major* constitutional reform of the Union. Both reforms indeed represented a constitutional 'bricolage' of pragmatic political compromises.[142]

(i) The Amsterdam Treaty: dividing the Third Pillar

What will the Treaty of Amsterdam be remembered for?[143] In addition to minor changes within the First and Second Pillar,[144] its central reform lay

---

[140] Article K.1 EU (old).

[141] This was – partly – qualified by the Court of Justice in Case C-105/03, *Pupine*, [2005] ECR I-5285. For a discussion of this case, see: S. Peers, 'Salvation Outside the Church: Judicial Protection in the Third Pillar after the "Pupino" and "Segi" Judgments' [2007] 44 CML Rev, 883; as well as: E. Spaventa, 'Opening Pandora's Box: Some Reflections on the Constitutional Effects of the Decision in "Pupino"' [2007] 3 *European Constitutional Law Review* 5.

[142] P. Pescatore, 'Nice: Aftermath' [2001] 38 CML Rev 265.

[143] Until 2009, European lawyers might have been tempted to mention the renumbering of the Treaties affected by the Amsterdam Treaty. However, this – dubious – achievement has now been lost, as the Lisbon Treaty has changed the numbering for the second time.

[144] Within the First Pillar, the Amsterdam Treaty extends and reforms the co-decision procedure (L. Gormley, 'Reflections on the Architecture of the European Union after the Treaty of Amsterdam' in: P. Twomey and D. O'Keeffe (eds.), *Legal Issues of the Amsterdam Treaty* (Hart, 1999), 57). The notable change in the Second Pillar was the creation of the new post of

in the changes brought to the Third Pillar – that is: Justice and Home Affairs.

The Amsterdam Treaty 'split asunder' what the Maastricht Treaty had joined together.[145] Indeed, from the subject areas originally falling within the Third Pillar, only those dealing with criminal law survived into the 'new' Third Pillar. The remainder was transferred to the First Pillar, as a more supranational approach for these matters had become favourable. The breaking up of the (old) 'Justice and Home' pillar left the new Third Pillar with a radically limited scope. The latter now only covered 'common actions among the Member States in the field of police and judicial cooperation in criminal matters and preventing and combating racism and xenophobia'.[146] After the Amsterdam amputation, the 'new' Third Pillar therefore came to be known as the 'Police and Judicial Cooperation in Criminal Matters' (PJCC) pillar. This shortened pillar remained an intergovernmental pillar – even if there were some minor supranational additions.[147]

What happened to the 'amputated' part of the (old) Third Pillar? The Amsterdam Treaty inserted it into the First Pillar, and thus transformed this *Union* policy to a *Community* policy. The new title introduced into the EC Treaty thus granted the Community powers in the area of 'visa, asylum, immigration and other policies related to free movement of persons'.[148] This was a supranational policy, albeit with intergovernmental traits.[149]

'High Representative for the Common Foreign and Security Policy' (cf. Article 1 (10) TA – inserting new Article J.16 EU (old).). Moreover, the Amsterdam Treaty brought the WEU closer to the EU in Part I, Article 1 (10) TA – inserting new Article J.7 EU (old): 'The Western European Union (WEU) is an integral part of the development of the Union providing the Union with access to an operational capability notably in the context of paragraph 2. It supports the Union in framing the defence aspects of the common foreign and security policy as set out in this Article. The Union shall accordingly foster closer institutional relations with the WEU with a view to the possibility of the integration of the WEU into the Union, should the European Council so decide. It shall in that case recommend to the Member States the adoption of such a decision in accordance with their respective constitutional requirements.'

[145] S. Peers, 'Justice and Home Affairs: Decision-making after Amsterdam' [2000] 25 EL Rev 183.

[146] Article 1 (11) TA (new) – Article K.1 EU (old).

[147] On this point, see the excellent analysis by J. Monar, 'Justice and home affairs in the Treaty of Amsterdam: reform at the price of fragmentation,' [1998] 23 EL Rev 320.

[148] Cf. Article 1 (15) TA – introducing the (new) Title III (a) into Part III of the EC Treaty. The price for this 'supranationalisation' was differential integration. Indeed, the United Kingdom and Ireland opted out of this new title (cf. Protocol on the Position of the United Kingdom and Ireland). And according to the 'Protocol on the application of certain aspects of Article 7a establishing the European Community to the United Kingdom and to Ireland', border controls for persons travelling into these two states would continue to be legal (*ibid.*, Article 1), and this would also hold true with regard to border controls for persons coming from these two States (*ibid.*, Article 3). On the complex position of Denmark, see: 'Protocol on the Position of Denmark'.

[149] On this point, see: K. Hailbronner, 'European Immigration and Asylum Law under the Amsterdam Treaty' [1998] 35 CML Rev 1047 at 1053 et seq.

But this was not all. The Member States finally agreed to 'incorporate' the Schengen Agreement and its legal offspring into the European Union.[150] The incorporation of the Schengen *acquis* under the roof of the European Union was legally complex for three reasons. First, not all Member States were parties to the international agreements and a legal solution had to be found for the non-participants.[151] Second, some *non*-Member States of the Union had been associated with the Schengen Agreement and would thus wish to be associated with the incorporation and future development of the Schengen *acquis*.[152] Third, since the old Third Pillar had been split into two parts – one supranational and one intergovernmental – the Schengen *acquis* could not be incorporated in one piece. It would also need to be divided according to whether the subject matter fell into the (new) First or the (new) Third Pillar. For that reason, the Schengen Protocol left it to the Council to determine 'in conformity with the relevant provisions of the Treaties, the legal basis for each of the provisions or decisions which constitute the Schengen acquis'.[153] But as long as the Council had not taken any implementing measures, 'the provisions or decisions which constitute the Schengen acquis [would] be regarded as acts based on Title VI of the Treaty on European Union', that is, acts of the Third Pillar.[154]

(ii) The Nice Treaty: limited institutional reform

Despite the political prospect of Eastern enlargement, the Amsterdam Treaty had postponed a 'comprehensive review of the provisions of the Treaties on the composition and functioning of the institutions'.[155] In light of these 'Amsterdam leftovers',[156] the principal aim of the Nice Treaty was the – overdue – institutional reform of the European Union. Past amendments had not

---

[150] Cf. 'Protocol Integrating the Schengen acquis into the framework of the European Union' – Preamble 2. The Annex to the Protocol identifies the 'Schengen Acquis' with the Schengen Agreement, the Schengen Convention, the Accession Protocols and Agreements, and the decisions and declarations adopted by the (Schengen) Executive Committee or bodies established under it.

[151] Articles 3 and 4 of the Schengen Protocol.

[152] The two non-Member States are the Republic of Iceland and the Kingdom of Norway, whose legal status is determined by Article 6 of the Schengen Protocol.

[153] *Ibid.*, Article 2 (1) – second indent; and see also: *ibid.*, Article 5.

[154] *Ibid.*, Article 2 (1) – fourth indent.

[155] Cf. Article 2 of the 'Protocol on the Institutions with the Prospect of Enlargement of the European Union'. The provision reads as follows: 'At least one year before the membership of the European Union exceeds twenty, a conference of representatives of the governments of the Member States shall be convened in order to carry out a comprehensive review of the provisions of the Treaties on the composition and functioning of the institutions.' The Protocol thereby envisaged that 'the Commission shall comprise one national of each of the Member States, provided that, by that date, the weighting of the votes in the Council has been modified, whether by re-weighting of the votes or by dual majority, in a manner acceptable to all Member States, taking into account all relevant elements, notably compensating those Member States which give up the possibility of nominating a second member of the Commission' (*ibid.*, Article 1).

[156] European Council (Helsinki, 10–11 December 1999), 'Presidency Conclusions' [1999] 12 *Bulletin of the European Communities*, 1 at paragraph 16: 'Following the Cologne Conclusions and in the light of the Presidency's report, the Conference will examine the size

changed the *structural* composition of its institutions. Each enlargement had simply increased their membership. This 'policy of pulling up chairs' would reach a limit with Eastern enlargement.[157] High expectations were therefore brought to the next amending Treaty. These heightened expectations, the Nice Treaty did *not* fulfil. The aim of a 'comprehensive review' of the institutional structure and decision-making system was not met. This substantial failure was soon seen as the result of the formal method of negotiation. The Nice Treaty had shown the procedural shortcomings of intergovernmental conferences for *major* Treaty reforms.[158]

What were the institutional changes nonetheless affected by the Nice Treaty? The Nice Treaty chiefly addressed the Amsterdam leftovers in a 'Protocol on the Enlargement of the European Union'. This contained provisions for the composition of the European Parliament,[159] the Council,[160] and the Commission.[161] With regard to the Court of Justice, the Nice Treaty also effected some changes in the EC Treaty as well as in the 'Protocol on the Statute of the European Court of Justice'. But importantly, the Court's jurisdiction would not be widened significantly. Finally, while the 'Charter of Fundamental Rights of the European Union' had been proclaimed at Nice,[162] its status would remain that of a non-binding instrument *outside* the European Union.

The Nice Treaty was self-conscious about its minor achievements. While they opened the way for Eastern enlargement, the 'comprehensive review' mandate had not been fulfilled. For that reason, the Member States added the Nice 'Declaration on the Future of the Union' that called for 'a deeper and wider debate about the future of the European Union'. Setting itself a deadline of its 2001 Laeken meeting, the European Council committed itself to 'a declaration

and composition of the Commission, the weighting of votes in the Council and the possible extension of qualified majority voting in the Council, as well as other necessary amendments to the Treaties arising as regards the European institutions in connection with the above issues and in implementing the Treaty of Amsterdam.'

[157] R. Barents, 'Some Observations on the Treaty of Nice', [2001] 8 *Maastricht Journal of European and Comparative Law* 121 at 122.

[158] Famously, after the prolonged and aggravated Nice Treaty negotiations, Tony Blair (former UK Prime Minister) is reported to have exclaimed: 'We cannot go on working like this!'

[159] Article 2 Enlargement Protocol.

[160] Article 3 Enlargement Protocol. The heart of this provision was the definition of what constitutes a qualified majority in the Council, and involved a re-weighing of the votes of the Member States.

[161] Article 4 Enlargement Protocol. The core of the provision was formed by two rules. Paragraph 1 reduced the number of Commissioners to 'one national of each of the Member States'. However, paragraph 2 qualified this, when the Union would reach twenty-seven Member States: 'The number of Members of the Commission shall be less than the number of Member States. The Members of the Commission shall be chosen according to a rotation system based on the principle of equality, the implementing arrangements for which shall be adopted by the Council, acting unanimously.'

[162] The Charter had been drafted by a special 'Convention' *outside* the Nice Intergovernmental Conference. On the drafting process, see: G. de Búrca, 'The Drafting of the European Union Charter of Fundamental Rights' [2001] 26 EL Rev 126.

containing appropriate initiatives for the continuation of this process'.[163] This process should thereby address the following questions:

- how to establish and monitor a more precise delimitation of powers between the European Union and the Member States, reflecting the principle of subsidiarity;
- the status of the Charter of Fundamental Rights of the European Union, proclaimed in Nice, in accordance with the conclusions of the European Council in Cologne;
- a simplification of the Treaties with a view to making them clearer and better understood without changing their meaning;
- the role of national parliaments in the European architecture.[164]

The Nice Treaty thus envisaged yet another intergovernmental conference to amend the Treaties, reflecting 'the need to improve and to monitor the democratic legitimacy and transparency of the Union and its institutions, in order to bring them closer to the citizens of the Member States'.[165] The Lisbon Treaty – eventually – fulfilled the mandate for a comprehensive reform. It would replace the old European Union with a new European Union.

4. From Nice to Lisbon: the (new) European Union

Whereas the 1957 Rome Treaty had been praised for 'its sober and precise legal wording',[166] every Treaty amendment since the Single European Act was criticised for the legal distortions it introduced into the constitutional order of the European Community.[167] While each political compromise advanced

---

[163] Cf. Declaration (No. 23) on the Future of the Union, paragraph 3.   [164] *Ibid.*, paragraph 5.

[165] *Ibid.*, paragraph 6.

[166] P. Pescatore, 'Some Critical Remarks on the "Single European Act"' [1987] 24 CML Rev 9, 15.

[167] The Single European Act was famously criticised by Pescatore: *ibid.*, at 15. The eminent former judge confessed: 'I am among those who think that forgetting about the Single Act would be a lesser evil for our common future than ratification of this diplomatic document.' This document was described as 'a flood of verbose vagueness'. The Treaty on European Union found a memorable criticism in D. Curtin's phrase of the 'Europe of bits and pieces'. The Maastricht Treaty amendments were said to have 'no overriding and consistent constitutional philosophy behind the proposed reforms'. On the contrary, the European legal order was 'tinkered with in an arbitrary and *ad hoc* fashion by the intergovernmental negotiators in a manner which defied, in many respects, its underlying *constitutional* character' (cf. 'The Constitutional Structure of the Union: A Europe of Bits and Pieces' [1993] 30 CML Rev 17, 17–18). For the Amsterdam Treaty it was said that 'the devil is not in the detail': 'The problem lies in the accumulation of texts, breeding ever deepening intransparency. Change which is not intelligible is likely to cause alienation' (cf. S. Weatherill, 'Flexibility or Fragmentation: Trends in European Integration' in J. Usher (ed.), *The State of the European Union* (Longman, 2000), p. 18). Finally, the Nice Treaty again encountered the strong voice of P. Pescatore, who raised the 'criticism of amateurishness' of the 'legal *bricolage* in the Nice documents' which constitute 'a patchwork of incoherent additions to the provisions of the EU and EC Treaties' (Guest Editorial, 'Nice – The Aftermath' [2001] 38 CML Rev 265).

European integration, two decades of legal pragmatism had turned Europe's constitution into an 'accumulation of texts, breeding ever deepening intransparency'.[168] The European Treaties had indeed become constitutional law full of historical experience – but without much legal logic.

This gloomy background provided the impulse for a major constitutional reform of the Union in the first decade of the twenty-first century. In the wake of the Nice Treaty's 'Declaration on the Future of the Union', the European Council convened in Laeken to issue a declaration on 'The Future of the European Union'.[169] Among the four desirable aims, the Laeken Declaration identified the need for '[a] better division and definition of competence in the European Union', a '[s]implification of the Union's instruments', '[m]ore democracy, transparency and efficiency in the European Union' and a move '[t]owards a Constitution for European citizens'.[170]

How was this to be achieved? To pave the way for a *major* Treaty reform, the European Council decided to convene a 'Convention on the Future of Europe'. The Convention was tasked 'to consider the key issues arising for the Union's future development and try to identify the various possible responses'. For that purpose it was asked to 'draw up a final document', which would evolve into the 2004 'Constitutional Treaty'. Yet the Constitutional Treaty would never enter into force. It failed to win the ratification battles in France and the Netherlands. Despite this failure, many of its provisions would survive into the 'Reform Treaty' concluded at Lisbon.

The Lisbon Treaty, while formally an amending Treaty, differs significantly from its predecessors. In substance, it is the – mildly moderated – 2004 Constitutional Treaty. And while the Lisbon Treaty did not formally place the European Union onto a new constitutional foundation, its opening provisions already announced a dramatic constitutional decision: 'The Union shall replace and succeed the European Community'.[171] Was this the end of the pillar structure? Did the establishment of the 'new' European Union dissolve the 'old' European Union? And what were the institutional and constitutional changes brought about by the Lisbon Treaty? Before answering these questions, we need first to look at the (failed) Constitutional Treaty.

(a) The (failed) Constitutional Treaty: formal 'total revision'

The Laeken European Council had charged a 'European Convention' with the task of identifying reform avenues for the future development of the Union.[172] The Convention would be chaired by a former French president, Valéry

---

[168] Weatherill, 'Flexibility or Fragmentation' (supra n. 167), 8.
[169] Laeken Declaration of 15 December 2001 on the Future of the European Union.   [170] *Ibid.*
[171] Article 1 (2) (b) Lisbon Treaty.
[172] On the work of the Convention and the 'accidental' creation of the Constitutional Treaty, see: P. Norman, *The Accidental Constitution: The Making of Europe's Constitutional Treaty* (EuroComment, 2003).

Giscard d'Estaing. It was to be composed of representatives from the Member States and the European institutions,[173] and led by a 'Praesidium'.[174] To facilitate its task, the convention organised a number of 'Working Groups',[175] which would prepare the intellectual ground for the plenary debate. The Convention eventually produced a '*Draft* Constitutional Treaty', which was presented to the European Council in 2003. The subsequent Intergovernmental Conference made significant changes to the Draft Treaty,[176] and agreed on a final version in 2004.

What was the constitutional structure of the (new) European Union? The 2004 Constitutional Treaty (CT) repealed all previous treaties,[177] and merged the pillar structure of the 'old' European Union to form a 'new' European Union.[178] The Constitutional Treaty thus created *one* Union, with *one* legal personality, on the basis of *one* Treaty. The Constitutional Treaty was divided into four parts. Part I defined the values and objectives, competences and institutions, as well as instruments and procedures of the Union. Part II incorporated the 'Charter of Fundamental Rights' into the Treaty. Part III spelled out the details of the various internal and external policies of the Union; and this included the former Second and Third Pillar policies of the 'old' Union. Finally, Part IV contained some general and final provisions.

The Constitutional Treaty would, as an international Treaty, need to be ratified by the Member States. Many of these States decided – in light of the 'constitutional' nature of the new Treaty – to submit their ratification to a referendum. This (national) constitutional choice was to provide direct

---

[173] In addition to the Chairman (V. Giscard d'Estaing) and two Vice-Chairmen (G. Amato and J. L. Dehaene), the Convention was composed of fifteen representatives from the national governments (one per State), thirty delegates from national parliaments (two per State), sixteen members of the European Parliament, and two Commission representatives. The (future) accession countries were represented in the same way as the Member States 'without, however, being able to prevent any consensus which may emerge among the Member States' (Cf. Laeken Declaration, supra n. 169).

[174] The Praesidium was composed of the Chairman and the Vice-Chairmen, three government representatives, two national parliament representatives, two European Parliament representatives and two Commission representatives.

[175] The Convention established eleven 'Working Groups': (I) 'Subsidiarity', (II) 'Charter/ECHR', (III) 'Legal Personality', (IV) 'National Parliaments', (V) 'Complementary Competences', (VI) 'Economic Governance', (VII) 'External Action', (VIII) 'Defence', (IX) 'Simplification', (X) 'Freeedom, Security and Justice', and (XI) 'Social Europe'. For the working documents and final reports of the Convention Working Groups, see: http://european-convention.eu.int/doc_wg.asp?lang=EN.

[176] On these changes, see: P. Craig, *The Lisbon Treaty: Law, Politics, and Treaty Reform* (Oxford University Press, 2010), 16–20.

[177] Article IV-437 CT. This would have simplified matters significantly. In the words of J.-C. Piris, *The Lisbon Treaty: A Legal and Political Analysis* (Cambridge University Press, 2010), 20: 'Up until 2004, the original 1957 Treaties had been amended and complemented fifteen times. As a result, there were about 2,800 pages of primary law contained in seventeen Treaties or Acts[.]'

[178] Article IV-438 (1) CT: 'The European Union established by this Treaty shall be the successor to the European Union established by the Treaty on European Union and to the European Community.'

democratic legitimacy to the European Union.[179] Yet, the strategy led to failure. The peoples of France and the Netherlands rejected the Constitutional Treaty in 2005. After the negative referenda, the Constitutional Treaty was put into a coma from which it was not to reawaken. Yet after a reflection period, the European Council agreed that 'after two years of uncertainty over the Union's treaty reform process, the time ha[d] come to resolve the issue and for the Union to move on'.[180] To this end, it called for an Intergovernmental Conference with the following mandate:

> The IGC is asked to draw up a Treaty (hereinafter called the 'Reform Treaty') amending the existing Treaties with a view to enhancing the efficiency and democratic legitimacy of the enlarged Union, as well as the coherence of its external action. The constitutional concept, which consisted in repealing all existing Treaties and replacing them by a single text called 'Constitution', is abandoned. The Reform Treaty will introduce into the existing Treaties, which remain in force, the innovations resulting from the 2004 IGC, as set out below in a detailed fashion.
>
> The Reform Treaty will contain two substantive clauses amending respectively the Treaty on the European Union (TEU) and the Treaty establishing the European Community (TEC). The TEU will keep its present name and the TEC will be called Treaty on the Functioning of the Union, the Union having a single legal personality. The word 'Community' will throughout be replaced by the word 'Union'; it will be stated that the two Treaties constitute the Treaties on which the Union is founded and that the Union replaces and succeeds the Community.[181]

The idea behind the mandate was simple. It consisted of abandoning the *form* of the Constitutional Treaty,[182] while rescuing its *substance*.[183] The idea of a formal re-founding of the European Union on the basis of a new Treaty was thus replaced with the idea of a substantive amendment of the existing Treaties. The Constitutional Treaty had to drop its constitutional garb. In political terms, this window (un)dressing was necessary to justify a second attempt at Treaty

---

[179] Apart from two Member States that were constitutionally compelled to organise referenda (namely, Denmark and Ireland), seven additional Member States decided to go down the direct constitutional democracy road (i.e., France, Luxembourg, Poland, Portugal, Spain, the Netherlands, United Kingdom).

[180] European Council (Brussels, 21–2 June 2007), 'Presidency Conclusions' [2007] 3 *EU Bulletin* 1 at 8.

[181] *Ibid.*, Annex I, paragraphs 1–2.

[182] This idea was spelled out in *ibid.*, paragraph 3: 'The TEU and the Treaty on the Functioning of the Union will not have a constitutional character. The terminology used throughout the Treaties will reflect this change: the term "Constitution" will not be used, the "Union Minister for Foreign Affairs" will be called High Representative of the Union for Foreign Affairs and Security Policy and the denominations "law" and "framework law" will be abandoned, the existing denominations "regulations", "directives" and "decisions" being retained. Likewise, there will be no article in the amended Treaties mentioning the symbols of the EU such as the flag, the anthem or the motto. Concerning the primacy of EU law, the IGC will adopt a Declaration recalling the existing case law of the EU Court of Justice.'

[183] *Ibid.*, paragraph 4.

reform. In legal terms, by contrast, 'none of the changes identified by the European Council were significant'.[184] Indeed, apart from some hasty and amateurish repackaging, the final 'Reform Treaty' would be 'the same in most important respects as the Constitutional Treaty'.[185]

The Reform Treaty was signed in December 2007 in Lisbon and was consequently baptised as the 'Lisbon Treaty'. After ratification problems in Ireland,[186] Germany,[187] and the Czech Republic,[188] the Lisbon Treaty entered into force in December 2009.

(b) The Lisbon Treaty: substantive 'total revision'

It had been 'a long road from Nice to Lisbon'.[189] After four years lost on the Constitutional Treaty and four more years of suspension, the Lisbon Treaty embodied the strong desire 'to complete the process started by the Treaty of Amsterdam and by the Treaty of Nice with a view to enhancing the efficiency and democratic legitimacy of the Union and to improving the coherence of its action'.[190]

The Lisbon Treaty had reverted to the amendment technique. Instead of a formal 'total revision', it chose to build on the *acquis constitutionnel* created by the Rome Treaty establishing the European Community and the (Maastricht) Treaty establishing the European Union. But while the Lisbon Treaty merged both into a 'new' European Union, it retained a *dual* Treaty base. This was – presumably – to underline its (formal) difference from the 2004 Constitutional Treaty. But importantly, the dual Treaty base no longer distinguished between a

---

[184] Craig, *The Lisbon Treaty* (supra n. 176), 23.

[185] *Ibid.*, 24. According to Craig, the Reform Treaty 'replicated 90 per cent of what had been in the Constitutional Treaty' (*ibid.*, 31). The repacking was a result of the (political) compromise of keeping the 2004 Constitutional Treaty substantially intact, while producing a new Treaty that formally looked different. On this dilemma, see: *ibid.*, 26: 'The drafters of the Lisbon Treaty were therefore caught in a dilemma: the natural desire to frame the revised TEU so as to embrace the EU's important constitutional principles had to be tempered by the political need to produce a document that did not simply replicate Part I of the Constitutional Treaty.'

[186] After a first referendum had failed, the European Council promised Ireland a number of concessions (see European Council (Brussels, 11–12 December 2008), 'Presidency Conclusions' [2008] 12 *EU Bulletin* 8). The most significant of these is the promise that 'a decision will be taken, in accordance with the necessary legal procedures, to the effect that the Commission shall continue to include one national of each Member State' (*ibid.*, paragraph 2).

[187] On the Lisbon Decision of the German Constitutional Court, see: D. Thym, 'In the Name of Sovereign Statehood: a Critical Introduction to the "Lisbon" Judgment of the German Constitutional Court' [2009] 46 CML Rev 1795.

[188] In order to remove the last hurdle to ratification, the European Council had to promise the Czech Republic an amendment to Protocol No. 30 on the Application of the Charter of Fundamental Rights (see European Council (Brussels, 29–30 October 2009), 'Presidency Conclusions' (http://european-council.europa.eu/council-meetings/conclusions.aspx), Annex I – Article 1: 'Protocol No. 30 on the application of the Charter of Fundamental Rights of the European Union to Poland and the United Kingdom shall apply to the Czech Republic'; and Article 3: 'This Protocol shall be annexed to the Treaty on European Union and to the Treaty on the Functioning of the European Union').

[189] Craig, *Lisbon Treaty* (supra n. 176), 1.   [190] Lisbon Treaty – Preamble 1.

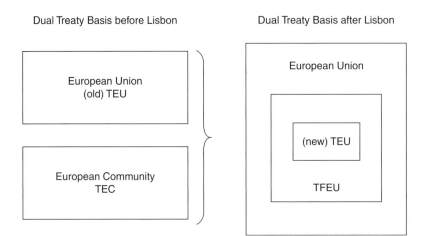

Figure 4 Dual Treaty basis before and after Lisbon

Community-Treaty and a *Union*-Treaty, as the new Union would be a single organisation. Substantively, *both* Treaties concern the European Union.

The division into two European Treaties followed a functional criterion. While the (new) Treaty on European Union contains the *general* provisions defining the Union, the Treaty on the Functioning of the European Union spells out specific provisions with regard to the Union institutions and policies. The structure of the Treaties is shown in Table 1.

This dual structure was (mis)shaped by the attempt of the Member States formally to 'repackage' the substance of the Constitutional Treaty. This 'restructuring' has led to a number of systemic inconsistencies. First, the institutional provisions are split over the two Treaties. Thus, Parts I and II as well as sections of Parts VI and VII of the TFEU should have been placed into the TEU. Second, because the Member States wished to underline the special status of the CFSP, this policy was not placed in Part V of the TFEU but instead inserted, as a separate title, into the TEU. This constitutional splitting of the Union's external relations provisions is unfortunate, and – oddity of oddities – places a single policy outside the TFEU. Third, instead of being an integral part of the TEU, the Charter of Fundamental Rights remains 'external' to the Treaties, while being recognised to 'have the same legal value as the Treaties'.[191]

Yet, despite its choice for a dual treaty base, the Lisbon Treaty also contains elements that underline the 'unity' of the Treaty structure. First, both Treaties expressly confirm that they have the *same* legal value.[192] Second, the Protocols are attached to *both* Treaties – a break with a traditional constitutional technique. But most importantly, the new European Union, while having two Treaties, has one single legal personality.[193]

---

[191] Article 6 (1) (new) TEU.   [192] Cf. Article 1 TEU and Article 1 TFEU.
[193] Article 47 (new) TEU.

Table 1 Structure of the TEU and TFEU

European Union			
EU Treaty		**FEU Treaty**	
Title I	Common Provisions	Part I	Principles
Title II	Democratic Principles	Part II	Citizenship (Non-Discrimination)
Title III	Institutions	Part III	Union (Internal) Policies
Title IV	Enhanced Cooperation	Part IV	Overseas Associations
Title V	External Action, and CFSP	Part V	External Action
Title VI	Final Provisions	Part VI	Institutions & Finances
		Part VII	General & Final Provisions

Charter of Fundamental Rights
Protocols (37)[194]
Declarations (65)[195]

What are the principal institutional and substantive changes brought about by the Lisbon Treaty? In line with the Laeken Declaration, the 2004 Constitutional Treaty and the 2007 Lisbon Treaty aimed at a better division and definition of Union competences. For that purpose, the TFEU contained a new title on 'categories and areas of Union competence'.[196] However, as a critical review of the title shows,[197] this reform objective has not been achieved. This negative outcome is however partly compensated for by the positive results with regard to the remaining three reform objectives. The Lisbon Treaty has satisfactorily simplified the Union instruments and law-making procedures. For it has indeed abolished the 'old' Union instruments, such as 'common positions'; and it eliminated the 'cooperation' procedure that had existed since the Single European Act.

What about the third Laeken mandate, that is, '[m]ore democracy, transparency and efficiency in the European Union'? The Lisbon Treaty represents a dramatic step towards political union. The (new) Treaty on European Union now contains a separate title on 'democratic principles'.[198] The central provision here is Article 10 TEU, according to which '[t]he functioning of the

---

[194] According to Article 51 (new) TEU: 'The Protocols and Annexes to the Treaties shall form an integral part thereof.' And the best way to make sense of a Protocol is to see it as a legally binding 'footnote' to a particular provision of the Treaties.

[195] Declarations are *not* an integral part of the Treaties, and are *not* legally binding. They only clarify the 'context' of a particular provision and, as such, may offer an interpretive aid. On the status of Declarations, see: A. G. Toth, 'The Legal Status of the Declarations Annexed to the Single European Act' [1986] 23 CML Rev 803.

[196] Title I of Part I (Articles 2–6) TFEU.

[197] R. Schütze, 'Lisbon and the Federal Order of Competences: a Prospective Analysis' [2008] 33 EL Rev, 709.

[198] Cf. Title II of the (new) TEU.

Union shall be founded on representative democracy'.[199] Democratic representation is offered directly and indirectly. European citizens are 'directly represented at Union level in the European Parliament';[200] whereas they are indirectly represented through their Member States in the (European) Council.[201] This *dual* democratic legitimacy of the Union corresponds to its *federal* nature.[202] The Lisbon Treaty thereby enhances the direct representation of European citizens by significantly widening the powers of the European Parliament. Not only has 'co-decision' become the 'ordinary legislative procedure',[203] Parliament's decision-making powers with regard to executive, external, and budgetary powers have also been significantly increased.[204]

Finally, what about the move '[t]owards a Constitution for European citizens'? The (Maastricht) European Union and the (Rome) European Community have now been merged into the (Lisbon) European Union. And while the Union is still not formally based on a single Treaty, the Lisbon Treaty has successfully abolished the pillars of the (Maastricht) Union. The former 'Second Pillar' on the CFSP has been integrated into the (new) TEU. And in its substance, the CFSP has been strengthened with regard to the Union's defence policy.[205] (The strengthened role of a European defence policy induced the Western European Union to dissolve.[206]) With regard to the Third Pillar, the Lisbon Treaty transfered PJCC to the former First Pillar. The (Amsterdam) Third Pillar is thus 'reunited' with the rest of the original (Maastricht) pillar on Justice and Home Affairs, and both are now under the supranational roof of Title V of Part Three of the TFEU.[207]

---

[199] Article 10 (1) (new) TEU.   [200] Article 10 (2) (new) TEU.   [201] Article 10 (3) (new) TEU.

[202] On this federal understanding, see: Chapter 2 – Section 3 below.   [203] Article 289 TFEU.

[204] For an analysis of these various powers, see: Chapter 3 – Section 2(d) below.

[205] Article 42 (2) (new) TEU: 'The common security and defence policy shall include the progressive framing of a common Union defence policy. This will lead to a common defence, when the European Council, acting unanimously, so decides.' And see also: Article 42 (7) (new) TEU: 'If a Member State is the victim of armed aggression on its territory, the other Member States shall have towards it an obligation of aid and assistance by all the means in their power, in accordance with Article 51 of the United Nations Charter.'

[206] Statement of the Presidency of the Permanent Council of the WEU on behalf of the High Contracting Parties to the Modified Brussels Treaty – Belgium, France, Germany, Greece, Italy, Luxembourg, The Netherlands, Portugal, Spain and the United Kingdom (Brussels, 31 March 2010): 'The Western European Union has made an important contribution to peace and stability in Europe and to the development of the European security and defence architecture, promoting consultations and cooperation in this field, and conducting operations in a number of theatres, including the Petersberg tasks. Building on the achievements of the WEU and the principle of European solidarity, the EU has taken on crisis management tasks since 2000 and has now developed a Common Security and Defence Policy. With the entry into force of the Lisbon Treaty, a new phase in European security and defence begins . . . The WEU has therefore accomplished its historical role. In this light we the States Parties to the Modified Brussels Treaty have collectively decided to terminate the Treaty, thereby effectively closing the organization, and in line with its article XII will notify the Treaty's depositary in accordance with national procedures.'

[207] This supranational roof came at the price of some intergovernmental characteristics, transitional provisions (cf. Title VII of Protocol No. 36 on 'Transitional Provisions'), and 'differential

Conclusion

In the first sixty years of its history, the European Union has evolved from a humble Community on coal and steel to an assured Union that is involved in almost all areas of modern life. The Union has, however, not only widened its jurisdictional and geographic scope, it has considerably deepened its supranational character – in relation to *both* normative *and* decisional supranationalism.[208]

This chapter has looked at four historical periods in the Union's evolution. The first period alone covered forty years, and this is no accident, since the last twenty years have been a period of accelerated constitutional change. Treaty amendment followed Treaty amendment! The Lisbon Treaty is the last chapter in this constitutional chain novel. However, as Section 4 has tried to show, it is a decisive chapter that has – if not in form, then in substance – reconstituted the European Union. This 'new' European Union differs in significant respects from the 'old' European Union founded by the Maastricht Treaty. Not only has the pillar structure disappeared, the Union's institutions as well as its powers and procedures have considerably changed. The European Union of today constitutes a fairly 'compact' constitutional object. The sole satellite that still orbits around it is the European Atomic Energy Community;[209] and it is hoped that the Member States will – sooner rather than later – integrate that Community into the European Union.

The Lisbon Treaty will not be the last chapter of the European Union. For the evolution of the European Union will of course continue. Constitutional change will need to follow social change. The Union must recognise this; or else, it will be punished by life. What is remarkable, however, is that the method of constitutional change has itself changed over time. While at first organised by means of the Union's general competences,[210] formal Treaty amendment has

---

integration' (cf. Protocol No. 21 'On the Position of the United Kingdom and Ireland in respect of the Area of Freedom, Security and Justice'). On the – complex – status of this policy area, see: S. Peers, 'Mission Accomplished? EU Justice and Home Affairs Law After the Treaty of Lisbon' [2011] 48 CMLRev. 661.

[208] A historical analysis of the evolution of the Union thus contradicts Professor Weiler's interesting – but mistaken – thesis about the essential constitutional balance between normative supranationalism and decisional intergovernmentalism (cf. J. Weiler, 'The Community System: the Dual Character of Supranationalism' [1981] 1 YEL 267). This thesis was already hard to defend before the Single European Act, but thereafter – and especially after the Maastricht Treaty – it became untenable.

[209] The Convention Working Group on 'Legal Personality' had argued in favour of merging Euratom into the new European Union (Final Report, CONV 305/02, 5): 'The underlying case for merging the Euratom Treaty is the same as for merging the TEC. The Euratom merger would in addition allow a large number of Euratom Treaty provisions that are identical or similar to the TEC to be deleted. However, in view of certain specific problems relating to the Euratom Treaty, it was felt that the possible implications of merging this Treaty needed to be further investigated.' However, a minority in the Working Group had argued that the integration of Euratom was 'not absolutely essential given the specific nature of that Treaty' (*ibid.*, 3), while noting that the treaty-making powers of the Commission within the sectoral Community may justify institutional separation.

[210] Cf. R. Schütze, 'Organized Change Towards an "Ever Closer Union": Article 308 EC and the Limits to the Community's Legislative Competence' [2003] 22 YEL 79.

become the preferred route after the Single European Act. The procedural hurdles for this are comparatively high,[211] but the Lisbon Treaty tries to make that task a little easier. The Union legal order now recognises two 'simplified revision procedures' in addition to the 'ordinary revision procedure'.[212] The ordinary revision thereby continues to require, after a complex preparatory stage,[213] the ratification of Treaty amendments 'by all the Member States in accordance with their respective constitutional requirements'.[214] The insistence on the express consent of all national parliaments or – where a referendum is constitutionally required – the national peoples will make this a steep route towards constitutional change.[215] The two simplified revision procedures try to provide for an easier passage. But the first simplified procedure hardly makes matters much simpler.[216] By contrast, the second simplified procedure allows – for a qualified part of primary law[217] – the European Union to change its constitutional Treaties if backed up by the *tacit* consent of national *parliaments*.[218] This route not only allows for parliamentary *inaction* but also expressly excludes national referenda. This should indeed make future constitutional change easier, and thus facilitates the constitutional capacity of the Union to adapt to social change.

---

[211] Cf. B. de Witte, 'Rules of Change in International Law: How Special is the European Community?' [1994] 25 *Netherlands Yearbook of International Law* 299.

[212] Article 48 (new) TEU.

[213] This process may, or may not, involve the calling of a 'Convention' – depending on the extent of the proposed Treaty amendments, cf. Article 48 (3) (new) TEU, and will be followed by an intergovernmental conference.

[214] Article 48 (4) (new) TEU.

[215] The Lisbon Treaty did not replace the unanimity requirement by a qualified majority requirement. It only committed itself to a procedural obligation to 'rethink' Treaty amendments, where 'four fifths of the Member States have ratified it and one or more Member States have encountered difficulties in proceeding with ratification' (*ibid.*, paragraph 5).

[216] *Ibid.*, paragraph 6. The paragraph has been used by the European Council for the first time in March 2011, cf. European Council Decision 2011/199 amending Article 136 TFEU with regard to a stability mechanism for Member States whose currency is the euro ([2011] OJ L91/1).

[217] Article 48 (7) (new) TEU. The paragraph only applies in two situations. First, '[w]here the Treaty on the Functioning of the European Union or Title V of this Treaty provides for the Council to act by unanimity in a given area or case, the European Council may adopt a decision authorising the Council to act by a qualified majority in that area or in that case.' (This however excludes decisions with military or defence implications.) Second, '[w]here the Treaty on the Functioning of the European Union provides for legislative acts to be adopted by the Council in accordance with a special legislative procedure, the European Council may adopt a decision allowing for the adoption of such acts in accordance with the ordinary legislative procedure'. However, it is important to note that Article 353 TFEU sets external limits to Article 48 (7) (new) TEU.

[218] Article 48 (7) (new) TEU third indent.

2

Constitutional Nature: A Federation of States

Contents

Introduction		47
1.	The American constitutional tradition: federalism as (inter)national law	49
2.	The European constitutional tradition: international versus national law	53
	(a) Conceptual polarisation: 'Confederation' versus 'Federation'	54
	(b) Early criticism: the European tradition and the (missing) federal genus	56
3.	The European Union in light of the American constitutional tradition	59
	(a) The foundational dimension: Europe's 'Constitutional Treaty'	60
	(b) The institutional dimension: a European Union of States and people(s)	62
	(c) The functional dimension: the division of powers in Europe	64
	(d) Overall classification: the European Union on federal 'middle ground'	65
4.	The European Union in light of the European constitutional tradition	66
	(a) The *sui generis* 'theory': the 'incomparable' European Union	67
	(b) The international law theory: the 'Maastricht Decision'	68
	(c) Europe's statist tradition unearthed: three constitutional denials	71
	(d) *Excursus*: Europe's democratic 'deficit' as a 'false problem'?	74
Conclusion		77

Introduction

The rise of the modern State system after the seventeenth century was a celebration of political pluralism. Each State was entitled to its own 'autonomous' existence. The rise of the absolute idea of State sovereignty led to an absolute denial of all supranational legal authority above the State. This way of thinking introduced a distinction that still structures our understanding of the legal world: the distinction between national and international law. The former was the sphere of subordination and compulsory law; the latter constituted the sphere of coordination and voluntary contract. International law was thus not 'real' law, as it could not be enforced. From the perspective of classic international law, a 'public law' between sovereigns was indeed a contradiction in terms for it required an authority above the States; but if sovereignty was the defining characteristic of the modern State, there could be no such higher authority. All relations between States must be voluntary and, as such, 'beyond' any public legal force.[1]

From the very beginning, the idea of State sovereignty hindered an understanding of the nature of the European Union. The latter was said to have been 'established on the most advanced frontiers of the [international] law of peaceful co-operation'; and its principles of solidarity and integration had even taken it 'to the boundaries of federalism'.[2] But was the Union inside those federal boundaries or outside them? For while the European Union was not a Federal State, it had assumed 'statist' features and combined – like a chemical compound – international and national elements. But how should one conceptualise this 'middle ground' between international and national law? In the absence of a theory of federalism beyond the State, European thought invented a new word – supranationalism – and proudly announced the European Union to be *sui generis*. The Union was 'incomparable' and its nature 'unique'. And the belief that Europe was incomparable ushered in the dark ages of European constitutional theory.[3] Indeed, the *sui generis* idea is not a theory. It is an *anti*-theory, for it refuses to search for commonalities; yet, theory *must* search for what is generic.[4]

How, then, should we view and analyse the nature and structure of the European Union? This chapter presents two alternative answers to this question by looking at two different constitutional traditions. Section 1 begins by introducing the American constitutional tradition that understood the (American) Union as a structure between international and national law. Section 2 moves to the European constitutional tradition, which has traditionally insisted on the indivisibility of sovereignty. This has led to a conceptual polarisation, according to which a 'Union of States' is either an international organisation – like the United Nations – or a Federal State – like Germany. Sections 3 and 4 then apply the two alternative theories to the European Union. Suffice to say that the American constitutional tradition is able to view the European Union as a Federation of

---

[1] In this context, see: the famous opening remarks by E. de Vattel, *The Law of Nations* (translated: J. Chitty) (Johnson & Co, 1883), xiii: 'I acknowledge no other natural society between nations than that which nature has established between mankind in general. It is essential to every civil society (civitati) that each member have resigned a part of his right to the body of the society, and that there exist in it an authority capable of commanding all the members, of giving them laws, and of compelling those who should refuse to obey. Nothing of this kind can be conceived or supposed to subsist between nations. Each sovereign state claims, and actually possesses an absolute independence on all the others.'

[2] P. Pescatore, 'International Law and Community Law – A Comparative Analysis' [1970] 7 CML Rev 167 at 182.

[3] While the 'classics' of European law had actively searched for comparisons with international and national phenomena (cf. E. Haas, *The Uniting of Europe* (Stanford University Press, 1968)), the legal comparative approach fell, with some exceptions, into a medieval slumber in the course of the 1980s.

[4] K. Popper, *The Logic of Scientific Discovery* (Routledge, 2002).

States, whereas Europe's own constitutional theory reduces it to a (special) international organisation. Which is the better theory? We shall see below that the second view runs into serious explanatory difficulties and should consequently be discarded. The European Union is indeed best understood as a 'Federation of States'.

1. The American constitutional tradition: federalism as (inter)national law

The American federal tradition emerged with the 1787 Constitution of the United States of America. Having realised the 'vices' and weaknesses of the 1777 Constitution, deliberations on a 'more perfect union' were held by a Constitutional Convention meeting in Philadelphia. The Convention proposed a more 'consolidated' Union. But the project triggered a heated debate on the nature of the new Union. Those advocating greater national consolidation thereby styled themselves as 'federalists'; and the papers that defended the new constitutional structure would become known as *The Federalist*.[5] By contrast, those insisting on the 'international' legal nature of the American Union became known as '*anti*-federalists'. They were opposed to the new constitution and complained that the Convention had been charged to 'preserve[] the [*international*] form, which regards the Union as a *confederacy* of sovereign states'; 'instead of which, they have framed a *national* government, which regards the Unions as a *consolidation* of the States'.

It was the response to this accusation that would provide the starting point of a novel understanding of sovereignty and its place within a Union of States. This American tradition claimed that that the 1787 Constitution had created a United States of America that was 'in between' an international and a national structure. This view was immortalised in *The Federalist No. 39* – written by James Madison.[6] This grand master of constitutional analysis here explored the nature of the Union's legal order. Refusing to concentrate on the metaphysics of sovereignty, Madison singled out three analytical dimensions which – for convenience – may be called: the foundational, the institutional, and the functional dimension. The first relates to the origin and character of the 1787 Constitution; the second concerns the composition of its governmental institutions; while the third deals with the scope and nature of the federal government's powers.

As regards the *foundational* dimension, the 1787 Constitution was an *international* act. What did this mean? It meant that the Constitution would need to be ratified 'by the people, not as individuals composing one entire nation, but as composing the distinct and independent States to which they respectively belong'. The '*unanimous* assent of the several States' that wished to become parties was required. The Constitution would thus result 'neither from the

---

[5] A. Hamilton, J. Madison and J. Jay, *The Federalist* (T. Ball, ed.) (Cambridge University Press, 2003).

[6] For an extended extract from *The Federalist No. 39*, see: Appendix 4 of this book.

decision of a *majority* of the people of the Union, nor from that of a *majority* of the States'.[7] 'Each State, in ratifying the Constitution, is considered as a sovereign body, independent of all others, and only to be bound by its own voluntary act.' The 1787 Constitution would thus 'be a [*international*], and not a *national* act'.[8] However, the new legal order differed from an international organisation in an important respect. For while the latter will ordinarily be ratified by the State *legislatures*, the proposed Constitution was to be validated by 'the assent and ratification of the several States, *derived from the supreme authority in each State, the authority of the people themselves*'.[9] Instead of the State *governments* – the delegates of the people – each State *people* itself would have to ratify the Constitution. This was the meaning behind the famous 'We, the people'. However, it was not the 'American people', but the people(s) of the several States that would ordain the 1787 Constitution.[10] The direct authority from the (State) people(s) would set the Constitution above the State *governments*. And in having the peoples of each State ratify the Constitution, the 1787 document would be a 'constitutional' – and not a mere 'legislative' – treaty.

What authority could amend the new Constitution once it had been 'ordained'? The 1787 Constitution would not require unanimity for amendment. The new amendment procedure was set out in Article V of the 1787 Constitution.[11] The

---

[7]   Madison, *The Federalist No. 39*, 184 (supra n. 5). To bring the point home, Madison continues (*ibid.*, 185): 'Were the people regarded in this transaction as forming one nation, the will of the majority of the whole people of the United States would bind the minority, in the same manner as the majority in each State must bind the minority; and the will of the majority must be determined either by a comparison of the individual votes, or by considering the will of the majority of the States as evidence of the will of a majority of the people of the United States. Neither of these rules have been adopted.'

[8]   *Ibid.*, 185.   [9]   *Ibid.*, 184 (emphasis added).

[10]   The phrase 'We, the people of the United States' simply referred to the idea that the people(s) in the States – not the State legislatures – had ratified the Constitution. Thus, the preamble of the 1780 Massachusetts Constitution, to offer an illustration, read: 'We, therefore, the people of Massachusetts'. The original 1787 draft preamble indeed read: 'We, the people of the States of New Hampshire, Massachusetts, Rhode-Island and Providence Plantations, Connecticut, New-York, New-Jersey, Pennsylvania, Delaware, Maryland, Virginia, North-Carolina, South-Carolina, and Georgia, do ordain, declare and establish the following constitution for the government of ourselves and our posterity.' However, due to the uncertainty which of the thirteen States would succeed in the ratification (according to Article VII of the Constitution-to-be only nine States were required for the Constitution to enter into force), the enumeration of the individuals States was dropped by the 'Committee of Style' (cf. M. Farrand, *The Framing of the Constitution of the United States* (Yale University Press, 1913), 190–1). Even as staunch a nationalist as Chief Justice J. Marshall admitted that 'the people' had ratified the 1787 Constitution as 'state peoples' (cf. *McCulloch* v. *Maryland*, 17 US 316 (1819), 403: 'No political dreamer was ever wild enough to think of breaking down the lines which separate the States, and of compounding the American people into one common mass. Of consequence, when they act, they act in their States. But the measures they adopt do not, on that account, cease to be the measures of the people themselves, or become the measures of the State governments.').

[11]   Article V reads: 'The Congress, whenever two thirds of both Houses shall deem it necessary, shall propose Amendments to this Constitution, or, on the Application of the Legislatures of two thirds of the several States, shall call a Convention for proposing Amendments, which, in either

provision stipulated that each proposed amendment would have to be ratified by three-quarters of the States – represented by a State convention or by its State legislature.[12] Once the Constitution would enter into force, the power of amending it was thus 'neither wholly *national* nor wholly [*international*]'. 'Were it wholly national, the supreme and ultimate authority would reside in the *majority* of the people of the Union; and this authority would be competent at all times, like that of a majority of every national society, to alter or abolish its established government. Were it wholly [international], on the other hand, the concurrence of each State in the Union would be essential to every alteration that would be binding on all.'[13]

Having analysed the origin and nature of the 1787 Constitution, Madison then moved to the second aspect of the 1787 constitutional structure. In relation to the *institutional* dimension, the following picture emerged. The legislature of the new Union was composed of two branches. The House of Representatives was elected by all the people of America as individuals and therefore was the 'national' branch of the central government.[14] The Senate, on the other hand, would represent the States as 'political and coequal societies'.[15] And in respecting their sovereign equality, the Senate was viewed as a international organ. Every law required the concurrence of a majority of the people and a majority of the States. Overall, the structure of the central government thus had 'a mixed character, presenting at least as many [*international*] as *national* features'.[16]

Case, shall be valid to all Intents and Purposes, as part of this Constitution, when ratified by the Legislatures of three fourths of the several States, or by Conventions in three fourths thereof, as the one or the other Mode of Ratification may be proposed by the Congress; Provided that no Amendment which may be made prior to the Year One thousand eight hundred and eight shall in any Manner affect the first and fourth Clauses in the Ninth Section of the first Article; and that no State, without its Consent, shall be deprived of its equal Suffrage in the Senate.'

[12] The structure of the amendment power led Dicey to conclude that 'the legal sovereignty of the United States resides in the States' governments as forming one aggregate body represented by three-fourths of the several States at any time belonging to the Union' (cf. A. V. Dicey, *Introduction to the Study of the Law of the Constitution* (Liberty Fund, 1982), 81).

[13] Madison, *The Federalist No. 39* (supra n. 5), 186–7.

[14] The 'national' structure of the House of Representatives would not be immediately created by the 1787 Constitution. Article I, Section 4 stated: 'The Times, Places and Manner of holding Elections for Senators and Representatives, shall be prescribed in each State by the Legislature thereof; but Congress may at any time make or alter such Regulations, except as to the Place of choosing Senators.' In the words of H. Wechsler (cf. 'The Political Safeguards of Federalism: The Role of States in the Composition and Selection of the National Government' [1954] 54 *Columbia Law Review*, 543 at 546: 'Though the House was meant to be the "grand depository of the democratic principle of the government," as distinguished from the Senate's function as the forum of the states, the people to be represented with due reference to their respective numbers were the people of the states.'). The first national electoral law for the House would only be adopted in 1842.

[15] Madison (supra n. 5), 185. In *The Federalist No. 62*, Madison adds (*ibid.*, 301): 'In this spirit it may be remarked, that the equal vote allowed to each State is at once a constitutional recognition of the portion of sovereignty remaining in the individual States, and an instrument for preserving that residuary sovereignty. So far the equality ought to be no less acceptable to the large than to the small States; since they are not less solicitous to guard, by every possible expedient, against an improper consolidation of the States into one simple republic.'

[16] *Ibid.*, 185.

Finally, *The Federalist* analysed a third dimension of the new constitutional order. In terms of substance, the powers of the central government showed both international and national characteristics. In relation to their *scope*, they were surely not national, since the idea of a national government implied competence over all objects of government. Thus, 'the proposed government cannot be deemed a *national* one; since its jurisdiction extends to certain enumerated objects only, and leaves to the several States a residuary and inviolable sovereignty over all other objects'.[17] However, the *nature* of the powers of the central government was 'national' in character. The distinction between an (international) confederacy and a national government was that 'in the former the powers operate on the political bodies composing the Confederacy, in their political capacities; in the latter, on the individual citizens composing the nation, in their individual capacities'.[18] The 1787 Constitution allowed the central government to operate directly on individuals and thus fell on the national side.

In light of these three constitutional dimensions, *The Federalist* concluded that the overall constitutional structure of the 1787 Constitution was 'in strictness, neither a national nor a [international] Constitution, *but a composition of both*'.[19] The central government was a 'mixed government'.[20] It stood on 'middle ground'.[21]

It was this *mixed* format of the constitutional structure of the United States of America that would come to be identified with the federal principle. A famous account was thereby offered by Alexis de Tocqueville, who introduced the new ideas to a broader European audience.[22] His influential account of the nature of the American Union described it as a 'middle ground' between an international league and a national government. The mixed nature of the American Union was, according to de Tocqueville, particularly reflected in the composition of the central legislator. The Union was neither a pure international league, in

---

[17] *Ibid.*, 186. *The Federalist No. 45* could justly claim that '[t]he powers delegated by the proposed Constitution to the federal government, are few and defined', whereas '[t]hose which are to remain in the State governments are numerous and indefinite' (*ibid.*, 227).

[18] *Ibid.*, 185. In *The Federalist No. 15*, we hear Hamilton say (*ibid.*, 67): 'The great and radical vice in the construction of the existing Confederation is in the principle of LEGISLATION for STATES or GOVERNMENTS, in their CORPORATE or COLLECTIVE CAPACITIES, and as contradistinguished from the INDIVIDUALS of which they consist. Though this principle does not run through all the powers delegated to the Union, yet it pervades and governs those on which the efficacy of the rest depends.' And in the words of the same author in *The Federalist No. 16* (*ibid.*, 74): 'It must stand in need of no intermediate legislations; but must itself be empowered to employ the arm of the ordinary magistrate to execute its own resolutions. The majesty of the national authority must be manifested through the medium of the courts of justice.'

[19] *Ibid.*, 187.   [20] *The Federalist No. 40* – Title.

[21] Letter of J. Madison to G. Washington of 16 April 1787: 'Conceiving that an individual independence of the States is utterly irreconcileable with their aggregate sovereignty; and that a consolidation of the whole into one simple republic would be as inexpedient as it is unattainable, I have sought for some middle ground, which may at once support a due supremacy of the national authority, and not exclude the local authorities wherever they can be subordinately useful.'

[22] A. de Tocqueville, *Democracy in America* (P. Bradley, ed.) (Vintage, 1954), vol. I.

which the States would have remained on a footing of perfect – sovereign – equality, nor was it a national government; for if 'the inhabitants of the United States were to be considered as belonging to one and the same nation, it would be natural that the majority of the citizens of the Union should make the law'. The 1787 Constitution had chosen a 'middle course', '*which brought together by force two systems theoretically irreconcilable*'.[23] This middle ground had also been reached in relation to the powers of government: 'The sovereignty of the United States is shared between the Union and the States, while in France it is undivided and compact'. 'The Americans have a Federal and the French a national Government.'[24] In fact, the unique aim of the 1787 Constitution 'was to divide the sovereign authority into two parts': 'In the one they placed the control of all the general interests of the Union, in the other the control of the special interests of its component States'.[25] The cardinal quality of the Union's powers was their direct effect: like a State government, the Union government could act directly on individuals.

Sovereignty – while ultimately residing somewhere – was thus seen as delegated and divided between *two* levels of government. Each State had given up part of its sovereignty,[26] while the national government remained 'incomplete'. And because both governments enjoyed powers that were 'sovereign', the new federalism was identified with the idea that '[t]wo sovereignties are necessarily in presence of each other'.[27] Federalism implied *dual* government, *dual* sovereignty, and also *dual* citizenship.[28]

2. The European constitutional tradition: international versus national law

A victim of the nineteenth century's obsession with sovereign States,[29] European constitutional thought came to reject the idea of a divided or dual sovereignty. Sovereignty was indivisible. In a Union of States, it could either lie with the States, in which case the Union was an international organisation; or sovereignty would lie with the Union, in which case the Union was a Federal 'State'. Federalism was thus thought of in terms of a sovereign State. Within this European tradition, federalism came to refer to the constitutional devolution

---

[23] *Ibid.*, 122–3 (emphasis added).   [24] *Ibid.*, 128.   [25] *Ibid.*, 151.

[26] *The Federalist No. 42* ridiculed the theory according to which the absolute sovereignty had remained in the States: 'the articles of Confederation have inconsiderately endeavored to accomplish impossibilities; to reconcile a partial sovereignty in the Union, with complete sovereignty in the States; to subvert a mathematical axiom, by taking away a part, and letting the whole remain' (Hamilton et al. (supra n. 5), 206).

[27] de Tocqueville, *Democracy in America* (supra n. 22), 172.

[28] On the concept of dual citizenship in federal orders, see: O. Beaud, 'The Question of Nationality within a Federation: a Neglected Issue in Nationality Law' in R. Hansen and P. Weil (eds.), *Dual Nationality, Social Rights, and Federal Citizenship in the U.S. and Europe* (Berghahn Books, 2002), 314.

[29] M. Koskenniemi, *From Apology to Utopia* (Cambridge University Press, 2005), Chapter 4.

of power within a sovereign *nation*.[30] A federation was a Federal *State*. This 'national' reduction of the federal principle censored the very idea of a 'Federation *of States*'. To explain the philosophical origins of the European tradition,[31] we shall first analyse the conceptual polarisation between (international) Confederation and (national) Federation that occurred as a result of the idea of State sovereignty. Thereafter, this section presents two early critics of the European constitutional tradition.

(a) Conceptual polarisation: 'Confederation' versus 'Federation'

European constitutionalism insisted on the indivisibility of sovereignty.[32] This *absolute* idea of sovereignty came to operate as a prism that would ignore all *relative* nuances within a mixed or compound legal structure. The result was a conceptual polarisation expressed in a distinction between two idealised categories: *either* a Union of States was a 'Confederation of *States*' *or* it was a 'Federal *State*'. *Tertium non datur*: any third possibility was excluded.[33]

How did European federal thought define a 'confederation' or 'international organisation'? An (international) Union of States was said to be formed on the basis of an ordinary international treaty. Because it was an international treaty, the States had retained sovereignty and, therewith, the right to nullification and secession. 'Nullification and secession, absolutely prohibited within a unitary or federal State, follow logically from the nature of the Confederation as a treaty creature. A sovereign State cannot be bound unconditionally and permanently.' 'The Confederation is a creature of international law. However, international law knows no other legal subjects than States. The Confederation is not a State

---

[30] D.J. Elazar, *Constitutionalizing Globalization: The Postmodern Revival of Confederal Arrangements* (Rowman & Littlefield, 1998), 39: 'Federation, indeed, is federalism applied to constitutionally defuse power within the political system of a single nation. Federation became synonymous with modern federalism because the modern epoch was the era of the nation-state when, in most of the modern world, the ideal was to establish a single centralized state with indivisible sovereignty to serve single nations or peoples.'

[31] In the nineteenth century, Germany and Switzerland were Europe's 'federal' entities. Austria and Belgium would be added in the twentieth century. On the constitutional history of German federal thought, see: E. Deuerlein, *Föderalismus: Die historischen und philosophischen Grundlagen des föderativen Prinzips* (List, 1972). On the constitutional history of Swiss federalism, see: A. Kölz, *Neue Schweizerische Verfassungsgeschichte* (Stämpfli, 1992 and 2004). The following section concentrates on German constitutional history.

[32] One British, one French and one German 'representative' will suffice to support this point: cf. Dicey, *Introduction to the Study of the Law of the Constitution* (supra n. 12), 3: 'Parliament is, under the British Constitution, an absolutely sovereign legislature'; R. Carré de Malberg, *Contribution à la Théorie Générale de l'État* (E. Maulin, ed.) (Dalloz, 2003), 139–40: 'La souveraineté est entière ou elle cesse de se concevoir. Parler de souveraineté restreinte, relative ou divisée, c'est commettre une contradiction in adjecto ... Il n'est donc pas possible d'admettre dans l'État fédéral un partage de la souveraineté[.]'; and P. Laband, *Das Staatsrecht des Deutschen Reiches* (Scientia, 1964), 73: 'die Souveränität eine Eigenschaft absoluten Charakters ist, die keine Steigerung und keine Verminderung zuläßt'.

[33] The logical device is also known as the 'law of the excluded middle'.

and can, consequently, not constitute a subject of international law.'[34] Since the Confederation was not a legal subject, it could not be the author of legal obligations; and it thus followed that the Member States *themselves* were the authors of the Union's commands.[35] The Union was thus regarded as possessing no powers of its own. It only 'pooled' and exercised *State* power. From this international law perspective, the Confederation was not an autonomous 'entity', but a mere 'relation' between sovereign States.

How did European federal thought define the concept of the 'Federal State'? The Federal State was regarded as a *State*; and, as such, it was sovereign – even if national unification had remained 'incomplete'. Because the Federal State was as sovereign as a unitary State, constitutional differences between the two States were downplayed to superficial 'marks of sovereignty'. It indeed became the task of European scholarship to make the 'Federal State' look like its unitary sisters. This was achieved through ingenious feats of legal 'reasoning'. A first argument asserted that when forming the Union, the States had lost all their sovereignty. They had been 're-established' as '*Member* States' *by the Federal Constitution*. These Member States were non-sovereign States.[36] But if the criterion of sovereignty could no longer be employed as the emblem of statehood, what justified calling these federated units 'States'? The search for a criterion that distinguished 'Member *States*' from 'administrative units' led European constitutional thought to insist on the existence of *exclusive* legislative powers.[37] In the succinct words of one of the most celebrated legal minds of the nineteenth century: 'To the extent that the supremacy of the Federal State reaches, the Member States lose their character as States.' And conversely: 'To the extent that the Member States enjoy an exclusive sphere, but only to this extent, will they retain their character as States.'[38]

Let us look at a second argument that was developed to downplay the constitutional differences between a Federal State and a unitary State. In a Federal State powers are divided between the Federal State and its Member States. But if the characteristic element of a Member *State* was the possession of exclusive legislative power, how could the Federal State be said to be sovereign? The European answer to this question was that all powers were ultimately derived from the Federal State, since it enjoyed 'competence-competence' (*Kompetenz-Kompetenz*).[39] This idea translated the unitary concept of sovereignty into a federal context: 'Whatever the actual distribution of competences, the Federal State retains its character as a sovereign State; and, as such, it potentially contains within itself all sovereign powers, even those whose

---

[34] G. Jellinek, *Die Lehre von den Staatenverbindungen* (W. Pauly, ed.) (Keip, 1996), 175 and 178 (translated: R. Schütze).

[35] *Ibid.*, 176.   [36] A. Hänel, *Deutsches Staatsrecht* (Duncker & Humblot, 1892), 802–3.

[37] Jellinek (supra n. 34), 43–4.

[38] G. Jellinek, *Allgemeine Staatslehre* (Springer, 1922), 771–2 (translated: R. Schütze).

[39] One of the best discussions of the concept of Kompetenz-Kompetenz can be found in: Hänel, *Deutsches Staatsrecht* (supra n. 36), 771–806.

autonomous exercise has been delegated to the Member States'.[40] If the Federal State is sovereign, it must be empowered to *unilaterally* amend its constitution. '[T]he power to change its constitution follows from the very concept of the sovereign State.' 'A State, whose existence depends on the good will of its members, is not sovereign; for sovereignty means independence.'[41]

The Federal State was, consequently, deemed to be empowered to 'nationalise' competences that were exclusively reserved to the Member States under the Federal Constitution – even against the will of the federated States. Through this process of 'unitarisation', the Member States would gradually lose their 'statehood'; and since the power to unilaterally amend the constitution was unlimited,[42] the Federal State was said to enjoy the magical power of 'competence-competence' with which it could legally transform itself into a unitary State. 'The existence of the Member States in the Union is, as such, no absolute barrier to the federal will. Indeed, the option to transform the Member States into mere administrative units reveals, in the purest way, the sovereign nature of the Federal State.' 'The negation of this legal option to transform the Federal State into a unitary State by means of constitutional amendment entails with it the negation of the sovereign and, therefore, state character of the Federal State.'[43] In the final analysis, the European tradition thus equated the Federal State with a decentralised unitary State.[44] Federalism was a purely 'national' phenomenon.

(b) Early criticism: the European tradition and the (missing) federal genus

The conceptual polarisation of the federal principle into two specific manifestations – (international) confederation and (national) federation – would structure much of the twentieth-century European debate. And yet, there were two remarkable early critics of that tradition. They could not be more different as regards their legal outlook. Hans Kelsen *legally* approached the federal principle with the tools of his 'pure theory of law', while Carl Schmitt concentrated on the *political* nature of federal orders.[45]

---

[40] Jellinek, *Die Lehre von den Staatenverbindungen* (supra n. 34), 290–1 (translated: R. Schütze).

[41] *Ibid.*, 295–6 (translated: R. Schütze).   [42] Hänel (supra n. 36) 776.

[43] Jellinek (supra n. 34) 304 and 306 (translated: R. Schütze). This has never been accepted by American constitutionalism, see: *Texas* v. *White* (1868) 74 US 700 at 725: 'The Constitution, in all its provisions, looks to an indestructible Union composed of indestructible States.' The rejection of an omnipotent Federal State can now also be found in the modern German Constitution. According to its Article 79 (3), constitutional '[a]mendments to this Basic Law affecting the division of the Federation into Länder, their participation on principle in the legislative process . . . shall be inadmissible'.

[44] H. Triepel, *Unitarismus und Föderalismus im Deutschen Reiche* (Mohr, 1907), 81.

[45] Neither of these two brilliant critiques of traditional European constitutional thought enjoyed much influence outside Germany after the Second World War. This is perhaps not surprising in the light of Schmitt's disgraceful post-Weimar biography. In Kelsen's case, the reason may lie in the lack of a translation of *Das Problem der Souveränität und die Theorie des Völkerrechts* and the

In 1920, Kelsen torpedoed the inconsistencies and tautologies inherent in European federal thought in a path-breaking analysis of the principle of sovereignty and the nature of international law.[46] While remaining loyal to the idea of indivisible sovereignty,[47] Kelsen attacked the categorical distinction between confederation and Federal State. Legally, they had a similar structure. What distinguished the one from the other was only their degree of (de)centralisation. A Federal State was simply a more 'consolidated' or 'centralised' union than a confederation. One federal species blends continuously into the other.[48]

But what did this mean for the distinction between 'treaty' and 'constitution'? For Kelsen, 'treaty and constitution are not mutually exclusive concepts', since the content of a treaty may be a constitution. 'The Federal State may thus have a constitution and yet be founded on an international treaty as much as the confederation has its constitution that may also be created through a treaty.'[49] There was thus no objective or inherent distinction between 'treaty' and 'constitution' as regards their origin; what differed was the *emotional* feeling brought towards them. Sovereignty lay in the eye of the beholder; and for social communities, this was a question of social psychology. Sovereignty and supremacy were 'emotional' questions; and, as such, beyond normative analysis.[50] The categorical distinction between 'treaty' and 'constitution', which was advocated by the European federal tradition, was based on a tautology:

> What matters is not, whether the treaty creates a legal order – every treaty does – but whether the legal order so created is considered as a partial legal order or as a total legal order. The decisive difference between the two lies in whether the juristic construction of the binding force of the treaty . . . is considered to derive from a 'higher', that is a more general, legal order – in our case: from the legal norm 'pacta sunt servanda' of the international legal order; or, whether the juristic construction posits the legal order created by the treaty itself as the highest source. In the latter case, the binding force of the treaty order is derived from an 'originality hypothesis'. Thereby, one must not overlook that the treaty as such, that is, a meeting of wills, is never 'constitutive'. 'Constitutive', that is, the final source of legal validity and force, is in the former case the 'international law hypothesis', in other words, the idea that above the contracting parties stands a higher international legal order; and in the latter case the 'originality hypothesis'.
>
> When some refer to a treaty creating a Federal State as 'constitutive', this signifies nothing but a desire to dissociate the treaty from the international legal order – standing above all States and consequently also above the central legal order created by the Member States – by denying its foundational quality for the legal order of the Federal State. Better still, the hypothesis of the primacy of international law is rejected so as to posit the concrete treaty and the legal order it

---

disappointingly reductionist translation of the relevant chapter of his *Allgemeine Staatslehre* in *The General Theory of Law and State*.

[46] H. Kelsen, *Das Problem der Souveränität und die Theorie des Völkerrechts* (Mohr, 1920).

[47] *Ibid.*, 64–6.   [48] *Ibid.*, 195: 'eine Form kontinuierlich in die andere übergeht'.   [49] *Ibid.*

[50] This is, in my opinion, the very essence of Kelsen's theory of sovereignty and the 'basic' norm (*ibid.*, 15).

creates – a legal order, which from the perspective of international law, would only be a partial legal order – as sovereign, that is, as a State in the sense of the dominant sovereignty dogma. The primacy of this State legal order is thus presumed from the start . . .[51]

This attack on the tautological nature of European federal thought was joined by a second – equally brilliant – critique: the federal theory of Carl Schmitt.[52] Schmitt agreed with Kelsen that the European debate had unduly concentrated on idealised differences between two *species* of the federal principle.[53] It had thereby forgotten to pay attention to the federal *genus* from which both species sprang. What were the *general* characteristics shared by the two *specific* manifestations of the federal principle? What had 'con*federation*' and '*Federal* State' in common? These questions centred on the 'federal' principle as such.

What, then, was federalism? A Federal Union was 'a permanent union based on a *voluntary* agreement whose object is the political preservation of its members'. The normative foundation for such a Federal Union was a 'federal treaty'. The 'federal treaty' was a '*constitutional*' treaty'. It was a treaty that 'changes the overall political status of each federated member in respect of this common aim'. A federal treaty was an international treaty of a constitutional nature.[54] 'Its conclusion is an act of the *pouvoir constituant*. Its content establishes the federal constitution and forms, at the same time, a *part of the constitution of every Member State*.'[55] The dual nature of each federation, standing on the middle ground between international and national order, was thus reflected in the dual nature of its foundational document. The 'federal treaty' stood in between an international treaty and a national constitution. Each federation was thus a creature of international *and* national law.[56]

What, then, distinguished a federation from an ordinary international organisation? Unlike an international league, every Federal Union had 'a common will and, thus, its own *political* existence'.[57] What distinguished a federation from an ordinary State? Unlike a unitary State, the federation was characterised by a political *dualism*. 'In each federal union, two kinds of political bodies co-exist: the existence of the whole federation and the individual existence of each federal member. Both kinds of political existence must remain coordinate in order for the federal union to remain alive.' Each Federal Union permanently lives in an 'existential equilibrium'. 'Such an existential limbo will lead to many

---

[51] H. Kelsen, *Allgemeine Staatslehre* (Springer, 1925), 197–8 (translated: R. Schütze).

[52] C. Schmitt, *Verfassungslehre* (Duncker & Humblot, 2003), Part IV: 'Verfassungslehre des Bundes', 361–91.

[53] *Ibid.*, 366.

[54] *Ibid.*, 367 and 368 (translated: R. Schütze): 'zwischenstaatlicher Statusvertrag', 'Bundesvertrag' and 'Verfassungsvertrag'.

[55] *Ibid.*

[56] *Ibid.*, 379: 'Jeder Bund ist als solcher sowohl völkerrechtliches wie staatsrechtliches Subjekt'.

[57] *Ibid.*, 371 (translated: R. Schütze, emphasis added). For Schmitt, the federation and its members are 'political' bodies. On Schmitt's definition of the 'political', see: C. Schmitt, *Der Begriff des Politischen* (Duncker & Humblot, 1996).

conflicts calling for decision.' Yet, for the political equilibrium to remain alive, the conflict over the locus of sovereignty must remain 'suspended'. The question of sovereignty may be posed, but it must never be answered. Only constitutional silence over the locus of sovereignty *perpetuates* the federal equilibrium.[58] Where the sovereignty question is – definitely – answered in favour of the Union, only it has political existence. The 'Union' is transformed into a sovereign State, whose legal structure may be federal but whose substance is not. Conversely, where the sovereignty question is – definitely – answered in favour of the Member States, the political existence of the federation disappears and the Union dissolves into an international league. The normative ambivalence surrounding the location of sovereignty lay thus at the core of all – real – federations.[59]

3. The European Union in light of the American constitutional tradition

The American tradition had identified the 1787 United States with the middle ground between an international and a national legal structure. Within the classic period of European law, the European Union was indeed described as a hybrid that was placed 'between international and municipal law'.[60] 'The [Union] is a new structure in the marches between internal and international law.'[61] It 'is neither an international Confederation, nor a Federal State'. 'It simultaneously combines characteristics from both types of State relations and thus forms a *mixtum compositum*.'[62] How did this mixed format express itself? What were its 'international' and 'national' features?[63] American

---

[58] Schmitt, *Verfassungslehre* (supra n. 52), 376–8 (translated: R. Schütze). For that silence to remain, a homogeneity of interests must be fostered. This had already been pointed out by de Tocqueville (supra n. 22), 175–6: 'Since legislators cannot prevent such dangerous collisions as occur between the two sovereignties which coexist in the Federal system, their first object must be, not only to dissuade the confederate States from warfare, but to encourage such dispositions as lead to peace.' 'A certain uniformity of civilization is not less necessary to the durability of a confederation than a uniformity of interests in the States which compose it.'

[59] Schmitt, *Verfassungslehre* (supra n. 52), 378

[60] C. Sasse, 'The Common Market: Between International and Municipal Law', [1965–6] 75 *Yale Law Journal*, 695; as well as P. Hay, 'The Contribution of the European Communities to International Law' [1965] 59 *Proceedings of the American Society of International Law*, 195 at 199: 'The contribution of the Communities for legal science is the breaking-up of the rigid dichotomy of national and international law'.

[61] E. Van Raalte, 'The Treaty Constituting the European Coal and Steel Community', [1952] 1 *International and Comparative Law Quarterly* 73 at 74.

[62] L.-J. Constantinesco, *Das Recht der Europäischen Gemeinschaften* (Nomos, 1977), 332 (translated: R. Schütze).

[63] In the following subsection, the terms 'international' and 'national' will be used as analytical terms. The former refers to a voluntary and horizontal structure recognising the sovereign equality of the States; the latter stands for the hierarchical and vertical structure within a unitary State. Even if the notion of 'unitary' is less charged with symbolic connotations than 'national', we shall use the latter term to facilitate a comparison with Madison's discussion of the mixed structure of the American Union.

constitutionalism offered a potent analytical approach to these questions. Refusing to concentrate on the metaphysics of sovereignty, three analytical dimensions had been singled out: the foundational, the institutional, and the functional dimension. The first relates to the origin and nature of the new legal order; the second concerns the composition of its 'government'; while the third deals with the scope and nature of the federation's powers. This approach may also prove fruitful for a legal analysis of the European Union.

(a) The foundational dimension: Europe's 'Constitutional Treaty'

The European Union was conceived as an international organisation. Its birth certificate was an international treaty. Its formation had been 'international' – just like the American Union. However, unlike the American Union, the European treaties have been ratified by the national *legislatures* – not the national peoples – of its Member States. Genetically, they are 'legislative' – not constitutional – treaties.[64] Would this (legislative) 'treaty' origin categorically rule out the idea of a European 'constitution'? This is not a matter of logical necessity. And as soon as we accept that the status of a legal norm depends on the function a society gives it,[65] it is hard to deny that the European treaties have been elevated to a constitutional status. They have evolved into a 'Treaty–Constitution'.[66] The European Court of Justice has insisted on the normative 'autonomy' of the European legal order and this 'originality hypothesis' severed the umbilical cord with the international legal order.[67]

This emancipation manifested itself in the following legal facts. First, in contrast to the normative regime governing international treaties, the European Court of Justice insisted on the 'unilateral' nature of European law: a Member State could not invoke the breach of European law by another Member State to justify a derogation from its own obligations under the Treaties.[68] Second, the European Court of Justice insisted on the supremacy of Union law over all

---

[64] It is difficult – if not impossible – to accept that 'the founding treaties as well as each amendment agreed upon by the governments appear as the direct expression of the common will of the [national] peoples of the Union' (I. Pernice, 'Multilevel Constitutionalism and the Treaty of Amsterdam: European Constitution-Making Revisited?' [1999] 36 CML Rev 703 at 717 (emphasis added)). National ratifications are – with the exception of a few Member States – only indirect expressions of the common will of the national peoples of the Union. National consent is typically expressed through national legislatures. It is equally difficult to agree that these national ratifications should be regarded 'as a *common* exercise of constitution-making power by the peoples of the participating State' (*ibid.*, 717 (emphasis added)). This theory does not explain how each unilateral national act ultimately transforms itself into a collective act.

[65] On this point, see the analysis by Kelsen (supra n. 51).

[66] E. Stein uses the compound 'Treaty-Constitution' (see 'Toward Supremacy of Treaty-Constitution by Judicial Fiat: on the Margin of the Costa Case' [1964–5] 63 *Michigan Law Journal*, 491).

[67] On Case 6/64, *Costa* v. *ENEL*, [1964] ECR 585, see: Chapter 1 – Section 2 above.

[68] Cf. Case 90–91/63, *Commission* v. *Luxemburg and Belgium*, [1963] ECR 625.

national law, including national constitutional law.[69] This contrasts with classic international law doctrine of which the supremacy doctrine forms no part.[70] However, the absolute supremacy of European law has not been accepted by all Member States. In parallel with a *European* perspective, there co-exists a *national* perspective on the supremacy issue.[71] But will the existence of a national perspective on the supremacy of European law rule out the 'constitutional' or 'federal' character of the European Union? This is not the case. The ambivalence surrounding supremacy and sovereignty can be viewed as part and parcel of Europe's *federal* nature. The 'suspension' of the supremacy question in the European Union is the very proof of the *political* co-existence of *two* political bodies and thus evidence of Europe's living federalism. Third, in establishing a direct link with individuals, Europe's constitutional order recognised from the very start an incipient form of European citizenship.[72] The latter was to be expressly acknowledged with the official introduction of a 'citizenship of the Union' in the Maastricht Treaty. According to Article 9 TEU '[e]very national of a Member State shall be a citizen of the Union'. And in accord with federal theory, every European will thus be a citizen of *two* political orders: 'Citizenship of the Union shall be additional to and not replace national citizenship.'

To conclude: in the eyes of the European Court of Justice and the majority of European scholars, the normative force of European law derives no longer from the normative foundations of international law. The ultimate normative base within Europe – its 'originality hypothesis' or '*Grundnorm*' – are the European Treaties as such. '[T]he E[U] Treaty, albeit concluded in the form of an international agreement, none the less constitutes the constitutional charter of a [Union] based on a rule of law[.]'[73] While 'international' in formation, the European Treaties have assumed 'national' characteristics.

Would this 'national' semi-nature not be put into question by the 'international' nature of the amendment process or the States' ability voluntarily to leave the Union? Indeed, Treaty amendment continues to (ordinarily) require the ratification of all the Member States according to their respective national constitutional requirements.[74] But whereas the Member States – in the

---

[69] Cf. Case 11/70, *Internationale Handelsgesellschaft mbH* v. *Einfuhr- und Vorratsstelle für Getreide und Futtermittel*, [1970] ECR 1125.

[70] On this point, see: Chapter 10 – Section 1 (a)(i) below.

[71] On this dual perspective on the supremacy question, see: Chapter 10 – Sections 1 and 2 below.

[72] For the opposite view, see: H. P. Ipsen, *Europäisches Gemeinschaftsrecht* (Mohr, 1972), 251.

[73] Opinion 1/91 (EFTA), [1991] ECR I-6079, para. 21. See also, Case 294/83, '*Les Verts*' v. *Parliament*, [1986] ECR 1339, para. 23: 'basic constitutional charter'.

[74] On the amendment provisions, see: Chapter 1, Conclusion. The introduction of simplified revision procedures by the Lisbon Treaty has recently been associated with Union Kompetenz-Kompetenz (see: G. Barrett, 'Creation's Final Laws: The Impact of the Treaty of Lisbon on the "Final Provisions" of the Earlier Treaties' [2008] 27 YEL, 3 at 15: 'From the theoretical standpoint, all of these are of interest in that they confer a form of *Kompetenz Kompetenz* on the European Union in that, for the first time they empower an institution of the Union itself – vis, the European Council – to amend the Treaties.')

collective plural – remain the 'Masters of the Treaties', *individual* Member States have lost their 'competence-competence'.[75] Legally, Member States are no longer competent to determine *unilaterally* the limits of their own competences themselves.[76] And as regards the right to withdrawal from the Union,[77] this is not an argument against the federal nature of the European *Union*, but an argument against the Union being a Federal *State*. For it is sovereign States that typically prohibit secession on the ground that it violates their sovereign integrity.[78]

(b) The institutional dimension: a European Union of States and people(s)

How are we to analyse the institutional dimension of the European Union? The Union's principal law-making organs are the European Parliament and the Council. How should we characterise each of them alongside the international versus national spectrum; and what will it tell us about the nature of the European legislator?

The composition of the European Parliament has changed over time. Originally, it was an assembly of 'representatives of the *peoples of the States* brought together in the Community'.[79] This designation was adequate as long as the Parliament consisted of 'delegates who shall be designated by the respective Parliaments from among their members in accordance with the procedure laid down by each Member State'.[80] However, the composition of the Parliament dramatically changed with the introduction of direct elections.[81] While there remain 'international' elements, its composition steadily evolved towards the 'national' pole. Today, the European Parliament *directly* represents – even if in a distorted

---

[75] H. P. Ipsen, 'Europäische Verfassung – Nationale Verfassung' [1987] 22 *Europarecht*, 195 at 202: 'Die staatliche Kompetenz-Kompetenz hat sich durch den Beitritt zur Gemeinschaft selbst beschränkt.'

[76] A. von Bogdandy and J. Bast, 'The European Union's Vertical Order of Competences: The Current Law and Proposals for its Reform' [2002] 39 CML Rev 227 at 237: '[T]he individual Member State has forfeited its right to determine its own competences (Kompetenz-Kompetenz) insofar as it is not permitted to extend its powers unilaterally to the detriment of the Union. While the Member States acting jointly as the Contracting Parties may amend the Treaties, transferring powers back to the Member States, they are bound by the procedures provided for in Article 48 TEU.'

[77] The right to withdrawal is now expressly enshrined in Article 50 (1) TEU: 'Any Member State may decide to withdraw from the Union in accordance with its own constitutional requirements.'

[78] On secession in (inter)national law, see: L. C. Buchheit, *Secession: The Legitimacy of Self-Determination* (Yale University Press, 1978).

[79] Article 137 EEC (emphasis added). France preferred this symbolic formulation. And to safeguard the indivisibility of the French Republic guaranteed under Article 1 of the 1958 Constitution, the idea of a 'representative mandate' was also rejected by the Constitutional Council in its 1977 decision on the 1976 European Parliament Election Act (J. P. Jacqué, 'La Souveraineté française et l'élection du Parlement Européen au suffrage universel direct' in A. Bleckmann and G. Ress (eds.), *Souveränitätsverständnis in den Europäischen Gemeinschaften* (Nomos, 1980), 71).

[80] Article 138 EEC   [81] On this point, see: Chapter 3 – Section 2(a) below.

way – a European people.[82] The Lisbon Treaty now expressly recognises this in Article 10 (2) TEU: 'Citizens are directly represented at Union level in the European Parliament.' It is thus wrong to claim that the European Parliament represents the national *peoples* in their collective capacity. It represents a – constitutionally posited – European people.[83] The Parliament's 'national' composition is reflected in its decision-making mode, which is majority voting.[84]

In terms of its composition, the Council is an 'international' organ. 'The Council shall consist of a representative of each Member State at ministerial level, who may commit the government of the Member State in question and cast its vote.'[85] Each national minister thus represents 'its' State government; and where decision-making is by unanimity, the sovereign equality of the Member States is respected. Yet, the European Treaties also envisage procedures that would break with the international idea of sovereign equality. From the very beginning, they permitted the Union to act by a (qualified) majority of States; and where a qualified majority sufficed, the Member States had weighed votes depending – roughly – on the size of their populations.[86] (Strictly speaking, the Council therefore will not represent the Member *States* – a notion that implies their *equality* – but it represents the national *peoples*.[87]) To act by qualified majority, the Council traditionally needs a 'triple majority': a majority of the *States* must obtain a majority of the votes from the *national peoples*; and the last-mentioned must also represent a majority of the *European people*.[88] Formally then, decision-making within the Council is neither completely international nor completely national, but a combination of both. It stands on federal middle ground.

The composition and operating mode of the European Parliament and the Council having been analysed, what – then – is the nature of the European legislator? Depending on the legislative procedure applicable, there are a number of European legislators. Where the Council operates on the basis of unanimity, the legislative procedure will still be predominantly of an 'international' nature:

---

[82] To this day, the European Treaties allocate a – neither equal nor proportional – number of parliamentary mandates to the Member States and there is still no uniform European electoral procedure. On the details, see: *ibid.*

[83] In the words of Habermas: 'The ethical-political self-understanding of citizens in a democratic community must not be taken as an historical-cultural a priori that makes democratic will-formation possible, but rather as flowing contents of a circulatory progress that is generated through the legal institutionalization of citizens' communication. This is precisely how national identities were formed in modern Europe. Therefore it is to be expected that the political institutions to be created by a European constitution would have an inducing effect.' See: J. Habermas, 'Remarks on Dieter Grimm's "Does Europe need a Constitution?"' [1995] 1 *European Law Journal* 303 at 306.

[84] Article 231 TFEU: 'Save as otherwise provided in the Treaties, the European Parliament shall act by a majority of the votes cast.'

[85] Article 16 (2) TEU.   [86] On this point, see: Chapter 3 – Section 4(c) below.

[87] For a similar conclusion albeit from a different perspective, see: A. Peters, *Elemente einer Theorie der Verfassung Europas* (Duncker & Humblot, 2001), 563 and 566.

[88] On the traditional voting rules in the Council and the Lisbon amendments, see: Chapter 3 – Section 4(c) below.

after all each State guards its sovereign equality in the form of a decisional veto power. According to the 'ordinary' legislative procedure, on the other hand, the Council decides by a qualified majority and the European Parliament acts as 'co-legislator'.[89] The European legislator is here 'bicameral' and this constitutional structure 'reflects a subtle federal balance': 'Legislation comes into being through majority voting in the two houses of the legislature and only after the approval by both of them. One house represents the people in their capacity as citizens of the Union, the other house represents the component entities of the federation, the Member States, and – through them – the people in their capacity as citizens of the Member States.'[90] Europe's prevailing legislator is consequently a combination of 'national' and 'international' elements. While the Parliament represents a – constitutionally posited – European people, the Council represents the Member States. This institutional arrangement reflects the *dual* basis of democratic legitimacy in the European Union.

(c) The functional dimension: the division of powers in Europe

What about the allocation of the functions of government? What kind of powers does the European Union enjoy? Within the internal sphere, Europe clearly enjoys significant legislative powers.[91] This is equally the case in the external sphere.[92] However, the European Union's powers remain enumerated powers. Its scope of government is 'incomplete'. The reach of Europe's powers is thus *not* 'national' – that is: sovereign – in scope.

But what is the nature of Europe's powers? When the European Union was born, the Treaties envisaged two instruments with direct effect on individuals. Regulations were to have direct and general application in all Member States.[93] Decisions allowed the Union to adopt directly effective measures addressed to particular persons.[94] In making regulations and decisions directly applicable in domestic legal orders, the European Treaties thus recognised two 'national' instruments – one legislative, the other executive. The European Union also possessed an 'international' instrument: the directive. In order to operate on individuals, the European command would need to be incorporated by the States. However, through a series of courageous rulings, the European Court of

---

[89] A. Dashwood, 'Community Legislative Procedures in the Era of the Treaty on European Union' [1994] 19 EL Rev 343 at 362–3. 'The "product" of the procedure is an act adopted jointly by the European Parliament and the Council – in contrast to that of the consultation or co-operation-procedures, which is simply an act of the Council … [T]he acts in question shall be signed by both the President of the European Parliament and the President of the Council, symbolising in the most concrete way possible the joint character of such acts.'

[90] K. Lenaerts, 'Federalism: Essential Concepts in Evolution – the Case of the European Union' [1998] 21 *Fordham International Law Journal* 746 at 763.

[91] On this point, see: Chapter 5 – Section 1 below.

[92] On this point, see: Chapter 6 – Section 1 below.

[93] Cf. Article 249 (2) EC, and now: Article 288 (2) TFEU.

[94] Cf. Article 249 (4) EC, and now: Article 288 (4) TFEU.

Justice partly transformed the directive's morphology by injecting 'national' elements. Directives thus combine 'international' and 'national' features.[95] They are a form of 'incomplete legislation' and thus symbolically represent Europe's 'federal' middle ground.

What about Europe's *executive* powers? While the Union had established its own enforcement machinery in some sectors,[96] the direct administration of European legislation has remained an exception – even if Europe has enlarged its executive presence in recent years. Indirect Union administration still characterises the European federation which continues to largely rely on its Member States to apply and implement European law.[97] The decentralised application of European law is effected through the supremacy principle: all organs of a Member State's administration – executive *and* judicial – must disapply conflicting national law in every individual case before them. Supremacy, in fact, primarily concerns the executive application of European law.[98] Unlike contemporary American federal doctrine,[99] European federalism even imposes a positive obligation on national administrations to implement European law. Thus, although national administrations are – from an institutional perspective – not integrated into the European administrative machinery, national administrations operate – from a functional perspective – as a decentralised European administration. However, there is an important caveat. The obligation to execute European law is on the Member States as 'corporate' entities. Where a national administration refuses to give effect to European law, the only road open for the European Union to enforce its laws is to bring an action before the European Court of Justice. In the execution of its legislative choices, European law thus still 'largely follows the logic of state responsibility in public international law'.[100]

(d) Overall classification: the European Union on federal 'middle ground'

In light of these three dimensions, how should we classify the European Union? Its formation was clearly international and its amendment still is. However, its international birth should not prejudge against the 'federal' or 'constitutional' status of the European Treaties. Was not the 1787 American *Federation* the result of an international act? And had not the 1949 German *Constitution* been ratified

---

[95] On the instrumental format of directives, see: Chapter 9 – Section 3 below.
[96] On this point, see: Chapter 7 – Section 3 below.   [97] *Ibid.*
[98] On this point, see: Chapter 10 – Section 1(b) below.
[99] On the 'no-commandeering rule' in US federalism, see: D. Halberstam, 'Comparative Federalism and the Issue of Commandeering' in K. Nikolaidis and R. Howse (eds.), *The Federal Vision: Legitimacy and Levels of Governance in the United States and the European Union* (Oxford University Press, 2001), 213.
[100] S. Kadelbach, 'European Administrative Law and the Law of a Europeanized Administration' in C. Joerges and R. Dehousse (eds.), *Good Governance in Europe's Integrated Market* (Oxford University Press, 2002), 167 at 176.

by the State legislatures?[101] The fact remains that the European legal order has adopted the 'originality hypothesis' and cut the umbilical cord with the international legal order. The Treaties *as such* – not international law – are posited at the origin of European law. Functionally, then, the European Union is based on a 'constitutional treaty' that stands on federal middle ground. The same conclusion was reached when analysing Europe's 'government'. The European Union's dominant legislative procedure strikes a federal balance between 'international' and 'national' elements. And while the scope of its powers is limited, the nature of the Union's powers is predominantly 'national'. Overall then, the legal structure of the European Union is 'in strictness, neither a national nor a[n] international Constitution, *but a composition of both*'.[102]

4. The European Union in light of the European constitutional tradition

European constitutionalism has, as we saw above, historically insisted on the indivisibility of sovereignty. It focuses on the locus of sovereignty. The *absolute* idea of sovereignty operates as a prism that ignores all *relative* nuances within a mixed or dual legal structure. Where States form a union but retain their sovereignty, the object thereby created is an international organisation (confederation) regulated by international law. By contrast, where States transfer sovereignty to the centre, a new State emerges. Within this State – a Federal State if powers are territorially divided – the centre is solely sovereign and (potentially) omnicompetent. This fourth section analyses the European Union in light of this second tradition.

When European thought began to apply its conceptual apparatus to the European Union, it noted that its theoretical categories could not explain the legal reality of European law. In the absence of a theory of federalism beyond the State, European thought invented a new word – supranationalism – and proudly announced the European Union to be *sui generis*. But in times of constitutional conflict, Europe's philosophical heritage returned to the fore and insisted on the international nature of the European Union. The 'international law theory' received its classic expression in the legal debate surrounding the ratification of the Maastricht Treaty.[103] The identification of the European Union with an international organisation[104] led to three constitutional denials:

---

[101] Article 144 (1) of the German Constitution states: 'This Basic Law shall require ratification by the *parliaments* of two thirds of the German Länder in which it is initially to apply' (emphasis added).

[102] Hamilton et al., *The Federalist* (supra n. 5), 187.

[103] J. Baquero-Cruz, 'The Legacy of the Maastricht-Urteil and the Pluralist Movement' [2008] 14 *European Law Journal* 389.

[104] For this thesis, see: D. Wyatt, 'New Legal Order, or Old' [1982] 7 *European Law Review* 147; T. Schilling, 'The Autonomy of the Community Legal Order' [1996] 37 *Harvard International Law Journal* 389.

the European Union could have no people, no constitution, and no constitutionalism.

(a) The *sui generis* 'theory': the 'incomparable' European Union

Europe's quest for a new word to describe the middle ground between 'international' and 'national' law would – at first – be answered by a novel concept: supranationalism. Europe was said to be a *sui generis* legal phenomenon. It was incomparable for 'it cannot be fitted into traditional categories of international or constitutional law'.[105]

Was the European Union really a species without a genus? There are serious problems with the *sui generis* argument. First of all, it lacks explanatory value for it is based on a conceptual tautology.[106] Worse, the *sui generis* theory 'not only fails to analyze but in fact asserts that no analysis is possible or worthwhile, it is in fact an "unsatisfying shrug"'.[107] Second, it only views the Union in *negative* terms – it is *neither* international organisation *nor* Federal State – and thus indirectly perpetuates the conceptual foundations of the European tradition.[108] Third, in not providing any external standard, the *sui generis* formula cannot detect, let alone measure, the European Union's evolution. Thus, even where the European Community lost some of its 'supranational' features – as occurred in the transition from the ECSC to the E(E)C – *both* would be described as *sui generis*. But worst of all: the *sui generis* 'theory' is historically unfounded. All previously existing Unions of States lay between international and national law.[109] More concretely, the power to adopt legislative norms binding on individuals – this acclaimed *sui generis* feature of Europe – cannot be the basis of its claim to specificity.[110] The same lack of 'uniqueness' holds true for other normative or institutional features of the European Union.[111] And even if one sees Europe's *Sonderweg* – yet another way of celebrating the *sui generis* idea – in 'the combination of a "confederal"

---

[105] H. L. Mason, *The European Coal and Steel Community: Experiment in Supranationalism* (Martinus Nijhoff, 1955), 126.

[106] P. Hay, *Federalism and Supranational Organisations* (University of Illinois Press, 1966), 37: 'It should be clear, however, that the term has neither analytic value of its own nor does it add in analysis: the characterization of the Communities as supranational and of their law as "supranational law" still says nothing about the nature of that law in relation either to national legal systems or to international law.'

[107] *Ibid.*, 44.

[108] For this brilliant point, see: C. Schönberger, 'Die Europäische Union als Bund' [2004] 129 *Archiv des öffentlichen Rechts* 81 at 83.

[109] J. B. Westerkamp, *Staatenbund und Bundesstaat: Untersuchungen über die Praxis und das Recht der modernen Bünde* (Brockhaus, 1892).

[110] Schönberger (supra n. 108) 93.

[111] To give but one more illustration: Europe's supremacy principle is, in its structure, not unique. The Canadian doctrine of 'federal paramountcy' also requires only the 'disapplication' and not the 'invalidation' of conflicting provincial laws.

institutional arrangement and a "federal" legal arrangement',[112] this may not be too special after all.[113]

The *sui generis* 'theory' is indeed an introverted and unhistorical 'theory' that is tacitly based on the idea of undivided sovereignty. This poses – unsolvable – problems for an analysis of the political and constitutional *dualism* that characterises the European Union. For a tradition that (tacitly or expressly) relies on the – unitary – concept of sovereignty, the constitutional pluralism within the Union must be seen as a 'novelty' or 'aberration'. The absence of an 'Archimedean point' from which all legal authority can be explained is thus – wrongly – hailed as a *sui generis* quality of the European Union.[114] Why not see the normative ambivalence surrounding the sovereignty principle in the European Union as part and parcel of Europe's *federal* nature? The *sui generis* 'theory' and the theory of constitutional pluralism indeed speak federal prose,[115] without – like Molière's Monsieur Jourdain – being aware of it.

In any event, the *sui generis* 'theory' of the European Union had always been a semantic tranquiliser. For it could not prevent classificatory wars in times of constitutional conflict. Whenever the sovereignty question was posed, Europe's statist tradition would brush this pseudo-theory aside and insist on the international law nature of the Union.

(b) The international law theory: the 'Maastricht Decision'

The ratification of the Maastricht Treaty was *the* 'constitutional moment' when the symbolic weight of European integration entered into the collective

---

[112] J. Weiler, 'Federalism without Constitutionalism: Europe's Sonderweg' in K. Nikolaidis and R. Howse (eds.), *The Federal Vision: Legitimacy and Levels of Governance in the United States and the European Union* (Oxford University Press, 2001), 54 at 58.

[113] On this point, see: P. Pescatore, *The Law of Integration: Emergence of a New Phenomenon in International Relations, Based on The Experience of the European Communities* (Sijthoff, 1974), 58.

[114] Cf. N. Walker, 'The Idea of Constitutional Pluralism' [2002] 65 *Modern Law Review* 317 at 338. This is how Walker, a leading figure of the 'constitutional pluralists', describes the origin of this 'new' constitutional philosophy: 'It is no coincidence that this literature has emerged out of the study of the constitutional dimension of EU law, for it is EU law which poses the most pressing paradigm-challenging test to what we might call constitutional monism. Constitutional monism merely grants a label to the defining assumption of constitutionalism in the Westphalian age . . . namely the idea that the sole centres or units of constitutional authorities are states. Constitutional pluralism, by contrast, recognizes that the European legal order inaugurated by the Treaty of Rome has developed beyond the traditional confines of inter-*national* law and now makes its own independent constitutional claims exist alongside the continuing claims of states' (*ibid.*, 337). This – 'Eurocentric' – view strikingly ignores the American experience, in which the Union *and* the States were seen to have 'constitutional' claims and in which the 'Union' was – traditionally – not (!) conceived in statist terms (cf. E. Zoeller, 'Aspects Internationaux du Droit Constitutionnel. Contribution à la Théorie de la Féderation d'Etats' [2002] 194 *Recueil des Cours de l'Académie de la Haye* 43).

[115] The family resemblance between federalism and constitutional pluralism was identified by a former President of the European Commission. When Europe 'turn[ed] to the principles of federalism in a bid to find workable solutions, it is precisely because they provide all the necessary guarantees on *pluralism* and the efficiency of the emergent institutional machinery' (see Address by Jacques Delors at the College of Europe (17 October), [1989] 10 *Bulletin of the European Communities* 110 at 114–15 (emphasis added)).

consciousness of European society. The ensuing legal debate crystallised into national constitutional reviews of the nature of the European Union. The most controversial and celebrated review was the 'Maastricht Decision' of the German Constitutional Court.[116] The Maastricht battle has structured the European constitutional debate for two decades. The German Supreme Court here posed the sovereignty question. Its central contestation was this: Europe's present *social* structure would set limits to the *constitutional* structure of the Europe Union. As long as there was no European equivalent to national peoples, there would be a legal limit to European integration. And in this moment of constitutional conflict, European federal thought was forced to reveal its deeper intellectual structure.

How did the German Constitutional Court derive national limits to European integration? The Court based its reasoning on the democratic principle – *the* material principle of modern constitutional thought. How could European laws be legitimised from a democratic point of view? Two options existed. First, European laws could be regarded as legitimised – directly or indirectly – through national democracy. Second, they could be legitimised by the existence of European democracy. As regards the first option, national democracy could only be *directly* safeguarded through unanimity voting in the Council. However, the rise of majority voting in the Council increasingly allowed the European Union to adopt legislation against the will of national peoples.[117] European integration indeed imposed formidable limits on the effectiveness of *national* democracy. Yet, majority voting was necessary for European integration;[118] and this had been recognised by Germany's choice to transfer sovereign powers to Europe. The situation in which a Member State was outvoted in the Council could thus still be *indirectly* legitimised by reference to the national decision to open up to European integration. (That argument works only where the national decision is of a constitutional nature – as in the case of Article 23 of the German Constitution.) But even this decision was subject to the fundamental boundaries set by the national Constitution.[119]

How did the German Constitutional Court assess the second option – legitimation through a European democratic structure? The Court readily admitted that 'with the building-up of the functions and powers of the Union, it becomes increasingly necessary to allow the democratic legitimation and influence provided by way of national parliaments *to be accompanied* by a representation of the

---

[116] BVerfGE 89, 155 (Maastricht Decison). The following discussion refers to the English translation of the judgment: [1994] CMLR 57 (Maastricht Decision).

[117] *Ibid.*, 78.

[118] *Ibid.*, 86: 'Unanimity as a universal requirement would inevitably set the wills of the particular States above that of the Community of States itself and would put the very structure of such a community in doubt.'

[119] Article 79 (3) of the German Constitution states: 'Amendments to this Basic Law affecting the division of the Federation into Länder, their participation on principle in the legislative process, or the principles laid down in Articles 1 and 20 shall be inadmissible.'

peoples of the Member States through a European Parliament as the source of
a *supplementary* democratic support for the policies of the European Union'.
Formal progress in this direction was made by the establishment of European
citizenship. This citizenship created a legal bond between Europe and its subjects,
which 'although it does not have a tightness comparable to the common nationality of a single State, provides a legally binding expression of the degree of *de
facto* community already in existence'.[120] But would this *constitutional* structure
correspond to Europe's *social* structure? The existing democratic structure of
the European Union would only work under certain social or '*pre*-legal' conditions. And these social pre-conditions for constitutional democracy did not
(yet) exist in Europe.[121]

The very purpose behind the European Union was to realise a 'Union of
States' as 'an *ever closer union of the peoples of Europe (organised as States) and
not a State based on the people of one European nation*'.[122] The European Union
was never to become a (federal) State. And from this negation, the German
Constitutional Court drew its dramatic and (in)famous conclusions. First, the
Union would need to recognise that the primary source of democratic legitimacy for European laws had remained the *national peoples*. Second, all legal
authority of the European Union derived thus from the Member States. Third,

---

[120] Maastricht Decision (supra n. 116) 86 (emphasis added).

[121] Let us quote the contested para. 41 (*ibid.*, 87) in full. 'Democracy, if it is not to remain a merely
formal principle of accountability, is dependent on the presence of certain pre-legal conditions,
such as a continuous free debate between opposing social forces, interests and ideas, in which
political goals also become clarified and change course and out of which comes a public opinion
which forms the beginnings of political intentions. That also entails that the decision-making-
processes of the organs exercising sovereign powers and the various political objectives pursued
can be generally perceived and understood, and therefore that the citizen entitled to vote can
communicate in his own language with the sovereign authority to which he is subject. Such
factual conditions, in so far as they do not yet exist, can develop in the course of time within the
institutional framework of the European Union . . . Parties, associations, the press and broad-
casting organs are both a medium as well as a factor of this process, out of which a European
public opinion may come into being[.]' The idea that no political system can operate without a
broad consensus on the purposes of government by members of the polity is generally accepted.
Only in passing did the German Constitutional Court seemingly define the substantive pre-
conditions of democracy by a relative 'spiritual[], social[] and political[]' homogeneity of a
people' (*ibid.*, 88). The reference to Heller was designed to express – opposing Schmitt – the
Court's belief in the necessity of a common set of civic values (!) as the basis of parliamentari-
anism (cf. H. P. Ipsen, 'Zehn Glossen zum Maastricht Urteil' [1994] 29 *Europarecht*, 1 at 6).
There is no trace in the judgment of an insistence on racial or ethnic homogeneity. Suggestions
to the contrary, describing the German Court's position as one of 'organic ethno-culturalism'
and as a 'worldview which ultimately informs ethnic cleansing' (cf. J. Weiler, 'Does Europe Need
a Constitution: Demos, Telos and the German Maastricht Decision' [1995] 1 *European Law
Journal* 219 at 251–2) are uninformed and unfair. Ironically, much of what Weiler pronounces
to be 'his' civic theory of social and political commitment to shared values (*ibid.*, 253) is what we
read in the German Constitutional Court's judgment.

[122] Maastricht Decision, 89 (emphasis added). The Court continues the theme a little later: 'In any
event the establishment of a "United States of Europe", in a way comparable to that in which the
United States of America became a State, is not at present intended.' Incidentally, the German
Supreme Court did, superficially, acknowledge the *sui generis* characteristics of the European
Union by inventing a new term for the European Union – the 'Staatenverbund'.

European laws could consequently 'only have effects within the German sovereign sphere by virtue of the German instruction that its law is applied'. European norms required a national 'bridge' over which to enter into the domestic legal order.[123] Fourth, where a European law went beyond this national scope, it could have no effects in the national legal order. Fifth, the ultimate arbiter of that question would be national Supreme Courts.

In conclusion, *each* Member State had remained a master of the Treaties. Each of them had preserved 'the quality as a sovereign State in its own right and the status of sovereign equality with other States within the meaning of Article 2 (1) of the United Nations Charter'.[124] European law was international law.[125]

(c) Europe's statist tradition unearthed: three constitutional denials

The constitutional conflict over the Maastricht Treaty on European Union had awoken old spirits: Europe's statist tradition. The reactions to the Maastricht challenge were manifold and ranged from the placid and guided to the aggressive and misguided.[126] But underneath superficial differences, much of the ensuing constitutional debate would not escape the conceptual heritage of Europe's statist tradition. The latent presence of the federal tradition manifested itself in three 'constitutional denials': Europe was said to have *no* people, *no* constitution, and *no* constitutionalism. These denials derived from a deep-seated belief in the indivisibility of sovereignty. Because sovereignty could not be divided, it had to be in the possession of *either* the Union *or* the Member States; that is: *either* a European people *or* the national peoples. Depending on the locus of sovereignty, the European Union would be *either* based on a (national) constitution *or* an (international) treaty. And even if Europe had a constitutional treaty, the lack of a 'constitutional demos' denied it a constitutionalism of its own.

Let us look at the underlying philosophical rationale for each of these denials, before subjecting each to constructive criticism.

Will a people – the 'constituency' for constitutional politics – precede its polity, or be a product of it? This question has received different philosophical and constitutional answers. To some, the 'people' will emerge only through subjection to a common sovereign.[127] To others, the 'people' will precede the State for it is

---

[123] On the bridge metaphor, see: C. U. Schmid, 'From Pont d'Avignon to Ponte Vecchio: the Resolution of Constitutional Conflicts between the European Union and the Member States Through Principles of Public International Law' [1998] 18 YEL 415.

[124] Maastricht Decision (supra n. 116), 91.

[125] Cf. Pernice, 'Multilevel Constitutionalism' (supra n. 64), 711: 'internationalist' view of the Court that 'treats [European] law as any other rule of international law'.

[126] For a moderate and informed analysis in English, see: U. Everling, 'The Maastricht Judgment of the German Federal Constitutional Court and its Significance for the Development of the European Union' [1994] 14 YEL 1. For the opposite, see: Weiler (supra n. 121).

[127] Cf. T. Hobbes, *Leviathan* (R. Tuck, ed.) (Cambridge University Press, 1996), 114 and 120: 'A Multitude of men, are made One Person, when they are by one man, or one Person,

they who invest the government with its powers.[128] Most early modern European States were 'supra-national' in character in that they housed multiple 'nations' under one governmental roof.[129] However, with the rise of nationalism in the nineteenth century States would come to be identified by their nation.[130] Multiple nations within one State came to be seen as an anomaly. This anomalous status was equally attached to the idea of 'dual citizenship': an individual should only be part of one political body.[131] (National) peoples thus came to be seen as mutually exclusive. Transposed to the context of the European Union, this meant that a European people could not exist alongside national peoples. (And European citizenship could not exist alongside national citizenship.) Both peoples would exclude – not complement – each other; and as long as national peoples exist – as they do – a European people could not.

This brings us to the second denial: the absence of a European constitution. Under the doctrine of popular sovereignty, only a 'people' can formally 'constitute' itself into a legal sovereign. A constitution is regarded as a unilateral act of the '*pouvoir constituant*'.[132] Thus, 'it is inherent in a constitution in the full sense of the term that it goes back to an act taken by or at least attributed to the people, in which they attribute political capacity to themselves'.[133] This normative – or, better: democratic – notion of constitutionalism is said to have emerged with the American and French Revolutions and, since then, to have become the *exclusive* meaning of the concept. 'There is no such source for primary Union law. It goes back not to a European people but to the individual Member States, and remains dependent on them even after its entry into force. While nations give themselves a constitution, the European Union is given a constitution by third parties.'[134] And assuming, hypothetically, that a European people would in the future give the Union a constitution? Then, 'the Union would acquire competence to decide about competences (*Kompetenzkompetenz*)'. It

---

Represented; so that it be done with the consent of every one of that Multitude in particular. For it is the Unity of the Represented, not the Unity of the Represented, that Maketh the Person One ... This done, the Multitude so united in one Person, is called a COMMONWEALTH, or in latine CIVITAS. This is the generation of that great LEVIATHAN, or rather (to speake more reverently) of that Mortall God, to which wee owe under the Immortal God, our peace and defence.' I am grateful to Q. Skinner for shedding much light on these passages.

[128] The theory of popular sovereignty will typically distinguish between a 'people' (nation), on the one hand, and a 'subject' (citizen) on the other. The former refers to a community characterised by an emotion of solidarity that gives the group consciousness and identity. The latter refers to an individual's legal relation to his or her State. On these issues, see: J. W. Salmond, 'Citizenship and Allegiance' [1901] 17 *Law Quarterly Review* 270.

[129] Before the 1789 French Revolution, French kings would refer to the 'peoples' of France (see: B. Voyenne, *Histoire de l'Idée Fédéraliste: les Sources* (Presses d'Europe, 1973), 165). The United Kingdom is still a multi-demoi State that comprises the English, Scottish, Welsh and a part of the Irish nation (cf. M. Keating, *Plurinational Democracy: Stateless Nations in a Post-Sovereign Era* (Oxford University Press, 2001), 123: 'one of the most explicitly plurinational States in the world').

[130] On these issues generally, see: E. Gellner, *Nations and Nationalism* (Wiley Blackwell, 2006).

[131] Beaud, 'The Question of Nationality' (supra n. 28), 317.

[132] On the theory, see: E. Zweig, *Die Lehre vom Pouvoir Constituant* (Mohr, 1904).

[133] D. Grimm, 'Does Europe Need a Constitution?' [1995] 1 *European Law Journal* 282 at 290.

[134] *Ibid.*

would have the power to unilaterally change its constitution and would thus have turned itself from a confederation of States into a Federal State.[135] However, for the time being, the Union is no State.[136] And failing that, the European Union has no constitution.

Let us finally look at a third – milder – denial: 'The condition of Europe is not, as is often implied, that of constitutionalism without a constitution, but of a constitution without constitutionalism.'[137] (Paradoxically, this very same denial had been made in relation to the American Union in the eighteenth century.[138]) 'In federations, whether American or Australian, German or Canadian, the institutions of a federal state are situated in a constitutional framework which presupposes the existence of a "constitutional demos", a single *pouvoir constituant* made of the citizens of the federation in whose sovereignty, as a constituent power, and by whose supreme authority the specific constitutional arrangement is rooted.' 'In Europe, that precondition does not exist. Simply put, Europe's constitutional architecture has never been validated by a process of constitutional adoption by a European constitutional *demos*[.]'[139] And in the absence of a unitary constitutional demos, Europe could have no constitutionalism.

What is common to these three denials? Each is rooted in Europe's statist tradition and based on the idea of indivisible sovereignty: a *unitary* people forms a *unitary* State on the basis of a *unitary* constitution. The inability to accept shared or divided sovereignty thus blinds the European tradition to the possibility of *federal* arrangements or a *duplex regimen* between peoples, States and constitutions. It is unable to envisage *two* peoples living in the same territory – yet, this is generally the case in federal unions.[140] It is unable to envisage *two* constitutional orders existing within the same territory – yet, this is generally the case in federal unions.[141] It is unable to envisage *two* governments operating in the same territory – yet, this is generally the case in federal unions. Finally, it is unable to envisage a compound *pouvoir constituant* of multiple *demoi* – yet, this is generally the case in federal unions.[142]

---

[135] *Ibid.*, 299.

[136] This is universally accepted; see: BVerfGE 22, 293 (EWG Verordnungen), 296: 'Die Gemeinschaft ist selbst kein Staat, auch kein Bundesstaat'.

[137] Weiler, 'Does Europe Need a Constitution' (supra n. 121), 220.

[138] Schmitt, *Verfassungslehre* (supra n. 52), 78: 'Den amerikanischen Verfassungen des 18. Jahrhunderts fehlt es an einer eigentlichen Verfassungstheorie.'

[139] Weiler, 'Federalism without Constitutionalism: Europe's Sonderweg' (supra n. 112), 56–7.

[140] Cf. Beaud, 'The Question of Nationality' (supra n. 28), 320: 'Dual citizenship, essential to federations, is then nothing but the duplication of the fundamental law of duality of political entities constituting them. In contrast to the State, the federation here is characterised by a "political dualism".'

[141] Both American and German constitutionalism accept the idea of 'State Constitutions' in addition to the federal Constitution.

[142] When Professor Weiler confesses that 'I am unaware of any federal state, old or new, which does not presuppose the supreme authority and sovereignty of its federal demos' (Weiler, 'Federalism without Constitutionalism: Europe's Sonderweg' (supra n. 112), 57), we may draw his attention

The black and white logic of unitary constitutionalism is simply unable to capture the federal 'blue' on the international versus national spectrum. The European Union's constitutionalism therefore must, in the future, be (re)constructed in federal terms. It is half-hearted to – enigmatically – claim that Europe has a constitution, but no constitutionalism. For once we admit that Europe has a constitution, who tells us so? National legal theory? International legal theory? Since neither affirms the statement that 'Europe has a constitution', the proposition presupposes a system of thought that allows us to 'recognise' or 'verify' that statement as true. Logically, the affirmation of a 'constitution' presumes the existence of a 'constitutionalism'. But more importantly: the misguided insistence on a 'constitutional demos' shows that 'constitutionalism' is still identified with the legitimising theory underlying a – *unitary* – Nation State. But Europe's mixed constitutional system cannot be conceived in purely unitary – or 'national' – terms. Only a *federal* constitutionalism can explain and give meaning to normative problems that arise in compound systems like the European Union.[143] And once we apply a *federal* constitutionalism to the European Union, the above 'denials' are shown for what they are: *false problems*. They are created by a wrong constitutional theory. National constitutionalism simply cannot explain the 'dual nature' of federations as classical physics was unable to explain the dual nature of light.[144] By insisting that the European Union is *either* international *or* national, it denies its status as an (inter)national phenomenon.

(d) *Excursus*: Europe's democratic 'deficit' as a 'false problem'?

The classic illustration of the distorted European constitutional discourse is the debate on the European Union's 'democratic deficit'.[145] It is not difficult to find such a deficit if one measures decision-making in the Union against the unitary

to the United States of America. Neither of the two Constitutions of the United States was ratified by a 'federal demos' in the form of 'the' American people. The Articles of Confederation were ratified by the State legislatures, while the 1787 Constitution was ratified by the State peoples. And as regards constitutional amendment, Article V of the US Constitution still requires the concurrence of the federal demos – acting indirectly through its representatives – and three-fourths of the State demoi – acting either through their representatives or in conventions. More generally, in all (democratic) Federal Unions the *pouvoir constituant* should be a compound of the federal and the State demoi. Where the 'constitutional demos' is conceived in unitary terms, the federal Union loses its federal base (cf. Schmitt, *Verfassungslehre* (supra n. 52), 389).

[143] For a remarkable step towards a general theory of federal constitutionalism, see: O. Beaud, *Théorie de la Fédération* (Presses Universitaires de France, 2007).

[144] Classical physics insisted that a phenomenon must be either a particle or a wave; and it could not be both. Following the works of Einstein, modern physics now accepts the dual nature of light.

[145] The following discussion focuses on the constitutional aspect of the democratic deficit. It does not claim that there is no democratic deficit at the *social* level, such as the low degree of electoral participation or the quality of the public debate on Europe. Nor will it claim that the current constitutional structures could not be improved so as to increase democratic governance in the European Union. For the various dimensions of the question of democratic legitimacy in the European Union, see: D. Chalmers et al., *European Union Law: Text and Materials* (CUP, 2010), 125–35. For the argument that the EU does not suffer from any democratic deficit, see:

standard of a Nation State. There, all legislative decisions are theoretically legitimised by one source – 'the' people as represented in the national parliament. But is this – unitary – standard the appropriate yardstick for a *compound* body politic?

In a federal polity there are *two* arenas of democracy: the 'State demos' and the 'federal demos'. Both offer independent sources of democratic legitimacy; and a *federal* constitutionalism will need to take account of this *dual* legitimacy. One *functional* expression of this dualism is the division of legislative powers between the State demos and the federal demos. One *institutional* expression of this dual legitimacy is the compound nature of the central legislator. It is typically made up of *two* chambers;[146] and thus, every federal law is – ideally – legitimised by reference to *two* sources: the consent of the State peoples and the consent of the federal people. It is thus mistaken to argue that '[t]rue federalism is fundamentally a non-majoritarian, or even anti-majoritarian, form of government since the component units often owe their autonomous existence to institutional arrangements that prevent the domination of minorities by majorities'.[147] While federal systems may have 'a somewhat ambiguous standing in democratic ideas',[148] federalism is *not* inherently *non*-democratic.[149] It is – if based on the idea of government by the governed – inherently *demoi*-cratic. And '[t]to really celebrate the EU as a *demoicracy*, one must depart from mainstream constitutional thinking'.[150]

A. Moravcsik, 'In Defence of the "Democratic Deficit": Reassessing Legitimacy in the European Union' [2002] 40 *Journal of Common Market Studies* 603.

[146] Cf. A. Gerber, 'Les Notions de Représentation et de Participation des Régions dans les Etats Fédéraux', LLM thesis, European University Institute (1993).

[147] G. Majone, 'Europe's "Democratic Deficit": The Question of Standards' [1998] 4 *European Law Journal* 5 at 11.

[148] R. A. Dahl, 'Federalism and the Democratic Process' in J. R. Pennock and J. W. Chapman (eds.), *Nomos XXV: Liberal Democracy* (New York University Press, 1983) 95 at 96. Dahl continues (*ibid.*, 96 and 101): 'If one requirement of a fully democratic process is that the demos exercises final control over the agenda, and if in federal systems no *single* body of citizens can exercise final control, is it then the case that in federal systems the processes by which people govern themselves cannot even in principle ever be fully democratic?'. 'Some critics have so contended. But if this is so, then a transnational federal system like the European [Union] is necessarily undemocratic. Are we to conclude that however desirable it might be on other grounds, when a people who govern themselves under a unitary constitution enter into a larger federal order they must necessarily suffer some loss of democracy?'

[149] In this sense also, see: Dahl, *ibid.* at 107: '[A]lthough in federal systems no single body of citizens can exercise control over the agenda, federalism is not for this reason less capable than a unitary system of meeting the criteria of the democratic process[.]'

[150] K. Nicolaïdis, 'We the Peoples of Europe . . .' [2004] 83 *Foreign Affairs* 97 at 102. An example of such mainstream constitutional thinking is the idea that 'the most legitimating element (from a "social" point of view) of the [Union] was the Luxembourg Accord and the veto power' as 'this device enabled the [Union] to legitimate its program and its legislation' (J. Weiler, 'The Transformation of Europe' [1990–1] 100 *Yale Law Journal* 2403 at 2473). This is mistaken in two ways. First, how can a unanimous decision of national ministers legitimate directly effective European laws? If European legislation affects European citizens *directly*, how can an *indirect* legitimatisation through national *executives* be sufficient? To solve this dilemma, Weiler refers to the underlying formal legitimacy of the founding Treaties that received national parliamentary consent and to the claim that national parliaments control their governments' ministers in

Finally, one *foundational* expression of this dual legitimacy is the – typically – compound nature of the federation's constituent power. The point has been well made in relation to the United States of America:

> Half a century ago J. Allen Smith wrote a book in which he bitterly criticized the undemocratic spirit of the American Scheme of government. In it he argued that a true democracy had to embrace the principle of majority rule ... His criticism was justified, but only within his own frame of reference. It was phrased in the wrong terms. He was in fact criticising a federal system for serving the ends it was intended to serve ... What he ignored was that even in 1907 the United States was still composed of States. The amending clause was an excellent spot for his attack and the criticism he made of it would have been equally applicable to any federation. Nearly all governments that are called federal employ some device in the amending process to *prevent* a mere majority from changing the constitution ... Does this prove federalism i[s] undemocratic? Certainly it does, if democracy be defined in terms of majority rule ... They argue that the will of the majority is being thwarted and suggest by implication at least that this is ethically wrong; the term 'will of the majority' carries with it certain moral overtones in these days of enlightened democracy. But what the *ad hoc* majoritarians forget is that a federal state is a different thing, that it is not intended to operate according to a majority principle. We cannot apply the standard of unitary government to a federal state. If the opinion of a majority is a sufficient guide for public policy in a community then it is unlikely that a federal system will have been established in that community.[151]

How enlightening *comparative* constitutionalism can be! The discussion of the European Union's 'democratic deficit' indeed reveals a deficit in democratic theory.[152] The description of crisis reflects a crisis of description.[153] Indeed, '[t]he question about which standards should be employed to assess the democratic credentials of the EU crucially hinges on how the EU is conceptualized'.[154] The search for normative criteria to describe and evaluate the European Union will – eventually – lead to a *federal* constitutional theory. The European Union

---

the Council. However, the former argument cannot explain how an earlier parliament can bind its successors. (This normative problem may only be solved through the insertion of a clause into the national *constitution* that would legitimatise European integration.) And even if we were to assume absolute control of national ministers by their national parliaments, *social* legitimacy is in any event co-dependent on 'system capacity'. Dahl explains this point as follows ('Federalism', supra n. 148 at 105 – emphasis added): 'As Rousseau suggested long ago, it is necessarily the case that the greater the number of citizens, the smaller the weight of each citizen in determining the outcome ... On the other hand, if a system is more democratic to the extent that it permits citizens to govern themselves on matters that are important to them, then in many circumstances a *larger system would be more democratic than a smaller one, since its capacity to cope with certain matters – defense and pollution, for example –* would be greater.'

151 W. S. Livingston, *Federalism and Constitutional Change* (Clarendon Press, 1956), 311–14.
152 O. Beaud, 'Déficit Politique ou Déficit de la Pensée Politique?' [1995] 87 *Le Debat* 44.
153 A. Winckler, 'Description d'une Crise ou Crise d'une description?' [1995] 87 *Le Debat* 59.
154 B. Kohler-Koch and B. Rittberger, 'Charting Crowded Territory: Debating the Democratic Legitimacy of the European Union' in B. Kohler-Koch and B. Rittberger (eds.), *Debating the Democratic Legitimacy of the European Union* (Rowman & Littlefield, 2007), 1 at 4.

is 'based on a *dual* structure of legitimacy: the totality of the Union's citizens, and the peoples of the European Union'. 'Elections provide *two* lines of democratic legitimacy for the Union's organizational structure. The European Parliament, which is based on elections by the totality of the Union's citizens, and the European Council as well as the Council, whose legitimacy is based on the Member States' democratically organized peoples[.]'[155] Duplex regimen, dual democracy.

Conclusion

What is the nature of the European Union? Can the Union be described as a federal Union? We saw above that the American tradition easily classifies the European Union as a Federal Union. The European Union has a mixed or compound structure; and in combining international and national elements, it stands on federal 'middle ground'. The federal label is – ironically – denied by Europe's own intellectual tradition. In pressing the federal principle into a national (State) format, the concept of federation is reduced to that of a Federal State. And while the creation of a Federal State may have been a long-term aim of a few idealists in the early years of European integration, the failure of the European Political Community in the 1950s caused the demise of federal ideology.[156] The fall of federalism gave rise to the philosophy of (neo-)functionalism.[157] The latter remained agnostic on what kind of object the Union was. The Union was celebrated as a *process* – a 'journey to an unknown destination'.[158] But this agnosticism could not forever postpone the fundamental question: 'What is the European Union?'

Early commentators were aware that the new European construct had moved onto the 'middle ground' between international and national law. Yet, Europe's conceptual tradition blocked the identification of that middle ground with the federal idea. Europe was celebrated as *sui generis*. But how common exceptionalisms are![159] The *sui generis* 'theory' was, in any event, but a veneer. In times of constitutional conflict, Europe's old federal tradition returned from the depths

---

[155] A. von Bogdandy, 'A Disputed Idea Becomes Law: Remarks on European Democracy as a Legal Principle', in *ibid.*, 33 at 36–7 (emphasis added).

[156] M. Forsyth, 'The Political Theory of Federalism: the Relevance of Classical Approaches' in J. J. Hesse and V. Wright, *Federalizing Europe?: The Costs, Benefits, and Preconditions of Federal Political Systems* (Oxford University Press, 1996), 25 at 26.

[157] The functionalist classic is D. Mitrany, *A Working Peace System: an Argument for the Functional Development of International Organization* (National Peace Council, 1946). Neofunctionalism discards the belief in the automaticity of the integration process and emphasises the need to build new loyalties with strategic elites. The classic here is: E. Haas, *The Uniting of Europe: Political, Social and Economic Forces, 1950–1957* (supra n. 3).

[158] A. Shonfield, *Journey to an Unknown Destination* (Penguin, 1973).

[159] J. Calhoun described the 1787 American legal order as 'new, peculiar, and unprecedented' (see J. C. Calhoun, 'A Discourse on the Constitution and Government of the United States', in *Union and Liberty* (Liberty Fund, 1992), 117). The legal structure of the British Commonwealth has been described as *sui generis*. The Balfour Report (1926) stated: 'The Committee are of opinion that

and imposed its two polarised ideal-types: Europe was either an international organisation or a Federal State. And since it was not the latter, it must – by definition – be the former.

What is the explanatory power of the international law thesis? Can it satisfactorily explain the legal and social reality within the European Union? In the last half a century, 'Little Europe' has emancipated herself from her humble birth and has grown into a mature woman: the European Union. The international law thesis thus runs into a great many explanatory difficulties. *Unlike* international doctrine predicts, the obligations imposed on the Member States are not interpreted restrictively. *Unlike* international doctrine predicts, the Member States are not allowed a free hand in how to execute their obligations. *Unlike* international doctrine predicts, the Member States cannot modify their obligations *inter se* through the conclusion of subsequent international treaties. In order to defend the international law hypothesis, its adherents must denounce these legal characteristics as non-essential 'marks' of sovereignty. And in relegating the social reality of European law to a false appearance, European thought refuses comparing the *ideal* with the *real*. But facts are stubborn things!

The *sui generis* thesis and the international law thesis had *both* caused the Union to disappear from the federal map. How did the federal idea return? Its revival in discussions of the structure of the European Union was slow. As a first step, it was accepted that the Union had borrowed the federal principle from the public law of federal States.[160] The European Union was said to be the 'classic case of federalism without federation'.[161] It had 'federal' features, but it was no 'federation'. Federation thus still meant Federal State.[162] The word 'federal', by contrast, attached to a *function* and not to the *essence* of the organisation. The adjective was allowed – adjectives refer to *attributes*, not to *essences* – but the noun was not. In order for European constitutionalism to accept the idea of a 'Federation of States' a second step was required. Europe needed to abandon its obsession with the idea of undivided sovereignty. It needed to accept that '[t]he law of integration rests on a premise quite unknown to so-called "classical"

nothing would be gained by attempting to lay down a Constitution for the British Empire. Its widely scattered parts have very different characteristics, very different histories, and are at very different stages of evolution; while, considered as a whole, it defies classification and bears no real resemblance to any other political organization which now exists or has ever yet been tried.'

[160] Haas separated the idea of 'federation' from the notion of 'State' (Haas (supra n. 3) 37) and could, consequently, speak of the 'federal attributes' (*ibid.*, 42) of the ECSC. The ECSC was, overall, described as a 'hybrid form, short of federation' (*ibid.*, 51), for it did not satisfy all the federal attributes believed by the author to be necessary for a federation to exist (*ibid.*, 59): 'While almost all the criteria point positively to federation, the remaining limits on the ability to implement decisions and to expand the scope of the system independently still suggest the characteristics of international organisation.'

[161] M. Burgess, *Federalism and the European Union: the Building of Europe 1950–2000* (Routledge, 2000), 28–9.

[162] Cf. W. G. Friedmann, *The Changing Structure of International Law* (Stevens, 1964), 98: 'The [European] Treaties stop short of the establishment of a federation. They do not transfer to a federal sphere the general powers usually associated with a federal state[.]'

international law: that is the divisibility of sovereignty'.[163] The Union enjoys 'real powers stemming from a *limitation of sovereignty* or a transfer of powers from the States to the [Union]' through which, in turn, 'the Member States have *limited their sovereign rights*, albeit within limited fields'.[164] The European Union is indeed based on a conception of divided sovereignty and in strictness neither international nor national, 'but a composition of both'. It represents an (inter)national phenomenon that stands on – federal – middle ground.

The best way to characterise the nature of the European Union is thus as a Federation of States.

---

[163] Pescatore, *The Law of Integration* (supra n. 113), 30. This corresponds to J. Fischer's vision: 'The completion of European integration can only be successfully conceived if it is done on the basis of a division of sovereignty between Europe and the nation-state. Precisely this is the idea underlying the concept of "subsidiarity," a subject that is currently being discussed by everyone and understood by virtually no one': 'From Confederacy to Federation: Thoughts on the Finality of European Integration', Speech at the Humboldt University in Berlin (12 May 2000).

[164] Case 6/64, *Costa* v. *ENEL* (supra n. 67), 593 (emphasis added).

3

Governmental Structure: Union Institutions I

Contents

Introduction		81
1.	The 'separation-of-powers' principle and the European Union	83
2.	The European Parliament	87
	(a) Formation: electing Parliament	87
	(i) Parliament's size and composition	88
	(ii) Members of the European Parliament and political parties	91
	(b) Internal structure: parliamentary organs	93
	(c) Plenary decision-making and voting	94
	(d) Parliamentary powers	96
	(i) Legislative powers	96
	(ii) Budgetary powers	97
	(iii) Supervisory powers	98
	(iv) Elective powers	99
3.	The European Council	100
	(a) The President of the European Council	102
	(b) The European Council: functions and powers	103
4.	The Council	104
	(a) The Council: composition and configuration	105
	(b) Internal structure and organs	106
	(i) The Presidency of the Council	106
	(ii) 'Coreper' and specialised committees	107
	(iii) *Excursus*: the High Representative of Foreign Affairs and Security Policy	110
	(c) Decision-making and voting	111
	(d) Functions and powers	114

Introduction

The creation of governmental institutions is *the* central task of all constitutions. Each political community needs institutions to govern its society; as each society needs common rules and a method for their making, execution and arbitration. It is no coincidence that the first three articles of the 1787 American Constitution establish and define – respectively – the 'Legislative Department', the 'Executive Department' and the 'Judicial Department'.

The European Treaties establish a number of European institutions to make, execute and arbitrate European law. The Union's institutions and their core tasks are defined in Title III of the Treaty on European Union. The central provision here is Article 13 TEU:

1. The Union shall have an institutional framework which shall aim to promote its values, advance its objectives, serve its interests, those of its citizens and those of the Member States, and ensure the consistency, effectiveness and continuity of its policies and actions.
   The Union's institutions shall be:
   – the European Parliament,
   – the European Council,
   – the Council,
   – the European Commission (hereinafter referred to as 'the Commission'),
   – the Court of Justice of the European Union,
   – the European Central Bank,
   – the Court of Auditors.
2. Each institution shall act within the limits of the powers conferred on it in the Treaties, and in conformity with the procedures, conditions and objectives set out in them. The institutions shall practise mutual sincere cooperation . . .

The provision lists seven governmental institutions of the European Union. They constitute the core 'players' in the Union legal order.[1] What strikes the attentive eye first is the number of institutions: unlike a tripartite institutional structure, the Union offers more than twice that number. The two institutions that do not – at first sight – seem to directly correspond to 'national' institutions are the (European) Council and the Commission. The name 'Council' represents a reminder of the 'international' origins of the European Union, but the institution can equally be found in the governmental structure of Federal States. It will be harder to find the name 'Commission' among the public institutions of

---

[1] While the Treaties set up seven 'institutions', they also acknowledge the existence of other 'bodies'. First, according to Article 13 (4) TEU, the Parliament, the Council and the Commission 'shall be assisted by an Economic and Social Committee and a Committee of the Regions acting in an advisory capacity'. The composition and powers of the 'Economic and Social Committee' are set out in Articles 301–304 TFEU. The composition and powers of the 'Committee of the Regions' are defined by Articles 305–307 TFEU. In addition to the Union's 'Advisory Bodies', the Treaties equally acknowledge the existence of a 'European Investment Bank' (Articles 308–309 TFEU; as well as Protocol No. 5 on the Statute of the European Investment Bank).

Table 2 Treaty provisions on the institutions

Treaty Provisions on the Institutions			
EU Treaty – Title III		**FEU Treaty – Part VI – Title I – Chapter 1**	
Article 13	Institutional Framework	Section 1	European Parliament (Arts. 223–234)
Article 14	European Parliament	Section 2	European Council (Arts. 235–236)
Article 15	European Council	Section 3	Council (Arts. 237–243)
Article 16	Council	Section 4	Commission (Arts. 244–250)
Article 17	Commission	Section 5	Court of Justice (Arts. 251–281)
Article 18	High Representative	Section 6	European Central Bank (Arts. 282–284)
Article 19	Court of Justice	Section 7	Court of Auditors (Arts. 285–287)

Protocol (No. 3): Statute of the Court of Justice
Protocol (No. 4): Statute of the ESCB and the ECB
Protocol (No. 6): Location of the Seats of the Institutions etc.
(Internal) Rules of Procedure of the Institution

States, where the executive is typically referred to as the 'government'. By contrast, central banks and courts of auditors exist in many national legal orders.

Where do the Treaties define the Union institutions? The provisions on the Union institutions are split between the Treaty on European Union and the Treaty on the Functioning of the European Union as shown in Table 2.

What is the composition and task of each Union institution? Chapters 3 and 4 will provide an analysis of each institution alongside three dimensions: its *internal* structure, its *internal* decisional procedures and its *internal* powers.[2] The *external* interactions *between* the Union's institutions in the exercise of the Union's governmental functions will be discussed in Part II – dealing with the powers and procedures of the *Union*. The powers of the Union differ from the powers of each institution in that the former concern the relationship between the Union and its Member States. Can we nonetheless connect an *internal* perspective on the institutions as 'organs' of the Union with their *external* interaction in a governmental function? And what does Article 13 (2) TEU mean when insisting that each institution must act within the limits of its powers and according to the Treaties' procedures? Is this the separation of powers principle within the Union legal order? We shall look at this 'horizontal' question in Section 1 of this chapter, before analysing the 'internal' structure of each institution in turn.

---

[2] Many of these 'internal' issues will be found in an institution's 'Rules of Procedure'. On the status of these procedural rules, see: S. Lefevre, 'Rules of procedure do matter: the legal status of the institutions' power of self-organisation' [2005] 30 EL Rev 802.

1. The 'separation-of-powers' principle and the European Union

When in 1748, Baron Charles de Montesquieu published 'The Spirit of Laws',[3] the enlightened aristocrat espoused his views on the division of powers in a chapter dedicated to 'The Constitution of England'.[4] Famously, three powers were identified:

> In every government there are three sorts of power: the legislative; the executive in respect to things dependent on the law of nations; and the executive in regard to matters that depend on the civil law. By virtue of the first, the prince or magistrate enacts temporary or perpetual laws, and amends or abrogates those that have been already enacted. By the second, he makes peace or war, sends or receives embassies, establishes the public security, and provides against invasions. By the third, he punishes criminals, or determines the disputes that arise between individuals. The latter we shall call the judiciary power[.][5]

Having identified three governmental 'powers' or functions, Montesquieu moved on to advocate their 'distribution' between different institutions:

> When the legislative and executive powers are united in the same person, or in the same body of magistrates, there can be no liberty; because apprehensions may arise, lest the same monarch or senate should enact tyrannical laws, to execute them in a tyrannical manner. Again, there is no liberty, if the judicial power be not separated from the legislative and executive. Were it joined with the legislative, the life and liberty of the subject would be exposed to arbitrary control; for the judge would be then the legislator. Were it joined to the executive power, the judge might behave with violence and oppression.[6]

Would the distribution of power mean that each power would need to be given to a 'separate' institution? Did the distribution of power thus lead to a *separation* of powers? This reading of Montesquieu's oracular passage appears – at first sight – to have been chosen by the founding fathers of the United States of America.[7] The idea behind the American constitutional structure seems to be that different governmental powers correlate with different institutions. Legislative powers are thus vested in 'Congress',[8] the executive

---

[3] Charles de Secondat, Baron de Montesquieu, *The Spirit of Laws* (translated and edited by T. Nugent, and revised by J. Prichard) (Bell, 1914), available at www.constitution.org/cm/sol.htm.

[4] *Ibid.*, Book XI – Chapter 6.   [5] *Ibid.*   [6] *Ibid.*

[7] On the impact of Montesquieu on the American Constitution, see: J. Madison, 'Federalist No. 47' in J. Madison et al., *The Federalist* (T. Ball, ed.) (Cambridge University Press, 2003), 235: 'In order to form correct ideas on this important subject, it will be proper to investigate the sense in which the preservation of liberty requires that the three great departments of power should be separate and distinct. The oracle who is always consulted and cited on this subject is the celebrated Montesquieu.'

[8] Article I, Section 1 US Constitution: 'All legislative Powers herein granted shall be vested in a Congress of the United States, which shall consist of a Senate and House of Representatives.'

power is vested in a 'President',[9] while the judicial power is vested in the 'Supreme Court'.[10]

But there is a second possible reading of the famous Montesquieu passage. The distribution of powers here leads to a *combination* of powers. 'To form a moderate government, it is necessary to *combine* the several powers; to regulate, temper, and set them in motion; to give, as it were, ballast to one, in order to enable it to counterpoise the other.'[11] The exercise of the legislative function should thus ideally involve more than one institution.

> The legislative body being composed of two parts, they check one another by the mutual privilege of rejecting. They are both restrained by the executive power, as the executive is by the legislative. These three powers should naturally form a state of repose or inaction. But as there is a necessity for movement in the course of human affairs, they are forced to move, but still in concert.[12]

The idea behind this second conception of the 'separation-of-powers' principle is thus a system of checks and balances. And it is this second conception of the 'separation-of-powers' principle that informs the European Treaties. The European Treaties do not – unlike the US Constitution – discuss each institution within the context of one governmental function. Instead, the European Treaties have adopted the opposite technique. Each institution has 'its' article in the Treaty on European Union, whose first section describes the *combination* of governmental functions in which it partakes.[13] The European Treaties have thus 'set up a system for distributing powers among different [Union] institutions, assigning to each institution its own role in the institutional structure of the [Union] and the accomplishment of the tasks entrusted to the [Union]'.[14] It is this conception of the separation-of-powers principle that informs Article 13 (2) TEU. The provision is known as the principle of inter-institutional balance and reads:

> Each institution shall act within the limits of the powers conferred on it in the Treaties, and in conformity with the procedures, conditions and objectives set out in them. The institutions shall practice mutual sincere cooperation.

The provision contains three constitutional commands. First, each institution must act within its powers defined by the Treaties. It is thus not possible for an institution to unilaterally *extend* its powers through constitutional practice.[15]

---

[9] *Ibid.*, Article II – Section 1: 'The executive Power shall be vested in a President of the United States of America.'

[10] *Ibid.*, Article III – Section 1: 'The judicial Power of the United States, shall be vested in one Supreme Court, and in such inferior Courts as the Congress may from time to time ordain and establish.'

[11] de Montesquieu (supra n. 3), Book V – Chapter 14.   [12] *Ibid.*

[13] This is normally the first section of the TEU article dealing with the – respective – institution.

[14] Case C-70/88, *Parliament* v. *Council (Chernobyl)*, [1990] ECR I-2041, para. 21. The Court consequently rejected the argument that the 'Commission committed a breach of the very principles which govern the division of powers and responsibilities between the [Union] institutions' when exercising legislative powers granted under the Treaties.

[15] Case 149/85, *Wybot* v. *Faure*, [1986] ECR 2391, especially para. 23.

Nor may an institution consensually *transfer* its powers to another institution – unless the Treaties expressly allow for such delegations of power. The Union legal order has indeed permitted such delegations from the very beginning,[16] and thus never subscribed to the 'static' non-delegation doctrine that characterised nineteenth-century American constitutional thought.[17] (But when an institution transfers one of 'its' powers to another institution, the transferor is thereby entitled to impose 'conditions' on the transferee.[18]) Second, '[o]bservance of the institutional balance means that each of the institutions must exercise its powers with due regard for the powers of the other institutions'.[19] This principle of 'mutual sincere cooperation' between the institutions in Article 13 (2) TEU is the horizontal extension of the principle of sincere cooperation in Article 4 (3) TEU.[20] One manifestation of this principle is inter-institutional agreements, in which the institutions agree to exercise 'their' powers in harmony with each other.[21] Finally, each institution is embedded within the governmental procedures of the European Union. Thus, under the (ordinary) legislative procedure, three of the Union institutions will need to take part: the Commission must formally propose the legislative bill, and the Parliament as well as the Council must co-decide on its adoption. And even where an institution only needs to be 'consulted', this involvement through consultation 'represents an essential factor in the institutional balance intended by the Treat[ies]'.[22]

What types of governmental 'powers' or 'functions' may be identified for the European Union? Apart from defining what constitutes the legislative procedure(s), the European Treaties do not formally classify the Union's governmental functions according to a particular procedure. In line with classic constitutional thought, the Treaties thus continue to be based on a material conception of governmental powers. The legislative power thereby relates to the competence

---

[16] On the delegation of legislative power, see: Chapter 7 – Section 2(a) below.

[17] Cf. *Field* v. *Clark*, 143 US 649 (1892). For a brief overview of the evolution of the American non-delegation case law, see: R. Schütze, '"Delegated" Legislation in the (new) European Union: A Constitutional Analysis' [2011] 74 (5) *Modern Law Review* 661–693, Section II.

[18] For an analysis of the 'political safeguards' within the European delegation doctrine, see: Chapter 7 – Section 2 below.

[19] Case C-70/88, *Parliament* v. *Council (Chernobyl)*, [1990] ECR I-2041 para. 22.

[20] Article 4 (3) TEU only deals with the federal relations between the Union and its Member States. We shall analyse this provision in detail in Part II of the book.

[21] The Treaties envisage inter-institutional agreements for example in Article 295 TFEU, which states: 'The European Parliament, the Council and the Commission shall consult each other and by common agreement make arrangements for their cooperation. To that end, they may, in compliance with the Treaties, conclude inter-institutional agreements which may be of a binding nature.' For a list of inter-institutional agreements concluded between 1958–2005, see: W. Hummer, 'Annex: Interinstitutional Agreements concluded during the Period 1958–2005' [2007] 13 ELJ 92. On the various 'theories' of the nature of inter-institutional agreements, see: B. Driessen, 'Interinstitutional Conventions and institutional balance' [2008] 33 EL Rev 550 at 551: 'Although such arrangements often do no more than lubricate interinstitutional relations, in many cases they affect the effective balance of influence between the institutions.'

[22] Case 138/79, *Roquette Frères* v. *Council (Isoglucose)*, [1980] ECR 3333, para. 33.

of making laws. The executive power relates to the competence of proposing and implementing laws. The judicial power relates to the competence of arbitrating laws in court. In addition to the classic trinity, modern constitutions have come to recognise additional governmental powers. A separate 'fourth power' thus relates to the external competences of a body politic.[23] This fourth power must be located as lying in between the legislative and the executive department,[24] for it involves both the creation of 'laws' and – in the worst case – the execution of wars against an enemy. Finally, many modern States even acknowledge a 'fifth power' relating to the governmental control of financial markets.[25] The task of governmental banks is to regulate and stabilise a polity's money supply.

How do the Union's institutions (and 'bodies') correlate with these five governmental powers so identified? It is important to keep in mind that '[t]he principle of institutional balance does not imply that the authors of the treaties set up a balanced distribution of the powers, whereby the weight of each institution is the same as that of the others'.[26] It simply means that '[t]he Treaties set up a system for distributing powers among the different [Union] institutions, assigning each institution its own role in the institutional structure

Table 3 Union institutions correlating to governmental functions

Legislative	External	Executive	Judicial	Financial
Parliament	(European) Council	European Council	Court	Central Bank
Council	Parliament	Commission	Commission	Investment Bank

[23] The recognition of foreign affairs as a public function distinct from the gestation of domestic affairs received its classic formulation in the political philosophy of John Locke. Locke had identified the 'federative power' as 'the power of war and peace, leagues and alliances, and all the transactions with all persons and communities without the commonwealth' (J. Locke, *Two Treaties of Government* (P. Laslett, ed.) (Cambridge University Press, 1985) 365, § 146).

[24] Hamilton, 'Federalist No. 75' (supra n. 7), 365 (emphasis added): 'Though several writers on the subject of government place that power in the class of executive authorities, yet this is evidently an arbitrary disposition; for if we attend carefully to its operation, it will be found to partake *more of the legislative than of the executive character,* though it does not seem strictly to fall within the definition of either of them. The essence of the legislative authority is to enact laws, or, in other words, to prescribe rules for the regulation of the society; while the execution of the laws, and the employment of the common strength, either for this purpose or for the common defence, seem to comprise all the functions of the executive magistrate. The power of making treaties is, plainly, neither the one nor the other. It relates neither to the execution of the subsisting laws, nor to the enaction of new ones; and still less to an exertion of the common strength. Its objects are CONTRACTS with foreign nations, which have the force of law, but derive it from the obligations of good faith. They are not rules prescribed by the sovereign to the subject, but agreements between sovereign and sovereign. *The power in question seems therefore to form a distinct department, and to belong, properly, neither to the legislative nor to the executive.'*

[25] On the history of the Bank of England, see: R. Roberts and D. Kynaston, *The Bank of England: Money, Power and Influence 1694–1994* (Oxford University Press, 1995); and on the creation of the US 'Federal Reserve System' in 1913, see: A. Meltzer, *A History of the Federal Reserve* (University of Chicago Press, 2004), vol. 1, 1913–51.

[26] J.-P. Jacque, 'The Principle of Institutional Balance' [2004] 41 CML Rev 383.

of the [Union] and the accomplishment of the tasks entrusted to the [Union]'.[27] Table 3 simply provides an overview of the *major* institutional participants that combine in each function.

2. The European Parliament

Despite its formal place in the Treaties, the European Parliament has never been the Union's 'first' institution. For a long time it followed, in rank, behind the Council and the Commission. Its original powers were indeed minimal. It was an 'auxiliary' organ that was to assist the institutional duopoly of Council and Commission. This minimal role gradually increased from the 1970s onwards. The Budget Treaties gave it a say in the budgetary process, and subsequent Treaty amendments dramatically enhanced its role in the legislative process. Today the Parliament constitutes – with the Council – a chamber of the Union legislature. Directly elected by the European citizens,[28] Parliament constitutes not only the most democratic institution; in light of its elective 'appointment', it is also the most supranational institution of the European Union.

This section looks at four aspects of the European Parliament. First, we shall look at its formation through European elections. A second section analyses its internal structure. A third section presents its decision-making and voting rules. Finally, a fourth section provides an overview of Parliament's powers in the various governmental functions of the Union.

(a) Formation: electing Parliament

When the European Union was born, the 1952 Paris and 1957 Rome Treaty envisaged that its Parliament was to be composed of 'representatives of the peoples of the States'.[29] This characterisation corresponded to its formation for the European Parliament was not directly elected. It was to 'consist of delegates who shall be designated by the respective Parliaments from among their members in accordance with the procedure laid down by each Member State'.[30] European parliamentarians were thus – delegated – *national* parliamentarians. This formation method brought Parliament close to an (international) 'assembly', but the founding Treaties already breached the classic international law logic in two ways. First, they had abandoned the idea of sovereign equality of the Member States by recognising different sizes for national parliamentary delegations.[31] And more importantly: both Treaties already envisaged that Parliament would eventually be formed through

---

[27] Case C-70/88 (supra n. 19), para. 21.
[28] Article 10 (2) TEU: 'Citizens are directly represented at Union level in the European Parliament.'
[29] Article 137 EEC. See also: Article 20 ECSC.   [30] Article 138 EEC. See also: Article 21 ECSC.
[31] Originally, the EEC Treaty granted thirty-six delegates to Germany, France and Italy; fourteen delegates to Belgium and the Netherlands; and six delegates to Luxembourg.

'elections by direct universal suffrage in accordance with a uniform procedure in all Member States'.[32]

When did the transformation of the European Parliament from an 'assembly' of national parliamentarians into a directly elected 'parliament' take place? It took two decades before the Union's 1976 'Election Act' was adopted.[33] And ever since the first parliamentary elections in 1979, the European Parliament ceased to be composed of 'representatives of peoples of the states'. It constituted henceforth the representative of a European people. The Lisbon Treaty has – belatedly – recognised this dramatic constitutional change. It now characterises the European Parliament as being 'composed of representatives of the Union's citizens'.[34] But what is the size and composition of the European Parliament? How are elections conducted? And what is the status of a 'Member of the European Parliament' (MEP)? Let us look at these questions in turn.

(i) Parliament's size and composition

The Treaties stipulate the following on the size and composition of the European Parliament:

> The European Parliament shall be composed of representatives of the Union's citizens. They shall not exceed seven hundred and fifty in number, plus the President. Representation of citizens shall be degressively proportional, with a minimum threshold of six members per Member State. No Member State shall be allocated more than ninety-six seats.
>
> The European Council shall adopt by unanimity, on the initiative of the European Parliament and with its consent, a decision establishing the composition of the European Parliament, respecting the principles referred to in the first subparagraph.[35]

The European Parliament has a maximum size of 751 members.[36] While relatively large in comparison with the (American) House of Representatives,

---

[32] Article 138 (3) EEC: 'The [Parliament] shall draw up proposals for elections by direct universal suffrage in accordance with a uniform procedure in all Member States. The Council shall, acting unanimously, lay down the appropriate provisions, which it shall recommend to Member States for adoption in accordance with their respective constitutional requirements.' See also: Article 21 (3) ECSC.

[33] 'Act concerning the Election of the Members of the European Parliament by direct universal Suffrage'. The Act was adopted in 1976 ([1976] OJ L 278/5). The Act has been variously amended. For the consolidated version, see: Appendix 5 of this book.

[34] Article 14 (2) TEU.   [35] *Ibid.*

[36] The 2009 Parliamentary Elections were still held under the pre-Lisbon arrangement. Under that arrangement, there existed only 736 seats with Germany having 99 seats. To bring the number up to 751 and to reduce the German MEPs by three, Spain proposed a Treaty amendment to Protocol (No. 36) on Transitional Provisions. This proposal suggested adding 18 MEPs for the 2009–14 parliamentary term *without* reducing the mandate of the three (already) elected German MEPs. Parliament would thus – temporarily – have 754 members! This proposal has received the consent of the Commission, the Parliament, and the European Council (see: Decision of the European Council of 17 June 2010 on the examination by a conference of

it is still smaller than the (British) House of Lords.[37] The Treaties themselves no longer determine its composition.[38] It is the European Council that must decide on the national 'quotas' for the Union's parliamentary representatives. The distribution of seats must however be 'degressively proportional' within a range spanning from six to ninety-six seats. While the European Council has not yet taken a formal decision, it has given its political endorsement to a proposal by the European Parliament.[39] In its proposal, Parliament provided a definition of 'degressively proportional',[40] and has suggested the following concrete distribution of seats among Member States:

Table 4 Distribution of seats in the European Parliament (Member States)

Member State (Seats)		
Belgium (22)	Ireland (12)	Austria (19)
Bulgaria (18)	Italy (72+1[41])	Poland (51)
Czech Republic (22)	Cyprus (6)	Portugal (22)
Denmark (13)	Latvia (9)	Romania (33)
Germany (96)	Lithuania (12)	Slovenia (8)
Estonia (6)	Luxembourg (6)	Slovakia (13)
Greece (22)	Hungary (22)	Finland (13)
Spain (54)	Malta (6)	Sweden (20)
France (74)	Netherlands (26)	United Kingdom (73)

representatives of the governments of the Member States of the amendments to the Treaties proposed by the Spanish Government concerning the composition of the European Parliament and not to convene a Convention (2010/350/EU)). The additional 18 MEPs will not be elected. According to Article 1 of the European Council Decision '[b]y way of derogation from Article 14 (3) of the Treaty on European Union, the Member States concerned shall designate the persons who will fill the additional seats referred to in paragraph 1, in accordance with the legislation of the Member States concerned and provided that the persons in question have been elected by direct universal suffrage'.

[37] To compare: the (American) House of Representatives has 435 members. The (British) House of Commons has 648 members, while the (British) House of Lords has presently 829 members.

[38] This had always been the case prior to the Lisbon Treaty. The composition of the Parliament has thus been 'de-constitutionalised'.

[39] See: Declaration (No. 5) on the political agreement by the European Council concerning the draft Decision on the composition of the European Parliament: 'The European Council will give its political agreement on the revised draft Decision on the composition of the European Parliament for the legislative period 2009–2014, based on the proposal from the European Parliament.' For the draft decision, see: European Parliament Resolution (11 October 2007) on the composition of the European Parliament ([2008] OJ C 227/132).

[40] Ibid., para. 6: '[T]he principle of degressive proportionality means that the ratio between the population and the number of seats of each Member State must vary in relation to their respective populations in such a way that each Member from a more populous Member State represents more citizens than each Member from a less populous Member State and conversely, but also that no less populous Member State has more seats than a more populous Member State[.]'

[41] This additional seat was added, because of Italian intransigence, by the Lisbon Intergovernmental Council, see: Declaration (No. 4) on the composition of the European Parliament: 'The additional seat in the European Parliament will be attributed to Italy.'

The national 'quotas' for European parliamentary seats constitute a compromise between the *democratic* principle and the *federal* principle. For while the democratic principle would demand that each citizen in the Union has equal voting power ('one person, one vote'), the federal principle insists on the political equality of States. The result of this compromise was the rejection of a *purely* proportional distribution in favour of a *degressively* proportional system. The degressive element within that system unfortunately means that a Luxembourg citizen has ten times more voting power than a British, French or German citizen.

How are the *individual* members of Parliament elected? The Treaties solely provide us with the most general of rules: 'The members of the European Parliament shall be elected for a term of five years by direct universal suffrage in a free and secret ballot.'[42] More precise rules are set out in the (amended) 1976 Election Act. Article 1 of the Act commands that the elections must be conducted 'on the basis of proportional representation'.[43] This outlaws the traditionally British election method of 'first past the post'.[44] The specifics of the election procedure are however principally left to the Member States.[45] European parliamentary elections thus still do not follow 'a uniform electoral procedure in all Member States', but are rather conducted 'in accordance with principles common to all Member States'.[46] The Treaties nonetheless insist on one common constitutional rule: 'every citizen of the Union residing in a Member State of which he is not a national shall have the right to vote and to stand as a candidate in elections to the European Parliament in the Member State in which he resides, under the same conditions as nationals of that State'.[47]

---

[42] Article 14 (3) TEU.   [43] Article 1 (1) and (3) of the 1976 Election Act (supra n. 33).

[44] This condition had not been part of the original 1976 Election Act, but was added through a 2002 amendment. This amendment was considered necessary as, hitherto, the British majority voting system 'could alone alter the entire political balance in the European Parliament' (F. Jacobs et al., *The European Parliament* (Harper Publishing, 2005), 17). The best example of this distorting effect was the 1979 election to the European Parliament in which the British Conservatives won 60 out of 78 seats with merely 50 per cent of the vote (*ibid.*).

[45] Article 8 of the 1976 Election Act: 'Subject to the provisions of this Act, the electoral procedure shall be governed in each Member State by its national provisions.' Under the Act, Member States are free to decide whether to establish national or local constituencies for elections to the European Parliament (*ibid.*, Article 2), and whether to set a minimum threshold for the allocation of seats (*ibid.*, Article 3). Moreover, each Member State can fix the date and times for the European elections, but this date must 'fall within the same period starting on a Thursday morning and ending on the following Sunday' for all Member States (*ibid.*, Article 10 (1)).

[46] Both alternatives are provided for in Article 223 (1) TFEU: 'The European Parliament shall draw up a proposal to lay down the provisions necessary for the election of its Members by direct universal suffrage in accordance with a uniform procedure in all Member States or in accordance with principles common to all Member States. The Council, acting unanimously in accordance with a special legislative procedure and after obtaining the consent of the European Parliament, which shall act by a majority of its component Members, shall lay down the necessary provisions. These provisions shall enter into force following their approval by the Member States in accordance with their respective constitutional requirements.'

[47] Article 22 (2) TFEU. However, the provision adds: 'This right shall be exercised subject to detailed arrangements adopted by the Council, acting unanimously in accordance with a special

(ii) Members of the European Parliament and political parties

For a long time, the 1976 Election Act solely governed the status of a Member of the European Parliament (MEP). It determined, inter alia, that members would enjoy the privileges and immunities of officials of the European Union.[48] It also established that membership of the European Parliament was incompatible with a parallel membership in a national government or parliament,[49] or with being a member of another European institution.

After years of debate and discontent, Parliament belatedly adopted its 'Statute for Members of the European Parliament'.[50] The Statute 'lays down the regulations and general conditions governing the performance of the duties of members of the European Parliament'.[51] Accordingly, 'members shall be free and independent'.[52] They 'shall vote on an individual and personal basis', and shall thus 'not be bound by any instructions'.[53] Members are entitled to table proposals for Union acts,[54] and may form political groups.[55] They are entitled to receive an 'appropriate salary to safeguard their independence',[56] and might get a pension.[57]

Members of Parliament will, as a rule, be members of a political party. Yet despite a considerable effort to nurture *European* parties,[58] European

legislative procedure and after consulting the European Parliament; these arrangements may provide for derogations where warranted by problems specific to a Member State.'

[48] Article 6 (2) of the 1976 Election Act.   [49] *Ibid.*, Article 7.

[50] European Parliament, Decision 2005/684 adopting the Statute for Members of the European Parliament ([2005] OJ L262/1 (Annex 2)). The legal basis for this type of act can now be found in Article 223 (2) TFEU: 'The European Parliament, acting by means of regulations on its own initiative in accordance with a special legislative procedure after seeking an opinion from the Commission and with the consent of the Council, shall lay down the regulations and general conditions governing the performance of the duties of its Members.'

[51] Article 1 MEP Statute.

[52] *Ibid.*, Article 2. This is repeated in Article 6 (1) of the 1976 Act: 'Members of the European Parliament shall vote on an individual and personal basis. They shall not be bound by any instructions and shall not receive a binding mandate.'

[53] Article 3 MEP Statute.   [54] *Ibid.*, Article 5.   [55] *Ibid.*, Article 8.

[56] *Ibid.*, Article 9. Article 10 fixes the salary as follows: 'The amount of the salary shall be 38.5 per cent of the basic salary of a judge of the Court of Justice of the European [Union].'

[57] *Ibid.*, Article 14 et seq.

[58] According to Article 10 (4) TEU: 'Political parties at European level contribute to forming European political awareness and to expressing the will of citizens of the Union.' The Treaties even contain a legal basis in Article 224 TFEU for 'regulations governing political parties at European level referred to in Article 20 (4) of the Treaty on European Union and in particular rules regarding their funding'. The legal basis has been used in the form of Regulation 2004/2003 on the regulations governing political parties at European level and the rule regarding their funding ([2003] OJ L 297/1), as amended by Regulation 1524/2007 ([2007] OJ L343/5). The Regulation defines a 'political party' as an 'association of citizens', 'which pursues political objectives' (*ibid.*, Article 2), and which must satisfy four conditions: '(a) it must have legal personality in the Member State in which its seat is located; (b) it must be represented, in at least one quarter of Member States, by Members of the European Parliament or in the national Parliaments or regional Parliaments or in the regional assemblies, or it must have received, in at least one quarter of the Member States, at least three per cent of the votes cast in each of those Member States at the most recent European Parliament elections; (c) it must observe, in particular in its programme and in its activities, the principles on which the European Union is founded, namely the principles of liberty, democracy, respect for human rights and

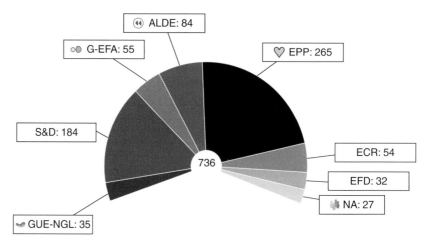

Figure 5 Distribution of Seats in the European Parliament (Political Parties)
Source: European Parliament

parliamentarians continue to be elected primarily as representatives of their *national* parties.[59] Members of Parliament will however often choose to join one of the European 'political groups'. (In reality, it is their national parties doing the joining for them.[60]) Parliament's Rules of Procedure stipulate that a political group must comprise a minimum number of twenty-five members and 'shall comprise Members elected in at least one-quarter of the Member States'.[61] The advantage of being within a political group is that they enjoy a privileged status within Parliament. There presently exist seven political groups within the European Parliament: the European People's Party (EPP),[62] the Progressive Alliance of Socialists and Democrats (S&D),[63] the Alliance of Liberals and

---

fundamental freedoms, and the rule of law; (d) it must have participated in elections to the European Parliament, or have expressed the intention to do so.' If these conditions are fulfilled, the political party can – under certain conditions (*ibid.*, Article 6) – apply for funding from the general budget of the European Union (*ibid.*, Article 4).

[59] This has led Hix to characterise European elections as 'second-order national contests' (S. Hix, *The Political System of the European Union* (Palgrave, 2005), 193).

[60] Each political group can itself decide on the membership in its Group Statute. For example, the European People's Parties Statute (see www.europeanpeoplesparty.eu/subsubpagina.php?hoofdmenuID=5&submenuID=38&subsubmenuID=84) is based on the membership of national parties and distinguishes between 'Ordinary Member Parties' and 'Associated Member Parties'. According to Article 5 of the Statute 'all members of the EPP Group in the European Parliament elected on a list of a member party are also members ex officio of the association'. However, parliamentarians who are not attached to any national party 'can become Individual Members of the association by decision of the Political Assembly on the proposal of the Presidency of the association' (*ibid.*).

[61] Rule 30 (2) Parliament Rules of Procedure.

[62] For example: the French Party 'Union for a Political Movement', as well as the German Party 'Christian Democratic Union' are members of this political group.

[63] For example: the British 'Labour Party', the German 'Social Democratic Party' and the French 'Socialist Party' are members of this European political group.

Democrats for Europe (ALDE),[64] the Greens-European Free Alliance (G-EFA), the European Conservatives and Reformists (ECR),[65] European United Left-Nordic Green Left (GUE-NGL), and the Europe of Freedom and Democracy (EFD). After the 2009 elections,[66] the distribution of seats among the political groups in the European Parliament is shown in Figure 5.

(b) Internal structure: parliamentary organs

Formally, Parliament always acts as the plenary. Yet it is entitled to organise itself internally and thus to establish a division of labour. According to Article 14 (4) TEU, '[t]he European Parliament shall elect its President and its officers from among its members'. The various officers and their duties are laid down in Chapter 2 of Parliament's Rules of Procedure. According to its Rule 13, Parliament elects by secret ballot a President, fourteen Vice-Presidents, and five Quaestors.[67]

The President is the 'Speaker' of the European Parliament, whose duties are set out in Rule 20: 'The President shall direct all the activities of Parliament and its bodies.'[68] S/he is entitled 'to open, suspend and close sittings; to rule on the admissibility of amendments, on questions to the Council and Commission'; s/he is also charged to 'maintain order, call upon speakers, close debates, put matters to the vote; and to refer to committees any communication that concerns them'.[69] Finally, the President represents Parliament in inter-institutional or international relations.[70]

Parliament is also supported by a number of internal parliamentary organs. The 'Bureau' is the body formed by the President and the Vice-Presidents.[71] It is charged with taking decisions on financial and administrative matters concerning the internal organisation of Parliament and its Members.[72] The 'Conference of Presidents' is the organ that consists of the President and the Chairs of the Political Groups.[73] Importantly, it is the body that 'shall take decisions on the organization of Parliament's work and matters of legislative planning'.[74] It will thereby 'draw up the draft agenda of Parliament's part-sessions', and constitutes 'the authority responsible for the composition and competence of committees'.[75]

Committees constitute the most important 'decentralised' organs of Parliament. The two principal committee types are 'standing committees' and

---

[64] For example: the British 'Liberal Democrats', the French 'Democratic Movement' and the German 'Free Democratic Party' are members of this European political group.
[65] The British Conservative Party is a member of this group.
[66] www.europarl.europa.eu/parliament/archive/elections2009/en/index_en.html
[67] The term of office for all three offices is two-and-a-half years (see Rule 17 Parliament Rules of Procedure).
[68] Rule 20 (1) Parliament Rules of Procedure.   [69] Ibid., Rule 20 (2).   [70] Ibid., Rule 20 (4).
[71] Ibid., Rule 22 (1).   [72] Ibid., Rule 23 – setting out the duties of the Bureau.
[73] Ibid., Rule 24 (1).   [74] Ibid., Rule 25 (2).
[75] Ibid., Rule 25 (6) and (7). On the 'draft agenda', see: Rule 137.

Table 5 Standing Committees of the European Parliament

Standing Committees			
Foreign Affairs	Economic and Monetary Affairs	Transport and Tourism	Legal Affairs
Development	Employment and Social Affairs	Regional Development	Civil Liberties, Justice and Home Affairs
International Trade	Environment	Agriculture and Rural Development	Constitutional Affairs
Budgets	Public Health and Food Safety	Fisheries	Women's Rights and Gender Equality
Budgetary Control	Industry, Research and Energy	Culture and Education	Petitions

'special committees'.[76] Standing committees are permanent committees. They are set up as thematically specialised bodies that concentrate on one area of parliamentary affairs.[77] With their mandates defined in the Rules of Procedure,[78] Table 5 lists Parliament's Standing Committees.

Importantly, as committees functionally operate like miniature parliaments, all committees must 'reflect the composition of Parliament'.[79] Committee members are elected after having been nominated by their political groups (or non-attached members). Standing committees have between forty and sixty members, are headed by a 'Committee Chair', and are coordinated by 'Committee Coordinators'.[80] The duties of standing committees are thereby defined as follows: 'Standing committees shall examine questions referred to them by Parliament or, during an adjournment of the session, by the President on behalf of the Conference of Presidents.'[81] Voting within committees is by show of hands – with the Chair *not* having a casting vote.[82] The responsibility for reporting back to the plenary is the task of a *rapporteur*. And this brings us to an important final point: committees only *prepare* decisions. For the tasks of deciding belongs – exclusively – to the plenary.

(c) The plenary: decision-making and voting

The plenary is the formal decision-making 'organ' of the European Parliament. It is through the plenary that Parliament formally acts. The Treaties –

---

[76] *Ibid.*, Rule 181. 'Special committees' must generally expire after one year. For the detailed rules on Committees of Inquiry, see: Rule 185 as well as Annex IX of the Rules of Procedure.

[77] *Ibid.*, Rule 183.   [78] *Ibid.*, Annex VII.   [79] *Ibid.*, Rule 186 (1).   [80] *Ibid.*, Rule 192.

[81] *Ibid.*, Rule 188 (1). According to Rule 188 (3): 'Should two or more standing committees be competent to deal with a question, one committee shall be named as the committee responsible and the others as committees asked for opinions.'

[82] *Ibid.*, Rule 195.

anachronistically – determine that Parliament is to meet, as plenary, at least once a year to hold its annual session.[83] Parliament decided early on to divide its annual session into twelve 'part-sessions' and to meet for a week every month. This choice has now been formally 'constitutionalised' by a Protocol attached to the Treaties.[84] These plenary sessions take place in Strasbourg – not in Brussels.

How does Parliament's plenary decide? Decision-making is governed by the general rule expressed in Article 231 TFEU: 'Save as otherwise provided in the Treaties, the European Parliament shall act by a majority of the *votes cast*. The Rules of Procedure shall determine the quorum.' These Rules define the quorum as 'one third of the component Members of Parliament'.[85] But what are the exceptions to the rule that Parliament decides by a majority of the votes cast? First, some Treaty articles qualify the majority by requiring that Parliament must decide by a majority of its *component* members. Thus, the nominated Commission President 'shall be elected by the European Parliament by a majority of its component members'.[86] Second, some Treaty provisions require a doubly qualified majority. A good example can be found in a parliamentary motion censuring the Commission. Such a motion of censure requires a '*two-third majority* of the *votes* cast, representing the *majority of the component Members* of the European Parliament'.[87]

The specifics of the voting procedure and the principles governing voting are set out in Rules 158–171 of the Parliament's Rules of Procedure. Parliament will generally vote by show of hands,[88] but 'voting by roll call' or electronic voting is also envisaged. In the former scenario, the individual votes of each parliamentarian will be recorded in the minutes.[89] In the latter scenario, 'only the numerical result of the vote shall be recorded'.[90] Exceptionally, a secret ballot is also possible.[91] But should a Parliament, which debates and votes in public, not also be required to record the votes of individual members? Two constitutional

---

[83] Article 139 EEC. Today, Article 229 TFEU states: 'The European Parliament shall hold an annual session. It shall meet, without requiring to be convened, on the second Tuesday in March. The European Parliament may meet in extraordinary part-session at the request of a majority of its component Members or at the request of the Council or of the Commission.'

[84] See Protocol (No. 6) on the Location of the Seats of the Institutions: 'The European Parliament shall have its seat in Strasbourg where the 12 periods of monthly plenary sessions, including the budget session, shall be held. The periods of additional plenary sessions shall be held in Brussels. The committees of the European Parliament shall meet in Brussels. The General Secretariat of the European Parliament and its departments shall remain in Luxembourg.'

[85] Rule 155 (2) Parliament Rules of Procedure. However, Rule 155 (3) establishes the quorate nature of Parliament as a rebuttable presumption: 'All votes shall be valid whatever the number of voters unless the President, on request made before voting has begun by at least 40 members, establishes at the time of voting that the quorum is not present.'

[86] See Article 17 (7) TEU. See also: Articles 48 and 49 TEU, as well as Articles 223 (1), 225, 226, 294 (7) and 314 (7) TFEU.

[87] Article 234 TFEU (emphasis added). See also: Article 354 TFEU – last indent: 'For the purposes of Article 7 of the Treaty on European Union, the European Parliament shall act by a two-thirds majority of the votes cast, representing the majority of its component Members.'

[88] Rule 165 (1) Parliament Rules of Procedure.   [89] *Ibid.*, Article 167 (2).

[90] *Ibid.*, Article 168 (2).   [91] *Ibid.*, Article 169.

rationales compete in answering this question. From a democratic perspective, the 'transparency' of the vote is important in that it allows citizens to monitor their representatives. And while the latter cannot be bound by instructions or a binding mandate,[92] citizens have at least a choice to 'de-select' their member of Parliament in the following elections. On the other hand, an impersonal vote may better protect the independence of members of Parliament from less legitimate influences. These may be party-political pressures within Parliament or organised civil society in the form of corporatist lobbies.

(d) Parliamentary powers

When the Paris Treaty set up the European Parliament, its sole function was to exercise 'supervisory powers'.[93] Parliament was indeed a passive onlooker in the decision-making process within the first Community. The Rome Treaty expanded Parliament's function to 'advisory and supervisory power'.[94] This recognised the active power of Parliament to be consulted on Commission proposals before their adoption by the Council.[95] After sixty years of evolution and numerous amendments, the Treaty on European Union today defines the powers of the European Parliament in Article 14 TEU as follows: 'The European Parliament shall, jointly with the Council, exercise legislative and budgetary functions. It shall exercise functions of political control and con-sultation as laid down in the Treaties. It shall elect the President of the Commission.'[96] This definition distinguishes between four types of powers: legislative and budgetary powers as well as supervisory and elective powers.

(i) Legislative powers

The European Parliament's principal power lies in the making of European laws. This involvement may take place at two moments in time. Parliament may informally propose new legislation.[97] However, it is not – unlike many national parliaments – entitled to formally propose bills. The task of making legislative proposals is, with minor exceptions, a constitutional prerogative of the Commission.[98]

The principal legislative involvement of Parliament thus starts after the Commission has submitted a proposal to the European legislature. Like other federal legal orders, the European legal order acknowledges a number of

---

[92] Article 3 MEP Statute states: 'Members shall vote on an individual and personal basis. They shall not be bound by any instructions and shall not receive a binding mandate. Agreements concerning the way in which the mandate is to be exercised shall be null and void.'

[93] Article 20 ECSC.   [94] Article 137 EEC.

[95] Case 138/79, *Roquette Frères* v. *Council* (supra n. 22).   [96] Article 14 (1) TEU.

[97] Article 225 TFEU: 'The European Parliament may, acting by a majority of its component Members, request the Commission to submit any appropriate proposal on matters on which it considers that a Union act is required for the purpose of implementing the Treaties. If the Commission does not submit a proposal, it shall inform the European Parliament of the reasons.'

[98] On this power, see: Chapter 5 – Section 3 below.

different legislative procedures. The Treaties now textually distinguish between the 'ordinary' legislative procedure and a number of 'special' legislative procedures. The former is defined as 'the joint adoption by the European Parliament and the Council' on a proposal from the Commission.[99] Special legislative procedures cover various degrees of parliamentary participation. Under the 'consent procedure' Parliament must give its consent before the Council can adopt European legislation.[100] This is a cruder form of legislative participation that essentially grants a negative power. Parliament cannot suggest positive amendments, but must take-or-leave the Council's position. Under the 'consultation procedure', by contrast, Parliament is not even entitled to do that. It merely needs to be consulted – a role that is closer to a supervisory than to a legislative function.[101] Exceptionally, a special legislative procedure may make Parliament the dominant legislative chamber.[102]

Importantly, Parliament's 'legislative' powers also extend to the external relations sphere. After Lisbon, Parliament has indeed become an important player in the conclusion of the Union's international agreements.

(ii) Budgetary powers

National parliaments have historically been involved in the budgetary process. For they were seen as legitimating the *raising* of revenue. In the words of the American colonists: 'No taxation without representation'. In the European Union, this picture is somewhat inverted. For since Union revenue is fixed by the Council and the Member States,[103] the European Parliament's budgetary powers have not focused on the income side but on the expenditure side. Its powers have consequently been described as the 'reverse of those traditionally exercised by parliaments'.[104]

Be that as it may, Parliament's formal involvement in the Union budget started with the 1970 and 1975 Budget Treaties. They distinguished between compulsory and non-compulsory expenditure, with the latter being expenditure that would not result from compulsory financial commitments flowing from the application of European law. Parliament's powers were originally

---

[99] Article 289 (1) TFEU.

[100] For example, Article 19 TFEU, according to which 'the Council, acting unanimously in accordance with a special legislative procedure and after obtaining the consent of the European Parliament, may take appropriate action to combat discrimination based on sex, racial or ethnic origin, religion or belief, disability, age or sexual orientation'.

[101] For example, Article 22 (1) TFEU, which states: 'Every citizen of the Union residing in a Member State of which he is not a national shall have the right to vote and to stand as a candidate at municipal elections in the Member State in which he resides, under the same conditions as nationals of that State. This right shall be exercised subject to detailed arrangements adopted by the Council, acting unanimously in accordance with a special legislative procedure and after consulting the European Parliament[.]'

[102] For example, Article 223 (2) TFEU – granting Parliament the power, with the consent of the Council, to adopt a Statute for its Members.

[103] See Article 311 TFEU on the 'Union's own resources'.

[104] D. Judge and D. Earnshaw, *The European Parliament* (Palgrave, 2008), 198.

confined to this second category. The Lisbon Treaty has, however, abandoned
the distinction between compulsory and non-compulsory expenditure, and
Parliament has thus become a equal partner in establishing the Union's annual
budget.[105]

(iii) Supervisory powers

A third parliamentary power is that of holding to account the executive.
Parliamentary supervisory powers typically involve the power to question,
debate and investigate.

A soft parliamentary power is the power to *debate*.[106] To that effect, the
European Parliament is entitled to receive the 'general report on the activities of
the Union' from the Commission,[107] which it 'shall discuss in open session'.[108]
And as regards the European Council, the Treaties require its President to
'present a report to the European Parliament after each of the meetings of the
European Council'.[109] Similar obligations apply to the European Central
Bank.[110] The power to *question* the European executive is formally enshrined
only for the Commission: 'The Commission shall reply orally or in writing to
questions put to it by the European Parliament or by its Members.'[111] However,
both the European Council and the Council have confirmed their willingness to
be questioned by Parliament.[112] Early on, Parliament introduced the institution
of 'Question Time' – modelled on the procedure within the British
Parliament.[113] And under its own Rules of Procedure, Parliament is entitled
to hold 'an extraordinary debate' on a 'matter of major interest relating to
European Union policy'.[114]

Parliament also enjoys the formal power to *investigate*. It is constitutionally
entitled to set up temporary Committees of Inquiry to investigate alleged
contraventions or maladministration in the implementation of European
law.[115] These temporary committees thus complement Parliament's standing

---

[105] Article 314 TFEU.

[106] In the area of the Union's common foreign and security policy, the parliamentary powers to
question and debate are now expressly enshrined in Article 36 (2) TEU: 'The European
Parliament may address questions or make recommendations to the Council or to the High
Representative. Twice a year it shall hold a debate on progress in implementing the common
foreign and security policy[.]'

[107] Article 249 (2) TFEU.   [108] Article 233 TFEU.   [109] Article 15 (6) (d) TEU.

[110] Article 284 (3) TFEU.   [111] Article 230 TFEU – second indent.

[112] The Council accepted this political obligation in 1973; see Jacobs, *The European Parliament*
(supra n. 44), 284.

[113] Rule 116 Parliament Rules of Procedure. For acceptance of that obligation by the Commission,
see: Framework Agreement on relations between the European Parliament and the European
Commission [2010] OJ L 304/47, para. 46.

[114] Rule 141 Parliament Rules of Procedure.

[115] Article 226 (1) TFEU. For a good overview of the history of these committees, see:
M. Shackleton, 'The European Parliament's New Committees of Inquiry: Tiger or Paper
Tiger' [1998] 36 *Journal of Common Market Studies* 115.

committees. They have been used, inter alia, to investigate the (mis)handling of the BSE crisis.[116]

Finally, European citizens have the general right to 'petition' the European Parliament.[117] And according to a Scandinavian constitutional tradition, the European Parliament will also elect an 'ombudsman'. The European Ombudsman 'shall be empowered to receive complaints' from any citizen or Union resident 'concerning instances of maladministration in the activities of the Union institutions, bodies or agencies'. S/he 'shall conduct inquiries' on the basis of complaints addressed to her or him directly or through a Member of the European Parliament.[118]

(iv) Elective powers

Modern constitutionalism distinguishes between 'presidential' and 'parliamentary' systems. Within the former, the executive officers are independent from Parliament, whereas in the latter the executive is elected by Parliament. The European constitutional order sits somewhere 'in between'. Its executive was for a long time selected without any parliamentary involvement. This continues to be the case for one branch of the Union executive: the European Council. However, as regards the Commission, the European Parliament has increasingly come to be involved in the appointment process. Today, Article 17 TEU describes the involvement of the European Parliament in the appointment of the Commission as follows:

> Taking into account the elections to the European Parliament and after having held the appropriate consultations, the European Council, acting by a qualified majority, shall propose to the European Parliament a candidate for President of the Commission. This candidate shall be elected by the European Parliament by a majority of its component members . . . The Council, by common accord with the President-elect, shall adopt the list of the other persons whom it proposes for appointment as members of the Commission. They shall be selected, on the basis of the suggestions made by Member States . . . The President, the High Representative of the Union for Foreign Affairs and Security Policy and the other members of the Commission shall be subject as a body to a vote of consent by the European Parliament. On the basis of this consent the Commission shall be appointed by the European Council, acting by a qualified majority.[119]

The appointment of the second branch of the European executive thus requires a dual parliamentary consent. Parliament must – first – 'elect' the President of the Commission. And it must – secondly – confirm the Commission as a

---

[116] For the Report of the 'BSE Committee of Inquiry' of the European Parliament, see: K. Vincent, '"Mad Cows" and Eurocrats – Community Responses to the BSE Crisis' [2004] 10 *European Law Journal* 499.

[117] According to Article 227 TFEU, any citizen or Union resident has the right to petition the European Parliament 'on any matter which comes within the Union's field or activity and which affects him, her or it directly'. See also: Article 20 (2) (d) TFEU.

[118] Article 228 TFEU.   [119] Article 17 (7) TEU.

collective body. (Apart from the President, the European Parliament has consequently not got the power to confirm each and every Commissioner.[120]) In light of this elective power given to Parliament, one is indeed justified to characterise the Union's governmental system as a 'semi-parliamentary democracy'.[121]

Once appointed, the Commission continues to 'be responsible to the European Parliament'.[122] Where this consent is lost, Parliament may vote on a motion of censure. If this vote of mistrust is carried, the Commission must resign as a body. The motion of collective censure mirrors Parliament's appointment power, which is also focused on the Commission *as a collective body*. This blunt 'atomic option' has never been used.[123] However, unlike the appointment power, Parliament has been able to sharpen its tools of censure significantly by concluding a political agreement with the Commission. Accordingly, if Parliament expresses lack of confidence in an *individual* member of the Commission, the President of the Commission 'shall either require the resignation of that Member' or, after 'serious' consideration, explain the refusal to do so before Parliament.[124] While this is a much 'smarter sanction', it has also never been used due to the demanding voting requirements in Parliament.

Parliament is also involved in the appointment of other European officers. This holds true for the Court of Auditors,[125] the European Central Bank,[126] the European Ombudsman,[127] as well as some European Agencies.[128] However, it is not involved in the appointment of judges to the Court of Justice of the European Union.

3. The European Council

The European Council originally developed outside the institutional framework of the European Union.[129] And for some time, the Member States even

---

[120] However, Parliament may request each nominated Commissioner to appear before Parliament and to 'present' his or her views. This practice thus comes close to 'confirmation hearings' (Judge and Earnshaw, *The European Parliament* (supra n. 104), 205).

[121] P. Dann, 'European Parliament and Executive Federalism: Approaching a Parliament in a Semi-Parliamentary Democracy' [2003] 9 *European Law Journal* 549.

[122] Article 17 (8) TEU.

[123] Once, however, the European Parliament came close to using this power when in 1999 it decided to censure the Santer Commission. However, the latter chose collectively to resign instead.

[124] Framework Agreement (supra n. 113), para. 5. However, this rule has been contested by the Council; see Council statement concerning the framework agreement on relations between the European Parliament and the Commission ([2010] OJ C287/1).

[125] Article 286 (2) TFEU.   [126] Article 283 (2) TFEU.   [127] Article 228 (2) TFEU.

[128] For example, Parliament is entitled to appoint two members to the Management Board of the European Environmental Agency; see Regulation No. 401/2009 on the European Environment Agency and the European Environment Information and Observation Network (Codified version), [2009] OJ L 126/13, Article 8 (1).

[129] On the historical evolution of the European Council, see: Chapter 1 Section 2(c) above.

tried to prevent the European Council from acting *within* the scope of the Treaties.[130] Since the 1992 Maastricht Treaty, the European Council has steadily moved inside the institutional framework of the Union. With the 2007 Lisbon Treaty, the European Council has finally become a formal institution of the European Union.[131] This formalisation recognises a substantive development in which the European Council had become 'the political backbone' of the European Union.[132]

The composition of the European Council is as simple as it is exclusive. It consists of the Heads of State or Government of the Member States.[133] With the Lisbon Treaty the European Council has its own President – who will be an additional member, as s/he cannot simultaneously serve as a Head of State or Government.[134] The President of the Commission shall also be a formal member.[135] However, neither the President of the European Council nor the Commission President enjoys a voting right.[136] They are thus not full members, but rather 'honorary' members of this Union institution. Their status is not so dissimilar to the High Representative of the Union for Foreign Affairs and Security Policy, who – while not even being a formal member of the European Council – shall nonetheless take part in its work.

The European Council shall meet twice every six months, but can have additional meetings when the situation so requires.[137] These regular meetings follow the seasons: there are spring, summer, autumn and winter meetings. These meetings were traditionally held in the Member State holding the Council presidency. However, the European Council now 'shall meet in Brussels'.[138]

How will it decide? The decision-making process within the European Council is shrouded in secrecy for its meetings are not public.[139] The default

---

[130] European Council, 'Solemn Declaration on European Union (Stuttgart, 1983)' reproduced in: A. G. Harryvan et al. (eds.), *Documents on European Union* (St. Martin's Press, 1997), 215 – para. 2.1.3: '[w]hen the European Council acts in matters within the scope of the European [Union], it does so in its capacity as the Council within the meaning of the Treaties'.

[131] Article 13 (1) TEU.   [132] J. Werts, *The European Council* (TMC Asser Institute, 1992), 296.

[133] Article 15 (2) TEU. The distinction between Heads of State or Government was originally made for France. For, under national constitutional law, the President, as Head of State, is principally charged with external relations powers. The situation is similar in Cyprus, Finland, Lithuania and – arguably – the Czech Republic and Poland.

[134] Article 15 (6) TEU – last indent: 'The President of the European Council shall not hold a national office.'

[135] Article 15 (2) TEU.

[136] Article 235 (1) TFEU: 'Where the European Council decides by vote, its President and the President of the Commission shall not take part in the vote.'

[137] Article 15 (3) TEU. In urgent situations, the physical meeting can be replaced by a 'written procedure' (see Article 7 European Council Rules of Procedure).

[138] Article 1 (2) European Council Rules of Procedure.

[139] *Ibid.*, Article 4 (3): 'Meetings of the European Council shall not be public.' However, according to Article 10, the European Council may decide 'to make public the result of votes, as well as the statements in its minutes and the items in those minutes relating to the adoption of that decision'.

principle is set out in Article 15 (4) TEU: 'Except where the Treaties provide otherwise, decisions of the European Council shall be taken by consensus.' The general rule is thus unanimity of all the Member States. However, there are some instances within the Treaties in which the European Council may act by a (qualified) majority of the Member States. In such a case, the Council's rules on what constitutes a qualified majority apply *mutatis mutandis* to the European Council.[140]

(a) The President of the European Council

Traditionally, the European Council had a rotating Presidency: every six months, the Head of State or Government of the State that held the Council Presidency was to be the President of the European Council.[141] The Lisbon Treaty has given the European Council its own – permanent – President.

The permanent President is elected by the European Council,[142] but cannot be elected from within the European Council. The period of office will be a (renewable) term of two-and-a-half years.[143] This is a – relatively – short time when compared with other governmental offices within the European Union. Nonetheless, the advantages of a permanent President over a rotating presidency are considerable. First, the rotating presidency of six months was *very* short. A permanent President thus promises – more – permanence. Second, the idea of having the President or Prime Minister of a Member State act as President of the European Council had always been incongruous. For how could the national loyalties of the highest *State* representative be harmoniously combined with the European obligation of standing above national interests? Third, the tasks of the President of the European Council have become far too demanding to be the subject of shared attention. The tasks of the President are today set out in Article 15 (6) TEU:

> The President of the European Council:
>
> (a) shall chair it and drive forward its work;
> (b) shall ensure the preparation and continuity of the work of the European Council in cooperation with the President of the Commission, and on the basis of the work of the General Affairs Council;
> (c) shall endeavour to facilitate cohesion and consensus within the European Council;
> (d) shall present a report to the European Parliament after each of the meetings of the European Council.
>
> The President of the European Council shall, at his level and in that capacity, ensure the external representation of the Union on issues concerning its

---

[140] Article 235 TFEU: 'Article 16 (4) of the Treaty on European Union and Article 238 (2) of this Treaty apply to the European Council when it is acting by a qualified majority.'
[141] On the rotating Presidency in the Council, see: Section 4 below.   [142] Article 15 (5) TEU.
[143] *Ibid.*

common foreign and security policy, without prejudice to the powers of the High Representative of the Union for Foreign Affairs and Security Policy.[144]

The tasks of the President are not very specific. The President has primarily coordinating and representative functions. S/he represents the European Council as an institution within the Union. Outside the Union, s/he ensures the external representation of the Union with regard to the Union's CFSP – a task that is however shared with the High Representative of Foreign Affairs and Security Policy.[145]

(b) The European Council: functions and powers

What are the functions and powers of the European Council? Article 15 TEU defines them as follows: 'The European Council shall provide the Union with the necessary impetus for its development and shall define the general political directions and priorities thereof.'[146] The political power to provide impulses and guidelines has been the traditional function of the European Council. It is the European Council that writes the Union's 'multiannual strategic programme'. And it is the European Council whose Presidency Conclusions offer specific and regular stimuli to the development of the Union and its policies.[147] We find numerous expressions of this executive power of political guidance in the Treaties.[148] However, the definition given in Article 15 TEU is reductionist in that it concentrates on the European Council's *executive* function. Yet the European Council also exercises three additional functions.

First, it is given a significant *constitutional* function. We have seen this above in relation to the simplified revision procedures.[149] And in limited areas, the European Council is even given the power unilaterally to 'bridge' the procedural or competence limits established by the Treaties.[150] These '*passerelles*' (little bridges) provide the European Council with a partial competence-competence. Finally, the European Council agrees on the eligibility conditions for States hoping to become members of the Union.[151]

---

[144] These powers are further defined in Article 2 of the European Council Rules of Procedure.

[145] On the High Representative, see: Section 4(b)(iii) below.   [146] Article 15 (1) TEU.

[147] On this point, see: Chapter 7 – Section 1 below.

[148] For example, Article 26 (1) TEU: 'The European Council shall identify the Union's strategic interests, determine the objectives of and define general guidelines for the common foreign and security policy, including for matters with defence implications. It shall adopt the necessary decisions.'

[149] On the European Council's role within Article 48 TEU, see: Chapter 1 – Conclusion.

[150] For an example of such a special 'bridge', see: Article 31 (3) TEU, as well as Article 86 (4) TFEU.

[151] Article 49 TEU. It is also charged to provide guidelines for the withdrawal of a Member State; see Article 50 (2) TEU.

Second, the European Council also has *institutional* functions. It can determine the composition of the European Parliament,[152] as well that of the European Commission.[153] It shall adopt the various Council configurations and determine that body's presidency.[154] It shall appoint the High Representative of the Union for Foreign Affairs and Security Policy,[155] as well as the President (and the executive board) of the European Central Bank.[156]

Third, the European Council exercises *arbitration* powers and thus functions like an appeal 'court' in – very – specific situations.[157] We can find an illustration of this power in the context of the Union competence in the 'Area of Freedom, Security and Justice'.[158] The European Council is here empowered to suspend the legislative procedure to arbitrate between the Council and a Member State claiming that the draft European law 'would affect fundamental aspects of its criminal justice system'.[159]

By contrast, one of the functions that the European Council cannot exercise is to adopt legislative acts. Article 15 TEU is clear on this point: the European Council 'shall not exercise legislative functions'.[160]

4. The Council

The 1957 Rome Treaty had charged the Council with the task of 'ensur[ing] that the objectives set out in this Treaty are attained'.[161] This task involved the exercise of legislative as well as executive functions. And while other institutions would be involved in these functions, the Council was to be the central institution within the European Union. This has dramatically changed with the rise of two rival institutions. On one side, the ascendancy of the European Parliament has limited the Council's legislative role within the Union. On the other side, the rise of the European Council has restricted the Council's executive powers. Today, the Council is best characterised as the 'federal' chamber within the Union legislature. It is the organ in which national ministers meet.

What is the composition of this federal chamber, and what is its internal structure? How will the Council decide – by unanimity or qualified majority?

---

[152] Article 14 (2) TEU: 'The European Council shall adopt by unanimity, on the initiative of the European Parliament and with its consent, a decision establishing the composition of the European Parliament, respecting the principles referred to in the first subparagraph.'
[153] Article 17 (5) TEU, as well as Article 244 TFEU.
[154] Article 236 TFEU. For a detailed analysis, see: Section 4 below.   [155] Article 18 (1) TEU.
[156] Article 283 (2) TFEU.   [157] Werts, *The European Council* (supra n. 132), 299.
[158] That is: Title V of Part III of the TFEU, Articles 67–89 TFEU.
[159] See Article 82 (3) TFEU: 'Where a member of the Council considers that a draft directive as referred to in paragraph 2 would affect fundamental aspects of its criminal justice system, it may request that the draft directive be referred to the European Council. In that case, the ordinary legislative procedure shall be suspended. After discussion, and in case of a consensus, the European Council shall, within four months of this suspension, refer the draft back to the Council, which shall terminate the suspension of the ordinary legislative procedure.'
[160] Article 15 (1) TEU.   [161] Article 145 EEC.

And what are the powers enjoyed by the Council? This fourth section addresses these questions in four subsections.

(a) The Council: composition and configuration

Within the European Union, the Council is the institution of the Member States. Its intergovernmental character lies in its composition. The Treaty on European Union defines it as follows: 'The Council shall consist of a representative of each Member State at ministerial level, who may commit the government of the Member State in question and cast its vote.'[162] Within the Council, each national minister thus represents the interests of his Member State. These interests may vary depending on the subject matter decided in the Council. And indeed, depending on the subject matter at issue, there are different Council configurations.[163] And for each configuration, a different national minister will be representing his State.[164] While there is thus – legally – but one single Council, there are – politically – ten different Councils.

The existing Council configurations are as follows:

Table 6 Council Configurations

Council Configurations
1 General Affairs
2 Foreign Affairs
3 Economic and Financial Affairs
4 Justice and Home Affairs
5 Employment, Social Policy, Health and Consumer Affairs
6 Competitiveness (Internal Market, Industry and Research)
7 Transport, Telecommunications and Energy
8 Agriculture and Fisheries
9 Environment
10 Education, Youth and Culture

---

[162] Article 16 (2) TEU.

[163] Article 16 (6) TEU: 'The Council shall meet in different configurations, the list of which shall be adopted in accordance with Article 236 of the Treaty on the Functioning of the European Union.' While the European Council has not yet adopted the list, the Council itself was entitled to lay down this list (see Article 4 of the Protocol (No. 36) on Transitional Provisions). This happened with Council Decision 2009/878, [2009] OJ L315/46.

[164] Under the Rome Treaty, the dividing line between the European Council and the Council was not very clear, since the Council could then meet in the formation of Heads of State or Government (cf. A. Dashwood, 'Decision-making at the Summit' [2000] 3 CYELS 79). The illustrious club could thus transform itself – in an instance – from the European Council to the Council. With the Lisbon Treaty, this problem has disappeared as the Treaties no longer expressly call for a Council configuration consisting of the Heads of State or Government.

What is the mandate of each Council configuration? The Treaties only define the task of the first two Council configurations.[165] The 'General Affairs Council' has one upward and one downward task. It must 'prepare and ensure the follow-up to meetings of the European Council'.[166] As regards its 'downward' task, it is charged to 'ensure consistency in the work of the different Council configurations' below the General Affairs Council.[167] The 'Foreign Affairs Council', on the other hand, is required to 'elaborate the Union's external action on the basis of strategic guidelines laid down by the European Council and ensure that the Union's action is consistent'.[168] The thematic scope and functional task of the remaining Council configurations is constitutionally open. They will generally deal with the subjects falling within their nominal ambit.

(b) Internal structure and organs

(i) The Presidency of the Council

The Council has no permanent President. For unlike the European Council, the Council operates in various configurations, and the task of presiding over these different configurations could not be given to one person. One therefore refers to the depersonalised office of the Council 'Presidency' as opposed to the President of the Council.

The Council Presidency is set out in Article 16 (9) TEU: 'The Presidency of Council configurations, other than that of Foreign Affairs, shall be held by Member State representatives in the Council on the basis of equal rotation.' The Council Presidency is thus a *rotating* presidency. The modalities of the rotating presidency have changed with time. Originally, a single Member State held it for six months. This has given way to 'troika presidencies'. The Lisbon Treaty codifies these team presidencies. The Council Presidency 'shall be held by pre-established groups of three Member States for a period of eighteen months'.[169] And within the team of three States, each member of the group shall chair the respective Council configurations for a period of six months.[170] The great exception to the rotating presidency in the Council is the 'Foreign Affairs Council'. Here, the Treaty contains a special rule in Article 18 TEU – dealing with the office of the High Representative of the Union for Foreign

---

[165] Article 16 (6) TEU.
[166] *Ibid*. For detailed rules on this task of the General Affairs Council, see: Article 2 (3) Council Rules of Procedure.
[167] Article 16 (6) TEU.   [168] *Ibid*.
[169] European Council Decision 2009/ 881 on the Exercise of the Presidency of the Council, [2009] OJ L315/50, Article 1 (1).
[170] *Ibid*., Article 1 (2). For a list of team presidencies, see: Council Decision 2009/908 Laying Down Measures for the Implementation of the European Council Decision on the Exercise of the Presidency of the Council, and on the Chairmanship of Preparatory Bodies of the Council, [2009] OJ L322/28. Extracts of the Council list can be found in Annex 6 of this book.

Affairs and Security Policy. 'The High Representative shall preside over the Foreign Affairs Council.'[171]

The tasks of the Presidency are twofold. Externally, it is to represent the Council.[172] Internally, it is to prepare and chair the Council meetings. The team presidency is thereby charged to write a 'draft programme' for eighteen months.[173] The individual Member State to hold office shall further establish 'draft agendas for Council meetings scheduled for the next six-month period' on the basis of the Council's draft programme.[174] Finally, the (relevant) chair of each Council configuration shall draw up the 'provisional agenda for each meeting'.[175] And while the Council will need to approve the agenda at the beginning of each meeting,[176] the power to set the provisional agenda is remarkable. The provisional agenda must thereby have the following form:

> The provisional agenda shall be divided into two parts, dealing respectively with deliberations on the legislative and non-legislative activities. The first part shall be entitled 'Legislative deliberations' and the second 'Non-legislative activities'. The items appearing in each part of the provisional agenda shall be divided into A items and B items. Items for which approval by the Council is possible without discussion shall be entered as A items[.][177]

The 'A items' constitute the vast majority of the agenda items.[178] They are effectively decided by the Council's committees, in particular the Committee of Permanent Representatives – to which we shall now turn.

(ii) 'Coreper' and specialised committees

The Council has, like the Parliament, developed committees to assist it. From the very beginning, a committee composed of representatives of the Member States would support the Council.[179] That committee was made permanent under the Rome Treaty.[180] The resultant 'Committee of *Permanent*

---

[171] Article 18 (3) TEU. According to Article 2 (5) Council Rules of Procedure, the High Representative may, however, 'ask to be replaced by the member of that configuration representing the Member State holding the six-monthly presidency of the Council'.

[172] Article 26 Council Rules of Procedure: 'The Council shall be represented before the European Parliament or its committees by the Presidency or, with the latter's agreement, by a member of the pre-established group of three Member States referred to in Article 1(4), by the following Presidency or by the Secretary-General.'

[173] *Ibid.*, Article 2 (6).   [174] *Ibid.*, Article 2 (7).   [175] *Ibid.*, Article 3 (1).

[176] *Ibid.*, Article 3 (7).   [177] *Ibid.*, Article 3 (6).

[178] According to F. Hayes-Renshaw and H. Wallace, *The Council of Ministers* (Palgrave, 2006), 77, some 85 per cent will be an 'A item'.

[179] The Committee beneath the ECSC Council was called 'Commission de Coordination du Conseil des Ministres' (Cocor). Its members were not permanently residing in Brussels.

[180] The Rome Treaty contained, unlike the Paris Treaty, an express legal basis for a Council Committee in Article 151 EEC: 'The Council shall adopt its rules of procedure. These rules of procedure may provide for the setting up of a committee consisting of representatives of the Member States.' While the provision did not expressly mention that these representatives would be permanent representatives, this had been the intention of the Member States (E. Noel, 'The Committee of Permanent Representatives' [1967] 5 *Journal of Common Market Studies* 219).

Representatives' became known under its French acronym: 'Coreper'. The Permanent Representative is the ambassador of a Member State at the European Union. S/he is based in the national 'Permanent Representation to the European Union'. Coreper has two parts: Coreper II represents the meeting of the ambassadors, while Coreper I – against all intuition – represents the meetings of their deputies. Both parts correspond to particular Council configurations. Coreper II prepares the first four Council configurations – that is the more important political decisions; whereas Coreper I prepares the more technical remainder.

The function of Coreper is vaguely defined in the Treaties: 'A Committee of Permanent Representatives of the Governments of the Member States shall be responsible for preparing the work of the Council.'[181] The abstract definition has been – somewhat – specified in the following way: 'All items on the agenda for a Council meeting shall be examined in advance by Coreper unless the latter decides otherwise. Coreper shall endeavour to reach agreement at its level to be submitted to the Council for adoption.'[182] In order to achieve that task, Coreper has set up 'working parties' below it.[183] (These working parties are composed of national civil servants operating on instructions from national ministries.) Where Coreper reaches agreement, the point will be classed as an 'A item' that will be rubberstamped by the Council. Where it fails to agree in advance, a 'B item' will need to be expressly discussed by the ministers in the Council. (But importantly, even for 'A items', Coreper is not formally entitled to take decisions itself. It merely 'prepares' and facilitates formal decision-making in the Council.)

The Treaties also acknowledge a number of specialised Council committees that complement Coreper. These committees are (primarily) advisory bodies. Five will be mentioned here. First, there is the 'Political and Security Committee' (PSC) established in the context of the Common Foreign and Security Policy.[184] According to the Treaties, it shall inter alia 'monitor the international situation' and 'contribute to the definition of policies by delivering opinions to the Council'.[185] The Committee has become so important that the Member State representative delegated to it has become the third person with ambassadorial rank within the Permanent Representations. Second, there exists the 'Article 207 Committee'. The latter receives its name from the article under which it is established. Article 207 TFEU stipulates that in international

The Merger Treaty formally established the Committee of Permanent Representatives (*ibid.*, Article 4).

[181] Article 16 (7) TEU and Article 240 (1) TFEU. See also: Article 19 of the Council Rules of Procedure.
[182] Article 19 (2) Council Rules of Procedure.
[183] *Ibid.*, Article 19 (3). Under this paragraph, the General Secretariat is under an obligation to produce a list of these preparatory bodies. For a recent version of this list, see: General Secretariat of the Council of the European Union, 20 July 2010, POLGEN 115.
[184] Cf. Article 38 TEU. See also: Council Decision 2001/78 Setting up the Political and Security Committee, [2001] OJ L27/1.
[185] Article 38 TEU.

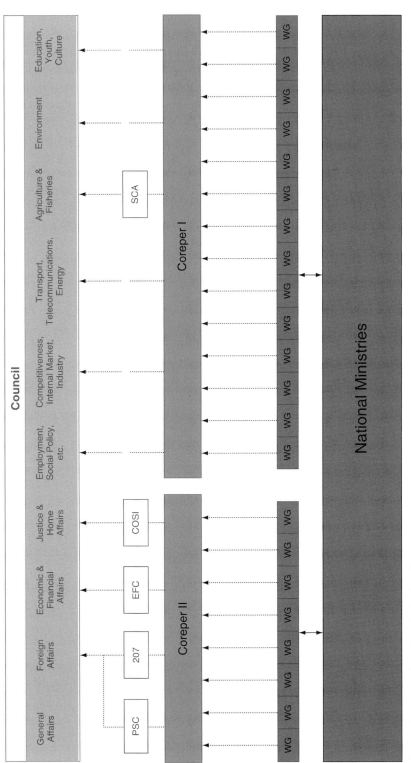

Figure 6 Preparatory Committees to the Council

negotiations between the European Union and third countries, the '[t]he Commission shall conduct these negotiations in consultation with a special committee appointed by the Council to assist the Commission'.[186] The following three committees deal with internal policies. A specialised Council committee is set up in the context of economic and monetary policy. The Economic and Financial Committee (EFC) is to 'promote coordination of the policies of Member States'.[187] Furthermore, '[a] standing committee shall be set up within the Council in order to ensure that operational cooperation on internal security is promoted and strengthened within the Union'.[188] This has happened recently.[189] There are also specialised committees with regard to Coreper I, the most important of which is the 'Special Committee on Agriculture' (SCA).

(iii) *Excursus*: the High Representative of Foreign Affairs and Security Policy

To help the Council Presidency within the Common Foreign and Security Policy, the Treaty of Amsterdam had added an 'assistant' office: the High Representative for the Common Foreign Security Policy (CFSP).[190] The Lisbon Treaty has changed its name into High Representative for *Foreign Affairs* and Security Policy. That change of name was designed to indicate a crucial institutional innovation: the 'personal union' of the (old) High Representative and the External Relations Commissioner. (This 'personal union' has not merged the two offices. It simply demands that the same person must hold *two* offices at once. Put colloquially, s/he will have to wear two institutional 'hats'.)

The High Representative shall conduct the Union's CFSP and chair the Foreign Affairs Council. In this capacity, s/he is subordinate to the Council.[191] The powers of the High Representative are defined in Article 27 TEU. The High Representative shall ensure the implementation of the decisions adopted by the European Council and the Council and make proposals for the

---

[186] Article 207 (3) TFEU.   [187] Article 134 (1) TFEU.   [188] Article 71 TFEU.

[189] Cf. Council Decision 2010/131 on setting up the Standing Committee on operational cooperation on internal security (COSI), [2010] OJ L52/50. According to Article 1: 'The Standing Committee on operational cooperation on internal security (hereinafter referred to as "the Standing Committee") foreseen in Article 71 of the Treaty is hereby set up within the Council.' Its tasks are defined in Article 3, whose first paragraph reads: 'the Standing Committee shall facilitate and ensure effective operational cooperation and coordination under Title V of Part Three of the Treaty, including in areas covered by police and customs cooperation and by authorities responsible for the control and protection of external borders.' 'It shall also cover, where appropriate, judicial cooperation in criminal matters relevant to operational cooperation in the field of internal security.'

[190] Cf. Article 18 (3) (old) EU: 'The Presidency shall be assisted by the Secretary-General of the Council who shall exercise the function of High Representative for the common foreign and security policy.'

[191] Cf. Article 18 (2) TEU: 'as mandated by the Council'. As the High Representative is also the Commissioner for External Relations, she or he will be subordinate to the Commission President. According to Article 18 (4) TEU (emphasis added): 'In exercising these responsibilities within the Commission, and only for these responsibilities, the High Representative shall be bound by Commission procedures *to the extent that this is consistent with paragraphs 2 and 3*.'

development of that policy.[192] The High Representative will represent the Union for CFSP matters and shall express the Union's position in international organisations.[193] And to help fulfil her mandate, the High Representative will be assisted by the – newly created – European External Action Service (EEAS).[194] This is the diplomatic corps of the European Union.

(c) Decision-making and voting

The Council must – physically – meet in Brussels to make decisions.[195] The meetings are divided into two parts: one dealing with legislative activities, the other with non-legislative activities. When discussing legislation, the Council must meet in public.[196] The Commission will attend Council meetings.[197] However, it is not a formal member of the Council and is thus not entitled to vote. The quorum within the Council is as low as it is theoretical: a majority of the members of the Council are required to enable the Council to vote.[198]

Decision-making in the Council will take place in two principal forms: unanimity voting and majority voting. Unanimity voting requires the consent of all national ministers and is required in the Treaties for sensitive political questions.[199] Majority voting, however, represents the constitutional norm. The Treaties here distinguish between a simple and a qualified majority. 'Where it is required to act by a simple majority, the Council shall act by a majority of its component members.'[200] This form of majority vote is rare.[201] The constitutional default is indeed the qualified majority: 'The Council shall act by a qualified majority except where the Treaties provide otherwise.'[202]

---

[192] Article 27 (1) TEU.   [193] Article 27 (2) TEU.

[194] Article 27 (3) TEU. The EEAS was established by Council Decision 2010/426 establishing the organisation and functioning of the European External Action Service, [2010] OJ L 201/30. On the establishment of the EEAS, see: P. Koutrakos, 'Habemus European External Action Service' [2010] 35 EL Rev 608, and B. van Vooren, 'A Legal-Institutional Perspective on the European External Action Service' [2011] 48 CML Rev 475.

[195] However, there exists an 'ordinary' and a 'simplified' written procedure established by Article 12 Council Rules of Procedure.

[196] Article 16 (8) TEU and Article 5 (1). According to Article 8, the deliberation of a non-legislative proposal must also be in public where 'an important new proposal' is at stake (*ibid.*, para.1). Importantly, Article 9 demands that 'the results of votes and explanations of votes by Council members', and the minutes, must always be made public.

[197] According to Article 5 (2) Council Rules of Procedure, the Council may however decide to deliberate without the Commission.

[198] *Ibid.*, Article 11 (4).

[199] Important examples of sensitive political issues still requiring unanimity are foreign affairs (cf. Chapter 6 – Section 3(a) below), and 'the harmonisation of legislation concerning turnover taxes, excise duties and other forms of indirect taxation' (see Article 113 TFEU).

[200] Article 238 (1) TFEU.

[201] For example, Article 150 TFEU. Most matters that allow for simple majority are (internal) procedural or institutional matters.

[202] Article 16 (3) TEU.

Table 7 Weighted Votes System within the Council

Member States: Votes	
Germany, France, Italy, United Kingdom	29
Spain, Poland	27
Romania	14
Netherlands	13
Belgium, Czech Republic, Greece, Hungary, Portugal	12
Austria, Bulgaria, Sweden	10
Denmark, Ireland, Lithuania, Slovakia, Finland	7
Cyprus, Estonia, Latvia, Luxembourg, Slovenia	4
Malta	3

Qualified Majority: 255/345

What constitutes a qualified majority of Member States in the Council? This has been one of the most controversial constitutional concepts in the European Union. From the very beginning, the Treaties had instituted a system of *weighted votes*. Member States would thus not be 'sovereign equals' in the Council, but would possess a number of votes that correlated with the size of their population. The system of weighted votes that applies today is set out in Table 7.

The weighting of votes is to some extent 'degressively proportional'. Indeed, the voting ratio between the biggest and the smallest state is ten to one – a ratio that is roughly similar to the degressively proportionate system for the European Parliament. However, the voting system also represents a system of symbolic compromises. For example: the four biggest Member States are all given the same number of votes – despite Germany's significantly greater demographic magnitude.[203]

In the past, this system of weighted votes has been attacked from two sides: namely from the smaller Member States as well as the bigger Member States. The smaller Member States have claimed that it favours the bigger Member States and have insisted that the 255 votes must be cast by a majority of the States. The bigger Member States, by contrast, have complained that the weighting unduly favours smaller Member States and have insisted on the political safeguard that the 255 votes cast in the Council correspond to 62 per cent of the total population of the Union. With these two qualifications taken into account, decision-making in the Council demands a *triple* majority: a *majority* of the weighted votes must be cast by a *majority* of the Member States representing a *majority* of the Union population.

---

[203] According to the Union's official census figures (see Council Decision 2010/795, [2010] OJ L 338/47), the German population exceeds that of France – the second most populous State of the Union – by about seventeen million people.

This triple majority system will govern decision-making in the Union until 2014. From 1 November 2014 a completely new system of voting is to apply in the Council. This revolutionary change is set out in Article 16 (4) TEU:

> As from 1 November 2014, a qualified majority shall be defined as at least 55 per cent of the members of the Council, comprising at least fifteen of them and representing Member States comprising at least 65 per cent of the population of the Union. A blocking minority must include at least four Council members, failing which the qualified majority shall be deemed attained. The other arrangements governing the qualified majority are laid down in Article 238(2) of the Treaty on the Functioning of the European Union.[204]

This new Lisbon voting system abolishes the system of weighted votes in favour of a system that grants each State a single vote. In a Union of twenty-seven States, 55 per cent of the Council members correspond to fifteen States. But this majority is again qualified from two sides. The bigger Member States have insisted on a relatively high population majority behind the State majority. The population threshold of 65 per cent of the Union population would mean that any three of the four biggest States of the Union could block a Council decision. The smaller Member States have thus insisted on a qualification of the qualification. A qualified majority will be 'deemed attained', where fewer than four States try to block a Council decision.

The new Lisbon system of qualified majority voting is designed to replace the triple majority with a simpler double majority.[205] And yet the Member States – always fearful of abrupt changes – have agreed on two constitutional compromises that cushion the new system of qualified majority voting. First, the Member States have revived the 'Ioannina Compromise'.[206] This was envisaged in a 'Declaration on Article 16 (4)',[207] and is now codified in a Council

---

[204] The Treaty recognises an express exception to this in Article 238 (2) TFEU, which states: 'By way of derogation from Article 16(4) of the Treaty on European Union, as from 1 November 2014 and subject to the provisions laid down in the Protocol on transitional provisions, where the Council does not act on a proposal from the Commission or from the High Representative of the Union for Foreign Affairs and Security Policy, the qualified majority shall be defined as at least 72 per cent of the members of the Council, representing Member States comprising at least 65 per cent of the population of the Union.'

[205] However, the 'Protocol on Transitional Provision' grants any Member State the right to choose between the 'old' Community and the 'new' Union system of voting in the period between 1 November 2014 and 31 March 2017 (*ibid.*, Article 3 (2)). See also: Declaration (No. 7) on Article 16(4) of the Treaty on European Union and Article 238(2) of the Treaty on the Functioning of the European Union, in particular (draft) Articles 1–3.

[206] The compromise was negotiated by the Member States' foreign ministers in Ioannina (Greece) – from where it takes its name. The compromise was designed to smooth the transition from the Union of twelve to a Union of fifteen Member States.

[207] Declaration (No. 7) on Article 16 (4) (supra n. 205) contains a draft Council Decision. And in order to protect their voting rights, the Member States have even insisted on Protocol (No. 9) on the Decision of the Council relating to the implementation of Article 16 (4) TEU and Article 238 (2) TFEU between 1 November 2014 and 31 March 2017 on the one hand, and as from 1 April 2017 on the other. The sole article of the Protocol states: 'Before the examination by the Council of any draft which would aim either at amending or abrogating the Decision or any of its

Decision.[208] According to the Ioannina Compromise, the Council is under an obligation – despite the formal existence of the double majority in Article 16 (4) TEU – to continue deliberations, where a fourth of the States or States representing a fifth of the Union population oppose a decision.[209] The Council is here under the procedural duty to 'do all in its power' to reach – within a reasonable time – 'a satisfactory solution' to address the concerns by the blocking Member States.[210]

This soft mechanism is complemented by a hard mechanism to limit qualified majority voting in the Council. For the Treaties also recognise – regionally limited – versions of the 'Luxembourg Compromise'.[211] A patent illustration of this can be found in the context of the Union's Common Foreign and Security Policy. This contains the following provision: 'If a member of the Council declares that, for vital and stated reasons of national policy, it intends to oppose the adoption of a decision to be taken by qualified majority, a vote shall not be taken.'[212] And even if the matter may be referred to the European Council,[213] that body will decide by unanimity.[214] A Member State can thus unilaterally block a Union decision on what it deems to be its vital interest.[215]

(d) Functions and powers

The Treaties summarise the functions and powers of the Council as follows: 'The Council shall, jointly with the European Parliament, exercise legislative and budgetary functions. It shall carry out policy-making and coordinating functions as laid down in the Treaties.'[216]

Let us look at each of these four functions. First, traditionally, the Council has been at the core of the Union's legislative function. Prior to the rise of the European Parliament, the Council indeed was the Union 'legislator'. The Council is today only a co-legislator, that is: a branch of the bicameral Union legislature.[217] And like Parliament, it must exercise its legislative function in

---

provisions, or at modifying indirectly its scope or its meaning through the modification of another legal act of the Union, the European Council shall hold a preliminary deliberation on the said draft, acting by consensus in accordance with Article 15(4) of the Treaty on European Union.'

[208] The Council formally adopted the decision in 2007 (see Council Decision 2009/857, [2009] OJ L314/73).

[209] *Ibid.*, Article 4.   [210] *Ibid.*, Article 5.

[211] On the 'Luxembourg Compromise', see: Chapter 1 – Section 2(b) above.

[212] Article 31 (2) TEU.

[213] On the appeal function of the European Council, see: Section 3(b) above.

[214] Article 31 (2) TEU.

[215] For example, see: Article 48 TFEU in the context of the free movement of workers and important aspects of a Member State's social security system. The provision states: 'Where a member of the Council declares that a draft legislative act referred to in the first subparagraph would affect important aspects of its social security system, including its scope, cost or financial structure, or would affect the financial balance of that system, it may request that the matter be referred to the European Council.'

[216] Article 16 (1) TEU.   [217] On this point, see: Chapter 5 – Section 3(a) below.

public.[218] Second, Council and Parliament also share in the exercise of the budgetary function. Third: what about the policy-making function? In this respect, the European Council has overtaken the Council. The former now decides on the general policy choices, and the role of the Council has consequently been limited to specific policy choices that implement the general ones.[219] Yet, these choices remain significant and the Council Presidency will set 'its' agenda.[220] Fourth, the Council has significant coordinating functions within the European Union. Thus, in the context of general economic policy, the Member States are required to 'regard their economic policies as a matter of common concern and shall coordinate them within the Council'.[221] The idea of an 'open method of coordination' indeed experienced a renaissance in the last decade.[222]

In addition to the four functions mentioned in Article 16 TEU, two additional functions must be added. First, the Council is still the dominant institution when it comes to the conclusion of international agreements between the European Union and third countries.[223] Second, it can – occasionally – still act as the Union's executive branch. The Union can delegate implementing powers to the Council 'in duly justified specific cases' in any area of European law.[224] From a constitutional viewpoint, the exercise of the executive function by the Council is highly problematic. For how can a part of the Union legislature exercise executive functions? This very possibility interferes with a foundational principle of modern constitutionalism: the separation of powers principle.

---

[218] Article 16 (8) TEU.

[219] On this point, in the context of external relations, see: Chapter 6 – Section 3(a) below.

[220] For a soft expression of this power, see: Article 241 TFEU that entitles the Council to request the Commission to undertake studies and to submit any appropriate legislative proposals.

[221] Article 121 (1) TFEU.

[222] On the open method of coordination, see: G. de Búrca, 'The Constitutional Challenge of New Governance in the European Union' [2003] 28 EL Rev 814.

[223] On this point, see: Chapter 6 – Section 3(b) below.   [224] Article 291 (2) TFEU.

4

Governmental Structure: Union Institutions II

Contents

1.	The Commission	116
	(a) Composition and structure	117
	(i) The President and 'his' college	118
	(ii) The Commission's administrative organs	119
	(b) Decision-making within the Commission	122
	(c) Functions and powers of the Commission	123
	(d) *Excursus*: European Agencies and the Commission	125
2.	The Court of Justice of the European Union	128
	(a) Judicial architecture: the European court system	129
	(i) The Court of Justice: composition and structure	130
	(ii) The General Court: composition and structure	131
	(iii) *Excursus*: the Advocates General	132
	(iv) The 'specialised court(s)': the Civil Service Tribunal	134
	(b) The judicial procedure(s)	135
	(c) Judicial reasoning: methods of interpretation	136
	(d) Jurisdiction and judicial powers	138
3.	The European Central Bank	139
	(a) The special status of the ECB	140
	(b) Organs and administrative structure	142
	(c) Internal divisions and decision-making	143
	(d) Functions and powers	144
4.	The Court of Auditors	145
	Conclusion	147

1. The Commission

The technocratic character of the early European Union expressed itself in the name of a fourth institution: the Commission. The Commission constituted the centre of the European Coal and Steel Community, where it was 'to ensure that the objectives set out in [that] Treaty [were] attained'.[1] In the European Union, the role of the Commission was, however, 'marginalised' by the Parliament and the Council. With these two institutions constituting the Union legislature, the Commission is now firmly located in the executive branch. In guiding the European Union, it – partly – acts like the Union's government (in the strict sense of the term). This section analyses the composition and structure of the Commission, before looking at its internal decision-making procedures. The functions and powers of the Commission will be discussed next, before an excursus briefly presents European Agencies as auxiliary organs of the Commission.

(a) Composition and structure

The Commission consists of one national of each Member State.[2] Its members are chosen 'on the ground of their general competence and European commitment from persons whose independence is beyond doubt'.[3] The Commission's term of office is five years.[4] During this term, it must be 'completely independent'. Its members 'shall neither seek nor take instructions from any Government or other institution, body, office or entity'.[5] The Member States are under a duty to respect this independence.[6] Breach of the duty of independence may lead to a Commissioner being 'compulsorily retired'.[7]

---

[1] Article 8 ECSC.

[2] Article 17 (4) TEU. The Lisbon Treaty textually limits this principle in a temporal sense: it will theoretically only apply until 31 October 2014. Thereafter, Article 17 (5) TEU states: 'As from 1 November 2014, the Commission shall consist of a number of members, including its President and the High Representative of the Union for Foreign Affairs and Security Policy, corresponding to two-thirds of the number of Member States, unless the European Council, acting unanimously, decides to alter this number.' The reduced Commission composition would be based on 'a system of strictly equal rotation between the Member States, reflecting the demographic and geographical range of all the Member States' (ibid., and see also: Article 244 TFEU). This provision had been a centrepiece of the Lisbon Treaty, as it was designed to increase the effectiveness of the Commission by decreasing its membership. However, after the failure of the first Irish ratification referendum, the European Council decided to abandon this constitutional reform in order to please the Irish electorate; see Presidency Conclusions of 11–12 December 2008 (Document 17271/1/08 Rev 1), para. 2: 'On the composition of the Commission, the European Council recalls that the Treaties currently in force require that the number of Commissioners be reduced in 2009. The European Council agrees that provided that the Treaty of Lisbon enters into force, a decision will be taken, in accordance with the necessary legal procedures, to the effect that the Commission shall continue to include one national of each Member State.' According to the Conclusions, the decision of the European Council will be translated into a (future) Protocol to be attached to the Treaties. The fate of Article 17 (5) TEU is the best illustration of the worst dependence of the Union on individual Member States. The unanimity requirement for Treaty amendment makes even the most intelligent Union reform dependent on unintelligible national desires. On the various guarantees given to Ireland before the second referendum, see: J.-C. Piris, *The Lisbon Treaty: A Legal and Political Analysis* (Cambridge University Press, 2010), 51–60.

[3] Article 17 (3) TEU.   [4] *Ibid.*   [5] *Ibid.*   [6] Article 245 TFEU – first indent.

[7] Article 245 TFEU – second indent. See also Article 247 TFEU: 'If any Member of the Commission no longer fulfils the conditions required for the performance of his duties or if he has been guilty of serious misconduct, the Court of Justice may, on application by the Council acting by a simple

But how is the Commission selected? Originally, the Commission was 'appointed'.[8] The appointment procedure has subsequently given way to an election procedure. This election procedure has two stages. In a first stage, the President of the Commission will be elected. The President will thereby be nominated by the European Council '[t]aking into account the elections to the European Parliament', that is: in accordance with the latter's political majority.[9] The nominated candidate must then be 'elected' by the European Parliament. If not confirmed by Parliament, a new candidate needs to be found by the European Council.[10] With the election of the Commission President begins the second stage of the selection process. By common accord with the President, the Council will adopt a list of candidate Commissioners on the basis of suggestions made by the Member States.[11] With the list being agreed, the proposed Commission is subjected 'as a body to a vote of consent by the European Parliament', and on the basis of this election, the Commission shall be appointed by the European Council.[12] This complex and compound selection process constitutes a mixture of 'international' and 'national' elements. The Commission's democratic legitimacy thus derives partly from the Member States, and partly from the European Parliament.

(i) The President and 'his' college

Whereas the Presidents of the Parliament and the Council are selected from 'within' the institution,[13] the Commission President helps in the selection of 'his' institution. This position as the 'Chief' Commissioner *above* 'his' college is clearly established by the Treaties.[14] 'The Members of the Commission shall carry out the duties devolved upon them by the President *under his authority*.'[15] In light of this political authority, the Commission is typically called after its President.[16]

The powers of the President are identified in Article 17 (6) TEU, which reads:

The President of the Commission shall:

(a) lay down guidelines within which the Commission is to work;
(b) decide on the internal organisation of the Commission, ensuring that it acts consistently, efficiently and as a collegiate body;

---

majority or the Commission, compulsorily retire him.' On the replacement procedure, see: Article 246 TFEU.

[8] Articles 9 and 10 ECSC.

[9] The terms of the Commission run in parallel with that of the Parliament.

[10] Article 17 (7) TEU – first indent.   [11] Article 17 (7) TEU – second indent.

[12] Article 17 (7) TEU – third indent.

[13] The same is true for the Court, see: Section 2(a) below. As regards the European Council, its President is also elected 'by' the institution, albeit not from 'within' the institution.

[14] N. Nugent, *The European Commission* (Palgrave, 2000), 68: 'The Commission President used to be thought of as *primus inter pares* in the College. Now, however, he is very much *primus*.'

[15] Article 248 TFEU (emphasis added).

[16] For example: the current Commission is called the (second) 'Barroso Commission'.

(c) appoint Vice-Presidents, other than the High Representative of the Union for Foreign Affairs and Security Policy, from among the members of the Commission.

A member of the Commission shall resign if the President so requests. The High Representative of the Union for Foreign Affairs and Security Policy shall resign, in accordance with the procedure set out in Article 18(1), if the President so requests.

The three powers of the President mentioned are formidable. First, s/he can lay down the political direction of the Commission in the form of strategic guidelines. This will normally happen at the beginning of a President's term of office.[17] The Presidential guidelines will subsequently be translated into the Commission's Annual Work Programme.[18] Second, the President is entitled to decide on the internal organisation of the Commission.[19] In the words of the Treaties: '[T]he responsibilities incumbent upon the Commission shall be structured and allocated among its members by its President.' The President is authorised to 'reshuffle the allocation of those responsibilities during the Commission's term of office',[20] and may even ask a Commissioner to resign. Third, the President can appoint Vice-Presidents from 'within' the Commission. Finally, there is a fourth power not expressly mentioned in Article 17 (6) TEU: 'The President shall represent the Commission.'[21]

What are the 'ministerial' responsibilities into which the present Commission is structured? Due to the requirement of one Commissioner per Member State, the (second) 'Barroso Commission' had to divide the tasks of the European Union into twenty-six (!) 'portfolios'. Reflecting the priorities of the Union's current President, they are as set out in Table 8.

Each Commissioner is responsible for his portfolio. Members of the Commission will thereby be assisted by their own cabinet.[22] And each cabinet will have an administrative head or *chef de cabinet*.

(ii) The Commission's administrative organs

The Commission has, just like the Parliament and the Council, an administrative infrastructure supporting the work of the College of Commissioners.

---

[17] On this, see: Chapter 7 – Section 1(a) below.

[18] For the Commission's Work Programme for 2011, see: *ibid*.

[19] Due to its dual constitutional role, some special rules apply to the High Representative of the Union. Not only do the Treaties determine the latter's role within the Commission, the President will not be able *unilaterally* to ask for his or her resignation (cf. Article 18 (4) TEU: 'The High Representative shall be one of the Vice-Presidents of the Commission. He shall ensure the consistency of the Union's external action. He shall be responsible within the Commission for responsibilities incumbent on it in external relations and for coordinating other aspects of the Union's external action.')

[20] Article 248 TFEU.   [21] Article 3 (5) Commission Rules of Procedure.

[22] Article 19 (1) Commission Rules of Procedure: 'Members of the Commission shall have their own cabinet to assist them in their work and in preparing Commission decisions. The rules governing the composition and operation of the cabinets shall be laid down by the President.'

Table 8 Commission College: President and Portfolios

	President
Agriculture and Rural Development	Health and Consumer Policy
Climate Action	Home Affairs
Competition	Industry and Entrepreneurship
Development	Inter-Institutional Relations and Administration
Digital Agenda	Internal Market and Services
Economic and Monetary Affairs	International Cooperation, Humanitarian Aid and Crisis Response
Education, Culture, Multilingualism and Youth	Justice, Fundamental Rights and Citizenship
Employment, Social Affairs and Inclusion	Maritime Affairs and Fisheries
Energy	Regional Policy
Enlargement and European Neighbourhood Policy	Research, Innovation and Science
Environment	Taxation and Customs Union, Audit and Anti-Fraud
Financial Programming and Budget	Trade
Foreign Affairs and Security Policy	Transport

The administrative substructure is designed to 'assist' the Commission 'in the preparation and performance of its task, and in the implementation of its priorities and the political guidelines laid down by the President'.[23] It is divided into 'Directorates-General' and 'Services'. The former are specialised in specific policy areas and thus operate 'vertically'. The latter operate 'horizontally' in providing specialised services across all policy areas.[24]

The best way to understand 'Directorates-General' is to consider them as the supranational equivalent of national ministries. Staffed with European civil servants, there are presently twenty-seven Directorates-General. Importantly, these Directorates-General do not necessarily correspond with one 'Commissioner portfolio'. While there is a direct correspondence in some areas, some Commissioner portfolios cut across the subject matter of two or even more Directorates-General. Commissioners are entitled to 'give instructions' to their Directorate(s)-General, with the latter being obliged to 'provide

---

[23] Article 21 Commission Rules of Procedure.

[24] This section will not look at the various services. The Commission distinguishes between 'General Services' (like the 'Secretariat General'), and 'Internal Services' (like the 'Legal Service' of the Commission). The functions of the former are set out in Article 23 (5) Commission Rules of Procedure. The functions of the latter are defined by Article 23 (4) Commission Rules of Procedure.

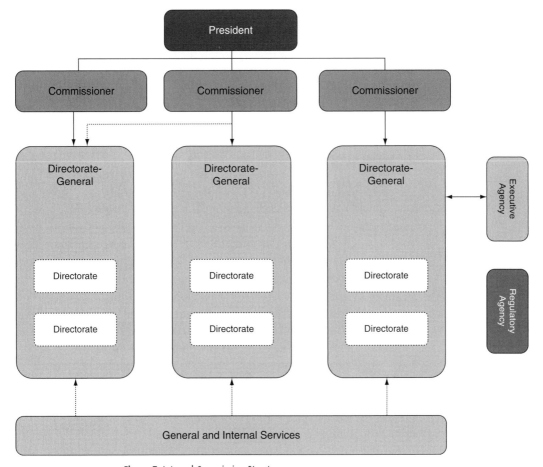

Figure 7 Internal Commission Structure

them with all the information on their area of activity necessary for them to exercise their responsibilities'.[25]

What is the structure *within* a Directorate-General? Each Directorate-General is headed by a Director-General, who represents the main contact between the Commission administration and the respective Commissioner(s). Each Directorate-General is divided into directorates, and each directorate is divided into units.[26] Units are headed by a Head of Unit and constitute the elementary organisational entity within the Commission administration.[27]

---

[25] Article 19 (2) Commission Rules of Procedure.
[26] Article 21 Commission Rules of Procedure – second indent.
[27] For an illustration of the internal structure of one Directorate-General, see Annex 7 of this book.

(b) Decision-making within the Commission

The Commission acts as a 'college', that is: as a collective body. The Treaties offer a single article on decision-making within the Commission: 'The Commission shall act by a majority of its Members.'[28] This is a devilishly simple and misleading picture. It is complemented and corrected by the Commission's Rules of Procedure, which define the various decision-making procedures and their voting arrangements. The Rules distinguish between four procedures: the 'oral procedure', the 'written procedure', the 'empowerment procedure' and the 'delegation procedure'.[29]

The first two procedures require a decision by the College as a *collective* body. The oral procedure stipulates a Commission meeting. Meetings are 'private' and confidential,[30] and take place, as a general rule, at least once a week.[31] Commissioners are required to attend, but the President can release them from this duty in certain circumstances.[32] (However, to be quorate at least half of the Commissioners must be present.[33]) Decisions are principally taken by tacit consensus. However, decisions may be taken by majority vote if that is requested by a member.[34] To save time within the meeting, the Commission Agenda will typically be divided into A-items and B-items.[35] To maximise time even further, the Commission is – under certain circumstances – entitled to dispense with a physical meeting and decide by means of the written procedure.[36] According to this procedure, a draft text is circulated to all Members of the Commission. Each Commissioner is entitled to make known any reservations within a time limit.[37] A decision is subsequently adopted if 'no Member has made or maintained a request for suspension up to the time limit set for the written procedure'.[38]

The oral and the written procedure are based on the principle of 'collegiality', that is, the collective decision-taking of the Commission. By contrast, the third and fourth procedure entitle the Commission to delegate power for the

---

[28] Article 250 TFEU.   [29] Article 4 Commission Rules of Procedure.   [30] *Ibid.*, Article 9.
[31] *Ibid.*, Article 5 (2).   [32] *Ibid.*, Article 5 (3).   [33] *Ibid.*, Article 7.
[34] *Ibid.*, Article 8 (2). Majority in this case requires the majority of its *component* members (*ibid.*, Article 8 (3)).
[35] Two days before the Commission College meets, the Commissioners' 'chiefs of cabinet' meet to discuss and resolve items in advance. The meeting of the 'chiefs of cabinets', which is chaired by the Secretary General of the Commission, thus operates like Coreper for the Council.
[36] Article 12 (1) Commission Rules of Procedure: 'The agreements of the Members of the Commission to a draft text from one or more of its Members may be obtained by means of written procedure, provided that the approval of the Legal Service and the agreement of the departments consulted in accordance with Article 23 of these Rules of Procedure has been obtained. Such approval and/or agreement may be replaced by an agreement between the Members of the Commission where a meeting of the College has decided, on a proposal from the President, to open a finalisation written procedure as provided for in the implementing rules.'
[37] Article 12 (2) Commission Rules of Procedure. Moreover, according to para. 3 '[a]ny Member of the Commission, may, in the course of the written procedure, request that the draft text be discussed'.
[38] *Ibid.*, Article 12 (4).

adoption of 'management or administrative measures' to individual officers. According to the 'empowerment procedure', the College can delegate power to one or more Commissioners.[39] According to the 'delegation procedure', it can even delegate power to a Director-General. While this decentralised form of decision-taking is much more efficient, it doubtless undermines the principle of collegiality behind the Commission. The Court of Justice has therefore insisted on a constitutional balance between the theoretical principle of 'the equal participation of the Members of the Commission in the adoption of decisions' on the one hand,[40] and the practical principle of preventing 'collective deliberation from having a paralysing effect on the full Commission' on the other.[41] It has thus insisted on 'procedural' as well as 'substantive' guarantees for delegations of power. The former requires that the decisions delegating authority are adopted at meetings of the Commission.[42] The latter insists that 'management of administrative measures' are not decisions of principle.[43]

(c) Functions and powers of the Commission

What are the functions and corresponding powers of the Commission in the governmental structure of the European Union? The Treaties provide a concise constitutional overview of its tasks in Article 17 TEU:

> The Commission shall promote the general interest of the Union and take appropriate initiatives to that end. It shall ensure the application of the Treaties, and of measures adopted by the institutions pursuant to them. It shall oversee the application of Union law under the control of the Court of Justice of the European Union. It shall execute the budget and manage programmes. It shall exercise coordinating, executive and management functions, as laid down in the Treaties. With the exception of the common foreign and security policy, and other cases provided for in the Treaties, it shall ensure the Union's external representation. It shall initiate the Union's annual and multiannual programming with a view to achieving interinstitutional agreements.[44]

The provision distinguishes six different functions. The first three functions constitute the Commission's core functions. First, the Commission is tasked to 'promote the general interest of the Union' through initiatives. It is thus to act as a 'motor' of European integration. In order to fulfil this – governmental – function, the Commission is given the (almost) exclusive right to *formally* propose legislative bills.[45]

---

[39] *Ibid.*, Article 13.   [40] Case 5/85, *AKZO Chemie v. Commission*, [1986] ECR 2585, para. 30.

[41] *Ibid.*, para. 31.   [42] *Ibid.*, para. 33.

[43] *Ibid.*, para. 37. In that case the Court of Justice found that a decision ordering an undertaking to submit to an investigation was a preparatory inquiry that was a measure of management (*ibid.*, para. 38). By contrast, in Case C-137/92P, *Commission v. BASF et al.*, [1994] ECR I-2555, the Court held that a decision finding an infringement of Article 114 TFEU was not a management decision (*ibid.*, para. 71).

[44] Article 17 (1) TEU.

[45] We saw above that the Parliament or the Council can informally suggest legislative bills to the Commission. Indeed, the great majority of Commission bills originate outside the Commission (cf. Nugent, *The European Commission* (supra n. 14), 236).

'Union acts may only be adopted on the basis of a Commission proposal, except where the Treaties provide otherwise.'[46] The Commission's prerogative to propose legislation is a fundamental characteristic of the European constitutional order. The right of initiative extends to (multi)annual programming of the Union,[47] and embraces the power to make proposals for law reform.[48]

The second function of the Commission is to '*ensure* the application' of the Treaties. This function covers a number of powers – legislative and executive in nature. The Commission may thus be entitled to apply the Treaties by adopting secondary legislation. This legislation may be adopted directly under the Treaties;[49] or, under powers delegated to the Commission from the Union legislature.[50] In some areas the Commission may be granted the executive power to apply the Treaties itself. The direct enforcement of European law can best be seen in the context of European competition law,[51] where the Commission enjoys significant powers to fine – private or public – wrongdoers. These administrative penalties sanction the non-application of European law.

The third function of the Commission is to act as guardian of the Union. It shall thus '*oversee* the application' of European law. The Treaties indeed grant the Commission significant powers to act as 'police' and 'prosecutor' of the Union. The policing of European law involves the power to monitor and to investigate infringements of European law. The powers are – again – best defined in the context of European competition law.[52] Where an infringement

---

[46] Article 17 (2) TEU. For an exception, see: Article 76 TFEU on legislative measures in the field of police and judicial cooperation in criminal matters.

[47] Under Article 314 (2) TFEU, the Commission is entitled to propose the draft budget: 'The Commission shall submit a proposal containing the draft budget to the European Parliament and to the Council not later than 1 September of the year preceding that in which the budget is to be implemented.'

[48] This is normally done through White Papers or Green Papers. For a famous White Paper, see: EU Commission, *Completing the Internal Market*: White Paper from the Commission to the European Council (COM(85) 310). For a famous Green Paper, see: EU Commission, *Damages Actions for Breach of the EC Antitrust Rules* (COM(2005) 672).

[49] See Article 106 (3) TFEU: 'The Commission shall ensure the application of the provisions of this Article and shall, where necessary, address appropriate directives or decisions to Member States.'

[50] On delegated legislation, see: Chapter 7 – Section 2 below.

[51] Cf. Article 105 (1) TFEU: '[T]he Commission shall ensure the application of the principles laid down in Articles 101 and 102. On application by a Member State or on its own initiative, and in cooperation with the competent authorities in the Member States, which shall give it their assistance, the Commission shall investigate cases of suspected infringement of these principles. If it finds that there has been an infringement, it shall propose appropriate measures to bring it to an end.'

[52] Cf. Regulation 1/2003 on the implementation of the rules on competition laid down in Articles 81 and 82 of the Treaty ([2003] OJ L1/1), Chapter V: 'Powers of Investigation', and in particular Article 17 (1): 'Where the trend of trade between Member States, the rigidity of prices or other circumstances suggest that competition may be restricted or distorted within the common market, the Commission may conduct its inquiry into a particular sector of the economy or into a particular type of agreements across various sectors. In the course of that inquiry, the Commission may request the undertakings or associations of undertakings concerned to supply the information necessary for giving effect to Articles 81 and 82 of the Treaty and may carry out any inspections necessary for that purpose.'

of European law has been identified, the Commission may bring the matter before the Court of Justice. The Treaties thus give the Commission the power to bring infringement proceedings against Member States,[53] and other Union institutions.[54]

The remaining three functions mentioned by Article 17 TEU are less central to the Commission. They can be characterised as budgetary, coordinating and representative functions. First, the Commission shall executive the Union budget,[55] and thus manages most Union programmes. Second, the Commission is tasked – like most other institutions – to coordinate Union activities in some areas.[56] Finally, the Commission shall 'ensure the Union's external representation'. This is a partial and partisan formulation. Indeed, the Commission is not the only external representative of the Union, as it must share this function with the President of the European Council as well as the High Representative of the Union. However, the Treaties do traditionally grant the Commission the power to act as external representative of the Union in the negotiation of international agreements.[57]

(d) *Excursus*: European Agencies and the Commission

With the rise of the 'administrative state',[58] many modern legal orders have had to transfer governmental tasks to bodies not expressly mentioned in their constitutions. The rise of 'agencies' was a significant feature in the constitutional development of the United States in the first half of the last century.[59]

---

[53] Article 258 TFEU: 'If the Commission considers that a Member State has failed to fulfil an obligation under the Treaties, it shall deliver a reasoned opinion on the matter after giving the State concerned the opportunity to submit its observations. If the State concerned does not comply with the opinion within the period laid down by the Commission, the latter may bring the matter before the Court of Justice of the European Union.' For an extensive discussion of this, see: Chapter 8 – Section 3(a) below.

[54] Article 263 TFEU. The provision will be extensively discussed in Chapter 8 – Section 1 below.

[55] Article 317 TFEU – first indent: 'The Commission shall implement the budget in cooperation with the Member States, in accordance with the provisions of the regulations made pursuant to Article 322, on its own responsibility and within the limits of the appropriations, having regard to the principles of sound financial management. Member States shall cooperate with the Commission to ensure that the appropriations are used in accordance with the principles of sound financial management.'

[56] For the Commission's powers of coordination, see for example: Article 168 (2) TFEU in the context of public health: 'The Commission may, in close contact with the Member States, take any useful initiative to promote such coordination, in particular initiatives aiming at the establishment of guidelines and indicators, the organisation of exchange of best practice, and the preparation of the necessary elements for periodic monitoring and evaluation.'

[57] On this point, see: Chapter 6 – Section 3(b) below.

[58] On this point, see: G. Lawson, 'The Rise and Rise of the Administrative State' [1993–94] 107 *Harvard Law Review* 1231.

[59] P. Strauss, 'The Place of Agencies in Government: Separation of Powers and the Fourth Branch' [1984] 84 *Columbia Law Review* 573.

Table 9 (Selected) European Agencies and Decentralised Bodies

(Selected) European Agencies and Decentralised Bodies	
European Fundamental Rights Agency (FRA)	Austria
European Defence Agency (EDA)	Belgium
European Environmental Agency (EEA)	Denmark
European Chemicals Agency (ECHA)	Finland
European Railway Agency (ERA)	France
European Aviation Safety Agency (EASA)	Germany
European Food Safety Authority (EFSA)	Italy
European Police Office (EUROPOL))	Netherlands
European External Border Agency (FRONTEX)	Poland
European Medicines Agency (EMEA)	United Kingdom

The European legal order followed this trend at the end of the twentieth century.[60] For contrary to a widespread and misleading myth, the Commission administration constitutes – compared with State administrations – a small bureaucracy.[61] And despite a healthy growth in personnel over the past decades, the Commission would not be able to achieve all the tasks under the Treaties. The European Union has therefore increasingly created 'European Agencies' to assist the Commission. For a long time these Agencies were not expressly acknowledged by the Treaties. The Lisbon Treaty only partially remedied this. For while Agencies are now mentioned in the Treaties,[62] they still do not properly represent Agencies as a fundamental part of the institutional system of the Union.

What and where are the Union's Agencies? The Agencies of the Union were not created overnight, yet there continues to be a nocturnal air around them. For if they are not expressly mentioned in the Treaties, where did they come from? The answer lies in the fact that they are creatures of secondary European law. The Union has created them by using its own legislative powers.[63] And

---

[60] While a few agencies had already emerged in the 1970s, there has been a real 'agencification' of the European legal order in the 1990s. Today, almost forty European Agencies exist in the most diverse areas of European law. For an inventory and functional typology of European Agencies, see: S. Griller and A. Orator, 'Everything Under Control? The "Way Forward" for European Agencies in the Footsteps of the Meroni Doctrine' [2010] 35 EL Rev 3 at Appendix. See also: E. Chiti, 'An Important Part of the EU's Institutional Machinery: Features, Problems and Perspectives of European Agencies' [2009] 46 CML Rev 1395.

[61] Nugent (supra n. 14), 162: '[T]he Commission employs far fewer people than do the national governments of even the small EU member states.'

[62] For example, Articles 9 and 15 TEU; as well as Article 263 TFEU.

[63] Agencies are typically created on the basis of Article 352 TFEU – the Union's residual power, which will be discussed in Chapter 5 – Section 1(b) below.

while there are severe constitutional limits to what powers can be delegated to European Agencies,[64] the Union has created many of them in the past decades.

What are the functions of European Agencies? Their primary function is to assist the Commission in its task to 'ensure' and 'oversee' the application of European law. Some Agencies are entitled to adopt binding decisions and thus apply European law directly.[65] Other Agencies are to prepare draft legislation for the Commission.[66] Many Agencies are simply information satellites: they are tasked to help the Commission in monitoring a policy area and to collect and coordinate information.[67] These three functions can be combined. This can be seen in the context of the European Aviation Safety Agency established by Regulation 216/2008, which states:

Establishment and functions of the Agency

1. For the purpose of the implementation of this Regulation, a European Aviation Safety Agency shall be established.
2. For the purposes of ensuring the proper functioning and development of civil aviation safety, the Agency shall:
   (a) undertake any task and formulate opinions on all matters covered by Article 1(1);
   (b) assist the Commission by preparing measures to be taken for the implementation of this Regulation. Where these comprise technical rules and in particular rules relating to construction, design and operational aspects, the Commission may not change their content without prior coordination with the Agency. The Agency shall also provide the Commission with the necessary technical, scientific and administrative support to carry out its tasks;
   (c) take the necessary measures within the powers conferred on it by this Regulation or other [Union] legislation;
   (d) conduct inspections and investigations as necessary to fulfil its tasks;
   (e) in its fields of competence, carry out, on behalf of Member States, functions and tasks ascribed to them by applicable international conventions, in particular the Chicago Convention.[68]

---

[64] On this point, see: Chapter 7 – Section 2(a)(i) below.

[65] For example: the European Aviation Safety Agency, see Regulation (EC) No. 216/2008 on common rules in the field of civil aviation and establishing a European Aviation Safety Agency ([2008] OJ L79/1).

[66] For example: the European Medicines Agency, see Regulation 726/2004 laying down Community procedures for the authorisation and supervision of medicinal products for human and veterinary use and establishing a European Medicines Agency ([2004] OJ L136/1). According to the Regulation, the Agency only conducts the preparatory stages of the decision, while the Commission is entitled to take the final decision (*ibid.*, Article 10 (2)).

[67] For example: the European Union Agency for Fundamental Rights, see Regulation 168/2007 establishing a European Union Agency for Fundamental Rights ([2007] OJ L 53/1). For a discussion of the powers and structure of the Agency, see A. von Bogdandy and J. von Bernstorff, 'The EU Fundamental Rights Agency within the European and International Human Rights Architecture: the Legal Framework and some Unsettled Issues in a New Field of Administrative Law' [2009] 46 CML Rev 1035.

[68] Article 17 of Regulation 216/2008 (supra n. 65).

What is the internal structure of a European Agency? And in what ways is it dependent on, or subordinate to, the Commission? The Union legal order has no single answer to these questions. With regard to the structure of Agencies, it generally distinguishes between two types of European Agencies: 'executive' Agencies and 'independent' Agencies. Executive Agencies are subordinate to the Commission and are governed by a single 'Statute'.[69] According to this Statute, executive Agencies fall under the control and responsibility of the Commission,[70] and will have a limited lifetime.[71] They consist of a 'Steering Committee' and a 'Director',[72] which are appointed by the Commission.[73] The Commission is entitled to supervise executive Agencies,[74] and it enjoys the power to 'review' and 'suspend' any of their acts.[75] By contrast, a second class of European Agencies is 'independent' from the Commission. This independence is both structural and functional. Independent Agencies will typically consist of a 'Management Board' composed of one representative of each Member State and one representative of the Commission.[76] They will be headed by an 'Executive Director', who is typically elected by the Management Board on a proposal from the Commission.[77] The Executive Director is, however, required to 'be completely independent in the performance of his/her duties', and this independence translates into a prohibition not to 'seek nor take instructions from any government or from any other body'.[78]

2. The Court of Justice of the European Union

'Tucked away in the fairyland Duchy of Luxembourg',[79] and housed in its 'palace', lies the Court of Justice of the European Union. The Court constitutes the judicial branch of the European Union. It is composed of various courts that are linguistically roofed under the name 'Court of Justice of the European Union'. This includes the 'Court of Justice', the 'General Court' and 'specialised courts'.[80]

The Court's task is to 'ensure that in the interpretation and application of the Treaties the law is observed'.[81] The Court of Justice of the European Union is, however, not the only one to interpret and apply European law.

---

[69] Regulation 58/2003 laying down the Statute for Executive Agencies to be entrusted with certain tasks in the management of Community Programmes ([2003] OJ L11/1).

[70] *Ibid.*, Article 1: 'This Regulation lays down the statute of executive agencies to which the Commission, under its own control and responsibility, may entrust certain tasks relating to the management of [Union] programmes.'

[71] *Ibid.*, Article 3.   [72] *Ibid.*, Article 7.   [73] *Ibid.*, Articles 8 and 10.   [74] *Ibid.*, Article 20.

[75] *Ibid.*, Article 22.

[76] For the European Aviation Safety Agency, see: Regulation 216/2008 (supra n. 65), Article 34. According to its Article 37 the Board will typically decide by a qualified majority.

[77] *Ibid.*, Article 39.   [78] *Ibid.*, Article 38 (1).

[79] E. Stein, 'Lawyers, Judges, and the Making of a Transnational Constitution' [1981] 75 *American Journal of International Law* 1.

[80] Article 19 (1) TEU.   [81] *Ibid.*

From the very beginning, the European legal order intended to recruit national courts in the interpretation and application of European law.[82] From a functional perspective, national courts are thus decentralised 'European' courts. From an institutional perspective, however, they are distinct and there is no institutional bridge from the national courts to the European Court of Justice.[83]

In concentrating on the institution of the Court of Justice of the European Union, the following section will start out by analysing its judicial architecture. Subsections 2 and 3 look inside the judicial process and decision-making, in particular judicial interpretation. Finally, subsection 4 briefly surveys the judicial powers of the Court.

(a) Judicial architecture: the European court system

When the European Union was born, its judicial branch consisted of a single court: the 'Court of Justice'. The (then) Court was a 'one stop shop'. All judicial affairs of the Union would need to pass through its corridors.

With its workload having risen to dizzying heights, the Court pressed the Member States to provide for a judicial 'assistant', and the Member States agreed to create a second court in the Single European Act. This granted the Council the power to 'attach to the Court of Justice a court with jurisdiction to hear and determine at first instance', that was 'subject to a right of appeal to the Court of Justice'.[84] Thanks to this definition, the newly created court was baptised the 'Court of First Instance'.[85] With the Lisbon Treaty, the court has now been renamed as the 'General Court'. The reason for this change of name lies in the fact that the court is no longer confined to first instance cases. Instead, '[t]he General Court shall have jurisdiction to hear and determine actions or proceedings brought against decisions of the specialised courts'.[86] What are the 'specialised courts' in the European Union? The Union has, at present, only one specialised court: the 'Civil Service Tribunal'.[87] And while the Commission had proposed a European 'Patent Court' as a second specialised court,[88] this has not yet been established.

---

[82] On this point, see: Chapter 8 – Section 4 below.
[83] There is no appeal from national courts to the European Courts. On this point, see again: *ibid.*
[84] Article 11 (1) Single European Act.
[85] The Court was set up by Council Decision 88/591 establishing a Court of First Instance of the European Communities ([1988] OJ L319/1).
[86] Article 256 (2) TFEU.
[87] Council Decision 2004/752 establishing the European Union Civil Service Tribunal ([2004] OJ L333/7). See also: N. Lavranos, 'The New Specialised Courts within the European Judicial System' [2005] 30 EL Rev 261.
[88] Commission Proposal for a Council Decision establishing the Community Patent Court and concerning appeals before the Court of First Instance (COM(2003) 828 final). For a discussion of this proposal, see: A. Arnull, *The European Court of Justice* (Oxford University Press, 2006), 151–2.

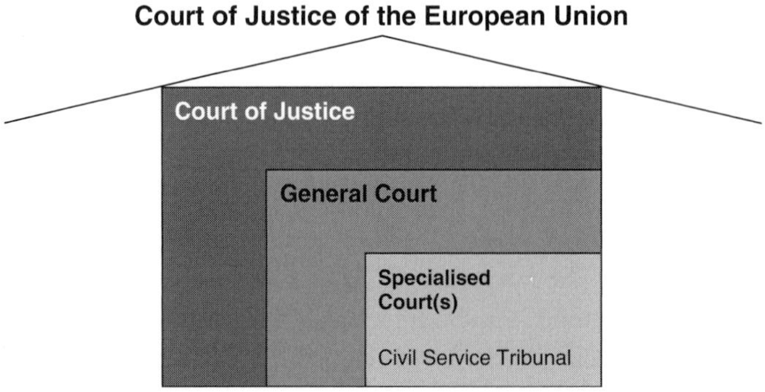

Court of Justice of the European Union

Figure 8 Structure of the Court of Justice of the European Union

The Court of Justice of the European Union has thus a three-tiered system of courts.[89] The architecture of the Union's judicial branch can be seen in Figure 8.

(i) The Court of Justice: composition and structure

'The Court of Justice shall consist of one judge from each Member State.'[90] They 'shall be chosen from persons whose independence is beyond doubt and who possess the qualifications required for appointment to the highest judicial office in their respective countries or who are jurisconsults of recognised competence'.[91] Judges are, however, not unilaterally appointed by their Member State. They are appointed by 'common accord of the governments of the Member States', and only after hearing an independent advisory panel.[92] Judges are indeed not representatives of their Member State and must be completely independent.[93] Their term of appointment is for six years – a relatively short term for judges – that can be renewed.[94] During their term of office they can only be dismissed by a unanimous decision of their peers.[95]

---

[89] In terms of the European Union's judicial reports, there are thus three different prefixes before a case. Cases before the Court of Justice are C-Cases, cases before the General Court are T-Cases (as the French name for the General Court is 'Tribunal'), and cases before the Civil Service Tribunal are F-Cases (stemming from the French 'fonction publique' for civil service).

[90] Article 19 (2) TEU.   [91] Article 253 TFEU.

[92] *Ibid.* According to Article 255 TFEU: 'A panel shall be set up in order to give an opinion on candidates' suitability to perform the duties of Judge and Advocate-General of the Court of Justice and the General Court before the governments of the Member States make the appointments referred to in Articles 253 and 254. The panel shall comprise seven persons chosen from among former members of the Court of Justice and the General Court, members of national supreme courts and lawyers of recognised competence, one of whom shall be proposed by the European Parliament. The Council shall adopt a decision establishing the panel's operating rules and a decision appointing its members. It shall act on the initiative of the President of the Court of Justice.'

[93] For detailed rules, see: Article 4 Court Statute.

[94] Article 253 (4) TFEU: 'Retiring Judges and Advocates-General may be reappointed.' According to paragraph [2]: '[e]very three years there shall be a partial replacement of the Judges and Advocates-General'. The relatively short term hardly constitutes a constitutional guarantee for independence but, as will be seen below, the independence of the Court is guaranteed by other devices, such as the collective and secret decision-making procedure.

[95] Article 6 Court Statute.

The judges compose the Court, but are not identical with it. The Court as a formal institution decides as a collective body, which has its own President. In theory, the principle of collegiality should mean that the Court of Justice only decides in plenary session, that is: as a 'full court' of all judges. However, from the very beginning the Court was entitled to set up 'chambers'. This organisational device allows the Court to multiply into a variety of 'miniature courts'. For the Court's chambers enjoy – unlike parliamentary committees vis-à-vis Parliament's plenary – the powers of the full Court. The division into chambers thus allows the Court to spread its workload. And indeed, the operation of the Court through chambers constitutes the norm for all categories of cases.[96] In the words of the Treaties: 'The Court of Justice *shall* sit in chambers or in a Grand Chamber', but exceptionally '*may also* sit as a full Court'.[97]

How many judges sit in a chamber, and how are they composed? Answers to these questions are provided in the 'Statute of the Court of Justice of the European Union', and the 'Rules of Procedure of the Court of Justice'. According to the former, the Court will normally sit in chambers consisting of three and five judges.[98] Exceptionally, the Court can sit in a 'Grand Chamber' consisting of thirteen judges, where a Member State or a Union institution as party to the proceedings so requests.[99] Very exceptionally, the Court shall sit as a 'full Court' in limited categories of constitutional cases.[100]

(ii) The General Court: composition and structure

'The General Court shall include at least one judge per Member State.'[101] The exact number is set by the Statute of the Court of Justice of the European Union at twenty-seven,[102] that is: one judge per Member State. The judges are to be chosen 'from persons whose independence is beyond doubt and who possess the ability required for appointment to *high* judicial office'.[103] Their (re)appointment is subject to the same rules as for the Court of Justice. The General Court also has its own President, whose election and functions are similar to his counterpart at the Court of Justice.

The General Court will – like the Court of Justice – also generally sit in chambers of three and five judges.[104] And in exceptionally difficult circumstances, it may sit as a 'full court' or as a 'Grand Chamber'.[105] However, in exceptionally easy circumstances, the General Court can also assign cases to a single-judge chamber.[106]

What is the jurisdiction of the General Court? Its jurisdiction has always been smaller than that of the Court of Justice. It was originally confined to cases brought directly by natural or legal persons.[107] Today, Article 256 TFEU

---

[96] The original Article 165 (2) EEC had limited the ability to set up chambers to 'particular categories of cases', but the Maastricht Treaty removed that constitutional limitation.
[97] Article 251 TFEU.   [98] Article 16 (1) Court Statute.   [99] *Ibid.*, Article 16 (2) and (3).
[100] *Ibid.*, Article 16 (4) and (5).   [101] Article 19 (2) TEU.   [102] Article 48 Court Statute.
[103] Article 254 (2) TFEU.   [104] Article 11 General Court Rules of Procedure.
[105] *Ibid.*, Article 14 (1).   [106] *Ibid.*, Article 14 (2).   [107] Article 11 (1) SEA.

distinguishes between three scenarios. First, the General Court will have jurisdiction to hear cases at first instance, with the exception of those cases assigned to a 'specialised court' or those cases reserved to the Court of Justice.[108] Second, the General Court will have jurisdiction to hear appeals against decisions of specialised courts. Third, the General Court may have jurisdiction for preliminary references from national courts in specific cases laid down by the Statute. (However, the General Court is entitled to decline jurisdiction and refer requests for a preliminary ruling to the Court of Justice, where it 'considers that the case requires a decision of principle likely to affect the unity or consistency of Union law'.[109])

Decisions of the General Court can be 'appealed' or 'reviewed'. Appeals can be launched by any party that was (partly) unsuccessful.[110] However, appeals are limited to points of law and must be on the grounds of 'lack of competence', 'breach of procedure', or infringement of European law by the General Court.[111] If the appeal is well founded, the Court of Justice will 'quash' the decision of the General Court.[112] It can then choose one of two options. It may act like a 'court of cassation', that is: cancel the previous judgment and refer the case back to the General Court. Alternatively, the Court of Justice can act as a 'court of revision' and give final judgment in the matter itself.[113] Similar – but nonetheless distinct – are reviews. The Court of Justice is indeed entitled to *review* a judgment of the General Court *on its own motion* in two situations. First, it can review a decision of the General Court, where that court acts in its own appellate capacity. Second, it can review a decision by the General Court where it gives a preliminary ruling for a national court.[114] However, in both situations review proceedings are limited to 'where there is a serious risk of the unity or consistency of Union law being affected'.[115]

(iii) *Excursus*: the Advocates General

The Court 'shall be assisted by Advocates General'.[116] The institution of Advocate-General is a trademark of the European judicial system.[117] Their

---

[108] Article 256 (1) TFEU. The exceptions are thus staff cases that fall within the first-instance jurisdiction of the Civil Service Tribunal. The Court of Justice is generally reserved first-instance jurisdiction for actions brought by a Member State or an institution for failure to act (cf. Article 51 Court Statute).

[109] Article 256 (3) TFEU – second indent.   [110] Article 56 (2) Court Statute.

[111] *Ibid.*, Article 58.   [112] *Ibid.*, Article 61.

[113] Decisions of the Court of Justice in appeal cases are suffixed by a 'P' for the French 'pourvoi' (i.e. appeal).

[114] Article 256 (2) and (3) TFEU.

[115] *Ibid.* For the 'Review of Decisions of the General Court', see: Articles 123 (a) et seq. of the Rules of Procedure of the Court of Justice.

[116] Article 19 (2) TEU.

[117] N. Burrows and R. Greaves, *The Advocate-General and EC Law* (Oxford University Press, 2007), 2.

number is currently set at eight, but the Council may increase this number.[118] Advocates General are appointed as officers of the Court,[119] but their duty is not to 'judge'. The Treaties define their function as follows: 'It shall be the duty of the Advocate General, acting with complete impartiality and independence, to make, in open court, reasoned submissions[.]'[120] According to this definition, an Advocate General is thus neither advocate nor general.[121] S/he is an independent advisor to the Court, who produces an 'opinion' that is not legally binding on the Court.[122] The opinion is designed to inform the Court of ways to decide a case and, in this respect, the Advocate General acts like an academic *amicus curiae*.

Until recently, each case before the Court of Justice was preceded by the opinion of an Advocate General. However, according to the Court's new Statute, the Court 'may decide, after hearing the Advocate General, that the case shall be determined without a submission from the Advocate General'.[123] For the General Court, absence is the constitutional rule. Only in exceptional cases will judgments of the General Court be preceded by the opinion of an Advocate General. The Rules of Procedure of the General Court indicate that the court 'shall' be assisted by an ad hoc Advocate General when in plenary session,[124] while it 'may' also be assisted by an Advocate General 'if it is considered that the legal difficulty or the factual complexity of the case so requires'.[125] And according to the Statute of the Court, it is the 'judges' of the General Court themselves who 'may be called to perform the task of an Advocate General'.[126]

---

[118] Article 252 (1) TFEU. The Declaration (No. 38) on Article 252 states: 'The Conference declares that if, in accordance with Article 252, first paragraph, of the Treaty on the Functioning of the European Union, the Court of Justice requests that the number of Advocates- General be increased by three (eleven instead of eight), the Council will, acting unanimously, agree on such an increase. In that case, the Conference agrees that Poland will, as is already the case for Germany, France, Italy, Spain and the United Kingdom, have a permanent Advocate-General and no longer take part in the rotation system, while the existing rotation system will involve the rotation of five Advocates-General instead of three.'

[119] Article 253 TFEU applies to judges as well as Advocates-General.

[120] Article 252 (2) TFEU.

[121] The title is thus 'a misnomer', since s/he 'is really no more an advocate than he is a general' (J. P. Warner as quoted in: N. Brown and T. Kennedy, *The Court of Justice of the European Communities* (Sweet & Maxwell, 2000), 64).

[122] Famous examples, where the Court went against the Advocate-General are Case 26/62, *Van Gend en Loos* v. *Netherlands Inland Revenue Administration*, [1963] ECR 1; as well as Case C-50/00P, *Unión de Pequeños Agricultores (UPA)* v. *Council*, [2002] ECR I-6677.

[123] Article 20 (4) of the Court Statute.   [124] Article 17 General Court Rules of Procedure.

[125] *Ibid.*, Article 18.

[126] Article 49 Court Statute. According to the fourth indent of that article '[a] member called upon to perform the task of Advocate-General in a case may not take part in the judgment of the case'. And according to Article 2 of the General Court Rules of Procedure, the President of the Court is not allowed to perform the function of the Advocate-General.

(iv) The 'specialised court(s)': the Civil Service Tribunal

Courts with special jurisdictions are common phenomena in national legal orders. Judicial specialisation allows judges to develop and employ legal expertise in an area that requires special knowledge. The Treaties do not expressly list the Union's specialised courts. However, Article 257 TFEU opens the way for specialised jurisdictions below the General Court, when it entitles the European legislator to establish 'specialised courts attached to the General Court to hear and determine at first instance certain classes of action or proceedings brought in specific areas'.[127] The jurisdiction of such a specialised court will thereby be defined in its constituting act, and its decisions may be subject to a right of appeal on points of law or fact as defined in the constituting act.

Judges for specialised courts shall 'be chosen from persons whose independence is beyond doubt and who posses the ability required for appointment to judicial office'.[128] Unlike the judges at the higher European courts, they will not be appointed by common accord of the Member States but by the (unanimous) Council.[129]

What specialised jurisdictions have been created in the European legal order? So far, only one specialised court has been established: the Civil Service Tribunal.[130] According to the Statute of the Court of Justice of the European Union, the Tribunal 'shall exercise at first instance jurisdiction in disputes between the Union and its servants'.[131] It shall consist of seven judges,[132] who are appointed for six years by the Council.[133] Due to the much smaller number of judges, the Council is obliged to 'ensure a balanced composition of the Civil Service Tribunal on as broad a geographical basis as possible from among nations of the Member States and with respect to the national legal systems represented'.[134] The Tribunal itself will normally sit in chambers of three judges.[135] Exceptionally, it may also sit as a full court or a chamber of five judges where the case is a hard one;[136] or, it may refer the case to a chamber of a single judge where the case is an easy one.[137] Appeals to the General Court are possible.[138] However, they are 'limited to points of law' and shall be confined to 'lack of jurisdiction', 'breach of procedure', and infringement of European law.[139]

---

[127] Article 257 TFEU – first indent.   [128] *Ibid.* – fourth indent.   [129] *Ibid.*

[130] Council Decision 2004/752 establishing the European Union Civil Service Tribunal ([2004] OJ L333/7).

[131] Annex I of the Court Statute, Article 1.

[132] *Ibid.*, Article 2. The number may be increased by the Council.

[133] Article 257 TFEU – fourth indent.   [134] Annex I of the Court Statute, Article 3.

[135] Article 12 Civil Service Tribunal Rules of Procedure.

[136] *Ibid.*, Article 13 (1). 'Whenever the difficulty of the questions of law raised or the importance of the case or special circumstances justify, a case may be referred to the full court or to the Chamber sitting with five Judges.'

[137] *Ibid.*, Article 14.   [138] *Ibid.*, Article 9.   [139] *Ibid.*, Article 11.

(b) The judicial procedure(s)

The procedure before the Court of Justice consists of two parts: a written part and an oral part.[140] The written part precedes the oral part and dominates the judicial procedure. A case begins when brought before the Court by a written application by the applicant.[141] The application will then be served on the defendant, who may lodge a defence.[142] Each party has the right to reply to the other.[143] Thereafter, the Court takes over the initiative. Two steps structure the written procedure. First comes the assignment of the case. The Court will assign the case to a Chamber or the Full Court – depending on the importance of the case.[144] It will also designate a 'Reporting Judge' and an Advocate General. They decide whether a preparatory inquiry needs to be held. This preparatory inquiry represents the second step. The Court may here, on its own motion or on application by a party, hear witnesses.[145] This leads to the oral part of the procedure. The hearing of the parties will normally be in public,[146] where the judges are allowed to put questions to the parties. After the hearing, the Advocate General will deliver his opinion. And the final step is the judgment itself. It ends the case.[147]

How will the Court make a judgment? Judicial decision-making takes place in 'closed session'.[148] The Court, in the formation that heard the case,[149] here deliberates in secret.[150] The basis of the deliberation is not the opinion of the Advocate General, but a draft judgment prepared by the 'Reporting Judge'. Every participating judge will state his or her opinion and the reasons behind it.[151] Voting will take place in reverse order of seniority – this is to prevent junior judges from being influenced by the opinion of their seniors. The final

---

[140] For a legal definition, see: Article 20 (2) Court Statute. This section will concentrate on the procedure(s) within the Court of Justice, and here in particular on direct actions.

[141] Article 21 Court Statute. The provision, as well as Article 38 of the Court Rules of Procedure, details the minimum information an application needs to contain.

[142] Article 39 Court Rules of Procedure.

[143] Article 41 Court Rules of Procedure. The provision defines the response by the applicant as 'reply' and the subsequent response by the defendant as 'rejoinder'.

[144] *Ibid.*, Article 44 (3). The Court may decide to 'join' cases on the ground that they concern the same subject-matter (*ibid.*, Article 43). A famous example here is: Joined Cases C-46/93 and C-48/93, *Brasserie du Pêcheur SA* v. *Bundesrepublik Deutschland* and *The Queen* v. *Secretary of State for Transport, ex parte Factortame Ltd and others*, [1996] ECR I-1029.

[145] Article 47 Court Rules of Procedure.

[146] See Article 31 Court Statute: 'The hearing in court shall be public, unless the Court of Justice, of its own motion or on application by the parties, decides otherwise for serious reasons.'

[147] Article 64 Court Rules of Procedure.   [148] *Ibid.*, Article 27 (1).

[149] *Ibid.*, Article 27 (2): 'Only those judges who were present at the oral proceedings and the Assistant Rapporteur, if any, entrusted with the consideration of the case may take part in the deliberations.'

[150] Article 35 Court Statute: 'The deliberations of the Court of Justice shall be and shall remain secret.'

[151] Article 27 (3) Court Rules of Procedure.

judgment will be reached by a majority of judges.[152] This 'majority' decision is the only decision of the Court. For unlike the US Supreme Court, no dissenting opinions by a minority of judges are allowed. All judicial differences must thus be settled in the (majority) decision of the Court.[153] This often turns a judgment into an 'edited collection', since disagreements within the Court must be settled by weaving diverse threads of reasoning into a single judicial texture. And the eclectic literary result may not be easy to understand! However, the collective and secret nature of the judgment is a shield protecting the independence of the European judiciary.

In addition to 'judgments', the Court also has the power to give 'orders' and 'opinions'. The former may result from an application for interim measures.[154] Interim measures are sometimes necessary, for actions brought before the Court have no suspensory effect.[155] An order will thus typically precede a judgment.[156] By contrast, 'opinions' of the Court can be requested in the context of international agreements.[157] Before the Union can conclude such an agreement, '[a] Member State, the European Parliament, the Council or the Commission may obtain the opinion of the Court of Justice as to whether an agreement envisaged is compatible with the Treaties'.[158] The Court's opinion is here more than advisory, for where it is adverse 'the agreement envisaged may not enter into force unless it is amended or the Treaties are revised'.[159] The Court's opinions have indeed shaped the external relations law of the European Union.

(c) Judicial reasoning: methods of interpretation

Courts are not democratic institutions. Their decision-making ought thus not to be based on political expediency. And in many modern societies, courts are therefore not allowed to make law.[160] They must only interpret and apply the

---

[152] *Ibid.*, Article 27 (5). There must always be an uneven number of voting judges. According to Article 17 (1) Court Statute, '[d]ecisions of the Court of Justice shall be valid only when an uneven number of its members is sitting in the deliberations'.

[153] Article 27 (6) Court Rules of Procedure.

[154] Article 279 TFEU: 'The Court of Justice of the European Union may in any cases before it prescribe any necessary interim measures.' See also: Article 86 Court Rules of Procedure.

[155] Article 278 TFEU.

[156] Orders are marked by an 'R' at the end of the case number, e.g., Case 27/76R, *United Brands* v. *Commission*, [1976] ECR 425 preceding the judgment of the Court in Case 27/76, *United Brands* v. *Commission*, [1978] ECR 207. Sometimes an 'order' may replace a judgment, see: Article 104 (3) Court Rules of Procedure: 'Where a question referred to the Court for a preliminary ruling is identical to a question on which the Court has already ruled, or where the answer to such a question may be clearly deduced from existing case-law, the Court may, after hearing the Advocate-General, at any time give its decision by reasoned order in which reference is made to its previous judgment or to the relevant case-law.'

[157] These 'Opinions' are not 'Cases' and consequently are numbered separately, such as 'Opinion 1/ 94'. For a list of the Court's 'Opinions', see: Table of Cases 1(b).

[158] Article 218 (11) TFEU.   [159] *Ibid.*

[160] Exceptionally, some modern States recognise the law-making function of courts. The English common law system is the best example.

law. The Court of Justice of the European Union stands in this 'civilian' tradition. For according to Article 19 TEU the Court shall 'ensure that in the interpretation and application of the Treaties the law is observed'.[161] The European Court is here portrayed as an 'active' interpreter and as a 'passive' applier of European law. It must apply European law where its meaning is clear, and must interpret it where its meaning is not clear.

The process of interpretation is a process of expressing implicit meaning. It lies between art and science. It is creative in its construction of meaning; yet, by insisting on judicial 'rules' of construction, it has a scientific soul. The interpretation of law is thus the creation of legal meaning according to a judicial methodology. The judicial method 'justifies' a decision of a court.[162] A court must give 'grounds' – legal grounds – for its decisions.[163]

There are four common methods that judges use to justify their decisions. They are: historical interpretation, literal interpretation, systematic interpretation, and teleological interpretation. There exists no hierarchy between these methods in the European legal order, and their parallel use may at times lead to conflicting results. Each method of interpretation grants a different degree of 'freedom' to the Court in deciding a case. The first two methods are 'conservative' methods, while the last two methods are 'progressive' methods of interpretation. A judicial preference for an interpretive method will thus prejudge the result of the interpretation.[164] Theoretically, the smallest interpretive room is given by the historical method. Historical interpretation searches for the original meaning of a rule. However, a commitment to 'originalism' encounters problems. It presumes that there was a clear meaning when the norm was created – which may not be the case.[165] And a historical reading of a norm may make it lose touch with the social reality to which it is to apply. Literal interpretation, by contrast, starts with the written text and gives it its (ordinary) contemporary meaning. The problem with the 'textualist' method in the European legal order is that there is not one single legal text. Systematic interpretation tries to construct the meaning of a norm by reference to its place within the general scheme of the legislative or constitutional system. Finally, teleological interpretation is the judicial method that allows a court to search for the purpose or spirit or useful effect – the *telos* – of a legal norm.

The European Court has used all four methods in its jurisprudence. But while occasionally using the historical method, the Court generally finds it

---

[161] Article 19 (1) TEU.

[162] On the notion of 'legal justification' in the European legal order, see: J. Bengoetxea, *The Legal Reasoning of the European Court of Justice. Towards a European Jurisprudence* (Clarendon Press, 1993), Chapter 5.

[163] Article 36 Court Statute: 'Judgments shall state the reasons on which they are based.'

[164] In the beautifully paradoxical words of G. Radbruch: 'The interpretation is the result of its result.' See G. Radbruch, *Einführung in die Rechtswissenschaft* (Meyer, 1925), 129.

[165] Constitutions (as well as legislation) are often the result of compromises. They take refuge in ambivalences and leave meaning to be defined in the future.

paramount 'to consider the spirit, the general scheme and the wording of those provisions'.[166] Teleological and systematic consideration have indeed often trumped even the clear wording of a provision. This 'activist' interpretation has attracted serve criticism – from academics and politicians alike.[167]

(d) Jurisdiction and judicial powers

The traditional role of courts in modern societies is to act as independent arbitrators between competing interests. Their jurisdiction may be compulsory, or not. The jurisdiction of the Court of Justice of the European Union is compulsory 'within the limits of the powers conferred on it in the Treaties'.[168] While compulsory, the Court's jurisdiction is thus limited. Based on the principle of conferral, the Court has no 'inherent' jurisdiction.

The functions and powers of the Court are classified in Article 19 (3) TEU:

> The Court of Justice of the European Union shall, in accordance with the Treaties:
>
> (a) rule on actions brought by a Member State, an institution or a natural or legal person;
> (b) give preliminary rulings, at the request of courts or tribunals of the Member States, on the interpretation of Union law or the validity of acts adopted by the institutions;
> (c) rule in other cases provided for in the Treaties.

The provision classifies the judicial tasks by distinguishing between direct and indirect actions. The former are brought directly before the European Court. The latter arrive at the Court indirectly through preliminary references from national courts. The powers of the Court under the preliminary reference procedure are set out in a single article.[169] By contrast, there exist a number of direct actions in the Treaty on the Functioning of the European Union. This Treaty distinguishes between enforcement actions brought by the Commission or a Member State,[170] judicial review proceedings for action and inaction of the Union institutions,[171] actions for damages for the (non-)contractual liability of the Union,[172] as well as a few minor jurisdictional heads.[173]

In light of its broad jurisdiction, the Court of Justice of the European Union can be characterised as a 'constitutional', an 'administrative', an 'international' court as well as an 'industrial tribunal'. Its jurisdiction includes public and

---

[166] *Van Gend en Loos* (supra n. 122), 12.
[167] See H. Rasmussen, *On Law and Policy in the European Court of Justice. A Comparative Study in Judicial Policymaking* (Nijhoff, 1986).
[168] Article 13 (2) TEU.
[169] Article 267 TFEU. The provision is analysed in Chapter 8 – Section 4 below.
[170] Articles 258–260 TFEU. The provisions are analysed in Chapter 8 – Section 3 below.
[171] Articles 263–266 TFEU. The provisions are analysed in Chapter 8 – Sections 1 and 3 below.
[172] Articles 268 and 340 TFEU. The provisions are analysed in Chapter 8 – Section 2 below.
[173] Articles 269–274 TFEU.

private matters. And while the Court claims to act like a 'continental' civil law court, it has been fundamental in shaping the structure and powers of the European Union as well as the nature of European law. The (activist) jurisprudence of the Court will be regularly encountered in the subsequent chapters of this book. The Court is indeed much more than the 'mouth of the law'.

Yet importantly, there are two constitutional gaps in the jurisdiction of the Court. First, the European Courts shall have no jurisdiction with respect to the Common Foreign and Security Policy.[174] The idea behind this exclusion is the – wrong – belief that courts have no role to play in political questions raised in the context of foreign affairs. Second, the Court 'shall have no jurisdiction to review the validity or proportionality of operations carried out by the police or other law-enforcement services of a Member State or the exercise of the responsibilities incumbent upon Member States with regard to the maintenance of law and order and the safeguarding of internal security'.[175] The exclusion of judicial review in this second instance is – perhaps – less problematic. For the provision will not exclude judicial review by *national* courts.

3. The European Central Bank

National Central Banks emerged in seventeenth-century Europe as public institutions to regulate money supply in the national market.[176] A European Central Bank had originally not been provided for in the Treaties. However, with the decision to move towards monetary union, a central institution was envisaged to regulate the money market in the European Union. The European Central Bank (ECB) came into formal existence in 1998, and assumed its formal functions on 1 January 1999 when the European currency – the 'euro' – was introduced. The status of the Bank within the institutional framework of the Union remained unclear for a long time. Prior to the Lisbon Treaty, it was not a formal 'institution' of the Union,[177] and its ambivalent legal status gave rise to a spirited academic debate. The debate has – partly – been ended by Article 13 (1) TEU, which expressly identifies the European Central Bank as an institution of the European Union. Nonetheless, the ECB is a 'special' institution that warrants a special analysis. Thereafter, we shall look at the composition and structure, decision-making procedure, and functions of the ECB respectively.

---

[174] *Ibid.*, Article 275.   [175] *Ibid.*, Article 276.

[176] Among the first 'central' banks to emerge were the Swedish 'Riksbank' (1664) and the 'Bank of England' (1694). On the legislative power of the US Congress to charter a national bank, see: *McCulloch* v. *Maryland*, 17 US 316 (1819).

[177] Prior to the Lisbon Treaty, the legal existence of the ECB was provided for not in the article dealing with the institutions, but in a separate article; see Article 8 EC: 'A European System of Central Banks (hereinafter referred to as "ESCB") and a European Central Bank (hereinafter referred to as "ECB") shall be established in accordance with the procedures laid down in this Treaty; they shall act within the limits of the powers conferred upon them by this Treaty and by the Statute of the ESCB and of the ECB (hereinafter referred to as "Statute of the ESCB") annexed thereto.'

(a) The special status of the ECB

Is the European Central Bank a *sui generis* institution of the Union? The argument has been made by reference to two 'special' characteristics. First, the European Central Bank must be 'independent'.[178] Second, it is embedded in the 'European System of Central Banks' (ESCB). This is a system composed of the European Central Bank and the National Central Banks of the Member States whose currency is the euro;[179] and the Treaties formally assign the tasks of monetary policy to the ESCB and not directly to the ECB.[180]

Let us start by looking at the 'independent' status of the ECB. The ECB 'shall be independent in the exercise of its powers and in the management of its finances'; and the Union as well as the Member States must respect that independence.[181] Unlike any other Union institution, the Bank has its own 'legal personality' distinct from the legal personality of the Union.[182] Moreover, the Bank has its own 'decision-making bodies' in the form of a 'Governing Council' and an 'Executive Board'. The Bank's special status gave rise to the theory that the ECB represented an 'independent specialised organisation of [Union] law' – like the European Atomic Community.[183] Yet the idea that the Bank was *legally* independent from the European Union has been thoroughly rejected by the European Court of Justice. In *Commission* v. *European Central Bank*,[184] the Bank had denied the applicability of European legislation on the ground that it was not an institution or body of the European Union. The Court unconditionally rejected the *legal* independence theory. The independence of the Bank only meant *political* independence.[185] And that political independence was not a unique feature of the Bank, but was shared by other Union institutions.[186]

What about the European Central Bank being part of a two-level structure within the European System of Central Banks? This – strange – constitutional

---

[178] Article 282 (3) TFEU.   [179] *Ibid.*, Article 282.   [180] *Ibid.*, Article 127 (2).
[181] *Ibid.*, Article 282 (3).   [182] *Ibid.*: 'The European Central Bank shall have legal personality.'
[183] C. Zilioli and M. Selmayr, *The Law of the European Central Bank* (Hart, 2001), 31. The practical consequence of that theory was that the ECB was assumed not to be directly bound by the objectives of the European Union. The sole 'Grundnorm' of the 'new Community' was price stability (*ibid.*, 35).
[184] Case C-11/00, *Commission* v. *European Central Bank*, [2003] ECR I-7147.
[185] *Ibid.*, para.134. For a criticism of that claim, see: R. Smits, 'The European Central Bank's Independence and Its Relations with Economic Policy Makers' [2007–08] 31 *Fordham International Law Journal* 1614 at 1625: 'In a self-professed democracy, the idea of central bankers not being influenced by [Union] and State government members is absurd.'
[186] Case C-11/00 (supra n. 184) para. 133: '[Union] institutions such as, notably, the Parliament, the Commission or the Court itself, enjoy independence and guarantees comparable in a number of respects to those thus afforded to the ECB. In that regard, reference may, for example, be made to Article [245 TFEU], which states that the Members of the Commission are, in the general interest of the [Union], to be completely independent in the performance of their duties. That provision states, in terms quite close to those used in [Article 130 TFEU], that in the performance of their duties the Members of the Commission are neither to seek nor to take instructions from any government or from any other body and, further, that each Member State undertakes not to seek to influence those Members in the performance of their tasks.'

structure must be understood against its historical background.[187] When the Member States decided to move towards monetary union, they had two alternatives. They could either dissolve the pre-existing National Central Banks and replace them with a single European Central Bank; or they could create a unitary monetary structure within which the National Central Banks acted as agents of the European Central Bank. The Treaties chose the second option – an option that has many advantages.[188] However, this second option is *not* a federal option. National Central Banks are not in a federal relationship with the European Central Bank. It is the European Central Bank that *exclusively* governs within the European System of Central Banks. It is the ECB that can – exclusively – decide whether to exercise the powers granted to it by the Treaties itself 'or *through* the national central banks'.[189] And when the ECB decides to 'have recourse to the national central banks',[190] the latter 'shall act in accordance with the guidelines and instructions of the ECB'.[191] National Central Banks are thus seen as a functionally integrated part of the European Central Bank. They enjoy only 'delegated' powers under an exclusive competence of the Union, and not 'autonomous' national powers.[192] Within the scope of the Treaties, they are consequently mere agents of the European Central Bank.[193] And the best way to characterise the status of the ECB in the ESCB is therefore to compare it to a *decentralised unitary* system – like the United Kingdom.[194]

In conclusion, how are we to characterise the European Central Bank? Textually and functionally, the ECB is a 'formal' institution of the Union, albeit endowed with its own special characteristics.[195] While it is organically separate from the National Central Banks, it functionally embraces them as decentralised agents of the ECB.

---

[187] For an excellent overview, see: Zilioli and Selmayr (supra n. 183), 54 et seq.

[188] *Ibid.*, 57: 'The maintenance of the national central Banks inside the ESCB was seen as an opportunity to found a new system on the experience, the traditions and the reputation of the national central banks[.]'

[189] Article 9 (2) ECB Statute (emphasis added).   [190] *Ibid.*, Article 12 (1) – third indent.

[191] *Ibid.*, Article 14 (3).

[192] According to Article 3 (c) TFEU, 'monetary policy for the Member States whose currency is the euro'. On exclusive competences and their meaning in the European legal order, see: Chapter 5 – Section 2(a) below.

[193] The 'ECB agent' theory is supported by two additional arguments. First, according to Article 35 (6) ECB Statute, the Court of Justice will 'have jurisdiction in disputes concerning the fulfilment by a national central bank of obligations under the Treaties and the Statute'. Second, while national central banks 'may' perform additional functions to those specified in the European Treaties, the European Central Bank can prohibit them if it considers that they interfere with the objectives and tasks of the ESCB (see: Article 14 (4) ECB Statute).

[194] On the constitutional 'devolution' of power from the Westminster Parliament, see: V. Bogdanor, *Devolution in the United Kingdom* (Oxford University Press, 2001).

[195] For a much stronger thesis, see: B. Krauskopf and C. Steven, 'The Institutional Framework of the European System of Central Banks: Legal Issues in the Practice of the First Ten Years of its Existence' [2009] 46 CML Rev 1143 at 1149: 'The ECB has institutional features which set it distinctly apart from all the other EU institutions.'

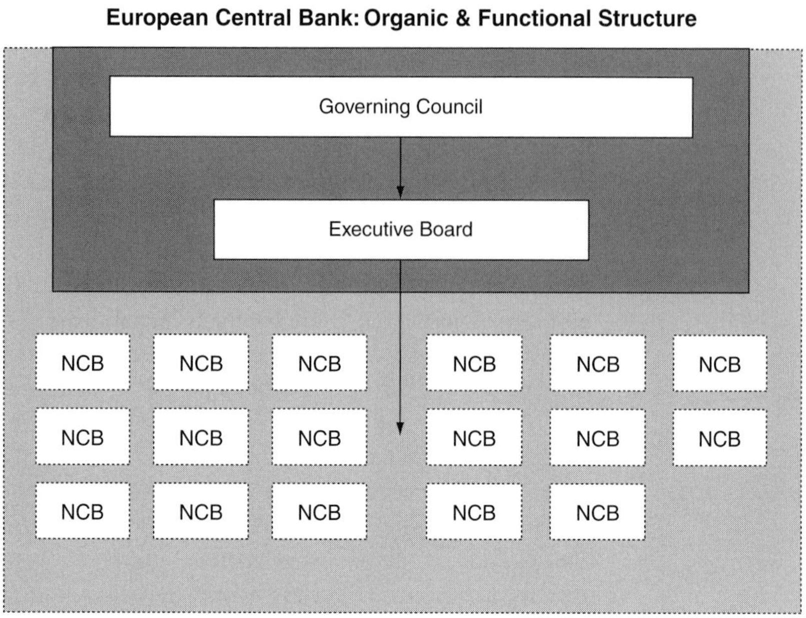

European Central Bank: Organic & Functional Structure

Figure 9 Structure of the European Central Bank

(b) Organs and administrative structure

The European Central Bank has two central organs and one President. The two organs are the 'Executive Board' and the 'Governing Council'.[196]

The Executive Board constitutes Europe's 'monetary executive'.[197] It comprises the President, the Vice-President and four additional members. The Executive Board is appointed by the European Council 'from among persons of recognised standing and professional experience in monetary or banking matters'.[198] The members of the Executive Board must perform their duties in complete independence.[199] Their term of office is eight years, and cannot be renewed.[200] The Governing Council is Europe's monetary regulator. It comprises the members of the Executive Board and the governors of the National Central Banks of the Euro-States.[201] Importantly, since the governors of the National Central Banks must not take instructions from their national governments,[202] they are *not* representatives of the Member States. They must act in the

---

[196] See Article 129 (1) TFEU as well as Article 9 (3) ECB Statute. The Treaties mention a third – transitory – organ: the 'General Council' (see Article 141 (1) TFEU). Article 43 of the ECB Statute defines the tasks of the General Council as those that were formerly exercised by the European Monetary Institute (the predecessor of the ECB), which are further spelled out in Article 46 of the ECB Statute.
[197] Zilioli and Selmayr (supra n. 183), 84.   [198] Article 283 (2) TFEU.
[199] Article 11 ECB Statute.   [200] *Ibid.*   [201] Article 283 (1) TFEU.   [202] Article 130 TFEU.

supranational interest of the European Union as a whole.[203] Governors of National Central Banks are thus unlike national ministers in the Council.

The central organs of the ECB are supported by a number of 'work units', and 'committees'.[204] Work units can be created by the Executive Board, and are 'under the managing direction' of the latter.[205] Work units within the ECB presently comprise 'Directorates-General' (for example: Financial Stability), and self-standing Directorates (for example: Internal Audit). With regard to committees, it is the Governing Council that will 'establish and dissolve' committees with particular mandates.[206] Committees are to be composed of up to two members from each of the National Central Banks (participating in the euro) and the European Central Bank. There are at present sixteen internal committees, such as the 'Banking Supervision Committee' and the 'Monetary Policy Committee'.

(c) Internal divisions and decision-making

Who governs within the European Central Bank? The Governing Council is the central policy-making organ, which is charged with ensuring that the tasks of the ECB are fulfilled. It will 'formulate the monetary policy of the Union, including, as appropriate, decisions relating to immediate monetary objectives, key interest rates and the supply of reserves in the ESCB, and shall establish the necessary guidelines for their implementation'.[207] Decision-making within the Governing Council is presently straightforward: each member has one vote.[208] (However, matters will become more complex when the number of Member States that adopt the euro exceeds eighteen. Here, the Statute envisages a rotating system among national governors.[209]) The right to vote must be exercised in person, but teleconferencing is possible. The Council will meet 'at least 10 times a year', and decisions are normally taken by simple majority.[210] Voting is confidential, but the Governing Council may decide to make

---

[203] H. K. Scheller, *The European Central Bank* (ECB, 2004), 54.

[204] See www.ecb.int/ecb/html/index.en.html

[205] Article 10 ECB Rules of Procedure (and see Decision of the European Central Bank 2004/257, [2004] OJ L 80/33).

[206] Article 9 ECB Rules of Procedure.   [207] Article 12 (1) ECB Statute – first indent.

[208] For particularly sensitive financial decisions, voting will be conducted through weighted votes. Votes will thereby 'be weighted according to the national central bank's shares in the subscribed capital of the ECB'. Obviously, the votes of the Executive Board will be zero (see Article 10 (3) ECB Statute).

[209] The rotating system is set out in Article 10 (2) of the ECB Statute, as well as in Article 3a of the ECB Rules of Procedure. It had been envisaged to apply when the number of national governors exceeds fifteen, but the Statute allowed the Governing Council to postpone its implementation until the number of Member States participating in monetary union exceeds eighteen. This decision to postpone was taken on 18 December 2008: see ECB Decision 2008/29 on postponing the start of the rotating system in the Governing Council of the European Central Bank (2009 OJ L 3/4), Article 1.

[210] Article 10 (2) ECB Statute. However, the Statute also envisages qualified majority voting.

the outcome of its deliberations public.[211] And if the Governing Council resolves not to decide itself, it 'may delegate its normative powers to the Executive Board for the purpose of implementing its regulations and guidelines'.[212]

What are the tasks of the Executive Board? The Executive Board is the 'executive' organ within the ECB. It 'shall implement monetary policy in accordance with the guidelines and decisions laid down by the Governing Council'; and, in that executive capacity, it will also be the primary instructor for National Central Banks.[213] It will moreover generally 'be responsible for the current business of the ECB'.[214] Decision-making in the Executive Board is also done in person, with each person having one vote. Save as otherwise provided, the Executive Board will thereby act by a simple majority of the votes cast, with the President having a casting vote in the event of a tie.[215]

Finally, what are the tasks of the ECB President? S/he will have to chair the Governing Council and the Executive Board, and will represent the ECB externally.[216] External representation includes participation in Council meetings that discuss matters falling within the competences of the Bank.[217]

(d) Functions and powers

The European Central Bank has not the constitutional honour of a separate article in the Treaty on European Union. This 'systemic' break in the arrangement of the institutional provisions is regrettable. In order to draw a picture of the functions and powers of the ECB, we must therefore look straight into the Treaty on the Functioning of the European Union. The latter defines the 'primary objective' of the European Central Bank as the maintenance of price stability.[218] This primary objective is not just a *primus inter pares*. While the ECB must also 'support the general economic policies in the Union', economic objectives are only secondary objectives that must be pursued '[w]ithout prejudice' to the monetary objective of price stability.[219] The primacy of price stability reflects modern economic thinking about the (limited) function of monetary policy.[220]

How is the ECB to achieve price stability? The Treaties answer this question indirectly by specifying a number of 'basic tasks'. The ECB must 'define and implement the monetary policy of the Union', 'conduct foreign-exchange operations', 'hold and manage the official foreign reserves of the Member States', and 'promote the smooth operation of payment systems'.[221] The most potent powers to achieve these tasks are the Bank's exclusive right to *authorise*

---

[211] Article 10 (4) ECB Statute.   [212] Article 17 ECB Rules of Procedure.
[213] Article 12 (1) ECB Statute.   [214] *Ibid.*, Article 11 (6).   [215] *Ibid.*, Article 11 (5).
[216] *Ibid.*, Article 13.   [217] Article 284 (2) TFEU.
[218] Article 127 (1) TFEU, as well as Article 282 (2) TFEU.   [219] Article 127 (1) TFEU.
[220] Scheller, *The European Central Bank* (supra n. 203), 45. But of course, economic thinking is cyclical.
[221] Article 127 (2) TFEU.

the issue of euro banknotes, and to set interest rates.[222] Money supply within the Union (or rather the Euro Group[223]) is thus *centrally* determined by the European Central Bank. And to partly regulate the demand side of the European currency, the Bank is equally involved in foreign exchange operations. However, the external relations powers of the Bank are subject to the special treaty making procedure set out in Article 219 TFEU.[224] This makes the Council – not the ECB – the central player in the external sphere. The Bank is however entitled to recommend 'formal agreements on an exchange-rate system for the euro in relation to the currencies of third States' to the Council,[225] and must generally be consulted on monetary agreements.[226] This consultation requirement is extended to common positions within international financial institutions 'to secure the euro's place in the international monetary system'.[227]

Are there other functions of the European Central Bank? A secondary function lies in its advisory role to other Union institutions on 'areas falling within its responsibilities'.[228] And the Bank must also contribute to the prudential supervision of credit institutions and the stability of the financial system.[229]

4. The Court of Auditors

Many constitutional orders subject public finances to an external audit.[230] In the Union legal order, the Court of Auditors was established by the 1975 Budget Treaty, and was elevated to a formal institution of the Union in the wake of the Maastricht Treaty. The name of this particular institution is partly misleading. The Court of Auditors is not a court in a judicial sense. It neither exercises judicial functions, nor is it staffed with lawyers.[231] The Court of Auditors is staffed with accountants, whose primary task is to 'carry out the Union's audit'.[232] Audit here means *external* audit, for each institution must internally audit itself.[233]

---

[222] *Ibid.*, Article 128 (1) (emphasis added). The Member States may, however, issue euro coins, but the volume of the issue of euro coins is still subject to the approval of the European Central Bank.

[223] That is the name for the Member States participating in monetary union. The status of the so-called 'Euro Group' is clarified in Protocol (No. 14) on the Euro Group. According to Article 1, '[t]he Ministers of the Member States whose currency is the euro shall meet informally'. According to Article 2, the Euro Group shall elect a president for two and a half years.

[224] On this point, see: Chapter 6 – Section 3(b) below.   [225] Article 219 (1) TFEU.

[226] *Ibid.*, Article 291 (3).   [227] *Ibid.*, Article 138 (1).

[228] *Ibid.*, Article 282 (5): 'within the areas within its responsibilities, the European Central Bank shall be consulted on all proposed Union acts, and all proposals for regulation at national level, and may give an opinion'.

[229] *Ibid.*, Article 127 (5).

[230] For the French 'Cour des Comptes', see: www.ccomptes.fr/fr/CC/Accueil.html.

[231] However, this is the case in some Member States, and this may explain the naming of the respective national institutions as 'courts' (see N. Price, 'The Court of Auditors of the European Communities' [1982] 2 YEL 239).

[232] Article 285 TFEU – first indent.

[233] Regulation 1605/2002 on the Financial Regulation applicable to the general budget of the European Communities ([2002] OJ L248/1), Chapter 3.

What is the structure and decision-making procedure of the Court? The Court consists of one national from each Member State. Members must be completely 'independent' and act 'in the Union's general interest'.[234] Membership is limited to persons who 'have belonged in their respective States to external audit bodies or who are especially qualified for this office'.[235] The Council – not the Member States – appoints members for a (renewable) term of six years.[236] The Court will – internally – elect its President.[237] The latter will 'call and chair the meetings of the Court', and 'represent the Court in its external relations'.[238] While the Court is divided into chambers,[239] it will normally act as a collegial body by a simple majority of its members.[240] Decisions of the Court shall be taken 'in formal session', but a written procedure may exceptionally apply.[241] However, for certain categories of reports the decision of a chamber might be sufficient.[242] Yet, all important reports must be adopted by the full Court.[243]

What are the functions and powers of the Court of Auditors? According to Article 287 TFEU, the Court of Auditors 'shall examine the accounts of all revenue and expenditure of the Union'.[244] And it shall additionally 'provide the European parliament and the Council with a statement of assurance as to the reliability of the accounts and the legality and regularity of the underlying transactions'.[245] To fulfil its task, the Court will primarily audit the financial records of the Union. However, it is also entitled to perform 'on the spot' investigations 'on the premises of any body, office or agency which manages revenue or expenditure on behalf of the Union and in the Member States, including on the premises of any natural or legal person in receipt of payments from the budget'.[246] This wide investigative power includes the Member States – in their function of Union executive – as well as any individual recipient

---

[234] Article 285 TFEU – second indent. The duty is further defined in Article 28 (3) and (4) TFEU: 'In the performance of these duties, the Members of the Court of Auditors shall neither seek nor take instructions from any government or from any other body. The Members of the Court of Auditors shall refrain from any action incompatible with their duties. The Members of the Court of Auditors may not, during their term of office, engage in any other occupation, whether gainful or not. When entering upon their duties they shall give a solemn undertaking that, both during and after their term of office, they will respect the obligations arising therefrom and in particular their duty to behave with integrity and discretion as regards the acceptance, after they have ceased to hold office, of certain appointments or benefits.'

[235] Article 286 (1) TFEU.   [236] Article 286 (2) TFEU.   [237] Ibid.

[238] Rules of Procedure of the Court of Auditors (CoA), Article 9 (a) and (e).

[239] Ibid., Article 10. According to Article 11 of Decision 26/2010 of the Court of Auditors implementing the Rules of Procedure, the Court has five chambers 'four Chambers with responsibility for specific areas of expenditure and for revenue (vertical Chambers), and one horizontal Chamber, known as the CEAD (Coordination, Communication, Evaluation, Assurance and Development) Chamber'.

[240] Article 287 (4) TFEU – third indent.   [241] Article 19 CoA Rules of Procedure.

[242] Ibid., Article 26.

[243] Article 64 of the Decision implementing the CoA Rules of Procedure (supra n. 239). This includes 'the Annual Report provided for in Article 287 (4) TFEU' (a), 'the Statement of Assurance' (b), as well as certain categories of 'specific annual reports' (c).

[244] Article 287 (1) TFEU.   [245] Ibid.   [246] Ibid., Article 287 (3).

of Union funds. Yet the audit must here be carried out 'in liaison' with the competent national authorities.[247]

In examining the accounts, what standard is the Court to apply? Two constitutional options exist. A *formal* review will solely require an examination of the 'legality' of the Union's financing, that is: whether the accounts reflect all the revenue received and all expenditure incurred. By contrast, a *substantial* review will additionally examine the 'soundness' of public spending decisions, that is: whether the financial priorities of the Union guarantee 'value for money'. Substantive review is more intrusive, as it involves questioning the underlying political choices behind the budget. The Union constitutional order has chosen this second option. The Court of Auditors must thus review whether the revenue and expenditure of the Union was 'lawful and regular', '*and* examine whether the financial management has been sound'.[248] The soundness of the Union's finances is thereby determined 'by reference to the principles of economy, efficiency and effectiveness'.[249]

The result of the audit will be published in an 'annual report' after the close of each financial year.[250] This annual report may be complemented by 'special reports' dealing with particular aspects of the Union budget.[251] The reports are designed to assist the European Parliament and the Council 'in exercising their powers of control over the implementation of the budget'.[252] And since the Commission is primarily charged with the implementation of the Union budget, the reports will be primarily addressed to this Union institution.[253] They constitute a 'declaration of good conduct',[254] which – if missing – may lead to the fall of the Commission.[255]

Conclusion

This chapter, and the previous chapter, analysed the governmental structure of the European Union. We saw above that the Union is not based on the classic tripartite structure that became famous in the eighteenth century. The Union has seven 'institutions': the European Parliament, the European Council, the Council, the Commission, the Court of Justice of the European Union, the European

---

[247] *Ibid.*   [248] *Ibid.*, Article 287 (2) (emphasis added).

[249] Article 27 (1) Financial Regulation (supra n. 233).   [250] Article 287 (4) TFEU.

[251] For example, see: Special Report 3/2011 on 'The efficiency and effectiveness of EU contributions channelled through United Nations Organisations in conflict-affected countries' (see http://eca. europa.eu/portal/pls/portal/docs/1/7913076.PDF).

[252] Article 287 (4) TFEU – fourth indent.

[253] According to Article 145 (1) Financial Regulation (supra n. 233), if the accounts are regular and sound, the Parliament shall, upon recommendation by the Council and before 15 May of year $n+2$, give a discharge to the Commission in respect for the implementation of the budget of year n.

[254] C. Kok, 'The Court of Auditors of the European Communities: "The other European Court in Luxembourg"' [1989] 26 CML Rev 345 at 350.

[255] It was the Court of Auditor's Report on the 1996 Union budget that led to the fall of the Santer Commission.

Central Bank, and the Court of Auditors. Each of these institutions is characterised by its distinct composition and its decision-making mode. According to these two dimensions, the Parliament, the Commission, the Court, the European Central Bank, and the Court of Auditors are closer to the 'national' end of the spectrum; whereas the European Council and the Council are closer to its 'international' end.

Importantly, since the Union is not based on the idea of an *institutional* separation of powers, each of the Union institutions shares in various governmental functions. This institutional power-sharing is the basis of the Union's system of checks and balances. What types of governmental 'powers' or 'functions' may be identified for the European Union? Chapter 3 identified five governmental functions: legislative, executive, judicial, external and financial functions. The legislative power relates to the competence of making laws. The executive power relates to the competence of proposing and implementing laws. The judicial power relates to the competence of arbitrating laws in court. A separate 'fourth power' relates to the external competences of a body politic. Finally, a 'fifth power' relates to the governmental control of financial markets.

Part II of this book will analyse four of these functions. What is the scope of the Union's powers and what legal procedures combine the various institutions into the exercise of these powers? The following four chapters will look at the powers and procedures within four branches of government.

Part II
Powers and Procedures

Having enumerated the 'values' and 'objectives' of the Union, the European Treaties do not enumerate the Union 'powers'. The Treaties pursue a different legal technique: they attribute legal power in substantive policy titles. Each policy area would contain a provision – sometimes more than one – on the basis of which the Union is entitled to act. These 'legal bases' not only define the material scope within which the Union can act, they also lay down the legal procedure to follow, and the legal instrument(s) to be used. Three dimensions thus characterise each legal base within the Treaties: competence, procedure and instrument. The first two dimensions will be discussed in Part II, while the third dimension concerns the normative quality of European law and will be discussed in Part III. In line with classic constitutional theory, four powers or functions will be discussed in four separate chapters.

Chapter 5 – Legislative Powers: Competences and Procedures

Chapter 6 – External Powers: Competences and Procedures

Chapter 7 – Executive Powers: Competences and Procedures

Chapter 8 – Judicial Powers: Competences and Procedures

5

Legislative Powers: Competences and Procedures

Contents

Introduction		151
1.	The scope of Union competences	152
	(a) Teleological interpretation	153
	(b) The general competences of the Union	157
	(i) The harmonisation competence: Article 114 TFEU	157
	(ii) The residual competence: Article 352 TFEU	160
2.	The categories of Union competences	162
	(a) Exclusive competences: Article 3 TFEU	164
	(b) Shared competences: Article 4 TFEU	166
	(c) Coordinating competences: Article 5 TFEU	167
	(d) Complementary competences: Article 6 TFEU	168
3.	Legislative procedures: ordinary and special	169
	(a) The 'ordinary' legislative procedure	171
	(i) Constitutional theory: formal text	171
	(ii) Constitutional practice: informal trilogues	174
	(b) The 'special' legislative procedures	176
4.	The principle of subsidiarity	177
	(a) Procedural standard: subsidiarity as a political safeguard of federalism	178
	(b) Substantive standard: subsidiarity as a judicial safeguard of federalism	181
Conclusion		184

Introduction

Each society needs common rules and mechanisms for their production. The concept of legislation is central to all modern societies. Legislation refers to the making of laws (*legis*).[1] But what is 'legislation'? Two competing conceptions of

---

[1] *Shorter Oxford English Dictionary.*

legislation have emerged in the modern era. The *formal* or *procedural* conception of legislation is tied to our modern understanding of *who* should be in charge of the legislative function. Legislation is formally defined as every legal act adopted according to the (parliamentary) *legislative procedure*. This procedural conception of legislation has traditionally shaped British constitutional thought.[2] By contrast, a second conception defines *what* legislation should be, that is: legal rules with *general application*. This *material* or functional conception of legislation has shaped continental constitutional thought.[3] A material definition of legislation underpins phrases like 'external legislation' through international agreements, and 'delegated legislation' adopted by the executive.

Which of these traditions has informed European constitutionalism? The Union has traditionally followed a material definition.[4] However, with the Lisbon Treaty, a formal definition of legislative power has been adopted. The Treaty on the Functioning of the European Union now constitutionally defines: 'Legal acts adopted by legislative *procedure* shall constitute *legislative* acts.'[5] The legislative procedure is thereby defined as a procedure that combines the European Parliament and the Council.

But what are the 'legislative' powers of the European Union? And what types of power can it enjoy? This chapter answers these questions in four sections. Section 1 analyses the scope of the Union's legislative competences. This scope is limited, as the Union is not a sovereign State. Section 2 analyses the different categories of Union competences. Depending on what competence category is involved, the Union will enjoy distinct degrees of legislative power. Section 3 analyses the identity of the Union legislator. Various legislative procedures thereby determine how the Union must exercise its 'legislative' competences. Section 4 finally scrutinises the principle of subsidiarity as a constitutional principle that controls the exercise of the Union's shared legislative powers.

1. The scope of Union competences

When the British Parliament legislates, it need not 'justify' its acts. It is considered to enjoy a competence to do all things.[6] This 'omnipotence' is inherent in the idea of a sovereign parliament in a 'sovereign state'. The European Union is neither 'sovereign' nor a 'state'. Its powers are *not inherent*

---

[2] For the British parliamentary definition of legislation, see: A. V. Dicey, *Introduction to the Study of the Law of the Constitution* (Liberty Fund, 1982), especially Chapters I and II.

[3] For an excellent overview, see H. Schneider, *Gesetzgebung* (C. F. Müller, 1982).

[4] R. Schütze, 'The Morphology of Legislative Power in the European Community: Legal Instruments and the Federal Division of Powers' [2006] 25 YEL 91.

[5] Article 289 (3) TFEU (emphasis added).

[6] In the words of Dicey (supra n. 2), 37–38: 'The principle of Parliamentary sovereignty means neither more nor less than this, namely that Parliament thus defined has, under the English constitution, the right to make or unmake any law whatever: and, further, that no person or body is recognised by the law of England as having a right to override or set aside the legislation of Parliament.'

powers. They must be *conferred* by its foundational charter: the European Treaties. This constitutional principle is called the 'principle of conferral'. The Treaty on European Union defines it as follows:

> Under the principle of conferral, the Union shall act only within the limits of the competences conferred upon it by the Member States in the Treaties to attain the objectives set out therein. Competences not conferred upon the Union in the Treaties remain with the Member States.[7]

The Treaties employ the notion of competence in various provisions. Nevertheless, there is no positive definition of the concept. So what is a legislative competence? The best definition is this: a legislative competence is the *material field* within which an authority is entitled to legislate. What are these material fields in which the Union is entitled to legislate? The Treaties do *not* enumerate the Union's 'competences' in a single list. Instead, the Treaties pursue a different technique: they attribute legal competence for each and every Union activity in the respective Treaty title. Each policy area contains a provision – sometimes more than one – on which Union legislation can be based. The various 'Union policies and internal actions' of the Union are set out in Part III of the Treaty on the Functioning of the European Union (Table 10).[8]

The Treaties present a picture of thematically limited competences in distinct policy areas. This picture is however – partly – misleading. Three legal developments have posed serious threats to the principle of conferral. First, the rise of teleological interpretation. The Union's competences are interpreted in such a way that they potentially 'spill over' into other policy areas. This 'spill over' effect can be particularly observed with regard to a second development: the rise of the Union's general competences. For in addition to thematic competences in specific areas, the Union enjoys two legal bases that horizontally cut across the various policy titles within the Treaties. These two competences are Articles 114 and 352 TFEU. The former can be found in Title VII and deals with the approximation of national laws; the latter is placed in the final provisions of the TFEU. Lastly, a third development would qualify the principle of conferral significantly: the doctrine of implied powers. However, that development will be looked at in Chapter 6 in the context of the Union's external powers.[9]

(a) Teleological interpretation

The Union must act 'within the limits of the competences conferred upon it *by the Member States*'.[10] Did this mean that the Member States would be able to

---

[7] Article 5 (2) TEU.
[8] And yet there exist some legal bases outside Part III of the TFEU, such as Article 16 (2) TFEU 'on rules relating to the protection of individuals with regard to the processing of personal data by Union institutions', and Article 352 TFEU – the Union's most famous legal base.
[9] On this point, see: Chapter 6 – Section 1(c) below.   [10] Article 5 (2) TEU (emphasis added).

Table 10 Union Policies and Internal Actions

Part III TFEU – Union Policies and Internal Actions			
Title I	The Internal Market	Title XIII	Culture
Title II	Free Movement of Goods	Title XIV	Public Health
Title III	Agriculture and Fisheries	Title XV	Consumer Protection
Title IV	Free Movement of Persons, Services and Capital	Title XVI	Trans-European Networks
Title V	Area of Freedom, Security and Justice	Title XVII	Industry
Title VI	Transport	Title XVIII	Economic, Social and Territorial Cohesion
Title VII	Common Rules on Competition, Taxation and Approximation of Laws	Title XIX	Research and Technological Development and Space
Title VIII	Economic and Monetary Policy	Title XX	Environment
Title IX	Employment	Title XXI	Energy
Title X	Social Policy	Title XXII	Tourism
Title XI	The European Social Fund	Title XXIII	Civil Protection
Title XII	Education, Vocational Training, Youth and Sport	Title XXIV	Administrative Cooperation

Title XX – Environment	
Article 191	Aims and Objectives
Article 192	**Legislative Competence**
Article 193	Powers of the Member States

Article 192

The European Parliament and the Council, acting in accordance with the ordinary legislative procedure and after consulting the Economic and Social Committee and the Committee of the Regions, shall decide what action is to be taken by the Union in order to achieve the objectives referred to in Article 191.(...)

determine the scope of the Union's competences? A *strict* principle of conferral would indeed deny the Union the power autonomously to interpret its competences. But this solution encounters serious practical problems: how is the Union to work if every legislative bill would need to gain the consent of every national parliament? Classic international organisations solve this dilemma between theory and practice by insisting that the interpretation of international treaties must be in line with the clear intentions of the Member States.[11] Legal

---

[11] In international law, this principle is called the 'in dubio mitius' principle. In case of a doubt, the 'milder' interpretation should be preferred.

competences will thus be interpreted restrictively. This restrictive interpretation is designed to preserve the sovereign rights of the States by preserving the historical meaning of the founding treaty.

By contrast, a *soft* principle of conferral allows for the teleological interpretation of competences. Instead of looking at the historical will of the founders, teleological interpretation asks what is the purpose – or *telos* – of a rule. It thus looks behind the legal text in search for a legal solution to a social problem that may not have been anticipated when the text was drafted. Teleological interpretation can therefore – partly – constitute a 'small' amendment of the original rule. It is potentially a method of incremental change that complements the – rare – qualitative changes following 'big' Treaty amendments.

Has the Union been able autonomously to interpret the scope of its competences, and if so how? After a brief period of following international law logic,[12] the Union embraced the constitutional technique of teleological interpretation. This technique can be seen in relation to the interpretation of the Union's *competences*, as well in relation to as the interpretation of European *legislation*. The first situation is famously illustrated in the controversy surrounding the adoption of the (first) Working Time Directive.[13] The Directive had been based on a provision within Title X on 'Social Policy'. That provision allowed the Union to 'encourage improvements, especially in the working environment, as regards the health and safety of workers'.[14] Would this competence entitle the Union to adopt legislation on the general organisation of working time?[15] The United Kingdom strongly contested this teleological reading. It claimed that there was no thematic link to health and safety, and that the Union legislator had therefore acted ultra vires. The Court, however, backed up the Union legislator. Its teleological reasoning was as follows:

> There is nothing in the wording of Article [153 TFEU] to indicate that the concepts of 'working environment', 'safety' and 'health' as used in that provision should, in the absence of other indications, be interpreted restrictively, and not as embracing all factors, physical or otherwise, capable of affecting the health and

---

[12] See, e.g., Case 8/55, *Fédération Charbonnière de Belgique* v. *High Authority of the European Coal and Steel Community*, [1955] ECR 245.

[13] Case C-84/94, *United Kingdom of Great Britain and Northern Ireland* v. *Council*, [1996] ECR I-5755.

[14] Ex-Article 118a (1) EEC. This competence is today Article 153 (1) (a) TFEU, which allows the Union to support and implement the activities of the Member States as regards the 'improvement in particular of the working environment to protect workers' health and safety'.

[15] Section II of Directive 93/104 regulated the minimum rest periods. Member States were obliged to introduce national laws to ensure that every worker is entitled to a minimum daily rest period of eleven consecutive hours per twenty-four hour period (*ibid.*, Article 3), and to a rest break where the working day is longer than six hours (*ibid.*, Article 4). Article 5 granted a minimum uninterrupted rest period of twenty-four hours in each seven-day period, and determined that this period should in principle include Sunday. Article 6 established a maximum weekly working time of forty-eight hours; and finally, the Directive established a four weeks' paid annual leave (*ibid.*, Article 7).

safety of the worker in his working environment, including in particular certain aspects of the organisation of working time.[16]

With one famous exception,[17] the European Court has indeed accepted all the teleological interpretations of Union competences by the Union legislator.

More than that, however, the Court itself interprets Union legislation in a teleological manner. The classic case in this context is *Casagrande*.[18] In order to facilitate free movement in the internal market, the Union had adopted legislation designed to abolish discrimination between workers of different Member States as regards employment, remuneration and other conditions of work.[19] And to facilitate the integration of the worker and his family into the host state, the Union legislation contained the following provision:

> The children of a national of a Member State who is or has been employed in the territory of another Member State *shall be admitted* to that State's general educational, apprenticeship and vocational training courses under the same conditions as the nationals of that State, if such children are residing in its territory. Member States shall encourage all efforts to enable such children to attend these courses under the best possible conditions.[20]

Would this provision entitle the son of an Italian worker employed in Germany to receive an educational grant for his studies? Literally interpreted, the provision exclusively covers the 'admission' of workers' children to the educational system of the host state. But the Court favoured a teleological interpretation that would maximise the useful effect behind the Union legislation. And since the purpose of the provision was 'to ensure that the children may take advantage on an equal footing of the educational and training facilities available', it followed that the provision referred '*not only to rules relating to admission*, but also to general measures intended to facilitate educational attendance'.[21] Thus, despite the fact that the (then) Treaties did not confer an express competence in educational matters to the Union, the Court considered that national educational grants fell within the scope of European legislation. The teleological interpretation of Union legislation had thus 'spilled over' into spheres that

---

[16] Case C-84/94 (supra n. 13), para. 15. The Court, however, annulled the second sentence of Article 5 of the Directive that had tried to protect, in principle, Sunday as a weekly rest period. In the opinion of the Court, the Council had 'failed to explain why Sunday, as a weekly rest day, is more closely connected with the health and safety of workers than any other day of the week' (*ibid.*, para. 37).

[17] Case C-376/98, *Germany* v. *Parliament and Council (Tobacco Advertising)*, [2000] ECR I-8419. This exception will be discussed below in the context of the Union's 'harmonisation competence'.

[18] Case 9/74, *Casagrande* v. *Landeshauptstadt München*, [1974] ECR 773.

[19] Regulation 1612/68 on freedom of movement for workers within the Community, [1968] OJ (Special English Edition) 475.

[20] *Ibid.*, Article 12 (emphasis added).

[21] Case 9/74, *Casagrande* (supra n. 18), paras. 8–9 (emphasis added).

the Member States had believed to have remained within their exclusive competences.

(b) The general competences of the Union

In principle, the Treaties grant special competences within each policy area.[22] Yet in addition to these thematic competences, the Union legislator enjoys two general competences: Article 114 and Article 352 TFEU. The former represents the Union's 'harmonisation competence'; the latter constitutes its 'residual competence'. Both competences cut *horizontally* through the Union's sectoral policies, and have even been used – or some might say abused – to develop policies not expressly mentioned in the Treaties.

(i) The harmonisation competence: Article 114 TFEU

On the basis of Article 114 TFEU, the European Union is entitled to adopt measures for the approximation of national laws 'which have as their object the establishment and functioning of the internal market'. The Union's competence to harmonise national laws thus applies where national laws affect the establishment *or* functioning of the internal market. The former alternative concerns obstacles to the fundamental freedoms of movement; the latter alternative captures distortions of competition resulting from disparities between national laws.

What was the scope of Article 114? In the past, the Union legislator has employed an extremely wide reading of this general competence. Its potentially unlimited scope is illustrated by *Spain* v. *Council*.[23] The European legislator had created a supplementary protection certificate, which could be granted under the same conditions as national patents by each of the Member States.[24] Three major constitutional hurdles seemed to oppose the constitutionality of this European law. First, Article 114 could theoretically not be used to create *new European* rights as it should only harmonise *existing national* rights. Second, the European law should theoretically further the creation of a single European market; yet, the supplementary certificate extended the duration of national patents and thus prolonged the compartmentalisation of the common market into distinct national markets. Finally, at the time of its adoption only *two* Member States had legislation concerning a supplementary certificate. Was this enough to trigger the Union's *harmonisation* power?

The Court took the first hurdle by force. It simply rejected the claim that the European law created a new right.[25] The same blind force would be applied to

---

[22] We thus find the Union's competence on environmental protection (Article 192 TFEU), in the Treaty's title dedicated to the environment (Title XX of Part III of the TFEU). On this point, see: Table 10 above.

[23] Case C-350/92, *Spain* v. *Council*, [1995] ECR I-1985.

[24] Regulation 1768/92 concerning the creation of a supplementary protection certificate for medicinal products, [1992] OJ L 182/1.

[25] Case C-350/92, *Spain* v. *Council* (supra n. 23), para. 27.

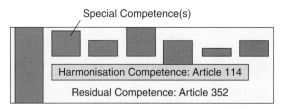

Figure 9a General and Special Competences

the second argument. The Court did not discuss whether the European law hindered the free circulation of pharmaceutical goods between States. Instead, the Court concentrated on the third hurdle in the form of the question as to whether Article 114 required the *pre*-existence of diverse national laws. In the eyes of the Court, this was not the case. The Court accepted that the contested European law aimed '*to prevent the heterogeneous development of national laws* leading to further disparities which would be likely to create obstacles to the free movement of medicinal products within the [Union] and thus directly affect the establishment and the functioning of the internal market'.[26] The European legislator was thus entitled to use its harmonisation power to prevent *future* obstacles to trade or a *potential* fragmentation of the internal market.

For a long time, the scope of the Union's harmonisation power appeared devoid of constitutional boundaries. Yet, the existence of constitutional limits was confirmed in *Germany* v. *Parliament and Council (Tobacco Advertising)*.[27] The bone of contention had been a European law that banned the advertising and sponsorship of tobacco products.[28] Could a prohibition or ban be based on the Union's internal market competence? Germany objected to the idea. It argued that the Union's harmonisation power could only be used to promote the internal market; and this was not so in the event, where the Union legislation constituted, in practice, a total prohibition of tobacco advertising.[29] The Court accepted – to the surprise of many – the argument. And it annulled, for the first time in its history, a European law on the ground that it went beyond the Union's harmonisation power. Emphatically, the Court pointed out that the latter could not grant the Union an unlimited power to regulate the internal market:

> To construe that article as meaning that it vests in the [Union] legislature a general power to regulate the internal market would not only be contrary to the express wording of the provisions cited above but would also be incompatible

---

[26] *Ibid.*, para. 35 (emphasis added).   [27] Case C-376/98, *Tobacco Advertising* (supra n. 17).

[28] Directive 98/43/EC on the approximation of the laws, regulations and administrative provisions of the Member States relating to the advertising and sponsorship of tobacco products, [1998] OJ L 213/9.

[29] Germany had pointed out that the sole form of advertising allowed under the Directive was advertising at the point of sale, which only accounted for 2 per cent of the tobacco industry's advertising expenditure (Case C-376/98, *Tobacco Advertising* (supra n. 17), para. 24).

with the principle embodied in Article [5 TEU] that the powers of the [Union] are limited to those specifically conferred on it. Moreover, a measure adopted on the basis of Article [114 TFEU] of the Treaty must genuinely have as its object the improvement of the conditions for the establishment and functioning of the internal market. If a mere finding of disparities between national rules and of the abstract risk of obstacles to the exercise of fundamental freedoms or of distortions of competition liable to result therefrom were sufficient to justify the choice of Article [114] as a legal basis, judicial review of compliance with the proper legal basis might be rendered nugatory.[30]

With *Tobacco Advertising*, the Court insisted on *three* constitutional limits on the Union's harmonisation power. First, the European law must *harmonise* national laws. Thus, Union legislation 'which leaves unchanged the different national laws already in existence, cannot be regarded as aiming to approximate the laws of the Member States'.[31] Second, a simple disparity in national laws will not be enough to trigger the Union's harmonisation competence. The disparity must give rise to obstacles in trade or appreciable distortions in competition. Thus, while Article 114 TFEU can be used to 'harmonise' *future* disparities in national laws, it must be 'likely' that the divergent development of national laws leads to obstacles in trade.[32] Third, the Union legislation must actually contribute to the elimination of obstacles to free movement or distortions of competition.[33] These three constitutional limits to the Union's 'harmonisation power' have been confirmed *in abstracto*;[34] yet subsequent jurisprudence has led to fresh accusations that Article 114 grants the Union an (almost) unlimited competence.[35]

---

[30] *Ibid.*, paras. 83–4.

[31] Case C-436/03, *European Parliament* v. *Council of the EU*, [2006] ECR I-3733, para. 44. The Court here confirmed and extended the point made in relation to intellectual property law (see Case C-350/92 *Spain* v. *Council* (supra n. 23); as well as Case C-377/98, *Netherlands* v. *Council and Parliament*, [2001] ECR I-7079) to 'new legal forms in addition to the national forms of cooperative societies' (*ibid.*, para. 40).

[32] Case C-376/98, *Tobacco Advertising* (supra n. 17), para. 86.

[33] Case C-491/01, *The Queen* v. *Secretary of State for Health, ex parte British American Tobacco*, [2002] ECR I-11453, para. 60.

[34] On this point, see: *ibid.*, as well as Case C-210/03, *Swedish Match*, [2004] ECR I-11893, Case C-380/03, *Germany* v. *Parliament and Council (Tobacco Advertising II)*, [2006] ECR I-11573.

[35] See Case C-380/03, *Tobacco Advertising II* (supra n. 34), para. 80: 'Recourse to Article [114 TFEU] as a legal basis does not presuppose the existence of an actual link with free movement between the Member States in every situation covered by the measure founded on that basis. As the Court has previously pointed out, to justify recourse to Article [114 TFEU] as the legal basis what matters is that the measure adopted on that basis must actually be intended to improve the conditions for the establishment and functioning of the internal market.' This statement explains why a total ban on the marketing of a product may still be justified under Article [114 TFEU] (see Case C-210/03, *Swedish Match* (supra n. 34). This has led D. Wyatt, 'Community Competence to Regulate the Internal Market' (Oxford University Faculty of Law Research Paper 9/2007), to query whether *Tobacco Advertising I* was a 'false dawn' (*ibid.*, 23). For a recent confirmation of this thesis, see: Case C-58/08, *The Queen, ex parte Vodafone et al* v. *Secretary of State*, (nyr).

(ii) The residual competence: Article 352 TFEU

Article 352 TFEU constitutes the most general competence within the Treaties. Comparable to the 'Necessary and Proper Clause' in the American Constitution,[36] it allows the Union to legislate or act where it is 'necessary, within the framework of the policies defined in the Treaties, to attain one of the objectives set out in the Treaties, and the Treaties have not provided the necessary powers'.

The legislative competence under Article 352 TFEU may be used in two ways. First, it can be employed in a policy title in which the Union is already given a specific competence, but where the latter is deemed insufficient to achieve a specific objective. Second, the residual competence can be used to develop a policy area that has no specific title within the Treaties. The textbook illustration for the second – and more dangerous – potential of Article 352 TFEU is provided by the development of a Union environmental policy *prior* to the Single European Act. For, stimulated by the political enthusiasm to develop such a European policy after the 1972 Paris Summit, the Commission and the Council faced the legal problem that environmental policy was not an official Union policy. There was therefore no specific legal title offered by the Treaties. And the way out of this dilemma was suggested by the Member States themselves. They called on the Union institutions to make the widest possible use of all provisions of the Treaties, especially Article 352.[37] The Member States thus favoured an extensive interpretation of the provision to cause a 'small amendment' of the Treaties.[38] The 'indirect' development of a European environmental competence was indeed impressive.[39]

Are there constitutional limits to Article 352 TFEU? The provision expressly mentions two limitations. First, '[m]easures based on this Article shall not entail harmonisation of Member States' laws or regulations in cases where the Treaties exclude such harmonisation'.[40] This precludes the use of the Union's

---

[36] According to Article I, Section 8, Clause 18 of the US Constitution, the American Union shall have the power '[t]o make all Laws which shall be necessary and proper for carrying into Execution the foregoing Powers, and all other Powers vested by this Constitution in the Government of the United States, or in any Department or Officer thereof'.

[37] The Declaration read: 'They [Heads of State or Government] agreed that in order to accomplish the tasks laid out in the different action programmes, it was advisable to use as widely as possible all the provisions of the Treaties *including [Article 352]*' (European Council, First Summit Conference of the Enlarged Community; [1972] 10 *Bulletin of the European Communities*, 9 at 23 (emphasis added)).

[38] This has been expressly recognised by the German Constitutional Court. According to the Court's Lisbon Decision (cf. BVerfGE 123, 267), Article 352 TFEU 'makes it possible to substantially emend [the] Treaty foundations of the European Union' (*ibid.* para. 328).

[39] Prior to the entry into force of the SEA, a significant number of environment-related measures were adopted on the basis of Articles 115 and 352, thus 'laying the foundation for the formation of a very specific [Union] environmental policy' (see F. Tschofen, 'Article 235 of the Treaty Establishing the European Economic Community: Potential Conflicts between the Dynamics of Lawmaking in the Community and National Constitutional Principles' [1991] 12 *Michigan Journal of International Law* 471 at 477).

[40] Article 352 (3) TFEU.

residual competence in policy areas in which the Union is limited to merely 'complement' national action.[41] Second, Article 352 'cannot serve as a basis for attaining objectives pertaining to the common foreign and security policy'.[42] This codifies past jurisprudence,[43] and is designed to protect the constitutional boundary drawn between the Treaty on European Union and the Treaty on the Functioning of the European Union.[44]

In addition to these two express boundaries, the European Court has also recognised an *implied* limitation to the Union's residual competence. While Article 352 could be used for 'small' amendments to the Treaties, it could not be used to effect 'qualitative leaps' that would change the constitutional identity of the European Union.[45] The Court confirmed this implied restriction in Opinion 2/94.[46] The European Court had here been requested to preview the Union's power to accede to the European Convention on Human Rights ('ECHR') – at a time when there was no express power to do so in the Treaties.[47] The Court characterised the relationship between the Union's residual competence and the principle of conferral as follows:

> Article [352] is designed to fill the gap where no specific provisions of the Treaty confer on the [Union] institutions express or implied powers to act, if such powers appear none the less to be necessary to enable the [Union] to carry out its functions with a view to attaining one of the objectives laid down by the Treaty. That provision, being an integral part of an institutional system based on the principle of conferred powers, cannot serve as a basis for widening the scope of [Union] powers *beyond the general framework* created by the provisions of the Treaty as a whole and, in particular, by those that define the *tasks* and the *activities* of the [Union]. On any view, Article [352] cannot be used as a basis for the adoption of provisions whose effect would, in substance, be to amend the Treaty without following the procedure which it provides for that purpose.[48]

---

[41] On 'complementary' competences in the Union legal order that exclude all harmonisation, see: Section 2 below.

[42] Article 352 (4) TFEU.

[43] See Case C-402/05P, *Kadi et al.* v. *Council and Commission*, [2008] ECR I-6351, paras. 198–9.

[44] See Article 40 TEU – second indent: '[T]he implementation of the policies listed in those Articles shall not affect the application of the procedures and the extent of the powers of the institutions laid down by the Treaties for the exercise of the Union competences under this Chapter.'

[45] A. Tizzano, 'The Powers of the Community' in Commission (ed.), *Thirty Years of Community Law* (Office for Official Publications of the EC, 1981) 43 at 58–9: 'To be more specific Article [352] cannot go beyond the bounds, described below, set by what has become known as the [European] constitution.' The author then lists three criteria, namely the 'observance of the principles essential to the organisation's structure', the 'observance of substantial principles of the [European] constitution', and the 'observance of the general principles of law laid down by the Court of Justice', thereby anticipating the ECJ's stance in Opinion 2/94.

[46] Opinion 2/94 (*Accession by the European Community to the European Convention of Human Rights*), [1996] ECR I-1759.

[47] After the Lisbon Treaty, the Union is now given the express competence to accede to the Convention (see Article 6 (2) TEU). On this point, see: Chapter 12 – Section 3(b) below.

[48] Opinion 2/94 (supra n. 46), paras. 29–30 (emphasis added).

The framework of the Treaty was thereby defined by the Union's tasks and activities. They would form the outer jurisdictional circle within which any legislative activity of the Union had to take place. However, instead of clarifying whether the protection of human rights constituted an 'objective' of the European Union,[49] the Court – prudently to some, in a cowardly manner to others – concentrated on the *external* constitutional limits which any interpretation of Article 352 would encounter. The judicial reasoning in the second part of the judgment was as follows: the accession of the Union to the ECHR would not cause a small (informal) amendment of the Union legal order, but one with '*fundamental institutional implications* for the [Union] and for the Member States, [which] would be of *constitutional significance* and would therefore be such as to go beyond the scope of Article [352]'. 'It could be brought about only by way of Treaty amendment.'[50] Article 352 would thus encounter an external border in the constitutional identity of the European legal order.

2. The categories of Union competences

The original Treaties did not specify the relationship between European and national competences.[51] They betrayed no sign of a distinction between different competence categories.

Two competing conceptions therefore emerged in the early childhood of the European legal order.[52] According to a first theory, all competences mentioned in the Treaties were exclusive competences. The Member States had fully 'transferred' their powers to the European Union,[53] and the division of powers

---

[49] According to the ECJ, human rights would only constitute a *condition* for the lawfulness of Union acts. The laconic reasoning on the part of the Court might be taken to mean that it did not exclude the possibility of considering a human rights policy as an autonomous objective or task of the Union (consider paras. 32–4 of Opinion 2/94 (supra n. 46)). Alston and Weiler assert that '[a]t no point in that Opinion did the Court suggest that the protection of human rights was not an objective of the [Union], nor did it say that the [Union] lacked competence to legislate in the field of human rights': see P. Alston and J. Weiler, 'An "Ever Closer Union" in Need of a Human Rights Policy: The European Union and Human Rights' in P. Alston, M. Bustelo, and J. Heenan (eds.), *The EU and Human Rights* (Oxford University Press, 1999), 3 at 24–5.

[50] Opinion 2/94 (supra n. 46), para. 35. This treaty amendment has taken place with the Lisbon Treaty, see Article 6 (2) TEU: 'The Union shall accede to the European Convention for the Protection of Human Rights and Fundamental Freedoms. Such accession shall not affect the Union's competences as defined in the Treaties.'

[51] J. V. Louis, 'Quelques Réflexions sur la Répartition des Compétences entre la Communauté Européenne et ses États Membres' [1979] 2 *Revue d'Intégration Européenne* 355, 357.

[52] For an early discussion of these two conceptions, see Tizzano, 'The Powers of the Community' (supra n. 45), 63–7. Tizzano calls the first conception the 'federalist' view, the second conception the 'internationalist' view.

[53] This is the term used in Case 6/64, *Costa* v. *ENEL*, [1964] ECR 585: 'By creating a [Union] of unlimited duration, having its own institutions, its own personality, its own legal capacity and capacity of representation on the international plane and, more particularly, *real powers stemming from a limitation of sovereignty or a transfer of powers from the States to the [Union]*, the Member States have limited their sovereign rights, albeit within limited fields, and have thus created a body of law which binds both their nationals and themselves' (emphasis added).

between the Union and the Member States was thus based on a strict separation of competences.[54] An alternative second conception of the nature of Union competences also emerged in those early days: all the Union's powers were shared powers.[55] Member States had only renounced *their* exclusive right to act within their territory by permitting the Union to share in the exercise of public functions. The constitutional development of the European legal order was to take place between these two extreme conceptions. Different categories of Union competence were 'discovered' in the course of the 1970s.[56]

What is the purpose of having different competence categories? Different types of competences constitutionally pitch the *relative degree of responsibility of public authorities* within a material policy field. The respective differences are of a relational kind: exclusive competences 'exclude' the other authority from acting within the same policy area, while non-exclusive competences permit the co-existence of two legislators. Importantly, in order to provide a clear picture of the federal division of powers, each policy area should ideally correspond to one competence category.

What then are the competence categories developed in the European legal order? The distinction between exclusive and non-exclusive competences had emerged early on.[57] The Treaties today distinguish between various categories of Union competence in Article 2 TFEU. The provision reads as follows:

1. When the Treaties confer on the Union exclusive competence in a specific area, only the Union may legislate and adopt legally binding acts, the Member States being able to do so themselves only if so empowered by the Union or for the implementation of Union acts.

2. When the Treaties confer on the Union a competence shared with the Member States in a specific area, the Union and the Member States may legislate and adopt legally binding acts in that area. The Member States shall exercise their competence to the extent that the Union has not exercised its competence. The Member States shall again exercise their competence to the extent that the Union has decided to cease exercising its competence.

3. The Member States shall coordinate their economic and employment policies within arrangements as determined by this Treaty, which the Union shall have competence to provide.

---

[54] The exclusivity thesis had been fuelled by early pronouncements of the European Court (see e.g., Case 30/59, *De Gezamenlijke Steenkolenmijnen in Limburg* v. *High Authority of the European Coal and Steel Community*, [1961] ECR 1, para. 22: 'In the Community field, namely in respect of everything that pertains to the pursuit of the common objectives within the Common Market, the institutions of the Community have been endowed with exclusive authority').

[55] See, e.g., H. P. Ipsen, *Europäisches Gemeinschaftsrecht* (J. C. B. Mohr, 1972), 432.

[56] On this development, see R. Schütze, *From Dual to Cooperative Federalism: The Changing Structure of European Law* (Oxford University Press, 2009), 157 et seq.

[57] *Ibid.*

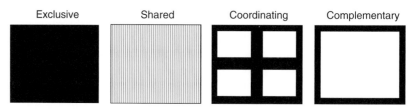

Figure 9b Competence Types

4. The Union shall have competence, in accordance with the provisions of the Treaty on European Union, to define and implement a common foreign and security policy, including the progressive framing of a common defence policy.

5. In certain areas and under the conditions laid down in the Treaties, the Union shall have competence to carry out actions to support, coordinate or supplement the actions of the Member States, without thereby superseding their competence in these areas. Legally binding acts of the Union adopted on the basis of the provisions of the Treaties relating to these areas shall not entail harmonisation of Member States' laws or regulations.

The Treaties thus expressly recognise four general competence categories: exclusive competences, shared competences, coordinating competences and complementary competences. And Articles 3–6 TFEU correlate the various Union policies to a particular competence category. In addition, Article 2 (4) TFEU acknowledges a separate competence category for the Union's common foreign and security policy.

Let us look at the Union's internal competence categories in this section, while the Union's CFSP competence will be discussed in Chapter 6.

(a) Exclusive competences: Article 3 TFEU

Exclusive powers are constitutionally guaranteed monopolies. Only one governmental level is entitled to act autonomously. Exclusive competences are thus double-edged provisions. Their positive side entitles one authority to act, while their negative side 'excludes' anybody else from acting autonomously within its scope. For the European legal order, exclusive competences are defined as areas, in which 'only the Union may legislate and adopt legally binding acts'. The Member States will only be enabled to act 'if so empowered by the Union or for the implementation of Union acts'.[58]

What are the policy areas of constitutional exclusivity? In the past, the Court had accepted a number of competences to qualify under this type. The first exclusive competence was discovered in the context of the Common Commercial

---

[58] Article 2 (1) TFEU.

Policy (CCP). In Opinion 1/75,[59] the Court found that the existence of a merely shared competence within the field would 'compromise[] the effective defence of the common interests of the [Union]'.[60] A second area of exclusive competence was soon discovered in relation to the conservation of biological resources of the sea. In *Commission* v. *United Kingdom*,[61] the Court found that Member States would be 'no longer entitled to exercise any power of their own in the matter of conservation measures in the waters under their jurisdiction'.[62]

Article 3 TFEU now expressly mentions five policy areas: (a) the customs union; (b) the establishment of the competition rules necessary for the functioning of the internal market; (c) monetary policy for the Member States whose currency is the euro; (d) the conservation of marine biological resources under the common fisheries policy; and (e) the common commercial policy.[63] In the light of the judicial status quo, this enumeration poses some definitional problems. First, there was arguably no need to expressly mention the exclusive competence for the establishment of a customs union. On the one hand, the competence to establish *intra*-Union customs has been 'abolished'.[64] And regarding the *external* aspect of the customs union competence, on the other hand, the adoption of a common customs tariff is already covered by the Union's Common Commercial Policy competence. Second, what distinguishes the competition rules from the establishment of *all other rules* 'necessary for the functioning of the internal market'? The constitutional drafters seem to have fallen victim to a logical fallacy: these rules will not necessarily require the exclusion of all national action within their scope.[65] Third, as regards monetary policy, the European Union is to enjoy an exclusive competence *only* in relation to the Member States whose currency is the euro.[66] Finally, subparagraph (d) codifies a constitutional chestnut that, in light of its subsequent judicial biog-

---

[59] Opinion 1/75 (*Draft understanding on a local cost standard*) [1975] ECR 1355

[60] *Ibid.*, para. 13.   [61] Case 804/79, *Commission* v. *United Kingdom*, [1981] ECR 1045.

[62] *Ibid.*, para. 18.   [63] Article 3 (1) TFEU.

[64] On the concept of 'abolished competences', see D. Simon, *Le Système Juridique Communautaire* (Presses Universitaires de France, 1998), 83.

[65] R. Schütze, 'Dual Federalism Constitutionalised: the Emergence of Exclusive Competences in the EC Legal Order' [2007] 32 EL Rev 3, 22–23. However, the Court has recently confirmed the existence of a partially exclusive competition law competence in Case C-550/07P, *Akzo Nobel Chemicals et al.* v. *Commission* (nyr), para. 116: 'As far as concerns the principle of conferred powers, it must be stated that the rules of procedure with respect to competition law, as set out in Article 14 of Regulation No 17 and Article 20 of Regulation No 1/2003, are part of the provisions necessary for the functioning of the internal market whose adoption is part of the exclusive competence conferred on the Union by virtue of Article 3(1)(b) TFEU.'

[66] Can an exclusive Union policy be subject to differential integration? There is an important objection to extending the concept of constitutional exclusivity to situations of differential integration: the fact that there is more than one public authority – the European Union and the national authorities of the *non-participating* Member States – within Europe could provide a theoretical argument against classifying monetary union as an exclusive competence *of the European Union*.

raphy,[67] could well have been (re)integrated into the European Union's *shared* agricultural competence.

(b) Shared competences: Article 4 TFEU

Shared competences are the 'ordinary' competences of the European Union. Unless the Treaties expressly provide otherwise, a Union competence will be shared.[68]

Within a shared competence, 'the Union and the Member States may legislate'.[69] However, according to the formulation in Article 2(2) TFEU both appear to be prohibited from acting at the same time: '[t]he Member States shall exercise their competence to the extent that the Union has not exercised its competence'. This formulation invokes the geometrical image of a divided field: the Member States may only legislate in that part which the European Union has not (yet) entered. Within one field, *either* the European Union *or* the Member States can exercise their shared competence.[70]

When viewed against the constitutional status quo ante, this is a mystifying conception of shared competences. For in the past fifty years, shared competences allowed the Union and the Member States to act in the same field at the same time. The exception to that rule concerned situations where the Union field preempted the Member States.[71] The formulation in Article 2 (2) TFEU is based on that exception. It appears to demand 'automatic [field] preemption of Member State action where the Union has exercised its power'.[72] Will the technique of European minimum harmonisation – allowing for higher national standards – thus be in danger? This seems doubtful, since the Treaties expressly identify minimum harmonisation competences as shared competences.[73]

---

[67] For the re-transformation of the 'conservation of marine biological resources' competence into a *de facto* shared competence, see Schütze, *From Dual to Cooperative Federalism* (supra n. 56), 179 et seq.

[68] Article 4 TFEU states that EU competences will be shared 'where the Treaties confer on it a competence which does not relate to the areas referred to in Article 3 and 6', that is: areas of exclusive or complementary EU competence.

[69] Article 2 (2) TFEU.

[70] The Union may, however, decide to 'cease exercising its competence'. This reopening of legislative space arises 'when the relevant EU institutions decide to repeal a legislative act, in particular better to ensure constant respect for the principles of subsidiarity and proportionality'. See: Declaration (No. 18) 'In relation to the delimitation of competences'.

[71] On the various preemption types, see: Chapter 10 – Section 3(a) below.

[72] P. Craig, 'Competence: Clarity, Conferral, Containment and Consideration' [2004] 29 EL Rev 323, 334. The Treaties however clarify that such field preemption would 'only' be in relation to the legislative act (see Protocol (No. 25) 'on the Exercise of Shared Competence': 'With reference to Article 2 of the Treaty on the Functioning of the European Union on shared competence, when the Union has taken action in a certain area, the scope of this exercise of competence only covers those elements governed by the Union act in question and therefore does not cover the whole [competence] area.').

[73] See Article 4 (2) (e) TFEU on the shared 'environment' competence.

Sadly, this preemption problem is not the only textual problem within Article 4 TFEU. For the provision recognises a special type of shared competence in Articles 4 (3) and (4) TFEU. Both paragraphs separate the policy areas of research, technological development and space, as well as development cooperation and humanitarian aid from the 'normal' shared competences. What is so special about these areas? According to paragraphs 3 and 4, the 'exercise of that competence shall not result in Member States being prevented from exercising theirs'. But since that qualification actually undermines the very essence of what constitutes a 'shared' competence, set out in Article 2 (2) TFEU, these policy areas should never have been placed there. This special type of shared competence has been described as parallel competence.[74]

(c) Coordinating competences: Article 5 TFEU

Coordinating competences are defined in the third paragraph of Article 2 TFEU; and Article 5 TFEU places 'economic policy', 'employment policy' and 'social policy' within this category. The inspiration for this third category was the absence of a political consensus in the European Convention. Whereas one group wished to place economic and employment coordination within the category of shared competences, an opposing view advocated their classification as complementary competence. The Presidium thus came to feel that 'the specific nature of the coordination of Member States' economic and employment policies merits a separate provision'.[75]

The constitutional character of coordinating competences remains largely undefined. From Articles 2 and 5 TFEU, we may solely deduce that the European Union has a competence to provide 'arrangements' for the Member States to exercise their competences in a coordinating manner. The Union's coordination effort may include the adoption of 'guidelines' and 'initiatives to ensure coordination'. It has been argued that the political genesis for this competence category should place it, on the normative spectrum, between shared and complementary competences.[76] If this systematic interpretation is

---

[74] But even this definition is problematic, for it is simply difficult to imagine that a Union *legal* act has no limiting effect whatsoever on the powers of the Member States. Assuming, for example, that the European Union takes a legal position within the area of development cooperation. Should we believe that *all national measures adopted within this area will be permitted*, even if they actually hinder or impede the EU scheme? For if this was the case, why was there any need for expressly requiring that 'in order to promote the complementarity and efficiency of their action, the Union and the Member States *shall* coordinate their policies on development cooperation and *shall* consult each other on their aid programmes' (Article 210 TFEU (emphasis added))? How can two parallels 'complement' each other and why emphasise a duty of cooperation for two levels that supposedly could never come into conflict?

[75] The Presidium CONV 724/03 (Annex 2), p. 68. Arguably, the addition of a new competence type was unnecessary in light of Article 2 (6) TFEU. The provision states: 'The scope of and arrangements for exercising the Union's competences shall be determined by the provisions of the Treaties relating to each area.'

[76] In this sense, see Craig, 'Competence' (supra n. 72), 338.

accepted, coordinating competences would have to be normatively stronger than complementary competences. This would imply that the adoption of Union acts resulting in *some* degree of harmonisation would be constitutionally permitted under these competences.

(d) Complementary competences: Article 6 TFEU

The term 'complementary competence' is not used in Article 2 (5) TFEU. However, it appears to be the best way generically to refer to 'actions to support, coordinate or supplement the actions of the Member States'.[77] Article 6 TFEU lists seven areas: the protection and improvement of human health; industry; culture; tourism; education, vocational training, youth and sport; civil protection; and administrative cooperation. Is this an exhaustive list? This should be the case in light of the residual character of shared competences.[78]

The contours of this competence type are – again – largely unexplored by jurisprudence. However, after the Lisbon reform, it appears to be a defining characteristic of complementary competences that they do 'not entail harmonisation of Member States' laws or regulations'.[79] But what exactly is the prohibition of 'harmonisation' supposed to mean? Two views can be put forward. According to the first, the exclusion of harmonisation means that Union legislation must not modify *existing* national legislation. However, considering the wide definition given to the concept of 'harmonisation' by the Court of Justice in *Spain* v. *Council*, any legislative intervention on the part of the Union will unfold a *de facto* harmonising effect within the national legal orders.[80] From this strict reading, the exclusion of harmonisation would consequently deny all preemptive effect to European legislation.[81] A second, less

---

[77] Article 2 (5) TFEU.

[78] Prior to the Lisbon Treaty, the concept of complementary competences could be employed to refer to *two* types of competences. In the first group were those competences that constitutionally limit the European legislator to the adoption of minimum standards that could then be 'complemented' by higher national standards. The second group of 'complementary competences' expressly described the function of the Union legislator as 'complementing', 'supplementing' or 'supporting' national action by means of 'incentive measures' that would exclude all harmonisation within the field. Article 2 (5) TFEU restricts the definition of complementary competences to this second group. This definitional *fait accompli* places the first group into the residual category of shared competences. On the disadvantages of this terminological choice, see: R. Schütze, 'Lisbon and the Federal Order of Competences: A Prospective Analysis' [2008] 33 EL Rev 709, and Conclusion below.

[79] Article 2 (5) TFEU – second indent.

[80] Case C-350/92, *Spain* v. *Council* [1995] ECR I-1985. In that judgment, the Court found the adoption of a Regulation not beyond the scope of Article 114 TFEU because it aimed 'to prevent the heterogeneous development of national laws leading to further disparities' in the internal market (*ibid.*, para. 35). The case was discussed in Section 1(b) above.

[81] Cf. A. Bardenhewer-Rating and F. Niggermeier, 'Artikel 152', para. 20, in H. von der Groeben and J. Schwarze, *Kommentar zum Vertrag über die EU* (Nomos, 2003).

restrictive, view argues that the Union's legislative powers are only trimmed so as to prevent the de jure harmonisation of national legislation.[82]

3. Legislative procedures: ordinary and special

British constitutionalism defines (primary) legislation as an act adopted by the Queen-in-Parliament. Behind this 'compound' legislator stands a legislative procedure. This legal procedure links the House of Commons, the House of Lords and the Monarchy. European constitutionalism also follows a procedural definition of legislative power. However, unlike British constitutional law, the Treaties distinguish between two types of legislative procedures: an ordinary legislative procedure and special legislative procedures. Article 289 TFEU indeed states:

1. The ordinary legislative procedure shall consist in the joint adoption by the European Parliament and the Council of a regulation, directive or decision on a proposal from the Commission. This procedure is defined in Article 294.
2. In the specific cases provided for by the Treaties, the adoption of a regulation, directive or decision by the European Parliament with the participation of the Council, or by the latter with the participation of the European Parliament, shall constitute a special legislative procedure.[83]

European 'legislation' is thus – formally – defined as an act adopted by the bicameral Union legislator. (The Commission will ordinarily be involved by making legislative proposals, but this is not – strictly – an absolute characteristic of Union legislation.[84]) According to the *ordinary* legislative procedure, the European Parliament and the Council act as co-legislators with *symmetric* procedural rights. European legislation is therefore seen as the product of a 'joint adoption' of both institutions. But the Treaties also recognise *special* legislative procedures. The defining characteristic of these special procedures is that they abandon the institutional equality of the European Parliament and the Council. Logically, then, Article 289 (2) TFEU recognises two variants. In the first variant, the European Parliament acts as the dominant institution, with the mere 'participation' of the Council in the form of 'consent'.[85] The

---

[82] For Lenaerts, 'incentive measures can be adopted in the form of Regulations, Directives, Decisions or atypical legal acts and are thus normal legislative acts of the [Union.]' '[T]he fact that a [European] incentive measure may have the indirect effect of harmonizing … does not necessarily mean that it conflicts with the prohibition on harmonization' (K. Lenaerts, 'Subsidiarity and Community Competence in the Field of Education' [1994–1995] 1 *Columbia Journal of European Law* 1 at 13 and 15).

[83] Article 289 (1) and (2) TFEU.

[84] There is no mention of the Commission in Article 289 (2) TFEU, and Article 289 (4) TFEU adds: 'In the specific cases provided for by the Treaties, legislative acts may be adopted on the initiative of a group of Member States or of the European Parliament, on a recommendation from the European Central Bank or at the request of the Court of Justice or the European Investment Bank.'

[85] See Articles 223 (2), 226 and 228 TFEU. The procedure for the adoption of the Union budget is laid down in Article 314 TFEU and will not be discussed here.

Ordinary Legislative Procedure   **Special Legislative Procedures**

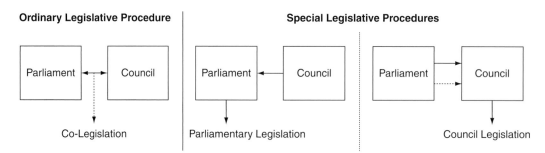

Figure 10 Structure of the Union Legislator

second variant inverts this relationship. The Council is here the dominant institution, with the Parliament either participating through its 'consent',[86] or in the form of 'consultation'.[87]

What tells us when *which* legislative procedure applies? There is no constitutional rationale or procedure catalogue. Each legal basis within a policy area determines which procedure applies,[88] and whether that procedure is of a legislative nature. For example, the Union's harmonisation power in Article 114 TFEU states that the European Parliament and the Council shall act 'in accordance with the *ordinary legislative* procedure'. And the Treaty defines the ordinary legislative procedure in a provision in a section dedicated to the 'Procedures for the Adoption of Acts and other Provisions'.[89] By contrast, there is no specific definition of what constitutes 'special' legislative procedures. They are thus defined in each specific legal basis. Thus, Article 352 TFEU – for example – allows for the adoption of Union measures 'in accordance with a *special legislative* procedure', and defines the latter as the Council acting unanimously on a proposal from the Commission and after obtaining the consent of the European Parliament.

The following two subsections will analyse the ordinary and special legislative procedures in more detail.

---

[86] See Articles 19 (1), 25, 86 (1), 223 (1), 311, 312 and 352 TFEU.
[87] See Articles 21 (3), 22 (1), 22 (2), 23, 64 (3), 77 (3), 81 (3), 87 (3), 89, 113, 115, 118, 126, 127 (6), 153 (2), 182 (4), 192 (2), 203, 262, 308, 311, 349 TFEU.
[88] Some legal bases require the consultation of an 'advisory' body. According to Article 300 TFEU, the Union has two advisory bodies: the 'Economic and Social Committee', and the 'Committee of the Regions'. The former 'shall consist of representatives of organisations of employers, of the employed, and of other parties representative of civil society, notably in socioeconomic, civic, professional and cultural areas' (*ibid.*, para. 2), and its advisory powers are defined in Article 304 TFEU. The Committee of the Regions consists of 'representatives of regional and local bodies who either hold a regional or local authority electoral mandate or are politically accountable to an elected assembly'. Its advisory powers are defined in Article 307 TFEU.
[89] This is Part Six – Title I – Chapter 2 – Section 2 – Article 294 TFEU.

(a) The 'ordinary' legislative procedure

(i) Constitutional theory: formal text

The ordinary legislative procedure has seven stages. Article 294 TFEU defines five stages; two additional stages are set out in Article 297 TFEU.

Proposal stage. Under the ordinary legislative procedure, the Commission enjoys – with minor exceptions – the exclusive right to submit a legislative proposal.[90] This (executive) prerogative guarantees a significant agenda-setting-power to the Commission. The Treaties – partly – protect this power from 'external' interferences by insisting that any amendment that the Commission dislikes will require unanimity in the Council – an extremely high decisional hurdle.[91]

First reading. The Commission proposal goes to the European Parliament. The Parliament will act by a majority of the votes cast,[92] that is: the majority of physically present members. It can reject the proposal,[93] approve it, or – as a middle path – amend it. The bill then moves to the Council, which will act by a qualified majority of its members.[94] Where the Council agrees with Parliament's position, the bill is adopted after the first reading. Where it disagrees, the Council is called to provide its own position and communicate it, with reasons, to Parliament.

Second reading. The (amended) bill lies for the second time in Parliament's court; and Parliament has three choices as to what to do with it. Parliament may positively approve the Council's position by a majority of the votes cast;[95] or reject it by a majority of its component members.[96] Approval is thus easier than rejection. (This tendency is reinforced by assimilating passivity to approval.[97]) However, Parliament has a third choice: it may propose, by the majority of its component members, amendments to the Council's position.[98] The amended

---

[90] Article 294 (2) TFEU. Paragraph 15 recognises exceptions to this rule in cases provided for in the Treaties. Perhaps the most significant exception is provided for by Article 76 TFEU referring to legislative measures in the field of police and judicial cooperation in criminal matters.

[91] Article 293 (1) TFEU, as well as Article 284 (9) TFEU. Moreover, until the conciliation stage the Commission may unilaterally alter or withdraw the proposal: Article 293 (2) TFEU.

[92] Article 294 (3) TFEU is silent on the voting regime within Parliament, and therefore Article 231 TFEU applies: 'Save as otherwise provided in the Treaties, the European Parliament shall act by a majority of the votes cast. The rules of procedure shall determine the quorum.'

[93] This option is not expressly recognised in the text of Article 294 (3) TFEU, but it is indirectly recognised in Rule 56 of the Parliament's Rules of Procedure.

[94] Article 294 (4) and (5) TFEU are silent on the voting regime, and therefore Article 16 (4) TEU applies: 'The Council shall act by a qualified majority except where the Treaties provide otherwise.'

[95] Article 294 (7) (a) TFEU.   [96] Article 294 (7) (b) TFEU.

[97] According to Article 294 (7) (a) TFEU – second alternative, where the Parliament does not act within three months, 'the act shall be deemed to have been adopted in the wording which corresponds to the position of the Council'.

[98] Article 294 (7) (c) TFEU. For an (internal) limitation on what types of amendments can be made, see: Rule 66 (2) of the Parliament's Rules of Procedure. The provision reads: 'An amendment to the Council's position shall be admissible only if it complies with Rules 156 and 157 and seeks: (a) to restore wholly or partly the position adopted by Parliament at its first reading; or (b) to reach a

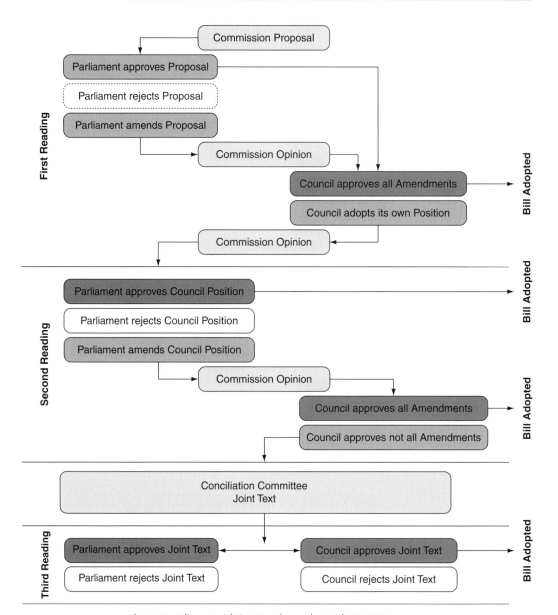

Figure 11 Ordinary Legislative Procedure under Article 294 TFEU

bill will be forwarded to the Council and to the Commission (that must deliver an opinion on the amendments). The bill is thus back in the Council's court,

compromise between the Council and Parliament; or (c) to amend a part of the text of a Council's position which was not included in – or differs in content from – the proposal submitted at first reading and which does not amount to a substantial change within the meaning of Rule 59; or (d) to take account of a new fact or legal situation which has arisen since the first reading. The President's discretion to declare an amendment admissible or inadmissible may not be questioned.'

and the Council has two options. Where it approves all (!) of Parliament's amendments, the legislative act is adopted.[99] (The Council thereby acts by a qualified majority, unless the Commission disagrees with any of the amendments suggested by the Council or the Parliament.[100]). But where the Council cannot approve all of Parliament's amendments, the bill enters into the conciliation stage.[101]

Conciliation stage. This stage presents the last chance to rescue the legislative bill. As agreement within the 'formal' legislature has proved impossible, the Union legal order 'delegates' the power to draft a 'joint text' to a committee. This Committee is called the 'Conciliation Committee'.[102] The mandate of the Committee is restricted to reaching agreement on a joint text 'on the basis of the positions of the European Parliament and the Council at second reading'.[103] This Committee is composed of members representing the Council,[104] and an equal number of members representing the European Parliament.[105] (The Commission will take part 'in' the committee, but is not a part 'of' the Committee. Its function is to be a mere catalyst for conciliation.[106]) The Committee thus represents a 'miniature legislature'; and like its constitutional

---

[99] Article 294 (8) (a) TFEU.   [100] Article 294 (9) TFEU.   [101] Article 294 (8) (b) TFEU.

[102] The Conciliation Committee is not a standing committee, but an ad hoc committee that 'is constituted separately for each legislative proposal requiring conciliation' (European Parliament, Codecision and Conciliation at: www.europarl.europa.eu/code/information/guide_en.pdf, 15).

[103] Article 294 (10) TFEU. However, the Court of Justice has been flexible and allowed the Conciliation Committee to find a joint text that goes beyond the common position after the second reading. (see, Case C-344/04, *The Queen on the application of International Air Transport Association et al.* v. *Department of Transport*, [2006] ECR I-403, paras. 57–9: '[O]nce the Conciliation Committee has been convened, it has the task not of coming to an agreement on the amendments proposed by the Parliament but, as is clear from the very wording of Article [294 TFEU], "of reaching agreement on a joint text", by addressing, on the basis of the amendments proposed by the Parliament, the common position adopted by the Council. The wording of Article [294 TFEU] does not therefore itself include any restriction as to the content of the measures chosen that enable agreement to be reached on a joint text. In using the term "conciliation", the authors of the Treaty intended to make the procedure adopted effective and to confer a wide discretion on the Conciliation Committee. In adopting such a method for resolving disagreements, their very aim was that the points of view of the Parliament and the Council should be reconciled on the basis of examination of all the aspects of the disagreement, and with the active participation in the Conciliation Committee's proceedings of the Commission of the European Communities, which has the task of taking "all the necessary initiatives with a view to reconciling the positions of the ... Parliament and the Council". In this light, taking account of the power to mediate thus conferred on the Commission and of the freedom which the Parliament and the Council finally have as to whether or not to accept the joint text approved by the Conciliation Committee, Article [294 TFEU] cannot be read as limiting on principle the power of that committee.'

[104] The Permanent Representative or his or her Deputy will typically represent the national ministers in the Council.

[105] The parliamentary delegation must reflect the political composition of the formal Parliament (see Rule 68 (2) of the Parliament's Rules of Procedure). It will normally include the three Vice-Presidents responsible for conciliation, the Rapporteur and Chair of the responsible parliamentary committee.

[106] Article 294 (11) TFEU. Formally, it will be the Commissioner responsible for the subject matter of the legislative bill, who will take part in the Conciliation Committee.

model, the Committee co-decides by a qualified majority of the Council representatives, and a majority of the representatives sent by Parliament. Where the Committee does not adopt a joint text, the legislative bill has failed. Where the Committee has managed to approve a joint text, the latter returns to the 'formal' Union legislator for a third reading.

Third reading. The 'formal' Union legislature must positively approve the joint text (without the power of amending it). The Parliament needs to endorse the joint text by a majority of the votes cast, whereas the Council must confirm the text by a qualified majority. Where one of the two chambers disagrees with the proposal made by the Conciliation Committee, the bill finally flounders. Where both chambers approve the text, the bill is adopted and only needs to be 'signed' and 'published'.

Signing and publication. The last two stages before a bill becomes law are set out in Article 297 TFEU which states: 'Legislative acts adopted under the ordinary legislative procedure shall be signed by the President of the European Parliament and by the President of the Council'; and they shall subsequently 'be published in the Official Journal of the European Union'.[107] The publication requirement is a fundamental element of modern societies governed by the rule of law. Only 'public' legislative acts will have the force of law. The Union legal order also requires that all legislative acts 'shall state the reasons on which they are based and shall refer to any proposals, initiatives, recommendations, requests or opinions required by the Treaties'.[108] This formal 'duty to state reasons' can be judicially reviewed, and represents a hallmark of legislative rationality.

(ii) Constitutional practice: informal trilogues

Constitutional texts often only provide a stylised sketch of the formal relations between institutions. And this formal picture will need to be coloured and revised by informal constitutional practices. This is – very – much the case for the constitutional text governing the ordinary legislative procedure. The rudimentary status of the constitutional text is – self-consciously – recognised by the Treaties themselves,[109] and the importance of informal practices has been expressly acknowledged by the European institutions.[110]

---

[107] Article 297 (1) TFEU. For legislation, this will be the 'L' Series.

[108] Article 296 TFEU – second indent.

[109] Article 295 TFEU states: 'The European Parliament, the Council and the Commission shall consult each other and by common agreement make arrangements for their cooperation. To that end, they may, in compliance with the Treaties, conclude interinstitutional agreements which may be of a binding nature.'

[110] See 'Joint Declaration on Practical Arrangements for the Codecision Procedure', [2007] OJ C 145/5. According to paragraphs 1 and 2: 'The European Parliament, the Council and the Commission, hereinafter referred to collectively as "the institutions", note that current practice involving talks between the Council Presidency, the Commission and the chairs of the relevant committees and/or rapporteurs of the European Parliament and between the co-chairs of the

Declining Democratic Representation

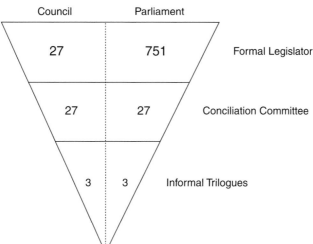

Figure 12 Declining Democratic Representation

The primary expression of these informal institutional arrangements are tripartite meetings ('trilogues'). They combine the representatives of the three institutions in an 'informal framework'.[111] Who are the respective representatives of the three institutions? This is a matter that can be decided by each institution itself. For the Parliament, it will usually involve the 'Rapporteur' and the Chair of the (standing) committee responsible. For the Council, its negotiating team has traditionally involved the Permanent Representative of the Member State holding the Council Presidency, as well as the Chair of the relevant Council Working Group. The Commission will typically be represented by a negotiating team headed by the relevant Director-General.

What is the task of institutional trilogues? The trilogues system is designed to create informal bridges during the formal legislative procedure that open up 'possibilities for agreements at first and second reading stages, as well as contributing to the preparation of the work of the Conciliation Committee'.[112] Trilogues may thus be held 'at all stages of the [ordinary legislative] procedure'.[113] Indeed, a 'Joint Declaration' of the Union institutions contains respective commitments for each procedural stage. In order to facilitate a formal agreement within the Union legislator during the first reading, informal agreements between the institutional representatives will thus be

Conciliation Committee has proved its worth. The institutions confirm that this practice, which has developed at all stages of the codecision procedure, must continue to be encouraged. The institutions undertake to examine their working methods with a view to making even more effective use of the full scope of the codecision procedure as established by the [TFEU].'
[111] *Ibid.*, para. 8.   [112] *Ibid.*, para. 7.   [113] *Ibid.*, para. 8.

forwarded to Parliament or Council respectively.[114] This equally applies to the second reading,[115] and to the conciliation stage.[116] The strategy of informality has proved extremely successful.[117] And yet, there are serious constitutional problems. For informal trilogues should not be allowed to short-circuit the formal legislative procedure. Were this to happen, democratic deliberation within a fairly representative European Union would be replaced by the informal government of a dozen representatives of the three institutions. And indeed, the democratic deficit of the Union would not lie in the *formal* structure of the Union legislator, but in its *informal* bypassing.

(b) The 'special' legislative procedures

In addition to the ordinary legislative procedure, the Treaties recognise three special legislative procedures. Unlike the ordinary procedure, the Union act will here not be the result of a 'joint adoption' of the European Parliament and the Council. It will be adopted by *one* of the two institutions. In the first variant of Article 289 (2) TFEU, this will be the Parliament; yet the Treaties here generally require the 'consent' of the Council. In the second variant of Article 289 (2) TFEU, the Council will adopt the legislative act; yet, the Treaties here require either the 'consent' or 'consultation' of the Parliament. The first two special procedures may be characterised as the 'consent procedure', the third special procedure can be referred to as the 'consultation procedure'.

What are the characteristics of the 'consent procedure' and the 'consultation procedure'? The former requires one institution to consent to the legislative bill of the other. Consent is less than co-decision, for only the dominant institution will be able to determine the substantive content of the bill. The non-dominant institution will be forced to 'take it or leave it'. But this veto power is still – much – stronger than mere consultation. For while the Court has recognised that consultation is 'an essential factor in the institutional balance intended by the Treaty',[118] consultation is nonetheless a mere 'formality'.[119] For the formal

---

[114] *Ibid.*, para. 14: 'Where an agreement is reached through informal negotiations in trilogues, the chair of Coreper shall forward, in a letter to the chair of the relevant parliamentary committee, details of the substance of the agreement, in the form of amendments to the Commission proposal. That letter shall indicate the Council's willingness to accept that outcome, subject to legal-linguistic verification, should it be confirmed by the vote in plenary. A copy of that letter shall be forwarded to the Commission.' For the inverted obligation, see: *ibid.*, para. 18.

[115] *Ibid.*, para. 23.   [116] *Ibid.*, paras. 24–5.

[117] According to the European Parliament, Codecision and Conciliation (supra n. 102), 14, in the period between 2004 and 2009, 72 per cent of legislative acts were agreed at first reading, and 23 per cent at second reading. This leaves only 5 per cent to pass through conciliation and the third reading.

[118] Case 138/79, *Roquette Frères* v. *Council (Isoglucose)*, [1980] ECR 3333, para. 33.

[119] The 'formality' still requires that the Council has to wait until Parliament has provided its opinion (see *ibid.*): 'In that respect it is pertinent to point out that observance of that requirement implied that the Parliament has expressed its opinion. It is impossible to take the view that the requirement is satisfied by the Council's simply asking for the opinion.' On this point, see

obligation to consult will not mean that the adopting institution must take into account the substantive views of the other.[120]

4. The principle of subsidiarity

Subsidiarity – the quality of being 'subsidiary' – derives from *subsidium*. The Latin concept evolved in the military context. It represented an 'assistance' or 'aid' that stayed in the background. Figuratively, an entity is subsidiary where it provides a 'subsidy' – an assistance of subordinate or secondary importance. In political philosophy, the principle of subsidiarity came to represent the idea 'that a central authority should have a subsidiary function, performing only those tasks which cannot be performed effectively at a more immediate or local level'.[121] The principle thus has a positive and a negative aspect.[122] It positively encourages 'large associations' to assist smaller ones, where they need help; and it negatively discourages 'to assign to a greater and higher association what lesser and subordinate organisations can do'. It is this dual character that has given the principle of subsidiarity its 'Janus-like' character.[123]

When did the subsidiarity principle become a constitutional principle of the European Union? The principle of subsidiarity surfaced in 1975,[124] but it would only find official expression in the context of the Union's environmental policy after the Single European Act (1986).[125] The Maastricht Treaty on European Union (1992) finally lifted the subsidiarity principle beyond its environmental confines. It became a general constitutional principle of the European Union. Today, the Treaty on European Union defines it in Article 5 whose third paragraph states:

> Under the principle of subsidiarity, in areas which do not fall within its exclusive competence, the Union shall act only if and in so far as the objectives of the proposed action cannot be sufficiently achieved by the Member States, either at central level or at regional and local level, but can rather, by reason of the scale or effects of the proposed action, be better achieved at Union level.

The definition clarifies that subsidiarity is only to apply within the sphere of non-exclusive powers and thus confirms that the European principle of

---

also: Case C-65/93, *Parliament* v. *Council*, [1995] ECR I-643. However, this case also established implied limitations on Parliament's prerogative (*ibid.*, paras. 27–8).

[120] This was confirmed in Case C-417/93, *Parliament* v. *Council*, [1995] ECR I-1185, esp. paras. 10–11.

[121] *Oxford English Dictionary*: 'subsidiary' and 'subsidiarity'.

[122] C. Calliess, *Subsidiaritäts- und Solidaritätsprinzip in der Europäischen Union* (Nomos, 1999), 26.

[123] V. Constantinesco, 'Who's Afraid of Subsidiarity?' [1991] 11 YEL 33 at 35.

[124] For a detailed textual genealogy of the subsidiarity principle in the European legal order, see Schütze, *From Dual to Cooperative Federalism* (supra n. 56), 247 et seq.

[125] The (then) newly inserted Article 130 r (4) EEC restricted Community environmental legislation to those actions whose objectives could 'be attained better at Community level than at the level of the individual Member States'.

subsidiarity is a principle of *cooperative* federalism.[126] The Treaty definition of subsidiarity recognises *two* tests. The first may be called the *national insufficiency test*. The Union can only act where the objectives of the proposed action could not be sufficiently achieved by the Member States (centrally or regionally). This appears to be an absolute standard. But how can this test be squared with the second test in Article 5 (3) TEU? That test is a *comparative efficiency test*. The Union should not act unless it can *better* achieve the objectives of the proposed action. Will the combination of these two tests mean that the Union would not be entitled to act where it is – in relative terms – better able to tackle a social problem, but where the Member States could – in absolute terms – still achieve the desired result? Worse, the formulation 'if and in so far' potentially offered *two* versions of the subsidiarity principle. The first version concentrates on the 'if' question by asking *whether* the Union should act. This has been defined as the principle of subsidiarity *in a strict sense*. The second version concentrates on the 'in-so-far' question by asking *how* the Union should act. This has been referred to as the principle of subsidiarity *in a wide sense*.[127]

The wording of Article 5 (3) TEU is indeed a textual failure. In the past two decades, two – parallel – approaches evolved to give meaning to the subsidiarity principle. The first approach concentrates on the political safeguards of federalism. The second approach focuses on subsidiarity as an objective judicial standard.

(a) Procedural standard: subsidiarity as a political safeguard of federalism

Despite its literary presence,[128] the principle of subsidiarity has remained a subsidiary principle of European constitutionalism. The reason for its shadowy existence has been its lack of conceptual contours. If subsidiarity was everything to everyone, how should the Union apply it? To limit this semantic uncertainty, constitutional clarifications have tried to 'proceduralise' the principle. This

---

[126] On the meaning of that concept, see: Schütze, *From Dual to Cooperative Federalism* (supra n. 56).

[127] K. Lenaerts, 'The Principle of Subsidiarity and the Environment in the European Union: Keeping the Balance of Federalism' [1994] 17 *Fordham International Law Journal* 846 at 875.

[128] From the – abundant – literature, see only: G. Berman, 'Taking Subsidiarity Seriously: Federalism in the European Community and the United States' [1994] 94 *Columbia Law Review* 331; N. Bernard, 'The Future of European Economic Law in the Light of the Principle of Subsidiarity' [1996] 33 CML Rev 633; G. de Búrca, 'Reappraising Subsidiarity Significance after Amsterdam', Harvard Jean Monnet Working Paper 1999/07; D. Z. Cass, 'The Word that Saves Maastricht? The Principle of Subsidiarity and the Division of Powers within the European Community' [1992] 29 CML Rev 1107; V. Constantinesco, 'Who's Afraid of Subsidiarity?' (supra n. 123); G. Davies, 'Subsidiarity: The Wrong Idea, in the Wrong Place, at the Wrong Time' [2006] 43 CML Rev 63; A. Estella, *The EU Principle of Subsidiarity and its Critique* (Oxford University Press, 2002); K. Lenaerts and P. van Ypersele, 'Le Principe de Subsidiarité et son Contexte: Étude de l'Article 3B du Traité CE' [1994] 30 *Cahier de Droit Européen* 3; T. Schilling, 'A New Dimension of Subsidiarity: Subsidiarity as a Rule and a Principle' [1994] 14 YEL 203; A. G. Toth, 'The Principle of Subsidiarity in the Maastricht Treaty' [1992] 29 CML Rev 1079.

attempt to develop subsidiarity into a political safeguard of federalism can be seen in Protocol (No. 2) 'On the Application of the Principles of Subsidiarity and Proportionality'. Importantly, the Protocol only applies to 'draft legislative acts',[129] that is: acts to be adopted under the ordinary or a special legislative procedure.[130]

The Protocol aims to establish 'a system of monitoring' the application of the principle. Each Union institution is called upon to ensure constant respect for the principle of subsidiarity.[131] And this means in particular that they must forward draft legislative acts to national Parliaments.[132] These draft legislative acts must 'be justified' with regard to the principle of subsidiarity and proportionality.[133] This (procedural) duty to provide reasons is defined as follows:

> Any draft legislative act should contain a detailed statement making it possible to appraise compliance with the principles of subsidiarity and proportionality. This statement should contain some assessment of the proposal's financial impact and, in the case of a directive, of its implications for the rules to be put in place by Member States, including, where necessary, the regional legislation. The reasons for concluding that a Union objective can be better achieved at Union level shall be substantiated by qualitative and, wherever possible, quantitative indicators. Draft legislative acts shall take account of the need for any burden, whether financial or administrative, falling upon the Union, national governments, regional or local authorities, economic operators and citizens, to be minimised and commensurate with the objective to be achieved.[134]

But how is this duty enforced? One solution would point to the European Court;[135] yet, the Protocol prefers a second solution: the active involvement of national parliaments in the legislative procedure of the European Union.[136] The Lisbon Treaty-makers hoped that this idea would kill two birds with one stone. The procedural involvement of national parliaments

---

[129] Article 3 Protocol (No. 2) 'On the Application of the Principles of Subsidiarity and Proportionality'.

[130] However, this will not mean that the judicial principle of subsidiarity does not apply to other types of acts. On the application of the principle of subsidiarity to executive acts, see: Chapter 7 – Section 3(b) below.

[131] Article 1 of the Protocol.   [132] *Ibid.*, Article 4.   [133] *Ibid.*, Article 5.   [134] *Ibid.*

[135] *Ibid.*, Article 8: 'The Court of Justice of the European Union shall have jurisdiction in actions on grounds of infringement of the principle of subsidiarity by a legislative act, brought in accordance with the rules laid down in Article 263 of the Treaty on the Functioning of the European Union by Member States, or notified by them in accordance with their legal order on behalf of their national Parliament or a chamber thereof.' For a discussion of the Court's deferential stance, see Section 4(b) below.

[136] This function is acknowledged in Article 12 (b) TEU, which requests national Parliaments to contribute to the good functioning of the Union 'by seeing to it that the principle of subsidiarity is respected in accordance with the procedures provided for in the Protocol on the application of the principles of subsidiarity and proportionality'.

promised to strengthen the federal *and* the democratic safeguards within Europe.

But if national parliaments are to be the Union's 'watchdogs of subsidiarity',[137] would they enjoy a veto right (hard constitutional solution) or only a monitoring right (soft constitutional solution)? According to the Subsidiarity Protocol, each national parliament may within eight weeks produce a reasoned opinion stating why it considers that a European legislative draft does not comply with the principle of subsidiarity.[138] Each parliament will thereby have two votes.[139] Where the negative votes amount to one-third of all the votes allocated to the national parliaments, the European Union draft 'must be reviewed'. This is called the 'yellow card' mechanism, since the Union legislator 'may decide to maintain, amend or withdraw the draft'.[140]

The yellow card mechanism is slightly strengthened in relation to proposals under the ordinary legislative procedure; albeit, here, only a majority of the votes allocated to the national parliaments will trigger it.[141] Under this 'orange card' mechanism, the Commission's justification for maintaining the proposal, as well as the reasoned opinions of the national parliaments, will be submitted to the Union legislator which will have to consider whether the proposal is compatible with the principle of subsidiarity. Where one of its chambers finds that the proposal violates the principle of subsidiarity, the proposal is rejected.[142] While this arrangement makes it – slightly – easier for the European Parliament to reject a legislative proposal on subsidiarity grounds, it might make it – ironically – more difficult for the Council to block a proposal on the basis of subsidiarity than on the basis of a proposal's lack of substantive merit.[143]

The Subsidiarity Protocol has rejected the idea of a 'red card' mechanism. This rejection has been bemoaned. The proposed procedural safeguards are

---

[137] I. Cooper, 'The Watchdogs of Subsidiarity: National Parliaments and the Logic of Arguing in the EU' [2006] 44 *Journal of Common Market Studies* 281.

[138] Article 6 Protocol (No. 2) 'On the Application of the Principles of Subsidiarity and Proportionality'.

[139] *Ibid.*, Article 7 (1).

[140] *Ibid.*, Article 7 (2). The threshold is lowered to a quarter for European laws in the area of freedom, security and justice.

[141] *Ibid.*, Article 7 (3).

[142] *Ibid.*, Article 7 (3) (b): 'if, by a majority of 55 per cent of the members of the Council or a majority of the votes cast in the European Parliament, the legislator is of the opinion that the proposal is not compatible with the principle of subsidiarity, the legislative proposal shall not be given further consideration'.

[143] For an analysis of this point, see G. Barrett, '"The King is Dead, Long live the King": the Recasting by the Treaty of Lisbon of the Provisions of the Constitutional Treaty concerning National Parliaments' [2008] 33 EL Rev 66 at 80–1. In the light of the voting threshold, 'it seems fair to predict that blockade of legislative proposals under Article 7(2) is likely to be a highly exceptional and unusual situation'.

said to 'add very little' to the federal control of the Union legislator.[144] Others have – rightly – greeted the fact that the subsidiarity mechanism will leave the political decision to adopt the legislative act ultimately to the *European* legislator. '[T]o give national parliaments what would amount to a veto over proposals would be incompatible with the Commission's constitutionally protected independence'.[145] '[A] veto power vested in national Parliaments would distort the proper distribution of power and responsibility in the EU's complex but remarkably successful system of transnational governance by conceding too much to State control.'[146] Indeed, to have turned national parliaments into 'co-legislators' in the making of European law would have aggravated the 'political interweaving' of the European and the national level and thereby deepened joint-decision traps.[147] The rejection of the hard veto solution is thus to be welcomed. The soft constitutional solution will indeed allow national parliaments to channel their scrutiny to where it can be most useful and effective: on their respective national governments.

(b) Substantive standard: subsidiarity as a judicial safeguard of federalism

Any substantive meaning of the subsidiarity principle is in the hands of the European Court of Justice. How has the Court defined the relationship between the national insufficiency test and the comparative efficiency test? And has the Court favoured the restrictive or the wide meaning of subsidiarity?

There are surprisingly few judgments that address the principle of subsidiarity. In *United Kingdom* v. *Council (Working Time)*,[148] the United Kingdom had applied for the annulment of the Working Time Directive. The applicant claimed 'that the [Union] legislature neither fully considered nor adequately demonstrated whether there were transnational aspects which could not be satisfactorily regulated by national measures, whether such measures would conflict with the requirements of the [Treaties] or significantly damage the interests of Member States or, finally, whether action at [European] level would provide clear benefits compared with action at national level'. The principle of subsidiarity would 'not allow the adoption of a directive in such wide and

---

[144] See the House of Commons, European Scrutiny Committee (Thirty-third Report: 2001–02): 'Subsidiarity, National Parliaments and the Lisbon Treaty', www.parliament.the-stationery-office.com/pa/cm200708/cmselect/cmeuleg/563/563.pdf, para. 35.

[145] A. Dashwood, 'The Relationship between the Member States and the European Union/Community' [2004] 41 CML Rev 355 at 369.

[146] S. Weatherill, 'Using National Parliaments to Improve Scrutiny of the Limits of EU Action' [2003] 28 EL Rev 909 at 912.

[147] On the concept and shortfalls of 'political interweaving' (*Politikverflechtung*), see: F. Scharpf, 'The Joint-Decision Trap: Lessons from German Federalism and European Integration' [1988] 66 *Public Administration* 239.

[148] Case C-84/94 (supra n. 13).

prescriptive terms as the contested directive, given that the extent and the nature of legislative regulation of working time vary very widely between Member States'.[149]

How did the Court respond? The Court offered an interpretation of subsidiarity that has structured the judicial vision of the principle ever since.

> Once the Council has found that it is necessary to improve the existing level of protection as regards the health and safety of workers and to harmonise the conditions in this area while maintaining the improvements made, achievement of that objective through the imposition of minimum requirements necessarily presupposes [Union]-wide action, which otherwise, as in this case, leaves the enactment of the detailed implementing provisions required largely to the Member States. The argument that the Council could not properly adopt measures as general and mandatory as those forming the subject-matter of the directive will be examined below in the context of the plea alleging infringement of the principle of proportionality.[150]

This judicial definition contained two fundamental choices. First, the Court assumed that where the Union had decided to 'harmonise' national laws, that objective necessarily presupposed Union legislation. This view answers the national insufficiency test with a mistaken tautology: only the Union can harmonise laws, and therefore the Member States already fail the first test. But assuming the 'whether' of European action had been affirmatively established, could the European law go 'as far' as it had? This was the second crucial choice of the Court. It decided against the idea of subsidiarity in a wider sense. Instead of analysing the intensity of the European law under Article 5 (3) TEU, it chose to review it under the auspices of the principle of proportionality under Article 5 (4) TEU. It is there that the Court made a third important choice. In analysing the proportionality of the European law, it ruled that 'the Council must be allowed a wide discretion in an area which, as here, involves the legislature in making social policy choices and requires it to carry out complex assessments'. Judicial review would therefore be limited to examining 'whether it has been vitiated by manifest error or misuse of powers, or whether the institution concerned has manifestly exceeded the limits of its discretion'.[151] The Court would thus apply a *low* degree of judicial scrutiny.[152]

In subsequent jurisprudence, the Court drew a fourth – procedural – conclusion from choices one and three. In *Germany* v. *Parliament and Council (Deposit Guarantee Scheme)*,[153] the German Government had claimed that the

---

[149] *Ibid.*, para. 46.   [150] *Ibid.*, para. 47.   [151] *Ibid.*, para. 58.

[152] On the development of the judicial review standard for Union acts in this context, see: G. de Búrca, 'The Principle of Proportionality and its Application in EC Law' [1993] 13 YEL 105.

[153] Case C-233/94, *Germany* v. *Parliament and Council (Deposit Guarantee Scheme)*, [1997] ECR I-2405.

Union act violated the *procedural* obligation to state reasons.[154] The European law had not explained how it was compatible with the principle of subsidiarity; and Germany insisted that it was necessary that 'the [Union] institutions must give detailed reasons to explain why only the [Union], to the exclusion of the Member States, is empowered to act in the area in question'. 'In the present case, the Directive does not indicate in what respects its objectives could not have been sufficiently attained by action at Member State level or the grounds which militated in favour of [Union] action.'[155]

The Court gave short shrift to that accusation. Looking at the recitals of the European law, the Court found that the Union legislator had given 'consideration' to the principle of subsidiarity. Having considered previous actions by the Member States insufficient, the European legislator had found it indispensable to ensure a harmonised minimum level. This was enough to satisfy the procedural obligations under the subsidiarity enquiry.[156] It was a *low* explanatory threshold indeed.

Choices one, three, and four have been confirmed in subsequent jurisprudence. By concentrating on the national insufficiency test, the Court has short-circuited the comparative efficiency test.[157] It has not searched for qualitative or quantitative benefits of European laws,[158] but confirmed its manifest error test – thus leaving subsidiarity to the political safeguards of federalism.[159] This is reflected in the low justificatory standard imposed on the Union legislator.[160] By contrast, as regards the second choice, the Court has remained

---

[154] On that duty to give reasons, see: Section 3 above. Germany made it an express point that it was this provision – and not the principle of subsidiarity as such – that it claimed had been violated (*ibid.*, para. 24).

[155] *Ibid.*, para. 23.   [156] *Ibid.*, paras. 26–8.

[157] See Case C-491/01, *The Queen* v. *Secretary of State for Health, ex parte British American Tobacco (Investments) Ltd and Imperial Tobacco Ltd et al.* (supra n. 33), paras. 181–3: '[T]he Directive's objective is to eliminate the barriers raised by the differences which still exist between the Member States' laws, regulations and administrative provisions on the manufacture, presentation and sale of tobacco products, while ensuring a high level of health protection, in accordance with Article [114 (3) TFEU]. Such an objective cannot be sufficiently achieved by the Member States individually and calls for action at [European] level, as demonstrated by the multifarious development of national laws in this case'; as well as: Case C-377/98, *Netherlands* v. *Parliament & Council* (supra n. 31), para. 32; Case C-103/01, *Commission* v. *Germany* [2003] ECR I-5369, paras. 46–7; as well as Joined Cases C-154 & 155/04 *The Queen, ex parte National Association of Health Stores and others* v. *Secretary of State for Health*, [2005] ECR I-6451, paras.104–8.

[158] See Article 5, Protocol on the Application of the Principles of Subsidiarity and Proportionality.

[159] See Case C-233/94 *Germany* v. *Parliament* (supra n. 153), para. 56; as well as: Case C-110/03, *Belgium* v. *Commission*, [2005] ECR I-2801, para. 68.

[160] See Case C-377/98 *Netherlands* v. *Council & Parliament* (supra n. 31), para. 33: 'Compliance with the principle of subsidiarity is necessarily implicit in the fifth, sixth and seventh recitals of the preamble to the Directive, which state that, in the absence of action at [European] level, the development of the laws and practices of the different Member States impedes the proper functioning of the internal market. It thus appears that the Directive states sufficient reasons on that point'.

ambivalent. While in some cases it has incorporated the intensity question into its subsidiarity analysis,[161] other jurisprudence has kept the subsidiarity and the proportionality principles at arm's length.[162]

What is the better option here? It has been argued that subsidiarity should be understood 'in a wider sense'.[163] For it is indeed impossible to reduce subsidiarity to 'whether' the Union should exercise one of its competences. The distinction between 'competence' and 'subsidiarity' – between Article 5 (2) and 5 (3) TEU – will only make sense if the subsidiarity principle concentrates on the 'whether' of *the specific act at issue*. But the 'whether' and the 'how' of the specific action are inherently tied together. The principle of subsidiarity will thus ask *whether* the European legislator has *unnecessarily* restricted national autonomy. A subsidiarity analysis that will not question the *federal* proportionality of a European law is bound to remain an empty formalism. Subsidiarity properly understood *is* federal proportionality.[164] In order to give substantive meaning to subsidiarity, the Court should therefore analyse the 'in-so-far' aspect within its subsidiarity calculus.

Conclusion

The Union is not a sovereign State. Its legislative competences are 'enumerated' competences that are 'conferred' by the European Treaties. The majority of the Union's legislative competences are spread across Part III of the Treaty on the Functioning of the European Union. In each of its policy areas, the Union will typically be given a specific competence. Its competence is thus thematically limited; yet, as we saw above, the Union legislator has made wide use of its powers by interpreting them teleologically. In the past, the Union has also extensively used its general competences. Articles 114 and 352 TFEU grant the Union two legislative competences that horizontally cut across its substantive policy areas. In their most dramatic form, they have allowed the Union to develop policies that were not expressly mentioned in the Treaties.

But not all legislative competences of the Union provide it with the same legal power. The Union legal order recognises various competence categories. The Treaties thus distinguish between exclusive, shared, coordinating and

---

[161] In Case C-491/01 *The Queen* v. *Secretary of State for Health, ex parte British American Tobacco (Investments) Ltd and Imperial Tobacco et al.* (supra n. 33), the Court identified the 'intensity of the action undertaken by the [Union]' with the principle of subsidiarity and not the principle of proportionality (supra n. 157, para. 184). This acceptance of subsidiarity *sensu lato* can also be seen at work in Case C-55/06, *Arcor* v. *Germany*, [2008] ECR I-2931, where the Court identified the principle of subsidiarity with the idea that 'the Member States retain the possibility to establish specific rules on the field in question' (*ibid.*, para. 144).

[162] See Case C-84/94, *United Kingdom* v. *Council (Working Time Directive)* (supra n. 13); as well as: Case C-103/01 *Commission* v. *Germany* (supra n. 157), para. 48.

[163] Schütze, *From Dual to Cooperative Federalism* (supra n. 56), 263 et seq.

[164] On the – liberal – principle of proportionality, see: Chapter 8 – Section 1(b)(ii) below.

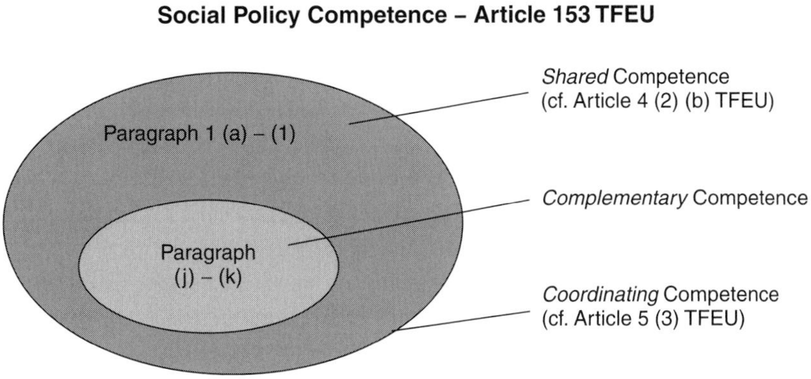

Social Policy Competence – Article 153 TFEU

Figure 13 Structure of the Social Policy Competence

complementary competences. Each competence category constitutionally dis-
tributes power between the Union and the Member States. Within its exclusive
competences, the Union is exclusively competent to legislate; whereas it shares
this power with the Member States under its non-exclusive powers. We saw
above that the Lisbon codification of the Union's competence categories is far
from perfect. Sadly, the Treaties do not deliver clear principles for the European
Union's federal order of competences.[165] The greatest disappointment for
lovers of constitutional logic is the existence of 'competence cocktails', that is:
policy titles that 'mix' various competence categories.[166] These 'mixed' policy
areas undermine the idea of a clear(er) division of power between the Union
and its Member States. One of the worst specimens of the split personality of
Union competences is Article 153 TFEU – a legal base within Title X on 'Social
Policy'.[167]

Who is the Union legislator? Like the British legislator, the Union legislator is
a compound legislator. However, unlike the British constitutional order, there
exists an 'ordinary' and three 'special' legislative procedures. All four procedures combine the European Parliament and the Council, but only under the
ordinary legislative procedure are they co-authors with symmetric

---

[165] Schütze, 'Lisbon and the Federal Order of Competences' (supra n. 78), 721.

[166] For these 'mixed' policy areas, the Working Group on 'Complementary Competences' had
proposed a 'centre of gravity' test. Where a policy area allowed generally for the adoption of
supporting measures and only exceptionally for legislative measures, it would be classified '*in
toto*' as an area of complementary competence (Final Report of Working Group V CONV 375/
1/02 Rev 1, p. 5). Where the respective balance tilted in the opposite direction, such as for
consumer protection, the area should be classified as a shared competence (*ibid.*, p. 9). However,
this approach has not been consistently applied, as the examples of fisheries, social policy and
public health demonstrate. Moreover, the approach in itself is a declaration of intellectual
bankruptcy in the light of the Laeken mandate: can the existence of 'mixed' legal competences be
squared with the attempt to strive for more transparency through a better definition and
division of competences?

[167] For an analysis of this point, see: Schütze, 'Lisbon and the Federal Order of Competences' (supra
n. 78), 720–1.

constitutional rights. The ordinary legislative procedure has a complex formal structure. It may, in the most extreme situation, comprise three readings. In the past, the Union has, however, tried to adopt legislation, as much as possible, after the first and the second reading; and, in order to achieve this result, it has used informal trilogues between the Parliament, the Council and the Commission. While these trilogues have been very successful, they contain the danger of short-circuiting the democratic representation underpinning the ordinary legislative procedure.

The Union legislator is – generally – a subsidiary legislator. The exercise of its non-exclusive competences is restricted by the principle of subsidiarity. The latter thus grants a constitutional advantage to national legislation in solving a social problem within the Union. In order to protect that constitutional advantage, the Union has pursued two mechanisms. The first mechanism concentrates on the procedural involvement of national parliaments in the (political) principle of subsidiarity. The second mechanism focuses on judicial limits to the (legal) principle of subsidiarity. Which mechanism should be preferred? It is uncontested that States might be protected by a procedural duty on the Union legislator to 'think hard' about subsidiarity.[168] However, procedural obligations only provide *some* protection of State autonomy.[169] The Court of Justice should thus be involved in setting a substantive subsidiarity standard. But would the setting of hard limits for the Union legislator not be inherently anti-democratic? This view is mistaken. For the democracy-centred rationale behind process constitutionalism is hard to apply to a federal context. Here the question is *not* whether a non-democratic court or a democratic parliament should decide, but whether the democratic majority of the *Union* or the democratic majority of a *State* should decide on the matter.[170] The parallel application of political and judicial safeguards of federalism should thus generally be accepted in the European legal order. And the Subsidiarity Protocol confirms this.[171]

---

[168] Let us remember the amusing anecdote of Agassiz as told by E. Pound, *ABC of Reading* (New Directions, 1960), 17–18: 'A post-graduate student equipped with honors and diplomas went to Agassiz to receive the final and finishing touches. The great man offered him a small fish and told him to describe it. Post-Graduate Student: "That's only a sunfish." Agassiz: "I know that. Write a description of it." After a few minutes the student returned with the description of the Ichthus Heliodiplodokus, or whatever term is used to conceal the common sunfish from vulgar knowledge, family of Heliichtherinkus, etc., as found in textbooks of the subject. Agassiz again told the student to describe the fish. The student produced a four-page essay. Agassiz then told him to look at the fish. At the end of three weeks the fish was in an advanced state of decomposition, but the student knew something about it.'

[169] For a – very – pessimistic view of the efficiency of the procedural safeguards established by the Subsidiarity Protocol, see: P. Kiiver, 'The Early-warning System for the Principle of Subsidiarity: the National Parliament as a Conseil d'Etat for Europe' [2011] EL Rev 98 at 100: 'it will never be triggered'.

[170] On this point, see: Chapter 2 – Section 4(d) above.   [171] See Article 8 of the Protocol.

6

External Powers: Competences and Procedures

Contents

Introduction		188
1. The external competences of the Union		190
(a) The Common Foreign and Security Policy		192
(b) The Union's special external powers		192
(c) The residual treaty power: Article 216 TFEU		194
(d) The relationship between the CFSP and the special external competences		197
2. The nature of external competences		199
(a) The *sui generis* nature of the CFSP competence		200
(b) Article 3 (2) TFEU: subsequent exclusive treaty powers		201
(i) Three lines of exclusivity: codifying constitutional practice?		201
(ii) Subsequent exclusivity: criticising constitutional theory		203
3. External decision-making procedures		204
(a) The 'specificity' of CFSP decision-making procedures		205
(i) Institutional actors and institutional balance		205
(ii) Voting arrangements in the Council		206
(b) The Union's (ordinary) treaty-making procedure		207
(i) Initiation and negotiation		208
(ii) Signing and conclusion		210
(iii) Modification, suspension (and termination)		211
(iv) Union succession to international agreements of the Member States		212
4. Sharing external power: constitutional safeguards of unitarianism		213
(a) Mixed agreements: an international and political safeguard		214
(b) The duty of cooperation: an internal and judicial safeguard		216
(i) Member States as 'trustees of the Union'		217
(ii) 'Reversed' subsidiarity: restrictions on the exercise of shared State power		218
Conclusion		220

Introduction

The constitutional distinction between internal and external affairs emerges with the rise of the territorial State. With political communities becoming defined by geographical borders, foreign affairs would refer to those matters that entailed an 'external' dimension.[1] The recognition of foreign affairs as a distinct public function received its classic formulation in the political philosophy of John Locke. Locke classified all external competences under the name 'federative' power, that is: 'the power of war and peace, leagues and alliances, and all the transactions with all persons and communities *without the commonwealth*'.[2] This definition reveals the classic scope of the foreign affairs power. It was the power to decide over war and peace. The treaty power is thereby principally perceived as an appendage to the right of war.[3] Foreign affairs were consequently considered part of the executive power. For relations between States were thought to have remained in a 'natural state'. And their 'law-less' character provided an argument against the allocation of external powers to the legislative branch.[4]

In the modern world, this reasoning is not as persuasive as three hundred years ago. The military connotations behind foreign affairs would partly be replaced by the rise of the international treaty as a regulatory instrument. With the internationalisation of trade and commerce in the eighteenth century, a new foreign affairs occupation became consolidated: regulatory international agreements. The amount of tariffs for goods needed to be regulated;[5] river navigation

---

[1] 'Foreign' partly derives from the Latin 'foris' meaning 'outside'.

[2] J. Locke, *Two Treatises of Government* (P. Laslett, ed.) (Cambridge University Press, 1988), 365 – § 146.

[3] See P. Haggenmacher, 'Some Hints on the European Origins of Legislative Participation in the Treaty-Making Function' [1991] 67 *Chicago-Kent Law Review* 313, 318–19: 'The treaty-making capacity was considered as an integral part of sovereignty. But mostly it appeared as a mere extension of the right of war ... The sovereign's power is shown to exert itself in two main directions, either to insure peace among the citizens within the State, or outside to warrant their security against threats from abroad. These external powers, comprising the right of legation as well as the faculty to enter treaties, tend to be subjoined to the power of war and peace.'

[4] The unruly character of international society dissuaded Locke from placing the federative power into the hands of the legislature (see Locke (supra n. 2, § 147). And in whose hands did Locke place the federative power? Locke allocates this public function to the institution that exercises the executive function – the monarch (*ibid.*, § 148): 'Though, as I said, the executive and federative power of every community be really distinct in themselves, yet they are hardly to be separated and placed at the same time in the hands of distinct persons. For both of them requiring the force of the society for their exercise, it is almost impracticable to place the force of the commonwealth in distinct and not subordinate hands, or that the executive and federative power should be placed in persons that might act separately, whereby the force of the public would be under different commands, which would be apt some time or other to cause disorder and ruin.' Locke here took lessons from the English civil war and its fiercest critic, T. Hobbes. To minimise the danger of an armed conflict within the commonwealth, the use of force is to be monopolised in the hands of *one* institution. While the powers of internal execution and foreign policy are functionally distinct, they are united in the same institution for the sake of securing internal peace.

[5] For example: 1860 Anglo-French Trade Agreement (Cobden–Chevalier Treaty).

had to be coordinated;[6] and intellectual property rights required to be protected.[7] This development led one of the drafters of the American constitution to suggest placing the treaty-making power 'in between' the rival constitutional claims of the executive and the legislative department.[8]

Globalisation and the economic interdependence of our time have much intensified the need for – peaceful – legal coordination between States. Yet, the Union is not a State – it is a Union of States. Is it nonetheless entitled to partake in the international affairs of the world? This depends – of course – on the structure of international law,[9] as well as the European Treaties themselves. The 1957 Treaty of Rome had already acknowledged the international personality of the European Community,[10] and the Treaty on European Union now grants such legal personality to the Union.[11]

This chapter looks at the external powers and procedures of the European Union. Sadly, the Union – even after Lisbon – suffers from a 'split personality' when it comes to the constitutional regime for foreign affairs. It has a general competence for its 'common foreign and security policy' (CFSP) within the TEU; and it enjoys various specific external powers within the TFEU. Sections 1 and 2 shall analyse each of these competences and their respective nature. Section 3 looks at the procedural dimension of the external relations of the Union. How will the Union act, and which institutions need to cooperate for it to act? This depends on which of the two constitutional regimes applies. For while the CFSP is still characterised by an 'executive' dominance, the procedures within the Union's special external powers are closer to the 'legislative' branch. Section 4 looks at two constitutional safeguards regulating the exercise of shared external competences: mixed agreements, and the duty of loyal cooperation.

---

[6] For example: 1868 Rhine Navigation Convention.

[7] For example: 1883 Paris Convention for the Protection of Industrial Property.

[8] For A. Hamilton's views, see: Chapter 3 – Section 1 above.

[9] The capacity of international organisations to be international actors has been recognised since 1949, see: Reparation for Injuries Suffered in the Service of the United Nations, Advisory Opinion (1949) ICJ Reports 174: 'Accordingly, the Court has come to the conclusion that the Organisation is an international person. That is not the same thing as saying that it is a State, which it certainly is not, or that its legal personality and rights and duties are the same as those of a State. Still less is it the same thing as saying that it is "a super-State", whatever that expression may mean. It does not even imply that all its rights and duties must be upon the international plane, any more than all the rights and duties of a State must be upon that plane. What it does mean is that it is a subject of international law and capable of possessing international rights and duties, and that it has capacity to maintain its rights by bringing international claims' (*ibid.*, 179).

[10] Ex-Article 281 EC. By contrast, the legal personality of the (Maastricht) European Union had been in doubt. In theory, it had no legal personality, as there existed no legal provision for it. In constitutional practice however, the (old) Union's international legal personality was implicit for it had been entitled to conclude international agreements under ex-Article 24 (old) EU. For this old debate, see: D. McGoldrick, *International Relations Law of the European Union* (Longman, 1997), Chapter 2.

[11] Article 47 TEU.

1. The external competences of the Union

What are the Union's objectives as an actor on the international scene? The external objectives are spelled out in Article 21 TEU. After a commitment to some 'universal' objectives,[12] the provision commits the Union to a number of 'particular' objectives. These 'Union-specific' objectives are as follows:

> The Union shall define and pursue common policies and actions, and shall work for a high degree of cooperation in all fields of international relations, in order to:
>
> (a) safeguard its values, fundamental interests, security, independence and integrity;
> (b) consolidate and support democracy, the rule of law, human rights and the principles of international law;
> (c) preserve peace, prevent conflicts and strengthen international security, in accordance with the purposes and principles of the United Nations Charter, with the principles of the Helsinki Final Act and with the aims of the Charter of Paris, including those relating to external borders;
> (d) foster the sustainable economic, social and environmental development of developing countries, with the primary aim of eradicating poverty;
> (e) encourage the integration of all countries into the world economy, including through the progressive abolition of restrictions on international trade;
> (f) help develop international measures to preserve and improve the quality of the environment and the sustainable management of global natural resources, in order to ensure sustainable development;
> (g) assist populations, countries and regions confronting natural or man-made disasters; and
> (h) promote an international system based on stronger multilateral cooperation and good global governance.

But in order to achieve these objectives, the Union cannot act as it pleases. For in accordance with the principle of conferral, the Union must act 'within the limits of the competences conferred upon it by the Member States in the Treaties'.[13] And this principle applies to 'both the internal action and the international action of the [Union]'.[14]

The competences of the Union on foreign affairs can generally be found in two constitutional sites. Title V of the Treaty on European Union deals with the 'Common Foreign and Security Policy',[15] whereas Part V of the Treaty on the

---

[12] Article 21 (1) TEU: 'democracy, the rule of law, the universality and indivisibility of human rights and fundamental freedoms, respect for human dignity, the principles of equality and solidarity, and respect for the principles of the United Nations Charter and international law'.

[13] Article 5 (2) TEU.   [14] Opinion 2/94 (*Accession to the ECHR*), [1996] ECR I-1759, para. 24.

[15] The TEU's common provisions also contain two external competences for the Union. Article 6 (2) TEU empowers the Union to accede to the European Convention for the Protection of Human Rights and Fundamental Freedoms. The Union's 'Neighbourhood Policy' finds its constitutional basis in Article 8 TEU. The Union is here entitled to develop a 'special relationship' with neighbouring countries so as to establish 'an area of prosperity and good neighbourliness'. To that effect, Article 8 (2) TEU allows the Union to conclude 'specific agreements

Table 11 Union External Policies

EU Treaty – Title V: CFSP	FEU Treaty – Part V: External Action	
Chapter 1 General Provisions	Title I	General Provisions
Chapter 2 Specific Provisions on the CFSP	Title II	Common Commercial Policy
Section 1 Common Provisions	Title III	Cooperation with Third Countries and Humanitarian Aid
Section 2 Common Security and Defence Policy	Title IV	Restrictive Measures
	Title V	International Agreements
	Title VI	Union's Relations with International Organisations and Third Countries and Union Delegations
	Title VII	Solidarity Clause

Functioning of the European Union enumerates various external policies within which the Union is entitled to act.[16] The relationship between both constitutional sites is complex and, in some ways, they are 'living apart together'. They are living apart, as Article 40 TEU draws a constitutional dividing line between them; yet, they are also living together under a common roof, as the 'General provisions on the Union's External Action' apply to both of them.[17] This means that all of the Union's external actions are guided by the same principles and objectives.[18]

This Section looks at the Union's general competence for its CFSP first of all, before analysing the main external competences conferred in the Treaty on the Functioning of the European Union. These competences are thematically

---

with the countries concerned'. For an analysis of the European Neighbourhood Policy, see: M. Cremona, 'The European Neighbourhood Policy: More than a Partnership?' in M. Cremona (ed.), *Developments in EU External Relations Law* (Oxford University Press, 2008), Chapter 7.

[16] A number of legal bases *outside* Part V of the TFEU also grant the Union external competences. For example, Article 168 (3) TFEU confers the power to adopt measures that foster cooperation with third countries and competent international organisations in the context of the Union's Public Health policy. For other express treaty-making competences, see only: Title XX on the environment, where the Union is given a competence to conclude environmental agreements with third States under Article 191 (4) TFEU.

[17] Title V – Chapter 1 (Articles 21 and 22) TEU. This is expressly confirmed for both constitutional sites in – respectively – Article 23 TEU and Article 205 TFEU. The latter states: 'The Union's action on the international scene, pursuant to this Part, shall be guided by the principles, pursue the objectives and be conducted in accordance with the general provisions laid down in Chapter 1 of Title V of the Treaty on European Union.'

[18] According to Article 21 (3) TEU: 'The Union shall respect the principles and pursue the objectives set out in paragraphs 1 and 2 in the development and implementation of the different areas of the Union's external action covered by this Title and by Part Five of the Treaty on the Functioning of the European Union, and of the external aspects of its other policies.'

arranged competences, yet there exists one exception: Article 216 TFEU. The provision grants the Union a 'residual' competence to conclude international agreements that horizontally cuts across all Union policies in the Treaty on the Functioning of the European Union. In some respects, it thus resembles Article 352 TFEU and warrants special attention. Finally, we shall look at the complex relationship between the two external relations regimes within the Treaties.

(a) The Common Foreign and Security Policy

The general competence of the Union on foreign affairs can be found in Title V of the Treaty on European Union. The second Chapter of this title deals with the 'Common Foreign and Security Policy'. Article 24 TEU here grants the Union 'competence in matters of common foreign and security policy [that] shall cover all areas of foreign policy and all questions relating to the Union's security, including the progressive framing of a common defence policy that might lead to a common defence'. This general competence is subsequently broken down into specific provisions dealing with the Union's power to adopt decisions. And with regard to the conclusion of international agreements, Article 37 TEU generally states that '[t]he Union may conclude agreements with one or more States or international organisations in areas covered by this Chapter'.

The Common Security and Defence Policy (CSDP) is seen as 'an integral part' of the CFSP.[19] What is the scope of the CSDP? The latter 'shall provide the Union with an operational capacity', which the Union may use 'on missions outside the Union for peace-keeping, conflict prevention and strengthening international security in accordance with the principles of the United Nations Charter'.[20] While already bearing the name, the CSDP shall – in the future – also include the 'progressive framing of a common Union defence policy'.[21] This will happen once the European Council so decides. Importantly however, Article 42 TEU contains a constitutional guarantee not to prejudice the neutrality of certain Member States, and to respect other Member States' obligations within the North Atlantic Treaty Organisation (NATO).[22]

(b) The Union's special external powers

Part V of the TFEU contains seven titles. After confirming the common principles and objectives of the Union's external action,[23] three Titles deal with special external policies,[24] two subsequent titles concern institutional

---

[19] Article 42 (1) TEU.   [20] *Ibid.*   [21] Article 42 (2) TEU – first indent.
[22] *Ibid.* – second indent.   [23] Article 205 TFEU.   [24] Part V – Titles II–IV of the TFEU.

matters,[25] and one Title establishes a 'Solidarity Clause'.[26] The majority of the Union's external competences are found in Titles II-IV. But we also find competences in the institutional provisions. Title V thus grants the Union a general competence to conclude international agreements,[27] and a special competence to conclude 'association agreements'.[28] Finally, Title VI grants the Union a horizontal competence to establish and maintain cooperative relations 'as are appropriate' with international organisations, in particular the United Nations and the Council of Europe.[29]

Let us briefly look at the three Titles dealing with specific external policies. Title II concerns the Union's Common Commercial Policy (CCP). This is the external expression of the Union's internal market. The Union is here tasked to represent the common commercial interests of the Member States on the international scene and to contribute to 'the harmonious development of world trade'.[30] Under Article 207 TFEU, the Union is thereby expressly entitled to adopt (unilateral) legislative acts,[31] and to conclude (bi- or multilateral) international agreements.[32] The scope of the CCP covers all matters relating to trade in goods and services, commercial aspects of intellectual property, and foreign direct investment.[33] However, the competence encounters two express limits – one specific and one general. First, international transport agreements are specifically excluded from the scope of the CCP.[34] And Article 207 TFEU establishes a second – general – limit to the CCP competence. It states that the exercise of the CCP competence 'shall not affect the delimitation of

---

[25] *Ibid.* – Titles I, V, and VI.

[26] *Ibid.* – Title VII. Despite its position within Part V of the TFEU, the solidarity clause is not a 'real' external policy of the Union. It imposes an obligation on the Union and its Member States to act jointly 'if a Member State is the object of a terrorist attack or the victim of a natural or man-made disaster' (Article 222 (1) TFEU); and this situation may not necessarily have foreign implications for the European Union. However, there are intimate constitutional links with the Union's CFSP. For example, the Union is entitled to mobilise military resources made available by the Member States (*ibid.*).

[27] See Article 216 TFEU (discussed below).

[28] See Article 217 TFEU. These agreements are special agreements in that they create 'special, privileged links with a non-member country which must, at least to a certain extent, take part in the [Union] system' (see Case 12/86, *Demirel* v. *Stadt Schwäbisch Gmünd*, [1987] ECR 3719, para. 9). The 'European Economic Area' Agreement between the European Union and Lichtenstein, Iceland and Norway is an association agreement.

[29] Article 220 TFEU. The European Union is a – full or partial – member of a number of international organisations. For a list of these organisations and the respective status of the Union, see: A. Missiroli, 'The New EU "Foreign Policy" System after Lisbon: A Work in Progress' [2010] 15 *European Foreign Affairs Review* 427 at 449 et seq.

[30] Article 206 TFEU.

[31] Article 207 (2) TFEU: 'The European Parliament and the Council, acting by means of regulations in accordance with the ordinary legislative procedure, shall adopt the measures defining the framework for implementing the common commercial policy.'

[32] Article 207 (3) TFEU.

[33] Article 207 (1) TFEU. For a brief constitutional history of the scope of the CCP, see: P. Eeckhout, *EU External Relations Law* (Oxford University Press, 2011), Chapter 2.

[34] Article 207 (5) TFEU.

competences between the Union and the Member States'.[35] This – odd – formulation is best understood as a – bad – attempt to say that the CCP competence should find a systemic limit in the internal competences of the Union. This prohibition is exemplified in the rule that the exercise of the Union's CCP competence 'shall not lead to harmonisation of legislative or regulatory provisions of the Member States in so far as the Treaties exclude such harmonisation'.[36]

Title III deals with three related but distinct external policies of the Union in three chapters. All three policies allow the Union to adopt unilateral measures,[37] and to conclude international agreements with third States.[38] Chapter 1 concerns 'Development Cooperation', whose primary objective is 'the reduction and, in the long term, the eradication of poverty' in developing countries.[39] Chapter 2 extends various forms of assistance to 'third countries other than developing counties'.[40] The Union's competence in respect of humanitarian aid can be found in Chapter 3 of this Title. It permits the Union to provide 'ad hoc assistance and relief and protection for people in third countries who are victims of natural or man-made disasters, in order to meet the humanitarian needs resulting from these different situations'.[41]

Finally, Title IV confers on the Union a competence to adopt economic sanctions. These are unilateral acts with a 'punitive' character. This competence has had an eventful constitutional history,[42] and still constitutes a strange animal. For according to Article 215 TFEU, the Union is not entitled to act on the basis of this competence alone. It can only exercise this competence *after* the Union has exercised its CFSP competence. The latter must have been exercised through a decision in favour of 'the interruption or reduction, in part or completely, of economic and financial relations with one or more third countries';[43] or, with regard to 'smart sanctions', against 'natural or legal persons and groups or non-State entities'.[44] In such a case, the Union is then entitled to implement this CFSP decision through the 'necessary measures' adopted under Article 215 TFEU. The provision indeed constitutes the central platform for the implementation of Resolutions of the Security Council of the United Nations.

(c) The residual treaty power: Article 216 TFEU

Under the 1957 Rome Treaty, the European Union only enjoyed two express treaty-making powers: one with regard to the Common Commercial Policy,

---

[35] Article 207 (6) TFEU.   [36] *Ibid.*   [37] See Articles 209 (1), 212 (2), 214 (3) TFEU.
[38] See Articles 209 (2), 212 (3), 214 (4) TFEU.   [39] Article 208 (1) TFEU.
[40] Article 212 (1) TFEU.   [41] Article 214 (1) TFEU.
[42] For a good account of that constitutional history, see: P. Koutrakos, *Trade, Foreign Policy and Defence in EU Constitutional Law: the Legal Regulation of Sanctions, Exports of Dual-use Goods and Armaments* (Hart, 2001), 58 et seq.
[43] Article 215 (1) TFEU.   [44] Article 215 (2) TFEU.

and the other with regard to Association Agreements.[45] And while subsequent Treaty amendments have – significantly – increased the number of specific treaty-making competences, there existed no general 'Treaty Power' of the European Union.[46] This absence was noted. And in an attempt to provide the Union with a general competence to conclude international agreements the European Court invented a doctrine of implied external powers.

The existence of implied powers was expressed in *ERTA*.[47] The Court here acknowledged, among other things,[48] that the competence to conclude international agreements 'arises not only from an express conferment by the Treaty', 'but may equally flow from other provisions of the Treaty and from measures adopted, within the framework of those provisions, by the [Union] institutions'.[49] The doctrine of implied treaty powers has had a complex constitutional history, and combines three jurisprudential lines.[50] The Lisbon Treaty has tried to codify the doctrine in Article 216 TFEU.[51] The provision states:

> The Union may conclude an agreement with one or more third countries or international organisations where the Treaties so provide or where the conclusion of an agreement is necessary in order to achieve, within the framework of the Union's policies, one of the objectives referred to in the Treaties, or is provided for in a legally binding Union act or is likely to affect common rules or alter their scope.[52]

While recognising the express treaty-making competences of the Union conferred elsewhere by the Treaties, the provision grants the Union a residual competence to conclude international agreements in three situations.

The first alternative mentioned in Article 216 (1) TFEU confers a treaty power to the Union 'where the conclusion of an agreement is necessary in order to achieve, within the framework of the Union's policies, one of the objectives referred to in the Treaties'. This formulation is – strikingly – similar to the one found in the Union's general competence in Article 352 TFEU. And if the Court decided to confirm this parallelism, the Union will have a residual competence to conclude international agreements that cuts across the jurisdictional scope of

---

[45] Ex-Articles 113 and 238 EEC.

[46] By contrast, Article 101 Euratom Treaty grants that Community a general competence in paragraph 1: 'The Community may within the limits of its powers and jurisdiction, enter into obligations by concluding agreements or contracts with a third State, an international organisation or a national of a third State.'

[47] Case 22/70, *Commission v. Council (ERTA)*, [1971] ECR 263.

[48] On the various aspects of this multi-layered ruling, see: R. Schütze, *From Dual to Cooperative Federalism: the Changing Structure of European Law* (Oxford University Press, 2009), 317 et seq.

[49] Case 22/70, *Commission v. Council* (supra n. 47), paras. 15–16.

[50] See Eeckhout (supra n. 33), Chapter 3; as well as: Schütze (supra n. 48), 290 et seq.

[51] See European Convention, 'Final Report Working Group VII – External Action' (CONV 459/02), para. 18: 'The Group saw merit in making explicit the jurisprudence of the Court[.]'

[52] Article 216 (1) TFEU.

the entire Treaty on the Functioning of the Union.[53] This competence would be wider than the judicial doctrine of parallel external powers. For past doctrine insisted that an external competence derived from an internal *competence* – and thus did not confer a treaty power to pursue any internal *objective*.[54] Yet the first alternative in Article 216 textually disconnects the Union's external competences from its internal competences. The latter might therefore no longer represent a constitutional limit to the Union's treaty powers.

Regardless of what the Court will eventually make of this first alternative, Article 216 mentions two additional situations. The Union will also be entitled to conclude international agreements, where this 'is provided for in a legally binding act or is likely to affect common rules or alter their scope'. Both alternatives make the existence of an external competence dependent on the existence of internal Union law. Two objections may be launched against this view. Theoretically, it is difficult to accept that the Union can expand its competences without Treaty amendment through the simple adoption of internal Union acts.[55] Practically, it is hard to see how either alternative will ever go beyond the first alternative.[56] And in any event, as we shall see in Section 2(b) below, it is likely that alternatives two and three were the result of a fundamental confusion within the Constitutional Convention drafting the text behind Article 216 TFEU.

---

[53] It is true that Article 216 TFEU – unlike Article 352 TFEU – has no fourth paragraph excluding its use 'for attaining objectives pertaining to the common foreign and security policy'. The problem therefore has been raised whether Article 216 is even wider than Article 352 in that it may also be used to pursue a CFSP objective (see M. Cremona, 'External Relations and External Competence of the European Union: the Emergence of an Integrated Policy' in P. Craig and G. de Búrca (eds.), *The Evolution of EU Law* (Oxford University Press, 2011), 217 at 226). However, even in the absence of an express limitation, Article 40 TEU should – in theory – operate as an implied limitation to the scope of Article 216 (1) TFEU. For a discussion of Article 40 TEU, see Section 1 (d) below.

[54] The classic doctrine of implied external powers, as defined in Opinion 1/76, thus stated that 'whenever [European] law has created for the institutions of the [Union] *powers* within its internal system for the purposes of attaining a specific objective, the [Union] has authority to enter into the international commitments necessary for the attainment of that objective even in the absence of an express provision in that connexion' (Opinion 1/76 (*Laying-up Fund*), [1977] ECR 741, para. 3 – emphasis added). And to make it even clearer, the Court continued to state that the external powers flowed 'by implication from the provisions of the Treaty creating the internal *power*' (*ibid.*, para. 4 – emphasis added).

[55] On the notion of *Kompetenz-Kompetenz*, see: Chapter 2 – Section 2(a) above.

[56] In any event, the existence of the first alternative next to the second alternative should now – finally – put to rest the idea that the existence of (implied) treaty power depends on the existence of internal legislation. For a long time the European Court was, however, undecided whether implied external powers were automatically implied from internal powers; or whether they were contingent on the actual exercise of these internal powers through the adoption of internal legislation. The better view had always insisted on parallel external powers running alongside the Union's internal powers without regard to European legislation (See E. Stein, 'External Relations of the European Community: Structure and Process' [1990] 1 *Collected Courses of the Academy of European Law* 115 at 146).

(d) The relationship between the CFSP and the special external competences

What is the constitutional relationship between the Union's general CFSP competence and its special competences listed in the external relations part of the Treaty on the Functioning of the European Union? While both are (now) housed under the same common provisions, the borderline between the CFSP and the other external policies has always been hotly contested. The reason for this contestation lies in the distinct procedural regime for each constitutional site. While the CFSP is still – principally – governed by an intergovernmental procedural regime, the Union's special external policies are supranational in character.[57] The key provision governing the borderline between the intergovernmental CFSP and the supranational external Union policies is Article 40 TEU. The provision states:

> The implementation of the common foreign and security policy shall not affect the application of the procedures and the extent of the powers of the institutions laid down by the Treaties for the exercise of the Union competences referred to in Articles 3 to 6 of the Treaty on the Functioning of the European Union.
>
> Similarly, the implementation of the policies listed in those Articles shall not affect the application of the procedures and the extent of the powers of the institutions laid down by the Treaties for the exercise of the Union competences under this Chapter.

The first indent protects the Union's supranational procedures and powers. It is designed to prevent the (European) Council from using the Union's CFSP competences, where recourse to one of the Union's supranational competences is possible. This is indeed the traditional – and, prior to Lisbon: exclusive – function of the provision.[58] The Court has interpreted this aspect of Article 40 in *ECOWAS*.[59] The case involved a legal challenge to the constitutionality of Union acts combating the spread of small arms and light weapons in the 'Economic Community of Western African States' (ECOWAS). Would these acts have to be adopted under the CFSP competence or the Union's competence in development cooperation? The Court found that the acts pursued a general foreign affairs aim and a specific development cooperation objective. However, as long as the CFSP objective was only *incidental*, the Union could adopt its acts

---

[57] On this point, see Section 3 below.

[58] In order to protect the *acquis communautaire*, the (old) TEU provided that 'nothing in this Treaty shall affect the Treaties establishing the European Communities' (ex-Article 47 (old) EU); and the Court of Justice was expressly called upon to police that border (see ex-Article 46 (f) (old) EU). For case-law under the old provision, see: Case C-170/96, *Commission* v. *Council (Airport Transit Visa)*, [1998] ECR I-2763; Case C-176/03, *Commission* v. *Council (Environmental Criminal Penalties)*, [2005] ECR I-7879; as well as Case C-440/05, *Commission* v. *Council (Ship-Source Pollution)*, [2007] ECR I-9097.

[59] Case C-91/05, *Commission* v. *Council (ECOWAS)*, [2008] ECR I-3651.

on the basis of its specific external competences. The decisive test was akin to a 'centre of gravity' test.[60]

Has this result been 'amended' by the Lisbon Treaty? The Lisbon Treaty added the second indent to Article 40 TEU. The provision now equally protects the intergovernmental CFSP from a supranational incursion through the Union's specific external competences. And as such it seems to 'codify' the *ECOWAS* solution. However, this might need to be qualified in one respect. *ECOWAS* had suggested that a Union act that equally pursued a CFSP and a non-CFSP objective would have to be split into two separate acts – with one act being adopted under the CFSP and the other under the special legal basis within the Treaties.[61] And while this prohibition of a dual legal basis for a single act may still apply to unilateral Union acts, it is harder to imagine for the conclusion of international agreements. For the Lisbon Treaty has established a single unified procedure for CFSP and non-CFSP agreements alike.[62]

How best to characterise the constitutional relationship between the CFSP competence and the Union's special external powers? The Lisbon Treaty has abandoned the idea that the Union's CFSP objectives form a separate set of Union objectives.[63] And in light of the general nature of these objectives, the CFSP should best be viewed as *lex generalis* to the *specialised* Union policies within Part V of the TFEU. This view will give priority – but not unconditional priority – to the special external competences of the Union. The latter will apply as a more refined constitutional mandate of Union foreign policy, wherever an action can be fully founded on that competence. By contrast, whenever a special Union objective is only incidental to the general foreign policy aim of a Union act, Article 40 TEU will henceforth protect the CFSP chapter. Thus a Union act that mainly pursues a general foreign policy objective, and only incidentally the objective of development cooperation, will have to be based on the Union's CFSP.

---

[60] On the 'centre of gravity' test, see: H. Cullen and A. Charlesworth, 'Diplomacy by other Means: the Use of Legal Basis Litigation as a Political Strategy by the European Parliament and Member States' [1999] 36 CML Rev 1243.

[61] Case C-91/05, *Commission* v. *Council* (supra n. 59), paras. 75–7: 'With regard to a measure which simultaneously pursues a number of objectives or which has several components, without one being incidental to the other, the Court has held, where various legal bases of the EC Treaty are therefore applicable, that such a measure will have to be founded, exceptionally, on the various corresponding legal bases. However, under [ex-]Article 47 [old] EU, such a solution [was] impossible with regard to a measure which pursues a number of objectives or which has several components falling, respectively, within development cooperation policy, as conferred by the EC Treaty on the Community, and within the CFSP, and where neither one of those components is incidental to the other. Since [ex-]Article 47 [old] EU precludes the Union from adopting, on the basis of the EU Treaty, a measure which could properly be adopted on the basis of the EC Treaty, the Union cannot have recourse to a legal basis falling within the CFSP in order to adopt provisions which also fall within a competence conferred by the EC Treaty on the Community.'

[62] On this point, see: Section 3(b) below.

[63] This view can still be seen in Case C-402/05P, *Kadi and Al Barakaat International Foundation* v. *Council and Commission*, [2008] ECR I-6351.

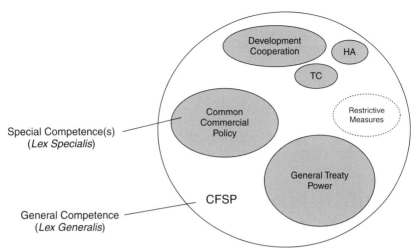

Figure 14 Relationship among Union External Competences

The characterisation of the CFSP competence as *lex generalis* turns it into a subsidiary competence – like Article 352 TFEU for the internal policies of the Union.[64] This subsidiary character establishes – with the exception of the Union competence on 'restrictive measures'[65] – a reciprocal relationship between the CFSP and the special external competences. The broader the interpretation given to the latter, the smaller the remaining scope of the CFSP competence.

2. The nature of external competences

What is the nature of the Union's external competences? What competence categories exist in the external sphere? With regard to their constitutional nature, the Treaties do not – as a rule – distinguish between internal and external competences. And indeed, within the areas of Union competences listed in Articles 3–6 TFEU, we find a number of external competences.[66]

---

[64] However, unlike Article 352 TFEU, the Union's general CFSP competence might not be open to be combined with a special competence. On the subsidiary character of Article 352 TFEU for the Union's internal policies, see: R. Schütze, 'Organized Change towards an "Ever Closer Union": Article 308 EC and the Limits to the Community's Legislative Competence' [2003] 22 YEL 79 at 95 et seq.

[65] The availability of this competence depends on the CFSP competence having first been exercised.

[66] For example, the common commercial policy is listed under the Union's exclusive competences (see Article 3 (1) (e) TFEU), environmental policy is listed as a shared competence (see Article 191 (4) TFEU: 'Within their respective spheres of competence, the Union and the Member States shall cooperate with third countries and with the competent international organisations. The arrangements for Union cooperation may be the subject of agreements between the Union and the third parties concerned'); and public health is listed as a complementary competence (see Article 6 (a) TFEU, and Article 168 (3) TFEU: "The Union and the Member States shall foster cooperation with third countries and the competent international organisations in the sphere of public health').

However, there are two exceptions to this rule. First, Article 2 TFEU specifically isolates the Union's CFSP competence from the ordinary competence categories – an arrangement that suggests a *sui generis* competence. Second, Article 3 (2) TFEU provides a source of exclusivity for the conclusion of international agreements that goes beyond the competence areas listed in Article 3 (1) TFEU.

Let us look at both derogations from the 'ordinary' competence categories discussed in Chapter 5.

(a) The *sui generis* nature of the CFSP competence

The nature of the Union's CFSP competence has been a legal problem ever since its inception. According to an early view, law adopted under a CFSP competence was 'classic' international law that contrasted with the supranational European law adopted under the 'ordinary' competences of the Union.[67] A second view, by contrast, argued that CFSP competences were part of one and the same European legal order.[68] The Lisbon Treaty has reinforced this second view. While recognising that the CFSP 'is subject to specific rules and procedures',[69] the Treaty on European Union and the Treaty on the Functioning of the European Union confirm that the two treaties 'have the same legal value'.[70] This includes secondary CFSP law. For indeed, CFSP competences will be exercised by the 'ordinary' legal instruments of the Union legal order,[71] yet unlike 'ordinary' Union law, the direct effect of CFSP law appears to be exceptional.[72]

How shall we then best characterise CFSP competences? The Treaties treat CFSP competences as distinct from the Union competences referred to in Articles 3–6 TFEU.[73] But what is their exact nature? We might find a first key to this question in Article 24 TEU dealing with the nature of the CFSP competence. The provision declares that '[t]he adoption of legislative acts shall be excluded' within the CFSP area. What will this mean? If the reference

---

[67] M. Pechstein and C. Koenig, *Die Europäische Union* (Mohr Siebeck, 2000), 5 et seq. The thesis that Union law differed from Community law had gained support from ex-Article 47 (old) EU, and Case C-402/05P, *Kadi* (supra n. 63), para. 202: 'integrated but separate legal orders'.

[68] K. Lenaerts and T. Corthaut, 'Of Birds and Hedges: the Role of Primacy in invoking Norms of EU law' (2006) 31 EL Rev 287 at 288.

[69] Article 24 (1) TEU.   [70] Article 1 TEU and Article 1 TFEU.

[71] That is: decisions and international agreements. Prior to the Lisbon Treaty, the CFSP competence was to be exercised by a number of special legal instruments, such as 'joint actions' and 'common positions'.

[72] On the doctrine of 'direct effect' of European law, see: Chapter 9 below. Direct effect is centrally determined by the European Courts. Yet the jurisdiction of the Court is generally excluded with respect to CFSP provisions and acts adopted on the basis of those provisions. The Treaties acknowledge only two express exceptions. First, CFSP law can be reviewed under Article 40 TEU. Second, the Court has jurisdiction to review the legality of 'decisions providing for restrictive measures against natural or legal persons adopted by the Council on the basis of Chapter 2 of Title V of the Treaty on European Union' (see Article 275 (2) TFEU).

[73] Article 40 TEU makes a clear distinction between the CFSP competence and 'the Union competences referred to in Articles 3–6 of the Treaty on the Functioning of the European Union'.

to 'legislative acts' were given a formal meaning, that is: referring to acts adopted under a legislative procedure, then Article 24 TEU would state the obvious. Indeed, neither the ordinary nor any of the special legislative procedures apply within the CFSP. By contrast, if the formulation is given a material meaning, then Article 24 TEU signalled the exclusion of *generally* applicable CFSP norms. A second key to the nature of CFSP competences might be found in Declaration 14 to the European Treaties, which underlines that the CFSP competence 'will not affect the existing legal basis, responsibilities, and powers of each Member State in relation to the formulation and conduct of its foreign policy, its national diplomatic service, relations with third countries and participation in international organisations'.[74] This formulation comes close to the idea of a parallel competence, but the better view insists that CFSP competences are 'special' or '*sui generis*' competences within the Union legal order.[75]

(b) Article 3 (2) TFEU: subsequent exclusive treaty powers

We find a second exception to the 'ordinary' competence categories of the Union in Article 3 (2) TFEU. The provision provides a special rule for the Union's competence to conclude international agreements. It states:

> The Union shall also have exclusive competence for the conclusion of an international agreement when its conclusion is provided for in a legislative act of the Union or is necessary to enable the Union to exercise its internal competence, or in so far as its conclusion may affect common rules or alter their scope.

In addition to the constitutionally fixed exclusive competences – mentioned in Article 3 (1) – the Union legal order thus acknowledges the possibility of a *dynamic* growth of its exclusive competences in the external sphere. We shall look at the constitutional practice of subsequently exclusive powers first, before criticising its underlying constitutional theory.

(i) Three lines of exclusivity: codifying constitutional practice?

According to Article 3 (2), the Union may subsequently obtain exclusive treaty-making power, where one of three situations is fulfilled. These three situations are said to codify three famous judicial doctrines. These doctrines were developed in the jurisprudence of the European Court prior to the Lisbon Treaty.[76]

According to the first situation, the Union will obtain a subsequently exclusive treaty-making power when the conclusion of an international agreement 'is provided for in a legislative act'. This formulation corresponds to the 'WTO

---

[74] Declaration (No. 14) concerning the Common Foreign and Security Policy.

[75] M. Cremona, 'The Draft Constitutional Treaty: External Relations and External Action' [2003] 40 CML Rev 1347 at 1354.

[76] On the three judicial doctrines, see: R. Schütze, 'Parallel External Powers in the European Community: from "Cubist" Perspectives towards "Naturalist" Constitutional Principles?' [2004] 23 YEL 225.

Doctrine'. In *Opinion 1/94* on the compatibility of the WTO Agreement with the Treaties,[77] the Court had stated: '[w]henever the [Union] has concluded in its internal legislative acts provisions relating to the treatment of nationals of non-member countries or expressly conferred on the institutions powers to negotiate with non-member countries, it acquires exclusive external competence in the spheres covered by those acts'.[78] Article 3 (2) codifies this judicial doctrine. However, the codification is more restrictive, as it excludes the first alternative ('provisions relating to the treatment of nationals of non-member countries') from its scope.

The second situation mentioned in Article 3 (2) TFEU grants the Union an exclusive treaty power, where this 'is necessary to enable the Union to exercise its internal competence'. This formulation appears to codify the 'Opinion 1/76 Doctrine',[79] albeit in a much *less* restrictive form. In its jurisprudence the Court had indeed confined this second line of subsequent exclusivity to situations 'where the conclusion of an international agreement is necessary in order to achieve Treaty objectives *which cannot be attained by the adoption of autonomous rules*',[80] and where the achievement of an internal objective is 'inextricably linked' with the external sphere.[81] None of these restrictions can be found in Article 3 (2) TFEU. And in its unqualified openness, the second situation comes close to the wording of the Union's 'residual' legislative competence: Article 352 TFEU. The almost identical wording of Article 3 (2) and Article 216 TFEU indeed suggests that 'implied shared competence would disappear'; yet, this would be 'a wholly undesirable departure from the case law'.[82]

Finally, the third situation in Article 3 (2) appears to refer to the Court's '*ERTA* doctrine'. Under the *ERTA* doctrine,[83] the Member States are deprived of their treaty-making power to the extent that their exercise affects internal European law. Each time the Union 'adopts provisions laying down common rules, whatever form these may take, the Member States no longer have the right, acting individually or even collectively, to undertake obligations with third countries *which affect those rules*'.[84] The principle behind *ERTA* is to prevent an international agreement concluded by the Member States from undermining 'the uniform and consistent application of the [Union] rules and the proper functioning of the system which they establish'.[85] Has Article 3 (2) properly codified this third judicial line of subsequently exclusive powers? The third alternative in Article 3 (2) – strangely – breaks the link between a

---

[77] Opinion 1/94 (*WTO Agreement*), [1994] ECR I-5267.   [78] *Ibid.*, para. 95.
[79] Opinion 1/76 (*Laying-Up Fund*), [1977] ECR 741. On the evolution of the Opinion 1/76 doctrine, see: Schütze (supra n. 76), 250 et seq.
[80] Opinion 2/92 (*Third Revised Decision of the OECD on national treatment*), [1995] ECR I-521, Part V – para. 4 (emphasis added).
[81] Case C-476/98, *Commission* v. *Germany* (*Open Skies*), [2002] ECR I-9855, para. 87.
[82] M. Cremona, 'A Constitutional Basis for Effective External Action? An Assessment of the Provisions on EU External Action in the Constitutional Treaty', EUI Working Paper 2006/30, 10.
[83] Case 22/70, *Commission* v. *Council* (supra n. 47).   [84] *Ibid.*, para. 18 – emphasis added.
[85] Opinion 1/03 (*Lugano Convention*), [2006] ECR I-1145, para. 133.

Member State agreement and internal European law, and replaces it with an analysis of the effect of a *Union* agreement on European rules. This simply must be an 'editorial mistake' on the part of the Treaty-makers, and it is hoped that the Court will correct this as soon as possible.

(ii) Subsequent exclusivity: criticising constitutional theory

The Treaties take great care to clarify that the question of competences is a 'constitutional' question. The competences of the Union should thus be increased solely by (ordinary) Treaty amendment.[86] Should we not expect that the nature of a competence – that is: the degree to which Member States remain entitled to act – is equally constitutionally fixed? In other words, is there not something strange in the idea that the Union can – without Treaty amendment – change its order of competences? As we saw above, this is not the position of the Lisbon Treaty, nor has it been that of the European Court. For the latter expressly subscribed to the theory of subsequently exclusive powers in Opinion 2/91:

> The exclusive or non-exclusive nature of the [Union]'s competence does not flow solely from the provisions of the Treaty but may also depend on the scope of the measures which have been adopted by the [Union] institutions for the application of those provisions and which are of such a kind as to deprive the Member States of an area of competence which they were able to exercise previously on a transitional basis.[87]

But even if Article 3 (2) and the European Court embrace the idea of subsequently exclusive powers, should we uncritically accept this theory? A number of theoretical objections may be advanced against it.[88] Indeed, identifying the effect of internal Union legislation with exclusive external competences raises serious objections from the perspective of the hierarchy of norms. The scope of the Union's exclusive competences is a constitutional question and, as such, it should – at least theoretically – only be extended by means of constitutional amendment. It thus seems a feat of legal alchemy to permit the Union to modify its order of competences, especially because this would allow the European legislator to escape the reach of the subsidiarity principle.[89] But the exclusionary effect in the first and third situation in Article 3 (2) stems from the effect of Union legislation. And this legislative 'exclusivity' is more fragile than constitutionally exclusive powers, since it can again be repealed by a legislative act.

The two phenomena of constitutional and legislative exclusivity should therefore be kept apart. And while the Lisbon Treaty-makers couched the effects mentioned in Article 3 (2) TFEU in terms of exclusive competences,

---

[86] On the idea of 'Kompetenz-Kompetenz', see: Chapter 2 – Section 2 above.
[87] Opinion 2/91 (*ILO Convention 170*), [1993] ECR I-1061, para. 9.
[88] Schütze (supra n. 48), 305 et seq.
[89] C. Calliess, *Subsidiaritäts- und Solidaritätsprinzip in der Europäischen Union* (Nomos, 1999), 95.

they should have been better expressed in the more nuanced vocabulary of the doctrine of legislative preemption.[90]

3. External decision-making procedures

How will the Union externally act, and through which procedures? This depends on the type of act adopted. An analysis of decision-making procedures within the Union's external powers must distinguish between unilateral acts and international agreements.[91] Unilateral external acts are acts that are single-handedly adopted by the European Union but directed at a third party.[92] By contrast, international agreements are agreements between the Union and a third party, and thus require the consent of the latter. We find *both* instruments within both constitutional sites for external relations. However, while the constitutional regime for unilateral acts is fundamentally different between the CFSP and the specialised TFEU external policies, both share the same treaty-making procedure.

This third section looks at the procedural regime for unilateral acts and international agreements. It will thereby concentrate on the decision-making procedure for unilateral CFSP decisions. The reason for this is that unilateral acts adopted under the specialised external competences generally follow the (ordinary) legislative procedure;[93] and, as formal Union legislation, their adoption was already discussed in Chapter 5. All international agreements on the other hand, are concluded according to procedures found in the Treaty on the Functioning of the European Union. The 'ordinary' treaty-making procedure is set out in Article 218 TFEU. The provision constitutes a *procedural* link between the two external relations sites, which – like the *personal* link in the form of the High Representative of FASP – has been introduced by the Lisbon Treaty.

Importantly, there is also an *institutional* link between the CFSP and the Union's specialised external policies. It is expressed in Article 22 TEU – placed in the Chapter on 'General Provisions on the Union's External Action'. According to this provision, the European Council must 'identify the strategic interests and objectives of the Union'. And these decisions on the strategic interests of the Union 'shall relate to the common foreign and security policy

---

[90] On the doctrine of preemption, see: Chapter 10 – Section 3 below.

[91] This section will not deal with 'positions' adopted within an international organisation.

[92] Such unilateral acts might range from development aid to economic sanctions. For an example of the latter, see: (Council) Regulation 204/2011 concerning restrictive measures in view of the situation in Libya ([2011] OJ L 58/1), as well as: (Council) Regulation 881/2002 imposing certain specific restrictive measures directed against certain persons and entities associated with Usama bin Laden, the Al-Qaida network and the Taliban ([2002] OJ L139/9).

[93] See Article 207 (2) TFEU (emphasis added): 'The European Parliament and the Council, acting by means of regulations in accordance with the *ordinary legislative procedure*, shall adopt the measures defining the framework for implementing the common commercial policy.'

and to other areas of the external action of the Union.[94] The European Council is thus the Union's – formal or informal – guide and pacemaker for all its external actions.[95]

(a) The 'specificity' of CFSP decision-making procedures

The decision-making procedures for unilateral CFSP acts are specific to the CFSP.[96] The specificity of CFSP procedures manifests itself in the institutional arrangements for decision-making, as well as the voting requirements in the Council. Their 'intergovernmental' character differs significantly from the supranational procedures governing all other external Union policies.

(i) Institutional actors and institutional balance

The original institutional arrangement within the CFSP has been described as 'confused'.[97] And while the Lisbon Treaty has simplified some matters, the constitutional principles governing the institutional dimension within the CFSP remain complex.

The central *policy* maker is the European Council, which identifies the strategic interests and general guidelines for the CFSP. It acts by means of decisions on a recommendation from the Council.[98] These decisions not only set the direction of the European foreign policy, but also its pace. (For decisions of the European Council will, as discussed below, have consequences for the voting arrangements in the Council.) The President of the European Council will 'at his level and in that capacity' ensure the external representation of the Union on issues concerning the CFSP without prejudice to the representational role of the High Representative of Foreign Affairs and Security Policy.[99]

The Council (here the Foreign Affairs Council) is the central *decision*-making body in the CFSP. It shall 'frame' the CFSP and 'take the decisions necessary for defining and implementing it' on the basis of the strategic interests and general guidelines adopted by the European Council.[100] This central decision-making role extends to the conclusion of international agreements.[101] The High Representative of Foreign Affairs and Security Policy, who will chair the Foreign Affairs Council, will generally assist the Council in its tasks.[102]

---

[94] Emphasis added
[95] The European Council indeed regularly decides on the strategic interests of the Union. It is interesting to note, however, that the European Council has come to prefer 'informal' strategies (see Strategy on Small Arms and Light Weapons) over 'formal' strategies (see Common Strategy 1999/414 on Russia, [1999] OJ L157/1). On this point, see: Eeckhout, *EU External Relations Law* (supra n. 33), 476–7.
[96] See Article 24 (1) TEU.
[97] P. Eeckhout, *External Relations of the European Union* (Oxford University Press, 2004), 420.
[98] See Articles 22 (1) and 26 (1) TEU.   [99] Article 15 (6) TEU.   [100] Article 26 (2) TEU.
[101] See Article 218 (2) TFEU: 'The Council shall authorise the opening of negotiations, adopt negotiating directives, authorise the signing of agreements and conclude them.'
[102] Article 27 (1) TEU.

What is the role of the supranational Union institutions? The role of the Commission within the CFSP is minimal and ill defined. It 'may', with the High Representative, make joint proposals to the European Council on the strategic interests of the Union;[103] and it 'may' support proposals by the High Representative to the Council, but this joint right of initiative is shared with any Member State.[104] What is the role of the European Parliament? The role of the European Parliament is even smaller than that of the Commission. Its principal prerogative lies in being regularly consulted 'on the main aspects and the basic choices' within the CFSP and having its views taken into consideration.[105] Parliament can ask questions and make recommendations to the Council, and it must hold a debate, twice a year, on the state of the CFSP.[106]

(ii) Voting arrangements in the Council

The Council is the central decision-taker within the CFSP. The Council voting rules are set out in Article 31 TEU. The general rule is that the Council acts unanimously. However, unlike other Union policies, the CFSP recognises the constitutional possibility of a 'constructive abstention'. It is constructive in that it allows the Council to act, despite an abstention, by unanimity. The abstaining Member State, having made a formal declaration, is not obliged to apply the Union decision.[107]

In derogation from the unanimity rule, Article 31 (2) enumerates a number of exceptional situations in which qualified majority voting applies. The Council can adopt a decision by qualified majority: (i) when it is based on a decision of the European Council; (ii) when it is based on a proposal from the High Representative following a specific request from the European Council; (iii) when it implements its own decisions; or (iv) when appointing a special representative (in accordance with Article 33 TEU).[108] This list of categories may be extended if the European Council so decides by unanimity.[109] Importantly, what constitutes a qualified majority under Article 31 TEU differs according to the category involved. This follows from Article 238 (2) TFEU,[110]

---

[103] Article 22 (2) TEU.

[104] Article 30 TEU. The Lisbon Treaty appears thus to have extinguished the Commission's autonomous right of initiative within the CFSP.

[105] Article 36 (1) TEU.   [106] Article 36 (2) TEU.

[107] This procedural mechanism finds a quantitative limit in one-third of the Member States comprising one-third of the population of the Union.

[108] Article 33 TEU states: 'The Council may, on a proposal from the High Representative of the Union for Foreign Affairs and Security Policy, appoint a special representative with a mandate in relation to particular policy issues. The special representative shall carry out his mandate under the authority of the High Representative.'

[109] Article 31 (3) TEU.

[110] The provision states: 'By way of derogation from Article 16(4) of the Treaty on European Union, as from 1 November 2014 and subject to the provisions laid down in the Protocol on transitional provisions, where the Council does not act on a proposal from the Commission or from the High Representative of the Union for Foreign Affairs and Security Policy, the qualified majority

which distinguishes between an 'ordinary' and a 'special' qualified majority for Council decisions, depending on whether the Council acts on a proposal from the High Representative. With the exception of category (ii), all CFSP decisions would thus seem to require a special qualified majority.

Finally, Article 31 TEU establishes two 'exceptions to the exception' of qualified majority voting. For it sets two absolute limits to decisional supranationalism. The first is of a political nature, the second of a constitutional nature. The political limit incorporates the 'Luxembourg Compromise' into the CFSP.[111] Any Member State may 'for vital and stated reasons of national policy' declare that it opposes a decision to be taken by qualified majority voting.[112] By contrast, the second limit is of a constitutional nature: any qualified majority voting can never apply to decisions having military or defence implications.[113]

(b) The Union's (ordinary) treaty-making procedure

The 'ordinary' procedure for the conclusion of international agreements by the Union is set out in Article 218 TFEU.[114] And the central institution within this procedure is the Council – not just as *primus inter pares* with Parliament, but simply as *primus*. Article 218 TFEU acknowledges the central role of the Council in all stages of the procedure: 'The Council shall authorise the opening of negotiations, adopt negotiating directives, authorise the signing of agreements and conclude them.'[115] The Council hereby acts by a qualified majority,[116] except in four situations. It shall act unanimously: when the agreement covers a field for which unanimity is required; for association agreements; with regard to Article 212 agreements with States that are candidates for Union

---

shall be defined as at least 72 per cent of the members of the Council, representing Member States comprising at least 65 per cent of the population of the Union.'

[111] On the 'Luxembourg Compromise', see: Chapter 1 – Section 2(b) above.

[112] Article 31 (2) TEU.   [113] Article 31 (5) TEU.

[114] Two special procedures are found in Articles 207 and 219 TFEU. The former deals with trade agreements within the context of the Union's common commercial policy. Article 207 (3) here expressly clarifies that 'Article 218 shall apply, subject to the special provisions in this Article'. Article 207 thus constitutes a *lex specialis* to the *lex generalis* of Article 218. The special rules within Article 207 principally concern the enhanced powers of the Commission and the special voting rules in the Council. A second express derogation from the 'ordinary' procedure in Article 218 is made for 'formal agreements on an exchange-rate system for the euro in relation to the currencies of third states' (see Article 219 (1): '[b]y way of derogation from Article 218'). The Council here acts, on a recommendation from the Commission or the European Central Bank, unanimously after consulting the European Parliament in accordance with the specific arrangements (to be decided under paragraph 3).

[115] Article 218 (2) TFEU.

[116] Importantly, the new Article 218 TFEU has not incorporated the old CFSP rule under ex-Article 24 (5) (old) EU, according to which a Member State would not be bound by an agreement to which its representative had not consented. However, the constitutional relationship between the general voting rules in Article 218 (8) TFEU and the special CFSP voting rules in Article 31 TEU is not yet clarified. Whether special CFSP arrangements, such as the 'constructive abstention' or the 'emergency break', will apply to CFSP agreements remains to be seen. (However, importantly, unlike Article 222 (3) TFEU, no express mention is made of the applicability of the voting arrangements in Article 31 TEU.)

accession; and, in respect of the Union's accession agreement to the ECHR.[117]

Having recognised the primary role of the Council, Article 218 TFEU then defines the secondary roles of the other EU institutions in the various procedural stages of treaty-making. The provision distinguishes between the initiation and negotiation of the agreement, its signing and conclusion, and also provides special rules for its modification and suspension. Exceptionally, the Union can become a party to international agreements without having concluded them. This – rare – phenomenon occurs, where the Union 'inherits' international agreements from its Member States through the doctrine of functional succession.

(i) Initiation and negotiation

Under Article 218 (3), the Commission holds the exclusive right to make recommendations for agreements that principally deal with non-CFSP matters. By contrast, as regards subjects that exclusively or principally fall within the CFSP, it is the High Representative who must submit recommendations to the Council. For matters falling partly within the CFSP and partly outside it, there is also the possibility of 'joint proposals'.[118]

On the recommendation, the Council may decide to open negotiations and nominate the Union negotiator 'depending on the subject matter of the agreement envisaged'.[119] This formulation is ambivalent. Textually, the phrase suggests a liberal meaning. The Council can – but need not necessarily – appoint the Commission as the Union negotiator for an agreement. According to this reading the Commission will not enjoy a prerogative to be the Union's negotiator for non-CFSP agreements. However, a systematic reading of the phrase leads to a more restrictive meaning. For if read in light of the jurisdictional division between the Commission and the High Representative at the recommendation stage, the Commission would be constitutionally entitled to be the Union negotiator for all Union agreements that 'exclusively or principally' fall into the Treaty on the Functioning of the European Union.[120]

The Council will be able to address directives to the negotiator and/or subject its powers to consultation with a special Council committee. Where the Commission is chosen as the Union negotiator, it will thus need to be 'authorised' by the Council and would conduct the negotiations under the control of the Council. The Commission's powers here are therefore between 'autonomous' and 'delegated' powers. The lower degree of institutional autonomy is justified by the fact that third parties are involved. (The subsequent rejection of the negotiated agreement by the Council would indeed have 'external' negative repercussions, and for that reason the ex ante involvement of the Council is a useful constitutional device.) On the other hand, the existence of an internal safeguard checking the Union negotiator creates, to some extent, a 'two-front

---

[117] Article 218 (8) TFEU.   [118] See Articles 22 (2) and 30 (1) TEU.
[119] Article 218 (3) TFEU.   [120] In this sense also: see Eeckhout (supra n. 33), 196.

war'. For the Union negotiator has not only to externally negotiate with the third party, but it also needs to internally deal with the Council.

Parliament is not formally involved in the negotiation. However, Article 218 (10) TFEU constitutionalises Parliament's right to be informed during all stages of the procedure. And this right has the potential of becoming an informal political safeguard that anticipates the interests of Parliament at the negotiation stage.[121]

Finally, any Union institution and the Member States are entitled to challenge the 'constitutionality' of a draft agreement *prior* to its conclusion. This judicial safeguard can be found in Article 218 (11) TFEU, which creates the jurisdiction of the Court for an 'Opinion'.[122] Where this 'Opinion' leads to a finding that the envisaged agreement is not compatible with the Treaties, the agreement may not enter into force – unless the Treaties themselves are amended.[123] The possibility of an ex ante 'review' of a draft agreement contrasts with the Court's ordinary ex post review powers.[124] However, the exception is – again – justified by the fact that third party rights under international law are involved. Indeed, it is a rule of international law that, once an agreement is validly concluded under international law, a contracting party generally cannot subsequently invoke internal constitutional problems to deny its binding effect.[125] Ex post review of an international agreement will thus be too late to negate the external effects of an international agreement.

---

[121] See Framework Agreement on Relations between the European Parliament and the European Commission, especially Annex III. According to paragraph 3 of the Annex, '[t]he Commission shall take due account of Parliament's comments throughout the negotiations'.

[122] Article 218 (11) TFEU. The Court has so far delivered fifteen Opinions on international agreements: Opinion 1/75 (*Local Cost Standard*), [1975] ECR 1355; Opinion 1/76 (*Laying-Up Fund*), [1977] ECR 741; Opinion 1/78 (*Natural Rubber Agreement*), [1979] ECR 2871; Opinion 1/91 (*EEA Draft Agreement*), [1991] ECR I-6079; Opinion 2/91 (*ILO Convention 170*), [1993] ECR I-1061; Opinion 1/92 (*EFTA Agreement II*), [1992] ECR I-2821; Opinion 2/92 (*Third Revised OECD Decision*), [1995] ECR I-521; Opinion 1/94 (*WTO Agreement*), [1994] ECR I-5267; Opinion 2/94 (*Accession to ECHR*), [1996] ECR I-1759; Opinion 3/94 (*Banana Framework Agreement*), [1995] ECR I-4577; Opinion 1/00 (*European Common Aviation Area*), [2002] ECR I-3493; Opinion 2/00 (*Cartagena Protocol*) [2002] ECR I-9713; Opinion 1/03 (*Lugano Convention*), [2006] ECR I-1145; Opinion 1/08 (GATS), (nyr); Opinion 1/09 (*European Patent Court*), (nyr).

[123] This happened, for example, with regard to the European Convention of Human Rights in 1996, see: Opinion 2/94 (*Accession to ECHR*), [1996] ECR I-1759. Prior to the Lisbon Treaty, accession to the Convention was thus unconstitutional. The Lisbon Treaty has amended the original Treaties, which now contain an express competence to accede to the ECHR in Article 6 (2) TEU.

[124] On (ex post) judicial review in the Union legal order, see: Chapter 8 – Section 1 below.

[125] See Article 46 Vienna Convention of the Law of Treaties: '(1) A State may not invoke the fact that its consent to be bound by a treaty has been expressed in violation of a provision of its internal law regarding competence to conclude treaties as invalidating its consent unless that violation was manifest and concerned a rule of its internal law of fundamental importance. (2) A violation is manifest if it would be objectively evident to any State conducting itself in the matter in accordance with normal practice and in good faith.'

(ii) Signing and conclusion

The Council will sign and conclude the agreement on a proposal by the negotiator.[126]

Prior to the formal conclusion of the agreement, the European Parliament must be actively involved, except where the agreement *exclusively* relates to the CFSP. (When compared with the Commission's involvement at the proposal stage,[127] the TFEU is here more generous for it expands parliamentary involvement to agreements that even principally relate to CFSP matters.) Article 218 (6) thereby distinguishes between two forms of parliamentary participation in the conclusion procedure: consultation and consent. The former is the residual category and applies to all agreements that do not require consent. The types of agreements where the Council needs to obtain parliamentary consent are enumerated in the form of five situations listed under Article 218 (6) (a) TFEU: (i) association agreements; (ii) the agreement on Union accession to the ECHR; (iii) agreements establishing a specific institutional framework; (iv) agreements with important budgetary implications for the Union; (v) agreements covering fields to which either the ordinary legislative procedure applies, or the special legislative procedure where consent by the European Parliament is required.

The first, second and third category may be explained by the constitutional idea of 'political treaties'.[128] For association agreements as well as institutional framework agreements, such as the ECHR, will by definition express an important *political* choice with long-term consequences. For these fundamental political choices Parliament – the representative of the European citizens – must give its democratic consent. The fourth category represents a constitutional reflex that protects the special role the European Parliament enjoys in establishing the Union budget.[129] The fifth category makes profound sense from the perspective of procedural parallelism. Under paragraph 6 (a) (v) of Article 218, Parliament is entitled to veto 'agreements covering fields' that internally require parliamentary co-decision or consent.[130] The parallelism between the internal and external sphere is however not complete: Parliament

---

[126] Article 218 (5) and (6) TFEU. The conclusion will usually be done by means of a Council Decision.

[127] Article 218 (3) TFEU: agreements relating 'exclusively *or principally*' to the CFSP (emphasis added).

[128] R. Jennings and S. Watts (eds.), *Oppenheim's International Law* (Oxford University Press, 2008), 211.

[129] For an extensive discussion of this category, see: Case 189/97, *Parliament* v. *Council (Mauritania Fisheries Agreement)*, [1999] ECR I-4741.

[130] The Lisbon reform of the provision removes two constitutional oddities that characterised ex-Article 300 EC. First, Parliament's prerogative to participate in the agreement is henceforth independent of the pre-existence of internal legislation. The consent requirement hinges on the internal decision-making procedure *as such*. Second, unlike ex-Article 300 EC, Article 218 has extended parliamentary consent for international agreements to all internal procedures that also require parliamentary consent. And again, this reform enhances the parallelism between the internal and the external sphere.

will indeed *not* enjoy the power of co-conclusion in areas in which the 'ordinary' legislative procedure applies. Its internal power to co-decision is here reduced to a mere power of 'consent'. It must 'take or leave' the negotiated international agreement. This structural 'democratic deficit' in the procedural regime for international agreements is however not a *sui generis* characteristic of the European Union, but can be found in other constitutional orders of the world.[131] It is generally justified by reference to the 'exceptional' nature of foreign affairs, and in particular their 'volatile' and 'secretive' nature.[132]

(iii) Modification, suspension (and termination)

Article 218 (7) TFEU deals with modifications of international agreements that have been successfully concluded. The Council may 'authorise the negotiator to approve on the Union's behalf modifications to the agreement where it provides for them to be adopted by a simplified procedure or by a body set up by the agreement'. (The Council can attach specific conditions to such an authorisation.) In the absence of such a specific authorisation for a simplified revision procedure, the ordinary treaty-making procedure will apply. This follows from a constitutional principle called *actus contrarius*. In order to modify an international agreement the same procedure needs to be followed that led to the conclusion of the international agreement in the first place.

Article 218 (9) TFEU deals with the suspension of an international agreement. The provision specifies that the Commission or the High Representative may propose to the Council the suspension of the agreement. (And while the provision does not expressly refer to the jurisdictional division between the two actors, as mentioned in Article 218 (3) TFEU for the proposal stage, we should assume that this rule would apply analogously. The High Representative should thus solely be entitled to recommend the suspension for international agreements that relate 'exclusively or principally' to the CFSP.) Parliament is not expressly mentioned and will thus only have to be informed of the Council decision. This truncated procedure allows the Union quickly to decide on the (temporary) suspension of an agreement. However, this 'executive' decision without parliamentary consent distorts to some extent the institutional balance in the external relations field.

How are Union agreements terminated? Unfortunately, Article 218 TFEU does not expressly set out a procedural regime for the termination of a Union agreement. Two views are possible. The first view is again based on the idea of *actus contrarius*: the termination of an agreement would need to follow the very same procedure for its conclusion. This procedural parallelism has been contested by reference to the constitutional traditions of the Union's Member

---

[131] It can be found, for example, in the United States. According to Article II, Section 2 of the US Constitution, it is the President who 'shall have Power, by and with the Advice and Consent of the Senate, to make Treaties, provided two thirds of the Senators present concur'. The American Parliament – the House of Representatives – is not formally involved.

[132] On this classic perception of foreign affairs, see: Introduction to this chapter, above.

States, which leave the termination decision principally in the hands of the executive.[133] A second view therefore reverts to the suspension procedure applied analogously.

(iv) Union succession to international agreements of the Member States

Can the Union be bound by agreements that it has not formally concluded? The counter-intuitive answer is positive: under European law, the Union can be bound by agreements of its Member States where the former has succeeded the latter.[134]

The doctrine of Union succession to international agreements of the Member States is a doctrine of *functional* succession.[135] It is not based on a transfer of territory, but on a transfer of *functions*. The European Court announced this European doctrine in relation to the General Agreement on Tariffs and Trade in *International Fruit*.[136] Formally, the Union was not a party to the international treaty, but the Court found that 'in so far as under the [European] Treat[ies] the [Union] has *assumed the powers previously exercised by Member States* in the area covered by the General Agreement, the provisions of that agreement have the effect of binding the [Union]'.[137] Functional succession thus emanated from the exclusive nature of the Union's powers under the Common Commercial Policy (CCP). Since the Union had assumed the 'functions' previously exercised by the Member States in this area, it was entitled and obliged to also assume their international obligations.

For a long time after *International Fruit*, the succession doctrine remained quiet. But in the last decade it experienced a constitutional revival. This allowed the Court better to define the doctrine's contours. Three principles seem to govern functional succession in the European legal order. First, for the succession doctrine to come into operation *all* the Member States must be parties to an international treaty.[138] Second, *when* the international treaty is concluded is irrelevant. It will thus not matter whether the international treaty was concluded before or after the creation of the European Community in 1958.[139]

---

[133] C. Tomuschat, 'Artikel 300 EG' in H. von der Groeben and J. Schwarze (eds.), *Kommentar zum Vertrag über die Europäische Union und zur Gründung der Europäischen Gemeinschaft* (Nomos, 2004), vol. IV, para. 61.

[134] For an overview, see: R. Schütze, 'The "Succession Doctrine" and the European Union' in A. Arnull et al. (eds.), *A Constitutional Order of States: Essays in Honour of Alan Dashwood* (Hart, 2011), 459.

[135] See P. Pescatore, *L'Ordre Juridique des Communautés Européennes* (Presse Universitaire de Liège, 1975), 147–8 (my translation): '[B]y taking over, by virtue of the Treaties, certain competences and certain powers previously exercised by the Member States, the [Union] equally had to assume the international obligations that controlled the exercise of these competences and powers[.]'

[136] Joined Cases 21–24/72, *International Fruit Company NV* v. *Produktschap voor Groenten en Fruit*, [1972] ECR 1219.

[137] *Ibid.*, paras. 14–18 (emphasis added).

[138] Case C-188/07, *Commune de Mesquer* v. *Total*, [2008] ECR I-4501.

[139] Case 308/06, *Intertanko and others* v. *Secretary of State for Transport*, [2008] ECR I-4057.

Third, the Union will only succeed to international treaties, where there is a '*full transfer of the powers* previously exercised by the Member States'.[140] The Union will thus not succeed to all international agreements concluded by all the Member States, but only to those where it has assumed an exclusive competence. Would the European succession doctrine thereby be confined to the sphere of the Union's *constitutionally* exclusive powers; or, would *legislative* exclusivity generated by Article 3 (2) TFEU be sufficient? The Court has shown a preference for a succession doctrine that includes legislative exclusivity. In *Bogiatzi*,[141] the Court indeed found that a 'full transfer' could take place where the Member States were completely preempted within the substantive scope of the international treaty.

4. Sharing external power: constitutional safeguards of unitarianism

States are sovereign subjects of international law.[142] From an international law perspective, they thus enjoy full external powers. But this – simple – solution might not apply to unions of States. Two constitutional traditions here co-exist. Within the American tradition, the Union is seen as the sole bearer of external sovereignty. It is the unitary external representative – with the Member States being 'closed' off from the international scene.[143] By contrast, according to the German tradition, the Union and its Member States may partake in international relations.[144] Within such an 'open federation', the external relations of the Union and its Member States need to be coordinated so as to safeguard diplomatic and political consistency. The European Union follows this second tradition. It is an open federation in which the Union and its Member States are active participants on the international scene.

How has the European legal order coordinated the (potentially) dual presence of the Union and its Member States? The Union has followed two mechanisms. The first mechanism is a political safeguard that brings the Union and its Member States to the same negotiating table for an international agreement. In the past fifty years, the Union indeed cultivated the international technique of mixed agreements. By contrast, a second mechanism is 'internal' to the Union and imposes a 'duty of cooperation' on the Member States that 'flows from the requirement of unity in the international representation of the [Union]'.[145] And while this duty – theoretically – operates on the Union as well

---

[140] *Ibid.*, para. 4 (emphasis added).

[141] Case C-301/08, *Bogiatzi* v. *Deutscher Luftpool and others*, (nyr).

[142] Article 6 of the 1969 Vienna Convention: 'Every State possesses capacity to conclude treaties.'

[143] For the American tradition of a 'closed federation', see: R. Schütze, 'Federalism and Foreign Affairs: Mixity as an (Inter)national Phenomenon' in C. Hillion and P. Koutrakos (eds.), *Mixed Agreements Revisited* (Hart, 2010), 57 at 59 et seq.

[144] For the German tradition of an 'open federation', see: *ibid.* at 65 et seq.

[145] Opinion 1/94 (supra n. 122), para.108.

as the Member States,[146] it has – practically – been solely used to facilitate the exercise of the Union's external powers on the international scene.

(a) Mixed agreements: an international and political safeguard

Who can conclude international agreements that do not entirely fall into the competence sphere of the Union or the Member States? The traditional answer to that question has been the Union and the Member States combined in the form of mixed agreements – that is: agreements to which both the Union and some or all of its Member States appear as contracting parties.[147] Mixity had originally been designed for a specific sector of European law.[148] However, it soon spread to become the hallmark of the European Union's foreign affairs federalism.[149]

The growth and success of mixed agreements in Europe's foreign affairs federalism may be accounted for by a number of reasons – internal and external to the Union legal order. First, mixed agreements would allow the Union and its Member States to complement their competences into a unitary whole that matched the external sovereignty of a third State. The division of treaty-making powers between them could then be reduced to an 'internal' Union affair.[150] Second, the uncertainty surrounding the nature and extent of the treaty-making powers of non-state actors under international law originally provided an additional reason.[151] As long as it remained uncertain whether or how the Union could fulfil its international obligations, mixed agreements would provide legal security for third States by involving the Member States as international 'guarantors' of the Union obligation.[152]

---

[146] *Ibid.*

[147] Mixity extends to all phases of an international agreement and may thus add a pluralist dimension to the negotiation, conclusion and implementation stage.

[148] Article 102 Euratom Treaty: 'Agreements or contracts concluded with a third State, an international organisation or a national of a third State to which, in addition to the Community, one or more Member States are parties, shall not enter into force until the Commission has been notified by all the Member States concerned that those agreements or contracts have become applicable in accordance with the provisions of their respective national laws.'

[149] The first mixed agreement concluded by the EEC was the 1961 Agreement establishing an association between the European Economic Community and Greece, [1963] OJ 26/294. For a relatively up-to-date registry, see J. Heliskoski, *Mixed Agreements as a Technique for Organizing the International Relations of the European Community and its Member States* (Kluwer, 2001), 252–77, listing 154 mixed agreements concluded between 1961 and 2000.

[150] See Ruling 1/78 *(IAEA Convention)*, [1978] ECR 2151, para. 35: 'It is sufficient to state to the other Contracting parties that the matter gives rise to a division of powers within the Community, it being understood that the exact nature of that division is a domestic question in which Third States have no need to intervene.'

[151] P. Pescatore, 'Les Relations Extérieures des Communautés Européennes: Contribution à la Doctrine de la Personnalité des Organisations Internationales' [1961] 103 *Recueil des Cours* 1, 105.

[152] M. J. Dolmans, *Problems of Mixed Agreements: Division of Powers within the EEC and the Rights of Third States* (Asser Instituut, 1985), 95.

The constitutional developments within the European legal order in the last four decades have weakened both rationales. Not only have the external powers of the Union been significantly expanded through the development of the doctrine of implied powers – now codified in Article 216 TFEU – its internal powers have been sharpened to guarantee the enforcement of Union agreements within the European legal order.[153] Today, the dominant – third – reason behind mixed agreements appears to be of a purely political nature: Member States insist on participating in their own name so as to remain 'visible' on the international scene.[154] Even for matters that fall squarely into the Union's competence, the Member States dislike being (en)closed behind a supranational veil.

How has the European Union reacted to the *internal* demand for mixed agreements? Shared competences do not constitutionally require mixed action.[155] Not every international agreement falling within an area of shared competences must therefore be mixed. Within shared competences, the Union or the Member States can both act autonomously and conclude independent agreements; or, if they so wish, they may act jointly.[156] It originally seemed that the European Court would demand specific *constitutional* justification for mixed external action in place of a pure Union agreement.[157] However, in the last three decades, the Court of Justice has given a judicial blessing to the uncontrolled use of mixed agreement in areas of shared competences.[158]

The widespread use of mixed external action evinces a remarkable Union tolerance towards the Member States' international powers, as the practice of

---

[153] On the direct and indirect effects of international agreement in the Union legal order, see: Chapter 9 – Section 4 below.

[154] C. D. Ehlermann, 'Mixed Agreements: A List of Problems' in O'Keeffe and Schermers (eds.), *Mixed Agreements* (Kluwer, 1983), 3 at 6: 'Member States wish to continue to appear as contracting parties in order to remain visible and identifiable actors on the international scene. Individual participation is therefore seen as a way of defending and enhancing the prestige and influence of individual Member States.'

[155] R. Schütze, 'The European Community's Federal Order of Competences: A Retrospective Analysis' in M. Dougan and S. Currie (eds.), *Fifty Years of the European Treaties – Looking Back and Thinking Forward* (Hart Publishing, 2009), 63, esp. 85–7.

[156] See Case 316/91, *Parliament v. Council*, [1994] ECR I-625, para. 26. In this sense, see also R. Holdgaard, *External Relations of the European Community: Legal Reasoning and Legal Discourses* (Kluwer, 2008), 152.

[157] Opinion 1/76 *(Laying-Up Fund)* [1977] ECR 741, paras. 6–8. The Court recognised that 'the danger of mixed agreements (and their attraction for Member States) lies in their tendency to over-emphasise at the expense of the [Union] the participation of the Member States as traditional international legal persons' (M. Cremona, 'The Doctrine of Exclusivity and the Position of Mixed Agreements in the External Relations of the European Community' [1982] 2 *Oxford Journal of Legal Studies* 393, 414).

[158] In the last thirty years, these 'facultative' mixed agreements – i.e., agreements in which the Union has competence to conclude the entire agreement – have become the prominent category of mixed agreements: 'Indeed, there is no decision from the Court under the EC Treaty where the explicit justification for recourse to the mixed procedure would have been the limited scope of [Union] competence – commonly regarded as the principal legal explanation for the practice of mixed agreements' (see Heliskoski (supra n. 149 at 68)).

mixed agreements entails a significant *anti*-Union consequence. According to a European 'constitutional convention', the Council concludes mixed agreements on behalf of the Union only once *all* the Member States have themselves ratified the agreement in accordance with their constitutional traditions.[159] The convention thus boils down to requiring 'unanimous' consent before the Union can exercise its competence. The conventional arrangement thus prolongs the (in)famous Luxembourg Accord in the external sphere. The constitutionally uncontrolled use of mixed agreements under the Union's shared powers has, unsurprisingly, been criticised as 'a way of whittling down systematically the personality and capacity of the [Union] as a representative of the collective interest'.[160] Others have celebrated the practice of mixed agreements as 'a near unique contribution to true federalism'.[161] The truth lies in between. Mixity should be confined to situations where solid constitutional reasons necessitate the doubling of the Member States on the international scene.

(b) The duty of cooperation: an internal and judicial safeguard

The Member States' duty to cooperate loyally and sincerely informs all areas of European law.[162] However, the duty is particularly important in the external sphere.[163] And this is especially so where the Union and the Member States must coordinate their international powers under a mixed agreement.[164]

---

[159] The inspiration for this constitutional convention appears to lie in Article 102 of the Euratom Treaty (supra n. 148). On the convention and ways to alleviate its consequences, see: P. Eeckhout, (supra n. 33), 258–9.

[160] P. Pescatore, 'Opinion 1/94 on "Conclusion" of the WTO Agreement: is there an Escape from a Programmed Disaster?' [1999] 36 CML Rev 387 at fn. 6. The criticism on mixed agreements has been rich from the very beginning, see: A. Barav, 'General Discussion' in C. W. A. Timmermans and E. L. M. Völker (eds.), *Division of Powers between the European Communities and their Member States in the field of External Relations* (Kluwer, 1981), 144: '[M]ixed agreements are probably a necessary evil, part of the integration process, but nobody would like to see any more of them.'

[161] J. H. H. Weiler, 'The External Relations of non-unitary Actors: Mixity and the Federal Principle' in Weiler (ed.), *The Constitution of Europe* (Cambridge University Press, 1999) at 130.

[162] For the general duty, see: Article 4 (3) TEU.

[163] For a special expression of the general duty of Article 4 (3) TEU in the CFSP area, see: Article 24 (3) TEU: 'The Member States shall support the Union's external and security policy actively and unreservedly in a spirit of loyalty and mutual solidarity and shall comply with the Union's action in this area. The Member States shall work together to enhance and develop their mutual political solidarity. They shall refrain from any action which is contrary to the interests of the Union or likely to impair its effectiveness as a cohesive force in international relations.' For even more specific duties of cooperation, see: Article 32 TEU (consultation and coordination of national policies within the European Council and the Council) and Article 34 TEU (coordination of Member States in international organisations).

[164] See Case 459/03, *Commission v. Ireland (Mox Plant)*, [2006] ECR I-4657, paras. 175–6: 'The Court has also emphasised that the Member States and the [Union] institutions have an obligation of close cooperation in fulfilling the commitments undertaken by them under joint competence when they conclude a mixed agreement. That is in particular the position in the case of a dispute which, as in the present case, relates essentially to undertakings resulting from a mixed agreement which relates to an area, namely the protection and preservation of the marine

However, while developed in the context of mixed agreements, this is not the only situation where the duty of cooperation has been given an active constitutional role.[165] For the Union legal order has equally employed the duty of cooperation to facilitate the (autonomous) exercise of the *Union's* external competences. This facilitating role has been expressed in a positive and a negative manner. The positive aspect of the duty of cooperation may demand that the Member States act as 'trustees of the Union interest'. By contrast, the negative aspect of the duty of cooperation can place a limit on the Member States exercising their shared external competences. In this second role, the duty of cooperation operates – partly – as the 'reverse' of the principle of subsidiarity.[166]

(i) Member States as 'trustees of the Union'

Classic international law is built on the idea of the sovereign State.[167] This State-centred structure of international law creates normative difficulties for non-State actors.[168] The European Union is a union of *States*, and as such still encounters normative hurdles when acting on the international scene. These normative hurdles have become fewer, but there remain situations in which the Union cannot externally act due to the partial blindness of international law towards compound subjects. And where the Union is – internationally – 'disabled' from exercising its competences, it will have to authorise its Member States to act on its behalf. This positive manifestation of the duty of cooperation is called the 'trustees doctrine'.[169]

environment, in which the respective areas of competence of the [Union] and the Member States are liable to be closely interrelated, as is, moreover, evidenced by the Declaration of [Union] competence and the appendix thereto.' For an analysis of the duty of cooperation within the (mixed) WTO Agreement, see: J. Heliskoski, 'The "Duty of Cooperation" between the European Community and its Member States within the World Trade Organisation' [1997] 7 *Finnish Yearbook of International Law* 59.

[165] See Case 266/03, *Commission v. Luxembourg*, [2005] ECR 4805, para. 58: 'That duty of genuine cooperation is of general application and does not depend either on whether the [Union] competence concerned is exclusive or on any right of the Member States to enter into obligations towards non-member countries.' For a general analysis of the duty in the external relations context, see: M. Cremona, 'Defending the Community Interest: the Duties of Cooperation and Compliance' in M. Cremona and B. de Witte (eds.), *EU Foreign Relations Law: Constitutional Fundamentals* (Hart, 2008), 125; as well as: E. Neframi, 'The Duty of Loyalty: Rethinking its Scope through its Application in the field of EU External Relations' [2010] 47 CML Rev 323.

[166] I am aware that this is a controversial formulation as the subsidiarity principle may theoretically operate downwards *and upwards*. However, in the past, European law has mainly identified subsidiarity as a mechanism for protecting the exercise of State competences. And for that reason 'reverse subsidiarity' tries to capture the idea that the Court here uses the duty of cooperation to protect the exercise of Union competences.

[167] M. Koskenniemi, *From Apology to Utopia: The Structure of International Legal Argument* (Cambridge University Press, 2006).

[168] See Jennings and Watts, *Oppenheim* (supra n. 128), 245 et seq.

[169] For a first analysis of this doctrinal construction in the external sphere, see: M. Cremona, 'Member States as Trustees of the Union Interest: Participating in International Agreements on Behalf of the European Union' in Arnull (supra n. 134), 435.

A good illustration of the trustees doctrine may be found in the context of the Union's inability to participate in international organisations. Many of these organisations still only allow States to become (active) members; and hence the European Union finds itself unable to exercise its competences in these international decision-making fora. An example of this state-centred membership is the International Labour Organisation (ILO). Here, the Union cannot itself conclude international conventions and must thus rely on its Member States. The obligation to act as trustee of the Union thereby derives from the duty of cooperation: 'In this case, cooperation between the [Union] and the Member States is all the more necessary in view of the fact that the former cannot, as international law stands at present, itself conclude an ILO convention and must do so *through the medium of the Member States*.'[170] The Union must here exercise its external competences indirectly, that is: through the Member States 'acting jointly in the [Union's] interest'.[171]

We find a more recent example of the trustees doctrine in the Council Decision 'authorising the Member States, in the interest of the [Union], to ratify or accede to the International Convention on Liability and Compensation for Damage in Connection with the Carriage of Hazardous and Noxious Substances at Sea'.[172] The Union could not accede to the Convention, as it was only open to sovereign States.[173] But since the relevant Convention was 'particularly important, given the interest of the [Union] and its Member States', the Union authorised and obliged its Member States to conclude the Convention.[174] The Union thus overcame its inability under international law by enabling and obliging its Member States to act in the common 'European' interest on the international scene.

(ii) 'Reversed' subsidiarity: restrictions on the exercise of shared State power

In an area of shared competences both the Union and the Member States are entitled to act externally by – for example – concluding an international agreement with the United States. But due to the various procedural obstacles in the Union treaty-making power, the Member States might be much quicker in exercising their shared competence. And third parties might indeed be more interested in twenty-seven bilateral agreements than one Union agreement on a matter.[175]

In order to safeguard the 'unity in the international representation of the [Union]',[176] the Court has therefore developed a 'negative' aspect to the duty of cooperation. Where the international actions of a Member State might jeopardise the conclusion of a Union agreement, the Court has imposed specific

---

[170] Opinion 2/91 (*ILO Convention 170*), [1993] ECR I-1061, para. 37 (emphasis added).
[171] *Ibid.*, para. 5.   [172] See Council Decision 2002/971/EC, [2002] OJ L 337/55.
[173] *Ibid.*, Preamble 4.   [174] *Ibid.*, Articles 1 and 3.
[175] This approach might be inspired by the classic Roman strategy of '*divide et impera*', that is: divide and rule.
[176] Opinion 1/94 (*WTO Agreement*), [1994] ECR I-5267, para. 108.

obligations on the Member States. These obligations limit the exercise of their shared powers, and thus – to some extent – mirror and invert the principle of subsidiarity. And like the principle of subsidiarity, the duty of cooperation has traditionally been thought to be of a 'procedural' nature.[177]

We find a good illustration of the negative duties imposed on the Member States when exercising their shared external competences in *Commission* v. *Luxembourg*.[178] Luxembourg had exercised its international treaty power to conclude a number of bilateral agreements with Eastern European States. The Commission was incensed, as it had already started its own negotiations for the Union as a whole. It thus complained that even if Luxembourg enjoyed a shared competence to conclude the agreements, '[t]he negotiation by the Commission of an agreement on behalf of the [Union] and its subsequent conclusion by the Council is inevitably made more difficult by interference from a Member State's own initiatives'.[179] The Union's position was claimed to have been weakened 'because the [Union] and its Member States appear fragmented'.[180] The Court adopted this view – but only partly:

> The adoption of a decision authorising the Commission to negotiate a multi-lateral agreement on behalf of the [Union] marks the start of a concerted [Union] action at international level and requires, for that purpose, *if not a duty of abstention on the part of the Member States, at the very least a duty of close cooperation* between the latter and the [Union] institutions in order to facilitate the achievement of the [Union] tasks and to ensure the coherence and consistency of the action and its international representation.[181]

Importantly, the Court did not condemn the exercise of the Member State's treaty power as such. Endowed with shared external power, Luxembourg could very well conclude bilateral agreements with third States. However, since the Commission had started a 'concerted [Union] action' for the conclusion of a Union agreement in this area, the Member State was under an obligation to cooperate and consult with the Commission. And in not consulting the Union, Luxembourg had violated the duty of cooperation.[182] The duty of cooperation was thus primarily seen as a duty of information. It appeared to be a *procedural* duty of conduct, and not a substantive duty of result.

The purely procedural character of the duty has however recently been put into question. In *Commission* v. *Sweden*,[183] the Union institution brought proceedings against Sweden for 'splitting the international representation of the [Union] and compromising the unity achieved … during the first

---

[177] Cremona, 'Defending the Community Interest' (supra n. 165), 168; as well as Neframi, 'The Duty of Loyalty' (supra n. 165), 355–6.

[178] Case 266/03, *Commission* v. *Luxembourg*, [2005] ECR 4805.   [179] *Ibid.*, para. 53.

[180] *Ibid.*   [181] *Ibid.*, para. 60 (emphasis added).   [182] *Ibid.*, para. 61.

[183] Case C-246/07, *Commission* v. *Sweden*, (nyr). For an extensive analysis, see: G. de Baere, '"O, Where is Faith? O, Where is Loyalty?" Some Thoughts on the Duty of Loyal Co-operation and the Union's External Environmental Competences in the light of the PFOS Case' [2011] 36 EL Rev 405.

Conference of the Parties to [the Stockholm Convention on Persistent Organic Pollutants]'.[184] What had happened? Sweden had not abstained from making a proposal within the international conference, and the Commission claimed that this unilateral action violated the duty of cooperation. Sweden counterclaimed that it had given sufficient information to and consulted with the Union and the other Member States.[185] But this time, this was not enough. After duly citing its case law, the Court moved to examine whether there existed a Union 'strategy' not to make a proposal.[186] And in finding that such a Union strategy existed, and that Sweden had 'dissociated itself from a concerted common strategy within the Council',[187] the Court found that Sweden had violated the duty of cooperation. In a remarkable feat of judicial creativity, the Court now found that its past case law stood for the proposition 'that Member States are subject to special duties of action *and abstention* in a situation in which the Commission has submitted to the Council proposals which, although they have not been adopted by the Council, represent a point of departure for concerted [Union] action'.[188]

This case might indeed be the beginning of a *substantive* duty of cooperation. For the Court was not satisfied with the procedural obligation to inform and consult, but prohibited the very exercise of a shared external competence by a Member State. Are there dangers in a substantive reading of the duty of cooperation? While such a reading better protects the unity of external representation of the Union and its Member States, there is a danger for the autonomous exercise of the States' international powers.[189] It all depends on how early the duty to abstain from international action departing from the Union position starts. The temporal aspect of the duty will thus principally determine its substantive effect.

Conclusion

The European Union has international personality and indeed represents a significant international actor. Unlike its Member States, the Union is not regarded as a sovereign State in international law. The European Union is a union of States and, as such, it is a compound subject of international law.

The Union's external competences are conferred competences. For in the absence of external sovereignty, the Union must have power transferred to it by its Member States. What is the scope of the Union's competences? Section 1 analysed the dual constitutional regime for external competences, as the latter are generally found in two constitutional sites. Title V of the Treaty on European Union confers a general competence on the Union to deal with the

---

[184] Case C-246/07, *Commission* v. *Sweden*, (supra n. 183), para. 44.   [185] *Ibid.*, para. 63.
[186] *Ibid.*, para. 76.   [187] *Ibid.*, para. 91.   [188] *Ibid.*, para. 103.
[189] Sweden rightly claimed that a substantive interpretation was 'likely to render shared competence in the case of mixed agreements meaningless' (*ibid.*, para. 63).

'Common Foreign and Security Policy'. By contrast, Part V of the Treaty on the Functioning of the European Union enumerates a number of special competences in particular policy areas. In addition to these thematic competences, the Union is also given a 'residual' treaty-making power: Article 216 TFEU. We saw above that the provision attempts to codify the Court's jurisprudence on the Union's implied treaty-making powers. This article is however a textual fiasco. For Article 216 (1) appears to be – mistakenly – shaped by three principles created by the European Court in the context of the European Union's *exclusive* competences.

What is the nature of the Union's external competences? Can they be classified by means of the same categories that apply to the Union's legislative competences? We saw in Section 2 that this is indeed generally the case. Yet, there are two constitutional exceptions. First, the character of the CFSP competence cannot be captured by the competence categories mentioned in Articles 3–6 TFEU. This follows implicitly from the – still – mysterious qualities of CFSP law, and expressly from Article 40 TEU. The CFSP competence is best seen as '*sui generis*' – a singular phenomenon that corresponds to the 'special' nature of the CFSP rules and procedures.[190] The second exception to the general competence categories of the Union is the idea of subsequently exclusive treaty-making powers. This idea derogates from the classification within the Union's legislative powers, whose exercise will not lead to an exclusive competence.[191] The idea of subsequent external exclusivity or 'exclusivity by exercise' had originally been developed by the European Court. The Lisbon Treaty has tried to codify past jurisprudence in the form of Article 3(2) TFEU. This codification is – again – not without problems, and it is – again – in the hands of the European judiciary to sharpen its contours in the future.

Section 3 analysed the decision-making procedures in the external relations of the Union. Which procedure thereby applies depends on two factors. First, is the measure to be adopted a unilateral act; or is it an international agreement? If it is an international agreement, then the Treaties follow common treaty-making procedures. If it is a unilateral measure, then the Treaties distinguish between the two constitutional regimes for external relations. While acts adopted under the Union's special competences principally follow the (ordinary) legislative procedure, the procedure for unilateral CFSP acts is 'special'.[192] It has a special nature both in relation to the constitutional balance between the institutional actors involved, and the special voting arrangements in the Council. Both features turn the CFSP into an 'intergovernmental' area of European law that contrasts with the rest of the Union's 'supranational' decision-making procedures. These 'intergovernmental' elements are however

---

[190] See Article 24 (1) TEU: 'The common foreign and security policy is subject to specific rules and procedures.'

[191] The supremacy of European law leads to the 'preemption' of conflicting national law. For a discussion of this point, see: Chapter 10 – Section 3 below.

[192] See Article 24 (1) TEU.

less obvious in the procedure for treaty-making. For the Lisbon Treaty has 'unified' the procedural regimes for CFSP and non-CFSP treaties in Article 218 TFEU. The provision distinguishes between various stages. The negotiation of international treaties is thereby principally left in the hands of the Commission and the High Representative. The conclusion of the agreement is the task of the Council. However, Parliament will need to give its consent on a wide range of agreements; yet, as we saw above, consent is not co-decision. The external powers of the Parliament are thus lower than its internal powers.

Section 4 finally looked at constitutional devices designed to safeguard a degree of 'unity' in the external actions of the Union and its Member States. These devices are necessary as the European Union is an 'open federation'. In order to ensure unity and consistency, the European legal order has principally had recourse to two constitutional mechanisms. Mixed agreements constitute an international law mechanism that brings the Union and the Member States (as well as third parties) to the same negotiating table. In an era of shared external powers,[193] mixed external action might not be mandatory; yet Member States have insisted on using mixed agreements as a political device. The second constitutional device is internal to the Union legal order. It is the duty of cooperation. While the duty is said to be reciprocal, it has principally been developed to facilitate the exercise of *Union* competences in the external sphere. The duty of cooperation has thereby been given a positive and a negative aspect. Positively, the Member States might be obliged to act as 'trustees of the Union interest' in international fora. Negatively, the duty has imposed obligations on the Member States when exercising their shared competences. This negative aspect is – to some extent – the opposite of the principle of subsidiarity. For the Member States are prevented from exercising their shared competence in order to prevent 'splitting the international representation of the [Union]'.[194]

---

[193] See J. de la Rochère, 'L'ère des Compétences Partagées de l'étendue des Compétences Extérieures de la Communauté Européenne' [1995] 390 *Revue Du Marché Commun et de l'Union Européenne* 461; as well as: Schütze, *From Dual to Cooperative Federalism* (supra n. 48), Chapter 6.

[194] Case C-246/07 (supra n. 183), para. 44.

7

Executive Powers: Competences and Procedures

Contents

Introduction   223
1. Governmental powers: the Union's dual executive   225
    (a) The legal instruments of political leadership   226
    (b) The informal procedure(s) of government   228
2. Law-making powers: delegated and implementing acts   230
    (a) The delegation of 'legislative' power: Article 290 TFEU   231
        (i)   Judicial safeguards: constitutional limits to delegated acts   233
        (ii) Political safeguards: control rights of the Union legislator   236
    (b) The 'conferral' of executive power: Article 291 TFEU   238
        (i)   The scope of Article 291 TFEU   238
        (ii) Constitutional safeguards for implementing legislation   240
3. Administrative powers I: centralised enforcement   243
    (a) The scope of the Union's administrative powers   244
    (b) Administrative powers and the subsidiarity principle   248
4. Administrative powers II: decentralised enforcement   250
    (a) The effects of national administrative acts   251
    (b) National administrative autonomy and its limits   253
Conclusion   256

Introduction

What are the 'executive' powers of the European Union? In many constitutions the executive branch has a residual character: anything that is *neither* legislative *nor* judicial is considered to fall within its scope. The *negative* definition of the executive function has historical reasons. For the original purpose of the separation of powers principle was to *remove* powers from an almighty monarch to a Parliament and the judiciary.

The problem with this negative definition however is its uncertain and relative nature; and serious attempts have been made positively to identify 'prerogatives' of executive power. Outside the field of external relations,[1] two such prerogatives have traditionally been recognised. First, the executive power is – naturally – identified with the task of executing laws, and thus with the aim of maintaining internal peace.[2] The task of law enforcement is complemented by a second – seemingly contradictory – demand.[3] Executive power is identified with the power to 'govern', that is: to lead and direct the political community. The executive branch is here the 'centre of impulse and decision'.[4] Despite their contradictory outlook, *both* traditional prerogatives of the executive – the reactive task to enforce laws and the active task to propose laws – are still based on a common idea: the executive enjoys the power of *decision*.

The power of decision is typically contrasted with the power to adopt legislative norms. For in the ideal 'legislative State' of the nineteenth century all legal norms are adopted by Parliament. And that Parliament cannot delegate power to the executive was seen as 'a principle universally recognized as vital to the integrity and maintenance of the [democratic] system of government ordained by the Constitution'.[5] Yet, this ideal would find limits in the normative needs of the 'administrative State' in the twentieth century.[6] Modern parliaments would simply have no time – or expertise – to 'master all the details of tea chemistry and packaging in order to specify the precisely allowable limits of dust, artificial coloring, and the like that would affect suitability for consumption'.[7] Industrial societies required a 'motorised legislator' that could accelerate the regulatory process.[8] And this secondary 'legislator' was to be the executive. In the administrative state, executive legislation would indeed become the numerical norm.[9] And the advent of the *legislating* executive indeed 'constitutes one of the most important transformations of

---

[1] On the 'executive' elements within the Union's external powers, see: Chapter 6 – Introduction.

[2] This is the reason why Locke (see J. Locke, *Two Treatises of Government* (Cambridge University Press, 1988), § 148), recognising the distinctive character of the executive and the external function, nonetheless places both powers into the hands of a single person – the monarch.

[3] E. Zoller, *Droit Constitutionnel* (Presses Universitaires de France, 1999), 425.

[4] L. Favoreu et al., *Droit Constitutionnel* (Dalloz, 2002), 537.

[5] *Field* v. *Clark*, 143 US 649 (1892), 692.

[6] See G. Lawson, 'The Rise and Rise of the Administrative State' [1993–4] 107 *Harvard Law Review* 1231.

[7] W. Gellhorn and C. Byse, *Administrative Law: Cases and Comments* (Foundation Press, 1974), 62.

[8] C. Schmitt, *Die Lage der Europäischen Rechtswissenschaft* (Universitätsverlag Tübingen, 1950), 18.

[9] H. W. R. Wade and C. F. Forsyth, *Administrative Law* (Oxford University Press, 2000), 839: 'there is no more characteristic administrative activity than *legislation*'; as well as: H. Pünder, 'Democratic Legitimation of Delegated Legislation – A Comparative View on the American, British and German Law' [2009] 58 *International and Comparative Law Quarterly* 353, esp. 355: 'in all countries compared, administrative law-making powers became the rule rather then the exception'. For a general overview, see also: A. von Bogdandy, *Gubernative Rechtsetzung* (Mohr Siebeck, 1999).

constitutionalism'.[10] In the administrative State the executive branch thus gains a third power: the power to adopt (delegated) legislation.

A modern treatment of executive power should then include three core functions of the executive, which – in descending order – are: the *political* power to govern, the *legislative* power to adopt executive norms, and the *administrative* power to enforce legislation. This chapter discusses all three types of 'executive' powers in the context of the European Union. Section 1 begins with an examination of the political power to act as government. We shall see that the 'steering' power of high politics belongs to two institutions within the Union: the European Council and the Commission. The Union 'government' (in a strict sense) is thus based on a 'dual executive'. Section 2 moves to an analysis of the (delegated) legislative powers of the Union executive. The central provisions here are Articles 290 and 291 TFEU. We shall see that the European legal order has allowed for wide delegations of power to the executive; while nonetheless insisting on substantive and procedural safeguards that protect two fundamental constitutional principles – federalism and democracy. Sections 3 and 4 look at the administrative powers of the Union. Based on the idea of 'executive federalism', the power to apply and enforce European law is divided between the Union and the Member States. The Union can – exceptionally – execute its own law; yet the centralised administration is limited by the subsidiarity principle. And as a rule, it is the Member States that execute Union law. This form of decentralised administration restricts the uniform effects of administrative decisions within the Union.

1. Governmental powers: the Union's dual executive

The notion of 'government' is used in a wide and in a strict sense. In the wide sense, political communities are 'governed' by the totality of constitutional institutions within society.[11] Yet in the strict sense of the word, they are 'governed' only by one of these institutions: the 'government'. The 'government' is that part of the executive that is charged with providing leadership and direction.[12] And depending on whether there exists one or two organs charged with political leadership within a society, we speak of a monist or a dualist executive.[13] The American constitution is based on a single executive: all executive power is vested in one organ – the President of the United States.[14] By contrast, Britain and France are based on the idea of a dual executive. There

---

[10] Zoller, *Droit Constitutional* (supra n. 3), 436.

[11] This wide sense is used by the US Constitution, see Article IV, Section 4: 'The United States shall guarantee to every State in this Union a Republican Form of Government'.

[12] For this strict sense: see: German Constitution, Chapter VI: 'The Federal Government'.

[13] Favoreu et al., *Droit Constitutionnel* (supra n. 4), 539.

[14] For the American debate surrounding the 'unitary' executive, see: S. Calabresi and K. Rhodes, 'The Structural Constitution: Unitary Executive, Plural Judiciary' [1992] 105 *Harvard Law Journal* 1153; as well as: L. Lessing and C. Sunstein, 'The President and the Administration' [1994] 94 *Columbia Law Review* 1.

The Union's 'Dual Executive'

Figure 15 Dual Executive of the Union

are two institutions that are regarded as 'leading' the country. In monarchical Britain this is the (hereditary) Crown and its Cabinet; whereas in republican France this is the (elected) President and his/her 'Government'.[15]

The European Union is based on the idea of a dual executive. There are thus two institutions charged with 'governing' the European Union: the European Council and the Commission. The former is charged with the task to 'provide the Union with the necessary impetus for its development' and to 'define the general political directions and priorities thereof'.[16] By contrast, the Commission is to 'promote the general interest of the Union and take appropriate initiatives to that end'.[17] *Both* institutions are consequently entitled and obliged to provide political leadership for the Union. What are the – respective – legal instruments for such leadership? And are there (in)formal procedures that combine the European Council and the Commission in the exercise of their governmental powers?

(a) The legal instruments of political leadership

What are the policy instruments in the hands of the European Council and the Commission? The task of analysing political leadership in legal categories is difficult. For while political mechanisms tend to be fluid and situational, legal categories tend to be solid and permanent. Let us nonetheless try to distil the permanent in the transient.

The task of the European Council is to act as 'initiator' and 'coordinator'. It will thereby principally express its views through 'Presidency Conclusions',[18] and 'decisions'.[19] The precise legal character of the 'Conclusions' is unclear. However, what *is* clear is that they represent the political agreement of the Heads of State or Government of the Member States, and as such constitute a formidable political instrument to provide impulses to the development of the European Union. They will cover both constitutional as well as substantive

---

[15] The 1958 French Constitution thus makes a clear distinction between the governmental powers of the President (Title II: Articles 5–19), and those of the Government (Title III: Articles 20–23).

[16] Article 15 (1) TEU.   [17] Article 17 (1) TEU.

[18] For a list of Presidency Conclusions, see: www.european-council.europa.eu/council-meetings/conclusions.aspx?lang=en.

[19] For important European Council decisions in the context of external relations, see e.g., Common Strategy of the European Council on the Mediterranean region (2000/458/CFSP), [2000] OJ L183/5; as well as: European Council Decision 2004/763/CFSP amending Common Strategy 2000/458/CFSP on the Mediterranean region in order to extend the period of its application, [2004] OJ L337/72.

themes. With regard to the former, the European Council has indeed been the primary mover behind Treaty reform. With regard to the latter, the European Council has a significant role in setting the legislative agenda for the Union. This can be illustrated by reference to the 'Stockholm Programme' – discussed below.

The Commission has traditionally used a sophisticated variety of policy instruments.[20] After its election, the new Commission would present its 'five-year strategic objectives',[21] which will be informed by the 'political guidelines' offered by its President.[22] These multi-annual strategic objectives will subsequently be translated into the Commission's annual 'policy strategy'.[23] This annual strategy is in turn the basis for the Commission's annual 'work programme'.[24] This work programme will go beyond abstract priorities and typically contains a detailed annex with concrete legislative initiatives to be presented in the course of the year. (In order to provide for a degree of interinstitutional cooperation, the Commission has agreed to present its work programme every year to the European Parliament and to 'take into account the priorities expressed by Parliament'.[25]) Finally, on the basis of the Commission's work programme, each Directorate-General will draft its own annual 'management plan'.[26] This ordinary policy cycle may – moreover – be complemented by extra-ordinary reform impulses through 'White Papers'. These typically express a particular reform effort for a specific sector. They have been frequently employed in the past.[27]

---

[20] For an overview, see: http://ec.europa.eu/atwork/strategy/index_en.htm.

[21] See 'Strategic Objectives 2005 – 2009; Europe 2010: A Partnership for European Renewal: Prosperity, Solidarity and Security, Communication from the President in agreement with Vice-President Wallström' (COM(2005) 12 final). The Commission appears to have replaced its five-year cycle with a ten-year cycle in the form of the 'Europe 2020' Programme. This represents the European Union's 'growth strategy for the coming decade' (see Commission, Communication 'Europe 2020': A Strategy for smart, sustainable and inclusive growth (COM (2010) 2020 final)). The Strategy comprises five objectives, which are addressed by seven 'flagship initiatives'. For one recent 'flagship initiative', see: Commission, Communication to the European Parliament, the Council, the European Economic and Social Committee and the Committee of the Regions: A resource-efficient Europe – Flagship initiative under the Europe 2020 Strategy (COM (2011) 21 final).

[22] According to Article 17 (6) (a) TEU, the President shall 'lay down guidelines within which the Commission is to work'. For the political guidelines of the second 'Barroso Commission', see: http://europa.eu/rapid/pressReleasesAction.do?reference=IP/09/1272.

[23] See Commission, Communication: Annual Policy Strategy for 2010, COM (2009) 73 final (available: http://ec.europa.eu/atwork/synthesis/doc/aps_2010_en.pdf).

[24] For the Commission's annual work programmes, see: http://ec.europa.eu/atwork/programmes/index_en.htm.

[25] See 2010 Framework Agreement on relations between the European Parliament and the European Commission, [2010] OJ L304/47, paras. 34 and 35. For a timetable of this cooperation, see: *ibid.*, Annex IV.

[26] For the annual management plan of DG Competition, see: http://ec.europa.eu/dgs/competition/index_en.htm.

[27] For a list of Commission 'White Papers', see: http://europa.eu/documentation/official-docs/white-papers/index_en.htm.

(b) The informal procedure(s) of government

How is the Union's dual executive working? Is there a strict division of powers between the European Council and the Commission; or are both institutions cooperating in the joint task of government? The European Union has followed the second route – even if the legal procedures connecting its dual executive are not as formalised and 'legal' as in other areas of European law.

Many of the major policy initiatives within the Union originate in the Commission, yet are addressed to the European Council. For example: the 'Europe 2020' agenda is to provide the Union with an economic growth strategy for the next decade. It was originally devised by the Commission;[28] yet the Commission admits that '[t]he European Council will have full ownership and be the focal point of the new strategy', and to that effect proposed to the European Council formally to endorse it. This indeed happened;[29] and had happened similarly in the past.[30]

This upward process may be complemented by a downward process. Thus, where the European Council has formally endorsed a general policy initiative, it may subsequently charge the Commission with the elaboration of specific policy initiatives. One prominent example of this institutional cooperation can be seen in the 'Stockholm Programme: An Open and Secure Europe Serving and Protecting Citizens'.[31] The Programme was established by the European Council, and constitutes a multi-annual programme (2010–2014) offering 'strategic guidelines for legislative and operational planning within the area of freedom, security and justice'.[32] One task within the Programme is 'Protecting Citizen's Rights in the Information Society',[33] in which the European Council recognised an individual's right to privacy. Acknowledging the executive prerogatives of the Commission within this area, the relevant passage of the Programme reads as follows:

> The European Council invites the Commission to:
>
> – evaluate the functioning of the various instruments on data protection and present, where necessary, further legislative and non-legislative initiatives to maintain the effective application of the above principles,
> – propose a Recommendation for the negotiation of a data protection and, where necessary, data sharing agreements for law enforcement purposes with the United States of America, building on the work carried out by the EU-US High

---

[28] Commission, Communication: A Strategy for smart, sustainable and inclusive growth, COM (2010) 2020 final.

[29] European Council, Presidency Conclusions (25/26 March 2010), and Presidency Conclusions (17 June 2010) – both available at website address, supra n. 18.

[30] The most famous illustration is the 1985 Commission White Paper 'Completing the Internal Market' (COM (1985) 310 final), which was formally addressed to the European Council.

[31] European Council, The Stockholm Programme – An Open and Secure Europe Serving and Protecting Citizens, [2010] OJ C115/01.

[32] *Ibid.*, 4.   [33] *Ibid.*, 10.

    Level Contact Group on Information Sharing and Privacy and Personal Data Protection,

– consider core elements for data protection agreements with third countries for law enforcement purposes, which may include, where necessary, privately held data, based on a high level of data protection, improve compliance with the principles of data protection through the development of appropriate new technologies, improving cooperation between the public and private sectors, particularly in the field of research . . .

The Commission has indeed followed the European Council's invitation and presented an 'Action Plan Implementing the Stockholm Programme',[34] where it has committed itself to a concrete timetable for each of these policy initiatives.[35] And first fruits of this can already be seen.[36]

The illustration of the Stockholm Programme demonstrates that policy initiatives are often the result of a *dual* and *combined* executive impulse: the European Council calls on the Commission, and the Commission calls on the European legislator.[37] The cooperative spirit between the European Council and the Commission will work particularly well where both follow similar political orientations. This may not necessarily be the case. For as we saw above,[38] the European Council is no longer constitutionally free to 'appoint' the Commission of its political tastes. With the Commission being 'elected' by the European Parliament, the possibility arises that the political orientation of the latter – and hence that of the Commission – will not 'coincide' with that of the European Council. A 'conservative' European Council may thus have to collaborate with a 'labour' Commission. In this situation, the European Union's dual government will be subject to a political dynamic that is known in French constitutional law as 'cohabitation', that is: the co-existence of two politically opposed executives.[39]

---

[34] Commission, Communication: Delivering an Area of Freedom, Security and Justice for Europe's Citizens – Action Plan Implementing the Stockholm Programme (COM (2010) 171 final). For the general invitation by the European Council, see: Presidency Conclusions (10/11 December 2009), 11 (para. 33): 'The European Council invites the Commission to present an Action Plan for implementing the Stockholm Programme, to be adopted at the latest in June 2010, and to submit a midterm review before 2012.'

[35] Commission, Action Plan (supra n. 34) – Annex.

[36] Commission, Communication: 'A comprehensive approach on personal data protection in the European Union', COM(2010) 609 final. And see also: Commission Decision 2010/87 on standard contractual clauses for the transfer of personal data to processors established in third countries under Directive 95/46/EC of the European Parliament and of the Council, [2010] OJ L39/5.

[37] For a constitutional link between the European Council and the Council, see: Article 16 (6) TEU. The General Affairs Council is here charged to liaise with the European Council. On this point, see: Chapter 3 – Section 4(a) above.

[38] On the selection of the Commission, see: Chapter 4 – Section 1(a) above.

[39] On this comparative constitutional point, see: Favoreu et al., *Droit Constitutionnel* (supra n. 4), 589 et seq.

2. Law-making powers: delegated and implementing acts

The advent of the legislating executive 'constitutes one of the most important transformations of constitutionalism'.[40] Executive legislation may thereby derive from two sources. It may be 'autonomous' regulatory power directly granted under the constitution;[41] or, it may be delegated to the executive on the basis of parliamentary legislation. In the latter scenario, the delegation 'distorts' the original balance of power and many constitutional orders therefore impose constitutional safeguards to control 'delegated legislation'.[42]

From the very beginning, the European Treaties allowed for autonomous and delegated regulatory powers of the Commission. Indeed, the Treaty makers had anticipated that the European legislator alone would not be able to legislate on all matters falling within the scope of the Treaties. The E(E)C Treaty thus provided for the possibility of a transfer of legislative power to the Commission.[43] Would there be constitutional controls around these delegated powers? After all, every delegation of power away from the *intergovernmental* Council to the *supranational* Commission would have a significant *unitary* effect on the decision-making in the European Union; and every delegation away from the *directly* elected European Parliament to the *indirectly* elected Commission would have a significant anti-democratic effect.

The European legal order has indeed developed two constitutional safeguards to protect its foundational principles of federalism and democracy. Judicially, the Court of Justice has endorsed a 'non-delegation' doctrine. The European legislator is constitutionally prohibited from delegating essential political choices to the executive. Yet even within these substantive limits, the European legislator has traditionally been unwilling to delegate power without some *political* control. From the very beginning, the Council – representing the Member States – would not delegate powers to the Commission – representing a supranational executive – without some intergovernmental control. It insisted on the establishment of committees as political safeguards of *federalism*. This system became known as 'Comitology', and was the sole political safeguard of federalism for *all* executive law-making under the Rome Treaty.[44]

---

[40] Zoller, *Droit Constitutionnel* (supra n. 3), 436.

[41] For example, the 1958 French Constitution recognises 'autonomous' regulatory powers of the executive. For an analysis of the distribution of legislative power between Parliament and the executive, see: J. Bell, *French Constitutional Law* (Clarendon Press, 1992), esp. Chapter 3 – 'The Division of Lawmaking Powers: The Revolution that Never Happened?'.

[42] B. Schwartz, 'Delegated Legislation in America: Procedure and Safeguards' [1948] 11 *Modern Law Review* 449.

[43] Ex-Article 211 EC entitled the Commission to 'exercise the powers conferred on it by the Council for the implementation of the rules laid down by the latter'.

[44] For almost three decades, comitology developed in the undergrowth of the Rome Treaty. It was only given textual foundations by the Single European Act. An amended ex-Article 202 EC expressly provided that the Council should – except in 'specific cases' – 'confer on the Commission, in the acts which the Council adopts, powers for the implementation of the rules

This has changed with the Lisbon Treaty. The Treaty has split the 'old' Union's constitutional regime for executive legislation into two halves. The 'new' Union legal order thus distinguishes between a delegation of 'legislative' power – that is: the power to *amend* primary legislation – and a delegation of 'executive' power – that is, the power to *implement* primary legislation. While both constitutional regimes identify the Commission as the principal delegee of Union power, they differ in the control mechanisms they establish over the exercise of delegated power. The delegation of legislative power is subject to the constitutional safeguards established in Article 290 TFEU. The delegation of implementing power is subject to the constitutional regime established by Article 291 TFEU.

This section analyses the respective constitutional regimes for 'delegated acts' and 'implementing acts'. How has the European Court defined the limits of the 'non-delegation' doctrine? What political control mechanisms protect the Union's foundational values of federalism and democracy against excessive executive legislation?

(a) The delegation of 'legislative' power: Article 290 TFEU

The constitutional regime for a delegation of power to the Commission to amend primary legislation is set out in Article 290 TFEU. The legal conditions and limitations for this delegation are defined as follows:

1. A legislative act may delegate to the Commission the power to adopt non-legislative *acts of general application to supplement or amend certain*

which the Council lays down'. The Council could thereby 'impose certain requirements in respect of the exercise of these powers'. This called for a comitology 'code' that would formally define the types of committees that could be used. The Council used this power three times: 1987, 1999 and 2006. For the 1987 Comitology Decision, see: Council Decision 87/373 laying down the procedures for the exercise of implementing powers conferred on the Commission (OJ 1987 L197/33). For the second Comitology Decision, see: (Council) Decision 1999/468 laying down the procedures for the exercise of implementing powers conferred on the Commission (OJ 1999 L184/23). The 2006 Comitology Decision did not repeal its predecessor but amended it substantially, see: (Council) Decision 2006/512 amending Decision 1999/468/EC laying down the procedures for the exercise of implementing powers conferred on the Commission (OJ 2006 L200/11). The most significant amendment here was the introduction of a new regulatory procedure: the 'regulatory procedure with scrutiny'. Article 2 (2) of the (amended) Comitology Decision defined its scope as follows: 'Where a basic instrument, adopted in accordance with the procedure referred to in Article 251 of the [EC] Treaty, provides for the adoption of measures of general scope designed to amend non-essential elements of that instrument, inter alia by deleting some of those elements or by supplementing the instrument by the addition of new non-essential elements, those measures shall be adopted in accordance with the regulatory procedure with scrutiny.' The procedure was thus to apply to legislative powers delegated to the Commission under co-decision, that is, where the Council and the Parliament act as co-legislators. Yet, not all acts adopted by co-decision would be subject to the new procedure. It only covered 'measures of general scope', which would 'amend non-essential elements' of the primary legislation. On the constitutional evolution of the Comitology system, see: R. Schütze, '"Delegated" Legislation in the (new) European Union: A Constitutional Analysis' [2011] 74 *Modern Law Review* 661.

non-essential elements of the legislative act. The objectives, content, scope and duration of the delegation of power shall be explicitly defined in the legislative act. The essential elements of an area shall be reserved for the legislative act and accordingly shall not be subject of a delegation of power.

2. Legislative acts shall explicitly lay down the conditions to which the delegation is subject; these conditions may be as follows:

    (a) the European Parliament or the Council may decide to revoke the delegation;

    (b) the delegated act may enter into force only if no objection has been expressed by the European Parliament or the Council within a period set by the legislative act.

   For the purposes of (a) and (b), the European Parliament shall act by a majority of its component members, and the Council by a qualified majority.[45]

What is the scope of Article 290 TFEU? Is the provision restricted to acts adopted under the 'ordinary' legislative procedure?[46] Textually, the Treaty does not mandate this restriction; and to increase the ability of the European legislator to concentrate on essential political matters, the better view therefore suggests a wide understanding of 'legislative act' that includes the special legislative procedures.[47] However, the scope of Article 290 is confined to situations where a Commission act amends *or* supplements primary legislation. Supplementation thereby ought to mean amendment through the inclusion of additional rules having the same status as primary legislation.[48] Article 290 TFEU confirms the hierarchical position of delegated legislation: it will be able to amend primary legislation and must therefore enjoy – at least relative to the

---

[45] Emphasis added.

[46] On the distinction between an 'ordinary' legislative procedure and various 'special' legislative procedures, see: Chapter 5 – Section 3 above.

[47] This position was advocated by the Commission; see Commission, Communication: 'Implementing Article 290 of the Treaty on the Functioning of the European Union', COM (2009) 673 final, 3: 'A delegation of power within the meaning of Article 290 is possible only in a legislative act. However, it makes little difference whether or not the legislative act was adopted jointly by Parliament and the Council, because Article 290 does not distinguish between the ordinary legislative procedure (formerly co-decision) and special legislative procedures.'

[48] This is the view of the Commission (*ibid.*, 4, emphasis added): 'Firstly, [the Commission] believes that by using the verb "amend" the authors of the new Treaty wanted to cover hypothetical cases in which the Commission is empowered formally to amend a basic instrument. Such a formal amendment might relate to the text of one or more articles in the enacting terms or to the text of an annex that legally forms part of the legislative instrument … Secondly, the Commission wishes to stress the importance that should be attached to the verb "supplement", the meaning and scope of which are less specific than those of the verb "amend". The Commission believes that in order to determine whether a measure "supplements" the basic instrument, the legislator should assess whether the future measure specifically adds new non-essential rules which change the framework of the legislative act, leaving a margin of discretion to the Commission. If it does, the measure could be deemed to "supplement" the basic instrument. *Conversely, measures intended only to give effect to the existing rules of the basic instrument should not be deemed to be supplementary measures.*'

amended act – hierarchical parity.[49] However, the ability to amend primary legislation is constitutionally limited in four ways. First, only the Commission – and not the Council[50] – may adopt delegating acts. Second, the Commission must adopt acts of 'general application', that is: acts that constitute material legislation.[51] Third, the scope of delegated powers must be 'explicitly defined'. Finally, the European legislature cannot delegate to the Commission the power to adopt 'essential elements' of the legislative act.[52]

The most important of these limits is the last one. Let us look at it in more detail.

(i) Judicial safeguards: constitutional limits to delegated acts

The 'essential elements' doctrine has had a long jurisprudential history in the Union legal order. Its classic shape was given in *Köster*.[53] A German farmer had challenged the legality of a legislative scheme established by the Commission that created import and export licences for cereals. It was alleged that 'the power to adopt the system in dispute belonged to the Council', which should have acted according to the 'normal' legislative procedure established in Article 43 TFEU.[54] The Court disagreed: while basic elements of the policy area must be decided in accordance with the institutional balance prescribed by the Treaty, non-essential elements could be delegated and adopted by a simpler procedure. This followed from the scheme of the Treaty, and the common constitutional traditions of all the Member States.[55]

But what was the dividing line between 'basic elements' and 'non-essential' elements? In *Rey Soda*,[56] the Court tackled this question. Pointing to the

---

[49] J. Bast, 'Legal Instruments and Judicial Protection' in A. von Bogdandy and J. Bast (eds.), *Principles of European Constitutional Law* (Hart Publishing, 2009), 345 at 391. For a similar conclusion derived from comparative constitutional law, see: J. P. Jacque, 'Introduction: Pouvoir Législatif et Pouvoir Exécutif Dans L'Union Européenne' in J.-B. Auby and J. Dutheil de la Rochère, *Droit Administratif Européen* (Bruylant, 2007), 25 at 45.

[50] This had been possible under the Rome Treaty. For an analysis of delegations to the Council, see: Schütze (supra n. 44), 672.

[51] In the past, 'implementation' under Article 202 EC comprised both general and specific acts; see Case 16/88, *Commission* v. *Council* [1989] ECR 3457, para. 11: 'The concept of implementation for the purposes of that article comprises both the drawing up of implementing rules and the application of rules to specific cases by means of acts of individual application.'

[52] Unfortunately, Article 290 TFEU contains the seeds for two possible definitions of the 'essential elements' doctrine. A first formulation refers to 'non-essential elements *of the legislative act*' (emphasis added), while the second formulation is broader and refers to the 'essential elements *of an area*' (emphasis added). This semantic ambivalence may well give rise to an uncertainty that has plagued the concept of 'minimum' standard in the context of shared competences. In that context it is not settled whether the Member States' power to adopt stricter measures must be viewed against each legislative act or against the policy area in general (cf. R. Schütze, *From Dual to Cooperative Federalism: The Changing Structure of European Law* (Oxford University Press, 2009), 272 et seq.).

[53] Case 25/70, *Einfuhr- und Vorratsstelle für Getreide und Futtermittel* v. *Köster et Berodt & Co,* [1970] ECR 1161.

[54] *Ibid.*, para. 5.   [55] *Ibid.*, para. 6.

[56] Case 23/75, *Rey Soda* v. *Cassa Conguaglio Zucchero,* [1975] ECR 1279.

institutional balance between Council and Commission, the Court held that the delegation mandate 'must be interpreted strictly'; yet, despite this limitation, the Court insisted that 'the concept of implementation must be given a wide interpretation'.[57] Only the Commission would be able to continuously follow trends in agricultural markets and regulate quickly if the situation so required. The Council was thus entitled 'to confer on the Commission *wide powers of discretion and action*'.[58] The scope of these – extensive – powers was to be judged in light of the objectives of the enabling act 'and less in terms of the literal meaning of the enabling word'.[59] However, 'provisions which are intended to give concrete shape to the fundamental guidelines of [Union] policy' were beyond delegation.[60]

What about a delegation to European agencies? Article 290 is silent on this point, and the reason for that can be found in a judgment that insists on the non-delegation of discretionary powers to agencies. This judicial decision was taken in *Meroni* v. *High Authority*.[61] The applicant had complained that the Commission had delegated to an agency 'powers conferred upon it by the Treaty, without subjecting their exercise to the conditions which the Treaty would have required if those powers had been exercised directly by it'.[62] The Court of Justice had little trouble in finding that this could not be done. Even if the delegation as such was constitutional, the Union 'could not confer upon the authority receiving the delegation powers different from those which the delegating authority itself received under the Treaty'.[63]

A second argument however moved to an analysis of the constitutional limits to a delegation of powers to agencies as such. While noting that Article 8 ECSC did not provide any power to delegate,[64] the Court nonetheless found that such a constitutional possibility 'cannot be excluded'. It was inherent in the powers of the Commission 'to entrust certain powers to such bodies subject to conditions to be determined by it and subject to its supervision' if such delegation was necessary for the performance of the Union's tasks. These tasks were set out in Article 3 ECSC – a provision that laid down 'very general objectives', which could not always be equally pursued. The Union thus had to make political choices, and these political choices could not be delegated to an agency:

> Reconciling the various objectives laid down in Article 3 [ECSC] implies a real discretion involving difficult choices, based on a consideration of the economic facts and circumstances in the light of which those choices are made. The consequences resulting from a delegation of powers are very different depending on whether it involves clearly defined executive powers the exercise of which can,

---

[57] *Ibid.*, paras. 9–10.   [58] *Ibid.*, para. 11 (emphasis added).   [59] *Ibid.*, para. 14.

[60] Case C-240/90, *Germany* v. *Commission*, [1992] ECR I-5383, para. 37.

[61] Case 9/56, *Meroni & Co, Industrie Metallurgische, SpA* v. *High Authority of the European Coal and Steel Community*, [1958] ECR 133.

[62] *Ibid.*, 146.   [63] *Ibid.*, 150.

[64] Article 8 ECSC read: 'The [Commission] shall be responsible for assuring the fulfilment of the purposes stated in the present Treaty under the terms thereof.'

therefore, be subject to strict review in the light of objective criteria determined by the delegating authority, *or whether it involves a discretionary power, implying a wide margin of discretion which may, according to the use which is made of it, make possible the execution of actual economic policy*. A delegation of the first kind cannot appreciably alter the consequences involved in the exercise of the powers concerned, whereas a delegation of the second kind, since it replaces the choices of the delegator by the choices of the delegate, brings about an actual transfer of responsibility.[65]

This judgment clarified two things. First, a delegation to bodies not mentioned in the Treaties – even 'bodies established under private law' – was constitutionally legitimate. However, such delegations 'can only relate to clearly defined executive powers, the use of which must be entirely subject to the supervision of the [Commission]'.[66] This followed from the 'balance of powers which is characteristic of the institutional structure of the [Union]'. To delegate 'a discretionary power' to 'bodies other than those which the Treaty has established' would render that guarantee ineffective.

Subsequent judicial and academic commentary has concentrated on this last passage. *Meroni* came to stand for a constitutional non-delegation doctrine according to which the European institutions could not delegate *any* discretionary power to European agencies.[67] And while this expansive reading may not have been originally intended,[68] constitutional folklore continues to pay homage to the 'Meroni Doctrine'. This constitutional choice has prevented European agencies from exercising *legislative* choices involving discretionary power. They may be entitled to adopt legally binding individual decisions implementing European norms.[69] But in general, they only assist the Commission in discharging *its* delegated powers.

---

[65] Case 9/56, *Meroni v. High Authority* (supra n. 61), 152 (emphasis added).   [66] *Ibid.*

[67] The most drastic expression of this expansive reading of *Meroni* is Case 98/80, *Romano v. Institut national d'assurance maladie-invalidité*, [1981] ECR 1241, para. 20: 'It follows both from Article [17] of the [EU] Treaty, and in particular by Articles [263] and [267] [TFEU], that a body such as the administrative commission may not be empowered by the Council to adopt acts having the force of law. Whilst a decision of the administrative commission may provide an aid to social security institutions responsible for applying [European] law in this field, it is not of such a nature as to require those institutions to use certain methods or adopt certain interpretations when they come to apply the [European] rules.'

[68] In Case 9/56, *Meroni* (supra n. 61), the Court – repeatedly – referred to the '*wide* margin of discretion' that was delegated to the agency (*ibid.*, 153 and 154; emphasis added). A close historical analysis could thus narrow the ruling to an early expression of the 'basic elements' principle: the Commission was simply not allowed to delegate *basic* choices to an agency. The Court has itself (occasionally) signalled its willingness to limit the *Meroni* doctrine to a 'basic elements' doctrine for agencies, see Case C-164/98P, *DIR International Film Srl et al. v. Commission*, [2000] ECR I-447; and albeit in a different context, Joined Cases C-154 and 155/04, *The Queen, ex parte National Association of Health Stores and others* v. *Secretary of State for Health*, [2005] ECR I-6451, especially para. 90.

[69] For an example of an agency of this type, see the 'Office for the Harmonisation of the Internal Market' (OHIM) established by Regulation 40/94 on the Community Trade Mark, [1994] OJ L11/1.

(ii) Political safeguards: control rights of the Union legislator

What are the political safeguards that the Union legislator can impose to control delegated 'legislative' power? These are defined in the second paragraph of Article 290 TFEU, which constitutionalises the political safeguards of federalism and democracy. Legislative acts may allow the European Parliament or the Council 'to revoke the delegation' (subparagraph a), or to veto the adoption of the specific delegated act (subparagraph b). The Parliament must thereby act by a majority of its component members – which makes the control of the delegation potentially harder than the adoption of primary legislation.[70] The Council, by contrast, will act by a 'normal' qualified majority – which will make, where the legal basis in the Treaties requires unanimity, revocation easier than the adoption of primary legislation. Article 290 thus grants a slight preference to the Council in enforcing the limits of delegation.[71]

From a democratic point of view, Article 290 represents a revolution, when compared with the constitutional status within the 'old' Union. The Rome Treaty had never acknowledged Parliament's *constitutional* right to control executive legislation.[72] That right was reserved to the Council. With the Lisbon Treaty, the Council *or* the European Parliament may – independently of each other – oppose or revoke delegated legislation. Moreover, the parliamentary objection is left in the institution's *political* discretion: Parliament need not point to special legal grounds to veto the Commission measure.[73] With regard to both alternatives mentioned in Article 290 (2) TFEU, the Lisbon amendments thus place the Parliament on a – roughly – equal footing with the Council in the political control of delegated acts amending primary legislation. The parliamentary control system over delegated legislation in the European Union is today more democratic than that in the American constitutional order.[74]

Are the political safeguards of democracy and federalism in Article 290 TFEU the only ones; or may the Union legislator also insist on the ex ante influence of 'committees'? The provision contains, unlike its predecessor,[75] no

---

[70] See Article 231 TFEU: 'Save as otherwise provided in the Treaties, the European Parliament shall act by a majority of the votes cast.' For the application of this rule to the context of the ordinary legislative procedure, see: Article 294 (13) TFEU.

[71] In this sense, see: K. Lenaerts and M. Desomer, 'Towards a Hierarchy of Legal Acts in the European Union? Simplication of Legal Instruments and Procedures' [2005] 11 *European Law Journal* 744 at 755.

[72] The 1999 Comitology system (as amended by the 2006 Comitology Decision) had provided for parliamentary involvement, but this had been a *legislative* concession by the Council (see Council Decision 2006/512 amending Decision 1999/468/EC laying down the procedures for the exercise of implementing powers conferred on the Commission, [2006] OJ L200/11).

[73] This had been the case under the 1999/2006 Comitology system (*ibid.*).

[74] Schütze, '"Delegated" Legislation in the (new) European Union' (supra n. 44).

[75] Ex-Article 202 EC stated that the Council shall 'confer on the Commission, in the acts which the Council adopts, powers for the implementation of the rules which the Council lays down. The Council may impose certain requirements in respect of the exercise of these powers. The Council may also reserve the right, in specific cases, to exercise directly implementing powers itself. The procedures referred to above must be consonant with principles and rules to be laid down in

legal basis for the adoption of a 'comitology law'. This constitutional absence should be seen as a deliberate choice. Admittedly, Article 290 (2) uses the conditional 'may' in relation to the two political safeguards discussed above. However, this should not be interpreted to allow the European legislator carte blanche to determine, in each legislative act, which conditions to impose.[76] The 'may' in Article 290 (2) should simply be seen as allowing for the constitutional option of using *both* mechanisms or *none* in a legislative act; or of excluding either the European Parliament or the Council – depending on the *special* legislative procedure used – as beneficiaries of these political safeguards.[77] Teleologically, then, we should assume that Article 290 TFEU is still based on the idea of a closed number of political safeguards that could be constitutionally imposed.[78] If this reading is accepted, Article 290 abandons the idea of committees of representatives that provide formal control over – not just informal advice on – the exercise of the Commission's delegated powers.[79]

---

advance by the Council, acting unanimously on a proposal from the Commission and after obtaining the opinion of the European Parliament.'

[76] To allow for a free choice beyond the control mechanisms expressly mentioned would be a serious constitutional retrogression. Ever since the Single European Act, the European legal order had insisted – in the pursuit of legal order and transparency – that the conditions imposed on delegated legislation be set *in advance* of the specific delegating act. From this teleological perspective, it is therefore problematic to claim that it would be 'perfectly open to the institutions concerned (the Commission, the Council, and the European Parliament) to agree among themselves more far-reaching conditions to apply to any basic act after the entry into force of the Treaty of Lisbon' (D. Curtin, *Executive Power of the European Union: Law, Practices, and the Living Constitution: Law, Practice, and Constitutionalism* (Oxford University Press, 2009), 123). If we accept that these additional conditions would need to be (exhaustively) defined *in advance*, on what legal basis should the 'Article 290 Comitology Regulation' be based? Article 291 TFEU? Article 352 TFEU appears to rule itself out on procedural grounds, since it does not allow for co-decision; and Article 114 TFEU would seem to exclude itself on substantive grounds for it is confined to the internal market.

[77] We should presume that where the primary legal base envisages the Council as the principal decision-maker, the (special) legislative act is unlikely to grant Parliament identical control powers for delegated acts.

[78] For the same conclusion, albeit by a wrong route, see: H. Hofmann, 'Legislation, Delegation and Implementation under the Treaty of Lisbon: Typology meets Reality' [2009] 15 *European Law Journal* 482 at 493: '[T]here are reasons to argue that Article 290 TFEU contains a closed enumeration. One of these arguments is the exceptional nature of the delegation of legislative powers to the executive body, the Commission. The delegation being the exception, indicates the necessity of a narrow interpretation of the exception *vis-à-vis* the rule.' The problem with this argument is that the control mechanisms in Article 290 (2) TFEU can be seen as political *limitations* to the 'exception' of executive legislation and should, following the author's argument, be interpreted widely.

[79] The Commission has already indicated its willingness to 'concede' influence to national authorities and experts; see Commission Communication (supra n. 47), 6–7 (emphasis added): 'Except in cases where this preparatory work does not require new expertise, the Commission intends systematically to consult experts from the national authorities of all the Member States, which will be responsible for implementing the delegated acts once they have been adopted. This consultation will be carried out in plenty of time, to give the experts an opportunity to make a useful and effective contribution to the Commission. The Commission might form new expert groups for this purpose, or use existing ones. The Commission attaches the highest importance to this work, which makes it possible to establish an effective partnership at the technical level

The abolition of comitology with regard to delegated acts will significantly reduce the ex ante control by the Union legislator. And while this decline is partly balanced by increasing the ex post control mechanisms, Article 290 appears to satisfy the Commission's demands to enhance its executive autonomy.[80] For the 'legislative veto' granted to the Council and the Parliament grants them solely the power to negate Commission acts. It will not include the positive power to amend executive legislation. This 'take it or leave it' choice of the Union legislator will thus increase the Commission's independence in formulating (non-essential) policy choices embedded in secondary legislation.

(b) The 'conferral' of executive power: Article 291 TFEU

The European Treaties' regime for executive legislation is based on the idea that the nature of the constitutional control mechanism should take account of the nature of the powers 'delegated' to the Commission.[81] But if a delegation of *legislative* power is subject to the political control of the legislature, who is to control the exercise of *executive* or 'implementing power'? And should there be constitutional limits to the scope of 'implementing' powers?

Before answering these – tricky – questions, we must first look at the scope of Article 291 TFEU. Will the provision overlap with Article 290 TFEU; or will the latter limit the scope of Article 291 TFEU?

(i) The scope of Article 291 TFEU

What will the scope of Article 291 be? Will it be limited by the scope of Article 290; or will the two provisions overlap? In other words, will the European legislator be able to choose whether it prefers the constitutional safeguards under Article 291 to those under Article 290? This freedom of choice would contradict the intention of the Treaty-makers.[82] Indeed, the better view is that '[t]he authors of the new Treaty clearly intended the two articles to be mutually exclusive'.[83]

What then are their respective spheres of application? The Commission has answered this question in the following way:

> [I]t should be noted that the authors of the new Treaty did not conceive the scope of the two articles in the same way. The concept of the delegated act is defined in

---

with experts in the national authorities. *However, it should be made clear that these experts will have a consultative rather than an institutional role in the decision-making procedure.*'

[80] See European Commission, European Governance: A White Paper, COM(2001) 428. For the academic view that sees the Commission as the 'winner' of the Lisbon reform, see: P. Craig, 'The Hierarchy of Norms' in T. Tridimas and P. Nebbia (eds.), *EU Law for the Twenty-First Century* (Oxford: Hart, 2004), vol. I, 75 at 81.

[81] Despite the formal(ist) distinction between 'delegated' and 'implementing power', the acts adopted under Article 291 TFEU are also the result of a delegation in a primary act. On the material notion of 'legislation', see: Chapter 5 – Introduction above.

[82] See Final Report of Working Group IX (Simplification), CONV 424/02.

[83] European Commission, Communication: Implementing Article 290 (supra n. 47), 3.

terms of its scope and consequences – as a general measure that supplements or amends non-essential elements – whereas that of the implementing act, although never spelled out, is determined by its rationale – the need for uniform conditions for implementation. This discrepancy is due to the very different nature and scope of the powers conferred on the Commission by the two provisions. When it receives the power to adopt delegated acts under Article 290 the Commission is authorised to supplement or amend the work of the legislator. Such a delegation is always discretionary: the legislator delegates its powers to the Commission in the interests of efficiency. In the system introduced by Article 291 the Commission does not exercise any 'quasi-legislative' power; its power is purely executive. The Member States are naturally responsible for implementing the legally binding acts of the European Union, but because it is necessary to have uniform conditions the Commission must exercise its executive power. Its intervention is not optional but compulsory, when the conditions of Article 291 are fulfilled.[84]

The argument advanced is that Articles 290 and 291 follow different constitutional rationales. The former concerns the *voluntary* delegation of legislative power in the interest of efficiency – and thus deals with the horizontal separation of powers. The latter concerns the *compulsory* delegation of executive power, where the national implementation leads to an unacceptable degree of diversity, and thus deals with the vertical separation of powers. Article 291 must therefore be placed within the constitutional context of 'executive federalism' within the European Union.[85]

But even if we accept that the constitutional logic underlying Articles 290 and 291 is fundamentally different, will this mean that the two provisions never overlap? Assuming that the European legislator establishes the essential elements in a legislative act, will it be entitled to immediately confer on the Commission the power to adopt 'implementing regulations' that flesh out the bare bones of the primary legislation?[86] Can the European legislator, in other words, freely choose between a 'delegated regulation' and 'implementing regulation' as the proper form of executive legislation? If so, there would be a functional overlap between Articles 290 and 291 TFEU. For while both regulations are – from the formal perspective – different acts,[87] they are – from the material perspective – identical. And to avoid a material overlap between Articles 290 and 291, one needs indeed to insist – with the

---

[84] *Ibid.*, 3–4.   [85] On this point, see: Section 3 below.

[86] This has happened in the recent Regulation 1093/2010 establishing a European Supervisory Authority (European Banking Authority), [2010] OJ L331/12. Article 11 of the Regulation not only delegates the power to adopt regulatory technical standards under Article 290 TFEU, but also grants the Commission the power to adopt 'implementing acts pursuant to Article 291 TFEU' under Article 15 of the Regulation.

[87] No implementing act can 'amend' the basic act – this function is now exclusively reserved to 'delegated acts'. Implementing acts can thus provide 'supplementary' rules, but these 'supplementary' (implementing) rules will not supplement *the legislative act*. They stand below the legislative act.

Commission – that it is *not* in the discretion of the European Union automatically to exercise its implementing power under Article 291. The exercise of implementing power under Article 291 must depend on something 'outside' the will of the EU executive; and that 'outside' is – has to be – nothing other than the Member States. Only where the Member States fail to execute European law in a sufficiently uniform manner will the Commission (or the Council) be entitled to exercise the Union's own executive power.

In sum, to avoid a functional overlap between Article 290 and Article 291, both provisions must be seen from different constitutional perspectives. Article 290 is designed directly to protect *democratic* values, while Article 291 is primarily designed to protect *federal* values. The European legislator can freely 'delegate' power to the Commission under both provisions. However, while the Commission has the right to use its delegated powers under Article 290 immediately as the principle of *legislative* subsidiarity will have been satisfied by the basic legislative act,[88] it would not be automatically able to act under Article 291 as every exercise of 'delegated' implementing power under Article 291 (2) will still be subject to the principle of (*executive*) subsidiarity.[89] Where the Union legislator thus chooses to delegate the power to adopt additional rules through 'implementing acts', instead of 'delegated acts', the Commission loses its right automatically to exercise its delegated power. Delegation under Article 291 is thus a constitutional minus.

(ii) Constitutional safeguards for implementing legislation

The constitutional regime for 'implementing acts' is set out in Article 291 TFEU. The provision states:

> Where uniform conditions for implementing legally binding Union acts are needed, those acts shall confer implementing powers on the Commission, or, in duly justified specific cases and in the cases provided for in Article 24 and 26 TEU, on the Council.[90]

The provision thus envisages the Commission *and the Council* as possible recipients of 'delegated' implementing power.[91] Importantly, Article 291 TFEU does not mention substantive limits to such a conferral. Will the 'essential elements' principle or the specificity principle thus not apply? And what are the 'specific cases' that allow the Council to 'delegate' implementing power to

---

[88] The argument goes as follows: as the 'delegated act' only concerns 'non-essential' elements and since the delegation mandate must expressly and clearly specify the 'objectives, content, scope and duration of the delegation' (Article 290 (1) TFEU), all future delegated acts should be seen as covered by the subsidiarity analysis of the basic legislative act.

[89] On this point, see: Section 3 (b) below.

[90] Article 291 (2) TFEU. Articles 24 and 26 TEU are part of Common Foreign and Security Policy.

[91] The confirmation of the constitutional option of a 'self-delegation' by the Council has been criticised as 'an anomaly in the overall picture of separation of functions' (see Lenaerts and Desomer (supra n. 71) 756).

itself? Did the drafters assume that the Union's constitutional *acquis* would automatically continue and thus extend to 'implementing acts'?[92] The better view answers this question in the negative. Article 291 TFEU should thus not be viewed from a *horizontal* separation of powers perspective, but – instead – be viewed from a *vertical* perspective that places Article 291 TFEU within the context of Europe's executive federalism. Once this is done, there is no need for an 'essential elements' doctrine for the provision.

What about the political safeguards that can be used to control the exercise of Union implementing power? To control the exercise of implementing power by the Commission – not the Council – the European legislator is called to 'lay down in advance the rules and general principles concerning mechanisms for control by Member States'.[93] This formulation stands in the constitutional tradition of the Rome Treaty; yet it appears to envisage different mechanisms of control. Article 291 TFEU indeed gives contradictory signals. On the one hand, it answered Parliament's wish to be involved in the adoption of a future Comitology 'law': Council *and* Parliament 'acting by means of regulations in accordance with the ordinary legislative procedure' shall adopt the political control mechanisms for delegated powers. This could have pointed to a future involvement of Parliament in controlling the implementation powers of the Commission.

On the other hand, the provision charges the European legislator to establish 'mechanisms for control by *Member States*'. This formulation appears to exclude – as ultra vires – any direct participation of Parliament (as well as the Council) in a future Comitology system.[94] This second view posed a dramatic challenge to the constitutionality of the old Comitology system. In that system the Member States were only *indirectly* involved in the control of executive legislation.[95] *Directly* involved in the control of the Commission's implementing powers were the *Union institutions* – not the Member States. And this would have to change as a result of the phrase 'mechanisms for control by the Member States'.

---

[92] In this sense, see: Hofmann (supra n. 78), 488: 'One of the weak points of this non-delegation-clause introduced into the new typology of acts is that it is explicitly only formulated for delegated acts under Article 290 TFEU. From a teleological point of view, however, it should also be applicable for the distinction between legislative and implementing acts under Article 291 TFEU.'

[93] Article 291 (3) TFEU.

[94] See P. Craig, 'The Role of the European Parliament under the Lisbon Treaty' in S. Griller and J. Ziller (eds.), *The Lisbon Treaty: EU Constitutionalism without a Constitutional Treaty?* (Springer, 2008), 109 at 123.

[95] See Case 25/70, *Köster* (supra n. 53), para. 9: 'The management committee does not therefore have the power to take decisions in place of the Commission or the Council. Consequently, without distorting the [Union] structure and the institutional balance, the management committee machinery enables the Council to delegate to the Commission an implementing power of appreciable scope, subject to its power to take the decision itself if necessary.'

The new Comitology Regulation has indeed abandoned the old Comitology Decision(s) and replaced it with a – radically – reformed Comitology system.[96] The new system distinguishes between two procedures – the advisory procedure and the examination procedure – according to which the Commission can adopt implementing acts.[97] The Commission is not free to choose which procedure applies. On the contrary, the Comitology Regulation sets out the scope of the examination procedure with the advisory procedure constituting the residual category.[98] The examination procedure thereby applies to 'implementing acts of general scope', but will also cover individual measures in important policy areas of the Union.[99]

In what ways are the two procedures controlling the Commission's power to adopt implementing acts? Both procedures oblige the Commission to 'be assisted by a committee composed of representatives of the Member States'.[100] The Commission will thus have to submit draft acts to a committee. Under the advisory procedure, the opinion of the Committee is only 'advisory'. Where the advisory committee has a negative opinion, the Commission must take 'the utmost account of the conclusions' but may still adopt the implementing act anyway.[101] This freedom is restricted under the examination procedure. For while the Commission can adopt the act, where there is a positive or no opinion,[102] the Committee can veto a Commission act through a negative opinion.[103] Yet the Commission – as chair of the committee – can then still refer the draft act to an 'appeal committee' for further deliberation.[104] The appeal committee is composed in the same way as the examination committee;[105] and where it delivers a positive opinion, 'the Commission shall adopt the draft legislative acts'.[106] By contrast, where the appeal committee confirms the negative opinion, 'the Commission shall not adopt the draft legislative act'.[107]

---

[96] Regulation 182/2011 laying down the rules and general principles concerning mechanisms for control by Member States of the Commission's exercise of implementing powers, [2011] OJ L55/13. For extensive extracts of the Comitology Regulation, see Appendix 8 to this book.

[97] *Ibid.*, Recital 8.   [98] *Ibid.*, Article 2.

[99] *Ibid.*, Article 2 (2). Subparagraph (b) enumerates, inter alia, the common agricultural and fisheries policies and the common commercial policy.

[100] *Ibid.*, Article 3 (2).   [101] *Ibid.*, Article 4 (2).

[102] The rules as to when the Commission can adopt the act, where there is no opinion of the examination committee, are fairly complex. Article 5 (4) distinguishes between the general rule (subparagraph 1) that allows the Commission to adopt the draft acts, and a number of exceptional cases (subparagraph 2) in which silence is taken to be a negative opinion. Finally, Article 5 (5) contains a (very) special procedure for antidumping or countervailing measures.

[103] *Ibid.*, Article 5 (3): 'if the committee delivers a negative opinion, the Commission shall not adopt the draft implementing act'.

[104] *Ibid.*

[105] According to Article 6 (1) of the Regulation, the appeals committee shall decide by the majority provided for in Article 5 (1) Regulation, that is: according to 'the majority laid down in Article 16(4) and (5) of the Treaty on European Union and, where applicable, Article 238(3) TFEU'; and '[t]he votes of the representatives of the Member States within the committee shall be weighted in the manner set out in those Articles'.

[106] *Ibid.*, Article 6 (3) – first indent.   [107] *Ibid.*, Article 6 (3) – third indent.

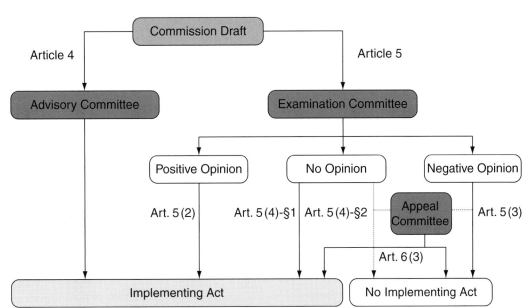

'Comitology' under Article 291 (3) TFEU: Regulation 182/2011

Figure 16 'Comitology' as defined by Regulation 182/2011

Schematically, the 'Comitology' regime under Article 291 (3) TFEU is shown in Figure 16.

What is the role of the European legislator in the control regime under Article 291 TFEU? The answer is that there is no direct role for either Parliament or Council. However, both are entitled to indicate to the Commission their belief that the draft act exceeds the implementing powers provided for in the primary act.[108] But this right of scrutiny is a 'soft' right. The Commission is not obliged to amend or withdraw its proposal. Yet, where the implementing act indeed exceeds the delegation mandate, both institutions will be entitled to apply for judicial review to have the act repealed on grounds of lack of competence.[109]

3. Administrative powers I: centralised enforcement

With regard to the enforcement of federal law, federal unions may follow one of two constitutional models. According to the 'centralisation model', the administration of federal law is left to federal administrative authorities. In order to

---

[108] *Ibid.*, Article 11.
[109] On the availability of judicial review for lack of competence, see: Chapter 8 – Section 1(b) below.

enforce its law, the Union thus establishes its own administrative infrastructure. This model has been adopted in the United States of America.[110] By contrast, the 'decentralisation model' leaves the execution of federal law to the Member States of the Union. The Union's executive competences are here smaller than its legislative competences. This system of decentralised execution is called 'executive federalism', and has traditionally been adopted in the Federal Republic of Germany.[111]

Which of the two models does the European Union follow? According to Article 291 (1) TFEU, 'Member States shall adopt all measures of national law necessary to implement legally binding Union acts'; but where 'uniform conditions for implementing legally binding Union acts are needed', the Union shall adopt the executive act.[112] In the enforcement of European law, it is thus – primarily – the Member States that are called upon to execute European law. However, the execution of European law by the Union constitutes a subsidiary – secondary – option. The European Union thus appears to combine *both* federal models in its own constitutional brand. It partly adopts the American solution in which the Union's legislative and executive spheres coincide; but unlike American federalism, the Union's executive powers are subsidiary to the administrative powers of the Member States. We shall look at both aspects of the centralised enforcement of European law in this section, while Section 4 analyses the constitutional principles governing the decentralised enforcement of European law.

(a) The scope of the Union's administrative powers

Administrative powers allow a public authority to apply a general norm to a specific situation. To what extent is the European Union empowered to apply its own legislative norms in specific situations?

In contrast to the 'administrative system' established by the ECSC, the European (Economic) Community had been conceived as a legislative system.[113] The vast majority of its competences were originally 'legislative' competences; and executive powers were expressly attributed in – very – few areas indeed.[114] Did this mean that in all areas that did not *expressly* mention the administrative power to adopt decisions, the Union would have to rely on the

---

[110] For an analysis of the centralisation model in the US, see: R. Schütze, 'From Rome to Lisbon: "Executive Federalism" in the (New) European Union' [2010] 47 CML Rev 1385 at 1387 et seq.

[111] For an analysis of the decentralisation model in Germany see: *ibid.*, 1389 et seq.

[112] Article 291 (2) TFEU.

[113] L. Azoulai, 'Pour un Droit de l'Execution de l'Union Européenne' in J. Dutheil de la Rochère (ed.), *L'Execution Du Droit de l'Union: Entre Méchanismes Communautaires et Droit Nationaux* (Bruylant, 2009), 1 at 2.

[114] The 1957 Rome Treaty expressly mentioned only the power to adopt 'decisions' addressed to individuals in three areas: agriculture (Article 43 EEC), transport (Articles 79 and 80 EEC) and competition (Articles 85 et seq. EEC). The power to adopt decisions under the common commercial policy was implicit in Article 113 (2) EEC.

State administrations to enforce European law? Or would the Union enjoy general or implied administrative powers to execute its law in individual situations?

Two powers do potentially provide the Union with general administrative competences. The Union's internal market competence under Article 114 TFEU allows the Union to adopt 'measures for the approximation of the provisions laid down by law, regulation or administrative action in Member States'. The power to adopt 'measures' appeared to include the power to adopt individual decisions. But how could a decision 'harmonise' national laws or administrative actions? In *Germany* v. *Council*,[115] this argument was placed on the judicial table in the context of the Product Safety Directive.[116] Germany argued that the power to 'harmonise' precluded the executive power to adopt decisions;[117] and since Article 9 of the relevant Directive granted such a power in certain situations, the provision had to be void.[118] The Court held otherwise:

> The measures which the Council is empowered to take under that provision are aimed at 'the establishment and functioning of the internal market'. In certain

---

[115] Case C-359/92, *Germany* v. *Council*, [1994] ECR I-3681.

[116] Directive 92/59/EEC on general product safety (OJ 1992 L228, 24). The Directive is now replaced by Directive 2001/95/EC on general product safety (OJ 2002 L11, 4).

[117] Germany's principal argument in this respect is quoted in para. 17: 'The German Government objects to that argument essentially on the ground that the sole aim of ... Article [114 (1)] TFEU] ... is the approximation of laws and that those articles do not therefore confer power to apply the law to individual cases in the place of the national authorities, as permitted by Article 9 of the directive. The German Government further observes that the powers conferred upon the Commission by Article 9 thus exceed those which, in a federal state such as the Federal Republic of Germany, are enjoyed by the Bund in relation to the Länder, since, under the German Basic Law, the implementation of federal laws rests with the Länder. Lastly, the German Government submits that Article 9 cannot be regarded as constituting an implementing power, within the meaning of the third indent of [ex-]Article [202] of the [EC] Treaty, since that article does not embody a substantive power of its own, but merely authorises the Council to confer implementing powers on the Commission where a legal base exists in primary [European] law for the act to be implemented and its implementing measures.' This view was – partly – shared by Advocate-General Jacobs, see Case C-359/92, *Germany* v. *Council* (supra n. 115) at 3693, esp. para. 36.

[118] Article 9 provided as follows: 'If the Commission becomes aware, through notification given by the Member States or through information provided by them, in particular under Article 7 or Article 8, of the existence of a serious and immediate risk from a product to the health and safety of consumers in various Member States and if: (a) one or more Member States have adopted measures entailing restrictions on the marketing of the product or requiring its withdrawal from the market, such as those provided for in Article 6(1)(d) to (h); (b) Member States differ on the adoption of measures to deal with the risk in question; (c) the risk cannot be dealt with, in view of the nature of the safety issue posed by the product and in a manner compatible with the urgency of the case, under the other procedures laid down by the specific [Union] legislation applicable to the product or category of products concerned; and (d) the risk can be eliminated effectively only by adopting appropriate measures applicable at [European] level, in order to ensure the protection of the health and safety of consumers and the proper functioning of the common market, the Commission, after consulting the Member States and at the request of at least one of them, may adopt a decision, in accordance with the procedure laid down in Article 11, requiring Member States to take temporary measures from among those listed in Article 6(1) (d) to (h).'

fields, and particularly in that of product safety, the approximation of general laws alone may not be sufficient to ensure the unity of the market. Consequently, the concept of 'measures for the approximation' of legislation must be interpreted as encompassing the Council's power to lay down measures relating to a specific product or class of products and, if necessary, individual measures concerning those products. So far as concerns the argument that the power thus conferred on the Commission goes beyond that which, in a federal State such as the Federal Republic of Germany, is enjoyed by the *Bund* in relation to the *Länder*, it must be borne in mind that the rules governing the relationship between the [Union] and its Member States are not the same as those which link the *Bund* with the *Länder*.[119]

Article 114 TFEU would thus entitle the Union to adopt administrative decisions. Yet, since the ruling dealt with a *State*-addressed decision, its constitutional impact might be confined to that category. But could Article 114 TFEU also be employed to adopt decisions addressed to private individuals; or even the creation of the Union's own administrative infrastructure? Subsequent jurisprudence has clarified that Article 114 TFEU could indeed be used for both purposes. For the adoption of decisions addressed to individuals, the *cause célèbre* is *United Kingdom* v. *Parliament and Council*.[120] The case concerned the validity of Regulation 2065/2003, which tried to ensure the effective functioning of the internal market through a European authorisation procedure. The legislative measure delegated the power to grant or reject authorisations to the Commission;[121] and its decisions were addressed to individual applicants.[122] The British government protested: 'The legislative power conferred by Article [114] is a power to harmonise national laws, not a power to establish [Union] bodies or to confer tasks on such bodies, or to establish procedures for the approval of lists of authorised products.'[123] Yet in its judgment, the Court

---

[119] Case C-359/92, *Germany* v. *Council* (supra n. 115), paras. 37–8. The Court also held Article 9 of the Directive to be a 'proportionate' executive power of the [Union] (*ibid.*, para. 46): 'Those powers are not excessive in relation to the objectives pursued. Contrary to the assertion made by the German Government, the infringement procedure laid down in Article [258] of the [FEU] Treaty does not permit the results set out in Article 9 of the directive to be achieved.'

[120] Case 66/04, *United Kingdom* v. *Parliament and Council*, [2005] ECR I-10553. In relation to Article 114 TFEU's use to create a Union body, see: Case C-217/04, *United Kingdom* v. *Parliament and Council (ENISA)*, [2006] ECR I-3771, especially para. 44: 'The legislature may deem it necessary to provide for the establishment of a [Union] body responsible for contributing to the implementation of a process of harmonisation in situations where, in order to facilitate the uniform implementation and application of acts based on that provision, the adoption of non-binding supporting and framework measures seems appropriate.'

[121] According to the authorisation procedure set out in Regulation 2065/2003 (OJ 2003 L309, 1), an individual applicant would need to send its application to the competent national authority, which would send the application to the European Food Safety Authority (EFSA) (*ibid.*, Article 7). The EFSA would then forward its opinion on the application to the Commission, the Member States and the applicant (*ibid.*, Article 8). The Commission would take the final decision (*ibid.*, Article 9), in accordance with the procedure set out in Article 19 (2) of the Regulation.

[122] Article 9 (1) (b) of the Regulation; and see also: Article 11 (1) of the Regulation.

[123] Case 66/04, *UK* v. *Parliament* (supra n. 120), para. 18.

confirmed this very power. Article 114 TFEU could be used as a legal base for the power to adopt individual administrative decisions.[124]

An even more general legal basis for the adoption of administrative measures may be available to the European Union: Article 352 TFEU. The Article allows the Union to 'adopt the appropriate measures', where this is necessary to attain one of the objectives set out in the Treaties. This power includes the competence to adopt administrative decisions; and the Court has clarified that this competence may also be used to complement a specific legislative competence that did not expressly provide for the centralised enforcement of European law.[125] The power to adopt administrative decisions could thus be derived – for almost every policy area within the scope of the Treaties – where this was deemed 'necessary'.[126] Article 352 thus provides an *executive* competence reservoir that coincides with the scope of the Union's legislative powers. This reading has been strengthened by the Lisbon Treaty. Indeed, Article 291 TFEU gives firmer constitutional foundations to the parallelism of legislative and executive powers in the European Union. For while the Member States will be primarily responsible for the enforcement of European law, the Union is considered to be entitled to implement its own law, '[w]here uniform conditions for implementing legally binding Union acts are needed'.[127]

The question left open by the Lisbon Treaty is this: should we see Article 291 (2) as an independent legal basis for Union administrative action? The wording of the provision provides an argument against this view, as its text refers to the horizontal relations between Union institutions. However, systemic and teleological considerations may lead to a different interpretation. Unlike its predecessor,[128] Article 291 TFEU is not confined to regulating the horizontal relationship between Union institutions but refers in paragraph 1 to the *vertical relations between the Union and the Member States*. A systemic reading of Article 291 TFEU might thus suggest that, while the Member States are principally responsible under paragraph 1, the Union will be competent under paragraph 2. The Union competence could thereby derive from Article 291 (2) *as such*, while the specific Union act only regulates the *delegation* of implementing power to the Commission (Council).[129] This systemic

---

[124] *Ibid.*, para. 64.

[125] On the constitutional availability of Article 352 TFEU in this situation, see: R. Schütze, 'Organized Change Towards an "Ever Closer Union": Article 308 EC and the Limits to the Community's Legislative Competence' [2003] 22 YEL 79 at 95: 'The Two Dimensions of Power: Regulatory Instruments and Article 308 EC'.

[126] On the (new) limits to Article 352 TFEU, see: Chapter 5 – Section 1(b) above.

[127] Article 291 (2) TFEU.   [128] On ex-Article 202 EC, see: supra n. 44.

[129] Some have even claimed that the Commission would enjoy an autonomous power under Article 291 (2) TFEU; see: J. P. Jacque, 'Le Traité de Lisbonne: Une Vue Cavalière' [2008] 44 *Revue Trimestrielle de Droit Européen* 439 at 480: 'le pouvoir d'exécution appartient à la Commission qui ne dispose plus, comme dans la situation actuelle, d'un pouvoir délégué, mais d'un pouvoir propre'.

interpretation is reinforced by teleological considerations. A competence read-ing of Article 291 TFEU would allow the Union to adopt any type of imple-menting act – including implementing decisions – without recourse to Article 352 TFEU.[130] This reading would provide the Union with a solid legal founda-tion for its administrative action. However, it is – as ever – a matter for the European Court to decide what the law is.

(b) Administrative powers and the subsidiarity principle

The subsidiarity principle is defined in Article 5 (3) TEU. It limits the exercise of a shared competence of the Union by insisting that national actions must be insufficient and that therefore the adoption of European measures is compara-tively more efficient.[131] The wording of the principle refers to any action by the Union. This has – from the very beginning – been understood to include *administrative* actions.[132] The executive principle of subsidiarity asks whether the Member States or the European Union will better achieve the enforcement of European law. Executive subsidiarity thereby operates *independently* from the principle's application in the legislative sphere. Thus, even when *centralised legislative* action by the Union is justified under the subsidiarity principle, the latter may nonetheless mandate the *decentralised execution* of European legis-lation by the Member States.

What criteria have the European legislator or the European Courts developed to clarify the contours of executive subsidiarity? We find a legislative mecha-nism for executive subsidiarity in the context of European competition law.[133]

---

[130] For example, Article 207 TFEU only permits the Union to exercise its Common Commercial Policy competence by means of two instruments: regulations and international agreements. All internal 'measures defining the framework for implementing the common commercial policy' must be adopted 'by means of regulations' and 'in accordance with the ordinary legislative procedure' (para. 2). Article 207 TFEU will not, as such, entitle the Union to adopt individual decisions. And this morphological limitation is to stay even if the Union legislator decides to delegate legislative power to the Commission, since Article 290 TFEU specifies that the Commission can only adopt 'non-legislative acts of *general application*' (para. 1). The Union may here only be able to base an individual decision on Article 352 TFEU.

[131] Are there exclusive executive competences of the EU? Textually, Article 2 TFEU applies the category of exclusive competence to areas in which the Union 'may legislate and adopt *legally binding acts*' (Article 2 (1) TFEU – emphasis added). The possibility of executive measures falling within this category is recognised. Has the Treaty tied the categorisation of all 'non-legislative' competences to the classification of the Union's 'legislative' competences? Article 2 (1) TFEU provides a strong textual argument against this view. For it mentions *two* alternatives when the Member States are entitled to act within an exclusive (legislative) competence, namely: where 'so empowered by the Union *or for the implementation of Union acts*' (emphasis added). While the former alternative thus refers to a *delegated* competence, the latter must constitute an *autonomous* competence of the Member States.

[132] C. D. Ehlermann, 'Quelques Réflexions sur la Communication de la Commission Relative au Principe de Subsidiarité' [1992] *Revue du marché unique européen*, 215.

[133] On the application of the principle of subsidiarity in the context of EU competition law, see: R. Wesseling, 'Subsidiarity in Community Antitrust Law: Setting the Right Agenda' [1997] 22 EL Rev 35.

The enforcement of European competition law is based on a system of shared competences spelled out in Regulation 1/2003.[134] It entitles the European Commission as well as the national competition authorities to apply European competition law; but 'the competition authorities of the Member States are automatically relieved of their competence if the Commission initiates its own proceedings'.[135] Is the discretion of the Commission to centralise enforcement here subject to a subsidiarity analysis? The principles governing the exercise of the Commission's administrative competences were partly clarified by its 'Notice on Cooperation within the Network of Competition Authorities'.[136] The Commission here specified when it wishes to centralise the administration of European competition law:

> The Commission is particularly well placed if one or several agreement(s) or practice(s), including networks of similar agreements or practices, *have effects on competition in more than three Member States* (cross-border markets covering more than three Member States or several national markets). Moreover, the Commission is particularly well placed to deal with a case if it is closely linked to other [Union] provisions which may be exclusively or more effectively applied by the Commission, if the [Union] interest requires the adoption of a Commission decision *to develop [Union] competition policy* when a new competition issue arises or *to ensure effective enforcement*.[137]

The centralised administration of European law would consequently be mandated, where one of three – alternative – criteria is met. The first criterion relates to the *geographical scale* of the competition law problem. Where more than three Member States are concerned, administrative centralisation is deemed to be justified. This trans-border element has close subsidiarity overtones in that it is associated with the 'national insufficiency' test.[138] The second criterion is, by contrast, of a *political* nature. Since the Commission is principally responsible for the development of European competition *policy*,[139] it must be able to decide important cases itself. The third criterion concerns the *effectiveness* of the competition law administration. This criterion is reminiscent of the 'comparative efficiency test' in Article 5 (3) TEU. What efficiency gains warrant

---

[134] Regulation 1/2003 on the implementation of the rules on competition laid down in Articles 81 and 82 of the [EC] Treaty (OJ 2003 L1/1).

[135] *Ibid.*, Recital 17.

[136] Commission Notice on Cooperation within the Network of Competition Authorities (OJ 2004 C101/43). The Notice is a 'soft law' measure that, as such, only binds the Commission. However, according to its paragraph 72, Member States' competition authorities may sign a statement that they will by abide the principles set out in the Notice; and the Notice has indeed been signed by all national competition authorities.

[137] Commission Notice (*ibid.*), paras. 14–15 (emphasis added).

[138] On the two tests within the legislative principle of subsidiarity, see: Chapter 5 – Section 4.

[139] Commission Notice (supra n. 136), recital 43: 'Within the network of competition authorities the Commission, as the guardian of the Treaty, has the ultimate but not the sole responsibility for developing policy and safeguarding consistency when it comes to the application of European competition law.'

administrative centralisation? We find some tentative answers in a later part of the Network Notice. The Commission may centralise decision-making, where the national administrative authorities envisage conflicting or substantively wrong decisions; or where a national authority unduly draws out proceedings in the case.[140] This definition of executive subsidiarity provides the Commission with an extremely favourable prerogative over the Member State administrations.

Have the European Courts insisted on an independent judicial control of the constitutional principle? In the past, the Courts have often deferred to the 'political' nature of the subsidiarity analysis and thus recognised a wide discretion for the European legislator.[141] Have the Courts extended this laissez-faire approach to the European executive? Or have the Courts insisted on a strict(er) judicial review of executive subsidiarity?

The issue arose in *France Télécom* v. *Commission*.[142] The French undertaking had been subject to a Commission investigation and challenged its legality on the ground that the French competition authority would have been better able to deal with the case. The Commission, on the other hand, insisted that the administrative system established by Regulation 1/2003 'preserve[d] the Commission's power to act at any time against any infringement of Articles [101 and 102 TFEU]'. Moreover, 'where the Commission has competence to apply the [FEU] Treaty directly in individual cases, the principle of subsidiarity cannot be interpreted in a manner that deprives it of such competence'.[143] In its judgment, the Court – wrongly – held that the subsidiarity principle could never limit the Commission's power to enforce the competition rules.[144] The judgment represents a serious blow to the idea of an independent judicial analysis of executive subsidiarity. The Court appears to leave the principle of executive subsidiarity completely in the hands of the European institutions. This reliance on the political safeguards of federalism is misplaced, especially in the context of the executive function. The European Courts should therefore look beyond the legislative expressions of subsidiarity and apply an independent judicial review of the question of executive subsidiarity.

4. Administrative powers II: decentralised enforcement

According to Article 291 (1) TFEU, 'Member States shall adopt all measures of national law necessary to implement legally binding Union acts'; and only where 'uniform conditions for implementing legally binding Union acts are

---

[140] Commission Notice (supra n. 136), para. 54.   [141] On this point, see: Chapter 5 – Section 4.
[142] Case T-339/04, *France Télécom SA* v. *Commission*, [2007] ECR II-521. The case is extensively discussed by F. Rizzuto, 'Parallel Competence and the Power of the EC Commission under Regulation 1/2003 according to the Court of First Instance' [2008] *European Competition Law Review* 286.
[143] Case T-339/04, *France Télécom* (supra n. 142), paras. 72–3.   [144] *Ibid.*, para. 89.

needed', shall the Union itself adopt an executive act.[145] In the enforcement of European law, it is thus the Member States that are primiarily called upon to execute European law.

This choice in favour of the decentralised application of European law has two potential consequences. First, administrative decisions taken by the national authorities implementing European law may only be valid in the national territory. Second, because the authorities that execute European law are national authorities, it is *national* administrative law that governs the case. The Union has tried to limit both consequences by placing them within a European constitutional frame. These constitutional limits make the decentralised application of European law by the Member States a form of executive *federalism*. The general constitutional principle governing the decentralised enforcement of European law is thereby laid down in Article 4 (3) TEU. The provision states: 'The Member States shall take any appropriate measure, general or particular, to ensure fulfilment of the obligations arising out of the Treaties or resulting from the acts of the institutions of the Union.' This general duty has become known as the duty of loyal cooperation.[146]

(a) The effects of national administrative acts

The decentralised execution of European law by the Member States means that administrative decisions taken by national authorities will, as such, only be binding within the Member State.[147] This follows from the territoriality principle, according to which national powers can only unfold their effects within the national territory. Administrative decisions within the Member States, even when executing European law, will therefore in principle be adopted in complete isolation from other Member States. The administrative decision within one Member State will thus have no automatic effects within another Member State.

The potential difficulties caused by diverse national administrative practices were soon realised. In the context of competition law, the Union was thus given the power to centralise the application of European law if there was a danger of administrative inconsistency between Member States. In other policy areas, the Union legislator has built cooperative relationships between national authorities. These horizontal relationships are to facilitate the mutual recognition of

---

[145] Article 291 (2) TFEU.

[146] The duty was an early signal in favour of executive federalism. And the Court of Justice has positively confirmed that reading (see Joined Cases 89 and 91/86, *L'Étoile Commerciale and Comptoir National Technique Agricole (CNTA)* v. *Commission*, [1987] ECR 3005, para.11). See also: Case C-476/93P, *Nutral* v *Commission*, [1995] ECR I-4125, para.14: 'according to the institutional system of the [Union] and the rules governing relations between the [Union] and the Member States, it is for the latter, in the absence of any contrary provision of [European] law, to ensure that [Union] regulations, particularly those concerning the common agricultural policy, are implemented within their territory.'

[147] This 'international' solution is not adopted in Germany, which has chosen the 'national' solution, cf. German Constitutional Court, BVerfGE 11, 6 (*Dampfkessel*), 18.

national administrative acts enforcing European law. While not required automatically to give validity to administrative decisions of other Member States, national authorities may nonetheless be subject to procedural and substantive duties imposed by European law.[148] For example, as regards medicinal products for human use, the relevant European directive establishes a '[m]ututal recognition procedure'.[149] In other areas, the Union legislator has even granted automatic *trans*-national validity to national administrative acts.[150] An illustration of this technique can be found in the Union Customs Code.[151] Its Article 250 – entitled 'Legal effects in a Member State of measures taken, documents issued and findings made in another Member State' – reads as follows:

> Where a customs procedure is used in several Member States,
>
> – the decisions, identification measures taken or agreed on, and the documents issued by the customs authorities of one Member State shall have the same legal effects in other Member States as such decisions, measures taken and documents issued by the customs authorities of each of those Member States;
> – the findings made at the time controls are carried out by the customs authorities of a Member State shall have the same conclusive force in the other Member States as the findings made by the customs authorities of each of those Member States.

We find similar investitures of transnational effects granted to national executive acts in other areas of European law.[152] However, national administrative acts with Union-wide effects constitute the exception.[153]

---

[148] This idea has been named 'reference model' and is extensively discussed by G. Sydow, *Verwaltungskooperation in der Europäischen Union* (Mohr Siebeck, 2004).

[149] Directive 2001/83 on the Community Code relating to medicinal products for human use, OJ 2001 OJL311/67.

[150] The term 'trans-national validity' was coined by E. Schmidt-Aßmann, 'Verwaltungskooperation und Verwaltungskooperationsrecht in der Europäischen Verwaltung' [1996] 31 *Europarecht* 270.

[151] Regulation 2913/92 establishing the Community Customs Code (OJ 1992 L 302/1).

[152] For example, Regulation 116/2009 on the export of cultural goods (Codified version) (OJ 2009 L39/1) makes the export of cultural goods outside the customs territory of the Union subject to an export licence and decrees that this licence shall be issued 'by a competent national authority' defined in Article 2 (2). Article 2 (3) then 'Europeanises' this national decision: 'The export licence shall be valid throughout the [Union]'. See also: Regulation 428/2009 setting up a [Union] regime for the control of exports, transfer, brokering and transit of dual-use items (OJ 2009 L134/1), whose Article 9 (2) states: 'For all other exports for which an authorisation is required under this Regulation, such authorisation shall be granted by the competent authorities of the Member State where the exporter is established. Subject to the restrictions specified in paragraph 4, this authorisation may be an individual, global or general authorisation. All the authorisations shall be valid throughout the [Union].'

[153] Could the European legislator decide to give such transnational effects to all national administrative acts? Article 291 (2) TFEU could not be used as a legal basis for such a – radical – decision, for it only entitles the Union to *replace* the Member States' indirect execution of European law by means of its direct involvement. Neither does Article 114 TFEU appear

(b) National administrative autonomy and its limits

In enforcing European law, national authorities are subject to the duty of loyal cooperation. How has the Court of Justice interpreted this duty in the context of the Union's executive federalism?

The Court has started out by recognising, in principle, the procedural autonomy of the Member States in the enforcement of European law: 'Although under Article [4] of the [FEU] Treaty the Member States are obliged to take all appropriate measures whether general or particular, to ensure fulfilment of the obligations arising out of the Treaty, it is for them to determine which institutions within the national system shall be empowered to adopt the said measures.'[154] More than that: '[w]here national authorities are responsible for implementing a [Union] regulation it must be recognised that in principle this implementation takes place with due respect for the forms and procedures of national law'.[155]

One expression of the principle of national procedural autonomy may be seen in the European 'no-commandeering' rule.[156] While not yet expressly confirmed by the European Courts, a Union decision may arguably never 'command' national executive officers directly. The formal addressee of a State-addressed decision always remains the *Member State as such*.[157] In the past, the Union judiciary has implicitly adopted this position. For the Court held that, under the decentralised enforcement, the Member States are entitled autonomously to interpret European rules, since 'the Commission has no power to take decisions on their interpretation but may only express an opinion which is not binding upon the national authorities'.[158] Textual ambivalences in European legislation thus appear to provide the national administrations – not

---

apposite for a decision to generally grant transnational effects to national executive action as the latter would not 'harmonise' national laws or administrative actions. The only possible contender is Article 352 TFEU. However, even this provision would find an external limit on the (present) constitutional identity of the Union; and this identity would be changed if the Union were to move – wholesale – from the decentralised enforcement of European law *pro statu* to the decentralised enforcement of European law *pro unione*.

[154] Joined Cases 51 to 54/71, *International Fruit Company NV and others* v. *Produktschap voor groenten en fruit*, [1971] ECR 1107, para. 3.

[155] Case 39/70, *Norddeutsches Vieh- und Fleischkontor GmbH* v. *Hauptzollamt Hamburg-St. Annen*, [1971] ECR 49, para. 4. See also: Joined Cases 205–15/82, *Deutsche Milchkontor GmbH and others* v. *Federal Republic of Germany*, [1983] ECR 2633, para. 17: 'the national authorities when implementing [European] regulations act in accordance with the procedural and substantive rules of their own national law'.

[156] For an analysis of the American principle of the same name, see D. Halberstam, 'Comparative Federalism and the Issue of Commandeering' in K. Nicolaidis and R. Howse (eds.), *The Federal Vision: Legitimacy and Levels of Governance in the US and the EU* (Oxford University Press, 2001).

[157] For an excellent analysis of this point, see: L. J. Constantinesco, *Das Recht der Europäischen Gemeinschaften* (Nomos, 1977), 299. For the opposite view, see: T. von Danwitz, *Europäisches Verwaltungsrecht* (Springer, 2008), 626.

[158] Case 133/79, *Sucrimex SA and Westzucker GmbH* v. *Commission*, [1980] ECR 1299, para. 16. On the power of the Commission to decide on 'binding' interpretations of European law, see also: Case 74/69, *Hauptzollamt Bremen-Freihafen* v. *Waren-Import-Gesellschaft Krohn & Co.*, [1970] ECR 451, para. 9.

the European administration – with the power to decide on the meaning of these provisions. This negative signal may be evidence of a general constitutional rule that prohibits the Commission from issuing formal commands to national administrations. If that view is accepted, it follows that national administrative organs are not part of a hierarchically structured 'integrated administration'.[159] And where a national administration fails to execute European law, the Commission will have to initiate judicial enforcement proceedings against the *Member State*.[160]

But even if the Union cannot penetrate into the administrative structures of its Member States, the procedural autonomy of the Member States is not absolute. It has to be reconciled with the need to apply European law uniformly. What then are the constitutional limits imposed on the principle of national procedural autonomy? National administrative rules are subject to the constitutional principles of equivalence and effectiveness.[161] And if these negative limits are not sufficient, the Union can harmonise national administrative procedures.[162] What legal bases will the Union have to adopt common administrative procedures? The power to harmonise national administrative law has always been part of the Union's harmonisation power. And the competence to structure national administrative procedures has been widely used in the past.[163]

---

[159] On the conceptual relation between the power to issue administrative instructions and an integrated administration, see the brilliant analysis by G. Biaggini, *Theorie und Praxis des Verwaltungsrechts im Bundesstaat* (Helbing & Liechtenhahn, 1996).

[160] S. Kadelbach, 'European Administrative Law and the Law of a European Administration' in C. Joerges and R. Dehousse (eds.), *Good Governance in Europe's Integrated Market* (Oxford University Press, 2002), 167.

[161] Discussion of these two principles is typically confined to the context of *judicial* remedies. (For their discussion in that context, see: Chapter 11 – Sections 2 and 3.) However, they equally apply – *mutatis mutandis* – to *administrative* remedies. The Court thus confirmed the principles of effectiveness and equivalence in Joined Cases 205-15/82, *Deutsche Milchkontor* (supra n. 155), paras. 22–3, as well as in Case C-201/02, *The Queen on the application of Delena Wells* v. *Secretary of State for Transport*, [2004] ECR I-723: '[U]nder Article [4(3) TEU] the competent authorities are obliged to take, within the sphere of their competence, all general or particular measures for remedying the failure to carry out an assessment of the environmental effects of a project as provided for in Article 2(1) of Directive 85/337. The detailed procedural rules applicable in that context are a matter for the domestic legal order of each Member State, under the principle of procedural autonomy of the Member States, provided that they are not less favourable than those governing similar domestic situations (principle of equivalence) and that they do not render impossible in practice or excessively difficult the exercise of rights conferred by the [European] legal order (principle of effectiveness).'

[162] Joined Cases 205-15/82, *Deutsche Milchkontor* (supra n. 155), para. 24: 'if the disparities in the legislation of Member States proved to be such as to compromise the equal treatment of producers and traders in different Member States or distort or impair the functioning of the Common Market, it would be for the [Union] institutions to adopt the provisions needed to remedy such disparities'.

[163] For a good illustration of this, see: Regulation 510/2006 on the protection of geographical indications and designations of origin for agricultural products and foodstuffs (OJ 2006 L93/12). According to its Article 5 (5) 'the Member State shall initiate a national objection procedure ensuring adequate publication of the application and providing for a reasonable period within which any natural or legal person having a legitimate interest and established or resident on its territory may lodge an objection to the application'. Moreover, 'The Member State shall ensure

The Lisbon Treaty has now inserted a new special constitutional base: Article 197 TFEU. This article constitutes by itself Title XXIV dealing with the 'Administrative Cooperation' between the European Union and the Member States. The provision states:

1. Effective implementation of Union law by the Member States, which is essential for the proper functioning of the Union, shall be regarded as a matter of common interest.
2. The Union may support the efforts of Member States to improve their administrative capacity to implement Union law. Such action may include facilitating the exchange of information and of civil servants as well as supporting training schemes. No Member State shall be obliged to avail itself of such support. The European Parliament and the Council, acting by means of regulations in accordance with the ordinary legislative procedure, shall establish the necessary measures to this end, *excluding any harmonisation of the laws and regulations of the Member States* . . .

The decentralised administration of European law is – unsurprisingly – of central interest to the Union. To guarantee an effective administration, the Union may decide to 'support the efforts of Member States to improve their administrative capacity to implement Union law'. But this Union support is entirely voluntary and the European legislation adopted under this competence must not entail 'any harmonisation of the laws and regulations of the Member States'.

This constitutional limitation is to be regretted. The trimming of the legal base to a 'complementary competence' may well have an ironic side-effect.[164] In blocking the European streamlining of (inefficient) national administrations, the provision protects their formal organisational autonomy.[165] However, the refusal to allow for the harmonisation of national administrative capacities through Union legislation may indirectly favour the centralised intervention by the Union under Article 291(2) TFEU. Thus, in excluding the Union's competence to harmonise national administrative law, the authors of the Lisbon Treaty placed procedural autonomy over substantive autonomy. This constitutional choice may – ironically –*reduce* the scope of the decentralised administration of Union law by the Member States.[166]

that its favourable decision is made public and that any natural or legal person having a legitimate interest has means of appeal.' See also: Directive 2002/21 on a common regulatory framework for electronic communications networks and services (Framework Directive) (OJ 2002 L108/33), esp. Articles 3 (2) and 4 (1).

[164] The competence is mentioned as a complementary competence in Article 6 (g) TFEU.

[165] However, this protection will not be absolute: see Article 197 (3) TFEU: 'This Article shall be without prejudice to the obligations of the Member States to implement Union law or to the prerogatives and duties of the Commission. It shall also be without prejudice to other provisions of the Treaties providing for administrative cooperation among the Member States and between them and the Union.'

[166] To add a footnote to this conclusion: Article 114 TFEU may – after Case C-376/98, *Germany v Parliament and Council (Tobacco Advertising)*, [2000] ECR I-8419 – still provide a legal basis for the harmonisation of national administrative provisions despite the existence of a 'saving clause'

Conclusion

This chapter analysed three core executive 'functions' within the European Union: the governmental, the legislative and the administrative function. We found that the distribution of governmental powers is based in the idea of a dual executive. Two institutions are thus responsible for proving political impulses to the Union: the European Council and the Commission. From an international perspective, the former offers the highest political authority in the Union, as it assembles the highest national decision-makers in a European institution. The Commission constitutes, by contrast, the 'national' branch of the Union's dual executive. And it has assumed a – functionally – subordinate position to the European Council. However, major policy initiatives originate, as we saw above, in the Commission before they are formally endorsed by the European Council, and they often subsequently return to the Commission. Both branches of the Union executive thus cooperate in a complex constitutional relationship. That relationship will work best if both executive branches follow similar political orientations.

Section 2 analysed the 'law-making' powers of the Union executive. These powers are firmly in the hands of the Commission. They are exceptionally granted directly by the Constitution, but in the vast majority of cases they result from a delegation of powers. The Union legal order thereby distinguishes between two constitutional regimes for delegating law-making powers: Article 290 and Article 291 TFEU. Within the former, the Union legislator is entitled to delegate the power to amend or supplement primary legislation. This power is, however, limited by the 'essential element' doctrine, and either branch of the Union legislator is entitled to veto the resulting delegated acts. By contrast, Article 291 TFEU allows for the conferral of 'implementing powers on the Commission'.[167] The provision does not mention any constitutional limits to the delegation mandate, but entitles the Union legislator to adopt 'the rules and general principles concerning mechanisms for control by Member States of the Commission's exercise of implementing powers'.[168] This power has been used in the form of Regulation 182/2011 – the 'Comitology Regulation'. Under that (new) comitology system, the Commission's implementing powers are subject to approval by a committee composed of Member State representatives. Depending on whether the advisory or examination procedure is applicable, the committee may or may not veto the Commission proposal.

under Article 197 (2) TFEU. (On the status of these 'saving clauses' and their relation to Article 114 TFEU, see: Schütze, *From Dual to Cooperative Federalism* (supra n. 52), 149 *et seq.*) However, it may be doubted whether Article 114 could ever be used to adopt a comprehensive 'European Administrative Code'. For a similar conclusion, albeit in the context of Article III-285 of the Constitutional Treaty, see: J. Schwarze, *EU Administrative Law* (Sweet & Maxwell, 2006), ccxix: 'a long way from being a possible future legal base for the creation of a comprehensive European administrative law or even just serving as a tool for the development of a general administrative procedural code'.

[167] Article 291 (2) TFEU.   [168] Article 291 (3) TFEU.

Finally, Sections 3 and 4 looked at the third core executive function within the European Union. The power to 'administer' European law in individual situations is shared between the Union and the Member States. Under this system of executive federalism, the Member States are primarily responsible for the administration of European law. However, the Union is entitled to establish a centralised enforcement machinery, '[w]here uniform conditions for implementing legally binding Union acts are needed'.[169] The Union's administrative powers are, however, subject to the principle of subsidiarity. This follows from Article 5 (3) TEU, which subjects all Union action to this constitutional safeguard of federalism. By contrast, in order to ensure a degree of uniformity in the decentralised enforcement of European law, the Union legal order has tried to place the national administrative autonomy into a Union constitutional frame. This has occasionally meant that national administrations must take the findings of other national administrations into account. Alternatively, the Court and the Union legislator have tried to establish European minimum standards that govern national administrative procedures. This has happened through positive harmonisation as well as the principles of equivalence and effectiveness. The two principles will be discussed in – much – more detail in Chapter 11 in the context of the judicial enforcement of European law by national courts.

---

[169] Article 291 (2) TFEU.

8

Judicial Powers: Competences and Procedures

Contents

Introduction		259
1. Annulment powers: judicial review		262
	(a) The existence of a 'reviewable' act	263
	(b) Legitimate grounds for review	264
	(i) 'Formal' and 'substantive' grounds	265
	(ii) In particular: the proportionality principle	267
	(c) Legal standing before the European Court	268
	(i) The Rome formulation and its judicial interpretation	270
	(ii) The Lisbon formulation and its interpretative problems	273
	(d) The indirect review of European law	275
	(i) Collateral review: the plea of illegality	275
	(ii) Indirect review through preliminary rulings	276
2. Remedial powers: liability actions		278
	(a) Procedural conditions: from dependent to independent action	279
	(b) Substantive conditions: from *Schöppenstedt* to *Bergaderm*	280
3. Adjudicatory powers I: enforcement actions		283
	(a) Enforcement actions against Member States	283
	(i) The procedural conditions under Article 258 TFEU	283
	(ii) Judicial enforcement through financial sanctions	286
	(b) Enforcement actions against the Union: failure to act	287
4. Adjudicatory powers II: preliminary rulings		289
	(a) Paragraph 1: the jurisdiction of the European Court	291
	(b) Paragraph 2: the conditions for a preliminary ruling	292
	(i) 'Who': national courts and tribunals	293
	(ii) 'What': necessary questions	295
	(c) Paragraph 3: the obligation to refer and '*acte clair*'	296
	(d) The legal nature of preliminary rulings	299
Conclusion		301

Introduction

When compared with the legislative and executive branches, the judiciary looks like their poor relation. The classic civil law tradition considers courts as 'the mouth that pronounces the words of the law, mere passive beings that can moderate neither its force nor its rigour'.[1] And even the common law tradition finds that '[w]hoever attentively considers the different departments of power must perceive, that in a government in which they are separated from each other, the judiciary, from the nature of its functions, will always be *the least dangerous* to the political rights of the constitution; because it will be least in a capacity to annoy or injure them'.[2] Both traditions thus see the judiciary as 'the least dangerous branch'.[3] This philosophy originates in the eighteenth-century view that reduced the judiciary to its *adjudicatory* function: courts merely decide disputes between private or public parties.

The subsequent rise of the judicial function in the nineteenth and twentieth century was the result of two constitutional victories.[4] Courts succeeded to impose their control over the executive branch.[5] And more importantly still, some States would allow for the constitutional review of legislation. In *Marbury* v. *Madison*,[6] the American Supreme Court thus claimed the power to 'un-make' a law adopted by the legislature. It justified its annulment power as follows: 'all those who have framed written constitutions contemplate them as forming the fundamental and paramount law of the nation, and consequently the theory of every such government must be that an act of the legislature, repugnant of the constitution is void'.[7] The judicial 'victories' over the executive and legislative branch reinforced the idea that a State should be governed by the 'rule of law', that is: a legal order that provides for judicial mechanisms to review the 'legality'

---

[1] C. Montesquieu, *The Spirit of the Laws* (A. M. Cohler et al.: transl. and ed.) (Cambridge University Press, 1989), 163.

[2] A. Hamilton, 'Federalist 78' in A. Hamilton et al., *The Federalist* (T. Ball, ed.) (Cambridge University Press, 2003), 377 at 378. The quote continues: 'The judiciary ... has no influence over either the sword or the purse; no direction either of the strength or of the wealth of the society, and can take no active resolution whatever. It may truly be said to have neither Force nor Will, but merely judgment; and must ultimately depend upon the aid of the executive arm even for the efficacy of its judgments.'

[3] For a famous analysis of this claim, see: A. Bickel, *The Least Dangerous Branch: Supreme Court at the Bar of Politics* (Yale University Press, 1986).

[4] For a comparative constitutional perspective on the rise of the judiciary, see: M. Cappelletti, *Judicial Review in the Contemporary World* (Bobbs-Merrill, 1971); and for a shorter version: Cappelletti, 'The "Mighty Problem" of Judicial Review and the Contribution of Comparative Analysis' [1979] 2 *Legal Issues of Economic Integration* 1.

[5] In some legal orders – like the United Kingdom – judicial review is limited to the review of executive law. Based on the idea of a 'sovereign Parliament', British courts are traditionally not entitled to annul parliamentary acts. On the classic British position, see: A. Dicey, *Introduction to the Study of the Law of the Constitution* (Liberty Fund, 1982).

[6] *Marbury* v. *Madison*, 5 US 137 (1803). For the historical context of the decision, see: W. E. Nelson, *Marbury v. Madison: The Origins and Legacy of Judicial Review* (University Press of Kansas, 2000).

[7] *Marbury* v. *Madison* (supra n. 6) 177.

of all governmental acts. And this idea would, in some legal orders, include the sanctioning power of the judiciary to order a State to make good a damage caused by a public 'wrong'.[8]

A modern definition of the judicial power will thus need to include three core functions, which – in descending order – are: the power to *annul* legislative or executive acts, the power to *remedy* public wrongs through governmental liability, and the power to *adjudicate* legal disputes between parties. This chapter discusses all three types of 'judicial' powers in the context of the European Union. Section 1 starts with an analysis of the annulment power of the European Court. The power of judicial review is the founding stone of a Union 'based on the rule of law'.[9] Section 2 moves to the remedial power of the European Court,[10] and the question when the Union will be liable to pay damages for an illegal action. Finally, Sections 3 and 4 investigate the Court's judicial power to adjudicate disputes between parties. The Treaties here distinguish between direct and indirect actions. Direct actions start directly in the European Court; whereas indirect actions start in the national courts and involve the European Court only indirectly in the dispute. The two direct actions discussed in Section 3 are both infringement actions designed to 'enforce' the Treaties against the Member States and the Union respectively. By contrast, the Treaties acknowledge an indirect action in the form of the preliminary reference procedure. The procedure is the judicial cornerstone of the Union's cooperative federalism. For it combines the *central* interpretation with the *decentralised* application of European law in a single case.

This chapter naturally cannot discuss all judicial competences of the European Court. A collection of them can be found in that part of the Treaty on the Functioning of the European Union dealing with the Court of Justice of the European Union.[11]

Within this part, we also find two general jurisdictional limitations on the European Court: Articles 275 and 276 TFEU. The former declares that the European Court 'shall *not* have jurisdiction with respect to the provisions relating to the common foreign and security policy nor with respect to acts

---

[8] This challenged the classic common law principle that the 'sovereign can do no wrong'. In the words of W. Blackstone, *Commentaries on the Laws of England* (Forgotten Books, 2010), Book III – Chapter 17, 254: 'That the king can do no wrong, is a necessary and fundamental principle of the English constitution: meaning only, as has formerly been observed, that, in the first place, whatever may be amiss in the conduct of public affairs is not chargeable.'

[9] See Case 294/83, *Parti écologiste 'Les Verts' v. European Parliament*, [1986] ECR 1339, para. 23: 'The European [Union] is a [union] based on the rule of law, inasmuch as neither its Member States nor its institutions can avoid a review of the question whether the measures adopted by them are in conformity with the basic constitutional charter, the [Treaties].'

[10] The remedial powers of the national courts for breaches of European law by the Member States will be discussed in Chapter 11 – Section 4 below.

[11] Part Six – Title I – Chapter 1 – Section 5 TFEU. The Section is – roughly – divided into an 'institutional' part (Articles 251–257 TFEU), and a 'competence and procedure' part (Articles 258–281 TFEU).

Table 12 Judicial Competences and Procedures

Judicial Competences and Procedures (Articles 258 – 281 TFEU)			
Article 258	**Enforcement Action brought by the Commission**	Article 269	Jurisdiction for Article 7 TEU
Article 259	Enforcement Action brought by another Member State	Article 270	Jurisdiction in Staff Cases
Article 260	**Action for a Failure to Comply with a Court Judgment**	Article 271	Jurisdiction for Cases involving the European Investment Bank and the European Central Bank
Article 261	Jurisdiction for Penalties in Regulations	Article 272	Jurisdiction granted by Arbitration Clauses
Article 262	(Potential) Jurisdiction for Disputes relating to European intellectual property rights	Article 273	Jurisdiction granted by Special Agreement between the Member States
Article 263	**Action for Judicial Review**	Article 274	Jurisdiction of national courts involving the Union
Article 265	**(Enforcement) Action for the Union's Failure to Act**	Article 275	Non-Jurisdiction for the Union's Common Foreign and Security Policy
Article 267	**Preliminary Rulings**	Article 276	Jurisdictional Limits within the Area of Freedom, Security and Justice
Article 268	**Jurisdiction in Damages Actions under Article 340**	**Article 277**	**Collateral (Judicial) Review for acts of general application**

adopted on the basis of those provisions'.[12] Yet, there are two exceptions within that exception. First, the Court is allowed to review acts adopted under the Union's CFSP, where it is claimed that they should have been adopted within one of the Union's special external policies.[13] Second, a CFSP act is reviewable, where it is claimed to restrict the rights of a natural or legal person.[14] By contrast, Article 276 TFEU decrees that the European Court 'shall have *no* jurisdiction to review the validity or proportionality of operations carried out by the police or other law-enforcement services of a Member State or the exercise of the responsibilities incumbent upon Member States with regard to the maintenance of law and order and the safeguarding of internal security'.[15] These two 'holes' in the judicial competences of the Court are deeply regrettable, for they both replace the 'rule of law' with the rule of the executive.[16]

---

[12] Article 275 (1) TFEU (emphasis added).

[13] Article 275 (2) TFEU. On the 'borderline' provision of Article 40 TEU, see: Chapter 6 – Section 1 (d) above.

[14] Article 275 (2) TFEU.   [15] Article 276 TFEU (emphasis added).

[16] For a third – but temporal – jurisdiction 'hole', see: Article 10 of Protocol (No. 36) 'On Transitional Provisions': 'the powers of the Court of Justice of the European Union under

1. Annulment powers: judicial review

The most powerful function of a court is the power to 'un-make' law, that is: to annul an act that was adopted by the legislative or executive branches. The competence and procedure for judicial review in the European Union legal order is set out in Article 263 TFEU. The provision reads:

> [1] The Court of Justice of the European Union shall review the legality of legislative acts, of acts of the Council, of the Commission and of the European Central Bank, other than recommendations and opinions, and of acts of the European Parliament and of the European Council intended to produce legal effects vis-à-vis third parties. It shall also review the legality of acts of bodies, offices or agencies of the Union intended to produce legal effects vis-à-vis third parties.
>
> [2] It shall for this purpose have jurisdiction in actions brought by a Member State, the European Parliament, the Council or the Commission on grounds of lack of competence, infringement of an essential procedural requirement, infringement of the Treaties or of any rule of law relating to their application, or misuse of powers.
>
> [3] The Court shall have jurisdiction under the same conditions in actions brought by the Court of Auditors, by the European Central Bank and by the Committee of the Regions for the purpose of protecting their prerogatives.
>
> [4] Any natural or legal person may, under the conditions laid down in the first and second paragraphs, institute proceedings against an act addressed to that person or which is of direct and individual concern to them, and against a regulatory act which is of direct concern to them and does not entail implementing measures . . .
>
> [6] The proceedings provided for in this Article shall be instituted within two months of the publication of the measure, or of its notification to the plaintiff, or, in the absence thereof, of the day on which it came to the knowledge of the latter, as the case may be.[17]

Where an action for judicial review is well founded, the Court of Justice 'shall declare the acts concerned to be void'.[18] The Union will henceforth 'be required

---

Title VI of the Treaty on European Union, in the version in force before the entry into force of the Treaty of Lisbon, shall remain the same, including where they have been accepted under Article 35(2) of the [old] Treaty on European Union'. However, this transitional regime for the area of police cooperation and judicial cooperation in criminal matters will definitely end five years after the entry into force of the Lisbon Treaty, that is, 1 December 2014.

[17] The omitted paragraph 5 lays down special rules for Union agencies and bodies. It states: 'Acts setting up bodies, offices and agencies of the Union may lay down specific conditions and arrangements concerning actions brought by natural or legal persons against acts of these bodies, offices or agencies intended to produce legal effects in relation to them.' The following Section will not deal with this special aspect of judicial review. For an overview, see: J. Saurer, 'Individualrechtsschutz gegen das Handeln der Europäischen Agenturen' [2010] 45 *Europarecht* 51.

[18] Article 264 (1) TFEU. However, according to Article 264 (2) TFEU, the Court can – exceptionally – 'if it considers this necessary, state which of the effects of the act which it has declared void shall be considered as definitive'.

to take the necessary measures to comply with the judgment of the Court of Justice of the European Union';[19] and may even be subject to compensation for damage caused by the illegal act.[20] But what are the procedural requirements for a judicial review action? Article 263 follows a complex structure; and the easiest way to understand its logic is to break it down into four constituent components. Paragraph 1 concerns the question *whether* the Court has the power to review particular types of Union acts. Paragraph 2 tells us *why* there can be judicial review, that is: on what grounds one can challenge the legality of a European act. Paragraphs 2–4 concern the question of *who* may ask for judicial review and thereby distinguishes between three classes of applicants. Finally, paragraph 6 tells us *when* an application for review must be made, namely, within two months. After that, a Union act should – theoretically – be immune and permanent. But matters are not that simple. For while direct review is henceforth expired, an applicant may still be entitled to challenge the legality of a Union act *indirectly*.

This section looks at the first three constitutional components before analysing two indirect routes to the judicial review of European law.

(a) The existence of a 'reviewable' act

Paragraph 1 determines whether there can be judicial review. This question has two dimensions. The first dimension relates to *whose* acts may be challenged; the second dimension clarifies *which* acts might be reviewed.

Whose acts can be challenged in judicial review proceedings? According to Article 263 (1) TFEU, the Court is entitled to review 'legislative acts', that is: acts whose joint authors are the European Parliament and the Council. It can also review unilateral acts of all Union institutions and bodies, except for the Court of Auditors. By contrast, the Court cannot judicially review acts of the Member States. And this prohibition includes unilateral national acts, as well as international agreements of the Member States. The European Treaties thus cannot – despite their being the foundation of European law – be reviewed by the Court. For as collective acts of the Member States, they cannot be attributed to the Union institutions,[21] and as such are beyond the review powers of the European Court.

Which acts of the Union institutions can be reviewed? Instead of a positive definition, Article 263 (1) only tells us which acts *cannot* be reviewed. Accordingly, there can be no judicial review for 'recommendations' or 'opinions'. The reason for this exclusion is that both instruments 'have no binding

---

[19] Article 266 TFEU.   [20] Articles 268 and 340 TFEU. On this point, see: Section 2 below.

[21] The European Treaties are not primary legislation of the Union! On the principles governing the 'authorship' of European law, see: R. Schütze, 'The Morphology of Legislative Power in the European Community: Legal Instruments and the Federal Division of Powers' [2006] 25 YEL 91.

force',[22] and there is thus no need to challenge their *legality*.[23] The provision equally excludes judicial review for acts of the European Parliament, the European Council, and of other Union bodies not 'intended to produce legal effects vis-à-vis third parties'. The rationale behind this limitation is that it excludes acts that are 'internal' to an institution. And despite being textually limited to *some* Union institutions, the requirement of an 'external' effect has been extended to all Union acts. The Court has thus clarified that purely preparatory acts of the Commission or the Council cannot be challenged. '[A]n act is open to review only if it is a measure definitely laying down the position of the Commission or the Council'.[24] In a legislative or executive procedure involving several stages, all preparatory acts are consequently considered 'internal' acts; and as such cannot be reviewed.[25] But apart from this insistence on a legal effect outside the Union institution(s), the Court has embraced a wide definition of which acts may be reviewed. The nature of the act would thereby be irrelevant. In *ERTA*,[26] the Court thus found:

> Since the only matters excluded from the scope of the action for annulment open to the Member States and the institutions are 'recommendations or opinions' – which by the final paragraph of Article [288 TFEU] are declared to have no binding force – Article [263 TFEU] treats as acts open to review by the Court all measures adopted by the institutions which are intended to have legal force. The objective of this review is to ensure, as required by Article [19 TEU], observance of the law in the interpretation and application of the Treaty. It would be inconsistent with this objective to interpret the conditions under which the action is admissible so restrictively as to limit the availability of this procedure merely to the categories of measures referred to by Article [288 TFEU]. An action for annulment must therefore be available in the case of all measures adopted by the institutions, whatever their nature or form, which are intended to have legal effects.[27]

The Court's wide review jurisdiction is however externally limited by Articles 275 and 276 TFEU – as discussed in the Introduction to this chapter, above.

(b) Legitimate grounds for review

Not every reason is a sufficient reason to request judicial review. While the existence of judicial review is an essential element of all political orders subject

---

[22] Article 288 (5) TFEU.

[23] Strangely, sometimes such 'soft law' may however have 'legal' effects. On this point see: L. Senden, *Soft Law in European Community Law* (Hart, 2004).

[24] Case 60/81, *International Business Machines (IBM)* v. *Commission*, [1981] ECR 2639, para.10.

[25] However, the Court clarified that preparatory acts can indirectly be reviewed once the (final) 'external act' is challenged (*ibid.*, para.12): 'Furthermore, it must be noted that whilst measures of a purely preparatory character may not themselves be the subject of an application for a declaration that they are void, any legal defects therein may be relied upon in an action directed against the definitive act for which they represent a preparatory step.'

[26] Case 22/70, *Commission* v. *Council (ERTA)*, [1971] ECR 263.   [27] *Ibid.*, paras. 39–42.

to the 'rule of law', the extent of judicial review will differ depending on whether a procedural or a substantive version is chosen. The British legal order has traditionally followed a *procedural* definition of the rule of law. Accordingly, courts are (chiefly) entitled to review whether in the adoption of an act the respective legislative or executive procedures have been followed.[28] The 'merit' or 'substance' of a legislative act is here beyond the review powers of the courts. By contrast, the American constitutional order has traditionally followed a *substantive* definition of the rule of law. Courts are here obliged to review the content of a legislative act, in particular, whether it violates fundamental human rights as guaranteed in the Constitution. A substantive rule of law entails the danger of a 'government of judges', that is: the government of philosophical guardians whose views might not reflect the democratic will of the political community. Yet many modern States recognise the need for non-majoritarian institutions to protect individual rights against the 'tyranny of the multitude'.[29]

For the European legal order, Article 263 (2) TFEU limits judicial review to four legitimate grounds: 'lack of competence', 'infringement of an essential procedural requirement', 'infringement of the Treaties or any rule of law relating to their application', and 'misuse of powers'. Do these reasons indicate whether the Union subscribes to a formal or substantive rule of law?

Let us look at this general question first, before analysing the principle of proportionality as a specific ground of review.

(i) 'Formal' and 'substantive' grounds

The Union legal order recognises three 'formal' grounds of review.

First, a European act can be challenged on the ground that the Union lacked the competence to adopt it. The ultra vires review of European law thereby extends to primary and secondary legislation. The review of the former originates in the principle of conferral.[30] Since the Union may only exercise those powers conferred on it by the Treaties, any action beyond these powers is ultra vires and thus voidable.[31] With regard to secondary legislation, the Court may not only review whether the delegate has acted within the scope of the powers delegated, but it must also ensure that the absolute limits to such a delegation have not been violated.[32] This follows not from the (vertical) principal of

---

[28] A. W. Bradley and K. D. Ewing, *Constitutional and Administrative Law* (Pearson, 2003), Chapters 30 and 31.

[29] The phrase is attributed to E. Burke. For an overview of Burke's thought, see: L. Gottschalk, 'Reflections on Burke's Reflections on the French Revolution' [1956] 100 *Proceedings of the American Philosophical Society* 417.

[30] On the principle of conferral, see: Chapter 5 – Section 1 above.

[31] The European Court has traditionally been reluctant to declare Union legislation void on the ground of lack of competence. This judicial passivity stemmed from the Court's unwillingness to interfere with a consensual decision of the Member States in the Council. On the 'culture of consent' after the Luxembourg compromise, see: Chapter 1 – Section 2(b) above.

[32] On the delegation doctrine in the Union legal order, see: Chapter 7 – Section 2(a) above.

conferral, but from the (horizontal) principle protecting the institutional balance of powers within the Union.[33]

Second, a Union act can be challenged if it infringes an essential procedural requirement. According to this second ground of review, not all procedural irregularities may invalidate a Union act but only those that are 'essential'. When are 'essential' procedural requirements breached? The constitutional principles developed under this jurisdictional head are the result of an extensive 'legal basis litigation'.[34] An essential procedural step is breached when the Union adopts an act under a procedure that leaves out an institution that was entitled to be involved.[35] Alternatively, the Union may have adopted an act on the basis of a wrong voting arrangement *within* one institution. Thus, where the Council voted by unanimity instead of a qualified majority, an essential procedural requirement is breached.[36] By contrast, no essential procedural requirement is infringed when the Union acts under a 'wrong' competence, which nonetheless envisages an identical legislative procedure.[37] One prominent provision in the context of essential procedural requirements moreover is Article 296 TFEU, which imposes a 'duty to state reasons' on the European Union when adopting European law.[38]

The third formal ground of review is 'misuse of powers', which has remained relatively obscure.[39] The subjective rationale behind it is the prohibition on pursuing a different objective from the one underpinning the legal competence.[40]

Finally, a Union act can be challenged on the ground that it represents an 'infringement of the Treaties or any other rule of law relating to their application'. This constitutes a 'residual' ground of review. The European Court has used this residual ground of review as a constitutional gate to import a range of 'unwritten' general principles into the Union legal order.[41] These principles include, inter alia, the principles of legal certainty and legitimate expectations.[42]

---

[33] On the principle of institutional balance, see: Chapter 3 – Section 1 (a) above.

[34] On the phenomenon of 'legal basis litigation' in the Union legal order, see: H. Cullen and A. Worth, 'Diplomacy by other Means: the Use of Legal Basis Litigation as a Political Strategy by the European Parliament and Member States' [1999] 36 CML Rev 1243.

[35] See Case 22/70, *Commission v. Council (ERTA)*, [1971] ECR 263, as well as: Case C-70/88, *Parliament v. Council (Chernobyl)*, [1990] ECR I-2041.

[36] See Case 68/86, *United Kingdom v. Council*, [1988] ECR 855; as well as: Case C-300/89, *Commission v. Council*, [1991] ECR I-2867.

[37] Case 165/87, *Commission v. Council*, [1988] ECR 5545, para.19: 'only a purely formal defect which cannot make the measure void'.

[38] Article 296 TFEU – second indent: 'Legal acts shall state the reasons on which they are based and shall refer to any proposals, initiatives, recommendations, requests or opinions required by the Treaties.' On this provision, see: Chapter 5 – Section 3(a) above.

[39] For a more extensive discussion of this ground of review, see: H. Schermers and D. Waelbroeck, *Judicial Protection in the European Union* (Kluwer, 2001), 402 et seq.

[40] See Joined Cases 18 and 35/65, *Gutmann v. Commission*, [1965] ECR 103.

[41] On the general principles in the Union legal order see: T. Tridimas, *The General Principles of EU Law* (Oxford University Press, 2007).

[42] For both principles, see: *ibid.*, Chapter 6.

And the introduction of these principles has added a *substantive* dimension to the rule of law in the European Union.[43] For it has been used to review the content of Union legislation against fundamental rights.[44] One expression of the Union's choice in favour of the substantive dimension of the rule of law is the principle of proportionality.

(ii) In particular: the proportionality principle

The constitutional function of the proportionality principle is to protect liberal values.[45] It constitutes one of the 'oldest' general principles of the Union legal order.[46] Beginning its career as an unwritten principle, the proportionality principle is now codified in Article 5 (4) TEU: 'Under the principle of proportionality, the content and form of Union action shall not exceed what is necessary to achieve the objectives of the Treaties.'[47] The proportionality principle has been characterised as 'the most far-reaching ground for review', and 'the most potent weapon in the arsenal of the public law judge'.[48] (But, as we saw above, the Treaties expressly limit its pervasive power in Article 276 TFEU with regard to police operations in the area of freedom, security and justice.[49])

How will the Court assess the proportionality of a Union act? In the past, the Court has developed a proportionality test. In its most elaborate form, the test follows a tripartite structure.[50] It analyses the *suitability*, *necessity*, and

---

[43] For an express confirmation that the Union legal order subscribes to the substantive rule of law version, see: Case C-367/95P, *Commission* v. *Sytraval and Brink's*, [1998] ECR I-1719, para. 67; as well as: Case C-378/00, *Commission* v. *Parliament and Council*, [2003] ECR I-937, para. 34.

[44] On the emergence of fundamental rights as general principles of Union law, see: Chapter 12 – Section 1 below.

[45] On the origins of the proportionality principle, see: J. Schwarze, *European Administrative Law* (Sweet & Maxwell, 2006), 678–9.

[46] An implicit acknowledgement of the principle may be found in Case 8/55, *Fédération Charbonnière de Belgique* v. *High Authority of the ECSC*, [1955] ECR (English Special Edition) 245 at 306: 'not exceed the limits of what is strictly necessary'.

[47] The provision continues: 'The institutions of the Union shall apply the principle of proportionality as laid down in the Protocol on the application of the principles of subsidiarity and proportionality.'

[48] Tridimas, *General Principles* (supra n. 41), 140.

[49] Article 276 TFEU states (emphasis added): 'In exercising its powers regarding the provisions of Chapters 4 and 5 of Title V of Part Three relating to the area of freedom, security and justice, the Court of Justice of the European Union shall have no jurisdiction to review the validity *or proportionality of operations* carried out by the police or other law-enforcement services of a Member State or the exercise of the responsibilities incumbent upon Member States with regard to the maintenance of law and order and the safeguarding of internal security.'

[50] See Case C-331/88, *The Queen* v. *Minister of Agriculture, Fisheries and Food and Secretary of State for Health, ex parte Fedesa and others*, [1990] ECR I-4023, para. 13: '[T]he principle of proportionality is one of the general principles of [Union] law. By virtue of that principle, the lawfulness of the prohibition of an economic activity is subject to the condition that the prohibitory measures are appropriate and necessary in order to achieve the objectives legitimately pursued by the legislation in question; when there is a choice between several appropriate measures recourse must be had to the least onerous, and the disadvantages caused must not be disproportionate to the aims pursued.'

proportionality (in the strict sense) of a Union act. (However, the Court does not always distinguish between the second and third prong.) Within its suitability review, the Court will check whether the European measure was suitable to achieve a given objective. This might be extremely straightforward.[51] The necessity test is, on the other hand, more demanding. The Union will have to show that the act adopted represents the least restrictive means to achieve a given objective. Finally, even the least restrictive means to achieve a public policy objective might disproportionately interfere with individual rights. Proportionality in a strict sense thus weighs whether the burden imposed on an individual is excessive or not.

While this tripartite test may – in theory – be hard to satisfy, the Court has granted the Union a wide margin of appreciation wherever it enjoys a sphere of discretion. The legality of a discretionary act will only be affected 'if the measure is manifestly inappropriate'.[52] This relaxed standard of review has meant that the European Court rarely finds a Union measure to be disproportionately interfering with fundamental rights. However, we find a good illustration of a disproportionate Union act in *Kadi*.[53] In its fight against international terrorism, the Union had adopted a Regulation freezing the assets of people suspected to be associated with Al-Qaeda. The applicant alleged, inter alia, that the Union act disproportionately restricted his right to property. The Court held that the right to property was not absolute and 'the exercise of the right to property may be restricted, provided that those restrictions in fact correspond to objectives of public interest pursued by the [Union] and do not constitute, in relation to the aim pursued, a disproportionate and intolerable interference, impairing the very substance of the right so guaranteed'.[54] And this required that 'a fair balance has been struck between the demands of the public interest and the interest of the individuals concerned'.[55] This fair balance had not been struck for the applicant;[56] and the Union act would, so far as it concerned the applicant,[57] have to be annulled.

(c) Legal standing before the European Court

The Treaties distinguish between three types of applicants in three distinct paragraphs of Article 263 TFEU.

---

[51] For a rare example, where the test is not satisfied, see: Case C-368/89, *Crispoltoni* v. *Fattoria autonoma tabacchi di Città di Castello*, [1991] ECR I-3695, esp. para. 20.

[52] Case C-331/88 (*supra* n. 50), para. 14. See also: Case C-122/95, *Germany* v. *Council (Bananas)*, [1998] ECR I-973, para. 79.

[53] Case C-402/05P, *Kadi and Al Barakaat International Foundation* v. *Council and Commission*, [2008] ECR I-6351.

[54] *Ibid.*, para. 355.   [55] *Ibid.*, para. 360.   [56] *Ibid.*, para. 371.

[57] *Ibid.*, para. 372. However, the Court found that the Union act as such could, in principle, be justified (*ibid.*, para. 366).

Paragraph 2 mentions the applicants that can always bring an action for judicial review. These 'privileged' applicants are: the Member States, the European Parliament,[58] the Council, and the Commission. The reason for their privileged status is that they are *ex officio* deemed to be affected by the adoption of a Union act.[59]

Paragraph 3 lists applicants that are 'semi-privileged'. These are the Court of Auditors, the European Central Bank and the Committee of the Regions.[60] They are 'partly privileged', as they may solely bring review proceedings 'for the purpose of protecting their prerogatives'.[61]

Paragraph 4 – finally – addresses the standing of natural or legal persons. These applicants are 'non-privileged' applicants, as they must demonstrate that the Union act affects them specifically. This fourth paragraph has been highly contested in the past fifty years. And in order to make sense of the European Court's past jurisprudence, we must start with a historical analysis of its 'Rome formulation', before moving to the current 'Lisbon formulation' of that paragraph.

---

[58] Under the original Rome Treaty, the European Parliament was not a privileged applicant. The reason for this lay in its mere 'consultative' role in the adoption of Union law. With the rise of parliamentary involvement after the Single European Act, this position became constitutionally problematic. How could Parliament cooperate or even co-decide in the legislative process, yet not be able to challenge an act that infringed its procedural prerogatives? To close this constitutional gap, the Court judicially 'amended' ex-Article 173 EEC by giving the Parliament the status of a 'semi-privileged' applicant (see Case 70/88, *Parliament v. Council (Chernobyl)*, [1990] ECR I-2041, paras. 24–7: '[T]he Court cannot, of course, include the Parliament among the institutions which may bring an action under [ex-]Article 173 of the EEC Treaty or Article 146 of the Euratom Treaty without being required to demonstrate an interest in bringing an action. However, it is the Court's duty to ensure that the provisions of the Treaties concerning the institutional balance are fully applied and to see to it that the Parliament's prerogatives, like those of the other institutions, cannot be breached without it having available a legal remedy, among those laid down in the Treaties, which may be exercised in a certain and effective manner. The absence in the Treaties of any provision giving the Parliament the right to bring an action for annulment may constitute a procedural gap, but it cannot prevail over the fundamental interest in the maintenance and observance of the institutional balance laid down in the Treaties establishing the European Communities. Consequently, an action for annulment brought by the Parliament against an act of the Council or the Commission is admissible provided that the action seeks only to safeguard its prerogatives and that it is founded only on submissions alleging their infringement.'). This status was codified in the Maastricht Treaty; and the Nice Treaty finally recognised Parliament's status as a fully privileged applicant under ex-Article 230 (2) EC.

[59] One notable absentee from the list of privileged applicants is the European Council. However, its interests are likely to be represented by the Council.

[60] On the right to consultation of the Committee of the Regions, see: Article 307 TFEU. And Article 8 (2) of Protocol (No. 2) 'On the Application of the Principles of Subsidiarity and Proportionality' states: 'In accordance with the rules laid down in the said Article, the Committee of the Regions may also bring such actions against legislative acts for the adoption of which the Treaty on the Functioning of the European Union provides that it be consulted.'

[61] For a definition of this phrase in the context of Parliament's struggle to protect its prerogatives before the Nice Treaty, see: Case C-316/91, *Parliament v. Council*, [1994] ECR I-625; as well as Case C-187/93, *Parliament v. Council*, [1994] ECR I-2857.

(i) The Rome formulation and its judicial interpretation

The Rome Treaty granted individual applicants the right to apply for judicial review in ex-Article 230 EC. Paragraph 4 of that provision allowed any natural or legal person to 'institute proceedings against a *decision* addressed to that person or against a *decision* which, although in the form of a regulation or *decision* addressed to another person, is of *direct and individual concern* to the former'.[62]

This 'Roman' formulation must be understood against the background of two constitutional choices. *First*, the drafters of the Rome Treaty had wished to confine the standing of private parties to challenges of individual 'decisions', that is: administrative acts. The Rome Treaty thereby distinguished between three types of decisions: decisions addressed to the applicant, decisions addressed to another person, and decisions 'in the form of a regulation'. This third decision was a decision 'in substance', which had been put into the wrong legal form.[63] Judicial review was here desirable to avert an abuse of powers. *Second*, not every challenge of a decision by private parties was permitted. Only those decisions that were of 'direct and individual concern' to a private party could be challenged. And while this effect was presumed for decisions addressed to the applicant, it had to be proven for all other decisions. Private applicants were thus 'non-privileged' applicants in a dual sense. Not only could they *not* challenge all legal acts, they were – with the exception of decisions addressed to them – not presumed to have a legitimate interest in challenging the act.

Both constitutional choices severely restricted the standing of private parties and were heavily disputed. In the Union legal order prior to Lisbon, they were subject to an extensive judicial and academic commentary.[64] In a first line of jurisprudence, the Court succeeded significantly to 're-write' ex-Article 230 (4) EC by deserting the text's insistence on a 'decision'. While it had originally paid

---

[62] Ex-Article 230 (4) EC (emphasis added).

[63] On the various instruments in the European legal order, see: Chapter 9 below. On the material distinction between 'decisions' and 'regulations', see: Joined Cases 16–17/62, *Confédération nationale des producteurs de fruits et légumes and others* v. *Council* [1962] ECR 471, where the Court found that the Treaty 'makes a clear distinction between the concept of a 'decision' and that of a 'regulation' (*ibid.*, 478). Regulations were originally considered the sole 'generally applicable' instrument of the European Union, and their general character distinguished them from individual decisions. The crucial characteristic of a regulation was the 'openness' of the group of persons to whom it applied. Where the group of persons was 'fixed in time', the Court regarded the European act as a bundle of individual decisions addressed to each member of the group (see Joined Cases 41–44/70, *International Fruit Company and others* v. *Commission*, [1971] ECR 411, esp. para. 17.)

[64] For the academic controversy (in chronological order), see: A. Barav, 'Direct and Individual Concern: an Almost Insurmountable Barrier to the Admissibility of Individual Appeal to the EEC Court' [1974] 11 CML Rev 191; H. Rasmussen, 'Why is Article 173 Interpreted Against Private Plaintiffs?' [1980] 5 EL Rev 112; N. Neuwahl, 'Article 173 Paragraph 4 EC; Past, Present and Possible Future' [1996] 21 EL Rev 17; A. Arnull, 'Private Applicants and the Action for Annulment since *Codorniu*' [2001] 38 CML Rev 8; and A. Ward, *Judicial Review and the Rights of Private Parties in EU law* (Oxford University Press, 2007).

homage to that text in denying private party review of generally applicable acts,[65] the Court famously abandoned its classic test and clarified that the general nature of the Union act was irrelevant. In *Codorniu*,[66] the Court thus found that '[a]lthough it is true that according to the criteria in the [fourth] paragraph of [ex-]Article [230] of the [EC] Treaty the contested provision is, by nature and by virtue of its sphere of application, of a legislative nature in that it applies to the traders concerned in general, that does not prevent it from being of individual concern to some of them'.[67] This judicial 'amendment' cut the Gordian knot between the 'executive' nature of an act and ex-Article 230 (4) EC. Private parties could thus challenge a single provision within *any* legal act – even generally applicable acts like regulations or directives – as long as they could demonstrate 'direct and individual concern'.

This brings us to the second famous battleground under ex-Article 230 (4) EC. What was the meaning of the 'direct and individual concern' formula? The criterion of direct concern was taken to mean that the contested measure *as such* would have to affect the position of the applicant.[68] Sadly, the criterion of 'individual concern' was less straightforward. It was given an authoritative interpretation in *the* seminal case on the standing of private parties under ex-Article 230 (4) EC: the *Plaumann* case. Plaumann, an importer of clementines, had challenged a Commission decision refusing to lower European customs duties on that fruit. But since the decision was not addressed to him – it was addressed to his Member State: Germany – he had to demonstrate that the decision was of 'individual concern' to him. The European Court defined the criterion as follows:

> Persons other than those to whom a decision is addressed may only claim to be individually concerned if that decision affects them by reason of certain attributes which are peculiar to them or by reason of circumstances in which they are

---

[65] The Court's classic test concentrated on whether – from a material point of view – the challenged act was a 'real' regulation. The 'test' is spelled out in Case 790/79, *Calpak* v. *Commission*, [1980] ECR 1949, paras. 8–9: 'By virtue of the second paragraph of Article [288] of the Treaty [on the Functioning of the European Union] the criterion for distinguishing between a regulation and a decision is whether the measure at issue is of general application or not ... A provision which limits the granting of production aid for all producers in respect of a particular product to a uniform percentage of the quantity produced by them during a uniform preceding period is by nature a measure of general application within the meaning of Article [288] of the Treaty. In fact the measure applies to objectively determined situations and produces legal effects with regard to categories of persons described in a generalised and abstract manner. The nature of the measure as a regulation is not called into question by the mere fact that it is possible to determine the number or even the identity of the producers to be granted the aid which is limited thereby.'

[66] Case C-309/89, *Codorniu* v. *Council*, [1994] ECR I-1853.

[67] *Ibid.*, para. 19. See also: Case 76/01P, *Eurocoton et al.* v. *Council*, [2003] ECR I-10091, para. 73: 'Although regulations imposing anti-dumping duties are legislative in nature and scope, in that they apply to all economic operators, they may nevertheless be of individual concern[.]'

[68] See Case 294/83, *Les Verts* (supra n. 9), para. 31: 'The contested measures are of direct concern to the applicant association. They constitute a complete set of rules which are sufficient in themselves and which require no implementing provisions.'

differentiated from all other persons and by virtue of these factors distinguishes them individually just as in the case of the person addressed.[69]

This formulation became famous as the 'Plaumann test'. If private applicants wish to challenge an act not addressed to them, it is not sufficient to rely on the adverse – absolute – effects that the act has on them. Instead, they must show that – relative to everybody else – the effects of the act are 'peculiar to them'. This *relational* standard insists that they must be 'differentiated from all other persons'. The applicants must be *singled* out as if they were specifically addressed. In the present case, the Court denied this *individual* concern, as Plaumann was seen to be only *generally* concerned 'as an importer of clementines, that is to say, by reason of a commercial activity which may at any time be practised by any person'.[70] The *Plaumann* test is therefore *very* strict: whenever a private party is a member of an 'open group' of persons – anybody could decide to become an importer of clementines tomorrow – legal standing under ex-Article 230 (4) EC was denied.[71]

Unsurprisingly, this restrictive reading of private party standing was heavily criticised as an unjustified limitation on an individual's fundamental right to judicial review.[72] And the Court would partly soften its stance in specific areas of European law.[73] However, it generally refused to introduce a more liberal approach to the standing of private applicants until the Lisbon Treaty. In *Unión de Pequeños Agricultores (UPA)*,[74] the Court indeed expressly rejected over-ruling its own jurisprudence on the – disingenuous[75] – ground that '[w]hile it is, admittedly, possible to envisage a system of judicial review of the legality of [Union] measures of general application different from that established by the founding Treaty and never amended as to its principles, it is for the Member States, if necessary, in accordance with Article 48 TEU, to reform the system currently in force'.[76]

---

[69] Case 25/62, *Plaumann* v. *Commission*, [1963] ECR 95 at 107.   [70] *Ibid.*

[71] Even assuming that Plaumann was the only clementine importer in Germany at the time of the decision, the category of 'clementine importers' was open: future German importers could wish to get involved in the clementine trade. Will there ever be 'closed groups' in light of this definition? For the Court's approach in this respect, see: Case 100/74, *CAM* v. *Commission*, [1975] ECR 1393; as well as: Case 11/82, *Piraiki-Patraiki and others* v. *Commission*, [1985] ECR 207.

[72] See Article 6 of the European Convention of Human Rights: 'In the determination of his civil rights and obligations or of any criminal charge against him, everyone is entitled to a fair and public hearing within a reasonable time by an independent and impartial tribunal established by law.'

[73] This had happened – for example – in the area of European competition law; see Case 26/76, *Metro-SB-Großmärkte* v. *Commission*, [1977] ECR 1875.

[74] Case C-50/00, *Unión de Pequeños Agricultores, (UPA)* v. *Council*, [2002] ECR I-6677.

[75] The *Plaumann* test is a result of the Court's own interpretation of what 'individual concern' means, and the Court could have therefore – theoretically – 'overruled' itself. This has indeed happened in other areas of European law; see Joined Cases C-267/91 and C-268/91, *Criminal proceedings against Keck and Mithouard*, [1993] ECR I-6097.

[76] Case C-50/00, *UPA* v. *Council* (supra n. 74), para. 45.

Has this – requested – constitutional reform taken place? Let us look at the Lisbon formulation dealing with the standing of private parties.

(ii) The Lisbon formulation and its interpretative problems

The Lisbon Treaty has substantially amended the Rome formulation. The standing of private parties is now enshrined in Article 263 (4) TFEU, which allows any natural or legal person to 'institute proceedings against an *act* addressed to that person or which is of *direct and individual concern* to them, and against a *regulatory act* which is of direct concern to them and does not entail implementing measures'.[77]

The new formulation of paragraph 4 textually recognises the judicial decoupling of private party standing from the nature of the Union act challenged. In codifying *Codorniu*, an individual can thus potentially challenge any Union 'act' with legal effects. However, depending on the nature of the act, Article 263 (4) TFEU still distinguishes three scenarios. Decisions addressed to the applicant can automatically be challenged. For 'regulatory' acts, the private party must prove 'direct concern'.[78] For all other acts, the applicant must continue to show 'direct *and* individual concern'. The Lisbon amendments thus abandoned the requirement of an 'individual concern' only for the second but not the third category of acts. The dividing line between the second and third category is indeed poised to become *the* post-Lisbon interpretative battlefield within Article 263 (4) TFEU.

What are 'regulatory acts'? The term is not defined in the Treaties. Two interpretative options exist. According to a first view, the concept of 'regulatory acts' is positively defined as all 'generally applicable acts'.[79] This reading liberalises the standing of private applicants significantly, as the second category would materially cover legislative as well as executive acts of a general nature. According to a second view, the concept must be negatively defined in contradistinction to 'legislative acts'. Regulatory acts are understood as

---

[77] Article 263 (4) TFEU (emphasis added).

[78] This should theoretically mean that no implementing act is needed. Why then does Article 263 (4) TFEU repeat this expressly? The answer might lie in the prior jurisprudence of the Court. On the criterion of direct concern, see here: Case C-417/04 P, *Regione Siciliana* v. *Commission*, [2006] ECR I-3881, para. 28: 'the fourth paragraph of [ex-]Article 230 EC, requires the contested [Union] measure to affect directly the legal situation of the individual and leave no discretion to its addressees, who are entrusted with the task of implementing it, such implementation being purely automatic and resulting from [Union] rules without the application of other intermediate rules'. The Court was thus not concerned whether there was a formal need for implementing measures. It was only interested in whether the act materially determined the situation of the applicant as such. Thus, even a Directive could be potentially of direct concern, see: Case T-135/96, *Union Européenne de l'artisanat et des petites et moyennes entreprises (UEAPME)* v. *Council*, [1998] ECR II-02335. From this perspective, new Article 263 (4) TFEU, and its insistence on the absence of an implementing act, might signal the wish of the Lisbon Treaty-makers to return to a more restrictive – formal – position.

[79] See M. Dougan, 'The Treaty of Lisbon 2007: Winning Minds, not Hearts' [2008] 45 CML Rev 617; and J. Bast, 'Legal Instruments and Judicial Protection' in A. von Bogdandy and J. Bast (eds.), *Principles of European Constitutional Law* (Hart, 2009), 345 at 396.

non-legislative general acts.[80] This view would place acts adopted under the – ordinary or special – legislative procedure outside the second category. The judicial review of formal legislation would consequently require 'direct *and* individual concern', and the latter would thus remain relatively immune from private party challenges. Which of the two options should be chosen by the Court? Legally, the drafting history of Article 263 (4) TFEU is inconclusive.[81] Nor do textual arguments clearly favour one view over the other.[82] And teleological arguments point in both directions – depending which *telos* one prefers. Those favouring individual rights will thus prefer the – wider – first view, whereas those wishing to protect democratic values will prefer the second view.

Regardless of how the Court eventually settles the meaning of 'regulatory acts', the third category of acts still requires a 'direct and individual concern'. Reports on the death of *Plaumann* may thus turn out to be greatly exaggerated.[83] If the Court were to continue its past jurisprudence, what substantive argument could be marshalled against it? The strongest critique of the Plaumann test has come from the pen of Advocate-General Jacobs. In *Unión de Pequeños Agricultores (UPA)*,[84] his learned opinion pointed to the test's anomalous logic. It is indeed absurd that 'the greater the number of persons affected the less likely it is that effective judicial review is available'.[85] What alternative test might then be suitable? 'The only satisfactory solution is therefore to recognise that an applicant is individually concerned by a [Union] measure where the measure has, or is liable to have, a *substantial adverse effect* on his interests.'[86] As we saw above, the Court rejected this reinterpretation on the formal ground that abandoning *Plaumann* would require Treaty amendment. However, the Court also provided a substantive ground to justify its restrictive stance towards private parties:

---

[80] A. Ward, 'The Draft EU Constitution and Private Party Access to Judicial Review of EU Measures' in T. Tridimas and P. Nebbia (eds.), *European Union Law for the Twenty-First Century* (Hart, 2005), 201 at 221; as well as A. Dashwood and A. Johnston, 'The Institutions of the Enlarged EU under the Regime of the Constitutional Treaty' [2004] 41 CML Rev 1481 at 1509.

[81] Final Report of the Discussion Circle on the Court of Justice (CONV 636/03). And see also: M. Varju, 'The Debate on the Future of Standing under Article 230 (4) TEC in the European Convention' [2004] 10 *European Public Law* 43.

[82] A comparison of the different language versions of Article 263 (4) TFEU is not conclusive. Systematic and textual arguments are equally inconclusive. For Article 277 TFEU (on collateral review) uses the term 'act of general application' – a fact that could be taken to mean that the phrase 'regulatory act' is different. However, Article 290 TFEU expressly uses the concept of 'non-legislative acts of general application' – which could, in turn, be taken to mean that 'regulatory act' in Article 263 (4) TFEU must mean something different here too.

[83] On the 'end' of *Plaumann*, see: S. Balthasar, 'Locus Standi Rules for Challenges to Regulatory Acts by Private Applicants: the New Article 263(4) TFEU' [2010] EL Rev 542 at 548; as well as: M. Kottmann, '*Plaumanns* Ende: ein Vorschlag zu Art. 263 Abs. 4 AEUV' [2010] 70 *Zeitschrift für ausländisches öffentliches Recht und Völkerrecht* 547.

[84] Case C-50/00, *UPA* (supra n. 74).

[85] Opinion of Advocate-General Jacobs, in: *ibid.*, para. 59.   [86] *Ibid.*, para. 102 (emphasis added).

By Article [263] and Article [277], on the one hand, and by Article [267], on the other, the Treaty has established a complete system of legal remedies and procedures designed to ensure judicial review of the legality of acts of the institutions, and has entrusted such review to the [Union] Courts. Under that system, where natural or legal persons cannot, by reason of the conditions for admissibility laid down in the fourth paragraph of Article [263] of the Treaty, directly challenge [Union] measures of general application, they are able, depending on the case, either indirectly to plead the invalidity of such acts before the [European] Courts under Article [277] of the Treaty or to do so before the national courts and ask them, since they have no jurisdiction themselves to declare those measures invalid, to make a reference to the Court of Justice for a preliminary ruling on validity.[87]

The Court here justified its restrictive stance on the *direct* review of European law by pointing to its expansive stance on the *indirect* review of European law.[88]

This claim will now be analysed.

(d) The indirect review of European law

(i) Collateral review: the plea of illegality

The first form of indirect review can be found in the 'plea of illegality'.[89] Its procedure is set out in Article 277 TFEU: 'Notwithstanding the expiry of the period laid down in Article 263, sixth paragraph, any party may, in proceedings in which an act of general application adopted by an institution, body, office or agency of the Union is at issue, plead the grounds specified in Article 263, second paragraph, in order to invoke before the Court of Justice of the European Union the inapplicability of that act.'

An applicant can thus invoke the illegality of a Union act in the course of proceedings for a – different – *direct action* under Article 263 TFEU. That is why this form of review is called 'collateral review'. The review is not an independent action, but the primary object of the review proceedings must be a *different* act. This will typically be an act that is related to the collaterally challenged 'parent' act. In the past, the constitutional advantage of the collateral review route was twofold. It not only bypassed the two-month time limit under

---

[87] *Ibid.*, para. 40.

[88] *Ibid.*, paras. 41–2: 'Thus it is for the Member States to establish a system of legal remedies and procedures which ensure respect for the right to effective judicial protection. In that context, in accordance with the principle of sincere cooperation laid down in Article [4(3)] of the [EU] Treaty, national courts are required, so far as is possible, to interpret and apply national procedural rules governing the exercise of rights of action in a way that enables natural and legal persons to challenge before the courts the legality of any decision or other national measure relative to the application to them of a [Union] act of general application, by pleading the invalidity of such an act.' This was confirmed in Case C-263/02P, *Commission* v. *Jégo-Quéré* [2004] ECR I-3425, paras. 31–2. Yet for arguments against this view, see: Opinion of Advocate-General Jacobs (supra n. 74), paras. 38–44.

[89] For an academic discussion of this plea, see: M. Vogt, 'Indirect Judicial Protection in EC Law – the Case of the Plea of Illegality' [2006] 31 EL Rev 364.

Article 263, but it could equally grant individuals the possibility of challenging generally applicable acts, where this would not have been possible under the restrictive reading of ex-Article 230 (4) EC.[90] However, it is unclear whether the non-reviewability of the parent act is a formal requirement for collateral review.[91]

(ii) Indirect review through preliminary rulings

The second form of indirect review of European law may take place under the preliminary reference procedure – discussed in Section 4 below. Under this procedure, the European Court may give rulings on 'the *validity* ... of acts of the institutions, bodies, offices or agencies of the Union'.[92] The complementary nature of the indirect review route of Article 267 TFEU was emphasised by the Court in *Les Verts*:

> Where the [Union] institutions are responsible for the administrative implementation of [European] measures, natural or legal persons may bring a direct action before the Court against implementing measures which are addressed to them or which are of direct and individual concern to them and, in support of such action, plead the illegality of the general measure on which they are based. Where implementation is a matter for the national authorities, such persons may plead the invalidity of general measures before the national courts and cause the latter to request the Court of Justice for a preliminary ruling.[93]

Individuals can thus challenge the legality of a Union act in national courts. Has the indirect review route thus led to a decentralised review system? The traditional answer is in the negative.[94] The European legal order indeed insists on the *exclusive* power of the European Court of Justice to declare European acts invalid. The exclusive jurisdiction is seen as inherent in the Treaties, and was clarified in *Foto-Frost*: 'Since Article [263] gives the Court exclusive jurisdiction to declare void an act of a [Union] institution, the coherence of the system

---

[90] Generally applicable acts could – prior to *Codorniu* – not be challenged, and the Court has thus explained the advantages of the collateral review route as follows (Case 92/78, *Simmenthal* v. *Commission*, [1979] ECR 777, paras. 37 and 41): 'Article [277] of the [FEU] Treaty gives expression to the general principle conferring upon any party to proceedings the right to challenge, for the purpose of obtaining the annulment of a decision of direct and individual concern to that party, the validity of previous acts of the institutions which form the legal basis of the decision which is being attacked, if that party was not entitled under Article [263] of the Treaty to bring a direct action challenging those acts by which it was thus affected without having been in a position to ask that they be declared void ... This wide interpretation of Article [277] derives from the need to provide those persons who are precluded by the [fourth] paragraph of Article [263] from instituting proceedings directly in respect of general acts with the benefit of a judicial review of them at the time when they are affected by implementing decisions which are of direct and individual concern to them.'

[91] See Case C-239/99, *Nachi Europe*, [2001] ECR I-1197.   [92] Article 267 (1) (b) TFEU.

[93] Case 294/83, *Les Verts* (supra n. 9), para. 23.

[94] For a 'modern' re-evaluation of the decentralised review system in the context of the CFSP, see: A. Hinarejos, *Judicial Control in the European Union: Reforming Jurisdiction in the Intergovernmental Pillars* (Oxford University Press, 2009).

requires that where the validity of a [Union] act is challenged before a national court the power to declare that act invalid must also be reserved to the Court of Justice.'[95]

How has the European Court organised the indirect review of European law? First, it has imposed an obligation on all national courts to make a reference to the Court of Justice if in doubt about the validity of the Union act.[96] Second, the Court has 'centralised' the effects of a declaration of invalidity under Article 267 TFEU. In the words of the Court in *International Chemical Corporation*:

> When the Court is moved under Article [267] to declare an act of one of the institutions to be void there are particularly imperative requirements concerning legal certainty in addition to those concerning the uniform application of [European] law. It follows from the very nature of such a declaration that a national court may not apply the act declared to be void without once more creating serious uncertainty as to the [European] law applicable. It follows therefrom that although a judgment of the Court given under Article [267 TFEU] declaring an act of an institution . . . to be void is directly addressed only to the national court which brought the matter before the Court, it is sufficient reason for any other national court to regard that act as void for the purposes of a judgment which it has to give.[97]

The indirect judicial review of Union acts through the preliminary reference procedure has become the Court's favoured option. Why has the Court favoured the indirect review of European law under Article 267 TFEU over its direct review under Article 263 TFEU? The arguments in favour of the indirect review route are straightforward. Indirect challenges may be brought against *any* Union act – even those of a non-binding nature.[98] They can be brought on *any* grounds – even those outside Article 263 (2) TFEU. They can be launched by *anyone* – without regard to 'direct and individual concern'. And – finally – they can be brought at (almost) *any* time.[99]

---

[95] Case 314/85, *Foto-Frost* v. *Hauptzollamt Lübeck-Ost*, [1987] ECR 4199, para. 17. See also: Case C-461/03, *Schul Douane-expediteur*, [2005] ECR I-10513. Under European law, national courts will thereby be entitled, under strict conditions, to grant interim relief (see Case C-466/93, *Atlanta Fruchthandelsgesellschaft mbH and others* v. *Bundesamt für Ernährung und Forstwirtschaft*, [1995] ECR I-3799).

[96] See Case C-344/04, *The Queen on the application of International Air Transport Association et al.* v. *Department of Transport*, [2006] ECR I-403, para. 30.

[97] Case 66/80, *International Chemical Corporation* v. *Amministrazione delle finanze dello Stato*, [1981] ECR 1191, paras. 12–13.

[98] Case 322/88, *Grimaldi* v. *Fonds des maladies professionnelles*, [1989] ECR 4407, paras. 7–9.

[99] However, there exists an important 'estoppel' exception that the Court has added. Where the applicant 'could without any doubt' have challenged the Union act directly under Article 263 TFEU, but failed to do so within the two-month time limit, it cannot subsequently ask for an indirect review of the measure (see Case C-188/92, *TWD* v. *Germany*, [1994] ECR I-833, para. 24). Where the standing is uncertain, the Court is, however, much more generous (see Case C-408/95, *Eurotunnel SA* v. *Sea France*, [1997] ECR I-6315).

However, there are also serious disadvantages in the indirect review route via the preliminary reference procedure.[100] First, the latter can only be used if a national court has jurisdiction, and this may not be the case where there are no national implementing acts to challenge.[101] Second, the applicant may need to *breach* European law before challenging the legality of the act on which the illegal behaviour rests. Third, individual applicants in national courts have no 'right' to demand the indirect review of Union law by the European Court. Where the relevant national court entertains no doubts as to the validity of the Union act, no private party appeal to the European Court will be possible. In light of these disadvantages, the Court might thus wish to reconsider its restrictive view on Article 263 (4) TFEU.

2. Remedial powers: liability actions

Where the Union has acted illegally, may the Court grant damages for losses incurred? The European Treaties do acknowledge an action for damages in Article 268 TFEU;[102] yet, for a strange reason the article refers to another provision: Article 340 TFEU, which reads:

> The contractual liability of the Union shall be governed by the law applicable to the contract in question.
>
> In the case of non-contractual liability, the Union shall, in accordance with the general principles common to the laws of the Member States, make good any damage caused by its institutions or by its servants in the performance of their duties.[103]

The provision distinguishes between contractual liability in paragraph 1, and non-contractual liability in paragraph 2. While the former is governed by national law, the latter is governed by European law. Paragraph 2 recognises that the Union can do 'wrong' either through its institutions or through its servants,[104] and that it will in this case be under an obligation to make good damage incurred.

What are the European constitutional principles underpinning an action for the non-contractual liability of the Union? Article 340 [2] TFEU has had a

---

[100] For a brilliant and extensive analysis, see: Opinion of Advocate-General Jacobs in Case C-50/00, *UPA* (supra n. 74), paras. 38–44.

[101] See Case C-263/02P, *Jégo Quéré* (supra n. 88).

[102] Article 268 TFEU: 'The Court of Justice of the European Union shall have jurisdiction in disputes relating to compensation for damage provided for in the second and third paragraphs of Article 340.'

[103] Article 340 (1) and (2) TFEU.

[104] This is equally true for the European Central Bank, but Article 340 (3) TFEU specifically clarifies that the Bank *as such* – not the European Union – will be called to pay damages. The ECB has an independent personality (see: Chapter 4 – Section 3 (a) above). As regards the Union's civil servants, only their 'official acts' will be attributed to the Union. With regard to their personal liability, Article 340 (4) TFEU states: 'The personal liability of its servants towards the Union shall be governed by the provisions laid down in their Staff Regulations or in the Conditions of Employment applicable to them.'

colourful and complex constitutional history. It has not only been transformed from a dependent action to an independent action, its substantial conditions have changed significantly. This section will briefly analyse the procedural and substantive conditions of Union liability actions.

(a) Procedural conditions: from dependent to independent action

The action for damages under Article 340 (2) TFEU started its life as a dependent action, that is: an action that hinged on the prior success of another action. In *Plaumann*, a case discussed in the previous section, a clementine importer had brought an annulment action against a Union decision while at the same time asking for compensation equivalent to the customs duties that had been paid as a consequence of the European decision. However, as we saw above, the action for annulment failed due to the restrictive standing requirements under Article 263 (4) TFEU. And the Court found that this would equally end the liability action for damages:

> In the present case, the contested decision has not been annulled. An administrative measure which has not been annulled cannot of itself constitute a wrongful act on the part of the administration inflicting damage upon those whom it affects. The latter cannot therefore claim damages by reason of that measure. The Court cannot by way of an action for compensation take steps which would nullify the legal effects of a decision which, as stated, has not been annulled.[105]

A liability action thus had to be preceded by a (successful) annulment action. The *Plaumann* Court insisted on a 'certificate of illegality' before even considering the substantive merits of Union liability. This dramatically changed in *Lütticke*.[106] The case constitutes the 'declaration of independence' for liability actions. 'Article [340] was established by the Treaty as an independent form of action with a particular purpose to fulfil within the system of actions and subject to conditions for its use, conceived with a view to its specific purpose.'[107] And according to the Court, it would be contrary to 'the independent nature' of this action as well as to 'the efficacy of the general system of forms of action created by the Treaty' to deny admissibility of the damages action on the ground that it might lead to a similar result as an annulment action.[108]

---

[105] Case 25/62, *Plaumann* (supra n. 69), 108.
[106] Joined Cases 31/62 and 33/62, *Lütticke et al.* v. *Commission*, [1962] ECR 501.
[107] *Ibid.*, para. 6.
[108] *Ibid.* In the present case, the Court dealt with an infringement action for failure to act under Article 265 TFEU (see: Section 3 below), but the same result applies to annulment actions; see Case 5/71, *Schöppenstedt* v. *Council*, [1971] ECR 975, para. 3: 'The action for damages provided for by Articles [268] and [340], paragraph 2, of the Treaty was introduced as an autonomous form of action with a particular purpose to fulfil within the system of actions and subject to conditions on its use dictated by its specific nature. It differs from an application for annulment in that its end is not the abolition of a particular measure, but compensation for damage caused by an institution in the performance of its duties.'

What are the procedural requirements for liability actions? The proceedings may be brought against any Union action or inaction that is claimed to have caused damage. The act (or omission) must however be an 'official act', that is: it must be attributable to the Union.[109] Unlike Article 263 TFEU, there are no limitations on the potential applicants: anyone who feels 'wronged' by a Union (in)action may bring proceedings under Article 340(2) TFEU.[110] And against whom? With the exception of the European Central Bank,[111] the provision only generically identifies the Union as the potential defendant. However, the Court has clarified that 'in the interests of a good administration of justice', the Union 'should be represented before the Court by the institution or institutions against which the matter giving rise to liability is alleged'.[112] When will the action have to be brought? Unlike the strict two-month limitation period for annulment actions, liability actions can be brought within a five-year period.[113] The procedural requirements for liability actions are thus much more liberal than the procedural regime governing annulment actions.

(b) Substantive conditions: from *Schöppenstedt* to *Bergaderm*

The constitutional regime governing the substantive conditions for liability actions may be divided into two historical phases. In the first phase, the European Court distinguished between 'administrative' and 'legislative'

---

[109] The Union must be the author of the act, and this means that the Treaties themselves – as collective acts of the Member States – cannot be the basis of a liability action (see Case 169/73, *Compagnie Continentale France* v. *Council*, [1975] ECR 117, para.16). For institutional acts, the Court has taken a teleological view on what constitutes the 'Union' (see Case C-370/89, *SGEEM & Etroy* v. *European Investment Bank*, [1993] ECR I-2583). Acts of Union civil servants must be 'official' acts that can be attributed to the Union (see Case 9/69, *Sayag et al.* v. *Leduc et al.*, [1969] ECR 329, para. 7: 'Article [268] indicates that the [Union] is only liable for those acts of its servants which, by virtue of an internal and direct relationship, are the necessary extension of the tasks entrusted to the institutions.'

[110] See Case 118/83, *CMC Cooperativa muratori e cementisti and others* v. *Commission*, [1985] ECR 2325, para. 31: 'Any person who claims to have been injured by such acts or conduct must therefore have the possibility of bringing an action, if he is able to establish liability, that is, the existence of damage caused by an illegal act or by illegal conduct on the part of the [Union].' This also included the Member States (see A. Biondi and M. Farley, *The Right to Damages in European Law* (Kluwer, 2009), 88).

[111] Article 340 (3) TFEU.

[112] Joined Cases 63–69/72, *Werhahn Hansamühle and others* v. *Council*, [1973] ECR 1229, para. 7.

[113] Article 46 Statute of the Court: 'Proceedings against the Union in matters arising from non-contractual liability shall be barred after a period of five years from the occurrence of the event giving rise thereto. The period of limitation shall be interrupted if proceedings are instituted before the Court of Justice or if prior to such proceedings an application is made by the aggrieved party to the relevant institution of the Union. In the latter event the proceedings must be instituted within the period of two months provided for in Article 263 of the Treaty on the Functioning of the European Union; the provisions of the second paragraph of Article 265 of the Treaty on the Functioning of the European Union shall apply where appropriate. This Article shall also apply to proceedings against the European Central Bank regarding non-contractual liability.'

Union acts.[114] The former were subject to a relatively low liability threshold. The Union would be liable for (almost) any illegal action that had caused damage.[115] By contrast, legislative acts were subject to the so-called '*Schöppenstedt* formula'.[116] This formula stated that 'where *legislative* action involving measures of economic policy is concerned, the [Union] does not incur non-contractual liability for damage suffered by individuals as a consequence of that action, by virtue of the provisions contained in Article [340], second paragraph, of the Treaty, *unless a sufficiently flagrant violation of a superior rule of law for the protection of the individual has occurred*'.[117] This formula made Union liability for legislative acts dependent on the breach of a 'superior rule' of Union law, whatever that meant,[118] which aimed to grant rights to individuals.[119] And the breach of that rule would have to be sufficiently serious.[120]

This test was significantly 'reformed' in *Bergaderm*.[121] The reason for this reform was the Court's wish to align the liability regime for breaches of European law by the Union with the liability regime governing breaches of European law by the Member States.[122] Today, European law confers a right to reparation:

> where three conditions are met: the rule of law infringed must be intended to confer rights on individuals; the breach must be sufficiently serious; and there must be a direct causal link between the breach of the obligation resting on the State and the damage sustained by the injured parties.[123]

---

[114] Tridimas, *General Principles* (supra n. 41), 478 et seq.

[115] See Case 145/83, *Adams* v. *Commission*, [1985] ECR 3539, para. 44: '[B]y failing to make all reasonable efforts … the Commission has incurred liability towards the applicant in respect of that damage.' On the liability regime for administrative acts in this historical phase, see: M. van der Woude, 'Liability for Administrative Acts under Article 215 (2) EC' in T. Heukels and A. McDonnell (eds.), *The Action for Damages in Community Law* (Kluwer, 1997), 109–28.

[116] Case 5/71, *Schöppenstedt* v. *Council*, [1971] ECR 975.

[117] *Ibid.*, para. 11 (emphasis added).

[118] On the concept of a 'superior rule', see: Tridimas, *General Principles* (supra n. 41), 480–2.

[119] Case C-282/90, *Vreugdenhil BV* v. *Commission*, [1992] ECR I-1937, paras. 20–21: 'In that context, it is sufficient to state that the aim of the system of the division of powers between the various [Union] institutions is to ensure that the balance between the institutions provided for in the Treaty is maintained, and not to protect individuals. Consequently, a failure to observe the balance between the institutions cannot be sufficient on its own to engage the [Union's] liability towards the traders concerned.'

[120] See Joined Cases 83 and 94/76, 4, 15 and 40/77, *Bayerische HNL Vermehrungsbetriebe and others* v. *Council and Commission*, [1978] ECR 1209, para. 6: 'In a legislative field such as the one in question, in which one of the chief features is the exercise of a wide discretion essential for the implementation of the common agricultural policy, the [Union] does not therefore incur liability unless the institution concerned has manifestly and gravely disregarded the limits on the exercise of its powers.'

[121] Case C-352/98P, *Bergaderm et al.* v. *Commission*, [2000] ECR I-5291.

[122] *Ibid.*, para. 41. This inspiration was 'mutual' for, as we shall see in Chapter 11 – Section 4 below, the Court used Article 340 (2) TFEU as a rationale for the creation of a liability regime for the Member States.

[123] *Ibid.*, para. 42.

Two important changes were reflected in the '*Bergaderm* formula'.[124] First, the Court abandoned the distinction between 'administrative' and 'legislative' acts. The new test would apply to all Union acts regardless of their nature.[125] Second, the Court dropped the idea that a 'superior rule' had to be infringed. Henceforth, it was only necessary to show that the Union had breached a rule intended to confer individual rights, and that the breach was sufficiently serious. And the decisive test for finding that a breach of European law was sufficiently serious was whether the Union 'manifestly and gravely disregarded the limits on its discretion'.[126]

One final questions remains: can the Union ever be liable for *lawful* actions that cause damage? Some legal orders indeed recognise governmental liability for lawful acts, where the latter demand a 'special sacrifice' from a limited category of persons.[127] The early Union legal order seemed averse to this idea.[128] Yet in *Dorsch Consult*,[129] the General Court flirted with the possibility of Union liability for lawful acts.[130] But the Court of Justice has put a – temporary – end to this, when it more recently held that by assuming 'the existence of a regime providing for non-contractual liability of the [Union] on account of the lawful pursuit by it of its activities falling within the legislative sphere, the [General Court] erred in law'.[131]

---

[124] See C. Hilson, 'The Role of Discretion in EC Law on Non-Contractual Liability' [2005] 42 CML Rev 676 at 682.

[125] Case C-352/98P, *Bergaderm* (supra n. 121), para. 46. See also: Case C-282/05P, *Holcim* v. *Commission*, [2007] ECR I-2941, para. 48: 'The determining factor in deciding whether there has been such an infringement is not the general or individual nature of the act in question. Accordingly, the applicant is not justified in submitting that the criterion of a sufficiently serious breach of a rule of law applies only where a legislative act of the [Union] is at issue and is excluded when, as in the present case, an individual act is at issue.'

[126] Case C-352/98P, *Bergaderm* (supra n. 121) para. 43. However, where there was no discretion, 'the mere infringement of [Union] law may be sufficient to establish the existence of a sufficiently serious breach' (*ibid.*, para. 44).

[127] For the German constitutional position, see: K. Hesse, *Grundzüge des Verfassungsrecht der Bundesrepublik Deutschland* (Müller, 1999), 196.

[128] In the words of Case 5/71, *Schöppenstedt* (supra n. 116), para. 11 (emphasis added): '[t]he non-contractual liability of the [Union] presupposes at the very least the *unlawful* nature of the act alleged to be the cause of the damage'.

[129] Case T-184/95, *Dorsch Consult* v. *Council and Commission*, [1998] ECR II-667.

[130] *Ibid.*, para. 80. '[I]n the event of the principle of [Union] liability for a lawful act being recognised in [European] law, such liability can be incurred only if the damage alleged, if deemed to constitute a "still subsisting injury", affects a particular circle of economic operators in a disproportionate manner by comparison with others (unusual damage) and exceeds the limits of the economic risks inherent in operating in the sector concerned (special damage), without the legislative measure that gave rise to the alleged damage being justified by a general economic interest.'

[131] Case C-120/06P *FIAMM et al.* v. *Council and Commission*, [2008] ECR I-6513, para. 179. For a discussion of the case in its external relations context, see: A. Thies, 'The Impact of General Principles of EC Law on its Liability Regime towards Retaliation Victims after FIAMM' [2009] EL Rev 889.

3. Adjudicatory powers I: enforcement actions

One of the essential tasks of courts is to apply the law in disputes between parties. This judicial form of law enforcement is 'reactive'. For, unlike the 'active' enforcement by administrative authorities, it needs to be initiated by a party outside the court.

The adjudication of European law follows, like the administration of European law, a central and a decentralised route. The central adjudication principally takes the form of two types of enforcement actions: enforcement actions against a Member State, and enforcement actions against the Union. With regard to the former, the Treaties allow the Commission or a Member State to bring proceedings, where they consider that a Member State has failed to fulfil an obligation under the Treaties. But the Treaties also establish an infringement procedure against the Union for an alleged failure to act.

(a) Enforcement actions against Member States

Where a Member State breaches European law,[132] the central way to 'enforce' the Treaties is to bring that State to the European Court.[133] The European legal order envisages two potential applicants for enforcement actions against a failing Member State: the Commission and another Member State. The procedure governing the former scenario is set out in Article 258 TFEU; and the – almost – identical procedure governing the second scenario is set out in Article 259 TFEU. Both procedures are – partly – inspired by international law logic. For not only are individuals excluded from enforcing their rights under that procedure, the European Court cannot repeal national laws that violate European law. Its judgment will simply 'declare' that a violation of European law has taken place. However, as we shall see below, this declaration may now be backed up by financial sanctions.

(i) The procedural conditions under Article 258 TFEU

Enforcement actions against a Member State are 'the *ultima ratio* enabling the [Union] interests enshrined in the Treat[ies] to prevail over the inertia and resistance of Member States'.[134] They are typically brought by the

---

[132] For a temporal exception to this rule for breaches of Union law in the field of police and judicial cooperation in criminal matters, see: Article 10 of Protocol (No. 36) on Transitional Provisions: 'the powers of the Commission under Article 258 of the Treaty on the Functioning of the European Union shall not be applicable'. However, according to Article 10 (3) of the Protocol, that limitation will definitely cease five years after the entry of the Lisbon Treaty, that is: on 1 December 2014.

[133] Exceptionally, it is not the Court but the 'political forum' of the European Council that is to 'determine the existence of a serious and persistent breach by a Member State', see: Article 7 (2) TEU. This determination may even lead to the suspension of membership rights: Article 7 (3) TEU. According to Article 269 TFEU, the Member State concerned can, however, challenge this determination before the Court, but the Court's jurisdiction is confined to procedural aspects.

[134] Case 20/59, *Italy* v. *High Authority*, [1960] ECR 325 at 339.

Commission.[135] For it is the Commission, acting in the general interest of the Union, that is charged with ensuring that the Member States give effect to European law.[136] The procedural regime for enforcement actions brought by the Commission is set out in Article 258 TFEU, which states:

> If the Commission considers that a Member State has failed to fulfil an obligation under the Treaties, it shall deliver a reasoned opinion on the matter after giving the State concerned the opportunity to submit its observations. If the State concerned does not comply with the opinion within the period laid down by the Commission, the latter may bring the matter before the Court of Justice of the European Union.

The provision clarifies that before the Commission can bring the matter to the Court, it must pass through an administrative stage. The purpose of this pre-litigation stage is 'to give the Member State concerned an opportunity, on the one hand, to comply with its obligations under [European] law and, on the other, to avail itself of its right to defend itself against the complaints made by the Commission'.[137] This administrative stage expressly requires a 'reasoned opinion', and before that – even if not expressly mentioned in Article 258 – a 'letter of formal notice'.[138] In the 'letter of formal notice', the Commission will notify the State that it believes it to violate European law, and ask it to submit its observations. Where the Commission is not convinced by the explanations offered by a Member State, it will issue a 'reasoned opinion'; and after that second administrative stage,[139] it will go to court.

---

[135] The following section therefore concentrates on proceedings brought by the Commission. The procedure under Article 259 TFEU, in any event, also requires Member States to bring the matter before the Commission (paragraph 2). However, unlike the procedural regime under Article 258 TFEU, the matter will go to the Court even in the absence of a reasoned opinion by the Commission (paragraph 4). Member States very rarely bring actions against another Member State, but see: Case C-145/04, *Spain* v. *United Kingdom*, [2006] ECR I-7917.

[136] Case C-431/92, *Commission* v. *Germany*, [1995] ECR I-2189, para. 21: 'In exercising its powers under Articles [17 TEU] and [258] of the [FEU] Treaty, the Commission does not have to show that there is a specific interest in bringing an action. Article [258] is not intended to protect the Commission's own rights. The Commission's function, in the general interest of the [Union], is to ensure that the Member States give effect to the Treaty and the provisions adopted by the institutions thereunder and to obtain a declaration of any failure to fulfil the obligations deriving therefrom with a view to bringing it to an end.'

[137] Case 293/85, *Commission* v. *Belgium*, [1988] ECR 305, para. 13.

[138] There are exceptions to this rule. The most important practical exception can be found in the shortened procedure in the context of the Union's state aid provisions, see: Article 108 (2) TFEU.

[139] The Court has insisted that the Member State must – again – be given a reasonable period to correct its behaviour; see Case 293/85, *Commission* v. *Belgium*, [1988] ECR 305, para.14: '[T]he Commission must allow Member States a reasonable period to reply to the letter of formal notice and to comply with a reasoned opinion, or, where appropriate, to prepare their defence. In order to determine whether the period allowed is reasonable, account must be taken of all the circumstances of the case. Thus very short periods may be justified in particular circumstances, especially where there is an urgent need to remedy a breach or where the Member State concerned is fully aware of the Commission's views long before the procedure starts.'

What violations of European law may be litigated under the enforcement procedure? With the general exceptions mentioned above,[140] the Commission can raise any violation of European law, including breaches of the Union's international agreements.[141] However, the breach must be committed by the 'State'. This includes its legislature, its executive and – in theory – its judiciary.[142] The Member State might also be responsible for violations of the Treaties by territorially autonomous regions.[143] And even the behaviour of its nationals may – exceptionally – be attributed to the Member State.[144]

Are there any defences that a State may raise to justify its breach of European law? Early on, the Court clarified that breaches of European law by one Member State cannot justify breaches of another. In *Commission* v. *Luxembourg and Belgium*,[145] the defendants had argued that 'since international law allows a party, injured by the failure of another party to perform its obligations, to withhold performance of its own, the Commission has lost the right to plead infringement of the Treaty'.[146] The Court did not accept this 'international law' logic of the European Treaties. The Treaties were 'not limited to creating reciprocal obligations between the different natural and legal persons to whom [they are] applicable, but establish[] a new legal order, which governs the powers, rights and obligations of the said persons, as well as the necessary procedures for taking cognisance of and penalising any breach of it'.[147] The binding effect of European law was thus comparable to the effect of 'national' or 'institutional' law.[148] The Court has also denied the availability of 'internal' constitutional problems,[149] or budgetary restraints, as justifications.[150] However, one of the arguments that the Court has accepted in the past is the idea of *force majeure* in an emergency situation.[151]

---

[140] See Articles 275 and 276 TFEU.

[141] Case C-61/94, *Commission* v. *Germany (IDA)*, [1996] ECR I-3989.

[142] The Court of Justice has been fairly reluctant to find that a national court has violated the Treaty. In the past, it has preferred to attribute the fact that a national judiciary persistently interpreted national law in a manner that violated European law to the *legislature's* failure to adopt clearer national laws; see Case C-129/00, *Commission* v. *Italy*, [2003] ECR I-14637. On this point, see: C. Timmermans, 'Use of the Infringement Procedure in Cases of Judicial Errors' in J. de Zwaan et al. (eds.), *The European Union – an Ongoing Process of Integration* (Asser Press, 2004), 155.

[143] See Case C-383/00, *Commission* v. *Germany*, [2002] ECR I-4219, para. 18: 'the Court has repeatedly held that, a Member State may not plead provisions, practices or situations in its internal legal order, including those resulting from its federal organisation, in order to justify a failure to comply with the obligations'.

[144] Case 249/81, *Commission* v. *Ireland (Buy Irish)*, [1982] ECR 4005.

[145] Joined Cases 90–91/63, *Commission* v. *Luxemburg and Belgium*, [1964] ECR 625.

[146] *Ibid.*, 631.   [147] *Ibid.*

[148] P. Pescatore, *The Law of Integration: Emergence of a New Phenomenon in International Relations Based on the Experience of the European Communities* (Sijthoff, 1974), 67 and 69.

[149] See Case C-39/88, *Commission* v. *Ireland*, [1990] ECR I-4271, para.11: 'a Member State may not plead internal circumstances in order to justify a failure to comply with obligations and time-limits resulting from [European] law'.

[150] See Case 30/72, *Commission* v. *Italy*, [1973] ECR 161.

[151] For an excellent discussion of the case law, see: L. Prete and B. Smulders, 'The Coming of Age of Infringement Proceedings' [2010] 47 CML Rev 9 at 44.

(ii) Judicial enforcement through financial sanctions

The European Court is not entitled to nullify national laws that violate European law. It may only declare national laws or practices incompatible with European law.[152] Where the Court has found that a Member State has failed to fulfil an obligation under the Treaties, 'the State shall be required to take the necessary measures to comply with the judgment of the Court'.[153] Inspired by international law logic, the European legal order here builds on the normative distinctiveness of European and national law. It remains within the competence of the Member States to remove national laws or practices that are incompatible with European law.

Nonetheless, the Union legal order may 'punish' violations by imposing financial sanctions on a recalcitrant State. The sanction regime for breaches by a Member State is set out in Article 260 (2) and (3) TFEU. Importantly, financial sanctions will not automatically follow from every breach of European law. According to Article 260 (2) TFEU, the Commission may only apply for a 'lump sum or penalty payment',[154] where a Member State has failed to comply with a *judgment of the Court*. And even in this limited situation, the Commission must bring a second (!) case before the Court.[155] There is only one exception to the requirement of a second judgment. This 'exceptional' treatment corresponds to a not too exceptional situation: the failure of a Member State properly to transpose a 'Directive'.[156] Where a Member State fails to fulfil its obligation 'to notify measures transposing a directive adopted under a legislative procedure',[157] the Commission can apply for a financial

---

[152] Cases 15 and 16/76, *France* v. *Commission*, [1979] ECR 32.   [153] Article 260 (1) TFEU.

[154] The Court has held that Article 265 allows it to impose a 'lump sum' *and* a 'penalty payment' at the same time. In the words of the Court in Case C-304/02, *Commission* v. *France (French Fisheries II)*, [2005] ECR I-6262, paras. 80–2: 'The procedure laid down in Article [260 (2) TFEU] has the objective of inducing a defaulting Member State to comply with a judgment establishing a breach of obligations and thereby of ensuring that [Union] law is in fact applied. The measures provided for by that provision, namely a lump sum and a penalty payment, are both intended to achieve this objective. Application of each of those measures depends on their respective ability to meet the objective pursued according to the circumstances of the case. While the imposition of a penalty payment seems particularly suited to inducing a Member State to put an end as soon as possible to a breach of obligations which, in the absence of such a measure, would tend to persist, the imposition of a lump sum is based more on assessment of the effects on public and private interests of the failure of the Member State concerned to comply with its obligations, in particular where the breach has persisted for a long period since the judgment which initially established it. That being so, recourse to both types of penalty provided for in Article [260 (2) TFEU] is not precluded, in particular where the breach of obligations both has continued for a long period and is inclined to persist.'

[155] The Court has softened this procedural requirement somewhat by specifically punishing 'general and persistent' infringements; see Case C-494/01 *Commission* v. *Ireland (Irish Waste)*, [2005] ECR I-3331. For an extensive discussion of this type of infringement, see: P. Wennerås, 'A New Dawn for Commission Enforcement under Articles 226 and 228 EC: General and Persistent (GAP) Infringements, Lump Sums and Penalty Payments' [2006] 43 CML Rev 31 at 33–50.

[156] On the legal instrument 'Directive', see: Chapter 9 – Section 3 below.

[157] Article 260 (3) TFEU.

sanction in the first enforcement action. The payment must take effect on the date set by the Court in its judgment, and is thus directed at this specific breach of European law.

(b) Enforcement actions against the Union: failure to act

Enforcement actions primarily target a Member State's failure to act (properly). However, infringement proceedings may also be brought against Union institutions. Actions for failure to act are thereby governed by Article 265 TFEU, which states:

> Should the European Parliament, the European Council, the Council, the Commission or the European Central Bank, in infringement of the Treaties, fail to act, the Member States and the other institutions of the Union may bring an action before the Court of Justice of the European Union to have the infringement established. This Article shall apply, under the same conditions, to bodies, offices and agencies of the Union which fail to act.
>
> The action shall be admissible only if the institution, body, office or agency concerned has first been called upon to act. If, within two months of being so called upon, the institution, body, office or agency concerned has not defined its position, the action may be brought within a further period of two months.
>
> Any natural or legal person may, under the conditions laid down in the preceding paragraphs, complain to the Court that an institution, body, office or agency of the Union has failed to address to that person any act other than a recommendation or an opinion.

An action for failure to act may thus be brought against any Union institution or body – with the exception of the Court of Auditors and the European Court. It can be brought by another Union institution or body, a Member State and even a private party; and unlike applications for judicial review, Article 265 TFEU makes no express distinctions between different types of applicants.[158]

---

[158] However, the Court appears to read the 'direct and individual concern' criterion into Article 265 TFEU; see Case 247/87, *Star Fruit Co* v. *Commission*, [1989] ECR 291, para. 13: 'It must also be observed that in requesting the Commission to commence proceedings pursuant to Article [258] the applicant is in fact seeking the adoption of acts which are not of direct and individual concern to it within the meaning of the [fourth] paragraph of Article [263] and which it could not therefore challenge by means of an action for annulment in any event.' And see also: Case C-68/95, *T. Port GmbH & Co. KG* v. *Bundesanstalt für Landwirtschaft und Ernährung*, [1996] ECR I-6065, para. 59: 'It is true that the third paragraph of Article [265] of the Treaty entitles legal and natural persons to bring an action for failure to act when an institution has failed to address to them any act other than a recommendation or an opinion. The Court has, however, held that Articles [263] and [265] merely prescribe one and the same method of recourse. It follows that, just as the fourth paragraph of Article [263] allows individuals to bring an action for annulment against a measure of an institution not addressed to them provided that the measure is of direct and individual concern to them, the third paragraph of Article [265] must be interpreted as also entitling them to bring an action for failure to act against an institution which they claim has failed to adopt a measure which would have concerned them in the same way. The possibility for individuals to assert their rights should not depend upon whether the institution concerned has acted or failed to act.'

What are the procedural stages of this action? As with enforcement actions against Member States, the procedure is divided into an administrative and a judicial stage. The judicial stage will only commence once the relevant institution has been 'called upon to act', and has not 'defined its position' within two months.[159]

What types of 'inactions' can be challenged? In its early jurisprudence, the Court appeared to interpret the scope of Article 265 TFEU in parallel with the scope of Article 263 TFEU.[160] This suggested that only those inactions with (external) legal effects might be challenged.[161] However, the wording of the provision points the other way – at least for non-private applicants. And this wider reading was indeed confirmed in *Parliament* v. *Council (Comitology)*,[162] where the Court found that '[t]here is no necessary link between the action for annulment and the action for failure to act'.[163] Actions for failure to act can thus also be brought in relation to 'preparatory acts'.[164] The material scope of Article 265 TFEU was, in this respect, wider than that of Article 263 TFEU.

However, in one important respect the scope of Article 265 TFEU is much smaller that that of Article 263 TFEU. The European Court has indeed added an 'unwritten' limitation that cannot be found in the text of Article 265 TFEU. It insists that a finding of a failure to act requires the existence of an *obligation to act*. Where an institution has 'the right, but not the duty' to act, no failure to act can be established.[165] This is, for example, the case with regard to the Commission's competence to bring enforcement actions under Article 258 TFEU. Under this article 'the Commission is not bound to commence the proceedings provided for in that provision but in this regard has a discretion which excludes the right for individuals to require that institution to adopt a specific position'.[166] The existence of institutional discretion thus excludes an obligation to act.

In *Parliament* v. *Council (Common Transport Policy)*,[167] the Court offered further commentary on what the existence of an obligation to act requires. Parliament had brought proceedings against the Council claiming that it had failed to lay down a framework for the common transport policy. The Council responded by arguing that a failure to act under Article 265 'was designed for

---

[159] On what may count as a 'defined' position, see: Case 377/87, *Parliament* v. *Council*, [1988] ECR 4017, and Case C-25/91, *Pesqueras Echebastar* v. *Commission*, [1993] ECR I-1719.

[160] Case 15/70, *Chevallery* v. *Commission*, [1970] ECR 975, para. 6: '[T]he concept of a measure capable of giving rise to an action is identical in Articles [263] and [265], as both provisions merely prescribe one and the same method of recourse.'

[161] On this point, see: Section 1(a) above.

[162] Case 302/87, *Parliament* v. *Council*, [1988] ECR 5615.

[163] *Ibid.*, para.16: 'There is no necessary link between the action for annulment and the action for failure to act . This follows from the fact that the action for failure to act enables the European Parliament to induce the adoption of measures which cannot in all cases be the subject of an action for annulment.'

[164] Case 377/87, *Parliament* v. *Council*, [1988] ECR 4017.

[165] Case 247/87, *Star Fruit Co* v. *Commission* (supra n. 158), esp. para. 12.   [166] *Ibid.*, para. 11.

[167] Case 13/83, *Parliament* v. *Council*, [1985] ECR 1513.

cases where the institution in question has a legal obligation to adopt a *specific* measure and that it is an inappropriate instrument for resolving cases involving the introduction of a whole system of measures within the framework of a complex legislative process'.[168] The Court joined the Council and rejected the idea that enforcement proceedings could be brought for the failure to fulfil the *general* obligation to develop a Union policy. The failure to act would have to be 'sufficiently defined'; and this would only be the case, where the missing Union act can be 'identified individually'.[169]

What are the consequences of an established failure to act on the part of the Union? According to Article 266, the institution 'whose failure to act has been declared contrary to the Treaties shall be required to take the necessary measures to comply with the judgment of the Court of Justice of the European Union'. And in the absence of an express time limit for such compliance, the Court requires that the institution 'has a reasonable period for that purpose'.[170]

4. Adjudicatory powers II: preliminary rulings

The European Court would not be able on its own to shoulder the adjudicatory task of deciding European law disputes. Yet, unlike the American constitutional order,[171] the European Union has not developed an extensive system of federal courts designed to apply federal law. The Union is based on a system of cooperative federalism: *all* national courts are entitled and obliged to apply European law to disputes before them.[172] The duty of national courts to apply European law derives from the general duty of loyal cooperation codified in Article 4 (3) TEU.[173] And this general duty is given a specific expression in the judicial sphere by Article 19 (1) TEU: 'Member States shall provide remedies sufficient to ensure effective legal protection in the fields covered by Union law.' This provision has been held to turn national courts into 'guardians' of the European legal order.[174]

---

[168] *Ibid.*, para. 29 (emphasis added).

[169] *Ibid.*, para. 37. The Court thus held in para. 53 that 'the absence of a common policy which the Treaty requires to be brought into being does not in itself necessarily constitute a failure to act sufficiently specific in nature to form the subject of an action under Article [265]'.

[170] *Ibid.*, para. 69.

[171] On American judicial federalism, see: R. H. Fallon et al., *Hart and Wechsler's The Federal Courts and the Federal System* (Foundation Press, 1996); as well as: E. Chemerinski, *Federal Jurisdiction* (Aspen, 2007).

[172] In Case 106/77, *Amministrazione delle Finanze dello Stato* v. *Simmenthal*, [1978] ECR 629 the European Court clarified that the duty applies to every national court (*ibid.*, para. 21): '[E]very national court must, in a case within its jurisdiction, apply [European] law in its entirety and protect rights which the latter confers on individuals[.]'

[173] Article 4 (3) TEU states: 'The Member States shall take any appropriate measure, general or particular, to ensure fulfilment of the obligation arising out of the Treaties or resulting from the acts of the institutions of the Union.'

[174] Opinion 1/09 (*Draft Agreement on the Creation of European and Community Patent Court*) (nyr), para. 66.

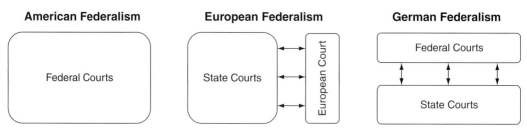

Figure 17 Judicial Federalism in Comparative Perspective

From a functional perspective, the decentralised adjudication of European law thus – partly – transforms national courts into 'European' courts. However, it is important to underline that national courts are not full European courts. First, they are not empowered to annul a Union act, as this is an *exclusive* competence of the European Court.[175] And second, unlike German judicial federalism, state courts are not hierarchically subordinated under the appeal jurisdiction of federal courts. The relationship between national courts and the European Court is based on their *voluntary* cooperation.

In the absence of an 'institutional' hierarchy between the European Court and the national courts, how has the European legal order guaranteed a degree of uniformity in the judicial application of European law? From the very beginning, the Treaties contained a mechanism for the interpretative assistance of national courts: the preliminary reference procedure. Where national courts encounter problems relating to the interpretation of European law, they could ask 'preliminary questions' to the European Court. The questions are 'preliminary', since they *precede* the application of European law by the national court. Thus, importantly, the European Court will not 'decide' the case. It is only *indirectly* involved in the judgment delivered by the national court; and for that reason preliminary rulings are called 'indirect actions'.

The preliminary rulings procedure constitutes the cornerstone of the Union's judicial federalism. This federalism is *cooperative* in nature: the European Court and the national courts collaborate in the adjudication of a single case. The procedure for preliminary rulings is set out in Article 267 TFEU, which reads:

[1] The Court of Justice of the European Union shall have jurisdiction to give preliminary rulings concerning:
(a) the interpretation of the Treaties;
(b) the validity and interpretation of acts of the institutions, bodies, offices or agencies of the Union;
[2] Where such a question is raised before any court or tribunal of a Member State, that court or tribunal may, if it considers that a decision on the question is necessary to enable it to give judgment, request the Court to give a ruling thereon.

---

[175] The Court of Justice has insisted on its 'exclusive' jurisdiction to nullify an act of a Union institution, see: Section 1(d)(ii) above.

[3] Where any such question is raised in a case pending before a court or tribunal of a Member State against whose decisions there is no judicial remedy under national law, that court or tribunal shall bring the matter before the Court.[176]

The provision establishes a constitutional nexus between the central and the decentralised adjudication of European law. This section looks at four aspects of the procedure. We start by analysing the jurisdiction of the European Court under the preliminary reference procedure, and then move to the conditions for a preliminary ruling. A third step investigates which national courts are obliged to make a reference. Finally, we shall analyse the nature and effect of preliminary rulings in the Union legal order.

(a) Paragraph 1: the jurisdiction of the European Court

The European Court's jurisdiction, set out in paragraph 1, is limited to *European* law. 'The Court is not entitled, within the framework of Article [267 TFEU] to interpret rules pertaining to national law.'[177] The Court's competence thereby extends to questions pertaining to the 'validity and interpretation' of European law. Preliminary references may thus be made in relation to *two* judicial functions. They can concern the *interpretation* of European law. This includes all types of European law – ranging from the deepest constitutional foundations to the loftiest soft law. But national courts can equally ask about the *validity* of European law.[178] And in exercising its judicial review function, the European Court will be confined to providing a ruling on the validity of acts *below* the Treaties.

The *application* of European law is not within the power of the Court. Article 267 TFEU 'gives the Court no jurisdiction to apply the Treat[ies] to a specific case'.[179] However, the distinction between 'interpretation' and 'application' is hard to make. The Court has tried to explain it as follows: 'When it gives an interpretation of the Treat[ies] in a specific action pending before a national court, the Court limits itself to deducing the meaning of the [European] rules from the wording and spirit of the Treat[ies], it being left to the national court

---

[176] The (omitted) fourth paragraph states: 'If such a question is raised in a case pending before a court or tribunal of a Member State with regard to a person in custody, the Court of Justice of the European Union shall act with the minimum of delay.' According to Article 23a of the Court's Statute, there may exist an 'urgent preliminary procedure' (in French: 'procedure préjudicielle d'urgence' or 'PPU') in the area of freedom security and justice. The Court has used this power and defined the procedure in Article 104b of the Court's Rules of Procedure. On the 'PPU', see: C. Barnard, 'The PPU: Is it Worth the Candle? An Early Assessment' [2009] 34 EL Rev 281.

[177] Case 75/63, *Hoekstra (née Unger)*, [1964] ECR 177, para. 3.

[178] On this point, see: Section 1(d)(ii) above.

[179] Case 6/64, *Costa* v. *ENEL*, [1964] ECR 585 at 592: 'This provision gives the Court no jurisdiction either to apply the Treaty to a specific case or to decide upon the validity of a provision of domestic law in relation to the treaty, as it would be possible for it to do under Article [258]'.

to apply in the particular case the rules which are thus interpreted.'[180] Theoretically, this should mean that the Court of Justice cannot decide whether a national law, in fact, violates the Treaties. And yet, the Court has often made this very assessment.[181]

A famous illustration of the blurred line between 'interpretation' and 'application' are the 'Sunday trading cases'.[182] Would the prohibition to trade on Sundays conflict with the Union's internal market provisions? Preliminary references had been made by a number of English courts to obtain an interpretation on the Treaties' free movement of goods provisions. The Court found that national rules governing opening hours could be justified on public interest grounds, but asked the referring national court 'to ascertain whether the effects of such national rules exceed what is necessary to achieve the aim in view'.[183] Yet the decentralised application of this proportionality test led to a judicial fragmentation of the United Kingdom. Simply put, different national courts decided differently. The Court thus ultimately took matters into its own hands and centrally applied the proportionality test.[184] And in holding that the British Sunday trading rules were not disproportionate interferences with the internal market, the Court crossed the line between 'interpretation' and 'application' of the Treaties.

(b) Paragraph 2: the conditions for a preliminary ruling

Article 267 (2) TFEU defines the competence of national courts to ask preliminary questions. The provision allows 'any court or tribunal of a Member State' to ask a European law question that 'is necessary to enable it to give judgment'.

---

[180] Joined Cases 28-30/62, *Da Costa et al.* v. *Netherlands Inland Revenue Administration*, Case 28/62, [1963] ECR 31 at 38.

[181] For two excellent analyses of this category of cases, see: G. Davies, 'The Division of Powers between the European Court of Justice and National Courts' *Constitutionalism Web-Papers* 3/2004 (SSRN Network: www.ssrn.com); as well as: T. Tridimas, 'Constitutional Review of Member State Action: the Virtues and Vices of an Incomplete Jurisdiction' [2011] 9 *International Journal of Constitutional Law* 737.

[182] See M. Jarvis, 'The Sunday Trading Episode: in Defence of the Euro-defence' [1995] 44 *International and Comparative Law Quarterly* 451.

[183] Case C-145/88, *Torfaen Borough Council*, [1989] ECR I-3851, para. 15.

[184] Case C-169/91, *Stoke-on-Trent* v. *B&Q*, [1992] ECR I-6635, paras. 12–14: 'As far as that principle is concerned, the Court stated in its judgment in the Torfaen Borough Council case that such rules were not prohibited by Article [34] of the [FEU] Treaty where the restrictive effects on [Union] trade which might result from them did not exceed the effects intrinsic to such rules and that the question whether the effects of those rules actually remained within that limit was a question of fact to be determined by the national court. In its judgments in the Conforama and Marchandise cases, however, the Court found it necessary to make clear, with regard to similar rules, that the restrictive effects on trade which might result from them did not appear to be excessive in relation to the aim pursued. The Court considered that it had all the information necessary for it to rule on the question of the proportionality of such rules and that it had to do so in order to enable national courts to assess their compatibility with [European] law in a uniform manner since such an assessment cannot be allowed to vary according to the findings of fact made by individual courts in particular cases.'

Are there conditions on 'who' can refer 'what' question to the European Court? The two conditions have been subject to an extended judicial and academic commentary and will be discussed in turn.

(i) 'Who': national courts and tribunals

The formulation 'court or tribunal' in Article 267 refers directly to *judicial* authorities, and thus indirectly excludes *administrative* authorities. But what exactly is a 'court or tribunal' that can refer questions to the Court of Justice? The Treaties provide no positive definition. Would the concept therefore fall within the competence of the Member States? Unsurprisingly, the European Court has not accepted this idea but has provided a European definition of the phrase. Its definition is extremely wide. In *Dorsch Consult*,[185] the Court stated that it will take account of a variety of factors 'such as whether the body is established by law, whether it is permanent, whether its jurisdiction is compulsory, whether its procedure is *inter partes*, whether it applies rules of law and whether it is independent[.]'[186] The last criterion is controlling.[187] Therefore, an authority that is not independent from the State's administrative branch is not a court or tribunal in the meaning of European law.[188]

The enormous breadth of this definition was illustrated in *Broekmeulen*.[189] The plaintiff had obtained a medical degree from Belgium and tried to register as a 'General Practitioner' in the Netherlands. The registration was refused on the ground that Dutch professional qualifications were not satisfied. The plaintiff appealed before the 'Appeals Committee for General Medicine' – a professional body set up under private law. This Appeals Committee was not a court or tribunal under Dutch law. But would it nonetheless be a 'court or tribunal' under European law; and, as such, be entitled to make a preliminary reference? The European Court found as follows:

> In order to deal with the question of the applicability in the present case of Article [267 TFEU], it should be noted that it is incumbent upon Member States to take the necessary steps to ensure that within their territory the provisions adopted by the [Union] institutions are implemented in their entirety. If, under the legal system of a Member State, the task of implementing such provisions is assigned to a professional body acting under a degree of governmental supervision, and if that body, in conjunction with the public authorities concerned, creates appeal

---

[185] Case C-54/96, *Dorsch Consult Ingenieugesellschaft* v. *Bundesbaugesellschaft Berlin*, [1997] ECR I-4961.

[186] *Ibid.*, para. 23.

[187] See Case C-210/06, *Cartesio*, [2008] ECR I-9641, esp. para. 57: 'Thus, where a court responsible for maintaining a register makes an administrative decision without being required to resolve a legal dispute, it cannot be regarded as exercising a judicial function.'

[188] Case C-53/03, *Syfait et al.* v. *GlaxoSmithKline*, [2005] ECR I-4609. On the general question, whether National Competition Authorities should be considered 'courts or tribunals' in the sense of Article 267, see: A. Komninos, 'Article 234 EC and National Competition Authorities in the Era of Decentralisation' [2004] 29 EL Rev 106.

[189] Case 246/80, *Broekmeulen* v. *Huisarts Registratie Commissie*, [1981] ECR 2311.

procedures which may affect the exercise of rights granted by [European] law, it is imperative, in order to ensure the proper functioning of [Union] law, that the Court should have an opportunity of ruling on issues of interpretation and validity arising out of such proceedings. As a result of all the foregoing considerations and in the absence, in practice, of any right of appeal to the ordinary courts, the Appeals Committee, which operates with the consent of the public authorities and with their cooperation, and which, after an adversarial procedure, delivers decisions which are recognised as final, must, in a matter involving the application of [European] law, be considered as a court of tribunal of a Member State within the meaning of Article [267 TFEU].[190]

Can higher national courts limit the power of a lower national court to refer prelimnary questions? The European legal order has given short shrift to the attempt to break the cooperative nexus between the European Court and *each level of the national judiciary*. In *Rheinmühlen*,[191] the Court thus held that 'a rule of national law whereby a court is bound on points of law by the rulings of a superior court cannot deprive the inferior courts of their power to refer to the Court questions of interpretation of [Union] law involving such rulings'.[192] For if inferior courts could not refer to the Court of Justice, 'the jurisdiction of the latter to give preliminary rulings and the application of [European] law *at all levels of the judicial systems* of the Member States would be compromised'.[193] A national court or tribunal, at any level of the national judicial hierarchy, and at any stage of its judicial procedure, is thus entitled to refer a preliminary question to the European Court of Justice.[194] National rules allowing for an appeal against the decision of the national court to refer a preliminary question to the European Court thus violate 'the autonomous jurisdiction which Article [267 TFEU] confers on the referring court'.[195]

---

[190] *Ibid.*, paras. 16–17.   [191] Case 166/73, *Rheinmühlen-Düsseldorf*, [1974] ECR 33.

[192] *Ibid.*, para. 4.

[193] *Ibid.* For a recent confirmation, see: Case C-173/09, *Elchinov* v. *Natsionalna zdravnoosiguritelna kasa*, (nyr), para. 27.

[194] This European entitlement cannot be transformed into a national obligation; see Case C-555/07, *Kücükdeveci* v. *Swedex*, (nyr), para. 54: 'The possibility thus given to the national court by the second paragraph of Article 267 TFEU of asking the Court for a preliminary ruling before disapplying the national provision that is contrary to European Union law cannot, however, be transformed into an obligation because national law does not allow that court to disapply a provision it considers to be contrary to the constitution unless the provision has first been declared unconstitutional by the Constitutional Court. By reason of the principle of the primacy of European Union law, which extends also to the principle of non-discrimination on grounds of age, contrary national legislation which falls within the scope of European Union law must be disapplied.'

[195] Case C-210/06, *Cartesio* (supra n. 187), para. 95: 'Where rules of national law apply which relate to the right of appeal against a decision making a reference for a preliminary ruling, and under those rules the main proceedings remain pending before the referring court in their entirety, the order for reference alone being the subject of a limited appeal, the autonomous jurisdiction which Article [267 TFEU] confers on the referring court to make a reference to the Court would be called into question, if – by varying the order for reference, by setting it aside and by ordering the referring court to resume the proceedings – the appellate court could prevent the referring court from exercising the right, conferred on it by the EC Treaty, to make a reference to the Court.'

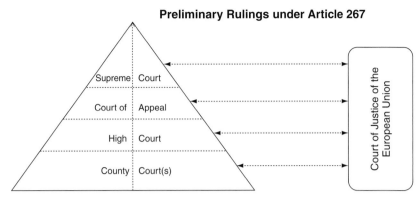

Figure 18 Preliminary Rulings under Article 267 TFEU

For the English judicial hierarchy, the judicial federalism constructed by the European Court thus looks like Figure 18.

(ii) 'What': necessary questions

National courts are entitled to request a preliminary ruling, where there is a 'question' that they consider 'necessary' to give judgment. In the past, the European Court has been eager to encourage national courts to ask preliminary questions. For these questions offered the Court formidable opportunities to say what the European constitution 'is'.[196] Thus, even where questions were 'imperfectly formulated', the Court was willing to extract the 'right' ones.[197] Moreover, the Court will generally not 'criticise the grounds and purpose of the request for interpretation'.[198] Nonetheless, in very exceptional circumstances the Court will reject a request for a preliminary ruling.

This happened in *Foglia* v. *Novello (No. 1)*,[199] where the Court insisted that questions referred to it must be raised in a 'genuine' dispute.[200] Where the parties to the national dispute agreed on the desirable outcome, the Court had no jurisdiction.[201] In a sequel to this case, the Court justified this jurisdictional limitation as follows:

---

[196] In the famous phrase by C. E. Hughes (as quoted by E. Corwin, 'Curbing the Court' [1936] 26 *American Labor Legislation Review* 85): 'We are under a Constitution, but the Constitution is what the judges say it is[.]'

[197] Case 6/64, *Costa* v. *ENEL*, [1964] ECR 585, 593: '[T]he Court has the power to extract from a question imperfectly formulated by the national court those questions which alone pertain to the interpretation of the Treaty.'

[198] *Ibid.*   [199] Case 104/79, *Foglia* v. *Novello*, [1980] ECR 745.

[200] G. Bebr, 'The Existence of a Genuine Dispute: an Indispensible Precondition for the Jurisdiction of the Court under Article 177 EEC?' [1980] 17 CML Rev 525.

[201] Case 104/79, *Foglia* (supra n. 199), paras. 11–13: 'The duty of the Court of Justice under Article [267] of the [FEU] Treaty is to supply all courts in the [Union] with the information on the interpretation of [European] law which is necessary to enable them to settle *genuine* disputes which are brought before them. A situation in which the Court is obliged by the expedient of

[T]he duty assigned to the Court by Article [267] is not that of delivering advisory opinions on general or hypothetical questions but of assisting in the administration of justice in the Member States. It accordingly does not have jurisdiction to reply to questions of interpretation which are submitted to it within the framework of procedural devices arranged by the parties in order to induce the Court to give its views on certain problems of [European] law which do not correspond to an objective requirement inherent in the resolution of a dispute.[202]

The Court of Justice has thus imposed some jurisdictional control on requests for preliminary rulings. To prevent an abuse of the Article 267 procedure, the European Court will be able 'to check, as all courts must, whether it has jurisdiction'.[203] Yet, it was eager to emphasise that it wished 'not in any way [to] trespass upon the prerogatives of the national courts'.[204] The Court thus pledged to 'place as much reliance as possible upon the assessment by the national court of the extent to which the questions submitted are essential'.[205] The Court will therefore decline jurisdiction 'only if it is manifest that the interpretation of [European] law or the examination of the validity of a rule of [European] law sought by that court bears no relation to the true facts or the subject-matter of the main proceedings'.[206] And, even if the question is not strictly speaking necessary, because the Court had already answered a very similar one in the past,[207] the Court will accept jurisdiction for questions raised under Article 267, paragraph 2.

(c) Paragraph 3: the obligation to refer and '*acte clair*'

While any national courts 'may' refer a question to the European Court under paragraph 2, Article 267 (3) TFEU imposes a obligation: 'Where any such question is raised in a case pending before a court or tribunal of a Member State against whose decisions there is no judicial remedy under national law, that court or tribunal shall bring the matter before the Court.' Certain courts therefore 'must' refer a question to the European Court. These courts are defined in Article 267 (3) as courts 'against whose decisions there is no judicial remedy under national law'.

---

arrangements like those described above to give rulings would jeopardise the whole system of legal remedies available to private individuals to enable them to protect themselves against tax provisions which are contrary to the Treaty. This means that the questions asked by the national court, having regard to the circumstances of this case, do not fall within the framework of the duties of the Court of Justice under Article [267] of the Treaty. The Court has accordingly no jurisdiction to give a ruling on the question asked by the national court.'

[202] Case 244/80, *Foglia* v. *Novello (2)*, [1981] ECR 3045, para. 18.   [203] *Ibid.*, para. 19.
[204] *Ibid.*, para. 18.   [205] *Ibid.*, para. 19.
[206] Case C-264/96, *Imperial Chemical Industries (ICI)* v. *Kenneth Hall Colmer (Her Majesty's Inspector of Taxes)*, [1998] ECR I-4695, para.15.
[207] In Case 28–30/62, *Da Costa et al.* v. *Netherlands Inland Revenue Administration*, [1963] ECR 31, the Court was presented with the identical scenario to Case 26/62, *Van Gend en Loos* and still held that Article 267 TFEU 'always allows a national court, if it considers it desirable, to refer questions of interpretation to the Court again' (*ibid.*, 38).

What will this formulation mean? Two theoretical options exist. Under the 'institutional' theory, the formulation refers to the highest judicial *institution* in the country. This would restrict the obligation to refer preliminary questions to a single court in a Member State – in the United Kingdom: the Supreme Court. By contrast, the 'procedural' theory links the definition of the court of last instance to the judicial *procedure* in the particular case. This broadens the obligation to refer to every national court whose decision cannot be appealed in the particular case. And the Court of Justice has – from the very beginning – favoured the second theory.[208] The key concept in Article 267 (3) TFEU is thereby the 'appeal*ability*' of a judicial decision. What counts is the *ability* of the parties to appeal to a higher court. The fact that the merits of the appeal are subject to a prior declaration of admissibility by the superior court may thereby not deprive the parties of a judicial remedy.[209] Where an appeal is thus *procedurally* possible, the obligation under Article 267 (3) TFEU will not apply.

Apart from the uncertainty as to what are courts 'against whose decisions there is no judicial remedy under national law', the wording of Article 267 (3) TFEU appears relatively clear. Yet, this picture is – very – deceptive. The European Court has indeed judicially 'amended' the provision in two significant ways. The first 'amendment' relates to references on the validity of European law. Despite the restrictive wording of paragraph 3, the European Court has insisted that *all* national courts must refer validity questions to the European Court.[210] This *expansion* of the scope of Article 267 (3) TFEU follows from the structure of the Union's judicial federalism, which grants the exclusive power to invalidate European law to the Court of Justice alone.

By contrast, a second 'amendment' has limited the obligation to refer preliminary questions. This *limitation* followed from constitutional common sense. For to ask a question implies uncertainty as to the answer. And where the answer is 'clear', there may be no need to raise a question. Yet on its textual

---

[208] The procedural theory received support in Case 6/64, *Costa* v. *ENEL*, [1964] ECR 585, where the ECJ treated an Italian court of *first* instance as a court against whose decision there was no judicial remedy.

[209] Case C-99/00, *Lyckeskog*, [2002] ECR I-4839, paras. 16–17: 'Decisions of a national appellate court which can be challenged by the parties before a supreme court are not decisions of a court or tribunal of a Member State against whose decisions there is no judicial remedy under national law within the meaning of Article [267 TFEU]. The fact that examination of the merits of such appeals is subject to a prior declaration of admissibility by the Supreme Court does not have the effect of depriving the parties of a judicial remedy. That is so under the Swedish system. The parties always have the right to appeal to the Hogsta domstol against the judgment of a hovratt, which cannot therefore be classified as a court delivering a decision against which there is no judicial remedy. Under Paragraph 10 of Chapter 54 of the Rattegangsbalk, the Hogsta domstol may issue a declaration of admissibility if it is important for guidance as to the application of the law that the appeal be examined by that court. Thus, uncertainty as to the interpretation of the law applicable, including [European] law, may give rise to review, at last instance, by the Supreme Court.'

[210] See Case C-344/04, *The Queen on the application of International Air Transport Association et al.* v. *Department for Transport*, (supra n. 96), para. 30.

face, Article 267 (3) treats national courts 'as perpetual children': they are forbidden from interpreting European law – even if the answers are crystal clear.[211] And in order to counter this, the European legal order imported a French legal doctrine under the name of *acte clair*.[212] The doctrine simply means that where it is *clear* how to *act*, a national court need not ask a preliminary question.

The doctrine of *acte clair* began its European career in *Da Costa*.[213] In this case, the Court held that 'the authority of an interpretation under Article [267] already given by the Court may deprive the obligation of its purpose and thus empty it of its substance'. 'Such is the case especially when the question raised is *materially identical* with a question which has already been the subject of a preliminary ruling in a similar case.'[214] The Court subsequently clarified that this covered a second situation. Where the European Court had already given a negative answer to a question relating to the *validity* of a Union act, another national court need not raise the same question again.[215] However, general guidelines on the constitutional scope of the *acte clair* doctrine were only offered in *CILFIT*.[216] The Court here widened the doctrine to situations 'where previous decisions of the Court have already dealt with the *point of law* in question, irrespective of the nature of the proceedings which led to those decisions, even though the questions at issue are not strictly identical'.[217] Yet national courts would only be released from their obligation to refer questions

---

[211] J.C. Cohen, 'The European Preliminary Reference and US Court Review of State Court Judgments: a Study in Comparative Judicial Federalism' [1996] *American Journal of Comparative Law* 421 at 438.

[212] There are different interpretations of the 'hidden' constitutional reasons behind the European *acte clair* doctrine. Some commentators have seen it in purely negative terms: the European Court finally become resigned to the fact that national supreme courts did not honour their obligation to refer questions under Article 267 (3) TFEU, and the invention of the *acte clair* doctrine 'legalised' a (previously) illegal national practice. A second interpretation sees the doctrine in a positive light: the European Court rejected the idea of considering national supreme courts as less reliable than lower national courts in interpreting European law. The obligation to refer would thus only arise where there was a real European law 'question'. A third interpretation has seen the doctrine of *acte clair* as part of a 'give and take' strategy, according to which the Court gave more power to national courts so as to develop a doctrine of precedent. On the various readings, see: H. Rasmussen, 'The European Court's Acte Clair Strategy in CILFIT' [1984] 10 EL Rev 242.

[213] Case 28-30/62, *Da Costa* (supra n. 207).   [214] *Ibid.*, 38.

[215] Case 66/80, *International Chemical Corporation*, [1981] ECR 1191, paras.12–13: 'When the Court is moved under Article [267] to declare an act of one of the institutions to be void there are particularly imperative requirements concerning legal certainty in addition to those concerning the uniform application of [European] law. It follows from the very nature of such a declaration that a national court may not apply the act declared to be void without once more creating serious uncertainty as to the [European] law applicable. It follows therefrom that although a judgment of the Court given under Article [267] of the Treaty declaring an act of an institution, in particular a Council or Commission regulation, to be void is directly addressed only to the national court which brought the matter before the Court, it is sufficient reason for any other national court to regard that act as void for the purposes of a judgment which it has to give.'

[216] Case 283/81, *CILFIT and others* v. *Ministry of Health*, [1982] ECR 3415.   [217] *Ibid.*, para. 14.

under Article 267 (3) TFEU, where the correct application of European law is 'so obvious as to leave no scope for any reasonable doubt as to the matter in which the question raised is to be resolved'.[218] This was an extremely high threshold, which the Court linked to the fulfilment of a number of very (!) restrictive conditions.[219]

(d) The legal nature of preliminary rulings

What is the nature of preliminary rulings from the European Court? Preliminary references are not appeals. They are – principally – discretionary acts of the national court asking for interpretative help from the European Court.[220] Once the European Court has given a preliminary ruling, this ruling will be binding. But *whom* will it bind – the parties to the national disputes or the national court(s)?

Preliminary rulings cannot bind the parties in the national dispute, since the European Court will not 'decide' their case. It is therefore misleading to even speak of a binding effect *inter partes* in the context of preliminary rulings.[221] The Court's rulings are addressed to the national court requesting the reference; and the Court has clarified that 'that ruling is binding on the national court as to the interpretation of the [Union] provisions and acts in question'.[222] Yet, will

---

[218] *Ibid.*, para. 16.

[219] *Ibid.*, paras. 16–20: 'Before it comes to the conclusion that such is the case, the national court or tribunal must be convinced that the matter is equally obvious to the courts of the other Member States and to the Court of Justice. Only if those conditions are satisfied, may the national court or tribunal refrain from submitting the question to the Court of Justice and take upon itself the responsibility for resolving it. However, the existence of such a possibility must be assessed on the basis of the characteristic features of [European] law and the particular difficulties to which its interpretation gives rise. To begin with, it must be borne in mind that [Union] legislation is drafted in several languages and that the different language versions are all equally authentic. An interpretation of a provision of [European] law thus involves a comparison of the different language versions. It must also be borne in mind, even where the different language versions are entirely in accord with one another, that [European] law uses terminology which is peculiar to it. Furthermore, it must be emphasised that legal concepts do not necessarily have the same meaning in [European] law and in the law of the various Member States. Finally, every provision of [European] law must be placed in its context and interpreted in the light of the provisions of [European] law as a whole, regard being had to the objectives thereof and to its state of evolution at the date on which the provision in question is to be applied.'

[220] Case C-2/06, *Kempter* v. *Hauptzollamt Hamburg-Jonas*, [2008] ECR I-411, para. 41: 'the system established by Article [267 TFEU] with a view to ensuring that [European] law is interpreted uniformly in the Member States instituted direct cooperation between the Court of Justice and the national courts by means of a procedure which is completely independent of any initiative by the parties'. And para. 42: 'the system of references for a preliminary ruling is based on a dialogue between one court and another, the initiation of which depends entirely on the national court's assessment as to whether a reference is appropriate and necessary'.

[221] Contra: A. Toth, 'The Authority of Judgments of the European Court of Justice: Binding Force and Legal Effects' [1984] 4 YEL 1.

[222] Case 52/76, *Benedetti* v. *Munari*, [1977] ECR 163, para. 26: 'that ruling is binding on the national court as to the interpretation of the [Union] provisions and acts in question'.

the binding effect of a preliminary ruling extend beyond the referring national court? In other words, is a preliminary ruling equivalent to a 'decision' addressed to a single court; or will the European Court's interpretation be generally binding on all national courts?

The Court has long clarified that a preliminary ruling is *not* a 'decision'; indeed, it is not even seen as an (external) act of a Union institution.[223] What then is the nature of preliminary rulings? The question has been hotly debated in the academic literature. And – again – we may contrast two views competing with each other. According to the common law view, preliminary rulings are – if not *de jure* at least *de facto* – legal precedents that generally bind all national courts. Judgments of the European Court are binding *erga omnes*.[224] This view typically links the rise of the doctrine of judicial precedent with the evolution of the doctrine of *acte clair*.[225] It is thereby claimed that the Court of Justice transformed its position vis-à-vis national courts from a *horizontal* and *bilateral* relationship to a *vertical* and *multilateral* one.[226]

The problem with this – masterful yet mistaken – theory is that the European Court subscribes to a second constitutional view: the civil law tradition. Accordingly, its judgments do not create 'new' legal rules but only clarify 'old' ones. In the words of the Court: 'The interpretation which, in the exercise of the jurisdiction conferred upon it by Article [267 TFEU], the Court of Justice gives to a rule of [European] law clarifies and defines where necessary the meaning and scope of that rule as it must be or ought to have been understood and applied from the time of its coming into force [.]'[227] The Court of Justice has thus adopted the – (in)famous – 'declaration theory'. And because 'the judgments are assumed to be declaring pre-existing law, their binding force applies to all relationships governed by the [positive] legal instrument since it entered into force'.[228] The vertical and multilateral effects of preliminary rulings are thus mediated through the positive law interpreted – and not, as the common law view asserts, through a doctrine of precedent.[229]

---

[223] Case 69/85 (Order), *Wünsche Handelsgesellschaft* v. *Germany*, [1986] ECR 947, para.16.

[224] See A. Trabucchi, 'L'Effet "Erga Omnes" des Décisions Préjudicielles Rendues par la Cour de Justice des Communautés Européennes' [1974] 10 RTDE 56.

[225] Ramussen, 'The European Court's *Acte Clair* Strategy' (supra n. 212).

[226] This view is popularised in: P. Craig and G. de Búrca, *EU Law: Text, Cases and Materials* (Oxford University Press, 2007), 461.

[227] Case 61/79, *Amministrazione delle finanze dello Stato* v. *Denkavit*, [1980] ECR 1205, para.16; and somewhat more recently: Case C-453/00, *Kühne & Heitz* v. *Productschap voor Pluimvee en Eieren*, [2004] ECR I-837, para. 21.

[228] D. Chalmers et al., *European Union Law* (Cambridge University Press, 2010), 171.

[229] Against this civilian background, the argument that the Treaty, by providing for the automatic operation of the obligation to refer, 'assumed that the Court's dicta under Article [267] were deprived of authority for any other court than the submitting one' (Ramussen, 'The European Court's *Acte Clair* Strategy' (supra n. 212) at 249), is flawed. And starting from this false premise, Rasmussen (over)interprets *CILFIT*.

In light of the 'civilian' judicial philosophy of the European Court, its judgments are *not* generally binding.[230] There is no vertical or multilateral effect of judicial decisions as 'judgments of the European Courts are *not sources* but *authoritative evidences* of [European] law'. '[A]n interpretation given by the Court becomes an integral part of the provision interpreted and cannot fail to affect the legal position of all those who may derive rights and obligations from that provision.'[231]

Are there constitutional problems with the Union's civil law philosophy? There are indeed 'temporal' problems. For the 'declaratory' effect of preliminary rulings generally generates 'retroactive' effects.[232] Indeed, in *Kühne & Heitz*,[233] the Court held that a (new) interpretation of European law must be applied 'even to legal relationships which arose or were formed before the Court gave its ruling on the question on interpretation'.[234] The Court has, however, recognised that its civil law philosophy must – occasionally – be tempered by the principles of legal certainty and financial equity.[235] It has therefore – exceptionally – limited the temporal effect of its preliminary rulings to an effect *ex nunc*, that is: an effect from the time of the ruling. However, at the same time, the Court has clarified that legal certainty will not prevent the retrospective application of a (new) interpretation, where the judgment of a court of final instance 'was, in the light of a decision given by the Court subsequent to it, based on a misinterpretation of [European] law which was adopted without a question being referred to the Court for a preliminary ruling under the third paragraph of Article [267]'.[236]

Conclusion

The Court of Justice of the European Union has never just been 'the mouth of the law'. The Court's judicial powers are extensive – and the Court has used them extensively. Yet while the Court's judicial activism has been subject to heavy criticism,[237] the Court continues to be a 'court'; and as a court its powers are essentially 'passive' powers. This chapter looked at three judicial powers in

---

[230] In this sense, see: Toth (supra n. 221), 60: 'in the cases under discussion the Court itself has never meant to attribute, as is sometimes suggested, a general binding force to interpretative preliminary rulings'.

[231] *Ibid.*, 70 and 74.

[232] On this point, see: G. Bebr, 'Preliminary Rulings of the Court of Justice: Their Authority and Temporal Effect' [1981] 18 CML Rev 475, esp. 491: 'The retroactive effect of a preliminary interpretative ruling is, according to the Court, the general rule.'

[233] Case C-453/00, *Kühne & Heitz* (supra n. 227).   [234] *Ibid.*, para. 22.

[235] For the former rationale, see: Case C-2/06, *Kempter* (supra n. 220); for the latter rationale, see: Case 43/75, *Defrenne* v. *Sabena*, [1976] ECR 455.

[236] Case C-2/06, *Kempter* (supra n. 220) para. 39. For a critical analysis of this case, see: A. Ward, 'Do unto Others as You Would Have Them Do unto You: "Willy Kempter" and the Duty to Raise EC Law in National Litigation' [2008] EL Rev 739.

[237] See H. Rasmussen, *On Law and Policy in the European Court of Justice. A Comparative Study in Judicial Policymaking* (Nijhoff, 1986).

the context of the Union legal order: the power to annul European law, the power to remedy illegal acts of the Union, and the power to enforce European law through adjudication, both directly in the European Court and indirectly through the national courts.

The Union is based on the rule of law inasmuch as the European Court is empowered to review the legality of European (secondary) law. The Union legal order has thereby opted for a strong 'rule of law' version. It allows the Court to review the formal and substantive legality of European law. However, in the past, there existed severe procedural limitations on the right of individual applicants to request judicial review proceedings. Under the Rome Treaty, private parties were only entitled to challenge 'decisions' that were of 'direct and individual concern to them'. And while subsequent jurisprudence broadened their standing to the review of any Union act, the *Plaumann* formula restricted the right to judicial review to an exclusive set of private applicants. The Lisbon Treaty has liberalised this procedural restriction for 'regulatory' acts, but whether this category covers all generally applicable acts – including formal legislation – is still unclear. In the past, the Court has justified its restrictive stance on *direct* judicial review with its preference for the *indirect* judicial review via the preliminary reference procedure.

Section 2 looked at the remedial powers of the European court, while Sections 3 and 4 analysed the application of European law through adjudication. The Union has here chosen a dual enforcement mechanism. First, it allows for the *central* adjudication of European law through actions directly brought before the European Court. The Treaties thereby distinguish between infringement proceedings against the Member States, and infringement proceedings against the Union for a failure to act. However, secondly, the Union legal order also provides for the decentralised adjudication of European law in the national courts. From a functional perspective, national courts are thus – partly – European courts. In order to guarantee a degree of uniformity in the interpretation of European law, the Treaties provide for a 'preliminary reference procedure'. This is not an appeal procedure, but allows national courts to ask – if they want to – questions relating to the interpretation of European law. This – voluntary – cooperative arrangement is replaced by a constitutional obligation for national courts of last resort. But even these courts cannot be forced to make a reference to the European Court *by the parties*. But where they violate their European obligations, a Member State may incur liability, and this liability might give rise to an individual claim for damages in national courts. This aspect will be looked at in detail in Chapter 11 of this book.[238]

---

[238] On this point, see: Chapter 11 – Section 4(a) below.

Part III
Rights and Remedies

What are the qualities of European law? In particular: what is the effect of European law in the national legal orders? While Part II looked at how European (secondary) law comes into being, this Part analyses the normative fabric of European law. The central quality of European law is its direct applicability and direct effect. Direct applicability means that a European norm need not be 'translated' into a national norm before it can apply in the Member States. The direct effect of a European norm means that individuals can enforce it as of right. What is the nature of European rights? European rights are supreme over national law. According to the supremacy principle, national authorities must thus disapply any conflicting national law. Moreover, they must provide effective (national) remedies to assist individuals in the enforcement of their European rights. These general normative aspects of European law are looked at in Chapters 9, 10 and 11 respectively, and the most 'foundational' European rights – that is: fundamental (human) rights – are finally analysed in Chapter 12.

Chapter 9 – European Law: Direct and Indirect Effect

Chapter 10 – European Law: Supremacy and Preemption

Chapter 11 – European Law: Remedies and Liabilities

Chapter 12 – In Particular: European Human Rights

9

European Law: Direct and Indirect Effect

Contents

Introduction	306
1. Constitutional law: the effect of European primary law	310
(a) Direct effect: from strict to lenient test	312
(b) The dimensions of direct effect: vertical and horizontal direct effect	315
2. Direct Union law: regulations and decisions	317
(a) Regulations: the 'legislative' instrument	317
(i) General application in all Member States	317
(ii) Direct application and direct effect	318
(b) Decisions: the executive instrument	320
(i) Specifically addressed decisions	321
(ii) Non-addressed decisions	322
3. Indirect Union law: directives	323
(a) Direct effect and directives: conditions and limits	323
(i) The no-horizontal-direct-effect rule	326
(ii) The limitation to the rule: the wide definition of State (actions)	327
(iii) The exception to the rule: incidental horizontal direct effect	329
(b) Indirect effects through national and (primary) European law	331
(i) The doctrine of consistent interpretation of national law	331
(ii) Indirect effects through the medium of European law	334
4. External Union law: international agreements	337
(a) Direct effects of Union agreements	338
(i) The conditions for direct effect	339
(ii) The dimensions of direct effect	341
(b) Indirect effects: the interpretation and implementation principles	342
Conclusion	344

Introduction

Classic international law holds that each State can choose the relationship between its 'domestic' law and 'international' law. Two – constitutional – theories thereby exist: monism and dualism.[1] Monist States make international law part of their domestic legal order. International law will thus directly apply *as if* it was domestic law.[2] By contrast, dualist States consider international law separate from domestic law. International law is viewed as the law *between* States; national law is the law *within* a State. While international treaties are thus binding 'on' States, they cannot be binding 'in' States. International law needs to be 'transposed' or 'incorporated' into domestic law and will here only have *indirect* effects through the medium of national law. The dualist theory is based on a basic division of labour: international institutions apply international law, while national institutions apply national law.

Did European law leave the choice between monism and dualism to its Member States? For dualist States, all European law would need to be 'incorporated' into national law before it could have domestic effects.[3] There would be no direct applicability of European law, as all European norms are mediated through national law. Individuals would here never come into *direct* contact with European law. And where a Member State violated European law, individuals could not invoke 'their' European rights as against national law. For the State's breach of European law could only be established and remedied at the

---

[1] The choice between monism and dualism is a 'national' choice. Thus, even where a State chooses the monist approach, monism in this sense only means that international norms are *constitutionally* recognised as an autonomous legal source of *domestic* law. Dualism, by contrast, means that international norms will not automatically, that is: through a constitutional incorporation, become part of the national legal order. Each international treaty demands a separate legislative act 'incorporating' the international norm into domestic law. The difference between monism and dualism thus boils down to whether international law is incorporated via the constitution, as in the United States; or whether international treaties need to be validated by a special parliamentary command, as in the United Kingdom. The idea that monism means that States have no choice but to apply international law is not accepted in international law.

[2] Article VI, Clause 2 of the United States Constitution (emphasis added): '[A]ll Treaties made, or which shall be made, under the Authority of the United States, *shall be the supreme Law of the Land*; and the Judges in every State shall be bound thereby, any Thing in the Constitution or Laws of any State to the Contrary notwithstanding.'

[3] For this dualist technique, see: (amended) European Communities Act (1972), Section 2(1): 'All such rights, powers, liabilities, obligations and restrictions from time to time created or arising by or under the Treaties, and all such remedies and procedures from time to time provided for by or under the Treaties, as in accordance with the Treaties are without further enactment to be given legal effect or used in the United Kingdom shall be recognised and available in law, and be enforced, allowed and followed accordingly; and the expression "enforceable EU right" and similar expressions shall be read as referring to one to which this subsection applies.' And see now also the 2011 European Union Act, Clause 18: 'Directly applicable or directly effective EU law (that is, the rights, powers, liabilities, obligations, restrictions, remedies and procedures referred to in section 2(1) of the European Communities Act 1972) falls to be recognised and available in law in the United Kingdom only by virtue of that Act or where it is required to be recognised and available in law by virtue of any other Act.'

Figure 19 Monism and Dualism

European level. And the European Treaties contained such an 'international' remedial machinery in the form of enforcement actions before the Court of Justice.[4]

Did this not signal that the European Treaties permitted the dualist approach? Not necessarily, for the Treaties also contained strong signals against the 'ordinary' international reading of European law. Not only was the Union entitled to adopt legal acts that were to be 'directly applicable *in* all Member States',[5] but from the very beginning, the Treaties also contained a constitutional mechanism that envisaged the direct application of European law by the national courts.[6] And even if a monist view had not been intended by the founding Member States, the European Court discarded any dualist leanings in the most important case of European law: *Van Gend en Loos*.[7] The Court here expressly cut the umbilical cord with classic international law by insisting that the European legal order was a 'new legal order'. In the famous words of the Court:

> The objective of the E[U] Treaty, which is to establish a common market, the functioning of which is of direct concern to interested parties in the [Union], implies that this Treaty is *more than an agreement which merely creates mutual obligations between the contracting States*. This view is confirmed by the preamble to the Treaty which refers not only to the governments but to peoples. It is also confirmed more specifically by the establishment of institutions endowed with sovereign rights, the exercise of which affects Member States and also their citizens. Furthermore, it must be noted that the nations of the States brought together in the [Union] are called upon to cooperate in the functioning of this [Union] through the intermediary of the European Parliament and the Economic and Social Committee.
>
> In addition the task assigned to the Court of Justice under Article [267 TFEU], the object of which is to secure uniform interpretation of the Treaty by national courts and tribunals, confirms that the States have acknowledged that [European] law has an authority which can be invoked by their nationals before those courts and tribunals. The conclusion to be drawn from this is that the [Union] constitutes a *new legal order of international law* for the benefit of which the States have limited their sovereign rights, albeit within limited fields, and the subjects of which comprise not only Member States but also their nationals. *Independently of*

---

[4] On this point, see: Chapter 8 – Section 3(a) above.   [5] Article 288 (2) TFEU.
[6] Article 267 TFEU. On the provision, see: Chapter 8 – Section 4 above.
[7] Case 26/62, *Van Gend en Loos* v. *Netherlands Inland Revenue Administration*, [1963] ECR (Special English Edition) 1.

the legislation of Member States, [European] law therefore not only imposes obligations on individuals but is also intended to confer upon them rights which become part of their legal heritage.[8]

All judicial arguments here marshalled to justify a monistic reading of European law are debatable.[9] But with a stroke of the pen, the Court confirmed the independence of the European legal order from classic international law. Unlike ordinary international law, the European Treaties were more than agreements creating mutual obligations between States. Individuals were subjects of European law and their rights and obligations would derive *directly* from European law. European law would thus be *directly* applicable in the national legal orders. And it was to be enforced in national courts – despite the parallel existence of an international enforcement machinery.[10] And because European law was directly applicable law, the European legal order could *itself* determine the nature and effect of European law within the national legal orders. The direct applicability of European law thus allowed the Court *centrally* to develop two foundational doctrines of the European legal order: the doctrine of direct effect and the doctrine of supremacy. The present chapter deals with the doctrine of direct effect; Chapter 10 deals with the doctrine of supremacy.

What is the relationship between direct applicability and direct effect? It is vital to understand that the Court's decision in favour of a monistic relationship between the European and the national legal orders did not mean that all European law could be enforced by national courts. To be enforceable, a norm must be 'justiciable' or 'executable',[11] that is: it must be capable of being applied by a public authority in a specific case. But not all legal norms have this quality. For example, where a European norm requires Member States

---

[8] *Ibid.*, 12 (emphasis added).

[9] For a critical overview, see T. Arnull, *The European Union and its Court of Justice* (Oxford University Press, 2006), 168 et seq.

[10] Case 26/62, *Van Gend en Loos* (supra n. 7), 13: 'In addition the argument based on Articles [258] and [259] of the [FEU] Treaty put forward by the three Governments which have submitted observations to the Court in their statements of the case is misconceived. The fact that these Articles of the Treaty enable the Commission and the Member States to bring before the Court a State which has not fulfilled its obligations does not mean that individuals cannot plead these obligations, should the occasion arise, before a national court, any more than the fact that the Treaty places at the disposal of the Commission ways of ensuring that obligations imposed upon those subject to the Treaty are observed, precludes the possibility, in actions between individuals before a national court, of pleading infringements of these obligations. A restriction of the guarantees against an infringement of Article [30] by Member States to the procedures under Articles [258 and 259] would remove all direct legal protection of the individual rights of their nationals. There is the risk that recourse to the procedure under these Articles would be ineffective if it were to occur after the implementation of a national decision taken contrary to the provisions of the Treaty. The vigilance of individuals concerned to protect their rights amounts to an effective supervision in addition to the supervision entrusted by Articles [258 and 259] to the diligence of the Commission and of the Member States.'

[11] On the application of the doctrine of direct effect to the national executive branch, see: Conclusion below.

to establish a public fund to guarantee unpaid wages for insolvent private companies, yet leaves a wide margin of discretion to the Member States on how to achieve that end, this norm is not intended to have direct effects in a specific situation. While it binds the national legislator, the norm is not self-executing. The concept of direct applicability is thus wider than the concept of direct effect. Whereas the former refers to the *internal* effect of a European norm within national legal orders, the latter refers to the *individual* effect of a binding norm in specific cases.[12] Direct effect requires direct applicability, but not the other way around. The direct applicability of a norm only makes its direct effect *possible*.

After all these terminological preliminaries, when will European law have direct effect? And are there different types of direct effect? May a norm without direct effect have indirect effects? This chapter explores the doctrine of (in)direct effect across the various sources of European law. It will start with the direct effect of the European Treaties in Section 1. The European Treaties are framework treaties in that they envisage the adoption of European secondary law. This secondary law may take various forms. These forms are defined in Article 288 TFEU.[13] The provision defines the Union's legal instruments, and states:

[1] To exercise the Union's competences, the institutions shall adopt regulations, directives, decisions, recommendations and opinions.
[2] A regulation shall have general application. It shall be binding in its entirety and directly applicable in all Member States.
[3] A directive shall be binding, as to the result to be achieved, upon each Member State to which it is addressed, but shall leave to the national authorities the choice of form and methods.
[4] A decision shall be binding in its entirety. A decision which specifies those to whom it is addressed shall be binding only on them.
[5] Recommendations and opinions shall have no binding force.

The provision thus acknowledges three binding legal instruments – regulations, directives, and decisions – and two non-binding instruments.[14] Why was there

---

[12] In this sense direct applicability is a 'federal' question as it relates to the effect of a 'foreign' norm in a domestic legal system, whereas direct effect is a 'separation-of-powers' question as it relates to the issue whether a norm must be applied by the legislature or the executive and judiciary.

[13] The institutional practice of Union decision-making has created a number of 'atypical' acts. For a discussion of atypical acts, see: J. Klabbers, 'Informal Instruments before the European Court of Justice' [1994] 31 CML Rev 997. But see also now: Article 296 TFEU – third indent: 'When considering draft legislative acts, the European Parliament and the Council shall refrain from adopting acts not provided for by the relevant legislative procedure in the area in question.'

[14] Logic would dictate that non-binding acts are not binding. Yet, the European Court has accepted the possibility of their having some 'indirect' legal effect. In Case 322/88, *Grimaldi* v. *Fonds des maladies professionelles*, [1989] ECR 4407, para. 18, the Court held that recommendations 'cannot be regarded as having no legal effect' as they 'supplement binding [European] provisions'. 'Non-binding' Union acts may, therefore, have legal 'side effects'. For an interesting overview, see L. Senden, *Soft Law in European Community Law: Its Relationship to Legislation* (Hart, 2004).

a need for three distinct binding instruments? The answer seems to lie in their specific – direct and indirect – effects in the national legal orders. While regulations and decisions were considered Union acts that directly established legal norms (Section 2), directives appeared to be designed as indirect forms of legislation (Section 3).

Sadly, Article 288 TFEU is incomplete, as it only mentions the Union's *internal* instruments. A fourth binding instrument indeed needs to be 'read into' the list: international agreements. For Union agreements are not only binding upon the institutions of the Union, but also '*on* its Member States'.[15] Did this mean that international agreements were an indirect form of external legislation, or could they be binding 'in' the Member States? Section 4 will analyse the (in)direct effects of international agreements in the national legal orders.

1. Constitutional law: the effect of European primary law

The European Treaties are framework treaties. They establish the objectives of the European Union, and endow it with the powers to achieve these objectives. Many of the European policies in Part III of the TFEU thus simply set out the competences and procedures for future Union secondary law. The Treaties, as primary European law, thereby offer the constitutional bones. But could this constitutional 'skeleton' itself have direct effect? Would there be Treaty provisions that were sufficiently precise to give rise to rights or obligations that national courts could apply in specific situations?

The European Court affirmatively answered this question in *Van Gend en Loos*.[16] The case concerned a central objective of the European Union: the internal market. According to that central plank of the Treaties, the Union was to create a customs union between the Member States. Within a customs union, goods can move freely without any pecuniary charges levied when crossing borders. The Treaties had chosen to establish the customs union gradually; and to this effect ex-Article 12 EEC contained a standstill obligation: 'Member States shall refrain from introducing between themselves any new customs duties on imports or exports or any charges having equivalent effect, and from increasing those which they already apply in their trade with each other.'[17] The Netherlands appeared to have violated this provision and, believing this to be the case, Van Gend & Loos – a Dutch importing company – brought proceedings in a Dutch court against the National Inland Revenue. The Dutch court had doubts about the admissibility and the substance of the case and referred a number of preliminary questions to the European Court of Justice.

---

[15] Article 216 (2) TFEU.   [16] Case 26/62, *Van Gend en Loos* (supra n. 7).

[17] The provision has been repealed. Strictly speaking, it is therefore not correct to identify Article 30 TEU as the successor provision, for the latter is based on ex-Articles 13 and 16 EEC. The normative content of ex-Article 12 EEC solely concerned the introduction of *new* customs duties; and therefore did not cover the abolition of existing tariff restrictions.

Could a private party enforce an international treaty in a national court? And if so, was this a question of national or European law? In the course of the proceedings before the European Court, the Netherlands government heavily disputed that an individual could enforce a Treaty provision against its own government in a national court. Any alleged infringements had to be submitted to the European Court by the Commission or a Member State under the 'international' infringement procedures set out in Articles 258 and 259 TFEU.[18] The Belgian government, having intervened in the case, equally claimed that the question of what effect an international treaty had within the national legal order 'falls exclusively within the jurisdiction of the Netherlands court'.[19] Conversely, the Commission countered that 'the effects of the provisions of the Treaty on the national law of Member States cannot be determined by the actual national law of each of them but by the Treaty itself'.[20] And since ex-Article 12 EEC was 'clear and complete', it was 'a rule of law capable of being effectively applied by the national court'.[21] The fact that the European provision was addressed to the Member States did 'not of itself take away from individuals who have an interest in it the right to require it to be applied in the national courts'.[22]

Two views thus competed before the Court. According to the 'international' view, legal rights of private parties could 'not derive from the [Treaties] or the legal measures taken by the institutions, but [solely] from legal measures enacted by Member States'.[23] According to the 'constitutional' view, by contrast, European law was capable of directly creating individual rights. The Court famously favoured the second view. It followed from the 'spirit' of Treaties that European law was no 'ordinary' international law. It would thus in itself be directly applicable in the national legal orders.

But when would a provision have direct effect, and thus entitle private parties to seek its application by a national court? Having briefly presented the general scheme of the Treaty in relation to customs duties,[24] the Court concentrated on the wording of ex-Article 12 EEC and found as follows:

> The wording of [ex-]Article 12 [EEC] contains a *clear and unconditional prohibition* which is not a positive but a *negative obligation*. This obligation, moreover, is *not qualified by any reservation on the part of the States, which would make its implementation conditional upon a positive legislative measure enacted under national law.* The very nature of this prohibition makes it ideally adapted to produce direct effects in the legal relationship between Member States and their subjects. The implementation of [ex-]Article 12 [EEC] does not require any legislative intervention on the part of the States. The fact that under this Article

---

[18] Case 26/62, *Van Gend en Loos*, (supra n. 7), 6. On enforcement actions by the Commission, see: Chapter 8 – Section 3(a) above.

[19] Case 26/62, *Van Gend en Loos* (supra n. 7), 6.   [20] *Ibid.*   [21] *Ibid.*, 7   [22] *Ibid.*

[23] This was the view of the German government (*ibid.*, 8).

[24] The Court considered ex-Article 12 EEC as an 'essential provision' in the general scheme of the Treaty as it relates to customs duties (*ibid.*, 12).

it is the Member States who are made the subject of the negative obligation does not imply that their nationals cannot benefit from this obligation.[25]

While somewhat repetitive, the test for direct effect is here clearly presented: wherever the Treaties contain a 'prohibition' that was 'clear' and 'unconditional', that prohibition would have direct effect. To be an unconditional prohibition thereby required two things. First, the European provision had to be an *automatic* prohibition, that is: it should not depend on subsequent positive legislation by the European Union. And second, the prohibition should ideally be *absolute*, that is: 'not qualified by any reservation on the part of the States'.

This was a – very – strict test. But ex-Article 12 EEC was indeed 'ideally adapted' to satisfy this triple test. It was a clear prohibition and unconditional in the double sense outlined above. However, if the Court had insisted on a strict application of all three criteria, very few provisions within the Treaties would have had direct effect. Yet the Court subsequently loosened the test considerably. And as we shall see below, it clarified that the Treaties could be vertically and horizontally directly effective.

(a) Direct effect: from strict to lenient test

The direct effect test set out in *Van Gend en Loos* was informed by three criteria. First, a provision had to be clear. Second, it had to be unconditional in the sense of being an automatic prohibition. And third, this prohibition would need to be absolute, that is: not allow for reservations. In its subsequent jurisprudence, the Court expanded the concept of direct effect on all three fronts.

First, how clear would a prohibition have to be to be directly effective? Within the Treaties' title on the free movement of goods, we find the following famous prohibition: 'Quantitative restrictions on imports and all measures having equivalent effect shall be prohibited between Member States.'[26] Was this a clear prohibition? While the notion of 'quantitative restrictions' might have been – relatively – clear, what about 'measures having equivalent effect'? The Commission had realised the open-ended nature of the concept and offered some early semantic help.[27] And yet, despite all the uncertainty involved, the Court found that the provision had direct effect.[28]

---

[25] *Ibid.*, 13 (emphasis added).   [26] Article 34 TFEU.

[27] Directive 70/50/EEC on the abolition of measures which have an effect equivalent to quantitative restrictions on imports and are not covered by other provisions adopted in pursuance of the EEC Treaty, [1970] OJ English Special Edition 17.

[28] Case 74/76, *Iannelli & Volpi SpA* v. *Ditta Paolo Meroni*, [1977] ECR 557, para. 13: 'The prohibition of quantitative restrictions and measures having equivalent effect laid down in Article [34] of the [FEU] Treaty is mandatory and explicit and its implementation does not require any subsequent intervention of the Member States or [Union] institutions. The prohibition therefore has direct effect and creates individual rights which national courts must protect[.]'

The same lenient interpretation of what 'clear' meant was soon applied to even wider provisions. In *Defrenne*,[29] the Court analysed the following prohibition: '[e]ach Member State shall ensure that the principle of equal pay for male and female workers for equal work or work of equal value is applied'.[30] Was this a clear prohibition of discrimination? Confusingly, the Court found that the provision might and might not have direct effect. With regard to indirect discrimination, the Court considered the prohibition indeterminate, since it required 'the elaboration of criteria whose implementation necessitates the taking of appropriate measures at [European] and national level'.[31] Yet in respect of direct discrimination, the prohibition was directly effective.[32]

What about the second part of the direct effect test? When was a prohibition automatic? Would this be the case where the Treaties expressly acknowledged the need for positive legislative action by the Union to achieve a Union objective? For example, the Treaty chapter on the right of establishment contains not just a prohibition addressed to the Member States in Article 49 TFEU,[33] the subsequent Article 50 states: 'In order to attain freedom of establishment as regards a particular activity, the European Parliament and the Council, acting in accordance with the ordinary legislative procedure and after consulting the Economic and Social Committee, shall act by means of directives.' Would this not mean that the freedom of establishment was conditional on legislative action? In *Reyners*,[34] the Court rejected this argument. Despite the fact that the general scheme within the chapter on freedom of establishment contained a set of provisions that sought to achieve free movement through positive Union legislation,[35] the Court declared the European right of establishment in Article 49 TFEU to be directly effective. And the Court had no qualms about giving direct effect to the general prohibition on 'any discrimination on grounds of nationality' – despite the fact that Article 18

---

[29] Case 43/75, *Defrenne v. Sabena*, [1976] ECR 455, para. 19.   [30] Article 157 (1) TFEU.

[31] Case 43/75, *Defrenne v. Sabena* (supra n. 29), para. 19.

[32] *Ibid.*, para. 24. This generous reading was subsequently extended to the yet wider prohibition on 'any discrimination on grounds of nationality'; see Case C-85/96, *Martínez Sala v. Freistaat Bayern*, [1998] ECR I-2691, para. 63.

[33] Article 49 (1) TFEU states: 'Within the framework of the provisions set out below, restrictions on the freedom of establishment of nationals of a Member State in the territory of another Member State shall be prohibited. Such prohibition shall also apply to restrictions on the setting-up of agencies, branches or subsidiaries by nationals of any Member State established in the territory of any Member State. Freedom of establishment shall include the right to take up and pursue activities as self-employed persons and to set up and manage undertakings, in particular companies or firms within the meaning of the second paragraph of Article 54, under the conditions laid down for its own nationals by the law of the country where such establishment is effected, subject to the provisions of the Chapter relating to capital.'

[34] Case 2/74, *Reyners v. Belgian State*, [1974] ECR 631. For an excellent discussion of this question, see: P. Craig, 'Once Upon a Time in the West: Direct Effect and the Federalisation of EEC Law' [1992] 12 *Oxford Journal of Legal Studies* 453 at 463–470.

[35] Case 2/74, *Reyners* (supra n. 34), para.32.

TFEU expressly called on the Union legislator to adopt rules 'designed to prohibit such discrimination'.[36]

Finally, what about the third requirement? Could *relative* prohibitions, even if clear, ever be directly effective? The prohibition on quantitative restrictions on imports, discussed above, is subject to a number of legitimate exceptions according to which it 'shall not preclude prohibitions or restrictions on imports, exports or goods in transit justified on grounds of public morality, public policy or public security'.[37] Was this then a prohibition that was 'not qualified by any reservation on the part of the States'? The Court found that this was indeed the case. For although these derogations would 'attach particular importance to the interests of Member States, it must be observed that they deal with exceptional cases which are clearly defined and which do not lend themselves to any wide interpretation'.[38] And since the application of these exceptions was 'subject to judicial control', a Member State's right to invoke them did not prevent the general prohibition 'from conferring on individuals rights which are enforceable by them and which the national courts must protect'.[39]

What, then, is the test for the direct effect of Treaty provisions in light of these – relaxing – developments? The simple test is this: a provision has direct effect when it is capable of being applied by a national court. Importantly, direct effect does *not* depend on a European norm granting a subjective right;[40] but on the contrary, the subjective right is a result of a directly effective norm.[41] Direct effect simply means that a norm can be 'invoked' in and applied by a court. And this is the case when the Court of Justice says it is! Today, almost all Treaty *prohibitions* have direct effect – even the most general ones. Indeed, in *Mangold*,[42] the Court held that an – unwritten and vague – *general* principle of European law could have direct effect. Should we embrace this development? We should, for the direct effect of a legal rule 'must be considered as being the normal condition of any rule of law'. The very questioning of the direct effect of European law was an 'infant disease' of the young European legal order.[43] And this infant disease has today – largely – been cured but for one area: the Common Foreign and Security Policy.

---

[36] Case 85/96, *Martínez Sala* v. *Freistaat Bayern* (supra n. 32).   [37] Article 36 TFEU.

[38] Case 13/68, *Salgoil* v. *Italian Ministry of Foreign Trade*, [1968] ECR 453 at 463.

[39] Case 41/74, *van Duyn* v. *Home Office*, [1974] ECR 1337, para. 7.

[40] For the opposite view, see: K. Lenaerts and T. Corthaut, 'Of Birds and Hedges: the Role of Primacy in Invoking Norms of EU' [2006] 31 EL Rev 287 at 310: direct effect 'is the technique which allows individuals to enforce a subjective right which is only available in the internal legal order in an instrument that comes from outside that order, against another (state or private) actor'.

[41] M. Ruffert, 'Rights and Remedies in European Community Law: a Comparative View' [1997] 34 CML Rev 307 at 315.

[42] For a long discussion of this case, see: Section 3(b)(ii) below.

[43] P. Pescatore, 'The Doctrine of "Direct Effect": an Infant Disease of Community Law' [1983] 8 EL Rev 155.

(b) The dimensions of direct effect: vertical and horizontal direct effect

Where a Treaty provision is directly effective, an individual can invoke European law in a national court (or administration). This will normally be as against the State. This situation is called 'vertical' effect, since the State is 'above' its subjects. But while a private party is in subordinate position vis-à-vis public authorities, it is in a coordinate position vis-à-vis other private parties. The legal effect of a norm between private parties is thus called 'horizontal' effect. And while there has never been any doubt that Treaty provisions can be invoked in a vertical situation, there has been some discussion on their horizontal direct effects.

Should it make a difference whether European law is invoked in proceedings against the Inland Revenue or in a civil dispute between two private parties? Should the Treaties be allowed to impose obligations on individuals? The Court in *Van Gend en Loos* had accepted this theoretical possibility.[44] And indeed, the horizontal direct effect of Treaty provisions has never been in doubt for the Court.[45] A good illustration of the horizontal direct effect of Treaty provisions can be found in *Familiapress* v. *Bauer*.[46] The case concerned the interpretation of Article 34 TFEU prohibiting unjustified restriction on the free movement of goods. It arose in a *civil* dispute before the Vienna Commercial Court between Familiapress and a German competitor. The latter was accused of violating the Austrian Law on Unfair Competition by publishing prize crossword puzzles – a sales technique that was deemed unfair under Austrian law. Bauer defended itself in the national court by invoking Article 34 TFEU – claiming that the directly effective European right to free movement prevailed over the Austrian law. And the Court of Justice indeed found that a national law that constituted an unjustified restriction of trade would have to be disapplied in the civil proceedings.

The question whether a Treaty prohibition has horizontal direct effect must, however, be distinguished from the question whether it also prohibits private actions. The latter is not simply a question of the *effect* of a provision, but rather of its personal scope. Many Treaty prohibitions are – expressly or implicitly – addressed to the State.[47] However, the Treaties equally contain provisions that are directly addressed to private parties.[48] The question whether a Treaty

---

[44] Case 26/62, *Van Gend en Loos* (supra n. 7), 12: '[European] law therefore not only imposes obligations on individuals . . .'.

[45] Indeed, the direct effect of Article 34 TFEU was announced in a 'horizontal' case between two private parties; see Case 74/76, *Iannelli & Volpi* v. *Paolo Meroni* (supra n. 28).

[46] Case C-368/95, *Vereinigte Familiapress Zeitungsverlags- und vertriebs GmbH* v. *Bauer Verlag*, [1997] ECR I-3689.

[47] For example, Article 157 TFEU states (emphasis added) that '[e]ach *Member State* shall ensure that the principle of equal pay for male and female workers for equal work or work of equal value is applied'; and Article 34 TFEU prohibits restrictions on the free movement of goods 'between Member States'.

[48] Article 102 TFEU prohibits 'all agreements between undertakings' that restrict competition within the internal market, and is thus addressed to private parties.

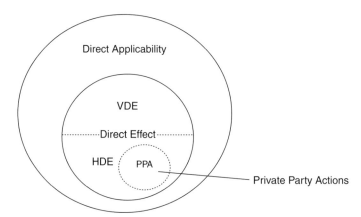

Figure 20 Direct Applicability, Direct Effect and Private Party Actions

prohibition covers public as well as private actions is controversial. Should the 'equal pay for equal work' principle or the free movement rules – both *expressly* addressed to the Member States – also *implicitly* apply to private associations and their actions? If so, the application of the Treaty will not just impose *indirect* obligations on individuals (when they lose their right to rely on a national law that violates European law); they will be *directly* prohibited from engaging in an activity. The Court has – in principle – confirmed that Treaty provisions, albeit addressed to the Member States, might cover private actions.[49] Thus in *Defrenne*, the Court found that the prohibition on pay discrimination between men and women could equally apply to private employers.[50] And while the exact conditions remain uncertain,[51] the Court has confirmed and reconfirmed the inclusion of private actions within the free movement provisions.[52]

To distinguish the logical relations between the various constitutional concepts of direct applicability, direct effect – both vertical (VDE) and horizontal (HDE) – and private party actions, Figure 20 may be useful.

---

[49] Case 36/74, *Walrave et al.* v. *Association Union cycliste international et al.*, [1974] ECR 1405, para. 19: 'to limit the prohibitions in question to acts of a public authority would risk creating inequality in their application'.

[50] Case 43/75, *Defrenne* (supra n. 29), para. 39: 'In fact, since Article [157 TFEU] is mandatory in nature, the prohibition on discrimination between men and women applies not only to the action of public authorities, but also extends to all agreements which are intended to regulate paid labour collectively, as well as to contracts between individuals.'

[51] The Court generally limits this application to 'private' rules that aim to regulate 'in a collective manner' (*ibid.*, para. 17). For somewhat more recent case law on the application of the free movement rules to private parties, see: Case C-415/93, *Union Royale Belge des Sociétés de Football Association ASBL* v. *Jean-Marc Bosman*, [1995] ECR I-4921.

[52] This has been confirmed for all four freedoms, with the possible exception of the provisions on goods. On the free movement of goods provisions in particular, see: P. Oliver et al., *Oliver on free movement of goods in the European Union* (Hart, 2010), Chapter 4, esp. 67 et seq.

2. Direct Union law: regulations and decisions

When the European Union was created, the Treaties envisaged two instruments that were directly applicable: regulations and decisions. A regulation would be an act of direct and general application in all Member States. It was designed as the legislative act of the Union. By contrast, a decision was originally seen as the executive instrument of the Union. It would directly apply to those to whom it was addressed.[53] Both instruments were predestined to have direct effects in the sense of allowing individuals to directly invoke them before national courts. Nonetheless, their precise effects have remained – partially – controversial. Would all provisions within a regulation be directly effective? And could decisions be generally applicable?

(a) Regulations: the 'legislative' instrument

'A regulation shall have general application. It shall be binding in its entirety and directly applicable in all Member States.'[54] This definition demands four things. First, regulations must be *generally* applicable. Second, they must be *entirely* binding. Third, they must be *directly* applicable, and that – fourth – in *all* Member States. This section starts by investigating characteristics one and four. It subsequently analyses the relationship between direct applicability and the question of direct effect.[55]

(i) General application in all Member States

Regulations were designed to be an instrument of (material) legislation.[56] Their 'general application' was originally meant to distinguish them from the 'specific application' of decisions.

In *Zuckerfabrik Watenstedt GmbH* v. *Council*,[57] the European Court defined 'general' applicability as 'applicable to objectively determined situations and involves legal consequences for categories of persons viewed in a general and abstract manner'; yet conceded that a regulation would not lose its general nature 'because it may be possible to ascertain with a greater or lesser degree of accuracy the number or even the identity of the persons to which it applies at any given time as long as there is no doubt that the measure is applicable as a result of an objective situation of law or of fact which it specifies'.[58] The crucial

---

[53] The original Article 189 EEC stated: 'A decision shall be binding in its entirety upon those to whom it is addressed.'

[54] Article 288 (2) TFEU.

[55] We shall analyse the 'second' element in Chapter 10 – Section 4(a)(i) when dealing with a regulation's preemptive capacity.

[56] Joined Cases 16–17/62, *Confédération Nationale des Producteurs de Fruits et de Légumes* v. *Council*, [1962] ECR 471, para. 2. On the material concept of legislation, see: Chapter 5 – Introduction.

[57] Case 6/68, *Zuckerfabrik Watenstedt GmbH* v. *Council*, [1968] ECR 409   [58] *Ibid.*, at 415.

characteristic of a regulation – a characteristic that would give it a 'legislative' character – is thus the 'openness' of the group of persons to whom it applies. Where the group of persons is 'fixed in time' the act would not constitute a regulation but a bundle of individual decisions.[59]

Would all provisions within a regulation have to satisfy the general applicability test? The European Court has clarified that this is not the case. Not all provisions of a regulation must be general in character. Some provisions may indeed constitute individual decisions 'without prejudice to the question whether that measure considered in its entirety can be correctly called a regulation'.[60] This laxer threshold has also been applied to the geographical scope of regulations. Article 288 TFEU tells us that they must be applicable in all the Member States. However, the European Court sees a regulation's geographical applicability from an abstract perspective: while normatively valid in all Member States, its concrete application can be confined to a limited number of States.[61]

(ii) Direct application and direct effect

By making regulations directly applicable, the Treaties recognised from the very beginning a monistic connection between that Union act and the national legal orders. Regulations would be automatically binding *within* the Member States – a characteristic that distinguished them from ordinary international law. Regulations were thus 'a *direct source of rights and duties* for all those affected thereby, whether Member States or individuals, who are parties to legal relationships under [European] law'.[62] In 1958, this was extraordinary: the Union had been given the power to directly legislate for all individuals in the Member States.[63]

Would the direct application of regulations imply their direct effect? Direct applicability and direct effect are, as we saw above,[64] distinct concepts. The former refers to the *normative* validity of regulations within the national legal order. Direct applicability indeed simply means that no 'validating' national act is needed for European law to have effects within the domestic legal orders: 'The direct application of a Regulation means that its entry into force and its application in favour of those subject to it are independent of any measure of reception into national law.'[65] Direct effect, on the other hand, refers to the

---

[59] Joined Cases 41–44/70, *International Fruit Company and others* v. *Commission*, [1971] ECR 411, esp. para. 17.

[60] Case 16 17/62, *Confédération Nationale des Producteurs de Fruits et Légumes* (supra n. 56), para. 2.

[61] Case 64/69, *Compagnie Française commerciale et financière* v. *Commission*, [1970] ECR 221.

[62] Case 106/77, *Amministrazione delle Finanze dello Stato* v. *Simmenthal SpA*, [1978] ECR 629, paras. 14–15 (emphasis added).

[63] J.-V. Louis, *Les Règlements de la Communauté Économique Européenne* (Presses universitaires des Bruxelles, 1969) at 16.

[64] See Introduction to this chapter.

[65] Case 34/73, *Fratelli Variola Spa* v. *Amministrazione delle Finanze dello Stato*, [1973] ECR 981, para. 10

ability of a norm to execute itself. Direct applicability thus only makes direct effect *possible*, but the former will not automatically imply the latter. The direct application of regulations thus 'leave[s] open the question whether a particular provision of a regulation has direct effect or not'.[66] In the words of an early commentator:

> Many provisions of regulations are liable to have direct effects and can be enforced by the courts. Other provisions, although they have become part of the domestic legal order as a result of the regulation's direct applicability, are binding for the national authorities only, without granting private persons the right to complain in the courts that the authorities have failed to fulfil these binding [Union] obligations. This is by no means an unrealistic conclusion. In every member State there consists quite a bit of law which is not enforceable in the courts, because these rules were not meant to give the private individual enforceable rights or because they are too vague or too incomplete to admit of judicial application.[67]

Direct effect is thus narrower than direct applicability. Not all provisions of a regulation will have to have direct effect. This has been expressly recognised by the Court.[68] In *Azienda Agricola Monte Arcosa*, the Court thus stated:

> [A]lthough, by virtue of the very nature of regulations and of their function in the system of sources of [European] law, the provisions of those regulations generally have immediate effect in the national legal systems without its being necessary for the national authorities to adopt measures of application, some of their provisions may none the less necessitate, for their implementation, the adoption of measures of application by the Member States ... In the light of the discretion enjoyed by the Member States in respect of the implementation of those provisions, it cannot be held that individuals may derive rights from those provisions in the absence of measures of application adopted by the Member States.[69]

Legislative discretion left to the national level will thus prevent provisions within regulations from having direct effect, 'where the legislature of a Member State has not adopted the provisions necessary for their implementation in the national legal system'.[70] Regulations often explicitly call for the adoption of implementing measures.[71] But even if there is no express provision,

---

[66] P. Pescatore, *The Law of Integration: Emergence of a New Phenomenon in International Relations, Based on the Experience of the European Communities* (Sijthoff, 1974), 164.

[67] G. Winter, 'Direct Applicability and Direct Effect. Two Distinct and Different concepts in Community Law' [1972] CML Rev 425–438 at 436.

[68] See Case 230/78, *SpA Eridania-Zuccherifici nazionali and SpA Societa Italiana per l'Industria degli Zuccheri* v. *Minister of Agriculture and Forestry, Minister for Industry, Trade and Craft Trades and SpA Zuccherifici Meridionali*, [1979] ECR 2749; Case 137/80, *Commission* v. *Belgium*, [1981] ECR 653, and Case 72/85, *Commission* v. *The Netherlands*, [1986] ECR 1219.

[69] Case C-403/98, *Azienda Agricola Monte Arcosa Srl*, [2001] ECR I-103, paras. 26, 28.

[70] *Ibid.*, para. 29.

[71] Article 2 (5) of Regulation 797/85 and Article 5 (5) of Regulation 2328/91 – at issue in *Azienda Agricola Monte Arcosa Srl* (supra n. 69) – indeed stated: 'Member States shall, for the purposes of

Member States are under a general duty to implement non-directly effective provisions within regulations.[72] Yet non-directly effective provisions might still have indirect effects. These indirect effects have been extensively discussed in the context of directives, and will be treated there. Suffice to say here that the European Court applies the constitutional doctrines developed in the context of directives – such as the principle of consistent interpretation – to provisions within regulations.[73]

(b) Decisions: the executive instrument

'A decision shall be binding in its entirety. A decision which specifies those to whom it is addressed shall be binding only on them.'[74] The best way to make sense of this definition is to contrast it with that for regulations. Like a regulation, a decision shall be binding in its entirety. And like a regulation it will be directly applicable. However, unlike a regulation, a decision was

---

this Regulation, define what is meant by the expression "farmer practising farming as his main occupation". This definition shall, in the case of a natural person, include at least the condition that the proportion of income derived from the agricultural holding must be 50% or more of the farmer's total income and that the working time devoted to work unconnected with the holding must be less than half the farmer's total working time. On the basis of the criteria referred to in the foregoing subparagraph, the Member States shall define what is meant by this same expression in the case of persons other than natural persons.' For another illustration of an express call for implementation measures, see: Regulation (EC) 318/2006 on the common organisation of the markets in the sugar sector, [2006] OJ L58/1, Article 7 (3): 'In case of allocation of a quota to a sugar undertaking having more than one production unit, the Member States shall adopt the measures they consider necessary in order to take due account of the interests of sugar beet and cane growers.' The legislative practice has attracted academic criticism: If 'the [Union] legislator intends to require implementing legislation on the part of the Member States, it would be clearer for anybody concerned with applying [European] law if the part of the Regulation, which certainly requires such [implementing] legislation were to be separated and to take the form of a *directive*' (G. Gaja, P. Hay and R. D. Rotunda, 'Instruments for Legal Integration in the European Community – A Review' in M. Cappelletti, M. Seccombe and J. Weiler (eds.), *Integration Through Law: Europe and the American Federal Experience* (de Gnyter, 1985), vol. I: 'Methods, Tools and Institutions', 113–160 at 125 (emphasis added)).

[72] For an implicit duty to adopt national implementing measures, see: Case C-177/95, *Ebony Maritime et al.* v. *Prefetto della Provincia di Brindisi et al.*, [1997] ECR I-1111, para. 35: '[T]he Court has consistently held that where a [Union] regulation does not specifically provide any penalty for an infringement or refers for that purpose to national laws, regulations and administrative provisions, Article [4 (3) TEU] requires the Member States to take all measures necessary to guarantee the application and effectiveness of [European] law. For that purpose, while the choice of penalties remains within their discretion, they must ensure in particular that infringements of [European] law are penalised under conditions, both procedural and substantive, which are analogous to those applicable to infringements of national law of a similar nature and importance and which, in any event, make the penalty effective, proportionate and dissuasive[.]'

[73] Case C-60/02, *Criminal proceedings against X*, [2004] ECR I-651, paras. 61–63, esp. para. 62 (emphasis added): 'Even though in the case at issue in the main proceedings the [Union] rule in question is a regulation, which by its very nature does not require any national implementing measures, and not a directive, Article 11 of Regulation No 3295/94 empowers Member States to adopt penalties for infringements of Article 2 of that regulation, thereby making it possible to *transpose to the present case the Court's reasoning in respect of directives*.'

[74] Article 288 (4) TFEU.

originally not designed to be generally applicable;[75] yet, with time, European constitutional practice developed a non-addressed decision. This development is now recognised in Article 288 [4] TFEU that allows for two types of decisions: decisions specifically applicable to those to whom it is addressed, and decisions that are generally applicable because they are not addressed to anybody specifically.

(i) Specifically addressed decisions

Decisions that mention an addressee shall only be binding on that person. Depending on whether the addressee(s) are private individuals or Member States, European law distinguishes between individual decisions and State-addressed decisions.

Individual decisions are similar to national administrative acts. They are designed to execute a Union norm by applying it to an individual situation. A good illustration can be found in the context of competition law, where the Commission is empowered to prohibit anti-competitive agreements that negatively affect the internal market.[76] A decision that is addressed to a private party will only be binding on the addressee. However, this will not necessarily mean that it has no *horizontal* effects on other parties. Indeed, the European legal order expressly recognises that decisions addressed to one person may be of 'direct and individual concern' to another.[77] In such a situation this 'third person' is entitled to challenge the legality of that decision.[78]

State-addressed decisions constitute the second group of decisions specifically applicable to the addressee(s).[79] We find again a good illustration of this Union act in the context of competition law. Here the Union is empowered to prohibit State aids to undertakings that threaten to distort competition within the internal market.[80] What is the effect of a State-addressed decision in the national legal orders? Binding on the Member State(s) addressed, may it give direct rights to individuals? In *Grad* v. *Finanzamt Traunstein*,[81] the Court answered this question positively. The German government had claimed that State-addressed decisions cannot, unlike regulations, create rights for private persons. But the response of the European Court went the other way:

> [A]lthough it is true that by virtue of Article [288], regulations are directly applicable and therefore by virtue of their nature capable of producing direct

---

[75] The old Article 189 EEC stated: 'A decision shall be binding in its entirety upon those to whom it is addressed.'

[76] Article 101 TFEU.

[77] Article 263 [4] TFEU: 'Any natural or legal person may, under the conditions laid down in the first and second paragraphs, institute proceedings against an act addressed to that person or which is of direct and individual concern to them, and against a regulatory act which is of direct concern to them and does not entail implementing measures.'

[78] For this point, see Chapter 8 – Section 1(c) above.

[79] On this type of decision, see: U. Mager, 'Die Staatengerichtete Entscheidung als supranationale Handlungsform' [2001] 36 *Europarecht* 661.

[80] Article 107 TFEU.   [81] Case 9/70, *Grad* v. *Finanzamt Traunstein*, [1970] ECR 825.

effects, it does not follow from this that other categories of legal measures mentioned in that Article can never produce similar effects. In particular, the provision according to which decisions are binding in their entirety on those to whom they are addressed enables the question to be put whether the obligation created by the Decision can only be invoked by the [Union] institutions against the addressee or whether such a right may possibly be exercised by all those who have an interest in the fulfilment of this obligation.

It would be incompatible with the binding effect attributed to decisions by Article [288] to exclude in principle the possibility that persons affected may invoke the obligation imposed by a decision. Particularly in cases where, for example, the [Union] authorities by means of a decision have imposed an obligation on a Member State or all the Member States to act in a certain way, the effectiveness ('*l'effect utile*') of such a measure would be weakened if the nationals of that State could not invoke it in the courts and the national courts could not take it into consideration as part of [European] law. Although the effects of a decision may not be identical with those of a provision contained in a regulation, this difference does not exclude the possibility that the end result, namely the right of the individual to invoke the measures before the courts, may be the same as that of a directly applicable provision of a regulation.[82]

State-addressed decisions could, consequently, create rights for private citizens. They could have direct effect in certain circumstances. What were those circumstances? The Court insisted that the direct effect of a provision depended on 'the nature, background and wording of the provision'.[83] And indeed, the provision in question was a prohibition that was 'unconditional and sufficiently clear and precise to be capable of producing direct effects in the legal relationships between the Member States and those subject to their jurisdiction'.[84] This test came close – remarkably close – to the Court's direct effect test for Treaty provisions. But would this also imply – like for Treaty provisions – their horizontal direct effect? State-addressed decisions here seem to follow the legal character of directives,[85] which will shall be discussed in Section 3 below.

(ii) Non-addressed decisions

While not expressly envisaged by the original Treaties, non-addressed decisions (decisions *sui generis*) became a widespread constitutional phenomenon within the European Union.[86] The Lisbon Treaty has now 'regularised' them in Article 288 TFEU. But what is the function of these decisions? In the past, the Union

---

[82] *Ibid.*, para. 5.   [83] *Ibid.*, para. 6.   [84] *Ibid.*, para. 9.

[85] See Cade C-80/06, *Carp* v. *Ecorad*, [2007] ECR I-4473, paras. 19 et seq., esp. para. 21: 'In accordance with Article [288], Decision 1999/93 is binding only upon the Member States, which, under Article 4 of that decision, are the sole addressees. Accordingly, the considerations underpinning the case-law referred to in the preceding paragraph with regard to directives apply *mutatis mutandis* to the question whether Decision 1999/93 may be relied upon as against an individual.'

[86] For a historical and systematic analysis, see the groundbreaking work by J. Bast, *Grundbegriffe der Handlungsformen der EU: entwickelt am Beschluss als praxisgenerierter Handlungsform des Unions- und Gemeinschaftsrechts* (Springer, 2006).

had recourse to these decisions – instead of regulations – to have an instrument that was directly applicable but lacked direct effect. The most famous illustrations of this were the old Comitology Decisions discussed in Chapter 7.[87]

3. Indirect Union law: directives

The third binding instrument of the Union is the most mysterious one: the directive. According to Article 288 (3) TFEU, '[a] directive shall be binding, as to the result to be achieved, upon each Member State to which it is addressed, but shall leave to the national authorities the choice of form and methods'.

This formulation suggested two things. First, directives appeared to be binding *on* States – not *within* States. On the basis of such a 'dualist' reading, directives would have no validity in the national legal orders. They seemed *not* to be directly applicable, and would thus need to be 'incorporated' or 'implemented' through national legislation. This dualist view was underlined by the fact that Member States were only bound as to the result to be achieved – for the obligation of result is common in classic international law.[88] Second, binding solely on the State(s) to which it was addressed, directives appeared to lack *general* application. Their general application could indeed only be achieved indirectly *via* national legislation transforming the European content into national form. Directives have consequently been described as 'indirect legislation'.[89]

But could this indirect Union law have direct effects? In a courageous line of jurisprudence, the Court confirmed that directives could – under certain circumstances – have direct effect and thus entitle individuals to have their European rights applied in national courts. But if this was possible, would directives not become instruments of direct Union law, like regulations? The negative answer to this question will become clearer in this third section. Suffice to say here that the test for direct effect of directives is subject to two additional limitations – one temporal, one normative. Direct effect would only arise *after* a Member State had failed properly to 'implement' the directive, and then only in relation to the State authorities themselves. We shall analyse the conditions and limits for the direct effect of directives, before exploring their indirect effects on national law.

(a) Direct effect and directives: conditions and limits

That directives could directly give rise to rights that individuals could claim in national courts was accepted in *Van Duyn* v. *Home Office*.[90] The case concerned

---

[87] For these 'decisions' *sui generis*, see: Chapter 7 – Section 2(b) above.

[88] For this view, see L.-J. Constantinesco, *Das Recht der Europäischen Gemeinschaften* (Nomos, 1977), 614.

[89] P. Pescatore, 'The Doctrine of "Direct Effect": an Infant Disease of Community Law' [1983] EL Rev 155–77 at 177.

[90] Case 41/74, *Van Duyn* v. *Home Office*, [1974] ECR 1337.

a Dutch secretary, whose entry into the United Kingdom had been denied on the ground that she was a member of the Church of Scientology. Britain had tried to justify this limitation on the free movement of workers by reference to an express derogation that allowed such restrictions on grounds of public policy and public security.[91] However, in an effort to harmonise national derogations from free movement, the Union had adopted a directive according to which '[m]easures taken on grounds of public policy or of public security shall be based exclusively on the personal conduct of the individual concerned'.[92] This outlawed national measures that limited free movement for generic reasons, such as membership in a disliked organisation. Unfortunately, the United Kingdom had not 'implemented' the directive into national law. Could Van Duyn nonetheless directly invoke the directive against the British authorities? The Court of Justice found that this was possible by emphasising the distinction between direct applicability and direct effect:

> [B]y virtue of the provisions of Article [288] regulations are directly applicable and, consequently, may by their very nature have direct effects, it does not follow from this that other categories of acts mentioned in that Article can never have similar effects. It would be incompatible with the binding effect attributed to a directive by Article [288] to exclude, in principle, the possibility that the obligation which it imposes may be invoked by those concerned. In particular, where the [Union] authorities have, by directive, imposed on Member States the obligation to pursue a particular course of conduct, the useful effect of such an act would be weakened if the individuals were prevented from relying on it before their national courts and if the latter were prevented from taking it into consideration as an element of [European] law. Article [267], which empowers national courts to refer to the Court questions concerning the validity and interpretation of all acts of the [Union] institutions, without distinction, implies furthermore that these acts may be invoked by individuals in the national courts.[93]

The Court – rightly – emphasised the distinction between direct applicability and direct effect, yet – wrongly – defined the relationship between these two concepts in order to justify its conclusion. To brush aside the textual argument that regulations are directly applicable while directives are not, it wrongly alluded to the idea that direct effect without direct application was possible.[94]

---

[91] Article 45 (1) and (3) TFEU.

[92] Article 3 (1) Directive 64/221 on the co-ordination of special measures concerning the movement and residence of foreign nationals which are justified on grounds of public policy, public security or public health, OJ (English Special Edition): Chapter 1963–1964/117.

[93] Case 41/74, *Van Duyn* (supra n. 90), para. 12.

[94] In the words of J. Steiner: 'How can a law be enforceable by individuals within a Member-State if it is not regarded as incorporated in that State?' (J. Steiner, 'Direct Applicability in EEC Law – A Chameleon Concept' [1982] 98 *Law Quarterly Review*, 229–248 at 234). The direct effect of a directive presupposes its direct application. And indeed, ever since *Van Gend en Loos*, all directives must be regarded as directly applicable (see S. Prechal, *Directives in EC Law* (Oxford University Press, 2005), 92 and 229. For the same conclusion, see also: C. Timmermans, 'Community Directives Revisited' [1997] 17 YEL 1–28 at 11–12.)

And the direct effect of directives was then justified by three distinct arguments. First, to exclude direct effect would be incompatible with the 'binding effect' of directives. Second, their 'useful effect' would be weakened if individuals could not invoke them in national courts. Third, since the preliminary reference procedure did not exclude directives, the latter must be capable of being invoked in national courts.

What was the constitutional value of these arguments? Argument one is a sleight of hand: the fact that a directive is not binding in *national law* is not 'incompatible' with its binding effect under *international law*. The second argument is strong, but not of a legal nature: to enhance the useful effect of a rule by making it more binding is a political argument. Finally, the third argument only begs the question: while it is true that the preliminary reference procedure generically refers to all 'acts of the institutions', it could be argued that only those acts that are directly effective can be referred. The decision in *Van Duyn* was right, but sadly without reason.

The lack of a convincing *legal* argument to justify the direct effect of directives soon prompted the Court to propose a fourth argument. 'A Member State which has not adopted the implementing measures required by the Directive in the prescribed periods may not rely, as against individuals, on its own failure to perform the obligations which the directive entails.'[95] This fourth reason has become known as the 'estoppel argument' – acknowledging its intellectual debt to English 'equity' law. A Member State that fails to implement its European obligations is 'stopped' from invoking that failure as a defence, and individuals are consequently – and collaterally – entitled to rely on the directive as against the State. Unlike the three original arguments, this fourth argument is *State*-centric. It locates the rationale for the direct effect of directives not in the nature of the instrument itself, but in the behaviour of the State.

This (behavioural) rationale would result in two important limitations on the direct effect of directives. Even if provisions within a directive were 'unconditional and sufficiently precise' 'those provisions may [only] be *relied upon by an individual against the State* where that State fails to implement the Directive in national law *by the end of the period prescribed or where it fails to implement the directive correctly*'.[96] This direct effect test for directives therefore differed from that for ordinary Union law, as it added a temporal and a normative limitation. *Temporally*, the direct effect of directives could only arise *after* the failure of the State to implement the directive had occurred. Thus, before the end of the implementation period granted to Member States, no direct effect could take place. And even once this temporal condition had been satisfied, the direct effect would operate only as against the State. This *normative* limitation on the direct effect of directives has become famous as the 'no-horizontal-direct-effect rule'.

---

[95] Case 148/78, *Ratti*, [1979] ECR 1629, para. 22.
[96] Case 80/86, *Kolpinghuis Nijmegen BV*, [1987] ECR 3969, para. 7 (emphasis added).

(i) The no-horizontal-direct-effect rule

The Court's jurisprudence of the 1970s had extended the direct effect of Union law to directives. An individual could claim his European rights against a State that had failed to implement it into national law. This situation was one of 'vertical' direct effect. Could an individual equally invoke a Directive against another private party? This 'horizontal' direct effect existed for direct Union law; yet should it be extended to directives? The Court's famous answer is a resolute 'no': directives could not have horizontal direct effects.

The 'no-horizontal-direct-effect rule' was first expressed in *Marshall*.[97] The Court based its negative conclusion on a textual argument:

> [A]ccording to Article [288 TFEU] the binding nature of a directive, which constitutes the basis for the possibility of relying on the directive before a national court, exists only in relation to 'each member state to which it is addressed'. It follows that a directive may not of itself impose obligations on an individual and that a provision of a directive may not be relied upon as such against such a person.[98]

The absence of horizontal direct effect was confirmed in *Dori*.[99] A private company had approached Ms Dori for an English language correspondence course. The contract had been concluded in Milan's busy central railway station. A few days later, she changed her mind and tried to cancel the contract. A right of cancellation had been provided by the European directive on consumer contracts concluded outside business premises,[100] but Italy had not implemented the directive into national law. Could a private party nonetheless directly rely on the unimplemented directive against another private party? The Court was firm:

> [A]s is clear from the judgment in Marshall ... the case-law on the possibility of relying on directives against State entities is based on the fact that under Article [288] a directive is binding only in relation to 'each Member State to which it is addressed'. That case-law seeks to prevent 'the State from taking advantage of its own failure to comply with [European] law' ... The effect of extending that case-law to the sphere of relations between individuals would be to recognise a power in the [Union] to enact obligations for individuals with immediate effect, whereas it has competence to do so only where it is empowered to adopt regulations. It follows that, in the absence of measures transposing the directive within the prescribed time-limit, consumers cannot derive from the directive itself a right of cancellation as against traders with whom they have concluded a contract or enforce such a right in a national court.[101]

---

[97] Case 152/84, *Marshall* v. *Southampton and South-West Hampshire Area Health Authority*, [1986] ECR 723.
[98] *Ibid.*, para. 48.   [99] Case C-91/92, *Faccini Dori* v. *Recreb*, [1994] ECR I-3325.
[100] Directive 85/577 concerning protection of the consumer in respect of contracts negotiated away from business premises (OJ 1985 L372/31).
[101] Case C-91/92, *Dori* (supra n. 99), paras. 22–5.

This denial of direct effect of directives in horizontal situations was grounded in three arguments.[102] First, a textual argument: a directive is binding in relation to each Member State to which it is addressed. But had the Court not used this very same argument to establish the direct effect of directives in the first place? Second, the estoppel argument: the direct effect for directives exists to prevent a State from taking advantage of its own failure to comply with European law. And since individuals were not responsible for the non-implementation of a directive, direct effect should not be extended to them. Third, a systematic argument: if horizontal direct effect was given to directives, the distinction between directives and regulations would disappear. This was a weak argument, for a directive's distinct character could be preserved in different ways.[103] In order to bolster its reasoning, the Court added a fourth argument in subsequent jurisprudence: legal certainty.[104] Since directives were not published, they must not impose obligations on those to whom they are not addressed. This argument has lost some of its force,[105] but continues to be very influential today.

All these arguments may be criticised.[106] But the Court of Justice has stuck to its conclusion: directives cannot *directly* impose obligations on individuals. They lack horizontal direct effect. This constitutional rule of European law has nonetheless been qualified by one limitation and one exception.

(ii) The limitation to the rule: the wide definition of State (actions)

One way to minimise the no-horizontal-direct-effect rule is to maximise the vertical direct effect of directives. The Court has done this by giving extremely extensive definitions to what constitutes the 'State', and what constitute 'public actions'.

What public authorities count as the 'State'? A minimal definition restricts the concept to a State's central organs. Because they failed to implement the directive, the estoppel argument suggested them to be vertically bound by the directive. Yet the Court has never accepted this consequence, and has endorsed a maximal definition of the State. It thus held that directly effective obligations 'are binding upon *all authorities of the Member States*'; and this included 'all

---

[102] The Court silently dropped the 'useful effect argument' as it would have worked towards the opposite conclusion.

[103] On this point, see: R. Schütze, 'The Morphology of Legislative Power in the European Community: Legal Instruments and Federal Division of Powers' [2006] 25 YEL 91.

[104] See Case C-201/02, *The Queen* v. *Secretary of State for Transport, Local Government and the Regions, ex parte Wells* [2004] ECR I-723, para. 56: 'the principle of legal certainty prevents directives from creating obligations for individuals'.

[105] The publication of directives is now, in principle, required by Article 297 TFEU.

[106] For an excellent overview of the principal arguments, see: P. Craig, 'The Legal Effect of Directives: Policy, Rules and Exceptions' [2009] 34 EL Rev 349. But why does Professor Craig concentrate on arguments one and four, instead of paying close attention to the strongest of the Court's reasons in the form of argument two?

organs of the administration, including decentralised authorities, such as municipalities',[107] even 'constitutionally independent' authorities.[108]

The best formulation of this maximalist approach was given in *Foster*.[109] Was the 'British Gas Corporation' – a statutory corporation for developing and maintaining gas supply – part of the British 'State'? The Court held this to be the case. Vertical direct effect would apply to any body 'whatever its legal form, which has been made responsible, pursuant to a measure adopted by the State, *for providing a public service under the control of the State and has for that purpose special powers* beyond those which result from the normal rules applicable in relations between individuals'.[110] This wide definition of the State consequently covers *private* bodies endowed with *public* functions.

This functional definition of the State, however, suggested that only 'public acts', that is: acts adopted in pursuit of a public function, would be covered. Yet there are situations where the State acts horizontally like a private person: it might conclude private contracts and employ private personnel. Would these 'private actions' be covered by the doctrine of vertical direct effect? In *Marshall*, the plaintiff argued that the United Kingdom had not properly implemented the Equal Treatment Directive. But could an *employee* of the South-West Hampshire Area Health Authority invoke the direct effect of a directive against this State authority in this *horizontal* situation? The British government argued that direct effect would only apply 'against a Member State *qua* public authority and not against a Member State *qua* employer'. 'As an employer a State is no different from a private employer'; and '[i]t would not therefore be proper to put persons employed by the State in a better position than those who are employed by a private employer'.[111] This was an excellent argument, but the Court would have none of it. According to the Court, an individual could rely on a directive as against the State 'regardless of the capacity in which the latter is acting, whether employer or public authority'.[112]

Vertical direct effect would thus not only apply to *private* parties exercising public functions, but also to public authorities engaged in *private* activities.[113] This double extension of the doctrine of vertical direct effect can be criticised for

---

[107] Case 103/88, *Costanzo SpA* v. *Comune di Milano*, [1989] ECR 1839, para. 31 (emphasis added).

[108] Case 222/84, *Johnston* v. *Chief Constable of the Royal Ulster Constabulary*, [1986] ECR 1651, para. 49.

[109] Case C-188/89, *Foster and others* v. *British Gas*, [1990] ECR I-3313.

[110] *Ibid.*, para. 20 (emphasis added). For a recent confirmation of that test, see: Case C-180/04, *Vassallo* v. *Azienda Ospedaliera Ospedale San Martino di Genova et al.*, [2006] ECR I-7251, para. 26.

[111] Case 152/84, *Marshall* (supra n. 97), para. 43.   [112] *Ibid.*, para. 49.

[113] *Ibid.*, para. 51: 'The argument submitted by the United Kingdom that the possibility of relying on provisions of the Directive against the respondent qua organ of the State would give rise to an arbitrary and unfair distinction between the rights of State employees and those of private employees does not justify any other conclusion. Such a distinction may easily be avoided if the Member State concerned has correctly implemented the Directive in national law.'

treating similar situations dissimilarly, for it creates a discriminatory limitation to the no-horizontal-direct-effect rule.

(iii) The exception to the rule: incidental horizontal direct effect

In the two previous situations, the Court respected the rule that directives could not have direct horizontal effects, but limited the rule's scope of application. Yet in some cases, the Court has found a directive *directly* to affect the horizontal relations between private parties. This 'incidental' horizontal effect of directives must, despite some scholastic effort to the contrary,[114] be seen as an *exception* to the rule. The incidental horizontal direct effect cases *violate* the rule that directives cannot directly impose obligations on private parties. The two 'incidents' chiefly responsible for the doctrine of incidental horizontal direct effects are *CIA Security* and *Unilever Italia*.

In *CIA Security* v. *Signalson and Securitel*,[115] the Court dealt with a dispute between three Belgian competitors whose business was the manufacture and sale of security systems. CIA Security had applied to a commercial court for orders requiring Signalson and Securitel to cease libel. The defendants had alleged that the plaintiff's alarm system did not satisfy Belgian security standards. This was indeed the case, but the Belgian legislation itself violated a European notification requirement established by Directive 83/189. But because the European norm was in a directive, this violation could – theoretically – not be invoked in a horizontal dispute between private parties. Or could it? The Court implicitly rejected the no-horizontal-direct-effect rule by holding the notification requirement to be 'unconditional and sufficiently precise' and finding that '[t]he *effectiveness of [Union] control will be that much greater if the directive is interpreted as meaning that breach of the obligation to notify constitutes a substantial procedural defect such as to render the technical regulations in question inapplicable to individuals'.*[116] CIA Security could thus rely on the directive as against its private competitors. And the national court 'must decline to apply a national technical regulation which has not been notified in accordance with the directive'.[117] What else was this but horizontal direct effect?

The Court confirmed the decision in *Unilever Italia* v. *Central Food.*[118] Unilever had supplied Central Food with olive oil that did not conform to Italian labelling legislation, and Central Food refused to honour the sales

---

[114] This phenomenon has been referred to as the: 'incidental' horizontal effect of directives (P. Craig and G. de Búrca, *EU Law* (Oxford University Press, 2011), 207 et seq.; 'horizontal side effects of direct effect' (S. Prechal, *Directives in EC Law* (supra n. 94), 261–70); and the 'disguised' vertical effect of directives (M. Dougan, 'The "Disguised" Vertical Direct Effect of Directives' [2000] 59 *Cambridge Law Journal*, 586–612). The argumentative categories that have been developed to justify when a directive can adversely affect a private party and when not, have degenerated into 'a form of sophistry which provide no convincing explanation for apparently contradictory lines of case law' (Craig and de Búrca, *ibid.*, at 226).

[115] Case C-194/94, *CIA Security* v. *Signalson and Securitel*, [1996] ECR I-2201.

[116] *Ibid.*, para. 48 (emphasis added).   [117] *Ibid.*, para. 55.

[118] Case C-443/98, *Unilever Italia* v. *Central Food*, [2000] ECR I-7535.

contract between the two companies. Unilever brought proceedings claiming that the Italian legislation – like in *CIA Security* – violated Directive 83/189. The case was referred to the European Court of Justice, where the Italian and Danish governments intervened. Both governments protested that it was 'clear from settled case-law of the Court that a directive cannot of itself impose obligations on individuals and cannot therefore be relied on as such against them'.[119] But the Court's – strange – answer was this:

> Whilst it is true, as observed by the Italian and Danish Governments, that a directive cannot of itself impose obligations on an individual and cannot therefore be relied on as such against an individual, that case-law does not apply where non-compliance with Article 8 or Article 9 of Directive 83/189, which *constitutes a substantial procedural defect*, renders a technical regulation adopted in breach of either of those articles inapplicable. In such circumstances, and unlike the case of non-transposition of directives with which the case-law cited by those two Governments is concerned, Directive 83/189 does not in any way define the substantive scope of the legal rule on the basis of which the national court must decide the case before it. It creates neither rights nor obligations for individuals.[120]

What did this mean? Could a 'substantial procedural effect' lead to the horizontal direct effect of the directive? And can a directive 'neutralise' national legislation without affecting the rights and obligations for individuals?

Let us stick to hard facts. In both cases, the national court was required to disapply national legislation in *civil* proceedings between *private* parties. Did CIA Security and Unilever Italia not 'win' a right from the directive to have national legislation disapplied? And did Signalson and Central Food not 'lose' the right to have national law applied? It seems impossible to deny that the directive *did* directly affect the rights and obligations of individuals. It imposed an obligation on the defendants to accept forfeiting their national rights. The Court thus *did* create an exception to the principle that a directly effective directive 'cannot of itself apply in proceedings exclusively between private parties'.[121] However, the exception to the no-horizontal-direct-effect rule has remained an exceptional exception. But, even so, there are – strong – arguments for the Court to abandon its constitutional rule altogether.[122] And as we shall see below, the entire debate surrounding directives might simply be the result of some linguistic confusion.[123]

---

[119] *Ibid.*, para. 35.   [120] *Ibid.*, paras. 50–1 (emphasis added).

[121] Joined Cases C-397/01 to C-403/01, *Pfeiffer et al.* v. *Deutsches Rotes Kreuz, Kreisverband Waldshut*, [2004] ECR I-8835, para. 109.

[122] See Opinion of Advocate-General Jacobs in Case C-316/93, *Vaneetveld* v. *Le Foyer*, [1994] ECR I-763, para. 31: '[I]t might well be conducive to greater legal certainty, and to a more coherent system, if the provisions of a directive were held in appropriate circumstances to be directly enforceable against individuals.'; as well as: Craig, 'Legal Effect of Directives' (supra n. 106), 390: 'The rationales for the core rule that Directives do not have horizontal direct effect based on the Treaty text, legal certainty and the Regulations/Directives divide are unconvincing.'

[123] On this point, see: Conclusion to this chapter.

(b) Indirect effects through national and (primary) European law

(i) The doctrine of consistent interpretation of national law

Norms may have direct and indirect effects. A provision within a directive lacking direct effect may still have certain indirect effects in the national legal orders. The lack of direct effect means exactly that: the directive cannot itself – that is *directly* – be invoked. However, the directive may still have indirect effects on the interpretation of national law. For the European Court has created a general duty on national courts (and administrations[124]) to interpret national law as far as possible in light of all European law. The doctrine of consistent interpretation was given an elaborate definition in *Von Colson*:

> [T]he Member States' obligation arising from a Directive to achieve the result envisaged by the Directive and their duty under Article [4(3) TEU] to take all appropriate measures, whether general or particular, to ensure the fulfilment of that obligation, is binding on all the authorities of Member States including, for matters within their jurisdiction, the courts. It follows that, in applying the national law in particular the provisions of a national law specifically introduced in order to implement [a Directive], national courts are required to interpret their national law in the light of the wording and the purpose of the Directive in order to achieve the result referred to in the third paragraph of Article [288].[125]

The duty of consistent interpretation is a duty to achieve the result by indirect means. Where a directive is not sufficiently precise, it is – theoretically – addressed to the national legislator. It is in the latter's prerogative to 'concretise' the directive's indeterminate content in line with its own national views. But where the legislator has failed to do so, the task is partly transferred to the national judiciary. For after the expiry of the implementation period,[126] national courts are under an obligation to 'implement' the directive judicially through a 'European' interpretation of national law. This duty of consistent interpretation applies regardless of 'whether the [national] provisions in question *were adopted before or after the directive*'.[127] The duty to interpret national

---

[124] Case C-218/01, *Henkel* v. *Deutsches Patent- und Markenamt*, [2004] ECR I-1725.

[125] Case 14/83, *Von Colson and Elisabeth Kamann* v. *Land Nordrhein-Westfalen*, [1984] ECR 1891, para. 26. Because this paragraph was so important in defining the duty of consistent interpretation, it is sometimes referred to as the 'Von Colson Principle'.

[126] National authorities are not required to interpret their national law in light of Union law before the expiry of the implementation deadline. After Case C-212/04, *Adeneler and Others* v. *Ellinikos Organismos Galaktos (ELOG)*, [2006] ECR I-6057, there is no room for speculation on this issue: '[W]here a directive is transposed belatedly, the general obligation owed by national courts to interpret domestic law in conformity with the directive exists only once the period for its transposition has expired' (*ibid.*, para. 115). However, once a directive has been adopted, a Member State will be under the immediate constitutional obligation to 'refrain from taking any measures liable seriously to compromise the result prescribed' in the directive, see: C-129/96, *Inter-Environnement Wallonie ASBL* v. *Region Wallonne*, [1997] ECR 7411, para. 45. This obligation is independent of the doctrine of indirect effect.

[127] Case C-106/89, *Marleasing* v. *La Comercial Internacional de Alimentacion*, [1990] ECR I-4135, para. 8 (emphasis added).

law as far as possible in light of European law would thus extend to all national law – irrespective of whether the latter was intended to implement the directive. However, where domestic law had been specifically enacted to implement the directive, the national courts must operate under the presumption 'that the Member State, following its exercise of the discretion afforded to it under that provision, had the intention of fulfilling entirely the obligations arising from the directive'.[128]

The duty of consistent interpretation may lead to the *indirect* implementation of a directive. For it can *indirectly* impose new obligations – both vertically and horizontally. An illustration of the horizontal *indirect* effect of directives can be seen in *Webb*.[129] The case concerned a claim by Mrs Webb against her employer. The latter had hired the plaintiff to replace a pregnant co-worker during her maternity leave. Two weeks after she had started work, Mrs Webb discovered that she was pregnant herself, and was dismissed for that reason. She brought proceedings before the Industrial Tribunal, pleading sex discrimination. The Industrial Tribunal rejected this on the ground that the reason for her dismissal had not been her sex but her inability to fulfil the primary task for which she had been recruited. The case went on appeal to the House of Lords, which confirmed the interpretation of national law but nonetheless harboured doubts about Britain's European obligations under the Equal Treatment Directive. On a preliminary reference, the European Court indeed found that there was sex discrimination under the directive and that the fact that Mrs Webb had been employed to replace another employee was irrelevant.[130] On receipt of the preliminary ruling, the House of Lords was thus required to change its previous interpretation of national law. Mrs Webb *won* a right, while her employer *lost* the right to dismiss her. The doctrine of indirect effect thus changed the horizontal relations between two private parties. The duty of consistent interpretation has consequently been said to amount to '*de facto* (horizontal) direct effect of the directive'.[131] Normatively, this horizontal effect is however an *indirect* effect. For it operates through the medium of national law.

Are there limits to the indirect effect of directives through the doctrine of consistent interpretation? The duty is very demanding: national courts are required to interpret their national law '*as far as possible, in the light of the wording and the purpose of the directive*'.[132] But what will 'as far as possible' mean? Should national courts be required to behave as if they were the national legislature? This might seriously undermine the (relatively) passive place reserved for judiciaries in the national constitutional orders. And the European legal order has indeed only asked national courts to adjust the interpretation of national law 'in so far as it is given discretion to do so *under*

---

[128] Joined Cases C-397/01 to C-403/01, *Pfeiffer* (supra n. 121), para. 112.
[129] Case C-32/93, *Webb* v. *EMO Air Cargo* [1994] ECR I-3567.   [130] *Ibid.*, paras. 26–8.
[131] Prechal, *Directives in EC Law* (supra n. 94), 211.
[132] Case C-106/89, *Marleasing* (supra n. 127), para. 8 (emphasis added).

national law.[133] The European Court thus accepts that there exist established national judicial methodologies and has permitted national courts to limit themselves to 'the application of interpretative methods recognised by national law'.[134] National courts are thus not obliged to 'invent' or 'import' novel interpretative methods.[135] However, within the discretion given to the judiciary under national law, the European doctrine of consistent interpretation requires the referring court 'to do whatever lies within its jurisdiction, having regard to the whole body of rules of national law'.[136]

But there are also European limits to this duty. The Court has clarified that the duty of consistent interpretation 'is limited by the general principles of law which form part of [European] law and in particular the principles of legal certainty and non-retroactivity'.[137] This has been taken to imply that the indirect effect of directives cannot aggravate the criminal liability of a private party, as criminal law is subject to particularly strict rules of interpretation.[138] But more importantly, the Court recognises that the clear and unambigous wording of a national provision constitutes an absolute limit to its interpretation.[139] National courts are thus not required to interpret national law *contra legem*.[140] The duty of consistent interpretation would thus find a boundary in the clear wording of a provision. In giving indirect effect to a directive, national courts are therefore not required to stretch the medium of national law beyond breaking point. They are only required to *interpret* the text – and not to *amend* it! Textual amendments continue to be the task of the national legislatures – and not the national judiciaries.

---

[133] Case C-14/83, *Von Colson* (supra n. 125), para. 28 (emphasis added).

[134] Joined Cases C-397/01 to C-403/01, *Pfeiffer* (supra n. 121), para. 116.

[135] See M. Klammert, 'Judicial Implementation of Directives and Anticipatory Indirect Effect: Connecting the Dots' [2006] 43 CML Rev 1251 at 1259. For the opposite view, see: Prechal, *Directives in EC Law* (supra n. 94), 213.

[136] Joined Cases C-397/01 to C-403/01, *Pfeffer* (supra n. 121), para. 118.

[137] Case 80/86, *Kolpinghuis*, (supra n. 96), para. 13.

[138] In Case C-168/95, *Arcaro*, [1996] ECR I-4705, the Court claimed that '[the] obligation of the national court to refer to the content of the directive when interpreting the relevant rules of its own national law reaches a limit where such an interpretation leads to the imposition on an individual of an obligation laid down by a directive which has not been transposed' (*ibid.*, para. 42). This ruling should, however, be interpreted restrictively. Indeed, P. Craig ('Directives: Direct Effect, Indirect Effect and the Construction of National Legislation' [1997] 22 EL Rev 519–538 at 527) has sceptically pointed out: 'If this is indeed so then it casts the whole doctrine of indirect effect into doubt.' In fact '[t]his was the whole point of engaging in the interpretive exercise'. 'Greater rights for the plaintiff will almost always mean commensurately greater obligations of the defendant.' The post-*Arcaro* jurisprudence appears to recognise this logical necessity (see S. Drake, 'Twenty Years after Von Colson: the Impact of "Indirect Effect" on the Protection of the Individual's Community Rights' [2005] 30 EL Rev 329–48 at 338).

[139] Case C-555/07, *Kücükdeveci* v. *Swedex*, (nyr), para. 49.

[140] Case C-212/04, *Adeneler* (supra n. 126), para. 110: 'It is true that the obligation on a national court to refer to the content of a directive when interpreting and applying the relevant rules of domestic law is limited by general principles of law, particularly those of legal certainty and non-retroactivity, and that obligation cannot serve as the basis for an interpretation of national law *contra legem*.'

The indirect horizontal effect of directives is consequently *limited* through the medium of national law. The duty of consistent interpretation is therefore a milder incursion on the legislative powers of the Member States than the doctrine of horizontal *direct* effect. For that doctrine may lead to the doctrine of supremacy, which requires national courts to disapply national laws that conflict with directly effective European law – regardless of their wording.[141]

(ii) Indirect effects through the medium of European law

The indirect effect of directives though the medium of national law encounters two limits – one temporal, one normative. Temporally, the duty of consistent interpretation only starts applying *after* the implementation period of the directive has passed. Normatively, the duty to interpret national law as far as possible with European law finds a limit in the express *wording* of a provision. Where one of these limits applies, national law cannot be used as a medium for the indirect effects of European law. But the European Court recently built an alternative avenue to promote the indirect effect of directives. Instead of mediating their effect through *national* law, it indirectly translates their content into European law. How so? The way the Court has achieved this has been to capitalise on the unwritten general principles of European law. For the latter may – as primary Union law – have horizontal direct effect.[142]

This new avenue was opened in *Mangold*.[143] The case concerned the German law on 'Part-Time Working and Fixed-Term Contracts'. The national employment law, transposing a European directive on the subject, permitted fixed-term employment contracts if the worker had reached the age of fifty-two. However, the German law seemed to violate a second directive: Directive 2000/78 establishing a general framework for equal treatment in employment and occupation adopted to combat discrimination in the workplace. According to Article 6 (1) of the directive, Member States could provide for differences in the workplace on grounds of age only if 'they are objectively and reasonably justified by a legitimate aim, including legitimate employment policy, labour market and vocational training objectives, and if the means of achieving that aim are appropriate and necessary'. In the present case, a German law firm had hired Mr Mangold, then aged fifty-six, on a fixed-term employment contract. A few weeks after commencing employment, Mangold brought proceedings against his employer before the Munich Industrial Tribunal, where he claimed

---

[141] Schütze, 'Morphology' (supra n. 103), 126: 'While the doctrine of consistent interpretation is a method to avoid conflicts, the doctrine of supremacy is a method to *solve* – unavoidable – conflicts.'

[142] On the normative quality of primary law, see: Section 1 above. The Court has recently used the normative qualities of regulations as a (secondary law) medium for directives; see Joined Cases C-37/06 and C-58/06, *Viamex Agrar Handels GmBH & Zuchtvieh-Kontor GmBH v. Hauptzollamt Hamburg-Jonas*, [2008] ECR I-69.

[143] Case C-144/04, *Mangold v. Helm*, [2005] ECR I-9981.

that the German law violated Directive 2000/78, as a disproportionate discrimination on grounds of age.

The argument was not only problematic because it was raised in *civil* proceedings between two *private* parties, which seemed to exclude the horizontal *direct* effect of Article 6 (1). More importantly, since the implementation period of Directive 2000/78 had not yet expired, even the horizontal *indirect* effect of the directive could not be achieved through a 'Europe-consistent' interpretation of *national* law. Yet having found that the national law indeed violated the *substance* of the directive,[144] the Court was out to create a new way to review the legality of the German law. Instead of using the directive as such – directly or indirectly – it found a general principle of European constitutional law that stood *behind* the directive. That principle was the principle of non-discrimination on grounds of age. And it was *that* general principle that would bind the Member States when implementing European law.[145] From there, the Court reasoned as follows:

> Consequently, observance of the general principle of equal treatment, in particular in respect of age, cannot as such be conditional upon the expiry of the period allowed the Member States for the transposition of a directive intended to lay down a general framework for combating discrimination on the grounds of age ... In those circumstances it is the responsibility of the national court, hearing a dispute involving the principle of non-discrimination in respect of age, to provide, in a case within its jurisdiction, the legal protection which individuals derive from the rules of [European] law and to ensure that those rules are fully effective, setting aside any provision of national law which may conflict with that law. Having regard to all the foregoing, the reply to be given to the [national court] must be that [European] law and, more particularly, *Article 6(1) of Directive 2000/78, must be interpreted as precluding a provision of domestic law such as that at issue in the main proceedings which authorises, without restriction, unless there is a close connection with an earlier contract of employment of indefinite duration concluded with the same employer, the conclusion of fixed-term contracts of employment once the worker has reached the age of 52.*[146]

This judgment has been – very – controversial. But it is less the individual components than their combination and context that was contentious. Past precedents had indeed established that the Union's (unwritten) general principles might dynamically derive from the constitutional traditions of the Member States.[147] And the Court had previously found that provisions in a directive

---

[144] *Ibid.*, para. 65.
[145] On the so-called 'implementation situation', see: Chapter 12 – Section 4(a) below.
[146] Case C-144/04, *Mangold* (supra n. 143), paras. 76–8 (emphasis added).
[147] On this point, see Chapter 12 – Section 1(a) below. In the present case the 'genesis' of a general principle prohibiting age discrimination was indeed controversial. Apparently, only two national constitutions recognised such a principle (see Advocate-General Mazák in Case C-411/05, *Palacios de la Villa*, [2007] ECR I-8531).

could be backed up by such a general principle.[148] It was also undisputed that the general principles could apply to the Member States implementing European law and thereby have direct effect.[149] However, to use all elements in *this* context was potentially explosive. For if this technique were generalised, the limitations inherent in the directive as an instrument of secondary law could be outflanked. The generalised use of primary law as the medium for secondary law was dangerous 'since the subsidiary applicability of the principles not only gives rise to a lack of legal certainty but also distorts the nature of the system of sources, converting typical [Union] acts into merely decorative rules which may be easily replaced by the general principles'.[150] Put succinctly: if a *special* directive is adopted to make a *general* principle sufficiently precise, how can the latter have direct effect while the former had not?

Yet to the chagrin of some,[151] the *Mangold* ruling was confirmed *and* consolidated in *Kücükdeveci*.[152] This time, Germany was said to have violated Directive 2000/78 by having discriminated against *younger* employees. The bone of contention was Article 622 of the German Civil Code, which established various notice periods depending on the duration of the employment relationship. However, the provision only started counting the duration after an employee had turned twenty-five.[153] After ten years of service to a private company, Ms Kücükdeveci had been sacked. Having started work at the age of 18, her notice period was thus calculated on the basis of a three-year period. Believing that this *shorter* notice period for young employees was discriminatory, she brought an action before the Industrial Tribunal. On reference to the Court of Justice, that Court found the German law to violate the directive.[154] And since the implementation period for Directive 2000/78 had now expired, there was no *temporal* limit to establishing the indirect effect of the directive through national law.

But the indirect effect of the directive through the interpretation of national law now encountered an – insurmountable – *normative* limit. Because of its clarity

---

[148] See Case 222/84, *Johnston* v. *Chief Constable* (supra n. 108), para. 18: 'The requirement of judicial control stipulated by that article [of the directive] reflects a general principle of law which underlies the constitutional traditions common to the Member States.'

[149] In the present case, the actual conclusion was controversial as 'the Court effectively ignored the limits placed upon the legal effects of Article 19 (1) TFEU, which had been consciously drafted by the Member States under the Treaty of Amsterdam so as to ensure that the various grounds of discrimination contained therein did not have direct effect. And would only produce legal effects (if at all) through the adoption of implementing measures by the Union legislature' (M. Dougan, 'In Defence of Mangold?' in A. Arnull (et al., eds.), *A Constitutional Order of States? Essays in EU Law in Honour of Alan Dashwood* (Hart, 2011), 219 at 226).

[150] Joined Case C-55 and C-56/07, *Michaeler et al.* v. *Amt für sozialen Arbeitsschutz Bozen*, [2008] ECR I-3135, para. 21.

[151] For a piece of German *angst*, consider the decision of the German Constitutional Court in *Honeywell* discussed in Chapter 10 – Section 2(b) below.

[152] Case C-555/07, *Kücükdeveci* v. *Swedex* (nyr).

[153] The last sentence of Article 622 (2) of the German Civil Code states: 'In calculating the length of employment, periods prior to the completion of the employee's 25th year of age are not taken into account.'

[154] Case C-555/07, *Kücükdeveci* (supra n. 152), para. 43.

and precision, the German legal provision was 'not open to an interpretation in conformity with Directive 2000/78'.[155] The indirect effect of the directive could thus not be established via the medium of national law, and the Court chose once more a general principle of European law as the medium for the content of the directive. The Court thus held that it was 'the general principle of European Union law prohibiting all discrimination on grounds of age, *as given expression in Directive 2000/78*, which must be the basis of the examination of whether European Union law precludes national legislation such as that at issue in the main proceedings'.[156] And where this general principle had been violated, it was the obligation of the national court to disapply any provision of national legislation contrary to that principle.[157] Yet crucially, the Court remained ambivalent about whether the general principle was violated *because* the directive had been violated.[158] The better view would here be that this is not the case. From a constitutional perspective, the threshold for the violation of a general principle ought to be higher than that for a specific directive.

4. External Union law: international agreements

In the 'globalised' world of the twenty-first century, international agreements have become important regulatory instruments. Instead of acting unilaterally, many States realise that the regulation of international trade or the environment requires a multilateral approach. And to facilitate international regulation, many legal orders have 'opened-up' to international law and adopted a monist position. Under monism, international treaties are *constitutionally* recognised sources of domestic law.[159] The European legal order has traditionally followed this monist approach. With regard to international agreements concluded by the Union, Article 216 (2) TFEU states: '[a]greements concluded by the Union are binding upon the institutions of the Union and on its Member States'.[160]

---

[155] *Ibid.*, para. 49.   [156] *Ibid.*, para. 27 (emphasis added), see also para. 50.
[157] *Ibid.*, para. 51.
[158] In *ibid.*, para. 43, the Court found that 'European Union law, more particularly the principle of non-discrimination on grounds of age as given expression by Directive 2000/78, must be interpreted as precluding national legislation, such as that at issue in the main proceedings'. But did this mean that the directive and the general principle were violated? In a later paragraph, the Court seems to leave the question to the national courts 'to ensure the full effectiveness of that law, disapplying *if need be* any provision of national legislation contrary to that principle' (para. 51, emphasis added).
[159] On this point, see: Introduction to this chapter.
[160] The same solution applied, *mutatis mutandis*, to international agreements originally concluded by the European Union under ex-Article 24 (old) EU. The binding nature of CFSP agreements within the Union legal order was confirmed by ex-Article 24 (6) (old) EU, which provided that those agreements would be binding on the institutions of the Union. Their binding effect on the Member States was indirectly expressed in ex-Article 24 (5) (old) EU, which suggested this view with the exception of Member States that needed to comply with domestic constitutional procedures. With regard to the direct applicability of international agreements, ex-Article 24 (old) EU and ex-Article 300 (7) (old) EC were thus 'in essence indistinguishable' (P. Eeckhout, *External Relations of the European Union* (Oxford University Press, 2005), 160).

This definition suggested two things. First, international agreements were binding *in* the European legal order. And indeed, the Court has expressly confirmed that international agreements 'form an integral part of the [European] legal system' from the date of their entry into force without the need for legislative acts of 'incorporation'.[161] Union agreements were external *Union* law. Second, these international agreements would also bind the Member States. And the Court here again favoured a monist philosophy. In treating international agreements as acts of the European institutions,[162] they would be regarded as European law; and as European law, they would be directly applicable 'in' the Member States. And as directly applicable sources of European law, international agreements have the capacity to contain directly effective provisions that national courts must apply. When would such direct effects arise? And would there also be indirect effects?

(a) Direct effects of Union agreements

Even in a monist legal order, not all international treaties will be directly effective.[163] The direct applicability of international agreements only makes them capable of having direct effects. Particular treaties may lack direct effect for 'when the terms of the stipulation import a contract, when either of the parties engages to perform a particular act, the treaty addresses itself to the political, not to the judicial department; and the legislature must execute the contract before it can become a rule for the Court'.[164] Where an international agreement asks for the adoption of implementing legislation it is indeed addressed to the legislative branch, and its norms will not be operational for the executive or the judiciary.

The question whether a Union agreement has direct effect has – again – been centralised by the European Court of Justice. The Court has justified this 'centralisation' by reference to the need to ensure legal uniformity in the European legal order. The effects of Union agreements may not be allowed to vary 'according to the effects in the internal legal order of each Member State which the law of that State assigns to international agreements'.[165] Once an agreement has thus been considered by the Court to unfold direct effects, it will be directly effective in the European as well as the national legal orders. What are the conditions for direct effect? Will they be similar to internal Union law? And will international agreements be directly effective vertically as well as horizontally?

---

[161] Case 181/73, *Haegemann* v. *Belgium*, [1974] ECR 449.
[162] Case C-192/89, *Sevince* v. *Staatssecretaris van Justitie*, [1990] ECR I-3461, para. 10.
[163] C. M. Vazquez, 'Treaties as Law of the Land: the Supremacy Clause and the Judicial Enforcement of Treaties' [2008] 122 *Harvard Law Review* 599.
[164] *Foster* v. *Neilson*, 27 US (2 Pet.) 253 at 314 (1829).
[165] Case 104/81, *Hauptzollamt Mainz* v. *Kupferberg & Cie*, [1982] ECR 3641, para. 14.

(i) The conditions for direct effect

When will an international treaty have direct effects? The Court has devised a two-stage test.[166] In a first stage, it examines whether the agreement *as a whole* is capable of containing directly effective provisions. The signatory parties to the agreement may have positively settled this issue themselves.[167] If this is not the case, the Court will employ a 'policy test' that analyses the nature, purpose, spirit or general scheme of the agreement.[168] This evaluation is inherently 'political', and the first part of the analysis is essentially a 'political question'. The conditions for the direct effect of external Union law here differ from the analysis of direct effect in the internal sphere. For internal law is automatically *presumed* to be *capable* of direct effect.

Where the 'political question' hurdle has been crossed, the Court will turn to examining the direct effect of a specific provision of the agreement.[169] The second stage of the test constitutes a classic direct effect analysis. Individual provisions must represent a 'clear and precise obligation which is not subject, in its implementation or effects, to the adoption of any subsequent measures'.[170] While the second stage of the test is thus identical to that for internal legislation, the actual results can vary. Identically worded provisions in internal and external legislation may not necessarily be given the same effect.[171]

In the past, the European Courts have generally been 'favourably disposed' towards the direct effect of Union agreements, and thus created an atmosphere of 'general receptiveness' to international law.[172] The classic exception to this constitutional rule is the WTO agreement.[173] The Union is a member of the World Trade Organization, and as such formally bound by its constituent agreements. Yet the Union Courts have persistently denied that agreement a safe passage through the first part of the direct effect test. The most famous judicial ruling in this respect is *Germany* v. *Council (Bananas)*;[174] yet, it was a

---

[166] For an excellent analysis, see: A. Peters, 'The Position of International Law within the European Community Legal Order' [1997] 40 *German Yearbook of International Law* 9–77 at 53–4 and 58–66.

[167] Case 104/81, *Kupferberg* (supra n. 165), para. 17.

[168] See Joined Case 21–24/72, *International Fruit Company NV and others* v. *Produktschap voor Groenten en Fruit*, [1972] ECR 1219, para. 20 as well as *Germany* v. *Council*, 280/93, [1993] ECR 4973, para. 105.

[169] The two prongs of the test can be clearly seen in Case 104/81, *Kupferberg* (supra n. 165). In paras. 18–22, the Court undertook the global policy test, while in paras. 23–7 it looked at the conditions for direct effectiveness of a specific provision.

[170] Case 12/86, *Demirel* v. *Stadt Schwäbisch Gmünd*, [1987] ECR 3719, para. 14.

[171] J. H. J. Bourgeois, 'Effects of International Agreements in European Community Law: Are the Dice Cast?' [1983–4] 82 *Michigan Law Review* 1250–73 at 1261. See also the discussion on the preemptive effect of international treaties in Chapter 10 – Section 4(a) below.

[172] P. Eeckhout, *External Relations of the European Union* (Oxford University Press, 2004), 301.

[173] P. Eeckhout, 'The Domestic Legal Status of the WTO Agreement: Interconnecting Legal System' [1997] 34 CML Rev 11.

[174] Case C-280/93, *Germany* v. *Council*, [1994] ECR I-4973.

later decision that clarified the constitutional rationale for the refusal to grant direct effect. In *Portugal* v. *Council*, the Court found it crucial to note that:

> Some of the contracting parties, which are among the most important commercial partners of the [Union], have concluded from the subject-matter and purpose of the WTO agreements that they are not among the rules applicable by their judicial organs when reviewing the legality of their rules of domestic law. Admittedly, the fact that the courts of one of the parties consider that some of the provisions of the agreement concluded by the [Union] are of direct application whereas the courts of the other party do not recognise such direct application is not in itself such as to constitute a lack of reciprocity in the implementation of the agreement[.]
>
> However, the lack of reciprocity in that regard on the part of the [Union's] trading partners, in relation to the WTO agreements which are based on reciprocal and mutually advantageous arrangements and which must *ipso facto* be distinguished from agreements concluded by the [Union] . . . may lead to disuniform application of the WTO rules. *To accept that the role of ensuring that [European] law complies with those rules devolves directly on the [Union] judicature would deprive the legislative or executive organs of the [Union] of the scope for manoeuvre enjoyed by their counterparts in the [Union's] trading partners.*[175]

In light of the economic consequences of a finding of direct effect, the granting of such an effect to the WTO agreement was too political a question for the Court to decide. Not only was the agreement too 'political' in that it contained few hard and fast legal rules,[176] a unilateral decision to grant direct effect within the European legal order would have disadvantaged the Union vis-à-vis trading partners that had refused to allow for the agreement's enforceability in their domestic courts. The judicial self-restraint thus acknowledged that the constitutional prerogative for external relations lay primarily with the legislative branch. Surprisingly, the Court's cautious approach to the WTO agreements, and their progeny,[177] has recently been extended into a second field.[178] And it seems likely that this less receptive approach will also apply to agreements

---

[175] Case C-149/96, *Portuguese Republic* v. *Council of the European Union*, [1999] ECR I-8395, paras. 43–6 (emphasis added).

[176] For the GATT Agreement, see: Joined Cases 21-24/72, *International Fruit Company* (supra n. 168), para. 21: 'This agreement which, according to its preamble, is based on the principle of negotiations undertaken on the basis of "reciprocal and mutually advantageous arrangements" is characterised by the great flexibility of its provisions[.]'.

[177] For the lack of direct effect of WTO rulings in the Union legal order, see: Case C-377/02, *Van Parys*, [2005] ECR I-1465. On the relationship between the European Courts and decisions by international tribunals, see: M. Bronckers, 'The Relationship of the EC Courts with other International Tribunals: Non-Committal, Respectful or Submissive?' [2007] 44 CML Rev 601.

[178] The Court dealt with the United Nations Convention on the Law of the Sea ('UNCLOS'), in Case C-308/06, *Intertanko et al.* v. *Secretary of State for Transport*, [2008] ECR I-4057 and found (paras. 64–5): '[I]t must be found that UNCLOS does not establish rules intended to apply directly and immediately to individuals and to confer upon them rights or freedoms capable of being relied upon against States, irrespective of the attitude of the ship's flag State. It follows that the nature and the broad logic of UNCLOS prevent the Court from being able to assess the validity of a [Union] measure in the light of that Convention.'

concluded within the Union's 'Common Foreign and Security Policy'. For in light of the latter's specificity,[179] the Court might well find that the 'nature and broad logic' of CFSP agreements prevent their having direct effects within the Union legal order.

(ii) The dimensions of direct effect

What are the dimensions of direct effect for the Union's international agreements? Will a directly effective Union agreement be vertically *and* horizontally directly effective?

Two constitutional options exist. First, international treaties can have horizontal direct effects. Then international agreements would come close to being 'external regulations'. Alternatively, the Union legal order could treat international agreements as 'external directives' and limit their direct effect to the vertical dimension. European citizens could then only invoke a directly effective provision of a Union agreement against the European institutions and the Member States, but they could not rely on a Union agreement in a private situation.

The Court has not expressly decided which option to follow. Yet, in *Polydor* v. *Harlequin* it seemed tacitly to assume the possibility of a horizontal direct effect of international agreements.[180] Doubts remained.[181] Yet the Court did not dispel them in *Sevince*.[182] However, the acceptance of the horizontal direct effect thesis has gained ground. In *Deutscher Handballbund eV* v. *Kolpak*,[183] the Court was asked whether rules drawn up by the German Handball Federation – a private club – would be discriminatory on grounds of nationality. The sports club had refused to grant Kolpak – a Slovakian national – the same rights as German players. This seemed to violate Article 38 of the Association Agreement between the Union and Slovakia stipulating that 'workers of Slovak Republic nationality legally employed in the territory of a Member State shall be free from any discrimination based on nationality, as regards

---

[179] On this point, see: Chapter 6 – Section 3(a) above.

[180] Case 270/80, *Polydor and others* v. *Harlequin and others*, [1982] ECR 329.

[181] These doubts inevitably gave rise to a good degree of academic speculation. In 1985, the following questions was put to H. J. Glaesner, the then Director General of the Legal Service of the Council, by the House of Lords Select Committee on the European Communities: 'You are well acquainted with the direct effect doctrine of internal provisions of the Treaty of Rome. As regards external provisions, [European] case law only supports direct effects which can be invoked against Member States. Is there any likelihood of it being extended to relations between private individuals . . .?' 'Would the distinction be likely to be that the Court would be more ready to grant an individual's right arising out of an external treaty . . . but would they hesitate to impose obligations on individuals arising out of those external treaties?' The Director-General could only answer: 'That is my feeling; it is not a philosophical consideration but a *feeling* of mine' (see Select Committee on the European Communities, 'External Competence of the European Communities' [1984–5] Sixteenth Report (Her Majesty's Stationery Office, 1985), 154 (emphasis added)).

[182] Case C-192/89, *Sevince* (supra n. 162).

[183] Case C-438/00, *Deutscher Handballbund eV* v. *Maros Kolpak*, [2003] ECR I-4135.

working conditions, remuneration or dismissal, as compared to its own nationals'. The question, therefore, arose whether this article had 'effects *vis-à-vis third parties inasmuch as it does not apply solely to measures taken by the authorities but also extends to rules applying to employees that are collective in nature*'.[184] The Court thought that this could indeed be the case.[185] And in allowing the rules to apply directly to private parties, the Court presumed that the international agreement would be horizontally directly effective.

This implicit recognition of the horizontal direct effect of Union agreements has been confirmed outside the context of association agreements.[186] And in the absence of any mandatory constitutional reason to the contrary, this choice seems preferable. Like US constitutionalism, the European legal order should not exclude the horizontal direct effect of international treaties. The problems encountered in the context of European directives would be reproduced – if not multiplied – if the European Court were to split the direct effect of international treaties into two halves. Self-executing treaties should thus be able 'to establish rights *and duties* of individuals directly enforceable in domestic courts'.[187]

(b) Indirect effects: the interpretation and implementation principles

A Union agreement lacking direct effect may – just like a regulation or a directive – nonetheless enjoy certain indirect effects in the European and national legal orders. The lack of direct effect simply means exactly what it says: the agreement has no *direct* effect. It cannot directly be relied upon as a source of rights and obligations. A Union agreement without such direct effect requires a medium – an internal Union act or a national law – to unfold its indirect effects in the European legal order. What types of indirect effects have been recognised?

Two constitutional principles spring to mind in this context. First, there is the principle of 'consistent interpretation'.[188] In *Commission v. Germany* (IDA),[189] the Court defined the principle in the following terms: '*When the wording of secondary [Union] legislation is open to more than one interpretation* ... the primacy of international agreements concluded by the [Union] over provisions of secondary legislation means that such provisions must, *so far as possible, be interpreted in a manner that is consistent with those agreements.*'[190] Second, there is the 'principle of implementation'.[191] In two

---

[184] *Ibid.*, para. 19 (emphasis added).   [185] *Ibid.*, paras. 32 and 37.
[186] See Case C-265/03, *Simutenkov* v. *Ministerio de Educacion y Cultura and Real Federacion Espanola de Futbol*, [2005] ECR I-2579, where the Court confirmed *Deutscher Handballbund* (supra n. 183) in the context of the Partnership and Cooperation Agreement between the EC and the Russian Federation.
[187] S. A. Riesenfeld, 'International Agreements' [1989] 14 *Yale Journal of International Law* 455–467 at 463 (emphasis added).
[188] For a discussion of the principle, see: Eeckhout, *External Relations* (supra n. 172) 314–16.
[189] Case C-61/94, *Commission* v. *Germany (IDA)*, [1996] ECR I-3989.
[190] *Ibid.*, para. 52 (emphasis added).   [191] Eeckhout, *External Relations* (supra n. 172), 316.

exceptional circumstances an international agreement that lacks direct effect – typically, an agreement relating to the WTO – can here provide an *indirect* standard of review for the legality of Union and national legislation. This indirect review occurs whenever the Union adopts internal legislation '*intended to implement a particular obligation* assumed in the context of the WTO, or where the *[Union] measure refers expressly to the precise provisions* of the WTO agreements'.[192]

This implementation principle has thus two prongs. According to the first prong, established in *Nakajima*,[193] an international agreement prevails over inconsistent European implementing legislation. The Court pointed out that the applicant was 'not relying on the direct effect' of the international agreement as such.[194] But since the Union measure had been adopted in order to comply with the international obligations of the Union, the Court was entitled 'to examine whether the Council went beyond the legal frame-work thus laid down'.[195] We encounter the second prong of the implementation principle in *FEDIOL*.[196] A Union regulation had been adopted, whose Article 2 (1) prohibited all 'illicit commercial practices' as 'any international trade practices attributable to third countries which are incompatible with international law or with the generally accepted rules'. The specific reference to international law in the Union act, so the Court claimed, did entitle it to review the actions of the Commission in light of the WTO rules. And as the Union legislator had instructed the Commission to let its action be guided by the international norms, judicial review of these actions would involve the interpretation and indirect application of the international rules.[197]

What is the constitutional rationale behind these cases? What is clear is that it was not the international agreements themselves that *directly* provided the basis for review. The treaties were only an *indirect* standard, since the Union measures were only reviewed 'in light of' these treaties. The international norms had thus been mediated through a Union measure. Could one, therefore, not argue that *through the act of implementation* the EU institutions have 'used and forfeited the international scope of manoeuvre'?[198] According to this view, it is the self-binding of the European institutions – manifested in a specific internal implementing act – that provides the intellectual basis for the judicial review. This approach may then be described as '*midway* between a monist and a dualist system of integrating international law'.[199]

---

[192] Case C-149/96, *Portugal* v. *Council*, [1999] ECR I-8395, para. 49 (emphasis added).
[193] Case C-69/89, *Nakajima All Precision* v. *Council*, [1991] ECR I-2069.   [194] *Ibid.*, para. 28.
[195] *Ibid.*, para. 32.   [196] Case 70/87, *FEDIOL* v. *Commission*, [1989] ECR 1781.
[197] *Ibid.*, para. 20.   [198] Eeckhout, *External Relations* (supra n. 172), 319.
[199] C. Timmermans, 'The EU and Public International Law' (1999) 4 *European Foreign Affairs Review*, 181–94 at 190 (emphasis added).

Conclusion

For a norm to be a legal norm it must be enforceable.[200] The very questioning of the direct effect of European law was indeed an 'infant disease' of a young legal order.[201] 'But now that [European] law has reached maturity, direct effect should be taken for granted, as a normal incident of an advanced constitutional order.'[202] The evolution of the doctrine of direct effect, discussed in this chapter, indeed mirrors this maturation. Today's test for the direct effect of European law is an extremely lenient test. A provision has direct effect, where it is 'unconditional' and thus 'sufficiently clear and precise' – two conditions that probe whether a norm can (or should) be applied in court or whether it first needs legislative concretisation. All sources of European law have been considered to be capable of producing law with direct effects. And this direct effect normally applies vertically as well as horizontally.

The exception to this rule is the 'directive'. For directives, the Union legal order prefers their indirect effects.[203] '[W]herever a directive is correctly implemented, its effects extend to individuals *through the medium of the implementing measures adopted*.'[204] The Court even insists on the mediated effect of directives for those parts of a directive that are directly effective.[205] The directive thus represents a form of 'background' or 'indirect' European law,[206] which is in permanent symbiosis with national (implementing) legislation.[207] Moreover, even when directives have direct effect, they are said to never have horizontal direct effects. But as we saw above, this is not an absolute truth. For the Court has implicitly accepted the incidental horizontal direct effect in some cases. Why has the Court shown such 'childish' loyalty to the no-horizontal-direct-effect rule? Has that rule not created more constitutional problems than it solves? And is the Court perhaps discussing a 'false problem'? For if the Court simply wishes to say that an (unimplemented) directive may never directly

---

[200] On the difference between (merely) 'moral' and (enforceable) 'legal' norms, see: H. L. A. Hart, *The Concept of Law* (Clarendon Press, 1997).

[201] P. Pescatore, 'The Doctrine of "Direct Effect": an Infant Disease of Community Law' [1983] 8 EL Rev 155.

[202] A. Dashwood, 'From Van Duyn to Mangold via Marshall: Reducing Direct Effect to Absurdity' [2006/07] 9 *Cambridge Yearbook of European Legal Studies* 81.

[203] Case 80/86, *Kolpinghuis* (supra n. 96), para. 15: 'The question whether the provisions of a directive may be relied upon as such before a national court arises only if the member State concerned has not implemented the directive in national law within the prescribed period or has implemented the directive incorrectly.'

[204] Case 8/81, *Becker* v. *Finanzamt Münster-Innenstadt*, [1982] ECR 53, para. 19 (emphasis added).

[205] In Case 102/79, *Commission* v. *Belgium*, [1980] ECR 1473, para. 12.

[206] Case C-298/89, *Gibraltar* v. *Council*, [1993] ECR I-3605, para. 16 (emphasis added): 'normally a form of *indirect regulatory or legislative measure*'.

[207] The indirect effect of directives thereby never stops. Directives will always remain in the background as a form of 'fall-back' legislation even where the national authorities have correctly implemented the directive; see Case 62/00, *Marks & Spencer plc* v. *Commissioners of Customs & Excise*, [2002] ECRI-6325, paras. 27–8.

prohibit *private* party actions, this does not mean that it cannot have horizontal direct effects in civil disputes challenging the legality of *State* actions.[208]

This brings us to a second important conclusion of this chapter. Not only can all European law be directly effective, all European law can also be indirectly effective. The doctrine of consistent interpretation – principally developed within the context of directives – indeed applies as a structural principle to all sources of European law.[209]

A third point needs to be raised. Will the – direct or indirect – effects of European law be confined to the *judicial* application of European law? This argument has been made,[210] and – despite strong criticism[211] – recently been re-made.[212] But this narrow view bangs its head against hard empirical facts,[213] and equally raises serious theoretical objections. For why should the recognition of an 'administrative direct effect' represent a 'constitutional enormity'?[214] The answer suggested is – with due respect – not convincing.[215] In most national legal orders the courts are as subordinate to national legislation as the executive branch. They may 'interpret' national legislation, but must not

---

[208] This – much – simpler reading of the substance of the case law would bring directives close to the normative character of Article 107 TFEU – prohibiting State aids. For while the provision can be invoked as against the State as well as against a private party, it cannot prohibit private aids by private companies.

[209] In the – brilliant – summary of Advocate-General Tizzano in Case C-144/04, *Mangold* (supra n. 143), para. 117: 'It must first be recalled that the duty of consistent interpretation is one of the "structural" effects of [European] law which, together with the more "invasive" device of direct effect, enables national law to be brought into line with the substance and aims of [European] law. Because it is structural in nature, the duty applies with respect to all sources of [European] law, whether constituted by primary or secondary legislation, and whether embodied in acts whose legal effects are binding or not. Even in the case of recommendations, the Court has held, "national courts *are bound* to take [them] into consideration in order to decide disputes submitted to them".'

[210] In this sense, see: B. de Witte, 'Direct Effect, Supremacy and the Nature of the Legal Order' in P. Craig and G. de Búrca (eds.), *The Evolution of EU Law* (Oxford University Press, 1999), 177 at 193.

[211] For a – direct – criticism of this view, see: Schütze, 'Morphology' (supra n. 103).

[212] B. de Witte, 'Direct Effect, Primacy and the Nature of the Legal Order' in: P. Craig and G. de Búrca (eds.), *Evolution* (supra n. 210), 323 at 333.

[213] Among the myriad judgments, see: Case 103/88, *Costanzo SpA* v. *Comune di Milano* [1989] ECR 1839, para. 31, where the Court found it 'contradictory to rule that an individual may rely upon the provisions of a directive which fulfil the conditions defined above in proceedings before the national courts seeking an order against the administrative authorities, and yet to hold that those authorities are under no obligation to apply the provisions of the directive and refrain from applying provisions of national law which conflict with them. It follows that when the conditions under which the Court has held that individuals may rely on the provisions of a directive before the national courts are met, all organs of the administration . . . are obliged to apply those provisions.'

[214] de Witte, 'Direct Effect, Supremacy' (supra n. 210), 193.

[215] de Witte 'Direct Effect, Primary' (supra n. 212), 333: 'In domestic law, executive authorities are normally subordinate to the legislator and cannot set aside, of their own motion, legislative norms conflicting with the constitution; only the appropriate (constitutional) courts can do so, if at all.'

amend it. And once we accept that European law entitles all national courts – even the lowest court in the remotest part of the country – to challenge an act of Parliament or the national constitution, is it really such an enormous step to demand the same of the executive? Would it not be absurd *not* to require national administrations to apply European law, but to allow for judicial challenges of the resulting administrative act? And while there may be no formal 'preliminary reference procedure' between the Union and the national administrations, there are indeed informal mechanisms to ensure the smooth operation within the Union's executive federalism. The conclusions of this chapter indeed extend to the administrative (in)direct effects of European law.

10

European Law: Supremacy and Preemption

Contents

Introduction	347
1. The European perspective: absolute supremacy	349
(a) The absolute scope of the supremacy principle	350
(i) Supremacy over internal laws of the Member States	350
(ii) Supremacy over international treaties of the Member States	352
(b) The 'executive' nature of supremacy: disapplication, not invalidation	355
2. The national perspective: relative supremacy	358
(a) Fundamental rights limits: the 'so-long' jurisprudence	359
(b) Competences limits: from *'Maastricht'* to *'Mangold'*	361
3. Legislative preemption: nature and effect	363
(a) Preemption categories: the relative effects of preemption	364
(i) Field preemption	365
(ii) Obstacle preemption	366
(iii) Rule preemption	366
(b) Modes of preemption: express and implied preemption	367
4. Constitutional limits to legislative preemption	368
(a) Union instruments and their preemptive capacity	369
(i) The preemptive capacity of regulations	369
(ii) the preemptive capacity of directives	371
(iii) The preemptive capacity of international agreements	372
(b) Competence limits to preemption	374
(i) Competences for minimum harmonisation	375
(ii) Complementary competences excluding harmonisation	376
Conclusion	378

Introduction

Since European law is directly applicable in the Member States, it must be applied alongside national law by national authorities. And since European law may have direct effect, it might come into conflict with national law in a specific situation.[1]

Where two legislative wills come into conflict, each legal order must determine *when* conflicts arise and *how* these conflicts are to be resolved. For the Union legal order, these two dimensions have indeed been developed for the relationship between European and national law. In Europe's constitutionalism they have been described as, respectively, the principle of preemption and the principle of supremacy: 'The problem of preemption consists in determining whether there exists a conflict between a national measure and a rule of [European] law. The problem of primacy concerns the manner in which such a conflict, if it is found to exist, will be resolved.'[2] Preemption and supremacy thus represent 'two sides of the same coin'.[3] They are like Siamese twins: different though inseparable. There is no supremacy without preemption.

This chapter begins with an analysis of the supremacy doctrine. How supreme is European law? Will European law prevail over all national law? And what is the effect of the supremacy principle on national law? We shall see that there are *two* perspectives on the supremacy question. According to the *European* perspective, all Union law prevails over all national law. This 'absolute' view is not shared by the Member States. Indeed, according to the *national* perspective, the supremacy of European law is relative: some national law is considered to be beyond the supremacy of European law. A third section then moves to the doctrine of preemption. This tells us to what extent national law conflicts with European law, that is: how much legal space a European law still leaves to the Member States. The Union legislator is generally free to choose to what extent it wishes to preempt national law. However, there are two potential constitutional limits to this freedom. First, the type of *instrument* used – regulation, directive or international agreement – might limit the preemptive effect of Union law. And, second: the type of *competence* on which the Union

---

[1] For the two main theories on the relationship between direct effect and supremacy, see: M. Dougan, 'When Worlds Collide! Competing Visions of the Relationship between Direct Effect and Supremacy' [2007] 44 CML Rev 931. The article is partly a response to K. Lenaerts and T. Corthaut, 'Of Birds and Hedges: the Role of Primacy in Invoking Norms of EU Law' [2006] 31 EL Rev 287, which has caused a lively debate. Nonetheless, why this 'German quarrel' – ironically not fought by Germans – has become so prominent is surprising, for it seems to have very few, if any, consequences on the relationship between European and national law. This chapter, as will become clearer below, favours the view that supremacy requires a concrete conflict between different norms. Where a European norm lacks direct effect, it cannot be applied in a specific case and for that reason cannot clash with a national norm. The supremacy principle is an 'executive' or 'judicial' principle.

[2] M. Waelbroeck, 'The Emergent Doctrine of Community Preemption – Consent and Redelegation' in T. Sandalow and E. Stein (eds.), *Courts and Free Markets: Perspectives from the United States and Europe* (Oxford University Press, 1982), vol. II, 548–80, at 551.

[3] S. Krislov, C.-D. Ehlermann and J. Weiler, 'The Political Organs and the Decision-Making Process in the United States and the European Community' in M. Cappelletti, M. Seccombe and J. Weiler (eds.), *Integration through Law: Europe and the American Federal Experience* (de Gruyter, 1986), vol. I, 3 at 90.

act is based – shared or complementary – might determine the capacity of the Union legislator to preempt the Member States.

1. The European perspective: absolute supremacy

The resolution of legislative conflicts requires a hierarchy of norms. Modern federal States typically resolve conflicts between federal and state legislation in favour of the former: federal law is supreme law over State law.[4] This 'centralist solution' has become so engrained in our constitutional mentalities that we tend to forget that the 'decentralised solution' is also possible: local law may reign supreme over central law.[5] Supremacy and direct effect are thus *not* different sides of the same coin. While the supremacy of a norm implies its direct effect, the direct effect of a norm will *not* imply its supremacy.[6] Each compound legal order must thus determine which law prevails in the case of a normative conflict. The simplest supremacy format is one that is absolute: all law from one legal order is superior to all law from the other. Absolute supremacy may here be given to the legal system of the smaller *or* the bigger political community. But between these two extremes lies a range of possible nuances.[7]

When the Union was born, the European Treaties did not expressly state the supremacy of European law.[8] Did this mean that supremacy was a matter to be determined by the national legal orders (decentralised solution)? Or was there a

---

[4] Article VI, Clause 2 of the US Constitution, for example, states: 'This Constitution, and the Laws of the United States which shall be made in pursuance thereof; and all treaties made, or which shall be made, under the Authority of the United States, shall be the supreme Law of the Land.'

[5] For a long time, the 'decentralised solution' structured federal relationships during the Middle Ages. Its constitutional spirit is best preserved in the old legal proverb: 'Town law breaks county law, county law breaks common law'. In the event of a legislative conflict, supremacy was thus given to the rule of the smaller political community.

[6] We can see direct effect without supremacy in the status given to customary international law in the British legal order. And the fact that there can be direct effect without supremacy is the reason why there are *two* variants of the monist theory of international law (see H. Kelsen, 'Sovereignty' in S.L. Paulson and B.L. Paulson (eds.), *Normativity and Norms: Critical Perspectives on Kelsenian Themes* (Clarendon Press, 1998), 525). For a monist theory that gives priority to national (constitutional) law, see: the United States. For a monist theory in which international law may even trump over national constitutional law, see: the Netherlands (A. Nollkaemper, 'The Netherlands' in D. Sloss (ed.), *The Role of Domestic Courts in Treaty Enforcement: a Comparative Study* (Cambridge University Press, 2009), 326).

[7] The status of international law in the German legal order depends on its legal source. While general principles of international law assume a hierarchical position between the German constitution and federal legislation, international treaties have traditionally been placed at the hierarchical rank of normal legislation.

[8] The Constitutional Treaty *would* have added an express provision (Article I-6 CT): 'The Constitution and law adopted by the institutions of the Union in exercising competences conferred on it shall have primacy over the law of the Member States.' However, the provision was not taken over by the Lisbon Treaty. Yet the latter has added Declaration 17 which states: 'The Conference recalls that, in accordance with well settled case law of the Court of Justice of the European Union, the Treaties and the law adopted by the Union on the basis of the Treaties have primacy over the law of Member States, under the conditions laid down by the said case law.'

Union doctrine of supremacy (centralised solution)? And if the latter, how supreme would European law be over national law? Would it adopt an absolute doctrine, or would it permit areas in which national law could prevail over conflicting European law? And would the supremacy of European law lead to the 'invalidation' of State law; or would it only demand its 'disapplication'?

Let us tackle these questions in two steps. We shall first look at the scope of the supremacy doctrine and see that the Union prefers an absolute principle: all European law prevails over all national law. However, the supremacy of European law will not affect the validity of national norms. This 'executive' nature of supremacy will be discussed in a second step.

(a) The absolute scope of the supremacy principle

The strong dualist traditions within two of the Member States in 1958,[9] posed a serious legal threat to the unity of the Union legal order. Within dualist States, the status of European law is seen as depending on the national act 'transposing' the European Treaties. Where this was a parliamentary act, any subsequent parliamentary acts could – expressly or implicitly – repeal the transposition law. Within the British tradition, this follows from the classic doctrine of parliamentary sovereignty: an 'old' Parliament cannot bind a 'new' one. Any 'newer' parliamentary act will thus theoretically prevail over the 'older' European Union Act. But the supremacy of European law could even be threatened in monist States. For even in monist States, the supremacy of European law will find a limit in the State's constitutional structures.

Would the European legal order insist that its law was to prevail over national law, including national constitutions? The Court of Justice did just that in a series of foundational cases. But while the establishment of the supremacy over internal national law was swift, its extension over the international treaties of the Member States was much slower.

(i) Supremacy over internal laws of the Member States
Frightened by the decentralised solution to the supremacy issue, the Court centralised the question of supremacy by turning it into a principle of European law. In *Costa* v. *ENEL*,[10] the European judiciary was asked whether national legislation adopted *after* 1958 could prevail over the Treaties. The litigation involved an unsettled energy bill owed by Costa to the Italian 'National Electricity Board'. The latter had been created by the 1962 Electricity Nationalisation Act, which was challenged by the plaintiff as a violation of the European Treaties. The Italian dualist tradition responded that the European Treaties – like ordinary international law – had been transposed by

---

[9] C. Sasse, 'The Common Market: Between International and Municipal Law' [1965–6] 75 *Yale Law Journal* 696–753.

[10] Case 6/64, *Costa* v. *ENEL*, [1964] ECR 585.

national legislation that could – following international law logic – be derogated by subsequent national legislation. Could the Member States thus unilaterally determine the status of European law in its national legal order? The Court rejected this reading and distanced itself from the international law thesis:

> By contrast with ordinary international treaties, the E[U] Treaty has created its own legal system which, on the entry into force of the Treaty, became an integral part of the legal systems of the Member States and which their courts are bound to apply . . . The integration into the laws of each Member State of provisions which derive from the [Union], and more generally the terms and the spirit of the Treaty, make it impossible for the States, as a corollary, to accord precedence to a unilateral and subsequent measure over a legal system accepted by them on a basis of reciprocity. Such a measure cannot therefore be inconsistent with that legal system. The *executive force* of [European] law cannot vary from one State to another in deference to subsequent domestic laws, without jeopardising the attainment of the objectives of the Treaty . . . It follows from all these observations that the law stemming from the Treaty, an independent source of law, could not, because of its special and original nature, be overridden by domestic legal provisions, however framed, without being deprived of its character as [European] law and without the legal basis of the [Union] itself being called into question.[11]

European law would reign supreme over national law, since its 'executive force' must not vary from one State to another. The supremacy of Union law could not be derived from classic international law;[12] and for that reason that Court had to declare the Union legal order autonomous from ordinary international law. But, how supreme was European law? The fact that the European Treaties prevailed over national legislation did not automatically imply that *all* secondary law would prevail over *all* national law. Would the Court accept a 'nuanced' solution for certain national norms, such as national constitutional law?

---

[11] *Ibid.*, 593–4 (emphasis added).
[12] Some legal scholars refer to the 'supremacy' of international law vis-à-vis national law (see F. Morgenstern, 'Judicial Practice and the Supremacy of International Law' [1950] 27 *British Yearbook of International Law* 42). However, the concept of supremacy is here used in an imprecise way. Legal supremacy stands for the priority of one norm over another. For this, two norms must conflict and, therefore, form part of the same legal order. However, classic international law is based on the sovereignty of States and that implied a dualist relation with national law. The dualist veil protected national laws from being overridden by norms adopted by such 'supranational' authorities as the Catholic Church or the Holy Roman Empire. (When a State opens up to international law, this 'monistic' stance is a *national* choice. International law as such has never imposed monism on a State. On the contrary, in clearly distinguishing between international and national law, it is based on a dualist philosophy.) Reference to the international law doctrine *pacta sunt servanda* will hardly help. The fact that a State cannot invoke its internal law to justify a breach of international obligations is not supremacy. Behind the doctrine of *pacta sunt servanda* stands the concept of legal responsibility: a State cannot – without legal responsibility – escape its international obligations. The duality of internal and international law is thereby maintained: the former cannot affect the latter (as the latter cannot affect the former).

The European Court never accepted the relative scope of the supremacy doctrine. This was clarified in *Internationale Handelsgesellschaft*.[13] A German administrative court had doubted that European legislation could violate fundamental rights granted by the German Constitution and raised this very question with the European Court of Justice. Were the fundamental structural principles of national constitutions, including human rights, beyond the scope of federal supremacy? The Court disagreed. 'Recourse to the legal rules or concepts of national law in order to judge the validity of measures adopted by the institutions of the [Union] would have an adverse effect on the uniformity and efficiency of [European] law. The validity of such measures can only be judged in the light of [European] law.'[14] The validity of European laws could not be affected – even by the most fundamental norms within the Member States. The Court's vision of the supremacy of European law over national law was an absolute one: 'The whole of [European] law prevails over the whole of national law.'[15]

(ii) Supremacy over international treaties of the Member States

While the European doctrine of supremacy had quickly emerged with regard to national legislation,[16] its extension to international agreements of the Member States was much slower. From the very beginning, the Treaties here recognised an express exception to the supremacy of European law. According to Article 351 TFEU:

> The rights and obligations arising from agreements concluded before 1 January 1958 or, for acceding States, before the date of their accession, between one or more Member States on the one hand, and one or more third countries on the other, shall not be affected by the provisions of the Treaties.[17]

Article 351 codified the 'supremacy' of *prior* international agreements of the Member States over conflicting European law. In the event of a conflict between the two, it was European law that could be disapplied *within the national legal*

---

[13] Case 11/70, *Internationale Handelsgesellschaft mbH* v. *Einfuhr- und Vorratsstelle für Getreide und Futtermittel*, [1970] ECR 1125.

[14] *Ibid.*, para. 3.

[15] R. Kovar, 'The Relationship between Community Law and National Law' in EC Commission (ed.), *Thirty Years of Community Law* (EC Commission, 1981), 109–149, at 112–13.

[16] On the establishment of the *social* acceptance of the doctrine, see: K. Alter, *Establishing the Supremacy of European Law: the Making of an International Rule of Law in Europe* (Oxford University Press, 2001).

[17] Paragraph 1. The provision continues (para. 2): 'To the extent that such agreements are not compatible with the Treaties, the Member State or States concerned shall take all appropriate steps to eliminate the incompatibilities established. Member States shall, where necessary, assist each other to this end and shall, where appropriate, adopt a common attitude.' On the scope of this obligation, see: J. Klabbers, 'Moribund on the Fourth of July? The Court of Justice on Prior Agreements of the Member States' [2001] 26 EL Rev 187, as well as: R. Schütze, 'The "Succession Doctrine" and the European Union' in A. Arnull (et al., eds.), *A Constitutional Order of States: Essays in Honour of Alan Dashwood* (Hart, 2011), 459 at 473 et seq.

orders. Indeed, Article 351 'would not achieve its purpose if it did not imply a duty on the part of the institutions of the [Union] not to impede the performance of the obligations of Member States which stem from a prior agreement'.[18] This was a severe incursion into the integrity of the European legal order, and as such had to be interpreted restrictively.[19]

But would there be internal or external limits to the 'supremacy' of prior international treaties of the Member States? The Court clarified that there existed internal limits to the provision. Article 351 (1) would only allow Member States to implement their *obligations* towards *third* States.[20] Member States could thus not rely on Article 351 to enforce their rights; nor could they rely on the provision to fulfil their international obligations between themselves. These internal limitations are complemented by external limitations. The Court clarified their existence in *Kadi*.[21] While admitting that Article 351 would justify even derogations from primary Union law, the Court insisted that the provision 'cannot, however, be understood to authorise any derogation from the principles of liberty, democracy and respect for human rights and fundamental freedoms enshrined in Article [2] [T]EU as a foundation of the Union'.[22] In the opinion of the Court, 'Article [351 TFEU] may in no circumstances permit any challenge to the principles that form part of the very foundations of the [Union] legal order'.[23] The Union's constitutional identity

---

[18] Case 812/79, *Attorney General* v. *Juan C. Burgoa*, [1980] ECR 2787, para. 9 (emphasis added). This was confirmed in Case C-158/91, *Criminal Proceedings against Jean-Claude Levy*, [1993] ECR I-4287, para. 22: 'In view of the foregoing considerations, the answer to the question submitted for a preliminary ruling must be that the national court is under an obligation to ensure [that the relevant European legislation] ... is fully complied with by refraining from applying any conflicting provision of national legislation, unless the application of such a provision is necessary in order to ensure the performance by the Member State concerned of obligations arising under an agreement concluded with non-member countries prior to the entry into force of the EEC Treaty.'

[19] Case C-324/93, *The Queen* v. *Secretary of State for Home Department, ex parte Evans Medical Ltd and Macfarlan Smith Ltd*, [1995] ECR I-563, para. 32.

[20] Case 10/61, *Commission* v. *Italy*, [1962] ECR 1, 10–11: '[T]he terms "rights and obligations" in Article [351] refer, as regards the "rights", to the rights of third countries and, as regards the "obligations", to the obligations of Member States and that, by virtue of the principles of international law, by assuming a new obligation which is incompatible with rights held under a prior treaty, a State ipso facto gives up the exercise of these rights to the extent necessary for the performance of its new obligation ... In fact, in matters governed by the [European] Treat[ies], th[ese] Treat[ies] take precedence over agreements concluded between Member States before [their] entry into force[.]'

[21] Case C-402/05P, *Kadi and Al Barakaat International Foundation* v. *Council and Commission*, [2008] ECR I-6351. The facts of the case will be discussed below.

[22] *Ibid.*, para. 303. The original provision at issue was ex-Article 6 (1) (old) EU, which stated: 'The Union is founded on the principles of liberty, democracy, respect for human rights and fundamental freedoms, and the rule of law, principles which are common to the Member States.' The provision is today enshrined in Article 2 TEU: 'The Union is founded on the values of respect for human dignity, freedom, democracy, equality, the rule of law and respect for human rights, including the rights of persons belonging to minorities ...'.

[23] Case C-402/05P, *Kadi* (supra n. 21), para. 304.

constituted a limit to the supremacy of prior international treaties concluded by the Member States.

But should the – limited – application of Article 351 TFEU be extended, by analogy, to *subsequent* international agreements?[24] The main constitutional thrust behind the argument is that it protects the effective exercise of the treaty-making powers of the Member States. For: 'otherwise the Member States could not conclude any international treaty without running the risk of a subsequent conflict with [European] law'.[25] This idea has been criticised: there would be no reason why the 'normal' constitutional principles characterising the relationship between European law and unilateral national acts should not also apply to subsequently concluded international agreements.[26] A middle position has proposed limiting the analogous application of Article 351 to situations where the conflict between post-accession international treaties of Member States and subsequently adopted European legislation was 'objectively unforeseeable' and could therefore not be expected.[27]

None of the proposals to extend Article 351 by analogy has however been mirrored in the jurisprudence of the European Court of Justice.[28] The Court has unconditionally upheld the supremacy of European law over international agreements concluded by the Member States after 1958. In light of the potential international responsibility of the Member States, is this a fair constitutional solution? Should it indeed make a difference whether a rule is adopted by means of a unilateral national measure or by means of an international agreement with a third State? Constitutional solutions still need to be found to solve the Member States' dilemma of choosing between the Scylla of liability under the European Treaties and the Charybdis of international responsibility for breach of contract. Should the Union legal order, therefore, be given an ex ante authorisation mechanism for Member States' international agreements? Or should the Union share financial responsibility for breach of contract with the Member State concerned?

These are difficult constitutional questions. They await future constitutional answers.[29]

[24] J. H. F. van Panhuys, 'Conflicts between the Law of the European Communities and Other Rules of International Law' [1965–6] 3 CML Rev 420, 434.
[25] E. Pache and J. Bielitz, 'Das Verhältnis der EG zu den völkerrechtlichen Verträgen ihrer Mitgliedstaaten' [2006] 41 *Europarecht* 316, 327 (my translation).
[26] E. Bülow, 'Die Anwendung des Gemeinschaftsrechts im Verhältnis zu Drittländern' in A. Clauder (ed.), *Einführung in die Rechtsfragen der europäischen Integration* (Europea Union Verlag, 1972), 52, 54.
[27] E.-U. Petersmann, 'Artikel 234' in H. Von der Groeben, J. Thiesing and C.-D. Ehlermann (eds.), *Kommentar zum EWG-Vertrag* (Nomos, 1991) 5725, 5731 (para. 6).
[28] See Joined Cases C-176 and 177/97, *Commission v. Belgium and Luxembourg*, [1998] ECR I-3557.
[29] For the time being, one legislative answer can be seen in the inclusion of 'express savings' clauses in the relevant Union legislation. A good illustration of this technique is Article 28 of Regulation 864/2007 on the law applicable to non-contractual obligations (Rome II) (OJ 2007 L199/40). This clause constitutes a legislative extension of Article 351 TFEU: the Union legislation will not

(b) The 'executive' nature of supremacy: disapplication, not invalidation

What are the legal consequences of the supremacy of European law over conflicting national law? Must a national court 'hold such provisions inapplicable to the extent to which they are incompatible with [European] law', or must it 'declare them void'?[30] This question concerns the constitutional effect of the supremacy doctrine in the Member States.

The classic answer to these questions is found in *Simmenthal II*.[31] The issue raised in the national proceedings was this: 'what consequences flow from the direct applicability of a provision of [Union] law in the event of incompatibility with a subsequent legislative provision of a Member State'?[32] Within the Italian constitutional order, national legislation could be *repealed* solely by Parliament or the Supreme Court. Would lower national courts thus have to wait until this happened and, in the meantime, apply national laws that violate Union laws? Unsurprisingly, the European Court rejected such a reading. Appealing to the 'very foundations of the [Union]', the European Court stated that national courts were under a direct obligation to give immediate effect to European law. The supremacy of European law meant that 'rules of [European] law must be fully and uniformly applied in all the Member States from the date of their entry into force and for so long as they continue in force'.[33] But did this mean that the national court had to *repeal* the national law? According to one view, supremacy did indeed mean that national courts must declare conflicting national laws void. European law would 'break' national law.[34] Yet the Court preferred a milder – second – view:

> [I]n accordance with the *principle of precedence* of [European] law, the relationship between provisions of the Treaty and directly applicable measures of the institutions on the one hand and the national law of the Member States on the other is such that those provisions and measures not only by their entry into force render *automatically inapplicable* any conflicting provision of current national law but – in so far as they are an integral part of, and take precedence in, the legal order applicable in the territory of each of the Member States – also preclude the valid adoption of new legislative measures to the extent to which they would be incompatible with [European] provisions.[35]

affect international agreements of the Member States with third States concluded after 1958 but before the time when the Regulation was adopted.

[30] This very question was raised in: Case 34/67, *Firma Gebrüder Luck* v. *Hauptzollamt Köln-Rheinau*, [1968] ECR 245.

[31] Case 106/77, *Amministrazione delle Finanze dello Stato* v. *Simmenthal SpA*, [1978] ECR 629. But see also: Case 48/71, *Commission* v. *Italy*, [1978] ECR 629.

[32] Case 106/77, *Simmenthal* (supra n. 31), para. 13.   [33] *Ibid.*, para. 14.

[34] This is the very title of a German monograph by E. Grabitz, *Gemeinschaftsrecht bricht nationales Recht* (L. Appel, 1966). This position was shared by Hallstein: '[T]he supremacy of [European] law means essentially two things: its rules take precedence irrespective of the level of the two orders at which the conflict occurs, and further, [European] law *not only invalidates previous national law but also limits subsequent national legislation*' (W. Hallstein quoted in Sasse, 'The Common Market' (supra n. 9), 696–753 at 717 (emphasis added)).

[35] Case 106/77, *Simmenthal* (supra n. 31), para.17 (emphasis added).

Where national measures conflicted with European law, the supremacy of European law would thus not render them void, but only 'inapplicable'.[36] Not 'invalidation' but 'disapplication' was required of national courts, where European laws came into conflict with pre-existing national laws. Yet, in the above passage, the effect of the supremacy doctrine appeared stronger in relation to future national legislation. Here, the Court said that the supremacy of European law would 'preclude the *valid adoption* of new legislative measures to the extent to which they would be incompatible with [European] provisions'.[37] Was this to imply that national legislators were not even *competent* to adopt national laws that would run counter to *existing* European law? Were these national laws void *ab initio*?[38]

In *Ministero delle Finanze* v. *IN.CO.GE.'90*,[39] the Commission picked up this second prong of the *Simmenthal* ruling and argued that 'a Member State has *no power whatever to [subsequently] adopt* a fiscal provision that is incompatible with [European] law, with the result that such a provision . . . must be treated as *non-existent*'.[40] But the European Court of Justice disagreed with this interpretation. Pointing out that *Simmenthal II* 'did not draw any distinction between pre-existing and subsequently adopted national law',[41] the incompatibility of subsequently adopted rules of national law with European law did not have the effect of rendering these rules non-existent.[42] National courts were thus only under an obligation to disapply a conflicting provision of national law – be it prior *or* subsequent to the Union law.[43]

---

[36] The Court's reference to 'directly applicable measures' was not designed to limit the supremacy of European law to regulations. The Union acts at issue in *Simmenthal* were, after all, directives. This point was clarified in subsequent jurisprudence: see Case 148/78, *Ratti*, [1979] ECR 1629; and Case 152/84, *Marshall* v. *Southampton and South-West Hampshire Area Health Authority*, [1986] ECR 723.

[37] Case 106/77, *Simmenthal* (supra n. 31) para. 17 (emphasis added).

[38] A. Barav, 'Les Effets du Droit Communautaire Directement Applicable' [1978] 14 CDE 265–86 at 275–6. See also, Grabitz, *Gemeinschaftsrecht* (supra n. 34) and Hallstein, quoted in Sasse, *The Common Market* (supra n. 34).

[39] Joined Cases C-10–22/97, *Ministero delle Finanze* v. *IN.CO.GE.'90 Srl and others*, [1998] ECR I-6307.

[40] *Ibid.*, para.18 (emphasis added).

[41] Arguably, the *Simmenthal* Court had not envisaged two different consequences for the supremacy principle. While paragraph 17 appears to make a distinction depending on whether national legislation existed or not, the operative part of the judgment referred to both variants. It stated that a national court should refuse of its own motion to 'apply any conflicting provision of national legislation' (Case 106/77, *Simmenthal* (supra n. 31), dictum).

[42] Joined Cases C-10-22/97, *IN.CO.GE.* (supra n. 39), paras. 20–1.

[43] The non-application of national laws in these cases is but a mandatory 'minimum requirement' set by the Union legal order. A national legal order can, if it so wishes, offer stricter consequences to protect the full effectiveness of European law: Case 34/67, *Firma Gebruder Luck* v. *Hauptzollamt Koln-Rheinau*, [1968] ECR 245, at 251: '[Although European law] has the effect of excluding the application of any national measure incompatible with it, the article does not restrict the powers of the competent national courts to apply, from among the various procedures available under national law, those which are appropriate for the purpose of protecting the individual rights conferred by [European] law'.

What will this tell us about the nature of the supremacy principle? It tells us that the supremacy doctrine is about the 'executive force' of European law. The Union legal order, while integrated with the national legal orders, is not a 'unitary' legal order. European law leaves the 'validity' of national norms untouched; and will not negate the underlying legislative competence of the Member States. The supremacy principle is thus not addressed to the State legislatures, but to the national executive and judicial branches. (And while in some situations the national *legislator* will be required to amend or repeal national provisions that give rise to legal uncertainty,[44] this secondary obligation is not a direct result of the supremacy doctrine but derives from Article 4 (3) TEU.[45]) The executive force of European law thus generally leaves the normative validity of national law intact. National courts are not obliged to 'break' national law. They must only not apply it when in conflict with European law in a specific case. Supremacy may then best be characterised as a 'remedy'. Indeed, it 'is the most general remedy which individuals whose rights have been infringed may institute before a national court of law'.[46]

This remedial supremacy doctrine has a number of advantages. First, some national legal orders may not grant their (lower) courts the power to invalidate parliamentary laws. The question of who may invalidate national laws is thus left to the national legal order.[47] Second, comprehensive national laws must only be disapplied to the extent to which they conflict with European law.[48]

---

[44] Case 167/73, *Commission* v. *French Republic*, [1974] ECR 359, para. 41: 'It follows that although the objective legal position is clear, namely that Article [45] and Regulation 1612/68 are directly applicable in the territory of the French Republic, nevertheless the maintenance in these circumstances of the wording of the *Code du Travail Maritime* gives rise to an ambiguous state of affairs by maintaining, as regards those subject to the law who are concerned, a state of uncertainty as to the possibilities available to them of relying on [European] law.' The Court now appears generally to assume that the presence of a national provision that conflicts with European law will *ipso facto* 'give . . . rise to an ambiguous state of affairs in so far as it leaves persons concerned in a state of uncertainty as to the possibilities available to them relying on [European] law'; see Case 104/86, *Commission* v. *Italy*, [1988] ECR 1799, para. 12. See also Case C-185/96, *Commission* v. *Hellenic Republic*, [1998] ECR 6601, para. 32: 'On that point, suffice it to recall that, according to established case-law, the maintenance of national legislation which is in itself incompatible with [European] law, even if the Member State concerned acts in accordance with [European] law, gives rise to an ambiguous state of affairs by maintaining, as regards those subject to the law who are concerned, a state of uncertainty as to the possibilities for them of relying on [European] law.'

[45] See e.g. *Commission* v. *Italy* (supra n. 44) para. 13, and Case 74/86, *Commission* v. *Germany*, [1988] ECR 2139, para. 12.

[46] W. van Gerven, 'Of Rights, Remedies and Procedures' [2000] 37 CML Rev 501 at 506.

[47] Case C-314/08, *Filipiak* v. *Dyrektor Izby Skarbowej w Poznaniu* (nyr), para. 82: 'Pursuant to the principle of the primacy of [European] law, a conflict between a provision of national law and a directly applicable provision of the Treaty is to be resolved by a national court applying [European] law, if necessary by refusing to apply the conflicting national provision, and not by a declaration that the national provision is invalid, the powers of authorities, courts and tribunals in that regard being a matter to be determined by each Member State.'

[48] B. de Witte, 'Direct Effect, Supremacy and the Nature of the Legal Order' in P. Craig and G. de Búrca (eds.), *The Evolution of EU Law* (Oxford University Press, 1999), 177–213 at 190.

They will remain operable in purely internal situations. Third, once the Union act is repealed, national legislation may become fully operational again.[49]

2. The national perspective: relative supremacy

The European Union is not a Federal State in which the sovereignty problem is solved. The European Union is a federal union of States. Each federal union is characterised by a political dualism in which each citizen is a member of *two* political bodies. These *two* political bodies will compete for loyalty – and sometimes, the 'national' view on a political question may not correspond with the 'European' view on the matter. What happens when the political views of a Member State clash with that of the federal Union? Controversies over the supremacy of federal law are as old as the (modern) idea of federalism.[50] And while the previous section exposed the European answer to the supremacy doctrine, this absolute vision is – unsurprisingly – not shared by the Member States. There does indeed exist a competing national view. And this national perspective accepts the supremacy of European law over *some* national law, but *not all* national law. The supremacy of European law is thus seen as relative, since it is granted and limited by national constitutional law.

The national limits to the supremacy of European law have traditionally been expressed in two contexts.[51] First, some Member States – in particular their Supreme Courts – have fought a battle over human rights within the Union legal order. It was claimed that European law could not violate *national* fundamental rights. The most famous battle over the supremacy of European law in this context is the conflict between the European Court of Justice and the German Constitutional Court. The German Constitutional Court has here insisted that it has the power to 'disapply' European law. The same power has been claimed in a second context: ultra vires control. This constitutional battleground became prominent in light of the expansive exercise of legislative and judicial competences by the Union. And again, while the Member States generally accept the supremacy of European law within *limited fields*, they contest that the European Union can exclusively delimit these fields. In denying

---

[49] *Ibid.*

[50] R. Schütze, 'Federalism as Constitutional Pluralism: Letter from America' in J. Kommarek and M. Avbelj (eds.), *Constitutional Pluralism in the European Union and Beyond* (Hart, 2012), Chapter 8.

[51] The following section concentrates on the jurisprudence of the German Constitutional Court. This court has long been the most pressing and – perhaps – prestigious national court in the Union legal order. For the reaction of the French Supreme Courts, see: R. Mehdi, 'French Supreme Courts and European Union Law: Between Historical Compromise and Accepted Loyalty' [2011] 48 CML Rev 439. For the views of the Central European Constitutional Courts, see: W. Sadurski, '"Solange, Chapter 3": Constitutional Courts in Central Europe – Democracy – European Union' [2008] 14 *European Law Journal* 1. For a historical overview of the relationship between European and national law, see: A. Oppenheimer, *The Relationship between European Community Law and National Law: the Cases* (Cambridge University Press, 1994).

the Union's *Kompetenz-Kompetenz*,[52] these States here insist on the last word with regard to the competences of the Union.

(a) Fundamental rights limits: the 'so-long' jurisprudence

A strong national view on supremacy crystallised around *Internationale Handelsgesellschaft*.[53] For after the European Court of Justice had espoused its absolute view on the supremacy of European law, the case moved back to the German Constitutional Court.[54] The German Court now defined its perspective on the question. Could national constitutional law, especially national fundamental rights, affect the application of European law in the domestic legal order?

Famously, the German Constitutional Court rejected the European Court's absolute vision and replaced it with the counter-theory of the *relative* supremacy of European law. The reasoning of the German Court was as follows: while the German Constitution expressly allowed for the transfer of sovereign powers to the European Union in its Article 24,[55] such a transfer was itself limited by the 'constitutional identity' of the German State. Fundamental constitutional structures were thus beyond the supremacy of European law:

> The part of the Constitution dealing with fundamental rights is an *inalienable essential feature of the valid Constitution of the Federal Republic of Germany and one which forms part of the constitutional structure of the Constitution*. Article 24 of the Constitution does not without reservation allow it to be subjected to qualifications. In this, the present state of integration of the [Union] is of crucial importance. The [Union] still lacks ... in particular a codified catalogue of fundamental rights, the substance of which is reliably and unambiguously fixed for the future in the same way as the substance of the Constitution ...
>
> *So long as* this legal certainty, which is not guaranteed merely by the decisions of the European Court of Justice, favourable though these have been to fundamental rights, is not achieved in the course of the further integration of the [Union], the reservation derived from Article 24 of the Constitution applies ... *Provisionally, therefore, in the hypothetical case of a conflict between [European] law and a part of national constitutional law or, more precisely, of the guarantees of fundamental rights in the Constitution, there arises the question of which system of law takes precedence, that is, ousts the other. In this conflict of norms, the guarantee of fundamental rights in the Constitution prevails so long as the*

---

[52] On this strange (German) notion, see: Chapter 2 – Section 2(a) above.

[53] Case 11/70, *Internationale Handelsgesellschaft mbH* v. *Einfuhr- und Vorratsstelle für Getreide und Futtermittel*, [1970] ECR 1125.

[54] BVerfGE 37, 271 (*Solange I (Re Internationale Handelsgesellschaft)*). For an English translation, see: [1974] 2 CMLR 540.

[55] Article 24 (1) of the German Constitution states: 'The Federation may by a law transfer sovereign powers to international organisations.' Prior to the Maastricht Treaty, a new article was inserted into the German Constitution expressly dealing with the European Union (see: Article 23 German Constitution).

competent organs of the [Union] have not removed the conflict of norms in accordance with the Treaty mechanism.[56]

'So long' as the European legal order had not developed an adequate standard of fundamental rights, the German Constitutional Court would 'disapply' European law that conflicted with the fundamental rights guaranteed in the German legal order.[57] There were thus *national* limits to the supremacy of European law. However, these national limits were also *relative*, as they depended on the evolution and nature of European law. This was the very essence of the 'so long' formula. For once the Union legal order had developed equivalent human rights guarantees, the German Constitutional Court would no longer challenge the supremacy of European law.

The Union legal order did indeed subsequently develop extensive human rights bill(s),[58] and the dispute over the supremacy doctrine was significantly softened in the aftermath of a second famous European case with a national coda. In *Wünsche Handelsgesellschaft,*[59] the German Constitutional Court not only recognised the creation of 'substantially similar' fundamental right guarantees, it drew a remarkably self-effacing conclusion from this:

> In view of those developments it must be held that, *so long as* the European [Union], and in particular the case law of the European Court, generally ensure an effective protection of fundamental rights as against the sovereign powers of the [Union] which is to be regarded as substantially similar to the protection of fundamental rights required unconditionally by the [German] Constitution, and in so far as they generally safeguard the essential content of fundamental rights, the Federal Constitutional Court will no longer exercise its jurisdiction to decide on the applicability of secondary [Union] legislation cited as the legal basis for any acts of German courts or authorities within the sovereign jurisdiction of the Federal Republic of Germany, and it will no longer review such legislation by the standard of the fundamental rights contained in the Constitution[.][60]

This judgment became known as 'So-Long II', for the German Constitutional Court again had recourse to this famous formulation in determining its relationship with European law. But importantly, this time the 'so-long' condition was inverted. The German Court promised not to question the supremacy of European law 'so long' as the latter guaranteed substantially similar

---

[56] *Solange I,* [1974] CMLR 540 at 550–1 (paras. 23–4, emphasis added).

[57] The German Constitutional Court here adopted the doctrine that the supremacy of the German Constitution could only lead to a 'disapplication' and not an 'invalidation' of European law. The German Court thus 'never rules on the validity or invalidity of a rule of [European] law'; but '[a]t most, it can come to the conclusion that such a rule cannot be applied by the authorities or courts of the Federal Republic of Germany as far as it conflicts with a rule of the Constitution relating to fundamental rights' (*ibid.,* 552).

[58] On this point, see: Chapter 12 below.

[59] BVerfGE 73, 339 (*Solange II (Re Wünsche Handelsgesellschaft)*). For an English translation, see: [1987] 3 CMLR 225.

[60] *Ibid.,* 265 (para. 48).

fundamental rights to those recognised by the German constitution. This was not an absolute promise to respect the absolute supremacy of European law, but a result of the Court's own relative supremacy doctrine having been fulfilled. 'So-Long II' thus only refined the national perspective on the limited supremacy of European law in 'So-Long I'.

(b) Competences limits: from 'Maastricht' to 'Mangold'

With the constitutional conflict over fundamental rights settled, a second concern emerged: the ever-growing competences of the European Union. Who was to control and limit the scope of European law? Was it enough to have the *European* legislator centrally controlled by the *European* Court of Justice? Or should the national constitutional courts be entitled to a decentralised ultra vires review? The European view on this is crystal clear: national courts cannot disapply – let alone invalidate – European law.[61] Yet unsurprisingly, this absolute view has not been shared by all Member States. And it was again the German Constitutional Court that has set the tone and the vocabulary of the constitutional debate. The ultra vires question was at the heart of its famous *Maastricht* decision that would subsequently be refined in *Honeywell* in reaction to the European Court's (in)famous decision in *Mangold*.

The German Court set out its ultra vires review doctrine in *Maastricht*.[62] Starting from the premise that the European Treaties adhere to the principle of conferred powers, the Court found that the Union ought not to be able to extend its own competences. While the Treaties allowed for teleological interpretation, there existed a clear dividing line 'between a legal development within the terms of the Treaties and a making of legal rules which breaks through its boundaries and is not covered by valid Treaty law'.[63] This led to the following conclusion:

> Thus, if European institutions or agencies were to treat or develop the Union Treaty in a way that was no longer covered by the Treaty in the form that is the basis for the Act of Accession, the resultant legislative instruments would not be legally binding within the sphere of German sovereignty. The German state organs would be prevented for constitutional reasons from applying them in Germany. Accordingly the Federal Constitutional Court will review legal instruments of European institutions and agencies to see whether they remain within the limits of the sovereign rights conferred on them or transgress them ...
>
> Whereas a dynamic extension of the existing Treaties has so far been supported on the basis of an open-handed treatment of Article [352] of the [FEU] Treaty as a 'competence to round-off the Treaty' as a whole, and on the basis of considerations relating to the 'implied powers' of the [Union], and of Treaty interpretation as allowing maximum exploitation of [Union] powers (*'effet utile'*), in

---

[61] On the *Foto-Frost* doctrine, see: Chapter 8 – Section 7(d)(ii) above.
[62] BVerfGE 89, 155 (*Maastricht Decision*). For an English translation, see: [1994] 1 CMLR 57.
[63] *Ibid.*, 105 (para. 98).

future it will have to be noted as regards interpretation of enabling provisions by [Union] institutions and agencies that the Union Treaty as a matter of principle distinguishes between the exercise of a sovereign power conferred for limited purposes and the amending of the Treaty, so that its interpretation may not have effects that are equivalent to an extension of the Treaty. Such an interpretation of enabling rules would not produce any binding effects for Germany.[64]

The German Constitutional Court thus threatened to disapply European law that it considered to have been adopted ultra vires.

This national review power was subsequently confirmed.[65] Yet, the doctrine was limited and refined in *Honeywell*.[66] The case resulted from a constitutional complaint that targeted the European Court's ruling in *Mangold*.[67] The plaintiff argued that the European Court's 'discovery' of a European principle that prohibited discrimination on grounds of age was ultra vires as it read something into the Treaties that was not there. In its decision, the German Constitutional Court confirmed its relative supremacy doctrine. It claimed the power to disapply European law that it considered not to be covered by the principle of conferral. The principle of supremacy was thus not unlimited.[68] However, reminiscent of its judicial deference in *So-Long II*, the Court accepted a presumption that the Union would generally act within the scope of its competences:

> If each member State claimed to be able to decide through their own courts on the validity of legal acts by the Union, the primacy of application could be circumvented in practice, and the uniform application of Union law would be placed at risk. If however, on the other hand the Member States were completely to forgo ultra vires review, disposal of the treaty basis would be transferred to the Union bodies alone, even if their understanding of the law led in the practical outcome to an amendment of a Treaty or an expansion of competences. That in the borderline cases of possible transgression of competences on the part of the Union bodies – which is infrequent, as should be expected according to the institutional and procedural precautions of Union law – the [national] constitutional and the

---

[64] *Ibid.*, 105 (para. 99).

[65] BVerfGE 123, 267 (*Lisbon Decision*). For an English translation, see: [2010] 3 CMLR 276. The Court here added a third sequel to its 'So-Long' jurisprudence (*ibid.*, 343): 'As long as, and insofar as, the principle of conferral is adhered to in an association of sovereign states with clear elements of executive and governmental co-operation, the legitimation provided by national parliaments and governments complemented and sustained by the directly elected European Parliament is sufficient in principle'.

[66] 2 BvR 2661/06 (*Re Honeywell*). For an English translation, see: [2011] 1 CMLR 1067. For a discussion of the case, see: M. Paydandeh, 'Constitutional Review of EU Law after *Honeywell*: Contextualising the Relationship between the German Constitutional Court and the EU Court of Justice' [2011] 48 CML Rev 9.

[67] For an extensive discussion of the case, see: Chapter 9 – Section 3(b) above.

[68] *Honeywell*, [2011] 1 CMLR 1067 at 1084 (para. 39): 'Unlike the primacy of application of federal law, as provided for by Article 31 of the Basic Law for the German legal system, the primacy of application of Union law cannot be comprehensive.' (It is ironic that this is said by a German *federal* court.)

Union law perspective do not completely harmonise, is due to the circumstance that the Member States of the European Union also remain the masters of the Treaties . . .

Ultra vires review by the Federal Constitutional Court can moreover *only be considered if it is manifest* that acts of the European bodies and institutions have taken place outside the transferred competences. A breach of the principle of conferral is only manifest if the European bodies and institutions have transgressed the boundaries of their competences *in a manner specifically violating the principle of conferral*, the breach of competences is in other words sufficiently qualified. This means that the act of the authority of the European Union *must be manifestly in violation of competences* and that the impugned act is highly significant in the structure of competences between the Member States and the Union with regard to the principle of conferral and to the binding nature of the statute under the rule of law.[69]

This limits the national review of European law to 'specific' and 'manifest' violations of the principle of conferral. There was thus a presumption that the Union institutions would generally act intra vires; and only for clear and exceptional violations would the German Constitutional Court challenge the supremacy of European law. This has – so far – never happened. But even if the German court's behaviour was again 'all bark and no bite',[70] the very act of articulating national limits to the supremacy of European law was an expression of the continued existence of a dual or plural perspective on the locus of sovereignty in the European Union. It proves the continued existence of two political levels that compete for the loyalty of their citizens.

Sovereignty thus continues to be contested.[71]

3. Legislative preemption: nature and effect

The contrast between the prodigious presence of the supremacy doctrine and the shadowy existence of the doctrine of preemption in the European law

---

[69] *Ibid.*, 1085–6 (paras. 42 and 46 (emphasis added)).

[70] C. U. Schmid, 'All Bark and No Bite: Notes on the Federal Constitutional Court's "Banana Decision"' [2001] 7 *European Law Journal* 95.

[71] In its '*Lisbon Decision*' (supra n. 65), the German Constitutional Court even added a third constitutional limit to European integration: the 'State identity limit'. Claiming that European unification could not be achieved in such a way 'that not sufficient space is left to the Member States for the political formation of the economic, cultural and social living conditions', the Court identified '[e]ssential areas of democratic formative action'. 'Particularly sensitive for the ability of a constitutional state to democratically shape itself are decisions on substantive and formal criminal law (1), on the disposition of the monopoly on the use of force by the police within the state and by the military towards the exterior (2), fundamental fiscal decisions on public revenue and public expenditure, the latter being particularly motivated, inter alia, by social policy considerations (3), decisions on the shaping of living conditions in a social state (4) and decisions of particular cultural importance, for example on family law, the school and education system and on dealing with religious communities (5).' See: [2010] 3 CMLR 276 at 340–1.

literature is arresting.[72] The assimilation of preemption problems to supremacy questions has been the cardinal cause for the under-theorised nature of the preemption phenomenon. But though related, the two doctrines ought to be kept apart. Supremacy denotes the superior hierarchical status of the Union legal *order* over the national legal *orders* and thus gives European law the *capacity* to preempt national law. The doctrine of preemption, on the other hand, denotes the *actual degree* to which national law will be set aside by European law. The supremacy clause thus does not determine 'what constitutes a conflict between state and federal law; it merely serves as a traffic cop, mandating a federal law's survival instead of a state law's'.[73] Preemption, on the other hand, specifies when such conflicts have arisen. The important question behind the doctrine of preemption is this: to what degree will European law leave national law on the same matter intact? The preemption doctrine is thus a 'relative' doctrine: not all European law preempts all national law.

(a) Preemption categories: the relative effects of preemption

The doctrine of preemption is essentially a doctrine of normative conflict. Conflicts arise where there is friction between two legal norms.[74] The spectrum of conflict is open-ended and ranges from purely hypothetical frictions to literal contradictions between norms. There is no easy way to measure normative conflicts; and, in an attempt to classify degrees of normative conflict, preemption categories have been developed. Most preemption typologies will, to a great extent, be arbitrary classifications. They will try to *reflect* the various judicial reasons and arguments created to explain why national law conflicts with European law. Sadly, unlike the American Supreme Court,[75] the European

---

[72] For an illustration of this point, see: P. Craig and G. de Búrca, *EU Law: Text, Cases & Materials* (Oxford University Press, 2011), which dedicates one (!) out of over 1,100 pages to the doctrine of preemption; yet spends 45 pages on the supremacy doctrine. And to make matters even clearer: the previous edition of that well-known textbook contained not a single page specifically dedicated to the doctrine of preemption.

[73] S. C. Hoke, 'Preemption Pathologies and Civic Republican Values' [1991] 71 *Boston University Law Review* 685 at 755.

[74] Normative conflicts have already been investigated in the context of public international law; see J. Pauwelyn, *Conflict of Norms in Public International Law: How WTO Law Relates to other Rules of International Law* (Cambridge University Press, 2003).

[75] The US Supreme Court has summarised the different types of preemption in *Pacific Gas & Electric Co* v. *State Energy Resources Conservation & Development Commission*, 461 US 190 (1983), at 203–4 (quotations and references omitted) in the following manner: 'Congress' intent to supersede state law altogether may be found from a scheme of the federal regulation so pervasive as to make reasonable the inference that Congress left no room to supplement it, because the Act of Congress may touch a field in which the federal interest is so dominant that the federal system will be assumed to preclude enforcement of state laws on the same subject, or because the object sought to be obtained by federal law and the character of obligations imposed by it may reveal the same purpose ... Even where Congress has not entirely displaced state regulation in a specific area, each state is preempted to the extent that it actually conflicts with

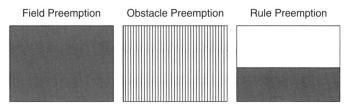

Figure 21 Preemption Types: Field, Obstacle, Rule Preemption

Court has yet to define and name a preemption typology for its legal order.[76] In linguistic alliance with US American constitutionalism, we shall, therefore, analyse the European Court's jurisprudence through the lens of the three preemption categories developed in that federation, that is: field preemption, obstacle preemption, and rule preemption.

(i) Field preemption

Field preemption refers to those situations where the Court does not investigate any *material* normative conflict, but simply excludes the Member States on the ground that the Union has exhaustively legislated for the field. This is the most powerful format of federal preemption: any national legislation within the occupied field is prohibited. The reason for the total exclusion lies in the perceived fear that *any* supplementary national action may endanger or interfere with the strict uniformity of Union law. The total prohibition for national legislators will thus to a certain extent reproduce the effects of a 'real' exclusive competence within the occupied field.[77] Underlying the idea of field preemption is a purely abstract conflict criterion: national legislation conflicts with the *jurisdictional* objective of the Union legislator to establish an absolutely uniform legal standard.

In order to illustrate the argumentative structure of field preemption, let us take a closer look at the jurisprudence of the European Court in the context of total harmonisation. In *Ratti*,[78] the ECJ found that Directive 73/173 preempted any national measures falling within its scope. Member States were therefore 'not entitled to maintain, parallel with the rules laid down by the Directive for imports, different rules for the domestic market'. It was a consequence of the

---

federal law. Such a conflict arises when compliance with both federal and state regulations is a physical impossibility . . . or where state law stands as an obstacle to the accomplishment and execution of the full purpose and objectives of Congress.' The three identified preemption types are, respectively, field preemption, rule preemption and obstacle preemption.

[76] Unfortunately, the European Court has not (yet) committed itself to a principled preemption statement like *Pacific Gas & Electric Co* v. *State Energy Resources Conservation & Development Commission* (supra n. 75). It came close in Case 218/85, *Association comité économique agricole régional fruits et légumes de Bretagne* v. *A Le Campion* (*CERAFEL*), [1986] ECR 3513. However, the Court has never extrapolated this preemption statement from its specific agricultural policy context. Moreover, not even in the agricultural context has *CERAFEL* become a standard point of reference in subsequent cases.

[77] On this point, see: Chapter 5 – Section 2(a) above.   [78] Case 148/78, *Ratti*, [1979] ECR 1629.

Union system that 'a Member State may not introduce into its national legislation conditions which are more restrictive than those laid down in the directive in question, or which are even more detailed *or in any event different*'.[79] The Union act represented an exhaustive set of rules and, thus, totally preempted national legislators.

(ii) Obstacle preemption

In contrast to field preemption, obstacle preemption – our second preemption category – requires some *material* conflict between European and national law. Unlike rule preemption, however, it refers to a form of argumentative reasoning that does not base the exclusionary effect of European law on the normative friction between a national law and *a particular European rule*. The Court will not go into the details of the legislative scheme, but will be content in finding that the national law somehow interferes with the proper functioning or impedes the objectives of the Union legislation. The burden of proof for finding a legislative conflict is, therefore, still relatively light.

Obstacle preemption reasoning can be found in *Bussone*.[80] In the '*absence of express provisions on the compatibility* with the organisation of the market established by [the] Regulation ... it is necessary to seek the solution to the question asked in the light of the aims and objectives of the regulations [as such]'. The Court noted that the Regulation did not seek to establish uniform prices, but that the organisation was 'based on freedom of commercial transactions under fair competitive conditions'. '[S]uch a scheme precludes the adoption of any national rules which may hinder, directly or indirectly, actually or potentially, trade within the [Union].'[81] The Court here employed a functional conflict criterion to oust supplementary national legislation: those national measures that limit the scope, impede the functioning or jeopardise the aims of the European scheme will conflict with the latter. While not as abstract and potent as field preemption, the virility of this functional conflict criterion is nonetheless remarkable. Where the Court selects the 'affect' or 'obstacle' criterion, European law will widely preempt national legislation. Any obstacle that reduces the effectiveness of the Union system may be seen to be in conflict with European law.

(iii) Rule preemption

The most concrete form of conflict will occur where national legislation literally contradicts a *specific European rule*. Compliance with both sets of rules is (physically) impossible. This scenario can be described as rule preemption. The violation of Union legislation by the national measure follows from its contradicting a Union rule 'fairly interpreted'. Put negatively, where the

---

[79] *Ibid.*, paras. 26–7 (emphasis added).
[80] Case 31/78, *Bussone v. Italian Ministry of Agriculture*, [1978] ECR 2429.
[81] *Ibid.*, paras. 43, 46–7.

national law does not contradict a specific Union provision, it will *not* be preempted.

We can find an illustration of this third type of preemption in *Gallaher*.[82] Article 3 (3) of Directive 89/622 concerned the labelling of tobacco products and required that health warnings should cover 'at least 4% of the corresponding surface'. Reading the 'at least' qualification as a provision allowing for stricter national standards, the British government had tightened the obligation on manufacturers by stipulating that the specific warning ought to cover 6% of the surfaces on which they are printed. Was this higher national standard supplementing the European rule preempted and, thus, to be disapplied? The European Court did not think so in an answer that contrasts strikingly with its previous ruling in *Ratti*. Interpreting Article 3 and 8 of the Directive, the European Court found that '[t]he expression "at least" contained in both articles must be interpreted as meaning that, if they consider it necessary, Member States are at liberty to decide that the indications and warnings are to cover a greater surface area in view of the level of public awareness of the health risks associated with tobacco consumption'.[83] The Court – applying a rule preemption criterion – allowed the stricter national measure. The national law did not contradict the Union rule and the national rules were, thus, not preempted by the European standard.

(b) Modes of preemption: express and implied preemption

It is important to distinguish between the categories of preemption, and the ways in which the European Union chooses one category over another. This second question concerns the modes of preemption; and one can here distinguish between express and implied preemption.

What are the modes in which a particular preemption category may be chosen? The fundamental starting point should be whether or not the Union legislator has spoken its mind. Where the Union has done so, 'express preemption' represents the most straightforward mode in doctrinal terms.[84] The Union legislation may itself define to what extent State law will be preempted.

---

[82] Case C-11/92, *The Queen* v. *Secretary of State for Health, ex parte Gallaher Ltd, Imperial Tobacco Ltd and Rothmans International Tobacco (UK) Ltd*, [1993] ECR I-3545.

[83] *Ibid.*, para. 20.

[84] For an example of express preemption, see Article 8 of Directive 73/173 on the classification, packaging and labelling of dangerous preparations (solvents), OJ 1973, L189/7 (discussed in *Ratti*, supra n. 78) which prohibited Member States from 'restrict[ing] or imped[ing] on the grounds of classification, packaging or labelling, the placing on the market of dangerous preparations which satisfy the requirements of the Directive'. See also: Article 2 (1) of Directive 76/756, as amended by Directive 83/276, OJ 1983, L151/47 (discussed in Case 60/86, *Commission* v. *United Kingdom (Dim-dip)*, [1988] ECR 3921): 'No Member State may: refuse, in respect of a type of vehicle, to grant [EU] type-approval or national type-approval, or refuse or prohibit the sale, registration, entry into service or use of vehicles, on grounds relating to the installation on the vehicles of the lighting and light-signalling devices.'

Conversely, the Union legislator may explicitly allow for the continued application of State law in certain areas in spite of some interference with the federal legislation. This form is called 'express saving' and constitutes the logical flip side of express preemption.[85]

Absent express legislative intent, when will Union legislation preempt State laws? Here it is the Union judiciary that must *imply* the type of preemption intended by the Union legislator. Implied preemption may involve controversial interpretative questions. It is best seen as a federal theory of statutory interpretation. For in federal unions, the interpretation of legislative acts will always involve a substantive *and* a federal dimension.[86] In federal orders, statutory interpretation must thus be seen from the perspective of the horizontal *as well as* the vertical separation of powers. The preemption doctrine thereby provides the analytical framework within which the historical sensitivities of a particular federal order are imputed in the interpretative process. For example, the US Supreme Court has developed a set of constitutional presumptions for or against implied preemption depending on the subject matter involved.[87] The preemption doctrine may, consequently, be conceived of as a *federal theory of interpretation*. It assembles those federal values that will influence and guide the federal judiciary in addition to the 'ordinary' canons of statutory interpretation.

4. Constitutional limits to legislative preemption

When exercising a shared competence, the Union legislator is generally free to determine to what extent it wishes to preempt national law. However, that constitutional freedom could be restricted in two ways. First, it could make a

---

[85] A typical express saving clause can be found in Article 8 of Directive 85/577 EC on the protection of consumers in respect of contracts negotiated away from business premises (discussed in *Dori*), OJ 1985, L372/31: 'This Directive shall not prevent Member States from adopting or maintaining more favourable provisions to protect consumers in the field which it covers.' See also Art. 14 (2) (a) of Directive 73/241, OJ 1973, L228/23: 'This directive shall not affect the provisions of national laws: (a) at present authorising or prohibiting the addition of vegetable fats other than cocoa butter to the chocolate products defined in Annex I.'

[86] 'On a substantive policy level, each [federal] court will have to calibrate the desirable balance between the competing social values at play in the federal legislation; while, at the same time, it will impute its global views on what it sees as the appropriate federal equilibrium.' See W. Cohen, 'Congressional power to define state power to regulate commerce: consent and preemption' in Sandalow and Stein (eds.), *Courts and Free Markets* (supra n. 2), 541.

[87] In *Boyle* v. *United Technologies*, 487 US 500 (1988), the Supreme Court ruled that field preemption is easily inferred where the subject matter concerns a 'uniquely federal interest', but for all other areas the 'clear statement rule' would apply. Advocates of federal preemption frequently argue that there is a 'dominant federal interest' in interstate or international activities – an argument based on a dictum in *Rice* v. *Santa Fe Elevator Corp*, 331 US 218 (1947). In *Hillsborough County Fla* v. *Automated Medical Laboratories*, 471 US 707 (1985), the Supreme Court gave a sobering definition by limiting 'dominant federal interests' to matters whose 'special features' would be of such an order as the responsibility of the national government for foreign affairs.

difference if the Union legislator used a regulation instead of a directive as a Union act. For a long time, it was indeed thought that a regulation would automatically lead to field preemption, while a directive could never do so. We shall examine the preemptive capacity of the Union's various legal instruments and see that this view is – presently – mistaken.[88] However, a second constitutional limit to the preemptive effect of Union legislation might be found in the competence category within a policy area. Will it make a difference, whether the Union uses an ordinary shared competence, or one that requires the adoption of minimum harmonisation? Can Union acts adopted on the basis of a complementary competence ever preempt national law?

Let us look at both (potential) limitations in turn.

(a) Union instruments and their preemptive capacity

When the Union was born, its various legal instruments were seen to structure the federal division of power between the European and the national level. Some early commentators thus argued that for each policy area the Treaty had fixed a specific format of legislative or regulatory intervention.[89] This competence reading of the various legal instruments has occasionally been expressed by the European Court of Justice.[90] Will this mean that the use of a particular instrument limits the Union legislator from preempting the Member States?

This section investigates the *preemptive* quality of the Union's three legislative instruments: regulations, directives and international agreements.

(i) The preemptive capacity of regulations

Regulations are binding in their entirety, and have been characterised as the 'most integrated form' of European legislation.[91] Typically considered to be the instrument of uniformity, will regulations automatically field-preempt national law within their scope of application?

The early jurisprudence of the European Court of Justice indeed emphasised their field-preemptive nature. In order to protect their normative autonomy and the uniform application of regulations within the national legal orders, the Court thus employed a strong preemption criterion. This initial approach is

---

[88] For an argument in favour of a re-federalisation of the directive, see: R. Schütze, 'The Morphology of Legislative Power in the European Community: Legal Instruments and the Federal Division of Powers' [2006] 25 YEL 91, Conclusion.

[89] See P. Pescatore, *The Law of Integration: Emergence of a New Phenomenon in International Relations, Based on the Experience of the European Communities* (Sijthoff, 1974), 62–3; and V. Constantinesco, *Compétences et Pouvoirs dans les Communautés Européennes: Contribution à l'étude de la Nature Juridique des Communautés* (Pichon & Durand-Auzias, 1974), 85.

[90] Case C-91/92, *Faccini Dori v. Recreb*, [1994] ECR I-3325.

[91] G. Gaja, P. Hay and R. D. Rotunda, 'Instruments for Legal Integration in the European Community – A Review' in M. Cappelletti, M. Seccombe, and J. Weiler (eds.), *Integration through Law: Europe and the American Federal Experience* (de Gruyter, 1986), vol. I, 113 at 124.

best illustrated in *Bollmann*.[92] Discussing the effect of a regulation on the legislative powers of the Member States, the ECJ found that since a regulation 'is directly applicable in all Member States, the latter, unless otherwise expressly provided, are precluded from taking steps, for the purposes of applying the regulation, which are *intended to alter its scope or supplement its provisions*'.[93] Early jurisprudence thus suggested that all national rules that fell within the scope of a regulation were automatically preempted.[94] Any supplementary national action would be prohibited. Provisions within regulations that permitted national action were, consequently, conceptualised as a re-delegation of legislative power to the national level.

It was this early jurisprudence that created the myth that regulations would automatically field-preempt national law. Their direct applicability was wrongly associated with field preemption.[95] But subsequent jurisprudence quickly disapproved of the simplistic correlation. In *Bussone*, the Court did not find the relevant regulation to field-preempt national law, but analysed whether national laws were '*incompatible with the provisions of that regulation*'.[96] And in *Maris* v. *Rijksdienst voor Weknemerspensioenen*,[97] the Court clarified that this incompatibility could sometimes require a material conflict as a regulation would only preclude 'the application of any provisions of national law to a *different or contrary effect*'.[98] Regulations thus do not automatically field-preempt. They will not always achieve 'exhaustive' legislation. On the contrary, a regulation may confine itself to laying down minimum standards.[99] Regulations may even replace directives, and thereby assume their predecessors' preemptive degree. It is thus misleading to classify regulations as instruments of strict uniformity.[100] While Member States are precluded from

---

[92] Case 40/69, *Hauptzollamt Hamburg Oberelbe* v. *Bollmann*, [1970] ECR 69.

[93] *Ibid.*, para. 4

[94] Case 18/72, *Granaria* v. *Produktschap voor Veevoeder*, [1972] ECR 1163, para. 16.

[95] 'This capacity to preempt or preclude national measures can be regarded as a characteristic peculiar to a Regulation (as opposed to any other form of [Union] legislation) and may shed some light on the nature of direct applicability under Article [288] of the Treaty' (M. Blumental, 'Implementing the Common Agricultural Policy: Aspects of the Limitations on the Powers of the Member States' [1984] 35 *Northern Ireland Legal Quarterly*, 28–51 at 39).

[96] Case 31/78, *Bussone* v. *Italian Ministry of Agriculture*, [1978] 2429, paras. 28–31.

[97] Case 55/77, *M. Maris, wife of R. Reboulet* v. *Rijksdienst voor Werknemerspensioenen*, [1977] ECR 2327.

[98] *Ibid.*, paras. 17–18 (emphasis added).

[99] Council Regulation No. 259/93 on the supervision and control of shipments of waste within, into and out of the European Community (OJ 1993 L30, p. 1) provides such an example of a 'minimum harmonisation' regulation. The regulation has been described as 'far from providing for a complete harmonisation of the rules governing the transfer of waste, and might in part even be regarded (in the words of one commentator) as an "organised renationalisation" of the subject.' (Advocate-General F. Jacobs, Case C-187/93, *Parliament* v. *Council*, [1994] ECR I-2857, para. 22).

[100] Contra: J. A. Usher, *EC Institutions and Legislation* (Longman, 1998), 130: 'In effect Regulations could be said simply, if inelegantly, to amount to a "keep out" sign to national legislation.'

unilateral 'amendment' or 'selective application',[101] these constitutional obligations apply to all Union acts and do not specifically characterise the format of regulations.

(ii) The preemptive capacity of directives

Directives shall be binding 'as to the result to be achieved' and 'leave to the national authorities the choice of form and methods'.[102] Binding as to the result to be achieved, the instrument promised to respect the Member States' freedom to select a national path to a European end. The very term 'directive' suggested an act that would confine itself to 'directions', and the instrument's principal use for the harmonisation of *national* law reinforced that vision.

Do directives thus represent broadbrush 'directions' that guarantee a degree of national autonomy? An early academic school indeed argued this view.[103] These voices championed a constitutional frame limiting the directive's preemptive effect. To be a 'true' directive, it would need to leave a degree of legislative freedom, and as such could never field-preempt national legislation within its scope of application.[104] This position thus interpreted the directive in competence terms: the Union legislator would act ultra vires, if it went beyond the constitutional frame set by a directive. But when precisely the preemptive Rubicon was crossed remained shrouded in linguistic mist.

In any event, past constitutional practice within the Union legal order has never endorsed a constitutional limit to the preemptive effect of directives. On the contrary, in *Enka* the Court of Justice expressly recognised a directive's ability to be 'exhaustive' or 'complete' harmonisation, wherever strict legislative uniformity was necessary.[105] Directives can – and often do – occupy a

---

[101] Case 39/72, *Commission v. Italy*, [1973] ECR 101, para. 20.   [102] Article 288 (3) TFEU.

[103] See R. W. Lauwaars, *Lawfulness and Legal Force of Community Decisions* (A. W. Sijthoff, 1973) 30–1 (emphasis added): 'But can this be carried so far that no freedom at all is left to the member States? In my opinion it follows from Article [288] that the directive *as a whole* must allow member States the possibility of carrying out the rules embodied in the directive in their own way. A directive that constitutes a uniform law is not compatible with this requirement because, by definition, it places a duty on the member States to take over the uniform text and does not allow any freedom as to choice of form and method.'; as well as: Gaja, Hay and Rotunda, 'Instruments for Legal Integration' (supra n. 91), 133 (emphasis added): 'The detailed character of many provisions may be inconsistent with the *concept of directive* as defined in the [FEU] Treaty [.]'; and P. E. Herzog, 'Article 189' in D. Campbell et al. (eds.), *The Law of the European Community: a Commentary on the EEC Treaty* (Matthew Bender, 1995), 613: 'The view that the definition of a directive given in [Article 288 (3) TFEU], has a limiting effect on the various grants of powers in substantive Treaty provisions authorizing the issuance of directives seems correct.'

[104] D. Oldekop, 'Die Richtlinien der Europäischen Wirtschaftsgemeinschaft' [1972] 21 *Jahrbuch des öffentlichen Rechts* 55–106 at 92–3.

[105] Case 38/77, *Enka BV v. Inspecteur der invoerrechten en accijnzen*, [1977] ECR 2203, paras. 11–12: 'It emerges from the third paragraph of Article [288] of the Treaty that the choice left to the Member States as regards the form of the measures and the methods used in their adoption by the national authorities depends upon the result which the Council or the Commission wishes to see achieved. As regards the harmonisation of the provisions relating to customs matters laid down in the Member States by law, regulation or administrative action, in order to

regulatory field.[106] Their preemptive *capacity* therefore equals that of regulations. The national choice, referred to in Article 288 [3] TFEU thereby only guarantees the power of Member States to implement the European *content* into national *form*: '[T]he choice is limited to the *kind* of measures to be taken; their *content* is entirely determined by the directive at issue. Thus the discretion as far as form and methods are concerned does not mean that Member States necessarily have a margin in terms of policy making.'[107]

(iii) The preemptive capacity of international agreements

The preemptive effect of Union agreements may be felt in two ways. First, directly effective Union agreements will preempt inconsistent *national* law.[108] But secondly, self-executing international obligations of the Union will also preempt inconsistent *European* secondary law. The preemptive potential of international agreements over internal European law follows from the 'primacy' of the former over the latter.[109] For the Court considers international agreements of the Union hierarchically above ordinary Union secondary law.

The first dimension of the preemptive ability of Union agreements relates to *national* law. Will the preemptive effect of an international norm be the same as that of an identically worded provision within a regulation or a directive? The Court has responded to this question in an indirect manner. In *Polydor*,[110] it was asked to rule on the compatibility of the 1956 British Copyright Act with the agreement between the European Union and Portugal. The bilateral free trade agreement envisaged that quantitative restrictions on imports and all measures having an equivalent effect to quantitative restriction should be abolished, but exempted all those restrictions justified on the grounds of the protection of intellectual property. Two importers of pop music had been charged with infringement of Polydor's copyrights and had invoked the directly effective provisions of the Union agreement as a sword against the British law.

Would the Union agreement preempt the national measure? If the Court had projected the 'internal' Union standard established by its jurisprudence in relation to Articles 34 TFEU et seq., the national measure would have been preempted. But the Court did not. It chose to interpret the identically worded

---

bring about the uniform application of the common customs tariff it may prove necessary to ensure the *absolute identity of those provisions*' (*ibid.*, paras. 11–12).

[106] E.g. Case 148/78, *Ratti*, [1979] ECR 1629.

[107] S. Prechal, *Directives in EC Law* (Oxford University Press, 2005), 73.

[108] E.g. Case C-61/94, *Commission v. Germany (IDA)*, [1996] ECR I-3989, where the European Court did find a national measure preempted by an international agreement. The agreement at stake was the international diary agreement and the Court found 'that Article 6 of the annexes precluded the Federal Republic of Germany from authorising imports of dairy products, including those effected under inward processing relief arrangements, at prices lower than the minimum' (*ibid.*, para. 39).

[109] *Ibid.*, para. 52.   [110] Case 270/80, *Polydor and others v. Harlequin and others*, [1982] ECR 329.

provision in the Union agreement more restrictively.[111] Identical text will, therefore, not guarantee identical interpretation: '[T]he fact that the provisions of an agreement and the corresponding [Union] provisions are identically worded does not mean that they must necessarily be interpreted identically. An international treaty is to be interpreted not only on the basis of its wording, but also in the light of its objectives.'[112] Context will thus prevail over text. The context or function of the international treaty will be decisive. Only where an international norm fulfils the 'same function' as the internal European norm, will the Court project the 'internal' preemptive effect to the international treaty.[113] But while the Court may apply a milder form of preemption to international agreements, it has not announced any constitutional limits to the preemptive capacity of international agreements.

Let us turn to the second dimension of the preemptive effect of Union agreements. The capacity of international agreements to preempt inconsistent internal Union legislation follows from the primacy of the former over the latter. The contours of this second preemption analysis can be evidenced in *The Netherlands v Parliament and Council*.[114] The dispute concerned the annulment of Directive 98/44 EC on the legal protection of biotechnological inventions. The Netherlands had, inter alia, argued that the Union measure violated Article 27 (3) (b) of the TRIPS Agreement. The directive prohibits Member States from granting patents for plants and animals other than micro-organisms, while the international treaty provides for such a legal option. The Dutch government claimed that Article 27 (3) (b) of the TRIPS agreement 'preempted' the higher European standard. The Court, while admitting that 'the Directive does deprive the Member States of the choice which the TRIPS

---

[111] *Ibid.*, paras. 15, 18–19.

[112] Opinion 1/91 (EEA Draft *Agreement*), [1991] ECR I-6079, para. 14. In relation to the EEA, the Court found that it was 'established on the basis of an international treaty which, essentially, *merely creates rights and obligations as between the Contracting Parties* and provides for no transfer of sovereign rights to the inter-governmental institutions which it sets up' (*ibid.*, para. 20, emphasis added). The EU Treaty, by way of contrast, constituted 'the constitutional charter of a [Union] based on the rule of law', one of whose particular characteristics would be 'the direct effect of a whole series of provisions which are applicable to their nationals' (*ibid.*, para. 21).

[113] An illustration can be found in Case 17/81, *Pabst & Richarz KG v. Hauptzollamt Oldenburg*, [1982] ECR 1331, where the ECJ was asked to compare Article 53 (1) of the association agreement between the Union and Greece with the relevant provision in the TFEU: 'That provision, the wording of which is similar to that of Article [110] of the Treaty, fulfils, within the framework of the association between the [Union] and Greece, the same function as that of Article [110] . . . It accordingly follows from the wording of Article 53(1), cited above, and from the objective and nature of the association agreement of which it forms part that that provision precludes a national system of relief from providing more favourable tax treatment for domestic spirits than for those imported from Greece' (*ibid.*, paras. 26–7). While the ECJ had still found that the European Treaties and EEA had different purposes and functions, the General Court seemed now to favour a parallel interpretation of the EEA Agreement with identically worded provisions of the European Treaties and secondary law in Case T-115/94, *Opel Austria GmbH v. Council*, [1997] ECR II-39.

[114] Case C-377/98, *Netherlands v. European Parliament and Council*, [2001] ECR I-7079.

Agreement offers to the parties to that agreement as regards the patentability of plants and animals', found that the Directive was 'in itself compatible with the Agreement'. The ECJ applied a conflict preemption criterion to determine whether a legislative conflict between the international treaty and the Union directive existed.

In sum, Union agreements have the capacity of double preemption: they can preempt inconsistent national law and conflicting internal Union legislation. The preemptive potential of international agreements appears to be milder than equivalently worded internal legislation. Only where the agreement has the same function as an internal European norm will the Court accept the same preemptive effect that would be triggered by identically worded European law. However, as regards their preemptive capacity, there are no constitutional limits that would restrict the choice of the Union to preempt the Member States.

(b) Competence limits to preemption

Within shared competences, the Union legislator is typically free to decide what preemption category to choose. Legislative discretion determines the degree to which national legislators are preempted by European legislation. However, there are competences that restrict this liberty. Within the Union's *shared* competences, certain policy areas restrict the Union legislator to setting minimum standards only. The method of constitutionally fixing minimum harmonisation emerged for the first time in relation to environmental and social policy. Subsequent amendments have extended this technique to other areas.[115] The constitutional relationship between the European and the national legislator is here relatively straightforward: the Treaty guarantees the ability of the national legislator to adopt *higher* standards. This particularity sets them apart from 'ordinary' shared competences. A second variant of constitutionally limited preemption flows from the Union's 'complementary competences'. They typically confine the Union legislator to adopt 'incentive measures' that exclude all harmonisation within the field.[116]

The central question for both types of competence is this: how much legislative space will the European Union need to leave to the national level? What is the frame of reference by which the 'minimum' nature of European laws will be evaluated? Do minimum harmonisation competences prevent the Union from ever laying down exhaustive standards with regard to a specific legislative *measure*? And can 'incentive measures' preempt national laws – even

---

[115] On this development, see: R. Schütze, *From Dual to Cooperative Federalism: The Changing Structure of European Law* (Oxford University Press, 2009), 265 et seq.

[116] On this point, see: Chapter 5 – Section 2(d) above.

though a complementary competence excludes all harmonisation within the field?

(i) Competences for minimum harmonisation

The constitutional regime for environmental policy is in many respects paradigmatic for the first type of limited competence. According to Article 193 TFEU, European legislation 'shall not prevent any Member State from maintaining or introducing more stringent protective measures'. European law must only lay down minimum standards and this permits national 'opt-ups'.[117] But are all measures adopted under Article 192 minimum harmonisation measures; or does Article 193 only 'softly' require the Union legislator to leave some – abstractly defined – legislative space to the national legislators? Surprisingly, after almost three decades of constitutional practice, the issue has not been definitely resolved.

Two views are possible. According to a first view, Article 193 will not constitutionally prevent the Union legislator from adopting single legislative acts that totally harmonise all matters within their scope.[118] This first view thus accepts a strong *presumption* against field preemption – codified in Article 193. However, the Union legislator faces no absolute *constitutional limitation* to exhaustively harmonise an environmental issue through a European law adopted under Article 192. Pointing to the insufficiency of this *soft* constitutional frame, a second view argues that Article 193 refers to every single piece of European legislation adopted under Article 192. The Union legislator will never be able to occupy a field. Each Union act will need to leave a degree of legislative space to the national legislators.

There are heavy legal arguments in favour of this *hard* constitutional solution for Article 192. First, the very wording of Article 193 points in that direction: the frame of reference for the higher national standard is not the Union environmental *policy*, but the specific Union *measure(s)*. Second, from a teleological perspective, the aim of achieving a high level of protection within the Union would be better served by always allowing Member States to go beyond the federal compromise represented in the European legislation.[119] Third, the 'minimum' quality of the Union's activities could be enforced for every single piece of legislation. Instead of an abstract standard – presumably measured against the totality of existing European environmental legislation – the frame of reference would be set by the scope of the specific piece(s) of legislation. Requiring the Union legislator to leave legislative space *within the scope of the*

---

[117] This is different from the 'opt-out' mechanism in Article 114 (4)–(9) TFEU, which allows for a *derogation* from European legislation.

[118] J. H. Jans, *European Environmental Law* (Europa Law Publishing, 2000), 118.

[119] G. Winter, 'Die Sperrwirkung von Gemeinschaftssekundärrecht für einzelstaatliche Regelungen des Binnenmarkts mit besonderer Berücksichtigung von Art. 130 t EGV' [1998] 51 *Die öffentliche Verwaltung* 377 at 380.

European act, would provide a more concrete 'jurisdictional' standard that would better safeguard the Member States' legislative autonomy.

What are the judicial guidelines from the European Court of Justice? The question about the nature of European legislation adopted under Articles 192 and 193 has – partly – been addressed in *Fornasar*.[120] The Court had to interpret the exhaustiveness of European legislation on hazardous waste, in particular Directive 91/689. The first part of the ruling signalled the Court's support for the hard constitutional solution. Indeed, the general tenor of the opening statement appears to endorse a hard frame around Article 192: '[European] rules do not seek to effect complete harmonisation in the area of the environment'. Isolated from the specific legislative measure on the judicial table, Article 193 would then always entitle national legislators to complement the common European standard. Had the Court stopped here, few doubts would have remained. However, the Court continued and the second part of the ruling represented a specific analysis of the legislative regime established for hazardous waste under the Directive. And since the Directive expressly entitled Member States to supplement the Union list, it could consequently be construed as a 'minimum harmonisation' measure. A narrow reading of the ruling could therefore characterise the minimum quality of the European intervention as a *legislative* choice embedded in the specific Union act. The evasive ambivalence of *Fornasar* shows that the Court still needs to make up its mind on whether to choose a 'soft' or a 'hard' constitutional solution for Article 192.[121]

(ii) Complementary competences excluding harmonisation

A number of Union competences only entitle the Union to adopt incentive measures and (thereby) 'exclude any harmonisation of the laws and regulations of the member States'.[122] Some complementary competences even expressly demand that European law must 'not affect' national provisions.[123] These formulations demonstrate the European Treaties' intent to reserve legislative

---

[120]   Case C-318/98, *Fornasar et al* v. *Sante Chiarcosso*, [2000] ECR I-4785.

[121]   The Court did not resolve this ambivalence in Case C-6/03, *Deponiezweckverband Eiterköpfe* v. *Land Rheinland-Pfalz*, [2005] ECR I-2753. The Court, again, started out with a broad constitutional statement (*ibid.*, para. 27): 'The first point to be noted is that the [European] rules do not seek to effect complete harmonisation in the area of the environment.' However, in a second step, the Court found – again – that the specific Directive only set minimum standards (*ibid.*, para. 31): 'The wording and broad logic of those provisions make it clearly apparent that they set a minimum reduction to be achieved by the Member States and they do not preclude the adopting by the latter of more stringent measures.' And – again – it found that 'Article [193 TFEU] *and the Directive* allow the Member States to introduce more stringent protection measures that go beyond the minimum requirements fixed by the Directive' (*ibid.*, para. 32 (emphasis added)).

[122]   On this point, see: Chapter 5 – Section 2(d) above.

[123]   See Article 153 (4) in the Title on 'Social Policy', which states: 'The provisions adopted pursuant to this Article: shall not affect the right of Member States to define the fundamental principles of their social security systems and must not significantly affect the financial equilibrium thereof; [and] shall not prevent any Member State from maintaining or introducing more stringent protective measures compatible with the Treaties.'

space to the national legislator. The invention of these competences was designed to constitutionally limit the ability of the Union to preempt national legislators. Let us look at each of these techniques in turn.

First, whatever the concept of 'incentive measure' is supposed to mean, one has to assume that it was designed to be a constitutional limitation to 'normal' measures. Literally, the concept suggests the desire to have the Union primarily encourage the coordination of national policies.

Second, what exactly is the prohibition of 'harmonisation' supposed to mean? Two views can be put forward. According to the first, the exclusion of harmonisation means that European legislation must not affect national legislation. However, considering the wide definition given to the concept of 'harmonisation' by the Court of Justice in *Spain* v. *Council*, any legislative intervention on the part of the Union will unfold a de facto harmonising effect within the national legal orders.[124] From this strict reading, the exclusion of harmonisation would deny all pre-emptive effects of European legislation.[125] A second – less restrictive – view argues that the Union's complementary competences are only trimmed so as to prevent the de jure harmonisation of national legislation.[126] *Both* views appear, however, problematic. National legislators are – still – quicker in passing legislation than the Union legislator. Will the Union therefore never be able to adopt a European standard for the social problem? Will Union action be confined to coordinating national policies without setting common European standards? If so, it would be difficult to speak of a truly independent Union *policy* as the European legislator simply cannot make its own *policy* choices.[127]

---

[124] Case C-350/92, *Spain* v. *Council*, [1995] ECR I-1985, where the Court found that the adoption of a Regulation would not go beyond the scope of Article 114 TFEU as it aimed 'to prevent the heterogeneous development of national laws leading to further disparities' in the internal market (*ibid.*, para. 35).

[125] A. Bardenhewer-Rating and F. Niggermeier, 'Artikel 152' in H. von der Groeben and J. Schwarze (eds.), *Kommentar zum Vertrag über die Europäische Union und zur Gründung der Europäischen Gemeinschaft* (Nomos, 2003), para. 20.

[126] For K. Lenaerts (see 'Subsidiarity and Community Competence in the Field of Education' [1994–5] 1 *Columbia Journal of European Law* 1) 'incentive measures' can be adopted in the form of Regulations, Directives, Decisions or atypical legal acts and are thus normal legislative acts of the Union. '[T]he fact that a [European] incentive measure may have the indirect effect of harmonizing . . . does not necessarily mean that it conflicts with the prohibition on harmonization' (*ibid.*, 15).

[127] The national 'preemption' of Union action would only be lifted where the diverse national laws create genuine obstacles to intra-European trade and/or distortions of competition. The Union would then be entitled to have recourse to Article 114 TFEU. However, in Case C-376/98, *Germany* v. *Parliament and Council (Tobacco Advertising)*, [2000] ECR I-8419, the Court clarified that Article 114 could not be used for a legislative measure whose principal aim was the protection of public health. Article 114 must not be used to circumvent the express exclusion of harmonisation found in Article 168. A 'health' measure adopted under Article 114 must therefore 'genuinely have as its object the improvement of the conditions for the establishment and functioning of the internal market'. A 'mere finding of disparities between national rules and of the abstract risk of obstacles to the exercise of fundamental freedoms or of distortions of competition' would not be sufficient (*ibid.*, paras. 79 and 84). For a discussion of the case, see: Chapter 5 – Section 1(b)(i).

Finally, what is the constitutional significance of 'shall not affect' provisions? The formulation sounds like an 'express saving clause', and would, if the Court decides to go down this road, mean that European law cannot 'preempt' any national legislation within the areas enumerated. These constitutional exemptions – some have called them 'negative competences' – must nonetheless not be confused with a constitutional recognition of exclusive national powers.

Conclusion

The doctrine of direct effect demands that a national court *applies* European law. And the doctrine of supremacy demands that a national court *disapplies* national law that conflicts with European law. Direct effect and supremacy are *not* twin doctrines. There can be direct effect without supremacy (but, admittedly, there can be no supremacy without direct effect). By contrast, supremacy and preemption are twin doctrines. There is no supremacy without preemption. The doctrine of preemption is a theory of legislative conflict. The doctrine of supremacy is a theory of conflict resolution. The two doctrines are vital for any federal legal order with overlapping legislative spheres.

For the European legal order, the absolute supremacy of European law means that all Union law prevails over all national law. The absolute nature of the supremacy doctrine is, however, contested by the Member States. While they generally acknowledge the supremacy of European law, they have insisted on national constitutional limits. Is this relative nature of supremacy a 'novelty' or 'aberration'?[128] This view is introverted and unhistorical when compared with the constitutional experiences of the United States.[129] Indeed, the normative ambivalence surrounding the supremacy principle in the European Union is part and parcel of Europe's *federal* nature.[130]

---

[128] See N. Walker, 'The Idea of Constitutional Pluralism' [2002] 65 *Modern Law Review* 317 at 338. This is how Walker, a leading figure of the 'constitutional pluralists', describes the origin of this 'new' constitutional philosophy: 'It is no coincidence that this literature has emerged out of the study of the constitutional dimension of EU law, for it is EU law which poses the most pressing paradigm-challenging test to what we might call constitutional monism. Constitutional monism merely grants a label to the defining assumption of constitutionalism in the Westphalian age . . . namely the idea that the sole centres or units of constitutional authorities are states. Constitutional pluralism, by contrast, recognizes that the European legal order inaugurated by the Treaty of Rome has developed beyond the traditional confines of inter-*national* law and now makes its own independent constitutional claims exist alongside the continuing claims of states' (*ibid.*, 337). This – 'Eurocentric' – view strikingly ignores the American experience, in which the Union *and* the States were seen to have 'constitutional' claims and in which the 'Union' was – traditionally – not (!) conceived in statist terms (see E. Zoeller, 'Aspects Internationaux du Droit Constitutionnel. Contribution à la Théorie de la Féderation d'états' [2002] 194 *Recueil des Cours de l'Académie de la Haye* 43).

[129] Schütze, 'Federalism as Constitutional Pluralism' (supra n. 50).

[130] On this point, see: Chapter 2 above.

In contrast with supremacy, preemption is a relative concept – even from the European perspective. The question is not whether European law preempts national law, but to what degree. Not all European law will thus preempt all national law. So, when will a conflict between European and national law arise? There is no absolute answer to this question. The Union legislator and the European Court of Justice will not always attach the same conflict criterion to all European legislation. Sometimes a purely 'jurisdictional' conflict will be enough to preempt national law. In other cases, some material conflict with the European legislative scheme is necessary. Finally, the Court may insist on a direct conflict with a specific Union rule. In parallel to American constitutionalism we consequently distinguished three preemption categories within the Union legal order: field preemption, obstacle preemption and rule preemption.

The constitutional nature of the preemption phenomenon was described as a theory of federal interpretation. The preemption doctrine acknowledges the federal dimension in the interpretation of federal legislation. In federal orders, the interpretative activity will not only affect the horizontal separation of powers – the judiciary acting as a quasi-legislator – but also the vertical separation of powers. Viewing the interpretation of European legislation as the 'objective' application of the supremacy principle de-federalises the interpretative process. This reductionist view has been responsible for the very slow emergence of a European doctrine of preemption.

11

European Law: Remedies and Liabilities

Contents

Introduction   380
1. The (consistent) interpretation principle   383
2. The equivalence principle   384
   (a) Non-discrimination: extending national remedies to European
       actions   385
   (b) 'Similar' actions: the equivalence test   386
3. The effectiveness principle   387
   (a) The historical evolution of the effectiveness standard   388
   (b) Procedural limits to the invocability of European law   393
4. The liability principle   396
   (a) State liability: the *Francovich* doctrine   397
       (i) The three conditions for State liability   399
       (ii) State liability for judicial breaches of European law   402
   (b) Private liability: the *Courage* doctrine   405
Conclusion   407

Introduction

Rights without remedies are like 'pie in the sky': a metaphysical meal. The Latin proverb is clear on this point: *ubi ius, ubi remedium*. Each right should have its remedi(es).[1]

Classic international law leaves the enforcement of its norms to the States themselves. The administrative and judicial remedies and procedures *within* States are beyond its reach. When founded, the European legal order followed

---

[1] Remedies might be said to fall into two broad categories. Ex ante remedies are to prevent the violation of a right (interim relief, injunctions), while ex post remedies are used to 'remedy' a violation that has already occurred (damages liability). On the many (unclear) meanings of 'remedy', see: P. Birks, 'Rights, Wrongs, and Remedies' [2000] 20 *Oxford Journal of Legal Studies* 1 at 9 et seq.

this logic. While it would subsequently 'centralise' the doctrines of direct effect and supremacy, both principles would only determine *that* national authorities must apply European law. However, they did not determine *which* national authorities must do so and according to *what* procedures. Were these national procedures beyond the scope of European law? Would the European Union, like the American Union, have to take State courts as it finds them?[2] And if not, to what extent would the European legal order require national procedural laws to *prevent* or *repair* violations of European rights?

The European legal order has traditionally recognised the procedural autonomy of the Member States in the enforcement of European law: 'Where national authorities are responsible for implementing [European law] it must be recognised that in principle this implementation takes place with due respect for the forms and procedures of national law.'[3] This formulation has become known as the principle of 'national procedural autonomy'.[4] The danger of this decentralised executive and judicial enforcement is that there may be a European *right*, but no national *remedy* to enforce that right. And for that reason, the autonomy of national enforcement powers was never absolute. National procedural powers were not exclusive powers of the Member States.[5] The Union has always recognised that it could harmonise national procedural laws where 'they are likely to distort or harm the functioning of the common market'.[6] National procedural rules are thus not 'off limits' for European law. Yet in the absence of positive harmonisation, the rights

---

[2] H. Hart, 'The Relations between State and Federal Law' [1954] 54 *Columbia Law Review*, 489 at 508. 'The general rule, bottomed deeply in belief in the importance of state control of state judicial procedure, is that federal law takes state courts as it finds them. For example, state rules about the ways in which claims for relief, or defences, or counter-defences, must be asserted may ordinarily be applied also to federal claims and defences and counter-defences, providing only that the rules are not so rigorous as, in effect, to nullify the asserted rights.'

[3] Case 39/70, *Norddeutsches Vieh- und Fleischkontor GmbH* v. *Hauptzollamt Hamburg-St. Annen*, [1971] ECR 49, para. 4.

[4] For a criticism of the notion, see: C. N. Kakouris, 'Do the Member States possess Judicial Procedural "Autonomy"?' [1997] 34 CML Rev 1389 (arguing that the Court has never referred to the principle in its case-law). However, the Court subsequently, and now regularly, recognised the principle in its case-law; see Case C-201/02, *The Queen* v. *Secretary of State for Transport, ex parte Wells*, [2004] ECR I-723, para. 67 (emphasis added): 'The detailed procedural rules applicable are a matter for the domestic legal order of each Member State, under the *principle of procedural autonomy of the Member States*[.]', as well as: Joined Cases C-392/04 and C-422/04, *i-21 Germany & Arcor* v. *Germany*, [2006] ECR I-8559, para. 57: 'principle of the procedural autonomy of the Member States'.

[5] Contra: D. Simon, *Le Système Juridique Communautaire* (Presses Universitaires de France, 2001), 156: 'les Etats membres ont une competence exclusive pour determiner les organes qui seront chargés d'exécuter le droit communautaire'.

[6] Case 33/76, *Rewe-Zentralfinanz eG and Rewe-Zentral AG* v. *Landwirtschaftskammer für das Saarland*, [1976] ECR 1989, para. 5: 'Where necessary, Articles [114 to 116 and 352 TFEU] enable appropriate measures to be taken to remedy differences between the provisions laid down by law, regulations or administrative action in Member States if they are likely to distort or harm the functioning of the common market. In the absence of such measures of harmonisation the right conferred by [European] law must be exercised before the national courts in accordance with the conditions laid down by national rules.'

conferred by European law 'must be exercised before the *national* courts in accordance with the conditions laid down by *national* rules'.[7]

But did this mean that, in the absence of positive harmonisation, the Member States were absolutely free to determine how individuals could invoke their European rights in national courts?[8] The Court has answered this question negatively. The core negative duty governing the decentralised enforcement of European law is Article 4 (3) TEU. This duty of 'sincere cooperation' imposes limitations on the procedural autonomy of the Member States.[9] The first constitutional limit to the autonomy of national courts has already been discussed in Chapter 9: the duty of consistent interpretation. However, the European Court would derive two additional constitutional obligations from the duty of sincere cooperation: the principle of equivalence and the principle of effectiveness. The classic expression of both limitations can be found in *Rewe*:

> [I]n the absence of [European] rules on this subject, it is for the domestic legal system of each Member State to designate the courts having jurisdiction and to determine the procedural conditions governing actions at law intended to ensure the protection of the rights which citizens have derived from the direct effect of [European] law, it being understood that such conditions cannot be less favourable than those relating to similar actions of a domestic nature … In the absence of such measures of harmonisation the right conferred by [European] law must [thus] be exercised before the national courts in accordance with the conditions laid down by national rules. The position would be different only if the [national rules] made it impossible in practice to exercise the rights which the national courts are obliged to protect.[10]

The procedural autonomy of the Member States, even in the absence of European harmonisation, was thus *relative*. First, national procedural rules could not make the enforcement of European rights less favourable than the

---

[7] *Ibid.* (emphasis added).

[8] This chapter concentrates on national courts. However, it is important to note that the same principles apply, *mutatis mutandis*, to national administrations; see R. Schütze, 'From Rome to Lisbon: "Executive Federalism" in the (New) European Union' [2010] 47 CML Rev 1385 at 1406. See also: M. Dougan, 'The Vicissitudes of Life at the Coalface: Remedies and Procedures for Enforcing Union Law Before the National Courts' in P. Craig and G. de Búrca, *The Evolution of EU Law* (Oxford University Press, 2011) 407 at 434: 'It thus appears that what we have traditionally thought of as the principles of effective *judicial* protection are in the course of being adopted – and surely also adapted – so as to establish minimum standards of good *administrative* process in cases involving Union law'. For relatively recent case law on this point, see Case C-120/05, *Schulze v. Hauptzollamt Hamburg-Jonas*, [2006] ECR I-10745.

[9] Article 4 (3) TEU states: 'Pursuant to the principle of sincere cooperation, the Union and the Member States shall, in full mutual respect, assist each other in carrying out tasks which flow from the Treaties. The Member States shall take any appropriate measure, general or particular, to ensure fulfilment of the obligations arising out of the Treaties or resulting from the acts of the institutions of the Union. The Member States shall facilitate the achievement of the Union's tasks and refrain from any measure which could jeopardise the attainment of the Union's objectives.'

[10] Case 33/76, *Rewe*, (supra n. 6) para. 5. See also: Case 45/76, *Comet BV v. Produktschap voor Siergewassen*, [1976] ECR 2043. For the modern version, see: Case C-312/93, *Peterbroeck, Van Campenhout & Cie v. Belgian State*, [1995] ECR I-4599.

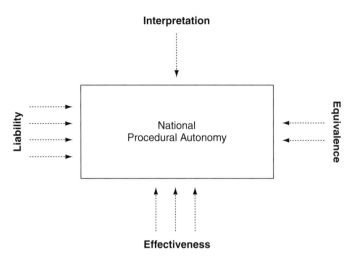

Figure 22 Limits on National Procedural Autonomy

enforcement of similar national rights. This prohibition of procedural discrimination was the principle of equivalence. Second, national procedural rules –
even if not discriminatory – ought not to make the enforcement of European
rights 'impossible in practice'. This would become known as the principle of
effectiveness. Both principles have led to a *judicial* harmonisation of national
procedural laws,[11] and this chapter analyses their evolution in Sections 2 and 3.
Section 4 turns to the most intrusive incursion of the procedural autonomy of
the Member States: the liability principle. While the previous two principles
depended on the existence of *national* remedies for the enforcement of
European law, this principle established a *European* remedy. Where an individual had not been able to enforce his European rights in a national court, he
could – under certain conditions – claim compensatory damages resulting from
a breach of European law.

1. The (consistent) interpretation principle

We have already encountered the first limitation on the procedural autonomy
of national courts: the duty of consistent interpretation.[12] According to this

---

[11] The Court expressly refers to both principles, see Joined Cases C-392/04 and C-422/04 *i-
21 Germany & Arcor* v. *Germany*, (supra n. 4), para. 57: '[A]ccording to settled case-
law, in the absence of relevant [European] rules, the detailed procedural rules designed to
ensure the protection of the rights which individuals acquire under [European] law are a
matter for the domestic legal order of each Member State, under the principle of the
procedural autonomy of the Member States, provided that they are not less favourable
than those governing similar domestic situations (principle of equivalence) and that they do
not render impossible in practice or excessively difficult the exercise of rights conferred by
the [Union] legal order (principle of effectiveness).'

[12] For a more extensive discussion of the duty, see: Chapter 9 – Section 3(b).

European principle, national courts (and administrations) must interpret national law as far as possible in light of European law.[13] The principle is rooted in Article 4 (3) TEU,[14] and is demanding: national courts are required to interpret their national law '*as far as possible*' in the light of the wording and the purpose of the European law.[15] However, as we saw above, the European legal order only asks national courts to adjust their interpretation of national law 'in so far as it is given discretion to do so *under national law*'.[16] The principle of consistent interpretation thus respects the (relative) autonomy of national judicial methods, for it permits national courts to limit themselves to 'the application of interpretative methods recognised by *national law*'.[17] National courts are not obliged to 'invent' or 'import' new interpretative methods.[18]

2. The equivalence principle

The idea behind the principle of equivalence is straightforward: national procedures and remedies for the enforcement of European rights 'cannot be less favourable than those relating to similar actions of a domestic nature'.[19] When applying European law, national courts must act *as if* they were applying national law. National procedures and remedies must not discriminate between national and European rights. The equivalence principle thus demands that similar situations are treated similarly. It will consequently not affect the substance of national remedies. It only requires the *formal* extension of those remedies to 'similar' or 'equivalent' actions under European law. And as such, the principle of equivalence is not too intrusive in the procedural autonomy of national courts.[20]

---

[13] Case C-218/01, *Henkel* v. *Deutsches Patent- und Markenamt*, [2004] ECR I-1725, para. 60: 'As the Court has held, the competent authorities called on to apply and interpret the relevant national law must do so, as far as possible, in the light of the wording and the purpose of the Directive so as to achieve the result it has in view and thereby comply with the third paragraph of Article [288 TFEU].' See also: Case C-109/09, *Deutsche Lufthansa* (nyr), para. 53: 'The requirement that national law be interpreted in conformity with EU law is inherent in the system of the FEU Treaty, since it permits national courts, for the matters within their jurisdiction, to ensure the full effectiveness of EU law when they determine the disputes before them.'

[14] Case 14/83, *Von Colson and Kamann* v. *Land Nordrhein-Westfalen*, [1984] ECR 1891, para. 26.

[15] Case C-106/89, *Marleasing SA* v. *La Comercial Internacional de Alimentacion SA*, [1990] ECR I-4135, para. 8 (emphasis added).

[16] Case 14/83, *Von Colson* (supra n. 14), para. 28 (emphasis added).

[17] Joined Cases C-397/01 to C-403/01, *Pfeiffer et al.* v. *Deutsches Rotes Kreuz, Kreisverband Waldshut eV*, [2004] ECR I-8835, para. 116 (emphasis added).

[18] See M. Klammert, 'Judicial Implementation of Directives and Anticipatory Indirect Effect: Connecting the Dots' [2006] 43 CML Rev 1251 at 1259. For the opposite view, see: S. Prechal, *Directives in EC Law* (Oxford University Press, 2005), 213.

[19] Case 33/76, *Rewe* (supra n. 6), para. 5.

[20] M. Dougan, *National Remedies before the Court of Justice: Issues of Harmonisation and Differentiation* (Hart, 2004), 26: 'Principles such as non-discrimination and equivalence implicitly assume that the remedies and procedural rules already provided under the domestic judicial orders are sufficient in scope and character to safeguard the exercise of the citizen's legal rights.'

(a) Non-discrimination: extending national remedies to European actions

A good example of the non-discrimination logic behind the equivalence principle can be seen in *i-21 Germany & Arcor* v. *Germany*.[21] The two plaintiffs were telecommunication companies that had paid licence fees to Germany. The national fees had been calculated on the anticipated administrative costs of the respective national authority over a period of thirty years and were charged in advance. The companies successfully challenged the national law determining the assessment method before the Federal Administrative Court, which declared it to violate German constitutional law. The plaintiff companies then sought repayment of the fees they had already paid. However, the national court dismissed this second action on the ground that the actual administrative decision had become final under national law. For under the German Administrative Procedure Act, a final administrative decision could only be challenged where the decision was 'downright intolerable'. For national law, this was not the case. But wondering whether it was required to apply a lower threshold for actions involving European law, the administrative court referred this question to the European Court. And analysing the equivalence principle within this context, the European Court held:

> [I]n relation to the principle of equivalence, this requires that all the rules applicable to appeals, including the prescribed timelimits, apply without distinction to appeals on the ground of infringement of [Union] law and to appeals on the ground of disregard of national law. It follows that, if the national rules applicable to appeals impose an obligation to withdraw an administrative act that is unlawful under domestic law, even though that act has become final, where to uphold that act would be 'downright intolerable', the same obligation to withdraw must exist under equivalent conditions in the case of an administrative act … Where, pursuant to rules of national law, the authorities are required to withdraw an administrative decision which has become final if that decision is manifestly incompatible with domestic law, that same obligation must exist if the decision is manifestly incompatible with [Union] law.[22]

In the present case, the question whether the national decision was 'downright intolerable' or 'manifestly incompatible' with European law depended on the degree of clarity of the Union law at issue, and was an interpretative prerogative of the national court.[23] The European Court thus accepted the high *national* threshold for judicial challenges of final administrative acts, but demanded that it would be applied, without discrimination, to European actions in national courts.

---

[21] Joined Cases C-392/04 and C-422/04, *i-21 Germany & Arcor* v. *Germany* (supra n. 4).
[22] *Ibid.*, paras. 62–3, 69.   [23] *Ibid.*, paras. 70–2.

(b) 'Similar' actions: the equivalence test

The logic of non-discrimination requires that similar actions be treated similarly. But what are 'equivalent' or 'similar' actions? The devil always lies in the detail, and much case law on the equivalence principle has concentrated on this devilish question. In *Edis*,[24] a company had been required to pay a registration charge. Believing the charge to be contrary to European law, the plaintiff applied for a refund that was rejected by the Italian courts on the ground that the limitation period for such refunds had expired. However, Italian law recognised various limitation periods – depending on whether the refund was due to be paid by public or private parties. The limitation period for public authorities was shorter than that for private parties. And this posed the following question: was the national court entitled to simply extend the national *public* refund procedure to charges in breach of European law; or was it required to apply the more generous *private* refund procedure? The Court answered as follows:

> Observance of the principle of equivalence implies, for its part, that the procedural rule at issue applies without distinction to actions alleging infringements of [Union] law and to those alleging infringements of national law, with respect to the same kind of charges or dues. *That principle cannot, however, be interpreted as obliging a Member State to extend its most favourable rules governing recovery under national law to all actions for repayment of charges or dues levied in breach of [European] law.* Thus, [European] law does not preclude the legislation of a Member State from laying down, alongside a limitation period applicable under the ordinary law to actions between private individuals for the recovery of sums paid but not due, special detailed rules, which are less favourable, governing claims and legal proceedings to challenge the imposition of charges and other levies. The position would be different only if those detailed rules applied solely to actions based on [European] law for the repayment of such charges or levies.[25]

In the present case, the 'equivalent' action was thus to be based on the national remedies that existed for refunds from *public* bodies. The existence of a more favourable limitation period for refunds from private parties was irrelevant, since the equivalence principle only required treating like actions alike. And the 'like' action in this case was the refund procedure applicable to a public body. The national procedural rules thus did not violate the principle of equivalence.

But matters might not be so straightforward. In *Levez*,[26] the Employment Appeal Tribunal in London had asked the Court of Justice about the compatibility of section 2(5) of the 1970 Equal Pay Act with the equivalence principle. The national law provided that, in proceedings brought in respect of a failure to comply with the equal pay principle, women were not entitled to arrears of

[24] Case C-231/96, *Edilizia Industriale Siderurgica Srl (Edis)* v. *Ministero delle Finanze*, [1998] ECR I-4951.
[25] *Ibid.*, paras. 36–7 (emphasis added).
[26] Case C-326/96, *Levez* v. *Jennings (Harlow Pools) Ltd*, [1998] ECR I-7835.

remuneration or damages of more than two years. The provision applied irrespective of whether a plaintiff enforced her *national* or *European* right to equal pay. Did this not mean that the equivalence principle was respected? The European Court did *not* think so, as it questioned the underlying comparative base. As the national legislation was designed to implement the European right to equal pay, the Court held that the national law 'cannot therefore provide an appropriate ground of comparison against which to measure compliance with the principle of equivalence'.[27] Remedies for equal pay rights needed to be compared with national remedies for 'claims similar to those based on the Act', such as remedies for breach of a contract of employment or discrimination on grounds of race.[28] The equivalence principle thus demanded the application of the more generous national remedies available under these more *general* national actions.

In conclusion, the equivalence principle requires national courts to ask, 'whether the actions concerned are similar as regards their purpose, cause of action and essential characteristics'.[29] This teleological comparability test might require the courts to look beyond the national procedural regime for a specific national or European right.

3. The effectiveness principle

From the very beginning, the European Court recognised the heightened tension between the (relative) procedural autonomy of the Member States and the principle of effectiveness. For while the equivalence principle simply required the *formal* extension of the *scope* of national remedies to equivalent European actions, the effectiveness principle appeared to ask national legal systems to provide for a *substantive* minimum *content* that would guarantee the enforcement of European rights in national courts. Thus, while the equivalence principle would be of no assistance where no similar national remedy existed, the effectiveness principle could require the strengthening of national remedies. This could potentially lead to a positive discriminatory situation in favour of the enforcement of European law. For thanks to the effectiveness principle, the enforcement of European rights could become easier than the enforcement of similar national rights.

The power of the effectiveness principle to interfere with the principle of national procedural autonomy was – from the start – much greater. The European Court consequently began to develop the principle from a minimal standard. National remedies would solely be found inefficient, where they 'made it *impossible* in practice to exercise the rights which the national courts

---

[27] *Ibid.*, para. 48.   [28] *Ibid.*, para. 49.
[29] Case C-78/98, *Preston et al.* v. *Wolverhampton Healthcare NHS Trust and Others*, [2000] ECR I-3201, para. 57: 'the national court must consider whether the actions concerned are similar as regards their purpose, cause of action and essential characteristics'.

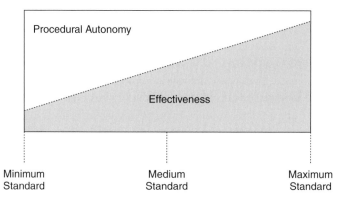

Figure 23 Standards of Effectiveness

are obliged to protect'.[30] This minimum standard has developed with time, and in various directions. For the sake of convenience, three standards may be distinguished. In addition to the minimum standard of practical impossibility, the Court has referred to the medium standard of an 'adequate' remedy,[31] and to the maximum standard guaranteeing the 'full effectiveness' of European law.[32] When and where do these three different standards apply? The Court's jurisprudence on this question is disastrously unclear. The best way to analyse the cases is to identify general historical periods in addition to a variety of specific thematic lines.[33] This section indeed cannot do justice to the subtlety – or chaos – within this area of European law. We shall confine ourselves to outlining the three broad temporal periods in the general development of the principle, and subsequently look inside one specific thematic line within the case law.

(a) The historical evolution of the effectiveness standard

The academic literature on the effectiveness principle typically distinguishes between three – broadly defined – periods of evolution. A first period of *restraint* is replaced by a period of *intervention*, which is in turn replaced by a period of *balance*.[34]

In the first period, the European Court showed much restraint towards the procedural autonomy of the Member States. The Court pursued a policy of

---

[30] Case 33/76, *Rewe* (supra n. 6), para. 5.   [31] Case 14/83, *Von Colson* (supra n. 14), para. 23.

[32] Case C-213/89, *The Queen* v. *Secretary of State for Transport, ex parte Factortame Ltd and others*, [1990] ECR I-2433, para. 21.

[33] For illustrations of this – brilliant and necessary – approach, see: Dougan, 'The Vicissitudes' (supra n. 8), Chapters 5 and 6; as well as T. Tridimas, *The General Principles of EU Law* (Oxford University Press, 2006), Chapter 9.

[34] A. Arnull, *The European Union and its Court of Justice* (Oxford University Press, 2006), 268; as well as Dougan, 'The Vicissitudes' (supra n. 8), 227, and Tridimas, *The General Principles* (supra n. 33), 420 et seq.

judicial minimalism.[35] The standard for an 'effective remedy' was low and simply required that the national procedures must not make the enforcement of European rights (virtually) impossible. This first period is exemplified by *Rewe*.[36] In that case, the plaintiff had applied for a refund of monies that had been charged in contravention of the European Treaties. The defendant accepted the illegality of the charges, but counterclaimed that the limitation period for a refund had expired. The Court accepted that the existence of a limitation period did not make the enforcement of European rights impossible and found for the defendant. The judgment was confirmed, in nearly identical terms, on the same day by a second case.[37] The Court's judicial minimalism was thereby premised on the hope of future legislative harmonisation by the Union.[38] And with the latter not forthcoming,[39] the Court moved into a second phase.

In this second period, the Court developed a much more demanding standard of 'effectiveness'. In *Von Colson*,[40] two female candidates for a warden position in an all-male prison had been rejected. The State prison service had indisputably discriminated against them on the ground that they were women. Their European right to equal treatment had thus been violated, and the question arose how this violation could be remedied. The remedy under German law exclusively allowed for damages, and these damages were furthermore restricted to the plaintiffs' travel expenses. Was this an effective remedy for the enforcement of their European rights? Or would European law require 'the employer in question to conclude a contract of employment with the candidate who was discriminated' against?[41] The Court rejected this specific remedy.[42] For the 'full implementation' of European law would 'not require any specific form of sanction for unlawful discrimination'.[43] The Court nonetheless clarified that the effectiveness principle required that the national remedy 'be

---

[35] A. Ward, *Judicial Review and the Rights of Private Parties in EC Law* (Oxford University Press, 2007), 87.

[36] Case 33/76, *Rewe* (supra n. 6).

[37] Case 45/76, *Comet BV* v. *Produktschap voor Siergewassen* (supra n. 10).

[38] Arnull, *The European Union and its Court of Justice* (supra n. 34), 276 – referring to Case 130/79, *Express Dairy Foods Limited* v. *Intervention Board for Agricultural Produce*, [1980] ECR 1887, para. 12: 'In the regrettable absence of [Union] provisions harmonising procedure and time-limits the Court finds this situation entails differences in treatment on a [European] scale. It is not for the Court to issue general rules of substance or procedural provisions which only the competent institutions may adopt.'

[39] For an exception to the rule, see: Article 6 of Directive 76/207 on the implementation of the principle of equal treatment for men and women as regards access to employment, vocational training and promotion, and working conditions (1976 OJ L39/40). The provision stated: 'Member States shall introduce into their national legal systems such measures as are necessary to enable all persons who consider themselves wronged by failure to apply to them the principle of equal treatment within the meaning of Articles 3, 4 and 5 to pursue their claims by judicial process after possible recourse to other competent authorities.'

[40] Case 14/83, *Von Colson* (supra n. 14).

[41] This was the first (preliminary) question asked by the German labour law court (*ibid.*, para. 6).

[42] *Ibid.*, para. 19.   [43] *Ibid.*, para. 23.

such as to guarantee real and effective judicial protection'.[44] The remedy would need to have 'a real deterrent effect on the employer', and in the context of a compensation claim this meant that the latter 'must in any event be *adequate* in relation to the damage sustained'.[45] And the German procedural rule that limited the compensation claim did not satisfy this standard of effectiveness.[46]

Instead of a minimum standard, the Court here generally moved to a standard that aspired *towards* the full effectiveness of European law. In *Dekker*,[47] the Court outlawed national procedural restrictions that 'weakened considerably'[48] the effectiveness of the European right to equal treatment; and in *Marshall II*,[49] it repeated its demand that where financial compensation was chosen to remedy a violation of European law, the compensatory damages 'must be *adequate*, in that it must enable the loss and damage actually sustained as a result of the discriminatory dismissal *to be made good in full*'.[50]

But the most famous intervention in the procedural autonomy of a Member State is undoubtedly reserved to a second English case: *Factortame*.[51] The facts of the case were as follows: the appellant company was incorporated under British law, but most of its shareholders were Spanish nationals. It had registered fishing vessels under the 1894 Merchant Shipping Act – a practice that allowed its Spanish shareholders to benefit from the fishing quota allocated to Great Britain under the Union's common fishing policy. This practice of 'quota hopping' was targeted by the 1988 Merchant Shipping Act. This Act aimed at stopping Britain's quota being 'plundered' by 'vessels flying the British flag but lacking any genuine link with the United Kingdom'.[52] The 1988 Act consequently limited the reregistration of all vessels to vessels that were 'British owned' and controlled from within the United Kingdom. But this nationality requirement violated the non-discrimination principle on which the European internal market is founded, and Factortame challenged the compatibility of the 1988 Act with European law. In order to protect its European rights in the meantime, it applied for interim relief, since it found that it would become insolvent if the national legislation was immediately applied.

The case went to the House of Lords. And the House of Lords did find that the substantive conditions for granting interim relief were in place, but held 'that the grant of such relief was precluded by the old common-law rule that an interim injunction may not be granted against the Crown, that is to say against the government, in conjunction with the presumption that an Act of Parliament

---

[44] *Ibid.* [45] *Ibid.* [46] *Ibid.*, para. 24.

[47] Case C-177/88, *Dekker* v. *Stichting Vormingscentrum voor Jong Volwassenen (VJV-Centrum) Plus*, [1990] ECR I-3941.

[48] *Ibid.*, para. 24.

[49] Case C-271/91, *Marshall* v. *Southampton and South-West Hampshire Area Health Authority*, [1993] ECR I-4367.

[50] *Ibid.*, para. 26 (emphasis added).

[51] Case C-213/89, *The Queen* v. *Secretary of State for Transport, ex parte Factortame Ltd and others*, [1990] ECR I-2433.

[52] *Ibid.*, para. 4.

is in conformity with [European] law until such time as a decision on its compatibility with that law has been given'.[53] Unsure whether this common law rule itself violated the effectiveness principle under European law, the House of Lords referred the case to Luxembourg. And the European Court answered as follows:

> [A]ny provision of a national legal system and any legislative, administrative or judicial practice which might impair the effectiveness of [European] law by withholding from the national court having jurisdiction to apply such law the power to do everything necessary at the moment of its application to set aside national legislative provisions which might prevent, even temporarily, [European] rules from having full force and effect are incompatible with those requirements, which are the very essence of [European] law. It must be added that the *full effectiveness* of [European] law would be just as much impaired if a rule of national law could prevent a court seised of a dispute governed by [European] law from granting interim relief in order *to ensure the full effectiveness of the judgment to be given on the existence of the rights claimed under [European] law*. It follows that a court which in those circumstances would grant interim relief, if it were not for a rule of national law, is obliged to set aside that rule.[54]

While short of creating a new remedy,[55] this came very close to demanding a maximum standard of effectiveness. Yet the Court soon withdrew from this highly interventionist stance and thereby entered into a third period in the evolution of the effectiveness principle.[56]

In this third period, the Court tried and – still – tries to find a balance between the minimum and the maximum standard of effectiveness.[57] The retreat from the second period of high intervention can be seen in

---

[53] *Ibid.*, para. 13.   [54] *Ibid.*, paras. 20–1 (emphasis added).

[55] A. G. Toth, 'Case Commentary' [1990] 27 CML Rev 573 at 586: 'It follows that the judgment does not purport to lay down substantive conditions for the grant of interim protection, nor to define the measures that may be ordered. Still less does it require the national courts to devise interim relief where none exists. What it requires is that national courts should make use of any interim measure that is normally available under national law, in order to protect rights claimed under [European] law.'

[56] This section will *not* discuss the (in)famous *Emmott* judgment (see Case C-208/90, *Emmott v. Minister for Social Welfare and Attorney General*, [1991] ECR I-4269), as the ruling should best be confined to the special context dealing with the nature of directives (*ibid.*, para. 17: 'Whilst the laying down of reasonable time-limits which, if unobserved, bar proceedings, in principle satisfies the two conditions mentioned above [i.e. the equivalence and effectiveness principles], account must nevertheless be taken of the particular nature of directives.') Moreover, the judgment was particularly motivated by a desire for substantive justice that clouded the judgment's formal legal value. The judgment's peculiar and special character was indeed quickly realised by the Court (see Case C-410/92, *Johnson v. Chief Adjudication Officer*, [1994] ECR I-5483, para. 26), which has, ever since, constructed it restrictively. On the – almost immediate – demise of *Emmott*, see: M. Hoskins, 'Tilting the Balance: Supremacy and National Procedural Rules' [1996] 21 EL Rev 365.

[57] F. G. Jacobs, 'Enforcing Community Rights and Obligations in National Courts: Striking the balance' in A. Biondi and J. Lonbay (eds.), *Remedies for Breach of EC Law* (Wiley, 1996). See also: Dougan, 'The Vicissitudes' (supra n. 8), 29: 'There has been a definite retreat back towards the orthodox presumption of national autonomy in the provision of judicial protection. But the

Steenhorst-Neerings,[58] where the Court developed a distinction between national procedural rules whose effect was to totally *preclude* individuals from enforcing European rights and those national rules that merely *restrict* their remedies.[59] In *Preston*,[60] the Court had again to deal with 1970 Equal Pay Act whose section 2 (4) barred any claim that was not brought within a period of six months following cessation of employment. And instead of concentrating on the 'full effectiveness' or 'adequacy' of the national remedy, the Court stated that '[s]uch a limitation period does not render impossible *or excessively difficult* the exercise of rights conferred by the [European] legal order and is not therefore liable to strike at the very essence of those rights'.[61] The Court here had recourse to a – stronger – alternative to the minimal impossibility standard: national procedures that would make the exercise of European rights 'excessively difficult' would fall foul of the principle of effectiveness.[62] This medium standard appeared to lie in between the minimum and the maximum standard.

When would this medium standard of effectiveness be violated? Instead of providing hard and fast rules, the Court has come to prefer a contextual test spelled out for the first time in *Peterbroeck*.[63] In order to discover whether a national procedural rule makes the enforcement of European rights 'excessively difficult', the Court analyses each case 'by reference to the role of that provision in the procedure, its progress and its special features, viewed as a whole, before the various national instances'.[64] It would thereby take into account 'the basic principles of the domestic judicial system, such as protection of the rights of the defence, the principle of legal certainty and the proper conduct of procedure'.[65] The results of this contextual test will be hard to predict as the Court emphasises the case-by-case nature of its analysis. Instead of hard rules, the Court's test is based on a balancing act between different procedural interests – not dissimilar to a proportionality analysis.

May this balanced approach sometimes require national courts to create 'new remedies' for the enforcement of European rights? The obligation to create new remedies had been expressly rejected in the first historical phase of the effectiveness principle.[66] However, the Court appears to have confirmed this possibility

---

contemporary principle of effectiveness surely remains more intrusive than the case law of the 1970s and early 1980s.'

[58] Case C-338/91, *Steenhorst-Neerings* v. *Bestuur van de Bedrijfsvereniging voor Detailhandel, Ambachten en Huisvrouwen*, [1993] ECR I-5475.

[59] On the distinction, see: Ward, *Judicial Review* (supra n. 35), 131. The distinction was elaborated in Case C-31/90, *Johnson* v. *Chief Adjudication Officer*, [1991] ECR I-3723.

[60] Case C-78/98, *Preston et al.* v. *Wolverhampton Healthcare NHS Trust and Others*, [2000] ECR I-3201.

[61] *Ibid.*, para. 34 (emphasis added).

[62] However, it is important to note that the 'excessively difficult' formula had already appeared on occasions in the second phase of the Court's case law; see Case 199/82, *Amministrazione delle Finanze dello Stato* v. *SpA San Giorgio*, [1983] ECR 3595, para.14.

[63] Case C-312/93, *Peterbroeck, Van Campenhout & Cie SCS* v. *Belgian State*, [1995] ECR I-4499.

[64] *Ibid.*, para. 14.   [65] *Ibid.*

[66] Case 158/80, *Rewe-Handelsgesellschaft Nord mbH and Rewe-Markt Steffen* v. *Hauptzollamt Kiel (Butter-Cruises)*, [1981] ECR 1805.

within its third historical phase. In *Unibet*,[67] the plaintiff sought a declaration by the national courts that Swedish legislation violated the EU Treaties' free movement provisions. However, there existed no Swedish court procedure that allowed for an *abstract* review of national legislation in light of European law. An individual who wished to challenge a national rule would have to break national law first and then challenge it in national proceedings brought against him. Did the non-existence of a freestanding European review procedure violate the principle that there must be an effective remedy in national law?[68] Synthesising the two previous periods of its case-law, the Court emphasised that the Treaties were 'not intended to create new remedies in the national courts to ensure the observance of [European] law other than those already laid down by national law', *unless* 'it were apparent from the overall scheme of the national legal system in question that no legal remedy existed which made it possible to ensure, even indirectly, respect for an individual's rights under [European] law'.[69] Using its *Peterbroeck* test,[70] the Court found that there existed various indirect ways that did not make it 'excessively difficult' to challenge the compatibility of Swedish legislation with European law.[71] The request for a freestanding action was consequently denied. And yet, the Court had expressly accepted – for the first time – that the creation of new national remedies might exceptionally be required by the effectiveness principle.

Has the Lisbon Treaty changed the balance between the principle of national procedural autonomy and the effectiveness principle once more? Has the newly introduced Article 19 (1) TEU further tilted the balance in favour of the effectiveness principle? The new Treaty provision states: 'Member States shall provide remedies sufficient to ensure effective legal protection in the fields covered by Union law'. This new article might indeed be seen as enhancing the standard of effectiveness along the lines set out in *Unibet* – but this is a matter for future European Courts.

(b) Procedural limits to the invocability of European law

Having looked at the general evolution of the effectiveness principle in the previous section, this section will concentrate on a special thematic line within the latest historical period of the principle. This jurisprudential line concerns national procedural regimes governing the invocation of European law in national proceedings.

---

[67] Case C-432/05, *Unibet* v. *Justitiekanslern*, [2007] ECR I-2271. But see also: Case C-253/00, *Muñoz & Superior Fruiticola* v. *Frumar & Redbridge Produce Marketing*, [2002] ECR I-7289.

[68] This was the first preliminary question in Case C-432/05, *Unibet* (supra n. 67), para. 36.

[69] *Ibid.*, paras. 40 and 41 (with reference to Case 158/80 *Rewe (Butter-Cruises)*, (supra n. 66)).

[70] Case 432/05, *Unibet* (supra n. 67), para. 54 (with reference to Case C-312/93, *Peterbroeck* (supra n. 63), para. 14).

[71] Case 432/05, *Unibet* (supra n. 67), para. 64.

In many legal orders, civil procedures are based on the principle that private parties are free to determine the content of their case.[72] The rationale behind this principle is private party autonomy. Unless a legal rule is seen as mandatorily applicable on grounds of public policy, the court may only apply those legal rules privately invoked. But even in administrative proceedings, a private party might be required to invoke its rights at the correct judicial stage. Where a party failed to invoke a favourable right at first instance, but discovers its existence on appeal, legal certainty might prevent it from invoking it subsequently. How have these principles been applied to the invocation of European law in national proceedings? (This *procedural* problem is distinct from the *structural* problem whether national courts might be prevented altogether from applying European law.[73]) Will the effectiveness principle require national courts to apply European law as a matter of public policy; or has the European legal order followed a balanced approach according to which the national procedures apply unless they make the enforcement of European law excessively difficult?

These complex procedural questions were tackled in *Peterbroeck*.[74] The plaintiff claimed that a Belgian law violated its free movement rights. Unfortunately, the plea had not been raised in the first instance proceedings; nor had it been invoked in the possible time prior to the appeal proceedings. Belgian procedural law consequently prevented the appeal court from considering the European law question; yet, thinking that this procedural limitation might itself violate European law, the national court referred a preliminary question to the Court of Justice. In its answer, the European Court developed its contextual test to discover whether the application of national procedures rendered the application of European law 'excessively difficult'.[75] And the Court held that this was the case in the present context. Finding that the first-instance court had been unable to make a preliminary reference as it was not a 'court or tribunal' in the sense of Article 267 TFEU,[76] the time limit for raising new pleas prior to appeals was considered excessively short. The obligation not to raise points of European law of its own motion thus did 'not appear to be reasonably justifiable by principles such as the requirement of legal certainty or the proper conduct of procedure'.[77]

But did this mean that national courts were positively required, as a matter of general principle, to invoke European law *ex officio*? In a judgment delivered on the very same day, the Court answered this question in the negative. In *Van Schijndel*,[78] the Court added an important caveat to the effectiveness principle. The Court held:

---

[72] On the distinction between 'adversarial' and 'inquisitorial' procedural systems, see: M. Glendon et al., *Comparative Legal Traditions* (Thomson, 2007).

[73] For this structural problem within Europe's judicial federalism, see Chapter 8 – Section 4.

[74] Case C-312/93, *Peterbroeck* (supra n. 63).   [75] On this point, see: *ibid.*   [76] *Ibid.*, para. 17.

[77] *Ibid.*, para. 20.

[78] Joined Cases C-430/93 and C-431/93, *Van Schijndel and Johannes Nicolaas Cornelis van Veen* v. *Stichting Pensioenfonds voor Fysiotherapeuten*, [1995] ECR I-4705.

[T]he domestic law principle that in civil proceedings a court must or may raise points of its own motion is limited by its obligation to keep to the subject-matter of the dispute and to base its decision on the facts put before it. That limitation is justified by the principle that, in a civil suit, it is for the parties to take the initiative, the court being able to act of its own motion only in exceptional cases where the public interest requires its intervention. That principle reflects conceptions prevailing in most of the Member States as to the relations between the State and the individual; it safeguards the rights of the defence; and it ensures proper conduct of proceedings by, in particular, protecting them from the delays inherent in the examination of new pleas.[79]

This suggests that while the equivalence principle may oblige national courts to raise European law of their own motion,[80] the effectiveness principle hardly ever will. The Court will here only challenge national procedural rules that make the enforcement of European rights 'virtually impossible or excessively difficult'.[81]

This medium standard of effectiveness was subsequently confirmed and refined.[82] And we find a good clarification and classification of the case law within this jurisprudential line in *Van der Weerd*.[83] The Court here expressly distinguished *Peterbroeck* as a special case 'by reasons of circumstances peculiar to the dispute which led to the applicant in the main proceedings being deprived of the opportunity to rely effectively on the incompatibility of a domestic provision with [European] law'.[84] But more importantly, the Court identified two key factors in determining whether it considers the effectiveness principle to demand the *ex officio* application of European law. First, it emphasised that it would be hesitant to interfere with the procedural autonomy of the national court, where the parties had 'a genuine opportunity to raise a plea based on [Union] law'.[85] However, it would thereby make its decision dependent on the importance of the respective European law in the Union legal order.

---

[79] *Ibid.*, paras. 20–1. See also: Case C-126/97, *Eco Swiss China Time Ltd* v. *Benetton International NV*, [1999] ECR I-3055, para. 46: 'Moreover, domestic procedural rules which, upon the expiry of that period, restrict the possibility of applying for annulment of a subsequent arbitration award proceeding upon an interim arbitration award which is in the nature of a final award, because it has become res judicata, are justified by the basic principles of the national judicial system, such as the principle of legal certainty and acceptance of res judicata, which is an expression of that principle.'

[80] Joined Cases C-430/93 and C-431/93, *Van Schijndel* (supra n. 78), para. 13: 'Where, by virtue of domestic law, courts or tribunals must raise of their own motion points of law based on binding domestic rules which have not been raised by the parties, such an obligation also exists where binding [European] rules are concerned.'

[81] Case C-40/08, *Asturcom Telecomunicaciones* v. *Rodríguez Nogueira* (nyr), para. 46.

[82] See Case C-126/97, *Eco Swiss China Time* (supra n. 79); Case C-240/98, *Océano Grupo Editorial* v. *Rocío Murciano Quintero*, [2000] ECR I-4941; Joined Cases C-397/98 and C-410/98, *Metallgesellschaft et al.* v. *Commissioners of Inland Revenue et al.*, [2001] ECR I-1727; as well as as well as Case C-2/06, *Kempter* v. *Hauptzollamt Hamburg-Jonas*, [2008] ECR I-411.

[83] Case C-222/05, *Van der Weerd et al.* v. *Minister van Landbouw, Natuur en Voedselkwaliteit*, [2007] ECR I-4233.

[84] *Ibid.*, para. 40.   [85] *Ibid.*, para. 41.

This second factor might explain why the Court has been more active in cases involving consumer protection.[86] For the Court appears to treat this area of European law as an expression of 'European public policy'.[87]

4. The liability principle

The international law spirit permeating the original European Treaties appeared to confine the Union to the use of national remedies for the enforcement of European law. Even if there existed a legislative power to harmonise national procedural law, this power was apparently 'not intended to create new remedies in the national courts to ensure the observance of [Union] law other than those already laid down by national law'.[88] This competence limit protected the procedural autonomy of the Member States. For even if the Court had pushed for a degree of uniformity in the decentralised enforcement of European law via the principles of equivalence and effectiveness, it would be *national* remedies whose scope or substance was extended. But what would happen if no national remedy existed? Would the non-existence of national remedies not be an absolute barrier to the enforcement of European law?

In what was perceived as a dramatic turn of events, the European Court renounced its earlier position and proclaimed the existence of a *European* remedy for breaches of European law in *Francovich*.[89] The Court here insisted that in certain situations the State was liable to compensate for losses caused by its violation of European law. This European remedy to sue a State for compensation contrasts strikingly with the absence of such a remedy in the American legal order.[90] But what are the conditions for State liability in the European Union? Will every breach trigger the liability principle? We shall look

---

[86] *Ibid.*, para. 40.

[87] For an excellent analysis of the cases, see: M. Ebers, 'From *Océano* to *Asturcom*: Mandatory Consumer Law, Ex Officio Application of European Union Law and Res Judicata' [2010] *European Review of Private Law* 823, esp. 843 et seq.

[88] Case 158/80, *Rewe (Butter-Cruises)* (supra n. 66). We saw above that the Court appears to have recently changed its view with regard to the principle of effectiveness.

[89] Joined Cases C-6/90 and C-9/90, *Francovich and Bonifaci et al.* v. *Italy*, [1991] ECR I-5357.

[90] In the United States, the doctrine of 'sovereign immunity' offers the Member States a shield against liability actions for damages resulting from a violation of Union law. The doctrine – partly – originates in the Eleventh Amendment: 'The Judicial power of the United States shall not be construed to extend to any suit in law or equity, commenced or prosecuted against one of the United States by Citizens of another State, or by Citizens or Subjects of any Foreign State.' And in *Alden* v. *Maine* 527 US 706 (1999) at 754, the Supreme Court considered 'sovereign immunity' to extend to private suits against States in their own courts. The contrast between the European and the American approaches to State liability seems indeed 'paradoxical' (see D. J. Melzer, 'Member State Liability in Europe and the United States' [2006] 4 *International Journal of Constitutional Law* 39 at 41): 'One might expect the United States – an older, more established, uncontroversial federal system, with a strong national government, an explicit principle of the supremacy of federal law, and an unquestioned national political community – to have fewer concerns about the imposition of state liability than the newer, less powerful, and far more fragile European polity. But the doctrinal pattern is just the opposite.'

at these questions first, before analysing whether the vertical dimension of the principle has been complemented by a horizontal dimension. The Court indeed appears to have extended the liability principle from violations of European law by public authorities to breaches of European law by private parties.

(a) State liability: the *Francovich* doctrine

Under the principle of effectiveness, national remedies must not make the enforcement of European law excessively difficult. But this did not necessarily mean that *States* would have to compensate all damages resulting from a breach of European law. The essential question thus was 'whether [European] law requires the national courts to acknowledge a right to damages vested in the victims of the violation of [European] law and to order public authorities, found to have infringed [European] law, to pay compensation to such persons, and if so, in which circumstances and according to which criteria'.[91]

For a long time, the Court had been ambivalent towards this question. While in one case it had positively found that a State's violation of European law required it '*to make reparation* for any unlawful consequences which may have ensued';[92] in another case it held that if 'damage has been caused through an infringement of [European] law the State is liable to the injured party of the consequences *in the context of the provisions of national law on the liability of the State*'.[93] Did this mean that the liability of the State depended on the existence of such a remedy in *national* law?[94] Or, did the Court have an independent *European* remedy in mind? This question was long undecided. For a clairvoyant observer there was 'little doubt that one future day the European Court will be asked to say, straightforwardly, whether [European] law requires a remedy in damages to be made available in the national courts'.[95] This day came on 8 January 1990. On this day, the Court received a series of preliminary questions in *Francovich and others* v. *Italy*.[96]

The facts of the case are memorably sad.[97] Italy had flagrantly flouted its obligations under the Treaties by failing to implement a European directive

---

[91] A. Barav, 'Damages in the Domestic Courts for Breach of Community Law by National Public Authorities' in H. G. Schermers et al. (eds.), *Non-Contractual Liability of the European Communities* (Nijhoff, 1988), 149.

[92] Case 6/60, *Humblet* v. *Belgium*, [1960] ECR (English Special Edition) 559 at 569 (emphasis added).

[93] Case 60/75, *Russo* v. *Azienda di Stato per gli interventi sul mercato agricolo*, [1976] ECR 45, para. 9 (emphasis added).

[94] For an (outdated) overview of the damages provisions in national law, see: N. Green and A. Barav, 'Damages in the National Courts for Breach of Community Law' [1986] 6 YEL 55.

[95] Barav, 'Damages in the Domestic Courts' (supra n. 91), 165.

[96] Joined Cases C-6/90 and C-9/90, *Francovich* (supra n. 89).

[97] Opinion of Advocate-General Mischo (*ibid.*, para.1): 'Rarely has the Court been called upon to decide a case in which the adverse consequences for the individuals concerned of failure to implement a directive were as shocking as in the case now before us.'

designed to protect employees in the event of their employer's insolvency.[98]
The Directive had required Member States to pass national legislation guaranteeing the payment of outstanding wages. Francovich had been employed by an
Italian company, but had hardly received any wages. Having brought proceedings against his employer, the latter had gone insolvent. For that reason he
brought a separate action against the Italian State to cover his losses. In the
course of these second proceedings, the national court asked the European
Court whether the State itself would be obliged to cover the losses of the
employees. The European Court found that the Directive had left the
Member States a 'broad discretion with regard to the organisation, operation
and financing of the guarantee institutions', and it therefore lacked direct
effect.[99] It followed that 'the persons concerned cannot enforce those rights
against the State before the national courts where no implementing measures
are adopted within the prescribed period'.[100]

But this was not the end of the story! The Court – unhappy with the negative
result flowing form the lack of direct effect – continued:

> [T]he principle whereby a State must be liable for loss and damage caused to
> individuals as a result of breaches of [European] law for which the State can be
> held responsible is inherent in the system of the Treaty. A further basis for the
> obligation of Member States to make good such loss and damage is to be found in
> Article [4(3)] of the Treaty [on European Union], under which the Member
> States are required to take all appropriate measures, whether general or partic-
> ular, to ensure fulfilment of their obligations under [European] law. Among these
> is the obligation to nullify the unlawful consequences of a breach of [European]
> law. It follows from all the foregoing that it is a principle of [European] law that
> the Member States are obliged to make good loss and damage caused to individ-
> uals by breaches of [European] law for which they can be held responsible.[101]

The European Court here took a qualitative leap in the context of remedies. Up
to this point, it could still legitimately be argued that the principle of national
procedural autonomy precluded the creation of European remedies, as the
principles of equivalence and effectiveness solely required the extension of
national remedies to violations of European law. With *Francovich* the Court
clarified that the right to reparation for such violations was 'a right founded
directly on [European] law'.[102] The action for State liability was thus a
European remedy that had to be made available in the national courts.[103]
How did the Court justify this 'revolutionary' result? It had recourse to the
usual constitutional suspects: the very nature of the European Treaties and the

---

[98] The Court had already expressly condemned this failure in: Case 22/87, *Commission* v. *Italian Republic*, [1989] ECR 143.
[99] Joined Cases C-6/90 and C-9/90, *Francovich* (supra n. 89), para. 25.   [100] *Ibid.*, para. 27.
[101] *Ibid.*, paras. 33–37.   [102] *Ibid.*, para. 41.
[103] On the application of this new principle in the United Kingdom, see: J. Convery, 'State Liability in the United Kingdom after *Brasserie du Pêcheur*' [1997] 34 CML Rev 603.

general duty under Article 4 (3) TEU. A more sophisticated justification was added by a later judgment. In *Brasserie du Pêcheur*,[104] the Court found:

> Since the Treaty contains no provision expressly and specifically governing the consequences of breaches of [European] law by Member States, it is for the Court, in pursuance of the task conferred on it by Article [19] of the [EU] Treaty of ensuring that in the interpretation and application of the Treaty the law is observed, to rule on such a question in accordance with generally accepted methods of interpretation, in particular by reference to the fundamental principles of the [Union] legal system and, where necessary, general principles common to the legal systems of the Member States. Indeed, it is to the general principles common to the laws of the Member States that the second paragraph of Article [340] of the [FEU] Treaty refers as the basis of the non-contractual liability of the [Union] for damage caused by its institutions or by its servants in the performance of their duties. The principle of the non-contractual liability of the [Union] expressly laid down in Article [340] of the [FEU] Treaty is simply an expression of the general principle familiar to the legal systems of the Member States that an unlawful act or omission gives rise to an obligation to make good the damage caused. That provision also reflects the obligation on public authorities to make good damage caused in the performance of their duties.[105]

The principle of State liability was thus rooted in the constitutional traditions common to the Member States and was equally recognised in the principle of *Union* liability for breaches of European law.[106] There was consequently a parallel between *State* liability and *Union* liability for tortious acts of public authorities. And this parallelism would have a decisive effect on the conditions for State liability for breaches of European law.

(i) The three conditions for State liability

Having created the liability principle for State actions, the *Francovich* Court nonetheless made the principle dependent on the fulfilment of three conditions:

> The first of those conditions is that the result prescribed by the directive should entail the grant of rights to individuals. The second condition is that it should be possible to identify the content of those rights on the basis of the provisions of the directive. Finally, the third condition is the existence of a causal link between the breach of the State's obligation and the loss and damage suffered by the injured parties. Those conditions are sufficient to give rise to a right on the part of individuals to obtain reparation, a right founded directly on [European] law.[107]

The original liability test was thus as follows: a European act must have been intended to grant individual rights, and these rights would – despite their lack

---

[104] Joined Cases C-46/93 and C-48/93, *Brasserie du Pêcheur SA* v. *Bundesrepublik Deutschland and The Queen* v. *Secretary of State for Transport, ex parte Factortame Ltd and others*, [1996] ECR I-1029.

[105] *Ibid.*, paras. 27–9.   [106] On this point, see: Chapter 8 – Section 2 above.

[107] Joined Cases C-6/90 and C-9/90, *Francovich* (supra n. 89), paras. 40–1.

of direct effect – have to be identifiable.[108] If this was the case, and if European law was breached by a Member State not guaranteeing these rights, any loss that was caused by that breach could be claimed by the individual.[109] On its face, this test appeared to be complete and was one of *strict* liability: any breach of an identifiable European right would lead to State liability. But the Court subsequently clarified that this was *not* the case, for the *Francovich* test was to be confined to the specific context of a flagrant non-implementation of a European Directive.

Drawing on its jurisprudence on *Union* liability, the Court subsequently introduced a more restrictive principle of State liability in *Brasserie du Pêcheur*.[110] The Court here clarified that State liability was to be confined to 'sufficiently serious' breaches. To cover up the fact that it had implicitly added a 'fourth' condition to its *Francovich* test, the Court replaced the new condition with the second criterion of its 'old' test. The new liability test could thus continue to insist on three – necessary and sufficient – conditions, but now read as follows:

> [European] law confers a right to reparation where three conditions are met: the rule of law infringed must be intended to confer rights on individuals; the breach must be sufficiently serious; and there must be a direct causal link between the breach of the obligation resting on the State and the damage sustained by the injured parties.[111]

The Court justified its limitation of State liability to 'sufficiently serious' breaches by reference to the wide discretion that Member States might enjoy, especially when exercising legislative powers. The 'limited liability' of the legislature is a common constitutional tradition of the Member States and equally applies to the Union legislature. Where legislative functions were concerned, Member States 'must not be hindered by the prospect of actions for damages'.[112] The special democratic legitimacy attached to parliamentary legislation thus provided an argument against public liability for breaches of private rights, 'unless the institution concerned has manifestly and gravely

---

[108] On an analysis of this criterion, see: Dougan, 'The Vicissitudes' (supra n. 8), 238 et seq. For a case in which the European Court found that a Directive did not grant rights, see: Case C-222/02, *Paul et al.* v. *Germany*, [2004] ECR I-9425, para. 51: 'Under those conditions, and for the same reasons as those underlying the answers given above, the directives cannot be regarded as conferring on individuals, in the event that their deposits are unavailable as a result of defective supervision on the part of the competent national authorities, rights capable of giving rise to liability on the part of the State on the basis of [European] law.'

[109] For an analysis of this criterion, see: Tridimas, *The General Principles* (supra n. 33), 529–33. See particularly: Case C-319/96, *Brinkmann Tabakfabriken GmbH* v. *Skatteministeriet*, [1998] ECR I-5255.

[110] Joined Cases C-46/93 and C-48/93, *Brasserie du Pêcheur* (supra n. 104), para. 42: 'The protection of the rights which individuals derive from [European] law cannot vary depending on whether a national authority or a [Union] authority is responsible for the damage.'

[111] *Ibid.*, para. 51.   [112] *Ibid.*, para. 45.

disregarded the limits on the exercise of its powers'.[113] And in analysing whether a breach was sufficiently serious in the sense of a 'manifest[] and grave[] disregard[]', the Court would balance a number of diverse factors,[114] such as the degree of discretion enjoyed by the Member States as well as the clarity of the Union norm breached.

Unfortunately, there are very few hard and fast rules to determine when a breach is sufficiently serious. Indeed, the second criterion of the *Brasserie* test has been subject to much uncertainty. Would the manifest and grave disregard test only apply to the legislative function? The Court appears to have answered this question in *Hedley Lomas*,[115] when dealing with the failure of the national *executive* to correctly apply European law. The Court found: 'where, at the time when it committed the infringement, the Member State in question was not called upon to make any legislative choices and had only considerably reduced, or even no, discretion, the mere infringement of [European] law may be sufficient to establish the existence of a sufficiently serious breach'.[116] The less the discretion, the less limited would be the liability of a State.[117] The Court here seemed to acknowledge two alternatives within the second *Brasserie* condition – depending whether the State violated European law via its legislative or executive branch. The existence of these two alternatives would find expression in *Larsy*,[118] where the Court found:

> [A] breach of [European] law is sufficiently serious where a Member State, in the exercise of its legislative powers, has manifestly and gravely disregarded the limits on its powers and, secondly, that where, at the time when it committed the infringement, the Member State in question had only considerably reduced, or even no, discretion, the mere infringement of [European] law may be sufficient to establish the existence of a sufficiently serious breach.[119]

For an executive failure, the threshold for establishing state liability is thus much lower than the liability threshold for legislative action. While the incorrect *application* of a clear European norm by the national executive will incur

---

[113] *Ibid.* See also: Case C-392/93, *The Queen* v. *HM Treasury, ex parte British Telecommunications*, [1996] ECR I-10631, para. 42.

[114] Joined Cases C-46/93 and C-48/93, *Brasserie du Pêcheur* (supra n. 104), para. 56: 'The factors which the competent court may take into consideration include the clarity and precision of the rule breached, the measure of discretion left by that rule to the national or [Union] authorities, whether the infringement and the damage caused was intentional or involuntary, whether any error of law was excusable or inexcusable, the fact that the position taken by a [Union] institution may have contributed towards the omission, and the adoption or retention of national measures or practices contrary to [European] law.'

[115] Case C-5/94, *The Queen* v. *Ministry of Agriculture, Fisheries and Food, ex parte Hedley Lomas*, [1996] ECR I-2553.

[116] *Ibid.*, para. 28.

[117] Case C-424/97, *Haim* v. *Kassenzahnärztliche Vereinigung Nordrhein*, [2000] ECR I-5123, para. 38. See also: Case C-470/03, *A. G. M.-COS.MET et al.* v. *Suomen Valtio et al.*, [2007] ECR I-2749.

[118] Case C-118/00, *Larsy* v. *Institut national d'assurances sociales pour travailleurs indépendants*, [2001] ECR I-5063.

[119] *Ibid.*, para. 38.

automatic liability, the incorrect *implementation* of a directive by the national legislature may not.[120] Nonetheless, the European Court distinguishes the *incorrect* implementation of a directive from its *non*-implementation. The use of a stricter liability regime for legislative *non*-action makes much sense, for the failure of the State cannot be excused by reference to the *exercise* of legislative discretion. The Court consequently held that the non-implementation of a directive could *per se* constitute a sufficiently serious breach.[121] But what about the third branch of government? Was the extension of State liability to national courts 'unthinkable'?[122] And if it were not, would the Court extend its ordinary constitutional principles to judicial breaches of European law? The unthinkable thought deserves a special section.

(ii) State liability for judicial breaches of European law

Common-sense intuition identifies the 'State' with its legislative and executive branches. The 'State' generally acts through its Parliament and its administration, but there exists a third power within the State: the judiciary. The benign neglect of the 'least dangerous branch' stems from two reductionist perceptions.[123] First, the judiciary is reduced to a passive organ that merely represents the 'mouth of the law'.[124] Second, its independence from the legislature and executive is mistaken as an independence from the State. Both perceptions are misleading: for in resolving disputes between private parties and in controlling the other State branches, the judiciary exercises *State* functions. And like the national executive, the national judiciary may breach European law by misapplying it in the national legal order. This misapplication could – theoretically – constitute a violation that triggers State liability.

---

[120] Joined Cases C-283 and C-291–2/94, *Denkavit et al.* v. *Bundesamt für Finanzen*, [1996] ECR I-4845.

[121] Case C-178/94, *Dillenkofer* v. *Germany*, [1996] ECR I-4845, para. 29: 'failure to take any measure to transpose a directive in order to achieve the result it prescribes within the period laid down for that purpose constitutes per se a serious breach of [European] law and consequently gives rise to a right of reparation for individuals suffering injury if the result prescribed by the directive entails the grant to individuals of rights whose content is identifiable and a causal link exists between the breach of the State's obligation and the loss and damage suffered'. Interestingly, as Tridimas points out, this may not necessarily be the case as a Member State may believe that its existing laws already fulfil the requirements of a directive (see Tridimas, *The General Principles* (supra n. 33), 506).

[122] H. Toner, 'Thinking the Unthinkable? State Liability for Judicial Acts after Factortame (III)' [1997] 17 YEL 165.

[123] On the judiciary being the least dangerous branch, see: A. Hamilton, 'Federalist No. 78', in A. Hamilton et al., *The Federalist* (T. Ball, ed.) (Cambridge University Press, 2003), 378: 'Whoever attentively considers the different departments of power must perceive that, in a government in which they are separated from each other, the judiciary, from the nature of its functions, will always be the least dangerous to the political rights of the Constitution; because it will be least in a capacity to annoy or injure them.'

[124] Charles de Secondat, Baron de Montesquieu, *The Spirit of Laws* (translated and edited by T. Nugent, and revised by J. Prichard) (Bell, 1914); available at: www.constitution.org/cm/sol.htm), Book XI – Chapter 6.

The theoretical possibility of State liability for judicial conduct had implicitly been recognised by the *Brasserie* Court.[125] And this practical possibility was confirmed in *Köbler*.[126] Austrian legislation had granted a special length-of-service increment to professors having taught for fifteen years at Austrian universities, without taking into account any service spent at universities of other Member States. The plaintiff – a university professor having taught abroad – brought an action before the Austrian Supreme Administrative Court, claiming that his free movement rights had been violated. Despite being a court 'against whose decision there is no judicial remedy under national law', the Supreme Administrative Court did not request a preliminary ruling from the Court of Justice as it – wrongly – believed the answer to the preliminary question to be clear.[127] As a consequence, it – wrongly – decided that the Austrian norm did not violate the plaintiff's directly effective free movement rights. Not being able to appeal against the final decision, Köbler brought a new action for damages in a (lower) civil court. In the course of these civil proceedings, the national court asked the European Court of Justice whether the principle of State liability for breaches of European law extended to (wrong) judicial decisions. And the positive response was as follows:

> In the light of the essential role played by the judiciary in the protection of the rights derived by individuals from [European] rules, the full effectiveness of those rules would be called in question and the protection of those rights would be weakened if individuals were precluded from being able, under certain conditions, to obtain reparation when their rights are affected by an infringement of [European] law attributable to a decision of a court of a Member State adjudicating at last instance. It must be stressed, in that context, that a court adjudicating at last instance is by definition the last judicial body before which individuals may assert the rights conferred on them by [European] law. Since an infringement of those rights by a final decision of such a court cannot thereafter normally be corrected, individuals cannot be deprived of the possibility of rendering the State liable in order in that way to obtain legal protection of their rights.[128]

The liability for damages would thereby not undermine the independence of the judiciary. For the principle of State liability 'concerns not the personal liability of the judge but that of the State'.[129] Nor would the idea of State liability

---

[125] The Court had here clarified that the principle of State liability 'holds good for any case in which a Member State breaches [European] law, *whatever the organ of the State* whose act or omission was responsible for the breach' (Joined Cases C-46/93 and C-48/93, *Brasserie du Pêcheur* (supra n. 104), para. 32, emphasis added).

[126] Case C-224/01, *Köbler* v. *Austria*, [2003] ECR I-10239. The facts of the case were slightly more complex than presented here. For a fuller discussion of the case, see: M. Breuer, 'State Liability for Judicial Wrongs and Community Law: the case of *Gerhard Köbler v Austria*' [2004] 29 EL Rev 243.

[127] On the obligation to refer preliminary questions for courts of last resort under Article 267 (3) TFEU and the *acte clair* doctrine, see Chapter 8 – Section 4(c).

[128] Case C-224/01, *Köbler* (supra n. 126), paras. 33–4.   [129] *Ibid.*, para. 42.

for wrong judicial decisions call into question the constitutional principle of *res judicata*. After all, the *Francovich* remedy would not revise the judicial decision of a court, but provide damages for the wrong – final – judgment. The principle of State liability meant 'reparation, but not revision of the judicial decision which was responsible for the damage'.[130] But what if revision through an appeal was still possible in the national legal order? Will State liability for judicial acts of lower courts provide a complementary remedy? In line with the general character of State liability as a remedy of last resort,[131] this should be denied. The *Köbler* Court indeed appeared to confine the liability principle to national courts against whose decision there was no appeal.[132]

Having thus confirmed the possibility of *Francovich* liability for final courts,[133] would the substantive conditions for this liability differ from the ordinary criteria established in *Brasserie du Pêcheur*? The Court found that this was not the case: State liability for judicial decisions would be 'governed by the same conditions'.[134] What did this mean for the second prong of the *Brasserie* test requiring a 'sufficiently serious' breach of European law? For the Court this meant that State liability for a judicial decision would only arise 'in the *exceptional* case where the court has manifestly infringed the applicable law'.[135] And this depended on, inter alia, 'the degree of clarity and precision of the rule infringed, whether the infringement was intentional, whether the error of law was excusable or inexcusable'.[136] The Court thus aligned its test for judicial acts with the test for (discretionary) legislative acts. For unlike (non-discretionary) executive acts, liability for judicial behaviour could not simply be established by a misapplication of European law. Liability was limited to exceptional circumstances, where a *manifest* infringement of European law had occurred. In the present case, these conditions were not met. Although the Supreme Administrative Court had wrongly interpreted European law, its incorrect application of the Treaty was not 'manifest in nature' and thus did not constitute a sufficiently serious breach of European law.[137]

---

[130] *Ibid.*, para. 39.   [131] On this point, see: Conclusion below.

[132] Case C-224/01, *Köbler* (supra n. 126), para. 53 (emphasis added): 'State liability for an infringement of [European] law by a decision of a national court adjudicating *at last instance* can be incurred only in the exceptional case where the court has manifestly infringed the applicable law.'

[133] The Court confirmed Case C-224/01, *Köbler* (supra n. 126) in Case C-173/03, *Traghetti del Mediterraneo* v. *Italy*, [2006] ECR I-5177.

[134] Case C-224/01, *Köbler* (supra n. 126) para. 52. And the Court clarified in Case C-173/03, *Traghetti del Mediterraneo* that 'under no circumstances may such criteria impose requirements stricter than that of a manifest infringement of the applicable law, as set out in paragraphs 53 to 56 of the *Köbler* judgment' (*ibid.* (supra n. 133), para. 44), and that European law thus 'precludes national legislation which limits such liability solely to cases of intentional fault' (*ibid.*, para. 46). For a discussion of this decision, see: B. Beutler, 'State Liability for Breaches of Community Law by National Courts: Is the Requirement of a Manifest Infringement of the Applicable Law an Insurmountable Obstacle?' [2009] 46 CML Rev 773.

[135] Case C-224/01, *Köbler* (supra n. 126), para. 53.   [136] *Ibid.*, para. 55.   [137] *Ibid.*, paras. 120–4.

(b) Private liability: the *Courage* doctrine

The idea of 'State liability' applies – it almost goes without saying – where the *State* is liable for a breach of European law. This *vertical* dimension of the liability principle has long been established, but what about the principle's *horizontal* dimension? While the principles of equivalence and effectiveness may require that breaches of European law by private parties be adequately compensated under *national* remedial law, will there be a *European* remedy according to which individuals are liable to pay damages for the losses suffered by other private parties?[138] From the very beginning, the Union legal order envisaged that European law could directly impose obligations on individuals.[139] Did this imply that a failure to fulfil these obligations could trigger the secondary obligation to make good the damage suffered by others?

The Court has given an ambivalent answer to this question in *Courage* v. *Crehan*.[140] The case concerned European competition law, which directly imposes obligations on private parties not to conclude anti-competitive agreements under Article 101 TFEU.[141] The plaintiff had brought an action against a public house tenant for the recovery of unpaid deliveries of beer. The tenant attacked the underlying beer-supply agreement by arguing that it was void as an anti-competitive restriction, and counterclaimed damages that resulted from the illegal agreement. However, under English law a party to an illegal agreement was not entitled to claim damages; and so the Court of Appeal raised the question whether this absolute bar to compensation violated European law. The European Court considered the issue as follows:

> The full effectiveness of Article [101] of the [FEU] Treaty and, in particular, the practical effect of the prohibition laid down in Article [101(1)] would be put at risk if it were not open to any individual to claim damages for loss caused to him by a contract or by conduct liable to restrict or distort competition. Indeed, the existence of such a right strengthens the working of the [European] competition rules and discourages agreements or practices, which are frequently covert, which are liable to restrict or distort competition. From that point of view, actions for damages before the national courts can make a significant contribution to the maintenance of effective competition in the [Union]. There should not therefore

---

[138] In favour of this proposition, see: Opinion of Advocate-General van Gerven in Case C-128/92, *H. J. Banks & Co Ltd* v. *British Coal Corporation*, [1994] ECR I-1209, paras. 40–1: '[T]he question arises whether the value of the *Francovich* judgment as a precedent extends to action by an individual (or undertaking) against another individual (or undertaking) for damages in respect of breach by the latter of a Treaty provision which also has direct effect in relations between individuals . . . In my view, that question must be answered in the affirmative[.]'

[139] On this point, see: Chapter 9 – Introduction above.

[140] Case C-453/99, *Courage* v. *Crehan*, [2001] ECR I-6297.

[141] Article 101 (1) TFEU states: 'The following shall be prohibited as incompatible with the internal market: all agreements between undertakings, decisions by associations of undertakings and concerted practices which may affect trade between Member States and which have as their object or effect the prevention, restriction or distortion of competition within the internal market[.]'

be any absolute bar to such an action being brought by a party to a contract which would be held to violate the competition rules.[142]

The Court here insisted on damages for losses suffered by a breach of European competition law by a private party. But was this a *national* or a *European* remedy? The original ambivalence surrounding the principle of State liability now embraced the principle of private liability.[143] Did *Courage* represent a horizontal extension of the liability principle? On a minimal reading, the ruling could be regarded as a simple application of the principle of effectiveness.[144] After all, the last sentence of the above passage seemed to outlaw a restriction to a *national* remedy. And the Court did not place its reasoning inside the *Brasserie* test. On a maximal reading, by contrast, *Courage* could be seen as a new constitutional doctrine that establishes a European remedy for private actions violating European law.[145] The constitutional language and spirit of the ruling indeed pointed towards a new and independent source of liability.[146] And the Court did not place its reasoning into the analytical framework governing the effectiveness principle.

If we accept the wider reading of *Courage*, what conditions would the Court apply to private violations of European law? If *Courage* was a private *Francovich*, then *Manfredi* is a private *Brasserie*. In *Manfredi*,[147] Italian consumers had brought an action against their insurance companies. They claimed that those companies engaged in anti-competitive behaviour; and, as a result of this breach of the European competition rules, their car insurance was on average 20 per cent higher than the normal price would have been. Could they ask for damages? The Court repeated that 'the practical effect of Article [101 (1)] would be put at risk if it were not open to any individual to claim damages for loss caused to him by a contract or by conduct liable to restrict or distort competition'; and concluded that therefore 'any individual can claim

---

[142] Case C-453/99, *Courage* (supra n. 140), paras. 26–7.

[143] For an early expression of this ambivalence, see: O. Odudu and J. Edelman, 'Compensatory Damages for Breach of Article 81' [2002] 27 EL Rev 327 at 336: 'Though, on its face, *Courage* does not suggest that a new remedy should be created to protect [European] rights, simply that existing national remedies should not be denied, *Courage* can be read as supporting the idea that compensatory damages must generally be provided for breach of Article [101], and must be available to all those who have suffered from the breach.'

[144] Dougan, 'The Vicissitudes' (supra n. 8), 379 (pointing to the absolute bar on one party seeking compensation).

[145] N. Reich, "The "Courage" Doctrine: Encouraging or Discouraging Compensation for Antitrust Injuries?' [2005] 42 CML Rev 35 at 38; as well as A. Komninos, 'Civil Antitrust Remedies Between Community and National Law' in C. Barnard and O. Odudu (eds.), *The Outer Limits of European Law* (Hart, 2009), 363 at 383: 'The enunciation of a [European] right in damages and, by implication, of a principle of civil liability of individuals for breaches of [European] law, is a logical consequence of the Court's abundant case law on state liability, and reflects a more general principle of [European] law that ,everyone is bound to make good loss or damage arising as a result of his conduct in breach of a legal duty.'

[146] Case C-453/99, *Courage* (supra n. 140), para. 19.

[147] Joined Cases C-295/04 to C-298/04, *Manfredi et al.* v. *Lloyd Adriatico Assicurazioni et al.*, [2006] ECR I-6619.

compensation for the harm suffered where there is a causal relationship between that harm and an agreement or practice prohibited under Article [101 TFEU]'.[148] This sounded like a strict liability test, for there was no express reference to a sufficiently serious breach. Did the Court here drop the second *Brasserie* criterion, because the European competition rules were unconditional and sufficiently clear so that 'the mere infringement of [European] law may be sufficient to establish the existence of a sufficiently serious breach'?[149] The Court has remained ambivalent on this issue. Indeed, it left the detailed procedural framework to national law.[150]

The existence of a general liability test for public and private violations of European law is thus in doubt. But even if *Courage* is eventually integrated into a unified liability test, it is important to underline that the private liability doctrine should be confined to breaches of obligations directly addressed to individuals.[151] Only where European law directly regulates private party actions should the *Courage* doctrine apply. Private liability ought thus never to originate in breaches of obligations addressed to public authorities – even if they have horizontal direct effect.[152] Not horizontal direct effect, but the narrower criterion of whether a European norm addresses private party actions should constitute the external limit to private party liability. The *Courage* doctrine should thus be confined to breaches of a – very – qualified part of European law.

Conclusion

The decentralised application of European law by national authorities means that the procedural regime for the enforcement of European rights is principally left to the Member States. However, the rule of 'national procedural autonomy' is be qualified by four principles. First, national courts (and administrations) are under an obligation to interpret national law as far as possible in light of European law. But more importantly, the European legal order has asked them to provide national remedies to prevent or discourage breaches of European law. The two constitutional principles judicially developed by the Court were the equivalence

---

[148] *Ibid.*, para. 61.   [149] Case C-5/94, *Hedley Lomas* (supra n. 115), para. 28.

[150] Joined Cases C-295/04 to C-298/04, *Manfredi* (supra n. 147), para. 62: 'In the absence of [European] rules governing the matter, it is for the domestic legal system of each Member State to designate the courts and tribunals having jurisdiction and to lay down the detailed procedural rules governing actions for safeguarding rights which individuals derive directly from [European] law, provided that such rules are not less favourable than those governing similar domestic actions (principle of equivalence) and that they do not render practically impossible or excessively difficult the exercise of rights conferred by [European] law (principle of effectiveness) [.]' The national autonomy to determine the specific rules included the question whether punitive damages could be awarded (*ibid.*, para. 92).

[151] Similarly: S. Drake, 'Scope of *Courage* and the Principle of "Individual Liability" for Damages: Further Development of the Principle of Effective Judicial Protection by the Court of Justice' [2006] 31 EL Rev 841 at 861.

[152] On the distinction between horizontal direct effect and private party actions, see: Chapter 9 – Section 1(b) above.

and the effectiveness principle. The former requests national courts to extend existing national remedies to similar European actions; while the latter demands that these national remedies must not make the enforcement of European law 'excessively difficult'. Traditionally, all three limitations on the principle of national procedural autonomy did not require national authorities to create new remedies. This absolute limitation was challenged by a fourth principle – the liability principle. The *Francovich* doctrine created a European remedy in national courts. They would have to provide for damages actions that compensate for losses resulting from (sufficiently serious) breaches of European law by a Member State. *Courage* may be seen as the horizontal extension of this liability principle, but the jury on this point is still out.

What is the relationship between national remedies and the *Francovich* remedy? The Court seems to treat the latter as a remedy of last resort.[153] We saw a specific expression of this relation in the *Köbler* rule that the availability of appeal procedures precludes State liability for judicial breaches of European law. However, this will not mean that national and European remedies do not complement each other. Indeed, the specific procedural regime for the European remedy of State liability is governed by national rules.[154]

Finally, what is the relationship between *Francovich* liability and direct effect? From the early days of this remedy, the Court has been clear that an individual may have a right to damages even for directly effective norms of European law.[155] Thus, the fact that an action can be brought to force a national administration to apply European law is no barrier for the availability of this secondary remedy.[156] This makes profound sense as the application of European law may only operate prospectively, whereas the compensation for past misapplications of European law works retrospectively. However, there can – of course – be liability without direct effect; and the State obligation to make good any damage caused by a serious breach of European law will often be the only option for an individual who cannot rely on the – vertical or horizontal – direct effect of European law.

---

[153] See Case C-91/92, *Faccini Dori v. Recreb*, [1994] ECR I-3325, para. 27: 'If the result prescribed by the directive cannot be achieved by way of interpretation, it should also be borne in mind that, in terms of the judgment in Joined Cases C-6/90 and C-9/90, *Francovich and Others v. Italy* [1991] ECR I-5357, paragraph 39, [European] law requires the Member States to make good damage caused to individuals through failure to transpose a directive, provided that three conditions are fulfilled.'

[154] On the *Francovich* remedy being put into a national procedural context, see: Ward, *Judicial Review* (supra n. 35), 233–49.

[155] Joined Cases C-46/93 and C-48/93, *Brasserie du Pêcheur* (supra n. 104), paras. 20 and 22: 'The Court has consistently held that the right of individuals to rely on the directly effective provisions of the Treaty before national courts is only a minimum guarantee and is not sufficient in itself to ensure the full and complete implementation of the Treaty . . . It is all the more so in the event of an infringement of a right directly conferred by a [European] provision upon which individuals are entitled to rely before the national courts. In that event the right to reparation is the necessary corollary of the direct effect of the [European] provisions whose breach caused the damage sustained.'

[156] See also: Case C-150/99, *Sweden v. Stockhold Lindöpark*, [2001] ECR I-493, para. 35.

12

In Particular: European Human Rights

Contents

Introduction	410
1. The 'unwritten' bill of rights: human rights as 'general principles'	411
(a) The birth of European fundamental rights	412
(i) The European standard – an 'autonomous' standard	414
(ii) Limitations, and 'limitations on limitations'	418
(b) United Nations law: external limits to European human rights?	419
2. The 'written' bill of rights: the Charter of Fundamental Rights	422
(a) The Charter: structure and content	423
(i) (Hard) rights and (soft) principles	425
(ii) Limitations, and 'limitations on limitations'	426
(b) Relations with the European Treaties (and the European Convention)	427
3. The 'external' bill of rights: the European Convention of Human Rights	429
(a) The Convention standard for Union acts	430
(i) Before accession: (limited) indirect review of Union acts	431
(ii) After accession: (full) direct review of Union acts	433
(b) Union accession to the European Convention: constitutional preconditions	434
4. The 'incorporation doctrine': European rights and national law	435
(a) Incorporation and general principles: implementation and derogation	436
(b) Incorporation and the Charter of Fundamental Rights	439
(i) General rules for all Member States	439
(ii) Special rules for Poland and the United Kingdom	441
(c) Incorporation and the European Convention of Human Rights?	443
(d) *Excursus*: incorporation and individuals – human rights and private actions	444
Conclusion	445

Introduction

The protection of human rights is a central task of many modern constitutions.[1] This protective task is principally transferred to the judiciary and involves the judicial review of governmental action.[2] The protection of human rights may thereby be limited to a judicial review of the executive.[3] But in its expansive form, it extends to the review of parliamentary legislation. And where this is the case, human rights will set *substantive* limits within which democratic government must take place.[4] The European Union follows this second constitutional tradition.[5] It considers itself to be 'founded on the values of respect for human dignity, freedom, democracy, equality, the rule of law and respect for human rights'.[6] Human rights are thus given a 'foundational' status in the Union. They are – literally – 'fundamental' rights amid the rights granted by European law.

What are the sources of human rights in the Union legal order? While there was no 'bill of rights' in the original Treaties,[7] three sources for European fundamental rights were subsequently developed. The European Court first began distilling general principles protecting fundamental rights from the constitutional traditions of the Member States. This *unwritten* bill of rights was inspired and informed by a second bill of rights: the European Convention of Human Rights. This *external* bill of rights was, decades later, matched by a *written* bill of rights specifically drafted for the European Union: the Charter of Fundamental Rights. These three sources of European human rights are now expressly referred to – in reverse order – in Article 6 of the Treaty on European Union:

1. The Union recognises the rights, freedoms and principles set out in the Charter of Fundamental Rights of the European Union of 7 December 2000, as adapted at Strasbourg, on 12 December 2007, which shall have the same legal value as the Treaties ...
2. The Union shall accede to the European Convention for the Protection of Human Rights and Fundamental Freedoms. Such accession shall not affect the Union's competences as defined in the Treaties.

---

[1] On human rights as constitutional rights, see: A. Sajó, *Limiting Government* (Central European University Press, 1999), Chapter 8.

[2] See M. Cappelletti, *Judicial Review in the Contemporary World* (Bobbs-Merrill, 1971).

[3] For the classic doctrine of parliamentary sovereignty in the United Kingdom, see: A. V. Dicey, *Introduction to the Study of the Law of the Constitution* (Liberty Fund, 1982).

[4] On the idea of human rights as 'outside' majoritarian (democratic) politics, see: Sajó, *Limiting Government* (supra n. 1), Chapter 2, esp. 57 et seq.

[5] On this point, see: Chapter 8 – Section 1 above; as well as: Case 294/83, *Parti écologiste 'Les Verts'* v. *European Parliament*, [1986] ECR 1339, para. 23: 'a [Union] based on the rule of law, inasmuch as neither its Member States nor its institutions can avoid a review of the question whether the measures adopted by them are in conformity with the basic constitutional charter, the Treaty'.

[6] Article 2 (1) TEU.

[7] P. Pescatore, 'Les Droits de l'Homme et l'Integration Européenne' [1968] 4 *Cahiers du Droit Européen* 629.

3. Fundamental rights, as guaranteed by the European Convention for the Protection of Human Rights and Fundamental Freedoms and as they result from the constitutional traditions common to the Member States, shall constitute general principles of the Union's law.

What is the nature and effect of each source of fundamental rights? This chapter investigates each of the Union's three bills of rights and the constitutional relations between them. Section 1 starts with the discovery of an 'unwritten' bill of rights in the form of general principles of European law. Section 2 analyses the Union's own 'written' bill of rights in the form of its Charter of Fundamental Rights. Section 3 investigates the relationship between the Union and the 'external' bill of rights in the form of the European Convention of Human Rights. While the co-existence of an external and internal human rights bill is not unusual,[8] the presence of two *internal* human rights regimes is a special feature of the Union legal order. But not only is the relationship between the two internal bills complex; they both enjoy a – highly – ambivalent relationship with the European Convention's external standard. Finally, what is the relationship between all three bills of rights and the Member States? Section 4 explores the last question. It will be seen that *each* of the three Union bills of rights will, at least to some extent, also apply to the Member States.

1. The 'unwritten' bill of rights: human rights as 'general principles'

Neither the 1952 Paris Treaty nor the 1957 Rome Treaty contained any express reference to human rights.[9] The silence of the former could be explained by its limited scope.[10] The silence of the latter, by contrast, could have its origin in the cautious climate following the failure of the 'European Political Community'.[11]

---

[8] K. Lenaerts and E. de Smijter, 'A "Bill of Rights" for the European Union' [2001] 38 CML Rev 273 at 292: 'It is not inconsistent for a – national or supranational – legal order to have its own catalogue of fundamental rights and at the same time to adhere to an international standard of protection of fundamental rights like the ECHR. As a matter of fact, all contracting parties to the ECHR have their own national catalogue of fundamental rights.'

[9] For speculations on the historical reasons for this absence, see: P. Pescatore, 'The Context and Significance of Fundamental Rights in the Law of the European Communities' [1981] 2 *Human Rights Journal*, 295; as well as: M. A. Dauses, 'The Protection of Fundamental Rights in the Community Legal Order' [1985] 10 EL Rev 399. For a new look at the historical material, see also: G. de Búrca, 'The Evolution of EU Human Rights Law' in P. Craig and G. de Búrca (eds.), *The Evolution of EU Law* (Oxford University Press, 2011), 465.

[10] J. Weiler, 'Eurocracy and Distrust: Some Questions Concerning the Role of the European Court of Justice in the Protection of Fundamental Human Rights within the Legal Order of the European Communities' [1986] 61 *Washington Law Review* 1103 at 1011 et seq.

[11] On the European Political Community, see: Chapter 1 – Section 1(b) above. This grand project had asked the (proposed) Community 'to contribute towards the protection of human rights and fundamental freedoms in the Member States' (Article 2), and would have integrated the European Convention on Human Rights into the Community legal order (Article 3). On the European Political Community, see: A. H. Robertson, 'The European Political Community' [1952] 29 BYIL 383.

With political union having failed, the 'grander' project of a human rights bill was replaced by the 'smaller' project of economic integration.[12]

Be that as it may, the European Court would – within the first two decades – develop an (unwritten) bill of rights for the European Union.[13] These fundamental rights would be *European* rights, that is: rights that were *independent* from national constitutions. The discovery of human rights as general principles of European law will be discussed first. Thereafter, this section discusses possible structural limits to European human rights in the form of international obligations flowing from the United Nations Charter.

(a) The birth of European fundamental rights

The birth of European fundamental rights did not happen overnight. The Court had been invited – as long ago as 1958 – to review the constitutionality of a European act in light of fundamental rights. In *Stork*,[14] the applicant had challenged a European decision on the ground that the Commission had infringed *German* fundamental rights. In the absence of a European bill of rights, this claim drew on the so-called 'mortgage theory'. According to this theory, the powers conferred on the European Union were tied to a human rights 'mortgage'. *National* fundamental rights would bind the *European* Union, since the Member States could not have created an organisation with more powers than themselves.[15] This argument was – correctly[16] – rejected by the Court. The task of the European institutions was to apply European laws 'without regard for their validity under national law'.[17] National fundamental rights could thus be *no direct* source of European human rights.

---

[12] Pescatore, 'Context and Significance' (supra n. 9), 296.

[13] The judicial motifs of the European Court in developing human rights are controversially discussed in the literature. It seems accepted that the Court discovered human rights as general principles – at least partly – in defence to national Supreme Courts challenging the absolute supremacy of European law (see Chapter 10 – Section 2 above). But apart from this 'defensive' use, the Court has been accused of an 'offensive use' in the sense of 'employ[ing] fundamental rights instrumentally' by 'clearly subordinat[ing] human rights to the end of closer economic integration in the [Union]' (see J. Coppel and A. O'Neill, 'The European Court of Justice: Taking Rights Seriously?' [1992] 29 CML Rev 669, 670 and 692). This 'offensive' thesis has – rightly – been refuted (see J. H. H. Weiler and N. Lockhart, '"Taking Rights Seriously" Seriously: the European Court and its Fundamental Rights Jurisprudence' [1995] 32 CML Rev 51 (Part I) and 579 (Part II)).

[14] Case 1/58, *Stork & Cie* v. *High Authority of the European Coal and Steel Community*, [1958] ECR (English Special Edition) 17.

[15] As the Latin legal proverb makes clear: 'Nemo dat quod non habet'.

[16] For a criticism of the 'mortgage theory', see: H. G. Schermers, 'The European Communities Bound by Fundamental Rights' [1990] 27 CML Rev 249, 251; as well as: R. Schütze, 'EC Law and International Agreements of the Member States – An Ambivalent Relationship?' [2006–07] 9 *Cambridge Yearbook of European Legal Studies*, 387 at 399–402.

[17] Case 1/58 *Stork* v. *High Authority* (supra n. 14), 26: 'Under Article 8 of the [ECSC] Treaty the [Commission] is only required to apply Community law. It is not competent to apply the national law of the Member States. Similarly, under Article 31 the Court is only required to

This position of the European Union towards *national* fundamental rights never changed. However, the Court's view evolved with regard to the existence of implied *European* fundamental rights. Having originally found that European law did 'not contain any general principle, *express or otherwise*, guaranteeing the maintenance of vested rights',[18] the Court subsequently discovered 'fundamental human rights enshrined in the general principles of [European] law'.[19]

This new position was spelled out in *Internationale Handelsgesellschaft*.[20] The Court here – again – rejected the applicability of national fundamental rights to European law. But the judgment now confirmed the existence of an 'analogous guarantee inherent in [European] law'.[21] Accordingly, 'respect for fundamental rights forms an integral part of the general principles of law protected by the Court of Justice'.[22] Whence did the Court derive these fundamental rights? The famous answer was that the Union's (unwritten) bill of rights would be '*inspired* by the constitutional traditions *common* to the Member States'.[23] While thus not a direct source, national constitutional rights constituted an *indirect* source for the Union's fundamental rights.

What was the nature of this indirect relationship between national rights and European rights? How would the former influence the latter? A constitutional clarification was offered in *Nold*.[24] Drawing on its previous jurisprudence, the Court held:

> [F]undamental rights form an integral part of the general principles of law, the observance of which it ensures. In safeguarding these rights, the Court is bound to

---

ensure that in the interpretation and application of the Treaty, and of rules laid down for implementation thereof, the law is observed. It is not normally required to rule on provisions of national law. Consequently, the [Commission] is not empowered to examine a ground of complaint which maintains that, when it adopted its decision, it infringed principles of German constitutional law (in particular Articles 2 and 12 of the Basic Law).' And in Joined Cases 36, 37, 38/59 and 40/59, *Geitling Ruhrkohlen-Verkaufsgesellschaft mbH, Mausegatt Ruhrkohlen-Verkaufsgesellschaft mbH and I. Nold KG* v. *High Authority of the European Coal and Steel Community*, [1959] ECR (English Special Edition) 423 at 438, the Court held: 'The applicant supports its arguments with German case-law on the interpretation of Article 14 of the Basic Law of the Federal Republic, which guarantees private property. It is not for the Court, whose function is to judge the legality of decisions adopted by the [Commission] and, as obviously follows, those adopted in the present case under Article 65 of the [ECSC] Treaty, to ensure that rules of internal law, even constitutional rules, enforced in one or other of the Member States are respected. Therefore the Court may neither interpret nor apply Article 14 of the German Basic Law in examining the legality of a decision of the [Commission].'

[18] *Ibid.*, 439 (emphasis added).

[19] Case 29/69, *Stauder* v. *City of Ulm*, [1969] ECR 419, para. 7. This approach had been suggested by Advocate-General Lagrange in Joined Cases 36, 37, 38/59 and 40/59, *Geitling* (supra n. 17), 450 (emphasis added): '[While] it is not for the Court, whose function it is to judge the legality of the authorisations, to apply, *or at least to do so directly* rules of national law, even constitutional rules, in force in one or other of the Member States. It may allow itself to be influenced by such rules in so far as, where appropriate, it may see in them the expression of a general principle of law which may be taken into consideration in applying the Treaty.'

[20] Case 11/70, *Internationale Handelsgesellschaft mbH* v. *Einfuhr- und Vorratsstelle für Getreide und Futtermittel*, [1979] ECR 1125.

[21] *Ibid.*, para. 4.   [22] *Ibid.*   [23] *Ibid.* (emphasis added).

[24] Case 4/73, *Nold* v. *Commission*, [1974] ECR 491.

draw *inspiration* from constitutional traditions common to the Member States, and it cannot therefore uphold measures which are incompatible with fundamental rights recognised and protected by the constitutions of those States. Similarly, international treaties for the protection of human rights on which the Member States have collaborated or of which they are signatories, can supply *guidelines* which should be followed within the framework of [European] law.[25]

In searching for fundamental rights inside the general principles of European law, the Court would thus draw 'inspiration' from the common constitutional traditions of the Member States. One – ingenious – way of identifying an 'agreement' between the various national constitutional traditions was to use international *agreements* of the Member States. One such international agreement was the European Convention of Human Rights. Having been ratified by all Member States and dealing specially with human rights,[26] the Convention would soon assume a 'particular significance' in identifying fundamental rights for the European Union.[27] And yet, none of this conclusively characterised the legal relationship between European human rights, national human rights and the European Convention of Human Rights.

Let us therefore look at the question of the Union human rights standard first, before analysing the constitutional doctrines governing limits to European human rights.

(i) The European standard – an 'autonomous' standard

Human rights express, together with the institutional structures of a polity, the fundamental values of a society. Each society may wish to protect distinct values and give them a distinct level of protection.[28] Not all societies may thus choose

---

[25] *Ibid.*, para. 13 (emphasis added).

[26] When the EC Treaty entered into force on 1 January 1958, five of its Member States were already parties to the European Convention for the Protection of Human Rights and Fundamental Freedoms, signed in Rome on 4 November 1950. Ever since France joined the Convention system in 1974, all EU Member States have also been members of the European Convention legal order. For an early reference to the Convention in the jurisprudence of the Court, see: Case 36/75, *Rutili* v. *Ministre de l'intérieur*, [1975] ECR 1219, para. 32.

[27] See Joined Cases 46/87 and 227/88, *Höchst* v. *Commission*, [1989] ECR 2859, para.13: 'The Court has consistently held that fundamental rights are an integral part of the general principles of law the observance of which the Court ensures, in accordance with constitutional traditions common to the Member States, and the international treaties on which the Member States have collaborated or of which they are signatories. The European Convention for the Protection of Human Rights and Fundamental Freedoms of 4 November 1950 (hereinafter referred to as "the European Convention on Human Rights") is of particular significance in that regard.'

[28] 'Constitutions are not mere copies of a universalist ideal, they also reflect the idiosyncratic choices and preferences of the constituents and are the highest legal expression of the country's value system.' See B. de Witte, 'Community Law and National Constitutional Values' [1991/2] 2 *Legal Issues of Economic Integration* 1 at 7.

to protect a constitutional 'right to work',[29] while most liberal societies will protect 'liberty'; yet, the level at which liberty is protected might vary.[30]

Which fundamental rights exist in the European Union, and what is their level of protection? From the very beginning, the Court of Justice was not completely free to invent an unwritten bill of rights. Instead, and in the words of the famous *Nold* passage, the Court was '*bound to* draw inspiration from constitutional traditions common to the Member States'.[31] But how binding would that inspiration be? Could the Court discover human rights that not all Member States recognise as a national human right? And would the Court consider itself under an obligation to use a particular standard for a human right, where a right's 'scope and the criteria for applying it vary'?[32]

The relationship between the European and the various national standards is not an easy one. Would the obligation to draw inspiration from the constitutional traditions *common* to the States imply a common *minimum* standard? Serious practical problems follow from this view. For if the European Union consistently adopted the lowest common denominator to assess the legality of its acts, it would run the risk of undermining its legitimacy. This would inevitably lead to charges that the European Court refuses to take human rights seriously. Should the Union thus favour the *maximum* standard among the Member States,[33] as 'the most liberal interpretation must prevail'?[34] This time, there are serious theoretical problems with this view. For the maximalist approach assumes that courts always balance private rights against public interests. But this is not necessarily the case;[35] and, in any event, the maximum standard is subject to a communitarian critique.[36] Finally, *both* the minimalist and the maximalist approach suffer from a fatal flaw: they subject the Union

[29] Article 4 of the Italian Constitution states: 'The Republic recognises the right of all citizens to work and promotes those conditions which render this right effective.'
[30] To illustrate this point with a famous joke: 'In Germany everything is forbidden, unless something is specifically allowed, whereas in Britain everything which is not specifically forbidden, is allowed.' (The joke goes on to claim that: 'In France everything is allowed, even if it is forbidden; and in Italy everything is allowed, especially when it is forbidden.')
[31] Case 4/73, *Nold* (supra n. 25), para.13 (emphasis added).
[32] Case 155/79, *AM & S Europe Limited* v. *Commission*, [1982] ECR 1575, para.19.
[33] In favour of a maximalist approach, see: L. Besselink, 'Entrapped by the Maximum Standard: on Fundamental Rights, Pluralism and Subsidiarity in the European Union' [1998] 35 CML Rev 629.
[34] This 'Dworkinian' language comes from Case 29/69, *Stauder* (supra n. 19), para. 4.
[35] The Court of Justice was faced with such a right-right conflict in Case C-159/90, *Society for the Protection of Unborn Children Ireland Ltd* v. *Stephen Grogan and others*, [1991] ECR I-4685, but (in)famously refused to decide the case for lack of jurisdiction.
[36] J. Weiler, 'Fundamental Rights and Fundamental Boundaries: On Standards and Values in the Protection of Human Rights', in N. Neuwahl and A. Rosas (eds.), *The European Union and Human Rights* (Brill, 1995), 51 at 61: 'If the ECJ were to adopt a maximalist approach this would simply mean that for the [Union] in each and every area the balance would be most restrictive on the public and general interest. A maximalist approach to human rights would result in a minimalist approach to [Union] government.'

legal order 'to the constitutional dictate of individual Member States',[37] and the Court has consequently rejected both approaches.[38]

What about the European Convention of Human Rights (ECHR) as a Union standard? The Convention has indeed developed into a standard that is (partly) independent from what the Court sees as the constitutional traditions of the Member States.[39] But what was the status of the Convention in the Union legal order? The relationship between the Union and the European Convention has remained ambivalent. The Court of Justice has not applied the 'succession theory' to the ECHR – and for good reasons.[40] Acceptance of the theory would have implied that the Union had 'replaced' the Member States through an exclusive transfer of power with regard to human rights. And in implicitly rejecting the 'succession theory',[41] the European Court has never considered itself materially bound by the interpretation given to the Convention by the European Court of Human Rights. And this interpretative freedom has created the possibility of a distinct *Union* standard.[42]

Have subsequent Treaty amendments transformed the indirect relationship between Union fundamental rights and the ECHR into a direct relationship? The argument had been made following the Maastricht Treaty. The (old) Article 6 (2) EU expressly called on the Union to respect fundamental rights 'as guaranteed by the European Convention for the Protection of Human Rights and Fundamental Freedoms'. Some commentators consequently began to argue that '[t]he ECHR is now *formally* integrated into EC law'.[43] More moderate voices limited the binding effect to its material de facto dimension.[44]

---

[37] *Ibid.*, 59.

[38] For an early (implicit) rejection of the minimalist approach, see: Case 44/79, *Hauer* v. *Land Rheinland-Pfalz*, [1979] ECR 3727, para. 32 (emphasis added) – suggesting that a fundamental right only needs to be protected in '*several* Member States'.

[39] For example, in Case 44/79, *Hauer* (supra n. 38), the Court began by looking at the ECHR (paras. 17–19) and only after a finding that the Convention would not generate a sufficiently precise standard would the Court turn to the 'constitutional rules and practices of the nine Member States' (paras. 20–1).

[40] On the succession theory, see: Chapter 6 – Section 3(d) above.

[41] See Case 4/73, *Nold* (supra n. 25). An early commentator – referring to *Nold* – thus argued: 'The Court could have followed the precedent of the *Third International Fruit Case* in which it decided that the [EU] was bound by the GATT. It should then have held that the [Union was] bound by the European Convention on Human Rights now that all its Member States were parties to it'. See: H. G. Schermers, 'Community Law and International Law' [1975] 12 CML Rev 77, 83.

[42] Yet it equally entailed the danger of diverging interpretations of the European Convention in Strasbourg and Luxembourg, see in particular: Joined Cases 46/87 and 227/88, *Höchst AG* v. *Commission*, [1989] ECR 2859. For an excellent analysis see: R. Lawson, 'Confusion and Conflict? Diverging Interpretations of the European Convention on Human Rights in Strasbourg and Luxembourg' in R. Lawson and M. de Blois (eds.), *The Dynamics of the Protection of Human Rights in Europe* (Martinus Nijhoff, 1994) vol. III, 219 esp. 234–50.

[43] L. B. Krogsgaard, 'Fundamental Rights in the European Community after Maastricht' [1993] 19 Legal Issues of Economic Integration 99, 108 (emphasis added).

[44] F. G. Jacobs, 'European Community Law and the European Convention on Human Rights' in D. Curtin and T. Heukels (eds.), *Institutional Dynamics of European Integration* (Martinus

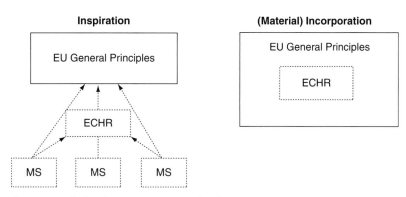

Figure 24 Inspiration Theory versus Incorporation Theory

However, neither view was accepted by the Court;[45] and – again – for good reasons.[46] Yet the Lisbon amendments might have changed this overnight. Today, there are strong textual reasons for claiming that the European Convention is *materially* binding on the Union. For according to the (new) Article 6(3) TEU, fundamental rights as guaranteed by the Convention 'shall constitute general principles of the Union's law'. Will this formulation not mean that all Convention rights *are* general principles of Union law? If so, the Convention standard would henceforth provide a direct standard for the Union. But if this route were chosen, the Convention standard would – presumably – only provide a *minimum* standard for the Union's general principles.[47]

Nijhoff, 1994), vol. II, 561 at 563 (emphasis added): 'As a result of the development of the case-law, now confirmed by the Single European Act and the Treaty on European Union, the [Union] can be said to be subject *in effect* to, if not bound formally by, the European Convention on Human Rights.'

[45] This position has been confirmed by the ECJ in Case C–112/00, *Schmidberger, Internationale Transporte und Planzüge* v. *Austria* [2003] ECR I–5659, paras. 71–2 (emphasis added): '[a]ccording to settled case-law, fundamental rights form an integral part of the general principles of law, the observance of which the Court ensures. For that purpose, the Court draws inspiration from the constitutional traditions common to the Member States and from the guidelines supplied by international treaties for the protection of human rights on which the Member States have collaborated or to which they are signatories. The ECHR has special significance in that respect ... *The principles established by that case-law were reaffirmed* in the preamble to the Single European Act and subsequently in [ex-]Article 6(2) of the [old] Treaty on European Union.'

[46] It had been argued that ex-Article 6 (2) (old) EU incorporated the ECHR by express reference (see R. Uerpmann-Wittzack, 'The Constitutional Role of Multilateral Treaty Systems' in A. von Bogdandy and J. Bast (eds.), *Principles of European Constitutional Law* (Hart, 2006) 145 at 172–4). However, the extension of the *Fediol* doctrine – developed in the *Community* legal order for *Community* agreements – seems hardly convincing. In the absence of a stronger reason, the better view therefore held that (old) Article 6(2) EU had not changed the constitutional status quo (see N. Neuwahl, 'The Treaty on European Union: A Step Forward in the Protection of Human Rights?', in Neuwahl and Rosas, *The European Union* (supra n. 36), 1 at 14).

[47] This is the solution which appears to have been chosen for the Charter, see: Section 2 below.

In conclusion, the Union standard for the protection of fundamental rights is an *autonomous* standard. While drawing inspiration from the constitutional traditions common to the Member States and the European Convention of Human Rights, the Court of Justice has – so far – not considered itself directly bound by a particular national or international standard. The Court has thus been free to distil and protect what it sees as the shared values among the majority of people(s) within the Union and thereby assisted – dialectically – in the establishment of a shared identity for the people(s) of Europe.[48]

(ii) Limitations, and 'limitations on limitations'

Within the European philosophical tradition, certain rights are absolute rights. They cannot – under any circumstances – be legitimately limited.[49] However, with the exception of the most fundamental of fundamental rights, human rights are *relative* rights that may be limited in accordance with the public interest. Private property may thus be taxed and individual freedom be restricted – *if* such actions are justified by the common good.

Nonetheless, liberal societies would cease to be liberal if they permitted unlimited limitations to human rights in pursuit of the public interest. Many legal orders consequently recognise limitations on public interest limitations. These 'limitations on limitations' to fundamental rights can be relative or absolute in nature. According to the principle of proportionality, each restriction of a fundamental right must be 'proportionate' in relation to the public interest pursued.[50] The principle of proportionality is thus a *relative* principle. It balances interests: the greater the public interest protected, the greater the right restrictions permitted. And in order to limit this relativist logic, a second principle may come into play. According to the 'essential core' doctrine,[51] any limitation of human rights – even proportionate ones – must never undermine the 'very substance' of a fundamental right. This sets an *absolute* limit to all governmental power by identifying an 'untouchable' core within a right.

Has the European legal order recognised limits to human rights? From the very beginning, the Court clarified that human rights are 'far from constituting unfettered prerogatives',[52] and that they may thus be subject 'to limitations laid down in accordance with the public interest'.[53] Yet the Court equally recognised 'limitations on limitations'. Yet while the principle of proportionality is

---

[48] T. Tridimas, 'Judicial Federalism and the European Court of Justice' in J. Fedtke and B. S. Markesinis (eds.), *Patterns of Federalism and Regionalism: Lessons for the UK* (Hart, 2006), 149 at 150 – referring to the contribution of the judicial process 'to the emergence of a European *demos*'.

[49] The European Court of Justice followed this tradition and recognised the existence of absolute rights in Case C-112/00, *Schmidberger* (supra n. 45), para. 80: 'the right to life or the prohibition of torture and inhuman or degrading treatment or punishment, which admit of no restriction'.

[50] Case 44/79, *Hauer* (supra n. 38), para. 23. On the proportionality principle in the Union legal order, see: Chapter 8 – Section 1(b)(ii) above.

[51] For the German constitutional order, see: Article 19 (2) German Constitution: 'The essence of a basic right must never be violated.'

[52] Case 4/73, *Nold* v. *Commission* (supra n. 24), para. 14.   [53] *Ibid.*

almost omnipresent in the jurisprudence of the Court,[54] the existence of an 'essential core' doctrine is still unclear. True, the Court has used formulations that come – very – close to the doctrine,[55] but its relationship to the proportionality principle is ambivalent.[56] The Court may, however, have recently confirmed the existence of the doctrine by recognising an 'untouchable' core of European citizenship rights in *Zambrano*.[57] Two Columbian parents had challenged the rejection of their Belgian residency permits on the ground that their children had been born in Belgium and thereby assumed Belgian and – thus – European citizenship.[58] The Court held that even if the Belgian measures were proportionate as such, they would 'have the effect of depriving citizens of the Union of the genuine enjoyment of the *substance of the rights* conferred by virtue of their status of citizens of the Union'.[59] The recognition of an untouchable 'substance' of a right indeed functions like the essential core doctrine.

(b) United Nations law: external limits to European human rights?

The European legal order is a constitutional order based on the rule of law.[60] This implies that an individual, where legitimately concerned,[61] must be able to challenge the legality of a European act on the basis that his human rights have been violated. Should there be exceptions to this constitutional rule? This

---

[54] On the proportionality principle, see: T. Tridimas, *The General Principles of EU Law* (Oxford University Press, 2007), Chapters 3–5.

[55] The European Courts appear to implicitly accept the doctrine; see: Case 4/73, *Nold* (supra n. 24), 14: 'Within the [Union] legal order it likewise seems legitimate that these rights should, of necessity, be subject to certain limits justified by the overall objectives pursued by the [Union], on condition that the substance of these rights is left untouched'; as well as: Case 5/88, *Wachauf* v. *Bundesamt für Ernährung und Forstwirtschaft*, [1989] ECR 2609, para. 18 : '[R]estrictions may be imposed on the exercise of those rights, in particular in the context of a common organisation of a market, provided that those restrictions in fact correspond to objectives of general interest pursued by the [Union] and do not constitute, with regard to the aim pursued, a disproportionate and intolerable interference, impairing the very substance of those rights.'

[56] This point is made by P. Craig, *The Lisbon Treaty: Law, Politics, and Treaty Reform* (Oxford University Press, 2010), 224, who argues that the Court often merges the doctrine of proportionality and the 'essential core' doctrine.

[57] Case C-34/09, *Zambrano* v. *Office national de l'emploi*, (nyr). Admittedly, there are many questions that this – excessively – short case raises (see: 'Editorial: Seven Questions for Seven Paragraphs' [2011] EL Rev 161). For a first analysis of this case, see: K. Hailbronner and D. Thym, 'Case Comment' [2011] 48 CML Rev 1253.

[58] According to Article 20 (1) TFEU. 'Citizenship of the Union is hereby established. Every person holding the nationality of a Member State shall be a citizen of the Union. Citizenship of the Union shall be additional to and not replace national citizenship.'

[59] Case C-34/09, *Zambrano* (supra n. 57), para. 42 (emphasis added); and see also para. 44: 'In those circumstances, those citizens of the Union would, as a result, be unable to exercise the substance of the rights conferred on them by virtue of their status as citizens of the Union.'

[60] Case 294/83, *Parti Écologiste 'Les Verts'* v. *European Parliament*, [1986] ECR 1339.

[61] On the judicial standing of private parties in the Union legal order, see: Chapter 8 – Section 1(c). Some have argued in favour of the creation of an 'Individual Human Rights Complaint Procedure' in addition to the classic judicial review procedure, see: B. de Witte, 'The Past and Future Role of the European Court of Justice in the Protection of Human Rights' in P. Alston (ed.), *The EU and Human Rights* (Oxford University Press, 1999), 859 at 893 et seq.

question is controversially debated in comparative constitutionalism.[62] And it has lately received much attention in a special form: will *European* fundamental rights be limited by *international* obligations flowing from the United Nations Charter?

The classic answer to this question was offered by *Bosphorus*.[63] The case dealt with a European regulation implementing the United Nations embargo against the Federal Republic of Yugoslavia.[64] Protesting that its fundamental right to property was violated, the plaintiff challenged the European legislation. And the Court had no qualms in judicially reviewing the European legislation – even if a lower review standard was applied.[65] The constitutional message behind the classic approach was clear: where the Member States decided to fulfil their international obligations under the United Nations *qua* European law, they would have to comply with the constitutional principles of the Union legal order and, in particular: European human rights.

This classic approach was challenged by the General Court in *Kadi*.[66] The applicant was a presumed Taliban terrorist, whose financial assets had been frozen as a result of European legislation that reproduced United Nations Security Council Resolutions.[67] Kadi claimed that his fundamental rights of due process and property had been violated. The Union organs intervened in the proceedings and argued – to the surprise of many – that 'the Charter of the United Nations prevail[s] over every other obligation of international, [European] or domestic law' to the effect that European human rights should

---

[62] For discussion of the idea of an 'emergency constitution' in a comparative constitutional perspective, see: C. L. Rossiter, *Constitutional Dictatorship: Crisis Government in the Modern Democracies* (Harcourt, Brace & World, 1963).

[63] Case C-84/95, *Bosphorus Hava Yollari Turizm ve Ticaret AS* v. *Minister for Transport, Energy and Communications and others*, [1996] ECR I-3953.

[64] Council Regulation (EEC) No. 990/93 of 26 April 1993 concerning trade between the European Economic Community and the Federal Republic of Yugoslavia (Serbia and Montenegro) (OJ 1993 L102, 14) was based on UN Security Council Resolution 820 (1993).

[65] For a critique of the standard of review, see I. Canor, '"Can Two Walk Together, Except They Be Agreed?" The Relationship between International Law and European Law: the Incorporation of United Nations Sanctions against Yugoslavia into European Community Law Through the Perspective of the European Court of Justice' [1998] 35 CML Rev 137–87 at 162: 'However, it can be sensed from the decision of the Court that it was so "impressed" by the importance of the aims of the Regulation, that it was prepared to justify *any* negative consequences . . . This attitude implies that no serious balancing test was carried out by the Court, and that it expressed an almost total indifference to the way the [Union] organs exercised their discretion in the political – foreign affairs – sphere when implementing the Resolution. It should not be the case that by invoking foreign affairs needs, the Council and the Commission is given *carte blanche* to infringe individual rights.'

[66] Case T-315/01, *Kadi* v. *Council and Commission*, [2005] ECR II-3649.

[67] The legal challenge principally concerned Council Regulation (EC) 881/2002 imposing certain specific restrictive measures directed against certain persons and entities associated with Usama bin Laden, the Al-Qaeda network and the Taliban, and repealing Regulation 467/2001, [2002] OJ L139/9. The Regulation aimed to implement UN Security Council Resolution 1390 (2002) laying down the measures to be directed against Usama bin Laden, members of the Al-Qaeda network and the Taliban and other associated individuals, groups, undertakings and entities.

be inoperative.[68] To the even greater surprise – if not shock – of European constitutional scholars,[69] the General Court accepted this argument. How did the Court come to this conclusion? It had recourse to a version of the 'succession doctrine',[70] according to which the Union may be bound by the international obligations of its Member States.[71] While this conclusion was in itself highly controversial,[72] the dangerous part of the judgment related to the consequences of that conclusion. For the General Court recognised 'structural limits, imposed by general international law' on the judicial review powers of the European Court.[73] In the words of the Court:

> Any review of the internal lawfulness of the contested regulation, especially having regard to the provisions or general principles of [European] law relating to the protection of fundamental rights, would therefore imply that the Court is to consider, indirectly, the lawfulness of those [United Nations] resolutions. In that hypothetical situation, in fact, the origin of the illegality alleged by the applicant would have to be sought, not in the adoption of the contested regulation but in the resolutions of the Security Council which imposed the sanctions. In particular, if the Court were to annul the contested regulation, as the applicant claims it should, although that regulation seems to be imposed by international law, on the ground that that act infringes his fundamental rights which are protected by the [Union] legal order, such annulment would indirectly mean that the resolutions of the Security Council concerned themselves infringe those fundamental rights.[74]

The General Court thus declined jurisdiction to directly review European legislation *because it would entail an indirect review of the United Nations resolutions*. The justification for this self-abdication was that United Nations law was binding on all Union institutions, including the European Courts.

From a constitutional perspective, this reasoning was prisoner to a number of serious mistakes.[75] And in its appeal judgment,[76] the Court of Justice remedied

---

[68] Case T-315/01, *Kadi* (supra n. 66), paras. 156 and 177.

[69] P. Eeckhout, *Does Europe's Constitution Stop at the Water's Edge: Law and Policy in the EU's External Relations* (Europa Law Publishing, 2005); as well as: R. Schütze, 'On "Middle Ground": The European Community and Public International Law', EUI Working Paper 2007/13.

[70] Case T-315/01, *Kadi* (supra n. 66), paras. 193 et seq.

[71] On the doctrine, see: Chapter 6 – Section 3(d) above.

[72] R. Schütze, 'The "Succession Doctrine" and the European Union' in A. Arnull *et al.* (eds.), *A Constitutional Order of States: Essays in Honour of Alan Dashwood* (Hart, 2011), 459.

[73] Case T-315/01, *Kadi* (supra n. 66), para. 212.   [74] *Ibid.*, paras. 215–16 (references omitted).

[75] First, even if one assumes that the Union succeeded the Member States and was thus bound by United Nations law, the hierarchical status of international agreements is *below* the European Treaties. It would thus be European human rights that limit international agreements – not the other way around. The Court's position was equally based on a second mistake: the General Court believed the United Nations Charter prevails over every international and domestic obligation (*ibid.*, para. 181). But this is simply wrong with regard to the 'domestic law' part. The United Nations has never claimed 'supremacy' within domestic legal orders, and after the constitutionalisation of the European Union legal order, the latter now constitutes such a 'domestic' legal order vis-à-vis international law.

[76] Case C-402/05P, *Kadi and Al Barakaat International Foundation* v. *Council and Commission*, [2008] ECR I-6351.

these constitutional blunders and safely returned to the traditional *Bosphorus* approach. The Court held:

> [T]he obligations imposed by an international agreement cannot have the effect of prejudicing the constitutional principles of the [European Treaties], which include the principle that all [Union] acts must respect fundamental rights, that respect constituting a condition of their lawfulness which it is for the Court to review in the framework of the complete system of legal remedies established by the Treat[ies].[77]

The United Nations Charter, while having 'special importance' within the European legal order,[78] would – in this respect – not be different from other international agreements.[79] Like 'ordinary' international agreements, the United Nations Charter might – if materially binding –have primacy over European legislation but '[t]hat primacy at the level of [European] law would not, however, extend to primary law, in particular to the general principles of which fundamental rights form part'.[80] European human rights would thus *not* find an external structural limit in the international obligations stemming from the United Nations.[81] The Union was firmly based on the rule of law, and this meant that all European legislation – regardless of its 'domestic' or international origin – would be limited by the respect for fundamental human rights.[82]

2. The 'written' bill of rights: the Charter of Fundamental Rights

The desire for a *written* bill of rights for the European Union first expressed itself in arguments favouring accession to the European Convention of Human Rights.[83] Yet an alternative strategy became prominent in the late twentieth century: the Union's own bill of rights. The initiative for a 'Charter of Fundamental Rights' came from the European Council, which transferred the drafting mandate to a 'European Convention'.[84] The idea behind an internal codification was to strengthen the protection of fundamental rights in Europe

---

[77] *Ibid.*, para. 285.   [78] *Ibid.*, para. 294.

[79] *Ibid.*, para. 300: '[I]mmunity from jurisdiction for a [Union] measure like the contested regulation, as a corollary of the principle of the primacy at the level of international law of obligations under the Charter of the United Nations, especially those relating to the implementation of resolutions of the Security Council adopted under Chapter VII of the Charter, cannot find a basis in the [European Treaties].'

[80] *Ibid.*, para. 308.   [81] *Ibid.*, para. 327.

[82] The Court in fact identified a breach of the right of defence, especially the right to be heard (*ibid.*, para. 353), as well as an unjustified violation of the right to property (*ibid.*, para. 370).

[83] Commission, 'Memorandum on the Accession of the European Communities to the European Convention for the Protection of Human Rights and Fundamental Freedoms' [1979] *Bulletin of the European Communities* – Supplement 2/79, especially 11 et seq.

[84] On the drafting process, see: G. de Búrca, 'The Drafting of the European Union Charter of Fundamental Rights' [2001] 26 EL Rev 126.

'by making those rights more visible in a Charter'.[85] The Charter was proclaimed in 2000, but it was then *not* legally binding. Its status was similar to the European Convention of Human Rights: it provided an informal *inspiration* but imposed no formal obligation on the European institutions.[86] This ambivalent status was immediately perceived as a constitutional problem.[87] But it took almost a decade before the Lisbon Treaty recognised the Charter as having 'the same legal value as the Treaties'.

This second section looks at the structure and content of the Charter, before investigating its relationship with the European Treaties (and the European Convention of Human Rights). The relationship is a problem, since Article 6 (1) TEU 'appends' the – amended[88] – Charter to the European Treaties. Not unlike the American 'Bill of Rights',[89] the Charter is thus placed *outside* the Union's general constitutional structure.

(a) The Charter: structure and content

The Charter 'reaffirms' the rights that result 'in particular' from the constitutional traditions common to the Member States, the European Convention of Human Rights and the general principles of European law.[90] This formulation suggested two things. First, the Charter aims to codify existing fundamental rights and was thus not intended to create 'new' ones.[91] And, second, it codifies European rights from *various* sources – and thus not solely the general principles found in the European Treaties.[92] To help identify the sources behind individual Charter articles, the Member States decided to give the Charter its

---

[85] Charter, Preamble 4. For a criticism of the idea of codification, see: J. Weiler, 'Does the European Union Truly Need a Charter of Rights' [2000] 6 ELJ 95 at 96: '[B]y drafting a list, we will be jettisoning one of the truly original features of the current constitutional architecture in the field of human rights – the ability to use the legal system of each of the Member States as an organic and living laboratory of human rights protection which then, case by case, can be adapted and adopted for the needs of the Union by the European Court in dialogue with its national counterparts.' However, not everybody may wish to live in a laboratory, and the criticism neglects the fact that, under Article 52 (2) of the Charter, the general principles continue to allow for the organic growth of unwritten human rights under the European Treaties.

[86] See: Case C-540/03, *Parliament* v. *Council*, [2006] ECR I-5769, para. 38: 'the Charter is not a legally binding instrument'.

[87] The Charter was announced at the Nice European Council, and its status was one of the questions in the 2000 Nice 'Declaration on the Future of the Union'.

[88] The 'Convention' drafting the 'Constitutional Treaty' amended the Charter. The amended version was first published in (2007) OJ C303/1 and can now be found in OJ (2010) C83/389.

[89] The American 'Bill of Rights' is the name given to the first ten amendments to the 1787 US Constitution.

[90] Charter, Preamble 5.

[91] See Protocol (No. 30) on the application of the Charter of Fundamental Rights of the European Union to Poland and to the United Kingdom, Preamble 6: 'the Charter reaffirms the rights, freedoms and principles recognised in the Union and makes those rights more visible, but does not create new rights or principles'.

[92] This might explain why the Charter contains fundamental rights that seem out of context when it comes to the competences of the European Union.

Table 13 Structure of the Charter of Fundamental Rights

Preamble	
Title I – Dignity	**Title IV – Solidarity**
Title II – Freedoms	**Title V – Citizens' Rights**
Title III – Equality	**Title VI – Justice**
Title VII – General Provisions Article 51 – Field of Application Article 52 – Scope and Interpretation of Rights and Principles Article 53 – Level of Protection Article 54 – Prohibition of Abuse of Rights	
Protocol No.30 on Poland & the United Kingdom	
Explanations	

own commentary: the 'Explanations'.[93] These 'Explanations' are not strictly legally binding, but they must be given 'due regard' in the interpretation of the Charter.[94]

The structure of the Charter is as shown in Table 13. The Charter divides the Union's fundamental rights into six classes. The classic liberal rights are covered by Titles I to III as well as Title VI. The controversial Title IV codifies the rights of workers; yet, provision is also made here for the protection of the family and the right to health care.[95] Title V deals with 'citizens' rights', that is: rights that a polity provides exclusively to its members.[96] This includes the right to vote and to stand as a candidate in elections.[97] The general principles on the interpretation and application of the Charter are finally set out in Title VII. These general provisions establish four fundamental principles. First, the Charter is addressed to the Union and will only exceptionally apply to the Member States.[98] Second, not all provisions within the Charter are 'rights', that is: directly effective entitlements to individuals. Third, the rights within the Charter can, within limits, be restricted by Union legislation.[99] Fourth, the Charter tries to establish

---

[93] Article 6 (1) TEU – second indent. These so-called 'Explanations' are published in [2007] OJ C303/17.

[94] Article 6 (1) TEU, and Article 52 (7) Charter: 'The explanations drawn up as a way of providing guidance in the interpretation of this Charter shall be given due regard by the courts of the Union and of the Member States.'

[95] See, respectively: Articles 33 and 35 of the Charter.

[96] Not all rights in this title appear to be citizens' rights. For example, Article 41 of the Charter protecting the 'right to good administration' states (emphasis added): '*Every person* has the right to have his or her affairs handled impartially, fairly and within a reasonable time by the institutions, bodies, offices and agencies of the Union.'

[97] Article 39 Charter.   [98] Article 51 Charter.   [99] Article 52 (1) Charter.

harmonious relations with the European Treaties and the European Convention, as well as constitutional traditions common to the Member States.[100]

In the context of the present section, principles two, three and four warrant special attention.[101]

(i) (Hard) rights and (soft) principles

It is important to note that the Charter makes a distinction between (hard) rights and (soft) principles.[102] Hard rights are rights that will have direct effect and can, as such, be invoked before a court. Not all provisions within the Charter are rights in this strict sense. Indeed, the Charter also recognises the existence of 'principles' in Title VII.[103]

What are these principles in the Charter, and what is their effect? The 'Explanations' offer a number of illustrations, in particular: Article 37 of the Charter dealing with 'Environmental Protection'. The provision reads: 'A high level of environmental protection and the improvement of the quality of the environment *must be integrated into the policies of the Union* and ensured in accordance with the principle of sustainable development.'[104] This wording contrasts strikingly with that of a classic right provision.[105] For it constitutes less a *limit* to governmental action than an *aim* for governmental action. Principles indeed come close to orienting objectives, which 'do not however give rise to direct claims for positive action by the Union institutions'.[106] They are not subjective rights, but objective guidelines that need to be observed.[107] Thus: 'The provisions of this Charter which contain principles may be implemented by legislative and executive acts taken by institutions[.]' 'They shall be judicially cognisable only in the interpretation of such acts and in the ruling on their legality.'[108] The difference between rights and principles is thus between a hard and a soft judicial claim. An individual will not have an (individual) right to a high level of environmental protection, but may claim that the Union violated the (governmental) principle when adopting too low a standard. And in line with the classic task of legal principles,[109] the courts must generally draw 'inspiration' from the Union principles when interpreting European law.

But how is one to distinguish between 'rights' and 'principles'? Sadly, the Charter offers no catalogue of principles. Nor are its principles neatly grouped

---

[100] Article 52 (2)-(4) as well as (6) of the Charter. But see also: Article 53 on the 'Level of Protection', which will be discussed in Section 4(b)(i) below.

[101] Principle one will also be discussed in Section 4(b) below.

[102] The distinction seems to contradict the jurisprudence of the Court with regard to fundamental *rights* as general *principles* in the context of the European Treaties. However, the best way to understand the distinction between 'rights' and 'principles' is not to see them as mutually exclusive, see: Dauses, 'Protection of Fundamental Rights' (supra n. 9), 406 and below.

[103] Article 51 (1) and 52 (5) of the Charter.   [104] Emphasis added.

[105] See Article 2 of the Charter: 'Everyone has the right to life.'

[106] 'Explanations' (supra n. 93), 35.

[107] Article 51 (1) of the Charter: 'respect the rights, observe the principles'.

[108] Article 52 (5) of the Charter.   [109] See R. Dworkin, *Taking Rights Seriously* (Duckworth, 1996).

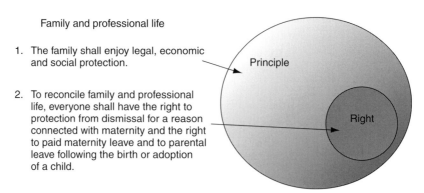

Family and professional life

1. The family shall enjoy legal, economic
    and social protection.

2. To reconcile family and professional
    life, everyone shall have the right to
    protection from dismissal for a reason
    connected with maternity and the right
    to paid maternity leave and to parental
    leave following the birth or adoption
    of a child.

Figure 25 Principles and Rights within the Charter

into a section within each substantive title. And even the wording of a particular article will not conclusively reveal whether it contains a right or a principle. But most confusingly, even a single article 'may contain both elements of a right and of a principle'.[110] How is this possible? The best way to make sense of this is to see rights and principles not as mutually exclusive concepts, but as distinct yet overlapping legal constructs.[111] 'Rights' are situational crystallisations of principles, and therefore derive from principles. A good illustration may be offered by Article 33 of the Charter on the status of the family and its relation to professional life as pictured by Figure 25.

(ii) Limitations, and 'limitations on limitations'

Every legal order protecting fundamental rights recognises that some rights can be limited to safeguard the general interest. For written bills of rights, these limitations are often specifically recognised for each constitutional right. While the Charter follows this technique for some articles,[112] it also contains a provision that establishes general rules for limitations to all fundamental rights. These general rules are set out in Article 52 of the Charter. The provision states:

> Any limitation on the exercise of the rights and freedoms recognised by this Charter must be *provided for by law* and *respect the essence of those rights and freedoms*. Subject to the principle of *proportionality*, limitations may be made

---

[110] 'Explanations' (supra n. 93), 35.

[111] In this sense, see: R. Alexy, *A Theory of Constitutional Rights* (Oxford University Press, 2002), 47 – using the Wittgensteinian concept of 'family resemblance' to describe the relationship between 'rights' and 'principles'.

[112] See Article 17 (Right to Property) of the Charter, which states in paragraph 1: 'No one may be deprived of his or her possessions, except in the public interest and in the cases and under the conditions provided for by law, subject to fair compensation being paid in good time for their loss. The use of property may be regulated by law in so far as is necessary for the general interest.'

only if they are necessary and genuinely meet objectives of general interest recognised by the Union or the need to protect the rights and freedoms of others.[113]

The provision presumes that each right within the Charter can be limited – a presumption that may be incorrect.[114] But be that as it may, any legitimate limitation must be provided for 'by law'. This (new) requirement seems to prohibit autonomous executive interventions into fundamental rights. However, the problem is this: will a limitation of someone's fundamental rights require the (democratic) legitimacy behind *formal* legislation, that is: a European law adopted under a 'legislative procedure'?[115] This view would significantly shift the balance between fundamental rights and the pursuit of the common good of the Union. The Court may thus favour a material concept of 'law' to widen the scope of legitimate limitations of fundamental rights.

In any event, Article 52 (1) of the Charter expressly mentions two constitutional limitations on right limitations. One limitation is relative, while the other is absolute in nature. According to the principle of proportionality, each restriction of fundamental rights must be necessary in light of the general interest of the Union or the rights of others. And, the provision now also confirms – it seems – the independent existence of an absolute limit by insisting that each limitation must always 'respect the essence' of the right in question.

(b) Relations with the European Treaties (and the European Convention)

The Charter is not 'inside' the Treaties, but 'outside' them. The question therefore arises as to its relationship with the European Treaties. According to Article 6 (1) TEU, the Charter has the same legal value as the Treaties and its relationship to them is governed by Title VII of the Charter. Within this Title, Article 52 (2) specifically governs the relationship between the Charter and the Treaties. It states: 'Rights recognised by this Charter for which provision is made in the Treaties shall be exercised under the conditions and within the limits defined by those Treaties.'

The Charter here adopts the Latin rule of *lex specialis derogat lex generalis*: the more specific law controls the more general law. Where the Charter codifies a fundamental right granted in the Treaties, the latter will have precedence. But this elegant theoretical solution suffers from a number of practical uncertainties. For how are we to identify the rights the Charter 'recognises' as (unwritten)

---

[113] Article 52 (1) Charter (emphasis added).

[114] Article 1 Charter expressly states: 'Human dignity is inviolable.'

[115] In favour of this view, see: D. Triantafyllou, 'The European Charter of Fundamental Rights and the "Rule of Law": Restricting Fundamental Rights by Reference' [2002] 39 CML Rev 53–64 at 61: 'Accordingly, references to "law" made by the Charter should ideally require a co-deciding participation of the European Parliament[.]' The exception the author allows relates to the 'solidarity rights' within the Charter.

fundamental rights within the European Treaties? The 'Explanations' are not of much assistance. A question to be resolved in future jurisprudence will thus be: has the Charter recognised rights from the constitutional traditions of the Member States *outside* those recognised as general principles within the European Treaties?[116] If that was the case, those Charter rights stemming directly from the common constitutional traditions of the Member States (and without equivalent general principle in the Treaties) would not be subject to the conditions and limits defined by the Treaties. And even where a Charter right does correspond to a general principle in the Treaties, the latter might have a narrower scope than the corresponding right in the Charter. In such cases, the question thus arises whether the entire Charter right is subject to the limitations established by the Treaties for the general principle.[117]

The Charter's relation to the European Convention is even more puzzling. The Charter seemingly offers a simple solution in its Article 52 (3):

> In so far as this Charter contains rights which correspond to rights guaranteed by the Convention for the Protection of Human Rights and Fundamental Freedoms, the meaning and scope of those rights shall be the same as those laid down by the said Convention. This provision shall not prevent Union law providing more extensive protection.

The provision appears to *materially* incorporate the European Convention of Human Rights into the Charter. On its surface, the first sentence of the provision thereby extends the *lex specialis* rule established in the previous paragraph for the European Treaties. It thus seems that for those Charter rights that correspond to Convention rights, the conditions and limits of the latter will apply.[118] But the logic of Convention precedence is contradicted by the second sentence. For if we allow Charter rights to adopt a higher standard of protection than that established in the European Convention,[119] it must be the Charter

---

[116] Article 52 (4) of the Charter states: 'In so far as this Charter recognises fundamental rights as they result from the constitutional traditions common to the Member States, those rights shall be interpreted in harmony with those traditions.' The 'Explanations' (supra n. 93), 34 tell us that Article 52 (4) has been based on the wording of Article 6 (3) TEU and demands that 'rather than following a rigid approach of "a lowest common denominator", the Charter rights concerned should be interpreted in a way offering a high standard of protection which is adequate for the law of the Union and in harmony with the common constitutional traditions'.

[117] This excellent point is made by Lenaerts and de Smijter, 'A Bill of Rights' (supra n. 8), 282–4. The authors compare the scope of the respective non-discrimination rights of the Charter (Article 21 of the Charter) with that of the Treaties (Article 19 TFEU). The scope of the former seems thereby broader than the scope of the latter. The question therefore arises whether the Court will subject the 'additional' scope of Article 21 of the Charter to the conditions set out in the TFEU.

[118] The 'Explanations' (supra n. 93), 33 contain a list of rights that 'at the present stage' must be regarded as corresponding to rights in the ECHR. For a recent case on the first sentence of Article 52 (3) Charter, see: Case C-279/09, *Deutsche Energiehandels- und Beratungsgesellschaft mbH* (nyr).

[119] It has been argued that this contradiction would dissolve if 'Union law' is understood as referring to the European Treaties or European legislation – and not to the Charter

that constitutes the *lex specialis* for the European Union. The wording of Article 52 (3) is thus – highly – ambivalent. The best way to resolve the textual contradiction is to interpret the provision to simply mean that 'the level of protection afforded by the Charter may never be lower than that guaranteed by the ECHR'.[120] Convention rights will thus offer a baseline – a minimum standard – for Charter rights.

3. The 'external' bill of rights: the European Convention of Human Rights

The discovery of an unwritten bill of rights and the creation of a written bill of rights for the Union had been 'internal' achievements. They did 'not result in any form of external supervision being exercised over the Union's institutions'.[121] Indeed, until recently,[122] the Union was not a party to a single international human rights treaty.[123] And by preferring *its* internal human

---

(T. Schmitz, 'Die Grundrechtscharta als Teil der Verfassung der Europäischen Union' [2004] *Europarecht* 691 at 710). But there are serious textual, historical and teleological arguments against this view. First, why should Article 52 (3) *of the Charter* not deal with the relationship between the Charter and the ECHR? Put differently, if the second sentence were confined to the higher standard established by the European Treaties, why was this not clarified in Article 6 (2) TEU or Article 6 (3) TEU? Second: historically, the European Convention Working Group had expressly argued for a higher standard within the Charter (see: Working Group II (Final Report), (2002) CONV 354/02, 7: 'The second sentence of Article 52 § 3 of the Charter serves to clarify that this article does not prevent more extensive protection already achieved or which may subsequently be provided for (i) in Union legislation and (ii) in some articles of the Charter which, although based on the ECHR, go beyond the ECHR because Union law acquis had already reached a higher level of protection (e.g., Article 47 on effective judicial protection, or Article 50 on the right not to be punished twice for the same offence). Thus, the guaranteed rights in the Charter reflect higher levels of protection in existing Union law.') Third, there are good teleological arguments for allowing a higher Charter standard, see: D. Chalmers et al., *European Union Law* (Cambridge University Press, 2010), 244: 'The ECHR covers forty-six states. It is committed to a less intense form of political integration and governs a more diverse array of situations than the European Union. It is not clear that the judgments of a court such as the European Court of Human Rights, operating in that context, should be accepted almost unquestioningly.'

[120] 'Explanations' (supra n. 93), 33. The 'Explanations' subsequently distinguish between a list of Charter rights 'where both the meaning and the scope are the same as the corresponding Articles of the ECHR', and those Charter rights 'where the meaning is the same as the corresponding Articles of the ECHR, but where the scope is wider' (*ibid.*, 33–4).

[121] I. De Jesús Butler and O. de Schutter, 'Binding the EU to International Human Rights Law' [2008] 27 YEL 277 at 278. This statement is correct only if limited to *direct* external supervision.

[122] The Union has now acceded to the United Nations Convention on the Rights of Persons with Disabilities, see: (2010) OJ L23/35. According to Article 1 of the Convention: 'The purpose of the present Convention is to promote, protect and ensure the full and equal enjoyment of all human rights and fundamental freedoms by all persons with disabilities, and to promote respect for their inherent dignity. Persons with disabilities include those who have long-term physical, mental, intellectual or sensory impairments which in interaction with various barriers may hinder their full and effective participation in society on an equal basis with others.' On the negotiating history of the Convention, see: G. de Búrca, 'The European Union in the Negotiation of the UN Disability Convention' [2010] 35 EL Rev 174.

[123] De Jesús Butler and de Schutter, 'Binding the EU' (supra n. 121), 298.

rights over any external international standard, the Court has even been accused of a 'chauvinist' and 'parochial' attitude.[124]

This bleak picture *is* distorted – at the very least, when it comes to one international human rights treaty that has always provided an external standard to the European Union: the European Convention of Human Rights. From the very beginning, the Court of Justice took the Convention very seriously,[125] sometimes even too seriously.[126] And for some time now, there has also been some form of external review of Union acts by the European Court of Human Rights. Nonetheless, there *are* many normative complexities with the European Convention as the Union's external bill of rights. This third section will look at the external standard imposed by the Convention prior to and after an eventual accession by the Union.

(a) The Convention standard for Union acts

The Union is (still) not a formal party to the European Convention. And the European Convention system has not found the European Union to have

---

[124] G. de Búrca, 'The European Court of Justice and the International Legal Order After *Kadi*' [2010] 51 *Harvard International Law Journal* 1 at 4. The author dislikes the Court's 'robustly dualist' (*ibid.*, 23) reasoning, which gave priority to the Union's own fundamental rules. Be that as it may, it is hard to see why a 'significant feature' of the *Kadi* judgment 'was the lack of direct engagement by the Court with the nature and significance of the international rules at issue in the case, or with other relevant sources of international law' (*ibid.*, 23). The accusation is, in my opinion, too harsh in light of the extensive discussion of the United Nations system in paragraphs 319 et seq. There the Court treated the matter as follows: 'According to the Commission, *so long as* under that system of sanctions the individuals or entities concerned have an acceptable opportunity to be heard through a mechanism of administrative review forming part of the United Nations legal system, the Court must not intervene in any way whatsoever ... [T]he existence, within that United Nations system, of the re-examination-procedure before the Sanctions Committee, even having regard to the amendments recently made to it, cannot give rise to generalised immunity from jurisdiction within the internal legal order of the [Union]. Indeed, such immunity, constituting a *significant derogation* from the scheme of judicial protection of fundamental rights laid down by the [EU Treaties], appears unjustified, for clearly that re-examination procedure does not offer the guarantees of judicial protection ...' (emphasis added). In a later publication, Professor de Búrca softens her charge that the European Union ignores or snubs international or regional human rights law, see: de Búrca, 'Evolution' (supra n. 9), 489.

[125] See S. Douglas-Scott, 'A Tale of Two Courts: Luxembourg, Strasbourg and the Growing European Human Rights Acquis' [2006] 43 CML Rev 629.

[126] See Case C-145/04, *Spain* v. *United Kingdom*, [2006] ECR I-7917. In that case, Spain had – rightly – argued that the extension of the right to vote in elections to the European Parliament to persons who are not citizens of a Member State violates Article 20 TFEU. Yet the Court, expressing '[a]t the outset' (*ibid.*, para. 60) its wish to comply with the judgment of the European Court of Human Rights in *Matthews* v. *United Kingdom*, [1999] 28 EHRR 361, misinterpreted the federal foundations of the European Union to pursue this aim to the end (paras. 94–5). On the idea that federal citizenship necessarily builds on the citizenship of the Member States, see: C. Schönberger, *Unionsbürger: Europas föderales Bürgerrecht in vergleichender Sicht* (Mohr Siebeck, 2006).

'succeeded' its Member States.[127] Unless the Union considered itself to be materially bound, the Convention's external supervision could not directly apply to the Union. Could the Member States thus escape their international obligations under the Convention by transferring decision-making powers to the European Union? In order to avoid a normative vacuum, the European Convention system has indeed accepted the *indirect* review of Union acts by establishing the doctrine of (limited) direct responsibility of Member States for acts of the Union. This complex construction is likely to disappear after accession.

(i) Before accession: (limited) indirect review of Union acts

Having originally found that the Union constituted an autonomous subject of international law whose actions could not be attributed to its Member States,[128] the European Commission of Human Rights and its Court subsequently changed views. In *M & Co v. Germany*,[129] the Commission found that, whereas 'the Convention does not prohibit a Member State from transferring powers to international organisations', 'a transfer of powers does not necessarily exclude a State's responsibility under the Convention with regard to the exercise of the transferred powers'.[130] This would not, however, mean that the State was to be held responsible for all actions of the Union: 'it would be contrary to the very idea of transferring powers to an international organisation to hold the Member States responsible for examining [possible violations] in each individual case'.[131]

What, then, were the conditions for this limited indirect review of Union acts? Consistent with its chosen emphasis on *State* responsibility, the Commission would not concentrate on the concrete decision of the Union, but on the State's decision to transfer powers to the Union. This transfer of powers was deemed 'not incompatible with the Convention provided that within that organisation fundamental rights will receive *an equivalent protection*'.[132] Member States would consequently not be responsible for every – compulsory – European Union act that violated the European Convention.[133]

---

[127] *Conféderation Française Démocratique Du Travail* v. *European Communities (alternatively, their Member States)* [1978] 13 DR 231, 240: 'In so far as the application is directed against the European [Union] as such the Commission points out that the European [Union] [is] not a Contracting Party to the European Convention on Human Rights (Art 66 of the Convention). To this extent the consideration of the applicant's complaint lies outside the Commission's jurisdiction ratione personae.'

[128] *Ibid.* The Commission held that the complaint was 'outside its jurisdiction ratione personae since the [Member] States by taking part in the decision of the Council of the European [Union] had not in the circumstances of the instant case exercised their "jurisdiction" within the meaning of Art 1 of the Convention'.

[129] *M & Co* v. *Federal Republic of Germany*, (1990) 64 DR 138.   [130] *Ibid.*, 145.

[131] *Ibid.*, 146.   [132] *Ibid.*, 145 (emphasis added).

[133] The decision thus introduced a distinction between the State execution of compulsory Union acts – for which there would only be limited review – and voluntary or discretionary State acts that would be subject to a full review. In *Matthews* v. *the United Kingdom* (1999) 28 EHRR 361,

In *Bosphorus*,[134] the European Court of Human Rights justified this 'middle ground' position as follows:

> The Convention does not, on the one hand, prohibit Contracting Parties from transferring sovereign power to an international (including a supranational) organisation in order to pursue co-operation in certain fields of activity. Moreover, even as the holder of such transferred sovereign power, that organisation is not itself held responsible under the Convention for proceedings before, or decisions of, its organs as long as it is not a Contracting Party. On the other hand, it has also been accepted that a Contracting Party is responsible under Article 1 of the Convention for all acts and omissions of its organs regardless of whether the act or omission in question was a consequence of domestic law or of the necessity to comply with international legal obligations. Article 1 makes no distinction as to the type of rule or measure concerned and does not exclude any part of a Contracting Party's 'jurisdiction' from scrutiny under the Convention.
>
> *In reconciling both these positions and thereby establishing the extent to which a State's action can be justified by its compliance with obligations flowing from its membership of an international organisation to which it has transferred part of its sovereignty, the Court has recognised that absolving Contracting States completely from their Convention responsibility in the areas covered by such a transfer would be incompatible with the purpose and object of the Convention ... In the Court's view, State action taken in compliance with such legal obligations is justified as long as the relevant organisation is considered to protect fundamental rights, as regards both the substantive guarantees offered and the mechanisms controlling their observance, in a manner which can be considered at least equivalent to that for which the Convention provides.* By 'equivalent' the Court means 'comparable'; any requirement that the organisation's protection be 'identical' could run counter to the interest of international co-operation pursued.[135]

In this indirect review of acts of the 'supranational' Union, the Convention Court would thus not apply its 'normal' standard.[136] Where the Union protected

---

the European Court of Human Rights declined to view Council Decision 76/787, [1976] OJ L278 and the 1976 Act concerning elections to the European Parliament as acts of the European Union. In the (correct) view of the Court they 'constituted international agreements which were freely entered into by the United Kingdom'. The Court consequently found that the UK, together with all the other Member States, was fully responsible under Article 1 of the Convention (*ibid.*, para. 33). The Court here dealt with European primary law that was 'authored' by the Member States – not the European Union. (On the European law principles governing the authorship of an act, see R. Schütze, 'The Morphology of Legislative Powers in the European Community: Legal Instruments and the Federal Division of Powers' [2006] 25 YEL 91, 98ff.) The same reasoning applies, *mutatis mutandis*, to discretionary national acts. Discretionary national acts are national acts – not Union acts – and therefore subject to a full review; see: *Bosphorus Hava Yollari Turizm ve Ticaret Anonim Sirketi* v. *Ireland*, [2006] 42 EHRR 1, paras. 148 and 157.

[134] *Bosphorus* (supra n. 133).   [135] *Ibid*, paras. 152–5 (emphasis added).

[136] For a criticism of this point, see Joint Concurring Opinion of Judges Rozakis et al. (*ibid.* paras. 3–4): 'The right of individual application is one of the basic obligations assumed by the States on ratifying the Convention. It is therefore difficult to accept that they should have been able to reduce the effectiveness of this right for persons within their jurisdiction on the ground that they have transferred certain powers to the European [Union]. For the Court to leave to the

human rights in an 'equivalent' manner to that of the Convention, the European Court of Human Rights would operate a 'presumption' that the States had not violated the Convention by transferring powers to the European Union. This presumption translates into a lower review standard for acts adopted by the European Union,[137] since the presumption of equivalent protection could only be rebutted where the actual treatment of human rights within the Union was 'manifestly deficient'.[138] The lower review standard represented a compromise between two extremes: no control, as the Union was not a member, and full control even in situations in which the Member States acted as mere agents of the Union. This compromise was 'the price for Strasbourg achieving a level of control over the EU, while respecting its autonomy as a separate legal order'.[139]

(ii) After accession: (full) direct review of Union acts

The present Strasbourg jurisprudence privileges the Union legal order in not subjecting it to the full external review by the European Court of Human Rights. However, this privilege is not the result of the Union being a 'model' member. Instead it results from the Union *not* being a formal member of the European Convention system.

Will the presumption that the Union – in principle – complies with the European Convention of Human Rights thus disappear with accession? It seems compelling that the *Bosphorus* presumption will cease once the Union accedes to the Convention. For '[b]y acceding to the Convention, the European Union will have agreed to have its legal system measured by the human rights standards of the ECHR', and will 'therefore no longer deserve special treatment'.[140] The replacement of an *indirect* review by a *direct* review should therefore – at least in theory – lead to the replacement of the *limited* review by a *full* review. Yet the life of law is not always logical, and the Strasbourg Court may well decide to cherish past experiences by applying a lower review standard to the (acceded) European Union. We must wait and see whether or not logic will trump experience.

> [Union's] judicial system the task of ensuring "equivalent protection" without retaining a means of verifying on a case-by-case basis that that protection is indeed "equivalent", would be tantamount to consenting tacitly to substitution, in the field of [European] law, of Convention standards by a [Union] standard which might be inspired by Convention standards but whose equivalence with the latter would no longer be subject to authorised scrutiny ... In spite of its relatively undefined nature, the criterion "manifestly deficient" appears to establish a relatively low threshold, which is in marked contrast to the supervision generally carried out under the European Convention on Human Rights.'

[137] J. Callewaert, 'The European Convention on Human Rights and European Union Law: A Long Way to Harmony' [2009] *European Human Rights Law Review* 768, 773: 'through the Bosphorus-presumption and its tolerance as regards "non manifest" deficiencies, the protection of fundamental rights under [European] law is policed with less strictness than under the Convention'.

[138] *Bosphorus* (supra n. 133), paras. 156–7.

[139] Douglas-Scott, 'A Tale of Two Courts' (supra n. 125), 639.

[140] T. Lock, 'EU Accession to the ECHR: Implications for Judicial Review in Strasbourg' [2010] 35 EL Rev 777 at 798.

However, what is certain already is that accession will widen the scope of application of the European Convention to include direct Union action. For in the past, the indirect review of Union acts was based on the direct review of Member State acts implementing Union acts. And this, by definition, required that a *Member State* had acted in some way.[141] Thus, in situations, where the Union institutions had acted directly upon an individual without any mediating Member State measures, this Union act could not – even indirectly – be reviewed.[142] In the absence of a connecting factor to one of the signatory States, the Union act was thus outside the Convention's jurisdiction.[143] This will definitely change once the Union accedes to the Convention. Henceforth all *direct* Union actions would fall within the jurisdiction of the Strasbourg Court. Thus, even if a lower external standard were to continue, it would henceforth apply to all Union acts – and not just acts executed by the Member States.

(b) Union accession to the European Convention: constitutional preconditions

To clarify the status of the European Convention in the European legal order, the Commission had, long ago, suggested that an accession to the Convention should be pursued.[144] But under the original Treaties, the European Union lacked the express power to conclude human rights treaties. The Commission thus proposed using the Union's general competence: Article 352 TFEU; yet – famously – the Court rejected this strategy in Opinion 2/94.[145] Since accession by the Union would have '*fundamental institutional implications*' for the Union and its Member States, it would go beyond the scope of Article 352 TFEU.[146] In the view of the Court only a subsequent Treaty amendment could provide the Union with the power of accession.

This power has now been granted by the Lisbon amendment. According to Article 6 (2) TEU, the European Union 'shall accede to the European Convention for the Protection of Human Rights and Fundamental Freedoms'. The 'shall' formulation indicates that the Union is even constitutionally obliged to become a member of this international organisation. However, the membership must not 'affect the Union's competences as defined in the Treaties',[147] and will need to pay due regard to the 'specific characteristics of the Union and Union law'.[148]

---

[141] *Ibid.*, 779.

[142] See *Connolly* v. *Fifteen Member States of the European Union* (Application No. 73274/01).

[143] Article 1 of the ECHR states: 'The High Contracting Parties shall secure to everyone within their jurisdiction the rights and freedoms defined in Section I of this Convention.'

[144] Commission, 'Memorandum on the Accession of the European Communities to the European Convention on the Protection of Human Rights and Fundamental Freedoms' (supra n. 83).

[145] Opinion 2/94 (*Accession to ECHR*), [1996] ECR I-1759.

[146] *Ibid.*, paras. 35–6 (emphasis added). On this point, see : Chapter 5 – Section 1(b)(ii) above.

[147] Article 6 (2) TEU.

[148] Protocol (No. 8) relating to Article 6 (2) of the Treaty on European Union on the Accession of the Union to the European Convention on the Protection of Human Rights and Fundamental

How and when will the Union accede to the Convention? Membership of the European Convention is now open to the European Union.[149] However, accession will principally depend on the Member States of the Union. For the Council will need to conclude the accession agreement by a unanimous decision of its member governments,[150] having previously obtained the consent of the European Parliament.[151] And unlike ordinary international agreements of the Union, the Union decision concluding the agreement will only enter into force 'after it has been approved by the Member States in accordance with their respective constitutional requirements'.[152] The Member States will thus be able to block Union accession twice: once in the Council and once outside it. And while they may be under a constitutional obligation to consent to accession as members of the Council, this is not the case for the second consent. For the duty to accede the Convention expressed in Article 6 (2) TEU will only bind the Union – and its institutions – but not the Member States.

4. The 'incorporation doctrine': European rights and national law

Will the fundamental rights of the European Union also bind the Member States? The question may come as a surprise. Yet just as not all provisions within the European Treaties are addressed to the Union,[153] not all European provisions may apply to the Member States. In fact, American constitutionalism traditionally considered the Bill of Rights exclusively addressed to the Union; and it therefore could not bind the States.[154] This partly changed with the Fourteenth Amendment in the second half of the nineteenth century,[155] but

---

Freedoms, Article 1. According to the provision, this duty includes in particular: '(a) the specific arrangements for the Union's possible participation in the control bodies of the European Convention'; and, '(b) the mechanisms necessary to ensure that proceedings by non-Member States and individual applications are correctly addressed to Member States and/or the Union as appropriate'. According to Article 2: 'The agreement referred to in Article 1 shall ensure that accession of the Union shall not affect the competences of the Union or the powers of its institutions. It shall ensure that nothing therein affects the situation of Member States in relation to the European Convention, in particular in relation to the Protocols thereto, measures taken by Member States derogating from the European Convention in accordance with Article 15 thereof and reservations to the European Convention made by Member States in accordance with Article 57 thereof.'

[149] For a long time, accession to the European Convention was confined to States (see: Article 4 of the Statute of the Council of Europe). This has recently changed with the amendment to Article 59 of the Convention, paragraph 2 of which now states: 'The European Union may accede to this Convention.' From the 'internal' perspective of European law, the new Art. 6 (2) TEU even imposes a constitutional obligation to accede: 'The Union shall accede to the European Convention for the Protection of Human Rights and Fundamental Freedoms.'

[150] Article 218 (8) TFEU – second indent.   [151] Article 218 (6) (a) (ii) TFEU.

[152] Article 218 (8) TFEU – second indent. While the procedure resembles that for the conclusion of mixed agreements, it differs from the latter in that it makes the validity of the Union decision *legally* dependent on its prior ratification by the Member States.

[153] For example, the Treaties prohibit *State* aids, but contain no prohibition of *Union* aid.

[154] *Barron* v. *Mayor of Baltimore*, 32 US (7 Pet.) 243 (1833).

[155] The (post-Civil War) Amendment states: 'No State shall make or enforce any law which shall abridge the privileges or immunities of citizens of the United States; nor shall any State deprive

it was only with the rise of the doctrine of incorporation in the early twentieth century that the Bill of Rights was considered to apply directly to the States.[156] The European legal order has, *mutatis mutandis*, followed this solution and accepted that European fundamental rights may – in certain circumstances – directly apply to the Member States.[157] This fourth – and final – section analyses those situations and circumstances in which the Courts have found the Union's three bills of rights to apply to national laws.

(a) Incorporation and general principles: implementation and derogation

Is there an incorporation doctrine within the Union's unwritten general principles? If the latter are a product of the common constitutional traditions of the Member States, how can there be a need for incorporation? The answer lies in the Union's autonomous human rights standard that may be higher than a particular national standard.[158] National legislation may thus respect national human rights, and yet violate the (higher) European standard. The Court has thus indeed invented an 'incorporation doctrine' for general principles of the Union legal order. However, this European incorporation doctrine is 'selective' in that it only applies in two situations. The first situation concerns the implementation of European law (implementation situation). The second situation concerns derogations from European law (derogation situation).

The Court expressly confirmed that European human rights bind national authorities when implementing European law in *Wachauf*.[159] European fundamental rights would be 'binding on the Member States when they *implement* [European] rules'.[160] What is the constitutional rationale behind this? Incorporation has here been justified on the ground that the Member States functionally act as the Union's decentralised executive branch.[161] It would be – black – magic, so the argument goes, if the Union could escape human rights

---

any person of life, liberty, or property, without due process of law; nor deny to any person within its jurisdiction the equal protection of the laws.'

[156] See *Gitlow* v. *New York* 268 US 652 (1925), 666: 'For present purposes we may and do assume that freedom of speech and of the press – which are protected by the First Amendment from abridgment by Congress – are among the fundamental personal rights and "liberties" protected by the due process clause of the Fourteenth Amendment from impairment by the States.' For the various theories on the (American) doctrine of incorporation, see: A. R. Amar, 'The Bill of Rights and the Fourteenth Amendment' [1991–2] 101 *Yale Law Journal* 1193.

[157] The question of incorporation is distinct from the question of direct effect. The doctrine of direct effect concerns the question whether provisions are sufficiently clear and precise. If they are, fundamental rights (like any ordinary European law) will have direct effect and need to be applied by the executive and judicial branches. By contrast, the doctrine of incorporation concerns the question *against whom* they can be applied, in this case: whether European human rights may – exceptionally – also provide a judicial review standard for *national laws*.

[158] On this point, see: Section 1(a)(i) above.

[159] Case 5/88, *Wachauf* v. *Bundesamt für Ernährung und Forstwirtschaft*, [1989] ECR 2609. The idea had been implicit in the (earlier) *Rutili* ruling, see: Case 36/75, *Rutili* v. *Ministre de l'intérieur*, (1975) ECR 1219.

[160] Case 5/88, *Wachauf* (supra n. 159), para. 19 (emphasis added).

[161] On the Member States acting as the Union executive, see: Chapter 7 – Section 4.

control by leaving the implementation of controversial European policies to the Member States. Individuals will thus be entitled to challenge national acts executing European law if they violate fundamental European rights. But while this is a reasonable rationale in situations in which the Member States strictly execute European law to the letter, should it extend to situations where the Member States are left with autonomous discretion? Will a Member State be bound to respect European fundamental rights in using *its* national competence when going beyond the floor set by European minimum harmonisation? This tricky question appears, in principle, to be answered in the positive.[162]

The Court has also come to accept a second situation in which European human rights are 'incorporated'. This is the case when Member States 'derogate' from European law. This 'derogation situation' was first accepted in *ERT*.[163] The plaintiff had been granted an exclusive licence under Greek law to broadcast television programmes, which had been violated by a local television station. In the course of national proceedings, the defendant claimed that the Greek law restricted its freedom to provide services protected under the European Treaties and also violated its fundamental right to freedom of expression. In a preliminary ruling, the European Court held that where a Member State relied on European law 'in order to justify rules which are likely to obstruct the exercise of the freedom to provide services, such justification, provided by [Union] law, must be interpreted in the light of the general principles of law *and in particular fundamental rights*'.[164] In this derogating

---

[162] Three cases support this point. In Case 5/88, *Wachauf* (supra n. 159), the Court expressly referred to the margin of appreciation left to the Member States in the implementation of European law (para. 22): 'The [Union] regulations in question accordingly leave the competent national authorities a sufficiently wide margin of appreciation to enable them to apply those rules in a manner consistent with the requirements of the protection of fundamental rights, either by giving the lessee the opportunity of keeping all or part of the reference quantity if he intends to continue milk production, or by compensating him if he undertakes to abandon such production definitively.' Second, in Case C-2/92, *The Queen* v. *Ministry of Agriculture, Fisheries and Food, ex parte Dennis Clifford Bostock*, [1994] ECR I-955), the plaintiff brought proceedings against the British Ministry of Agriculture, arguing that the United Kingdom had violated his property rights by failing to implement a compensation scheme for outgoing tenants and thus wrongly implementing European agricultural legislation. While finding that the European legislation did not require such a compensation scheme, the Court nonetheless examined whether European fundamental rights had been violated by the national legislation. This was confirmed in Case C-275/06, *Promusicae* v. *Telefónica de España*, [2008] ECR I-271. The case will be discussed in Section 4(b)(i) below. However, there are also judicial authorities against extending the implementing situation to cases where the Member States go beyond minimum harmonisation; see: Case C-2/97, *Società italiana petroli SPA (IP)* v. *Borsana*, [1998] ECR I-8597, esp. para. 40: 'Since the legislation at issue is a more stringent measure for the protection of working conditions compatible with the Treaty and results from the exercise by a Member State of the powers it has retained pursuant to Article [153] of the [FEU] Treaty, it is not for the Court to rule on whether such legislation and the penalties imposed therein are compatible with the principle of proportionality'; as well as: Case C-6/03, *Deponiezweckverband Eiterköpfe* v. *Land Rheinland-Pfalz*, [2005] ECR I-2753.

[163] Case C-260/89, *Elliniki Radiophonia Tiléorassi (ERT) et al.* v. *Dimotiki Etairia Pliroforissis and Sotirios Kouvelas and Nicolaos Avdellas et al.*, [1991] ECR I-2925.

[164] *Ibid.*, para. 43 (emphasis added).

situation, national rules would be subject to European fundamental rights, in this case: freedom of expression.

The Court's judgment in *ERT* was a silent revolution, since it implicitly overruled an earlier decision to the contrary.[165] Indeed, the constitutional rationale behind the derogation situation remains contested.[166] Moreover, the *ERT* judgment was – as many revolutions are – ambivalent about its ambit. Would European human rights apply to national measures outside the 'derogation situation'? A wider rationale had indeed been suggested in another part of the *ERT* judgment speaking of national rules falling within the scope of European law.[167] But while it is clear that a national law must first fall within the scope of European law,[168] the relationship between the derogation rationale and the wider scope rationale has never been conclusively resolved.[169] And even if the wider rationale is the right one, the question remains what exactly is meant by the phrase 'the scope of European law'. Various meanings here compete with each other. First, the Court may identify the scope of European law with the scope of existing European *legislation*.[170] Second, the formulation

---

[165] In Cases 60 and 61/84, *Cinéthèque SA and others* v. *Fédération nationale des cinémas français*, [1985] ECR 2605.

[166] See in particular: F. Jacobs, 'Human Rights in the European Union: the Role of the Court of Justice' [2001] EL Rev 331 at 336–7; and more recently: P. M. Huber, 'The Unitary Effect of the Community's Fundamental Rights: the *ERT*-Doctrine Needs to be Revisited' [2008] 14 *European Public Law* 323 at 328: 'Though this concept is approved from various sides, it is neither methodologically nor dogmatically convincing.'

[167] Case C-260/89, *ERT* (supra n. 163) para. 42: '[W]here such rules do fall within the scope of [European] law, and reference is made to the Court for a preliminary ruling, it must provide all the criteria of interpretation needed by the national court to determine whether those rules are compatible with the fundamental rights the observance of which the Court ensures and which derive in particular from the European Convention on Human Rights.' In the subsequent paragraph the Court then refers to the derogation rationale as a 'particular' expression of this wider rationale.

[168] See Case C-159/90 *Grogan*, (supra n. 35), in which the Court declared that the defendants could not invoke their European fundamental right to freedom of expression against Irish legislation prohibiting activities assisting abortion. According to the European Court, the defendants had not distributed information on abortion clinics on behalf of those clinics and it *thus followed that* 'the link between the activity of the students associations of which Mr Grogan and the other defendants are officers and medical terminations of pregnancies carried out in clinics in another Member State is too tenuous for the prohibition on the distribution of information to be capable of being regarded as a restriction within the meaning of [] the Treaty' (*ibid.*, para. 24). The national legislation thus lay outside the scope of European law (*ibid.*, para. 31).

[169] See Case C-299/95, *Kremzow* v. *Austria*, [1997] ECR I-2629, para. 16: 'The appellant in the main proceedings is an Austrian national whose situation is not connected in any way with any of the situations contemplated by the Treaty provisions on freedom of movement for persons. Whilst any deprivation of liberty may impede the person concerned from exercising his right to free movement, the Court has held that a purely hypothetical prospect of exercising that right does not establish a sufficient connection with [European] law to justify the application of [European] provisions[.]'

[170] See Case C-309/96, *Annibaldi* v. *Sindaco del Comune di Guidonia and Presidente Regione Lazio*, [1997] ECR I-7493, paras. 21 and 24: 'Against that background, it is clear, first of all, that there is nothing in the present case to suggest that the Regional Law was intended to implement a

could refer to the Union's *legislative competences*.[171] (This would broaden the applicability of incorporation to areas in which the Union has not yet adopted positive legislation.) Finally, the Court might wish to include all situations that fall within the scope of the Treaties, *period*.

(b) Incorporation and the Charter of Fundamental Rights

(i) General rules for all Member States

Will the 'Charter of Fundamental Rights *of the European Union*' be binding on the Member States?[172] The Charter answers this question in Article 51 establishing its field of application:

> The provisions of this Charter are addressed to the institutions, bodies, offices and agencies of the Union with due regard for the principle of subsidiarity *and to the Member States only when they are implementing Union law*. They shall therefore respect the rights, observe the principles and promote the application thereof in accordance with their respective powers and respecting the limits of the powers of the Union as conferred on it in the Treaties.[173]

The provision clarifies that the Charter is in principle addressed to the Union, and will only exceptionally apply to the Member States 'when they are *implementing* Union law'. This codifies the *Wachauf* jurisprudence. The article is, however, silent on the second scenario: the derogation situation. Will the incorporation doctrine under the Charter thus be more 'selective'?[174] The 'Explanations' relating to the Charter are inconclusive. They state: 'As regards the Member States, it follows unambiguously [sic] from the case-law of the Court of Justice that the requirement to respect fundamental rights defined in the context of the Union is only binding on the Member States *when they are in the scope of Union law*'.[175] The 'Explanations' substantiate this statement by

provision of [Union] law either in the sphere of agriculture or in that of the environment or culture ... Accordingly, as [European] law stands at present, national legislation such as the Regional Law, which establishes a nature and archaeological park in order to protect and enhance the value of the environment and the cultural heritage of the area concerned, applies to a situation which does not fall within the scope of [European] law.' And see also: Case C-323/08 *Rodríguez Mayor* v. *Herencia yacente de Rafael de las Heras Dávila*, (nyr), para. 59: 'However, as is clear from the findings relating to the first two questions, a situation such as that at issue in the dispute in the main proceedings does not fall within the scope of Directive 98/59, or, accordingly, within that of [Union] law.'; as well as Case C-555/07, *Kücükdevici* v. *Swedex* (nyr), esp. paras. 23–5.

171 This appears to be the meaning of the phrase in Cases 60 and 61/84, *Cinéthèque* (supra n. 165), para. 26: 'Although it is true that it is the duty of this Court to ensure observance of fundamental rights in the field of [European] law, it has no power to examine the compatibility with the European Convention of national legislation which concerns, as in this case, an area which falls within the jurisdiction of the national legislator.'

172 For an early analysis of this 'federal' question, see: P. Eeckhout, 'The EU Charter of Fundamental Rights and the Federal Question' [2002] 39 CML Rev 945.

173 Article 51 (1) of the Charter (emphasis added).

174 In favour of this view, see: M. Borowsky, 'Artikel 51' in J. Meyer (ed.), *Kommentar zur Charta der Grundrechte der Europäischen Union* (Lichtenhahn, 2006) 531 at 539.

175 'Explanations' (supra n. 93), 32 (emphasis added).

referring *both* to *Wachauf* and *ERT*; yet ultimately revert to a formulation according to which European fundamental rights 'are binding on Member States when they *implement* [Union] rules'.[176]

In light of this devilish inconsistency, the 'Explanations' have not much value. The wording of Article 51, on the other hand, is crystal clear and may prove an insurmountable textual barrier for the Court wishing to extend Charter incorporation to the 'derogation situation'.[177] Thus, unless the Court chooses to 'amend' the provision, the incorporation doctrine under the Charter would be smaller than the incorporation doctrine developed for the Union's general principles.

Be that as it may, what is the relationship between the (incorporated) European and a higher national standard of human rights? What happens where a Member State implementing European law respects the European standard, but violates the higher national standard? The problem seems to be addressed by Article 53 of the Charter. Accordingly, the Charter must not be interpreted to restrict human rights protected 'by the Member States' constitutions' 'in their respective fields of application'. The provision has been said to challenge the supremacy principle of European law,[178] and has consequently been explained away as a – legally – meaningless political 'inkblot'.[179] Yet this is not the only possible meaning of Article 53 of the Charter. An alternative reading may view the provision from the perspective of the principle of preemption. Article 53 here simply states that a higher national human rights standard will not be preempted by a lower European standard.

An illustration of the parallel application of European and national fundamental rights can be seen in *Promusicae* v. *Telefónica de España*.[180] Representing producers and publishers of musical recordings, the plaintiff had asked the defendant to disclose the identities and physical addresses of persons whom it provided with Internet services. These persons were believed to have used the KaZaA file exchange programme, thereby infringing intellectual property rights. The defendant refused the request on the ground that under Spanish law such a disclosure was solely authorised in criminal – not civil – proceedings. Promusicae responded that the national law implemented European law, and thus had to respect the European fundamental right to property. The question before the European Court therefore was: must Articles 17 and 47 of the

---

[176] *Ibid.* (emphasis added). The 'Explanations' here quote Case C-292/97, *Karlsson*, [2000] ECR I-2737, para. 37 (itself referring to Case C-2/92, *Bostock* (supra n. 162) para. 16).

[177] This view is taken by C. Barnard, 'The "Opt-Out" for the UK and Poland from the Charter of Fundmental Rights: Triumph of Rhetoric over Reality?' in S. Griller and J. Ziller (eds.), *The Lisbon Treaty : EU Constitutionalism Without a Constitutional Treaty*? (Springer, 2008), 256 at 263: 'Even if the explanations are wider, it is unlikely that they will be used to contradict the express wording of the Charter since the explanations are merely guidance on the interpretation of the Charter. The Charter will therefore apply to states only when implementing [European] law[.]'

[178] For a discussion of this point, see: J. B. Liisberg, 'Does the EU Charter of Fundamental Rights Threaten the Supremacy of Community Law?' [2001] 38 CML Rev 1171.

[179] *Ibid.*, 1198.   [180] Case C-275/06, *Promusicae* v. *Telefónica de España* (supra n. 162).

Charter 'be interpreted as requiring Member States to lay down, in order to ensure effective protection of copyright, an obligation to communicate personal data in the context of civil proceedings'?[181] Not only did the Court find that there was no such obligation,[182] it added that the existing European legislation would 'not preclude the possibility for the Member States of laying down an obligation to disclose personal data in the context of civil proceedings'.[183] A higher national standard for the protection of property was thus *not* prohibited. However, this higher national standard would need to be balanced against 'a further [European] fundamental right, namely the right that guarantees protection of personal data and hence of private life'.[184] And it was the obligation of the national court to reconcile the two fundamental rights by striking 'a fair balance' between them.[185]

In conclusion, as long as a higher national fundamental right does not clash with a different European fundamental right, the higher national standard is allowed. This permission may now be textually anchored in Article 53 of the Charter.

(ii) Special rules for Poland and the United Kingdom

The general rules governing the relationship between the Charter and the Member States are qualified for Poland and the United Kingdom.[186] The two States have a special Protocol that governs the application of the Charter to them.[187] The Protocol is not a full 'opt-out' from the Charter. It expressly requires 'the Charter to be applied and interpreted by the courts of Poland and the United Kingdom'.[188] However, opinions differ as to whether the Protocol constitutes a simple clarification for the two States – not unlike the 'Explanations';[189] or whether it does indeed represent a *partial* opt-out by establishing special principles for the two countries.[190]

---

[181] *Ibid.*, para. 41. Article 17 and Article 47 of the Charter protect, respectively, the right of property and the right of an effective remedy.

[182] *Ibid.*, para. 55.   [183] *Ibid.*, para. 54.   [184] *Ibid.*, para. 63.   [185] *Ibid.*, paras. 65 and 68.

[186] Protocol (No. 30) on the Application of the Charter of Fundamental Rights of the European Union to Poland and to the United Kingdom.

[187] The European Council has already agreed that the Czech Republic will be added to Protocol No. 30 when the Treaties are next amended; see: European Council (29–30 October 2009), Presidency Conclusions – Annex I: (Draft) Protocol on the Application of the Charter of Fundamental Rights of the European Union to the Czech Republic, esp. Article 1: 'Protocol No. 30 on the application of the Charter of Fundamental Rights of the European Union to Poland and to the United Kingdom shall apply to the Czech Republic.'

[188] Protocol No. 30, preamble 3.

[189] *Ibid.*, preamble 8: 'Noting the wish of Poland and the United Kingdom to clarify certain aspects of the application of the Charter'. For a sceptical view on the purpose of the Protocol, see: M. Dougan, 'The Treaty of Lisbon 2007: Winning Minds, Not Hearts' [2008] 45 CML Rev 617 at 670: '[T]he Protocol's primary purpose is to serve as an effective political response to a serious failure of public discourse. Indeed, the Protocol emerges as a fantasy solution to a fantasy problem[.]'

[190] Protocol No. 30, preamble 10: 'Reaffirming that references in this Protocol to the operation of specific provisions of the Charter are strictly without prejudice to the operation of other provisions of the Charter.'

The two Articles that make up the Protocol state:

Article 1

1. The Charter does not extend the ability of the Court of Justice of the European Union, or any court or tribunal of Poland or of the United Kingdom, to find that the laws, regulations or administrative provisions, practices or action of Poland or of the United Kingdom are inconsistent with the fundamental rights, freedoms and principles that it reaffirms.
2. In particular, and for the avoidance of doubt, nothing in Title IV of the Charter creates justiciable rights applicable to Poland or the United Kingdom except in so far as Poland or the United Kingdom has provided for such rights in its national law.

Article 2

To the extent that a provision of the Charter refers to national laws and practices, it shall only apply to Poland or the United Kingdom to the extent that the rights or principles that it contains are recognised in the law or practices of Poland or of the United Kingdom.

In what ways, if any, do the two articles establish special rules governing incorporation under Article 51 of the Charter? According to Article 1 (1) of the Protocol, the Charter must not *extend* the review powers of the national courts to find national laws of these States incompatible with European rights. This provision assumes that the Charter rights go beyond the status quo offered by the Union's unwritten bill of rights. This is not (yet) certain, but if the Court was to find Charter rights that did not correspond to human rights in the Treaties,[191] then Poland and the United Kingdom would not be bound by these 'additional' rights when implementing European law. The Protocol would consequently constitute a *partial* opt-out from the Charter. This is repeated 'for the avoidance of any doubt' in the context of the 'solidarity' rights in Article 1 (2).[192]

But what is the constitutional purpose behind Article 2 of the Protocol? In order to understand this provision, we need to keep in mind that some Charter rights expressly refer to 'national laws governing the exercise' of the European

---

[191] For an example of just where this might happen, see: supra n. 117.

[192] And yet, this might only be true for Britain as Declaration (No. 62) looks like a Polish 'opt-out' from the opt-out in Protocol No. 30. It states: 'Poland declares that, having regard to the tradition of social movement of "Solidarity" and its significant contribution to the struggle for social and labour rights, it fully respects social and labour rights, as established by European Union law, and in particular reaffirmed in Title IV of the Charter of Fundamental Rights of the European Union.'

right.[193] Take for example the 'right to marry and right to found a family' – a right of particular concern to Poland.[194] According to Article 9 of the Charter '[t]he right to marry and the right to found a family shall be guaranteed in accordance with the national laws governing the exercise of these rights'. Assume that the Court confirms the existence of a directly effective European right that would, in implementing situations, bind the Member States. Would twenty-seven different national laws govern the exercise of this right? Or would the Court revert to the *common* constitutional traditions of the Member States? And even if the former was the case, could a couple consisting of a Spaniard and a Pole claim a right to celebrate their same-sex marriage – a marriage that is allowed in Spain but prohibited in Poland? To avoid any normative confusion, Article 2 of the Protocol thus clarifies that any reference to national laws and practices only refers to 'law or practices of Poland or of the United Kingdom'.

(c) Incorporation and the European Convention of Human Rights?

All Member States are formal parties to the European Convention, and thus directly bound by it. Is there any need for an incorporation doctrine once the European Union accedes to the ECHR?

The answer is – surprisingly – 'Yes'. For while the substantive human rights standard established by the Convention is likely to be the same for the Union and its Member States, the formal legal effects of the Convention will differ. As an international agreement, the European Convention currently only binds the Member States under classic international law. Under classic international law, States remain free as to which domestic legal status to grant to an international treaty. For a majority of Member States,[195] the Convention indeed only enjoys a status equivalent to national legislation, that is: it is placed *below* the national

---

[193] The following Charter rights use this phrase: Article 9 – 'Right to marry and to found a family'; Article 10 – 'Freedom of thought, conscience, and religion'; Article 14 – 'Right to education'; Article 16 – 'Freedom to conduct a business'; Article 27 – 'Workers' right to information and consultation within the undertaking'; Article 28 – 'Right of collective bargaining and action'; Article 30 – 'Protection in the event of unjustified dismissal'; Article 34 – 'Social security and social assistance'; Article 35 – 'Health care'; and Article 36 – 'Access to services of general economic interest'.

[194] Declaration (No. 61) by the Republic of Poland on the Charter of Fundamental Rights of the European Union: 'The Charter does not affect in any way the right of Member States to legislate in the sphere of public morality, family law, as well as the protection of human dignity and respect for human physical and moral integrity.'

[195] On this point, see: N. Krisch, 'The Open Architecture of European Human Rights Law' [2008] 71 *Modern Law Review* 183 at 197: '[F]rom the perspective of the domestic courts national constitutional norms emerge as ultimately superior to European human rights norms and national courts as the final authorities in determining their relationship. This seems to hold more broadly: asked about their relationship to Strasbourg, 21 out of 32 responding European constitutional courts declared themselves not bound by ECtHR rulings.'

constitution. In the event of a conflict between a European Convention right and a national constitution, the latter will thus prevail.[196]

This normative hierarchy will change when the Union becomes a party to the European Convention. For once the Convention has become binding on the Union, it will also bind the Member States *qua* European law. This follows from Article 216 TFEU, according to which '[a]greements concluded by the Union are binding upon the institutions of the Union *and on its Member States*'.[197] The provision 'incorporates' all Union agreements into the national legal orders.[198] The European Convention will thus be *doubly* binding on the Member States: they are *directly* bound as parties to the Convention and *indirectly* bound as members of the Union. And with regard to the binding effect of the Convention *qua* European law, the Convention will have a hierarchical status *above* national constitutions.

(d) *Excursus*: incorporation and individuals – human rights and private actions

Traditionally, fundamental rights are solely addressed to public authorities. They are designed to protect private individuals against *public* power. Should these rights also apply to private parties? The philosophical answer should depend on the comparability of private and public conduct. For while State action generally covers the entire State territory, private action will in principle apply only locally. In light of this lower moral concern, classic constitutional doctrine generally denies the *direct* application of fundamental rights to private parties. Nonetheless, in seeing fundamental rights as the objective foundation of a constitutional order, some legal orders accept their *indirect* or *limited* direct application.[199]

How has the European constitutional order solved this question? Will its 'incorporation' entail an application to private parties? Some articles of the European Treaties have indeed been found to address private as well as public parties.[200] Some European fundamental rights will thus extend to actions by private parties. By contrast, the European Convention of Human Rights is not to address private actions directly. And the argument has been extended to the

---

[196] For the German legal order, see the relatively recent confirmation by the German Constitutional Court in *Görgülü* (2 BvR 1481/04) available at (English): www.bverfg.de/entscheidungen/rs20041014_2bvr148104en.html

[197] Emphasis added.

[198] A. Peters, 'The Position of International Law Within the European Community Legal Order' [1997] 40 *German Yearbook of International Law*, 9–78 at 34: 'transposing international law into [European] law strengthens international rules by allowing them to partake in the special effects of [European] law'.

[199] For German constitutionalism, see: BVerfGE 7, 198 (*Lüth*).

[200] See Article 157 TFEU on the right to equal pay, which the Court held to apply to private parties in Case 43/75, *Defrenne* v. *Sabena*, [1976] ECR 455, para. 39: 'The prohibition on discrimination between men and women applies not only to the action of public authorities, but also extends to all agreements which are intended to regulate paid labour collectively, as well as to contracts between individuals.'

Charter.[201] Yet even if the Charter would not directly apply to private parties, it may still have an indirect effect. This indirect or mediated effect of fundamental rights will express itself in a duty imposed on national courts to interpret European and national laws as far as possible in light of the Charter.

Conclusion

The protection of human rights is a central task of the European Constitution, where human rights are given a 'foundational' status. Unfortunately, the Union has not reserved one place for human rights, but has instead developed three bills of rights. Its unwritten bill of rights results from the general principles of Union law. The Charter of Fundamental Rights adds a written bill of rights for the Union. And the European Convention of Human Rights has always provided an external bill of rights – even prior to formal accession by the Union. This Chapter has analysed these three bills of rights and their respective relations to each other. The picture shown in Figure 26 has thereby emerged.

We saw above, that the complexity of the European human rights regime is not rooted in the existence of an external bill of rights. On the contrary, many legal problems will disappear once the Union becomes a formal party to the European Convention.[202] The main constitutional problems lie in the complex relationship between the Union's internal human rights bills. Why does the Union need two internal bills of rights? True, the existence of an unwritten bill of rights may provide a better ground for the 'organic' growth of future human

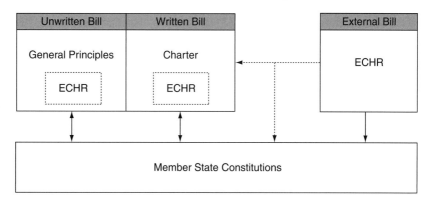

Figure 26 Relationship between the Union's three 'Bills of Rights'

---

[201] Craig, *The Lisbon Treaty* (supra n. 56), 207: '[The Charter] will not bind private parties such as employers.' If this view is accepted, there will indeed exist 'an uneasy tension in normative terms between the solely vertical scope of the Charter rights, when compared to the vertical and horizontal scope of some Treaty articles' (*ibid.*, 209).

[202] But why was there a need to 'materially' incorporate the European Convention – assuming this is what Article 6 (3) TEU and Article 52 (3) of the Charter are designed to do? Two reasons come to mind: one temporal and one normative. Temporally, a material incorporation precedes formal accession. The normative reason for a material incorporation may lie in the hierarchical status that the Convention will have once the Union has acceded to it. For even if the

rights, but why could this not have been achieved from within the Charter? The American Bill of Rights shows – with elegance and simplicity – how our Treaty drafters could have done it. For its penultimate provision states: 'The enumeration in the Constitution of certain rights shall not be construed to deny or disparage others retained by the people.'[203] The provision shows – once more – how much can be learnt from a little comparative constitutional law!

Convention eventually becomes formally binding on the Union, it will – as an international agreement of the Union – be placed below the European Treaties (and the Charter). And in an attempt to create as 'harmonious' relations as possible, the Lisbon Treaty materially incorporates the Convention into *primary* Union law.

[203] Ninth Amendment to the US Constitution.

Appendices

Contents

1. European Treaties (Chronology)   448
2. Territorial Evolution of the European Union   450
3. Extracts from the 'Luxembourg Compromise'   453
4. Extracts from James Madison's 'Federalist No. 39'   457
5. Extracts from the 1976 'European Parliament Direct Election Act'   460
6. Extracts from Decision 2009/908 on the Council Presidency   464
7. Directorate-General Home Affairs (Organigramme)   466
8. Extracts from the 'Comitology Regulation   467

1. European Treaties (Chronology)

Table 14 European Treaties

Signed	Name	Published	Entry
1951	Treaty establishing the European Coal and Steel Community	Founding Treaty[1]	1952
1952	European Defence Community	Founding Treaty	Failed
1957	Treaty establishing the European (Economic) Community	Founding Treaty[2]	1958
1957	Treaty establishing the European Atomic Energy Community	Founding Treaty	1958
1962	Protocol on the Netherlands Antilles (1962)	[1964] OJ 150	1964
1965	Protocol on the Privileges and Immunities of the European Communities	[1967] OJ 152	1967
1965	Treaty establishing a Single Council and a Single Commission of the European Communities (Merger Treaty)	[1967] OJ 152	1967
1970	Treaty amending certain Budgetary Provisions	[1971] OJ L2	1971
1972	Accession Treaty with Denmark, Ireland and the United Kingdom	[1972] OJ L73	1973
1977	Treaty amending certain financial Provisions	[1977] OJ L359	1977
1975	Treaty amending certain Provisions of the Protocol on the Statute of the European Investment Bank	[1978] OJ L91	1978
1979	Accession Treaty with Greece	[1979] OJ L291	1981
1984	Greenland Treaty	[1985] OJ L29	1985
1985	Accession Treaty with Spain and Portugal	[1985] OJ L302	1986
1986	Single European Act	[1987] OJ L169	1987
1992	Treaty on European Union	[1992] OJ C191[3]	1993
1994	Accession Treaty with Austria, Finland and Sweden	[1994] OJ C241	1995
1997	Treaty of Amsterdam	[1997] OJ C340	1999
2001	Treaty of Nice	[2001] OJ C80	2003

[1] The Treaty expired in 2002.
[2] For a consolidated version of the Treaty establishing the European Community, see: [2002] OJ C325.
[3] For a consolidated version of the Treaty on European Union, see: *ibid.*

Table 14 (cont.)

Signed	Name	Published	Entry
2003	Accession Treaty with the Czech Republic, Estonia, Cyprus, Latvia, Lithuania, Hungary, Malta, Poland, Slovenia and Slovakia	[2003] OJ L236	2004
2004	Treaty establishing a Constitution for Europe	[2004] OJ C310	Failed
2005	Accession Treaty with the Republic of Bulgaria and Romania to the European Union	[2005] OJ L157	2007
2007	Charter of Fundamental Rights of the European Union	[2007] OJ C303	2009
2007	Treaty of Lisbon amending the Treaty on European Union and the Treaty establishing the European Community	[2007] OJ C306	2009

Consolidated versions of the European Treaties

Treaty on European Union and the Treaty on the Functioning of the European Union	[2010] OJ 83
Charter of Fundamental Rights of the European Union	[2010] OJ 83
Treaty establishing the European Atomic Energy Community	[2010] OJ 84

2. Territorial Evolution of the European Union

Having started as the 'Europe of the Six', several enlargement 'waves' have increased the membership of the European Union significantly. Table 15 shows the geographical evolution of the Union.

Future membership is regulated in Article 49 TEU: '[a]ny European State' that respects the Union's values may apply to become a member of the Union. The conditions of eligibility are known as the 'Copenhagen Criteria' and state:

> Membership requires that the candidate country has achieved stability of institutions guaranteeing democracy, the rule of law, human rights and respect for and protection of minorities, the existence of a functioning market economy as well as the capacity to cope with competitive pressure and market forces within the Union. Membership presupposes the candidate's ability to take on the obligations of membership including adherence to the aims of political, economic and monetary union.[4]

Accession is not a unilateral act, but requires an accession agreement. Ultimately, the accession of a State into the Union is a *constitutional* choice left to the existing Member States. For the accession agreement, as a (material) Treaty amendment, needs to be ratified by '*all* the contracting States in accordance with their respective constitutional requirements'.[5]

Today the territorial scope of the European Union looks as in Figure 27.

---

[4] European Council, 'Conclusions of the Presidency (Copenhagen, 21–22 June 1993)' in A. G. Harryvan et al. (eds.), *Documents on European Union* (St. Martin's Press, 1997), 286–7.

[5] Article 49 TEU (emphasis added).

Table 15 Member States of the European Union (Evolution)

Founding Members	Northern Enlargement	Southern Enlargement	EFTA Enlargement	Eastern Enlargement	Candidate Countries
Belgium	Britain (1973)	Greece (1981)	Austria (1995)	Bulgaria (2007)	Croatia
France	Denmark (1973)	Portugal (1986)	Finland (1995)	Cyprus (2004)	FYRM
Germany	Ireland (1973)	Spain(1986)	Sweden (1995)	Czech Republic (2004)	Iceland
Italy				Estonia (2004)	Turkey
Luxembourg				Hungary (2004)	
Netherlands				Latvia (2004)	
				Lithuania (2004)	
				Malta (2004)	
				Poland (2004)	
				Romania (2007)	
				Slovakia (2004)	
				Slovenia (2004)	

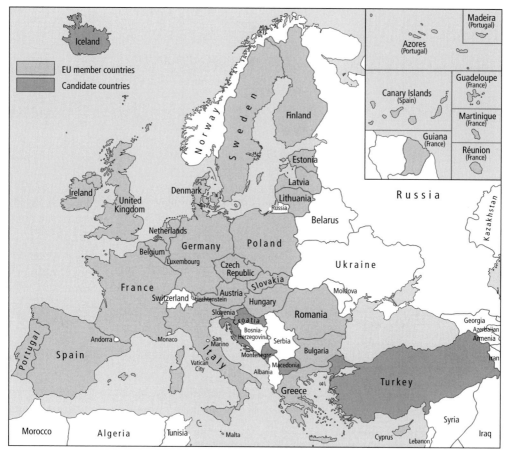

Figure 27 Territory of the European Union

3. Extracts from the 'Luxembourg Compromise'[6]

In the course of the two parts of its extraordinary session in Luxembourg on 17–18 and 28–29 January 1966, the EEC Council reached agreement on questions concerning the application of the majority rule and on relations with the Commission – questions raised by France following the crisis which began on 30 June 1965.

The texts of these Council agreements are given below in this Appendix.

It will be remembered that the Council, meeting on 30 November 1965 in the absence of the French member, examined the political aspects of the crisis and instructed its President, M. Colombo, Italian Minister of the Treasury, to inform the French Government of the joint position of the Five. At the same time the five delegations reiterated the appeal they had already made on 27 October 1965 that the French Government should take part in an extraordinary meeting, without the Commission, in order to resume its place within the Community institutions. A further meeting of the Council on 20 December 1965 afforded an opportunity to clarify various preliminary questions.

In a *note verbale* handed to the Italian Ambassador in Paris on 23 December 1965 by M. Couve de Murville, French Minister of Foreign Affairs, France made known her readiness to take part in a meeting of the Foreign Affairs Ministers in Luxembourg.

M. Werner, Prime Minister of Luxembourg and the new President of the Council, then convened the extraordinary Council session for 17 and 18 January in Luxembourg.

First part of the session (17 and 18 January 1966)

The Council first heard the French requests concerning the application of the majority rule and the role of the Commission.

In conformity with earlier French statements, M. Couve de Murville said that in questions of vital interest only unanimous agreement was politically

[6] Final Communiqué of the Extraordinary Session of the Council, Luxembourg, 17 to 18 and 28 to 29 January 1966, [1966] 3 *Bulletin of the European Communities*, 5–11.

conceivable. Without pressing for amendment of the Treaty the French Government suggested a sort of political agreement among the Six whereby the Council would abstain from deciding by majority vote if any member should so request because of the vital importance of the question for his country.

Discussion of this point revealed profound differences of opinion between the French and the other delegations. Various compromise proposals were however submitted (particularly by M. Colombo and M. Spaak). They aimed at giving the assurance that in such cases persistent efforts would be made to arrive at unanimous decisions without, however, excluding the ultimate possibility of a majority decision.

As regards the role of the Commission and its relations with the Council, M. Couve de Murville submitted the following *aide-mémoire* (later made public) as a suggestion to assist in subsequent discussions:

1. Cooperation between the Council and the Commission is the driving force of the Community and should be manifest at every stage. Consequently, before finally adopting a proposal of particular importance for all the States, the Commission should consult the Governments at an appropriate level. Such consultation would not impair the power of initiative and preparation with which the Commission is invested by the Treaty; it would simply oblige this institution to make judicious use of it.

2. It should be a rule that in no case may the Commission reveal the tenor of its proposals to the Parliament or to public opinion before they have been officially referred to the Council. *A fortiori*, the Commission may not take the initiative of publishing its proposals in the official gazette of the Communities.

3. a) The Commission often proposes to the Council decisions which, instead of dealing with the substance of the problems posed, merely give the Commission powers to act later but without specifying the measures which it will take if such powers are conferred upon it (1963 proposal of trade; certain commercial policy proposals).

   b) In certain cases the Commission can obtain authority from the Council to put into effect the rules which the latter lays down. This delegation of powers must not imply that the tasks entrusted to the Commission will then be outside the purview of the Council. True, in certain sectors such as agriculture, the Council can intervene at executive level through its representatives on the Management Committees. However, it must be noted that far from being content with this system the Commission is endeavouring to replace the Management Committees by simple advisory committees which have no hold over it (the case of Regulation 19/65 on cartels; Commission proposal of 1965 on transport).

   c) It is important that the executive powers thus vested in the Commission should be precisely circumscribed and leave no room for discretion or autonomous responsibility, failing which the balance of powers, which is a feature of the institutional structure of the Community and a basic guarantee provided by the Treaty, would not be respected.

4. The Treaty lays down that 'directives shall bind any Member State to which they are addressed as to the result to be achieved while leaving to domestic agencies competence as to the form and means'. But we cannot escape the fact that in practice the Commission very often proposes directives which set out in detail the rules to be applied. The only freedom then left to the States is to choose the form in which the contents will be clothed and to take the necessary implementing measures. It is evident that such practices constitute an attempt on the part of the Commission to cause the matters dealt with by such directives to slip out of national hands into the Community sphere of competence. Such methods should be avoided in future . . .

Second part of the session (28 and 29 January 1966)

At the meeting of 28 and 29 January the Six reached agreement and the following statements were issued:

a) Relations between the Commission and the Council

Close cooperation between the Council and the Commission is essential for the functioning and development of the Community.

In order to improve and strengthen this cooperation at every level, the Council considers that the following practical methods of cooperation should be applied, these methods to be adopted by joint agreement, on the basis of Article 162 of the EEC Treaty, without compromising the respective competences and powers of the two Institutions.

1. Before adopting any particularly important proposal, it is desirable that the Commission should take up the appropriate contacts with the Governments of the Member States, through the Permanent Representatives, without this procedure compromising the right of initiative which the Commission derives from the Treaty.
2. Proposals and any other official acts which the Commission submits to the Council and to the Member States are not to be made public until the recipients have had formal notice of them and are in possession of the texts. The 'Journal Officiel' (official gazette) should be arranged so as to show clearly which acts are of binding force. The methods to be employed for publishing those texts whose publication is required will be adopted in the context of the current work on the reorganisation of the 'Journal Officiel'.
3. The credentials of Heads of Missions of non-member States accredited to the Community will be submitted jointly to the President of the Council and to the President of the Commission, meeting together for this purpose.
4. The Council and the Commission will inform each other rapidly and fully of any approaches relating to fundamental questions made to either institution by the representatives of non-member States . . .

b) Majority voting procedure

    I. Where, in the case of decisions which may be taken by majority vote on a proposal of the Commission, very important interests of one or more partners are at stake, the Members of the Council will endeavour, within a reasonable time, to reach solutions which can be adopted by all the Members of the Council while respecting their mutual interests and those of the Community, in accordance with Article 2 of the [EEC] Treaty.

II. With regard to the preceding paragraph, the French delegation considers that where very important interests are at stake the discussion must be continued until unanimous agreement is reached.

III. The six delegations note that there is a divergence of views on what should be done in the event of a failure to reach complete agreement.

IV. The six delegations nevertheless consider that this divergence does not prevent the Community's work being resumed in accordance with the normal procedure.

The members of the Council agreed that decisions on the following should be by common consent:

a) The financial regulation for agriculture;
b) Extensions to the market organisation for fruit and vegetables;
c) The regulation on the organisation of sugar markets;
d) The regulation on the organisation of markets for oils and fats;
e) The fixing of common prices for milk, beef and veal, rice, sugar, olive oil and oil seeds.

Finally the Council drew up the following programme of work:

(1) The draft EEC and Euratom budgets will be approved by written procedure before 15 February 1966.
(2) The EEC Council will meet as soon as possible to settle as a matter of priority the problem of financing the common agricultural policy. Concurrently, discussions will be resumed on the other questions, particularly the trade negotiations in GATT and the problems of adjusting national duties on imports from non-member countries.
(3) The Representatives of the Member States' Governments will meet on the day fixed for the next Council meeting and will begin discussions on the composition of the new single Commission and on the election of the President and Vice-Presidents.

They will also agree on the date – in the first half of 1966 – when instruments of ratification of the Treaty on the merger of the institutions are to be deposited, on condition that the required parliamentary ratifications have been obtained and agreement has been reached on the composition and on the presidency and vice-presidency of the Commission.

4. Extracts from James Madison's 'Federalist No. 39'[7]

... But it was not sufficient, say the adversaries of the proposed Constitution, for the Convention to adhere to the republican form. They ought, with equal care, to have preserved the *federal* form, which regards the Union as a *confederacy* of sovereign States; instead of which, they have framed a *national* government, which regards the Union as a *consolidation* of the States. And it is asked by what authority this bold and radical innovation was undertaken? The handle which has been made of this objection requires that it should be examined with some precision.

Without enquiring into the accuracy of the distinction on which the objection is founded, it will be necessary to a just estimate of its force, first, to ascertain the real character of the government in question; secondly, to inquire how far the Convention were authorized to propose such a Government; and thirdly, how far the duty they owed to their country could supply any defect of regular authority.

First. In order to ascertain the real character of the government it may be considered in relation to the foundation on which it is to be established; to the sources from which its ordinary powers are to be drawn; to the operation of those powers; to the extent of them; and to the authority by which future changes in the Government are to be introduced.

On examining the first relation, it appears, on one hand, that the Constitution is to be founded on the assent and ratification of the people of America, given by deputies elected for the special purpose; but on the other, that this assent and ratification is to be given by the people, not as individuals composing one entire nation, but as composing the distinct and independent States to which they respectively belong. It is to be the assent and ratification of the several States, derived from the supreme authority in each State, the authority of the People themselves. The act, therefore, establishing the Constitution, will not be a *national* but a *federal* act.

That it will be a federal, and not a national act, as these terms are understood by the objectors, the act of the People, as forming so many independent States, not as forming one aggregate nation, is obvious from this single consideration, that it is to result neither from the decision of a *majority* of the people of the Union, nor from that of a *majority* of the States. It must result from the *unanimous* assent of

[7] See A. Hamilton (et al.), *The Federalist* (T. Ball, ed.) (Cambridge University Press, 2003), 184–7.

the several States that are parties to it, differing no otherwise from their ordinary assent than in its being expressed, not by the legislative authority, but by that of the people themselves. Were the People regarded in this transaction as forming one nation, the will of the majority of the whole people of the United States would bind the minority; in the same manner as the majority in each State must bind the minority; and the will of the majority must be determined either by a comparison of the individual votes; or by considering the will of the majority of the States, as evidence of the will of a majority of the people of the United States. Neither of these rules has been adopted. Each State, in ratifying the Constitution, is considered as a sovereign body, independent of all others, and only to be bound by its own voluntary act. In this relation, then, the new Constitution will, if established, be a *federal* and not a *national* Constitution.

The next relation is, to the sources from which the ordinary powers of Government are to be derived. The House of Representatives will derive its powers from the People of America, and the People will be represented in the same proportion, and on the same principle, as they are in the Legislature of a particular State. So far the government is *national*, not *federal*. The Senate, on the other hand, will derive its powers from the States, as political and co-equal societies; and these will be represented on the principle of equality in the Senate, as they now are in the existing Congress.[8] So far the government is *federal*, not *national*. The executive power will be derived from a very compound source. The immediate election of the President is to be made by the States in their political characters. The votes allotted to them are in a compound ratio, which considers them partly as distinct and co-equal societies; partly as unequal members of the same society. The eventual election, again, is to be made by that branch of the Legislature which consists of the national representatives; but in this particular act, they are to be thrown into the form of individual delegations, from so many distinct and co-equal bodies politic. From this aspect of the government, it appears to be of a mixed character, presenting at least as many *federal* as *national* features.

The difference between a federal and national Government, as it relates to the *operation of the Government*, is supposed to consist in this, that in the former, the powers operate on the political bodies composing the confederacy, in their political capacities; in the latter, on the individual citizens composing the Nation, in their individual capacities. On trying the Constitution by this criterion, it falls under the *national*, not the *federal* character; though perhaps not so completely as has been understood. In several cases and particularly in the trial of controversies to which States may be parties, they must be viewed and proceeded against in their collective and political capacities only. So far the national countenance of the Government on this side seems to be disfigured by a few federal features. But this blemish is perhaps unavoidable in any plan; and the operation of the Government on the People, in their individual capacities, in its ordinary and most essential proceedings, may, on the whole, designate it, in this relation, a *national* Government.

But if the Government be national with regard to the *operation* of its powers, it changes its aspect again when we contemplate it in relation to the *extent* of its

---

[8] That is, 'Congress' under the 1777 Articles of Confederation.

powers. The idea of a national Government involves in it, not only an authority over the individual citizens; but an indefinite supremacy over all persons and things, so far as they are objects of lawful Government. Among a People consolidated into one nation, this supremacy is completely vested in the national Legislature. Among communities united for particular purposes, it is vested partly in the general, and partly in the municipal Legislatures. In the former case, all local authorities are subordinate to the supreme; and may be controlled, directed, or abolished by it at pleasure. In the latter, the local or municipal authorities form distinct and independent portions of the supremacy, no more subject within their respective spheres to the general authority, than the general authority is subject to them, within its own sphere. In this relation, then, the proposed Government cannot be deemed a *National* one; since its jurisdiction extends to certain enumerated objects only, and leaves to the several States a residuary and inviolable sovereignty over all other objects. It is true, that in controversies relating to the boundary between the two jurisdictions, the tribunal which is ultimately to decide, is to be established under the General Government. But this does not change the principle of the case. The decision is to be impartially made, according to the rules of the Constitution; and all the usual and most effectual precautions are taken to secure this impartiality. Some such tribunal is clearly essential to prevent an appeal to the sword, and a dissolution of the compact; and that it ought to be established under the general, rather than under the local Governments, or, to speak more properly, that it could be safely established under the first alone, is a position not likely to be combated.

If we try the Constitution by its last relation, to the authority by which amendments are to be made, we find it neither wholly *national*, nor wholly *federal*. Were it wholly national, the supreme and ultimate authority would reside in the *majority* of the people of the Union; and this authority would be competent at all times, like that of a majority of every National society, to alter or abolish its established Government. Were it wholly federal, on the other hand, the concurrence of each State in the Union would be essential to every alteration that would be binding on all. The mode provided by the plan of the Convention is not founded on either of these principles. In requiring more than a majority, and particularly, in computing the proportion by *States*, not by *citizens*, it departs from the *national*, and advances towards the *federal* character: In rendering the concurrence of less than the whole number of States sufficient, it loses again the *federal*, and partakes of the *national* character.

The proposed Constitution, therefore, is, in strictness, neither a national nor a federal Constitution; but a composition of both. In its foundation it is federal, not national; in the sources from which the ordinary powers of the Government are drawn, it is partly federal, and partly national; in the operation of these powers, it is national, not federal: In the extent of them, again, it is federal, not National: And, finally, in the authoritative mode of introducing amendments, it is neither wholly federal nor wholly national.

5. Extracts from the 1976 'European Parliament Direct Election Act'[9]

Article 1

1. In each Member State, members of the European Parliament shall be elected on the basis of proportional representation, using the list system or the single transferable vote.
2. Member States may authorise voting based on a preferential list system in accordance with the procedure they adopt.
3. Elections shall be by direct universal suffrage and shall be free and secret.

Article 2

In accordance with its specific national situation, each Member State may establish constituencies for elections to the European Parliament or subdivide its electoral area in a different manner, without generally affecting the proportional nature of the voting system.

Article 3

Member States may set a minimum threshold for the allocation of seats. At national level this threshold may not exceed 5 per cent of votes cast.

Article 4

Each Member State may set a ceiling for candidates' campaign expenses.

Article 5

1. The five-year term for which members of the European Parliament are elected shall begin at the opening of the first session following each election. It may be extended or curtailed pursuant to the second subparagraph of Article 10 (2).
2. The term of office of each member of the European Parliament shall begin and end at the same time as the period referred to in paragraph 1.

Article 6

1. Members of the European Parliament shall vote on an individual and personal basis. They shall not be bound by any instructions and shall not receive a binding mandate.

---

[9] Act Concerning the Election of Members of the European Parliament by Direct Universal Suffrage, [1976] OJ L278/5. The Act has been amended several times. For an unofficial consodiated version, see: http://eur-lex.europa.eu/LexUriServ/LexUriServ.do?uri=CONSLEG:1976X1008:20020923:EN:PDF.

2. Members of the European Parliament shall enjoy the privileges and immunities applicable to them by virtue of the Protocol of 8 April 1965 on the privileges and immunities of the European Communities.

Article 7

1. The office of member of the European Parliament shall be incompatible with that of:
   - member of the Government of a Member State,
   - member of the Commission of the European Communities,
   - Judge, Advocate General or Registrar of the Court of Justice of the European Communities or of the Court of First Instance
   - member of the Board of Directors of the European Central Bank,
   - member of the Court of Auditors of the European Communities,
   - Ombudsman of the European Communities,
   - member of the Economic and Social Committee of the European Economic Community and of the European Atomic Energy Community,
   - member of committees or other bodies set up pursuant to the Treaties establishing the European Economic Community and the European Atomic Energy Community for the purpose of managing the Communities' funds or carrying out a permanent direct administrative task,
   - member of the Board of Directors, Management Committee or staff of the European Investment Bank,
   - active official or servant of the institutions of the European Communities or of the specialised bodies attached to them or of the European Central Bank.
2. From the European Parliament elections in 2004, the office of member of the European Parliament shall be incompatible with that of member of a national parliament.

   By way of derogation from that rule and without prejudice to paragraph 3:
   - members of the Irish National Parliament who are elected to the European Parliament at a subsequent poll may have a dual mandate until the next election to the Irish National Parliament, at which juncture the first subparagraph of this paragraph shall apply;
   - members of the United Kingdom Parliament who are also members of the European Parliament during the five-year term preceding election to the European Parliament in 2004 may have a dual mandate until the 2009 European Parliament elections, when the first subparagraph of this paragraph shall apply.
3. In addition, each Member State may, in the circumstances provided for in Article 7 extend rules at national level relating to incompatibility.
4. Members of the European Parliament to whom paragraphs 1, 2 and 3 become applicable in the course of the five-year period referred to in Article 3 shall be replaced in accordance with Article 12.

Article 8

Subject to the provisions of this Act, the electoral procedure shall be governed in each Member State by its national provisions.

These national provisions, which may if appropriate take account of the specific situation in the Member States, shall not affect the essentially proportional nature of the voting system.

Article 9

No one may vote more than once in any election of members of the European Parliament.

Article 10

1. Elections to the European Parliament shall be held on the date and at the times fixed by each Member State; for all Member States this date shall fall within the same period starting on a Thursday morning and ending on the following Sunday.
2. Member States may not officially make public the results of their count until after the close of polling in the Member State whose electors are the last to vote within the period referred to in paragraph 1.

Article 11

1. The Council, acting unanimously after consulting the European Parliament, shall determine the electoral period for the first elections.
2. Subsequent elections shall take place in the corresponding period in the last year of the five-year period referred to in Article 3.

   Should it prove impossible to hold the elections in the Community during that period, the Council acting unanimously shall, after consulting the European Parliament, determine, at least one year before the end of the five-year term referred to in Article 3, another electoral period which shall not be more than two months before or one month after the period fixed pursuant to the preceding subparagraph.
3. Without prejudice to Article 139 of the Treaty establishing the European Community and Article 109 of the Treaty establishing the European Atomic Energy Community, the European Parliament shall meet, without requiring to be convened, on the first Tuesday after expiry of an interval of one month from the end of the electoral period.
4. The powers of the outgoing European Parliament shall cease upon the opening of the first sitting of the new European Parliament.

Article 12

The European Parliament shall verify the credentials of members of the European Parliament. For this purpose it shall take note of the results declared officially by the Member States and shall rule on any disputes which may arise out of the provisions of this Act other than those arising out of the national provisions to which the Act refers.

Article 13

1. A seat shall fall vacant when the mandate of a member of the European Parliament ends as a result of resignation, death or withdrawal of the mandate.
2. Subject to the other provisions of this Act, each Member State shall lay down appropriate procedures for filling any seat which falls vacant during the five-year term of office referred to in Article 3 for the remainder of that period.

3. Where the law of a Member State makes explicit provision for the withdrawal of the mandate of a member of the European Parliament, that mandate shall end pursuant to those legal provisions. The competent national authorities shall inform the European Parliament thereof.

4. Where a seat falls vacant as a result of resignation or death, the President of the European Parliament shall immediately inform the competent authorities of the Member State concerned thereof.

Article 14

Should it appear necessary to adopt measures to implement this Act, the Council, acting unanimously on a proposal from the Assembly after consulting the Commission, shall adopt such measures after endeavouring to reach agreement with the Assembly in a conciliation committee consisting of the Council and representatives of the Assembly . . .

6. Extracts from Decision 2009/908 on the Council Presidency[10]

THE COUNCIL OF THE EUROPEAN UNION,

Having regard to the Treaty on European Union, and in particular Article 16 (9) thereof,

Having regard to the Treaty on the Functioning of the European Union, and in particular Article 236(b) thereof,

Having regard to the European Council Decision of 1 December 2009 on the exercise of the Presidency of the Council, and in particular Article 2, third subparagraph, and Article 4 thereof . . .

HAS ADOPTED THIS DECISION:

Article 1

The order in which the Member States shall hold the Presidency of the Council as from 1 January 2007 is set out in Council Decision of 1 January 2007 determining the order in which the office of President of the Council shall be held.

The division of this order of Presidencies into groups of three Member States, in accordance with Article 1(1) of the European Council Decision, is set out in Annex I to this Decision.

Article 2

1. Each member of a group as referred to in Article 1, second subparagraph, shall in turn chair for a six-month period all configurations of the Council, with the exception of the Foreign Affairs configuration. The other members of the group shall assist the Chair in all its responsibilities on the basis of the Council's 18-month programme.
2. The members of a group as referred to in Article 1 may decide upon alternative arrangements among themselves.
3. In either of the situations provided for in paragraphs 1 and 2, the Member States within each group shall by common accord determine the practical arrangements for their collaboration.

---

[10] Council Decision 2009/908 laying down measures for the implementation of the European Council Decision on the exercise of the Presidency of the Council, and on the chairmanship of preparatory bodies of the Council, [2009] OJ L322/28.

Article 3

The order in which the Member States will hold the Presidency as from 1 July 2020 shall be decided by the Council before 1 July 2017 . . .

ANNEX I

Germany | January-June | 2007 |
Portugal | July-December | 2007 |
Slovenia | January-June | 2008 |
France | July-December | 2008 |
Czech Republic | January-June | 2009 |
Sweden | July-December | 2009 |
Spain | January-June | 2010 |
Belgium | July-December | 2010 |
Hungary | January-June | 2011 |
Poland | July-December | 2011 |
Denmark | January-June | 2012 |
Cyprus | July-December | 2012 |
Ireland | January-June | 2013 |
Lithuania | July-December | 2013 |

Greece | January-June | 2014 |
Italy | July-December | 2014 |
Latvia | January-June | 2015 |
Luxembourg | July-December | 2015 |
Netherlands | January-June | 2016 |
Slovakia | July-December | 2016 |
Malta | January-June | 2017 |
United Kingdom | July-December | 2017 |
Estonia | January-June | 2018 |
Bulgaria | July-December | 2018 |
Austria | January-June | 2019 |
Romania | July-December | 2019 |
Finland | January-June | 2020 |

7. Directorate-General Home Affairs (Organigramme)

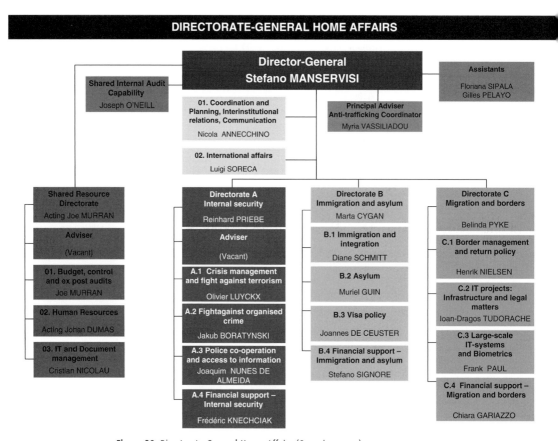

Figure 28 Directorate-General Home Affairs (Organigramme)

8. Extracts from the 'Comitology Regulation'[11]

THE EUROPEAN PARLIAMENT AND THE COUNCIL OF THE EUROPEAN UNION,

Having regard to the Treaty on the Functioning of the European Union, and in particular Article 291(3) thereof,

Having regard to the proposal from the Commission,

After transmission of the draft legislative act to the national parliaments,

Acting in accordance with the ordinary legislative procedure . . .

HAVE ADOPTED THIS REGULATION:

Article 1

Subject-matter

This Regulation lays down the rules and general principles governing the mechanisms which apply where a legally binding Union act (hereinafter a 'basic act') identifies the need for uniform conditions of implementation and requires that the adoption of implementing acts by the Commission be subject to the control of Member States.

Article 2

Selection of procedures

1. A basic act may provide for the application of the advisory procedure or the examination procedure, taking into account the nature or the impact of the implementing act required.
2. The examination procedure applies, in particular, for the adoption of:
   (a) implementing acts of general scope;
   (b) other implementing acts relating to:
       (i) programmes with substantial implications;
       (ii) the common agricultural and common fisheries policies;
       (iii) the environment, security and safety, or protection of the health or safety, of humans, animals or plants;
       (iv) the common commercial policy;
       (v) taxation.

---

[11] Regulation (EU) No 182/2011 laying down the rules and general principles concerning mechanisms for control by Member States of the Commission's exercise of implementing powers, [2011] OJ L55/13.

3. The advisory procedure applies, as a general rule, for the adoption of implementing acts not falling within the ambit of paragraph 2. However, the advisory procedure may apply for the adoption of the implementing acts referred to in paragraph 2 in duly justified cases.

Article 3

Common provisions

1. The common provisions set out in this Article shall apply to all the procedures referred to in Articles 4 to 8.
2. The Commission shall be assisted by a committee composed of representatives of the Member States. The committee shall be chaired by a representative of the Commission. The chair shall not take part in the committee vote.
3. The chair shall submit to the committee the draft implementing act to be adopted by the Commission.

   Except in duly justified cases, the chair shall convene a meeting not less than 14 days from submission of the draft implementing act and of the draft agenda to the committee. The committee shall deliver its opinion on the draft implementing act within a time limit which the chair may lay down according to the urgency of the matter. Time limits shall be proportionate and shall afford committee members early and effective opportunities to examine the draft implementing act and express their views.
4. Until the committee delivers an opinion, any committee member may suggest amendments and the chair may present amended versions of the draft implementing act.

   The chair shall endeavour to find solutions which command the widest possible support within the committee. The chair shall inform the committee of the manner in which the discussions and suggestions for amendments have been taken into account, in particular as regards those suggestions which have been largely supported within the committee.
5. In duly justified cases, the chair may obtain the committee's opinion by written procedure. The chair shall send the committee members the draft implementing act and shall lay down a time limit for delivery of an opinion according to the urgency of the matter. Any committee member who does not oppose the draft implementing act or who does not explicitly abstain from voting thereon before the expiry of that time limit shall be regarded as having tacitly agreed to the draft implementing act.

   Unless otherwise provided in the basic act, the written procedure shall be terminated without result where, within the time limit referred to in the first subparagraph, the chair so decides or a committee member so requests. In such a case, the chair shall convene a committee meeting within a reasonable time.
6. The committee's opinion shall be recorded in the minutes. Committee members shall have the right to ask for their position to be recorded in the minutes. The chair shall send the minutes to the committee members without delay.
7. Where applicable, the control mechanism shall include referral to an appeal committee.

The appeal committee shall adopt its own rules of procedure by a simple majority of its component members, on a proposal from the Commission.

Where the appeal committee is seised, it shall meet at the earliest 14 days, except in duly justified cases, and at the latest 6 weeks, after the date of referral. Without prejudice to paragraph 3, the appeal committee shall deliver its opinion within 2 months of the date of referral.

A representative of the Commission shall chair the appeal committee.

The chair shall set the date of the appeal committee meeting in close cooperation with the members of the committee, in order to enable Member States and the Commission to ensure an appropriate level of representation. By 1 April 2011, the Commission shall convene the first meeting of the appeal committee in order to adopt its rules of procedure.

Article 4

Advisory procedure

1. Where the advisory procedure applies, the committee shall deliver its opinion, if necessary by taking a vote. If the committee takes a vote, the opinion shall be delivered by a simple majority of its component members.
2. The Commission shall decide on the draft implementing act to be adopted, taking the utmost account of the conclusions drawn from the discussions within the committee and of the opinion delivered.

Article 5

Examination procedure

1. Where the examination procedure applies, the committee shall deliver its opinion by the majority laid down in Article 16(4) and (5) of the Treaty on European Union and, where applicable, Article 238(3) TFEU, for acts to be adopted on a proposal from the Commission. The votes of the representatives of the Member States within the committee shall be weighted in the manner set out in those Articles.
2. Where the committee delivers a positive opinion, the Commission shall adopt the draft implementing act.
3. Without prejudice to Article 7, if the committee delivers a negative opinion, the Commission shall not adopt the draft implementing act. Where an implementing act is deemed to be necessary, the chair may either submit an amended version of the draft implementing act to the same committee within 2 months of delivery of the negative opinion, or submit the draft implementing act within 1 month of such delivery to the appeal committee for further deliberation.
4. Where no opinion is delivered, the Commission may adopt the draft implementing act, except in the cases provided for in the second subparagraph. Where the Commission does not adopt the draft implementing act, the chair may submit to the committee an amended version thereof.

   Without prejudice to Article 7, the Commission shall not adopt the draft implementing act where:

(a) that act concerns taxation, financial services, the protection of the health or safety of humans, animals or plants, or definitive multilateral safeguard measures;

(b) the basic act provides that the draft implementing act may not be adopted where no opinion is delivered; or

(c) a simple majority of the component members of the committee opposes it.

In any of the cases referred to in the second subparagraph, where an implementing act is deemed to be necessary, the chair may either submit an amended version of that act to the same committee within 2 months of the vote, or submit the draft implementing act within 1 month of the vote to the appeal committee for further deliberation.

5. By way of derogation from paragraph 4, the following procedure shall apply for the adoption of draft definitive anti-dumping or countervailing measures, where no opinion is delivered by the committee and a simple majority of its component members opposes the draft implementing act.

The Commission shall conduct consultations with the Member States. 14 days at the earliest and 1 month at the latest after the committee meeting, the Commission shall inform the committee members of the results of those consultations and submit a draft implementing act to the appeal committee. By way of derogation from Article 3(7), the appeal committee shall meet 14 days at the earliest and 1 month at the latest after the submission of the draft implementing act. The appeal committee shall deliver its opinion in accordance with Article 6. The time limits laid down in this paragraph shall be without prejudice to the need to respect the deadlines laid down in the relevant basic acts.

Article 6

Referral to the appeal committee

1. The appeal committee shall deliver its opinion by the majority provided for in Article 5(1).

2. Until an opinion is delivered, any member of the appeal committee may suggest amendments to the draft implementing act and the chair may decide whether or not to modify it.

The chair shall endeavour to find solutions which command the widest possible support within the appeal committee.

The chair shall inform the appeal committee of the manner in which the discussions and suggestions for amendments have been taken into account, in particular as regards suggestions for amendments which have been largely supported within the appeal committee.

3. Where the appeal committee delivers a positive opinion, the Commission shall adopt the draft implementing act.

Where no opinion is delivered, the Commission may adopt the draft implementing act.

Where the appeal committee delivers a negative opinion, the Commission shall not adopt the draft implementing act.

4. By way of derogation from paragraph 3, for the adoption of definitive multilateral safeguard measures, in the absence of a positive opinion voted by the

majority provided for in Article 5(1), the Commission shall not adopt the draft measures.

5. By way of derogation from paragraph 1, until 1 September 2012, the appeal committee shall deliver its opinion on draft definitive anti-dumping or countervailing measures by a simple majority of its component members.

Article 7

Adoption of implementing acts in exceptional cases

By way of derogation from Article 5(3) and the second subparagraph of Article 5 (4), the Commission may adopt a draft implementing act where it needs to be adopted without delay in order to avoid creating a significant disruption of the markets in the area of agriculture or a risk for the financial interests of the Union within the meaning of Article 325 TFEU.

In such a case, the Commission shall immediately submit the adopted implementing act to the appeal committee. Where the appeal committee delivers a negative opinion on the adopted implementing act, the Commission shall repeal that act immediately. Where the appeal committee delivers a positive opinion or no opinion is delivered, the implementing act shall remain in force.

Article 8

Immediately applicable implementing acts

1. By way of derogation from Articles 4 and 5, a basic act may provide that, on duly justified imperative grounds of urgency, this Article is to apply.
2. The Commission shall adopt an implementing act which shall apply immediately, without its prior submission to a committee, and shall remain in force for a period not exceeding 6 months unless the basic act provides otherwise.
3. At the latest 14 days after its adoption, the chair shall submit the act referred to in paragraph 2 to the relevant committee in order to obtain its opinion.
4. Where the examination procedure applies, in the event of the committee delivering a negative opinion, the Commission shall immediately repeal the implementing act adopted in accordance with paragraph 2.
5. Where the Commission adopts provisional anti-dumping or countervailing measures, the procedure provided for in this Article shall apply. The Commission shall adopt such measures after consulting or, in cases of extreme urgency, after informing the Member States. In the latter case, consultations shall take place 10 days at the latest after notification to the Member States of the measures adopted by the Commission.

Article 9

Rules of procedure

1. Each committee shall adopt by a simple majority of its component members its own rules of procedure on the proposal of its chair, on the basis of standard rules to be drawn up by the Commission following consultation with Member States. Such standard rules shall be published by the Commission in the Official Journal of the European Union.

In so far as may be necessary, existing committees shall adapt their rules of procedure to the standard rules.

2. The principles and conditions on public access to documents and the rules on data protection applicable to the Commission shall apply to the committees.

Article 10

Information on committee proceedings

1. The Commission shall keep a register of committee proceedings which shall contain:
   (a) a list of committees;
   (b) the agendas of committee meetings;
   (c) the summary records, together with the lists of the authorities and organisations to which the persons designated by the Member States to represent them belong;
   (d) the draft implementing acts on which the committees are asked to deliver an opinion;
   (e) the voting results;
   (f) the final draft implementing acts following delivery of the opinion of the committees;
   (g) information concerning the adoption of the final draft implementing acts by the Commission; and
   (h) statistical data on the work of the committees.
2. The Commission shall also publish an annual report on the work of the committees.
3. The European Parliament and the Council shall have access to the information referred to in paragraph 1 in accordance with the applicable rules.
4. At the same time as they are sent to the committee members, the Commission shall make available to the European Parliament and the Council the documents referred to in points (b), (d) and (f) of paragraph 1 whilst also informing them of the availability of such documents.
5. The references of all documents referred to in points (a) to (g) of paragraph 1 as well as the information referred to in paragraph 1(h) shall be made public in the register.

Article 11

Right of scrutiny for the European Parliament and the Council

Where a basic act is adopted under the ordinary legislative procedure, either the European Parliament or the Council may at any time indicate to the Commission that, in its view, a draft implementing act exceeds the implementing powers provided for in the basic act. In such a case, the Commission shall review the draft implementing act, taking account of the positions expressed, and shall inform the European Parliament and the Council whether it intends to maintain, amend or withdraw the draft implementing act . . .

Index

acte clair doctrine 298–9
  see also preliminary reference procedure
adjudicatory powers *see under* judicial powers:
    competences and procedures
administrative powers *see under* executive
    powers: competences and procedures
Advocate-General 132–3
Amsterdam Treaty *see under* constitutional
    history: from Paris to Lisbon
annulment powers *see under* judicial powers:
    competences and procedures
army, European 16–18

budgets and budgetary powers 97–8, 115, 125,
    210
  Court of Auditors 146–7
    special reports 147

Charter of Fundamental Rights of the European
    Union 36, 42, 422–9
  binding status 423
  relations with European treaties (and the
    European Convention) 427–9
  structure and content 423–7
    (hard) rights and (soft) principles 425–6
    limitations and 'limitations on limitations'
      426–7
  see also European human rights
citizenship of the Union
  essential core of citizenship rights 418–19
  petitioning the European Parliament 99
  representation 31, 43–4, 61, 62–3, 64
  see also individuals and private parties
Civil Service Tribunal 128, 129, 134
Comitology 236–8
  new Comitology system 241–3
  non-addressed decisions 322–3
  old Comitology system, 230, 241, 322–3
Common Commercial Policy 193–4, 212
Common Foreign and Security Policy (CFSP)
    32, 42, 44, 103
  Common Security and Defence Policy 192
  competence of the Union 192
  decision-making and voting 114, 204–5
    institutional actors and institutional
      balance 205–6
    'specificity' of CFSP
      decision-making procedures 205–7
    voting arrangements in the Council 206–7

direct effect 314, 339–41
  economic sanctions 194
  European Courts having limited jurisdiction
    139, 260–1
  European External Action Service 110–11
  High Representative of Foreign Affairs and
    Security Policy 103, 110–11, 125, 205–6
    European Council appointing 104
    proposals developing policy of European
      Council and Council 110–11
    treaty-making and submitting
      recommendations to the Council 208
    treaty suspension proposals to the Council
      211
  relationship between CFSP and special
    external competences 195, 197–9
  sui generis nature of the CFSP competence
    200–1
Common Security and Defence Policy 192
compensation *see* damages/compensation
competences *see* executive powers:
    competences and procedures; external
    powers: competences and procedures;
    judicial powers: competences and
    procedures; legislative powers:
    competences and procedures
competition law 248–50, 251, 321, 405–7
complementary competences 168–9
conferral principle
  disapplication of European law not covered
    by the conferral principle 361–3
  review of 'specific' and 'manifest'
    violations of the principle 363
  scope of Union competences 153, 154–5, 190
consistent interpretation principle 331–4
  indirect effects: interpretation and
    implementation principles 342
  procedural autonomy of national courts
    331–4, 382, 383–4
constitutional history: from Paris to Lisbon
    9–43
  from Maastricht to Nice: the (Old) European
    Union 27–37
    Amsterdam Treaty: dividing the Third
      Pillar 33–5, 41
    decade of 'constitutional bricolage':
      Amsterdam and Nice 33–7
    First Pillar: the European Communities
      29–32, 34

constitutional history (cont.)
  Nice Treaty: limited institutional reform
    35–7, 38, 41
  Second Pillar: Common Foreign and
    Security Policy 32
  Temple structure: the three Pillars of the
    (Maastricht) Union 29–33
  Third Pillar: Justice and Home Affairs 33
  from Nice to Lisbon: the (new) European
    Union 37–44
  (failed) Constitutional Treaty: formal total
    revision 38–41, 42
  Lisbon Treaty: substantive 'total revision'
    37, 41–4
  origins of European cooperation and
    unification 7, 9–12
  from Paris to Rome: European Coal and Steel
    Community 10–18, 67, 116–17
  (failed) European Defence Community
    16–18, 24–5
  Schuman Plan 12–13
  (supranational) structure of the ECSC
    13–16, 19–20
  from Rome to Maastricht: European
    (Economic) Community 18–27, 67
  decisional supranationalism:
    governmental structure 20–3
  intergovernmental developments outside
    the EEC 23–6
  normative supranationalism: nature of
    European Law 19–20
  supranational /intergovernmental reforms
    through Single European Act 26–7
constitutional nature: a federation of States
    47–79
  American constitutional tradition:
    federalism as (inter)national law 49–53
  conclusion: the European Union as a
    'Federation of States' 77–9
  European constitutional tradition:
    international versus national law 53–9,
    213
  conceptual polarisation: 'confederation'
    versus 'federation' 54–6
  'confederations' and European federal
    thought 54–5
  early criticism: the European tradition and
    the (missing) federal genus 56–9
  federal States and European federal
    thought 55–6
  federalism as a sovereign State 53–9
  European Union in light of the American
    constitutional tradition 59–66, 213
  foundational dimension: Europe's
    'Constitutional Treaty' 60–2
  functional dimension: the division of
    powers in Europe 64–5
  institutional dimension: a European
    Union of States and peoples 62–4
  overall classification: the European Union
    on federal 'middle ground' 65–6
  European Union in light of the European
    constitutional tradition 66–77

    Europe's statist tradition unearthed: three
      constitutional denials 71–4
    excursus: Europe's democratic 'deficit' as a
      'false problem' 74–7
    international law theory: the 'Maastricht
      decision' 66–7, 68–71, 78
    sui generis theory: the 'incomparable'
      European Union 48, 66, 67–8
Constitutional Treaty see under constitutional
    history: from Paris to Lisbon
Constitutions 1–2
  creation of government institutions as central
    task of constitutions 81
  European Constitution 2–5
  and sovereignty see under sovereignty
  see also constitutional nature: a federation of
    States
coordinating competences 167–8
cooperation see duty of sincere cooperation
'Coreper' and specialised Council committees
    107–10
Council, the, 32, 104–15
  composition and configuration 20–1, 63, 99,
    105–6
    council configurations 105–6
  decision-making and voting 63, 111–14
    Ioannina Compromise 113–14
    Luxembourg Compromise 21–2, 114
    new voting /double majority system
      113–14
    qualified majority voting 21–2, 27, 31–2,
      64, 69, 111–14, 207–8
    simple majority voting 111
    triple majority system 63, 112–13
    unanimity voting 20–1, 63–4, 69, 111, 134,
      207–8
    weighed votes 63, 112–13
  European Parliament's supervisory powers
    98
  functions and powers 104, 114–15
    co-legislator 114–15, 169–70, 171–7
    controlling delegated 'legislative' and
      implementing power 236, 241–3
    judicial appointments 134
    treaty-making 207–12
  internal structure and organs 106–11
    'Coreper' and specialised Council
      committees 107–10
    excursus: High Representative of Foreign
      Affairs and Security Policy 110–11
    Presidency of the Council 104, 106–7
  review proceedings 269
Council of Europe 10, 193
Court of Auditors 100, 145–7, 263
  functions and powers 146–7
  review proceedings 269, 287
  structure and decision-making 146
Court of First Instance see General Court see
    under Court of Justice of the European
    Union
Court of Justice of the European Union 128–39
  competences
    administrative 245–7

ERTA doctrine 202–3
exclusive competences: Article 3 TFEU
    164–7
exclusive treaty powers 201–3
mixed agreements 215
Opinion 1/76 Doctrine 202
residual competence 161–2
shared competences 215
special external competences 197–8
WTO doctrine 201–2
constitutional limits to delegated acts 233–5
    delegation to European Agencies 234–5
    'essential elements' doctrine 233–4
    non-delegation doctrine/'Meroni doctrine'
        230, 235
doctrine of consistent interpretation of
    national law 331–4
draft international agreements, challenges to
    209
duty of cooperation, negative aspect to
    218–20
see also duty of sincere cooperation
effectiveness principle 387–96
enforcement of European law 65, 138
    infringement proceedings *see*
        infringement proceedings
    interim measures 136
    limiting consequences of decentralised
        enforcement 250–1
see also judicial powers: competences and
    procedures
equivalence principle 385, 386–7
European Central Bank, status and
    independence of 140
European legal order as 'new legal order'
    306–8
European primary law, effect of *see under*
    direct and indirect effect
executive subsidiarity 250
implied external powers 195, 197–9, 215
judicial appointments 100, 130, 131, 134
judicial architecture: European Court system
    129–34
    Court of Justice: composition and
        structure 130–1, 132
    creation of Court of First Instance/General
        Court 129
    excursus: Advocates-General 132–3
    General Court: composition and structure
        27, 128, 131–2, 133
    specialised court(s): Civil Service Tribunal
        128, 129, 134
judicial powers and jurisdiction *see* judicial
    powers: competences and procedures
judicial procedures 135–6
    orders and opinions 136
    voting and majority judgments 135–6
judicial reasoning: methods of interpretation
    136–8
    teleological interpretation 136–8, 153–7
judicial supranationalism 23
normative 'autonomy' of European legal
    order 60–1

preliminary rulings *see* preliminary reference
    procedure
role 128
    interpreting law 136–8, 153–7
state liability 396, 397–9
subsidiarity principle 181–4
succession doctrine 212–13, 416, 421, 430–1
supremacy of European law *see* supremacy of
    European law and preemption
'unwritten' Bill of Rights/human rights *see*
    under European human rights
unwritten general principles of European
    law, effects of 334–7
see also judicial powers: competences and
    procedures

damages/compensation 280–2, 396, 397–9,
    400–1
    state liability: the *Francovich* doctrine 396,
        397–402
        judicial breaches of European law 402–4
    see also individuals and private parties;
        liability principle
Davignon Report 24–5
decision-making and voting *see under*
    European Central Bank; European
    Commission; European Council;
    European Parliament; external powers:
    competences and procedures; Member
    States
decisions
    binding nature 309–10
    decisions: the executive instrument
        320–3
        non-addressed decisions 322–3
        specifically addressed decisions 321–2
    definition 320–1
    as direct Union law 317, 320–3
Delors Commission/Report 26, 27
democracy 2, 62–4
    degressively proportional system 90, 112
    democratic 'deficit' 74–7
    democratic legitimacy of parliamentary
        legislation 400–1
    democratic supranationalism/legitimacy
        31–2, 37, 38, 39–40, 41, 43–4
    dual democracy/legitimacy 75–7
    EU governmental system as a 'semi-
        parliamentary democracy' 99–100
    human rights setting substantive limits for
        democratic government 410
    '*Maastricht* decision' 68–71
        legitimation through European
            democratic structure 69–70
        national democracy 69
        national peoples as primary source of
            democratic legitimacy 70, 75
    voting transparency 96
    see also citizenship of the Union; European
        Parliament
development cooperation 194, 197–8
direct and indirect effect 3, 19, 305
    conclusion 344–6

direct and indirect effect (cont.)
  constitutional law: the effect of European
    primary law 310–16
    dimensions of direct effect: vertical and
      horizontal direct effect 315–16
    direct effect: from strict to lenient test
      312–14
    direct effect, strict test for 310–12
    direct applicability and direct effect 308–9,
      318–20, 324
    direct Union law: regulations and directives
      317–23
      decisions *see* decisions
      regulations *see* regulations
    external Union law: international agreements
      see international agreements
    indirect Union law: directives *see* directives
  directives 64–5, 323–37
    binding nature 309–10, 371
    definition 323
    direct effect and directives: conditions and
      limitations 323–30
    'estoppel argument' 325
    indirect effects through national and
      (primary) European law 331–7
    doctrine of consistent interpretation of
      national law 331–4
    indirect effects through the medium of
      European law 334–7
    as 'indirect legislation' 323
    no-horizontal-direct-effect rule 326–7
    exception to the rule: incidental horizontal
      direct effect 329–30
    limitation to the rule: wide definition of
      State (actions) 327–9
    preemptive capacity 368–9, 371–2
  duty of sincere cooperation
    and enforcement of European law *see*
      remedies and liabilities
    as an internal and judicial safeguard 213–14,
      216–20
      Member States as 'trustees of the union'
        217–18
      'reversed' subsidiarity: restrictions on the
        exercise of shared State power 218–20
    national courts applying European law
      289–90
    principle of mutual loyal and sincere
      cooperation 85, 216

economic sanctions 194
effectiveness principle 382–3, 387–96, 397, 398,
  405
  historical evolution of effectiveness standard
    388–93
  minimum standards 387–8
  procedural limits to the invocability of
    European law 393–6
enforcement
  enforcement actions *see under* judicial
    powers: competences and procedures
  individuals enforcing rights *see under*
    individuals and private parties

remedies and liabilities *see* remedies and
  liabilities
environmental policy 375–6, 425
equivalence principle 382–3, 384–7, 398, 405
  national courts raising European law of their
    own motion 394–5
  nature of 384
  non-discrimination: extending national
    remedies to European actions 385
  'similar' actions: the equivalence test 386–7
European Agencies 125–8
  delegation to 234–5
  functions 127
  structures and types of agencies 128
European Atomic Energy Community 12, 18, 45
European Central Bank 30, 139–45
  establishment 139
  European Council appointing President and
    Board 104, 142
  European Parliament's appointment powers
    100
  European Parliament's supervisory powers
    98
  functions and powers 144–5
  internal division of powers and decision-
    making 143–4
    voting 143–4
  organs and administrative structure 142–3
  review proceedings 269
  special status 140–1
European Coal and Steel Community *see under*
  constitutional history: from Paris to
  Lisbon
European Commission 116–28
  administrative organs 119–21
  composition and structure 117–21
    Commission's administrative organs
      119–21
    European Council determining
      composition 104
    President and 'his' college 118–19
    President elected by European Parliament
      99–100, 118
  decision-making and voting 122–3
    collective decision-making 122
    delegated powers 122–3
  and European agencies 125–8
  European Convention of Human Rights 434
  European Parliament
    appointment process, involvement in
      99–100, 229
    supervisory powers 98, 100, 227
  functions and powers 117, 123–5, 226
    delegated acts *see under* executive powers:
      competences and procedures
    infringement proceeding *see* infringement
      proceedings
    legal instruments of political leadership
      227
    legislation 123–4, 169, 171–3, 174–6
    see also executive powers: competences and
      procedures
    role within CFSP 206, 208

treaty-making and suspension 208–9, 211
informal procedures(s) of government 228–9
review proceedings 269
supranational nature 20–1, 26
European Commission of Human Rights 433–4
European Convention of Human Rights 429–35
external human rights standard for Union
acts 430–4
after accession: (full) direct review of
Union acts 433–4
before accession: (limited) indirect review
of Union acts 431–3
Union accession to the Convention:
constitutional preconditions 434–5
European Council 27, 32, 100–4
Charter of Fundamental Rights 422
composition 101
President 102–3, 125, 205
decision-making and voting 101–2, 114, 205
and development of the Union 36–7, 38–41
establishment as
semi-permanent 'government' 25–6
functions and powers 103–4
identifying interests/objectives of Union/
for CFSP 204–5, 226
law-making *see under* executive powers:
competences and procedures
legal instruments of political leadership
226–7
informal procedures(s) of government 228–9
infringement proceedings *see under* judicial
powers: competences and procedures
rise of European Council restricting
Council's executive powers 104
as a Union institution 26, 27, 28, 100–1
European Court of Human Rights 430, 433–4
European Defence Community 16–18
European Economic Community *see under*
constitutional history: from Paris to
Lisbon
European External Action Service *see under*
Common Foreign and Security Policy
(CFSP)
European human rights 162, 409–46
birth of fundamental European rights 412–19
European standard – an 'autonomous'
standard 414–18
limitations of human rights and
'limitations on limitations' 418–19
national fundamental rights 412–16
conclusions 445–6
'essential core' doctrine 418–19, 427
'external' Bill of Rights: European
Convention of Human Rights *see*
European Convention of Human Rights
fundamental rights limits and supremacy of
European law 358, 359–61
'incorporation doctrine': European Rights
and national limitations 435–45
incorporation and Charter of
Fundamental Rights 439–43
incorporation of European Convention of
Human Rights 443–4

incorporation of general principles:
implementation/derogation 436–9
incorporation and individuals – European
rights and private actions 444–5
special rules for Poland and the United
Kingdom 441–3
sources of human rights 410–11
'unwritten' Bill of Rights: human rights as
'general principles' 411–22
birth of fundamental European rights
412–19
United Nations' law: external limits to
European human rights 419–22
'written' Bill of Rights: Charter of
Fundamental Rights *see* Charter of
Fundamental Rights of the European
Union
European law
agencies as creatures of secondary European
law 126
binding legal instruments 309–10
see also decisions; directives; regulations
constitutional law 2–5
direct effect and indirect effect *see* direct and
indirect effect
direct Union law *see under* direct and indirect
effect
draft law, Member State challenging 104
enforcement of *see* remedies and liabilities
European Commission overseeing
application of European law 124–5, 127
European legal order as a 'new legal order'
306–8
European Parliament's legislative powers
96–7
indirect Union law *see under* direct and
indirect effect
interpretation *see* interpretation
and judicial powers *see* judicial powers:
competences and procedures
legal authority of the EU deriving from
Member States 70–1, 72–3
legislative powers *see* legislative powers:
competences and procedures
liabilities *see* liability principle
and monism and dualism 306–8, 318, 323,
337–8, 350, 363
national peoples as primary source of
democratic legitimacy for European
laws 70
non-binding legal instruments 309–10
normative 'autonomy' of European legal
order 60–1
European legal order adopting 'originality
hypothesis' 57–8, 61, 66
normative supranationalism: nature of
European law 19–20
preemption *see* legislative preemption
'primacy' of international agreements over
European law 372, 373–4
remedies and liabilities *see* remedies and
liabilities
secondary law 309–10

European law (cont.)
  supremacy of European law *see* supremacy of
    European law and preemption
  Treaty amendment 45–6, 61–2
    competences 203
    and the European Council 103
    'unilateral' nature of European law 60
European Monetary System 24, 27
European Parliament 87–100
  ascendancy limiting the Council's legislative
    role 104
  co-decision procedure 31–2, 43–4, 174–6
  and Commission *see under* European
    Commission
  composition 62–3
    European Council determining 104
  cooperation procedure 27, 31–2, 43
  decision-making and voting
    decisional supranationalism 22–3
    democratic support for EU policies 69–70
    plenary decision-making and voting 94–6,
      100
  formation: electing Parliament 87–93
    directly elected Parliament replacing an
      assembly 22, 62–3, 87–8
    Members of the European Parliament and
      political parties 91–3
    Parliament's size and composition 88–90
  internal structure: Parliamentary 'organs'
    93–4
    Committees 93–4, 98–9
    President and Vice-Presidents 93
  Parliamentary powers 96–100
    budgetary powers 97–8, 115
    controlling delegated 'legislative' and
      implementing power 236, 241–3
    elective powers: appointment of the Union
      officers 99–100
    legislative powers/co-legislator with
      Council 64, 96–7, 169–70, 171–7
    powers widened by treaties 43–4, 96
    role within CFSP 206
    supervisory powers 98–9, 100
    treaty-making 209, 210–11
    review proceedings 269
European Political Cooperation 24–5,
  26, 32
European Security and Defence Policy 32
European System of Central Banks 30, 140–1
  see also European Central Bank
European Union (EU)
  competences and legislation *see* legislative
    powers: competences and procedures
  constitutional history and origins *see*
    constitutional history: from Paris to
    Lisbon
  governmental structure *see* governmental
    structure: Union institutions
  nature of *see* constitutional nature: a
    federation of States
exclusive competences 164–6
executive powers: competences and procedures
  223–57

administrative powers: centralised
  enforcement 243–50
  administrative powers and the subsidiarity
    principle 248–50
  scope of the Union's administrative
    powers 244–8
administrative powers: decentralised
  enforcement 250–5
  effects of national administrative acts
    251–2
  national administrative autonomy and its
    limits 253–5
Article 290 TFEU: delegation of 'legislative'
  power 231–8
  judicial safeguards: constitutional limits to
    delegated acts 233–5
  political safeguards: control rights of the
    Union legislator 236–8
  scope of Article 290 TFEU 238–40
Article 291 TFEU: 'conferral' of executive
  power 238–43
  constitutional safeguards for
    implementing legislation 240–3
  scope of Article 291 TFEU 238–40
conclusion 256–7
governmental powers: the Union's dual
  executive 225–9
  informal procedures(s) of government
    228–9
  legal instruments of political leadership
    226–7
law-making powers: delegated and
  implementing acts 230–43
  autonomous and delegated regulatory
    powers 230–1
  'conferral' of executive power: Article 291
    TFEU 238–43
  delegation of 'legislative' power: Articles
    290 TFEU 231–8
nature of executive powers 223–5
see also legislative powers: competences and
  procedures
external powers: competences and procedures
  187–222
conclusion 220–2
external competences of the Union 190–9
  CFSP *see* Common Foreign and Security
    Policy (CFSP)
  competences of the Union on foreign
    affairs 190–2
  relationship between CFSP and special
    external competences 195, 197–9
  residual treaty power: Article 216 TFEU
    194–6
  Union's objectives 190
  Union's special external powers 192–4
external decision-making procedures 204–13
  CFSP decision-making *see* Common
    Foreign and Security Policy (CFSP)
  initiation and negotiation 208–9
  modification and suspension
    (termination) 211–12
  signing and conclusion 210–11

unilateral external acts and international
agreements 204–5
Union's (ordinary)
treaty-making procedure 207–13
Union succession to international
agreements of Member States 212–13
foreign affairs emerging as a distinct public
function 188
nature of external competences 199–204
Article 3 (2) TFEU: subsequent exclusive
treaty powers 201–4
subsequent exclusivity: criticising
constitutional theory 203–4
sui generis nature of the CFSP competence
200–1
three lines of exclusivity: codifying
constitutional practice 201–3
sharing external power: constitutional
safeguards for unity 213–20
duty of cooperation: an internal and judicial
safeguard 213–14, 216–20
Member States as 'Trustees of the Union'
217–18
mixed agreements: an international and
political safeguard 213, 214–16
'reversed' subsidiarity: restrictions on the
exercise of shared State power
218–20

federalism *see* constitutional nature: a
federation of States
France
Constitutional Treaty 38, 39–40
dual executive 225–6
'empty chair' policy 21–2
French Revolution 72
fundamental rights *see* European human rights

Gaulle, General Charles de 21
General Court *see under* Court of Justice of the
European Union
Germany 65–6, 213
administrative powers 244
disapplication of European law not covered
by the conferral principle 361–3
review of 'specific' and 'manifest'
violations of conferral principle 363
'*Maastricht* decision' 68–71, 361–2
relative supremacy of European law 359–61,
362
governmental structure: Union institutions
80–115, 116–48
Commission *see* European Commission
conclusion 147–8
Council *see* Council
Court of Auditors *see* Court of Auditors
Court of Justice *see* Court of Justice of the
European Union
European Central Bank *see* European Central
Bank
European Council *see* European Council
European Parliament *see* European
Parliament

European Treaties establishing institutions
81–2
'separation-of-powers' principle and the EU
83–7
principle of inter-institutional balance 84–5
types of governmental powers or functions
85–7

harmonisation 157–9, 245–6, 324
administrative cooperation 254–5
complementary competences excluding
harmonisation 376–8
field preemption 365–6
national procedural laws 381–3, 396
shared competences and fixing minimum
harmonisation 374
competences for minimum harmonisation
375–6
High Representative of Foreign Affairs and
Security Policy *see under* Common
Foreign and Security Policy (CFSP)
horizontal direct effect *see under* direct and
indirect effect
human rights *see* European human rights
humanitarian aid 194

implied powers, doctrine of 195, 197–9, 215
'incorporation doctrine' *see under* European
human rights
indirect actions *see* preliminary reference
procedure
indirect effect *see* direct and indirect effect
individuals and private parties
citizenship of the Union *see* citizenship of the
Union
enforcing international treaties 310–12
enforcing rights
direct effect 315–16, 318–20, 323–30
indirect union law: directives 323–37
monism and dualism 306–8
no-horizontal-direct-effect rule *see under*
directives
specifically addressed decisions 321–2
State liability: the *Francovich* doctrine 396,
397–402
see also remedies and liabilities
human rights *see* European human rights
instruments with direct effects on individuals
64–5, 67, 245–7, 317
see also decisions; regulations
judicial review 262, 265, 270–3, 283, 288
collateral review 275–6
indirect review through preliminary
rulings 276–8
proportionality principle 267–8
standing 273–5
substantive conditions for liability 280–2
see also judicial powers: competences and
procedures
privacy, right to 228–9
private liability: the *Courage* doctrine 405–7
rights from Treaty obligations 19
and the State 71–2

infringement proceedings 124–5, 254, 260
   brought by European Commission 124–5
   and Member States 283–5
   'international' infringement proceedings 311
   letters of formal notice and reasoned
      opinions 284
   and Union institutions 287–9
   see also judicial powers: competences and
      procedures
institutions *see* governmental structure: Union
   institutions
inter-institutional balance principle 84–5
internal market
   completing 26–7
   harmonisation competence 157–9
international agreements 115, 125, 136, 154–5,
   194
   Article 3 (2) TFEU: subsequent exclusive
      treaty powers 201–4
      subsequent exclusivity: criticising
         constitutional theory 203–4
      three lines of exclusivity: codifying
         constitutional practice 201–3
   definition 337–8
   direct effect of Union agreements 338–42
      conditions for direct effect 339–41
      dimensions of direct effect 341–2
   draft international agreements, challenges to
      209
   European Convention of Human Rights *see*
      European Convention of Human Rights
   external Union law 337–43
   indirect effects: interpretation and
      implementation principles 342–3
      principle of consistent interpretation 342
      principle of implementation 342–3
   preemptive capacity 372–4
      capacity of double preemption 374
   residual treaty power: Article 216 TFEU 193,
      194–6
   sharing external power: constitutional
      safeguards for unity 213–20
      duty of cooperation *see* duty of sincere
         cooperation
      mixed agreements: an international and
         political safeguard 213, 214–16
   supremacy of European law over
      international treaties of Member States
      352–4
   Union's (ordinary) treaty-making procedure
      204–5, 207–13
      initiation and negotiation 208–9
      modification and suspension
         (termination) 211–12
      signing and conclusion 210–11
      unilateral external acts and international
         agreements 204–5
      Union succession to international
         agreements of Member States 212–13,
         416, 421, 430–1
International Labour Organisation 218
international law

American constitutional tradition:
   federalism as (inter)national law 49–53
constitutions and treaties 56–9
enforcement of international law norms 380
European constitutional tradition *see*
   constitutional nature: a federation of
   States
and European law 19–20, 68–71
   independence of European legal order
      from classic international law 306–8
   'primacy' of international agreements over
      European law 372, 373–4
international agreements *see* international
   agreements/treaties
international law hypothesis and
   international legal order 57–8
international law theory and EU *see under*
   constitutional nature: a federation of
   States
international organisations *see* international
   organisations
and national law 47–8
   monism and dualism 306, 318, 323, 337–8
   see also under constitutional nature: a
      federation of States
recognising only States 54–5
States as sovereign subjects 213–20
unanimous decision-making and
   international law 20–1, 63–4, 69
international organisations 66, 110–11, 154–5,
   193
   EU's inability to participate in 217–18
interpretation
   application of law and interpretation of law
      291–2
   consistent interpretation of national law *see*
      consistent interpretation principle
   indirect effects: interpretation and
      implementation principles 342–3
      principle of consistent interpretation 342
      principle of implementation 342–3
   international agreements/treaties, 154–5,
      372–3
   interpretative prerogatives of national courts
      385
   preemption doctrine as a federal theory of
      interpretation 368
   preliminary references, interpretation of law
      on 291–2, 299–301
   principles and methods of interpretation of
      law 136–8
      teleological interpretation 136–8, 153–7

judges and the judiciary
   appointments 100, 130, 131, 134
   human rights, protecting 410
   powers *see* judicial powers: competences and
      procedures
   State liability for judicial breaches of
      European law 402–4
      independence of judiciary not undermined
         403

see also Court of Justice of the European
     Union; national courts
judicial powers: competences and procedures
     258–302
  adjudicatory powers: enforcement actions
     283–9
     enforcement actions against Member
        States *see under* Member States
     enforcement action against the Union:
        failure to act 287–9
  adjudicatory powers: preliminary rulings
     138, 276–8, 289–301
  annulment powers: judicial review 262–78
     acts which can/cannot be reviewed 263–4
     indirect review of European law 138, 260,
        275–8
     reviewable bodies 263
     the existence of a 'reviewable' act 263–4
     legal standing before the European Court
        268–75
     legitimate grounds for review 264–8
  conclusion 301–2
  definition of judicial power 260
  direct and indirect actions 138, 260
  indirect review of European law 138, 260,
     275–8
     collateral review: the plea of illegality
        275–6
     indirect review through preliminary
        rulings 276–8
  infringement proceedings *see* infringement
     proceedings
  jurisdiction and judicial powers 138–9
     direct and indirect actions 138, 260
     judicial competence and procedures 261–1
     jurisdictional gaps 139, 260–1
     preliminary references 291–2
  legal standing before the European Court
     268–75
     individual applicants/private parties
        270–5
     Lisbon formulation and its interpretative
        problems 273–5
     non-privileged applicants 269
     Plaumann test 271–2, 274–5
     privileged applicants 269
     Rome formulation and its judicial
        interpretation 270–3
     semi-privileged applicants 269
  legitimate grounds for review 264–8
     'formal' and 'substantive' grounds 265–7
     infringement of an essential procedural
        requirement 266
     infringement of the Treaties 266–7
     lack of competence 265–6
     misuse of powers 266
     proportionality principle: substantive
        grounds 267–8
  preliminary references *see* preliminary
     reference procedure
  remedial powers: liability actions 278–82
     procedural conditions: from dependent to
        independent action 279–80

     substantive conditions: from
        Schöppenstedt to *Bergaderm* 280–2
  judicial review *see under* judicial powers:
     competences and procedures
Justice and Home Affairs 33–5, 44

Kelsen, Hans 56–8

Laeken meeting and Declaration 36–7, 38, 43
law *see* European law; international law;
     national law
legislative powers: competences and procedures
     151–86
  categories of Union competence 162–9
     complementary competences: Article 6
        TFEU 168–9
     coordinating competences: Article 5 TFEU
        167–8
     exclusive competences: Article 3 TFEU
        164–6
     shared competences: Article 4 TFEU 164–7
  conclusion 184–6
  concept of legislation and approach of the EU
     151–2
  legislative procedures: ordinary and special
     169–77
     ordinary legislative procedure 171–6
     special legislative procedures 176–7
  ordinary legislative procedure 171–6
     constitutional practice: informal trilogues
        174–6
     constitutional theory: formal text 171–4
  principle of subsidiarity *see* subsidiarity
     principle
  scope of Union competences 152–62
     conferral principle 153, 154–5, 190
     general competences of the Union 157–62
     harmonisation competence 157–9
     legislative competence 153
     residual competence 160–2
     teleological interpretation 153–7
  see also executive powers: competences and
     procedures
legislative preemption 363–8
  competence limits to preemption 374–8
     competences for minimum harmonisation
        374, 375–6
     complementary competences excluding
        harmonisation 374, 376–8
  conclusion 378–9
  constitutional limits to legislative
     preemption 368–78
     competence limits to preemption 374–8
     Union instruments and their preemptive
        capacity 369–74
  meaning of doctrine of preemption 364
  modes of preemption: express and implied
     preemption 367–8
  preemption categories: relative effects of
     preemption 364–7
     field preemption 365–6, 369–71
     obstacle preemption 366
     rule preemption 366–7

legislative preemption (cont.)
  preemptive capacity of directives 368–9, 371–2
  preemptive capacity of international
    agreements 372–4
  preemptive capacity of regulations 368–71
  see also supremacy of European law and
    preemption
liability principle 396–407
  private liability: the *Courage* doctrine 405–7
  state liability: the *Francovich* doctrine 396,
    397–9
    three conditions for State liability 399–402
    State liability for judicial breaches of
      European law 402–4
Lisbon Treaty see under constitutional history:
  from Paris to Lisbon
Locke, John 188
loyal and sincere cooperation see duty of sincere
  cooperation
Luxembourg Compromise 21–2, 114, 207, 216

Madison, James 49–52
Maastricht Treaty
  international law theory: '*Maastricht*
    decision' 66–7, 68–71, 78
  from Maastricht to Nice see under
    constitutional history: from Paris to
    Lisbon
Member States
  Comitology system 241–3
  competences see legislative powers:
    competences and procedures
  courts see national courts
  decision-making and voting 63, 69
    Luxembourg Compromise 21–2
    ratification of Treaty amendments 45–6,
      61–2
    veto powers 63–4
    weighed votes 63, 112–13
  decisions 321–2
  directives 323–5, 327–9
    doctrine of consistent interpretation of
      national law 331–4
  economic policies, coordinating 115
  eligibility conditions for States seeking
    membership 103
  enforcement actions against Member States
    283–7
    judicial enforcement through financial
      sanctions 286–7
    procedural conditions under Article 258
      TFEU 283–5
  enforcement of European law see remedies
    and liabilities
  human rights/national fundamental rights
    412–16
  see also European human rights
  'incorporation doctrine': European rights
    and national limitations 435–45
    general rules for all Member States 439–41
    incorporation and Charter of
      Fundamental Rights 439–43
    incorporation of European Convention of
      Human Rights 443–4

  incorporation of general principles:
    implementation/derogation 436–9
    special rules for Poland and the United
      Kingdom 441–3
  infringement proceedings see infringement
    proceedings
  international agreements
    binding Member States 337–8
    challenging draft international agreements
      209
    duty of cooperation see duty of sincere
      cooperation
    and human rights 414
    law and order 139, 260–1
    mixed agreements 213, 214–16
    Union succession to international
      agreements of Member States 212–13,
      416, 421, 430–1
  see also international agreements
  legal authority of the EU deriving from
    Member States 70–1, 72–3
  national law 47–8
    American constitutional tradition:
      federalism as (inter)national law
      49–53
    constitutional tradition see constitutional
      nature: a federation of States
    federal treaty 58
    and preemption see legislative preemption
  no-horizontal-direct-effect rule and wide
    definition of State (actions) 327–9
  obligations to implement European law 64–5
  preliminary references see under judicial
    powers: competences and procedures
  regulations 317–20
  remedies see remedies and liabilities
  review proceedings 269
  role within CFSP 206
  sovereign equality and the EU 63–4, 70–1,
    78–9, 87, 112
  see also sovereignty
  State liability see liability principle
  supremacy of European law see under
    supremacy of European law and
    preemption
MEPs 91–3
mixed agreements 213, 214–16
Montesquieu, Baron Charles de 83–4
mutual recognition 23, 251–2

national courts 128–9, 132, 134, 139
  consistent interpretation of national law see
    consistent interpretation principle
  enforcement of European law see remedies
    and liabilities
  'executive' nature of supremacy:
    disapplication not invalidation 355–8
  see also supremacy and preemption
  interpretative prerogatives 385
  preliminary references from see preliminary
    reference procedure
  procedural autonomy of Member States see
    remedies and liabilities
  role in applying European law 289–90

national law 47–8
  American constitutional tradition:
    federalism as (inter)national law 49–53
  European constitutional tradition *see*
    constitutional nature: a federation of
    States
  federal treaty 58
national Parliaments 179–81
national procedural autonomy principle 381
negative integration 23
Netherlands and the Constitutional Treaty 38,
  39–40
Nice Treaty *see under* constitutional history:
  from Paris to Lisbon
no-horizontal-direct-effect rule *see under*
  directives
non-discrimination 312–14
  effectiveness principle 389–91
  extending national remedies to European
    actions 385
  'similar' actions: the equivalence test 386–7

Ombudsman, European 99
  appointment 100
open method of coordination 115
Organisation for European Economic
  Cooperation 10

passerelles 103
Pillars, First, Second and Third *see under*
  constitutional history: from Paris to
  Lisbon
Pléven Plan/René Pléven 16
Poland 441–3
Police and Judicial Cooperation in Criminal
  Matters (PJCC) 34, 44
political groups, European 92–3
positive integration 23, 26–7
preemption *see* legislative preemption
preliminary reference procedure 138, 260,
  289–301
  conditions for a preliminary ruling 292–6
    necessary questions 295–6
    national courts and tribunals 293–5
  indirect review through preliminary rulings
    276–8
  jurisdiction of the European Court 291–2
  legal nature of preliminary rulings 299–301
  obligation to refer and 'acte clair' 296–9
    acte clair doctrine 298–9
  rejecting preliminary ruling requests 295–6
proportionality principle 182, 184, 267–8
  'essential core' doctrine 418–19, 427
  limitations/restrictions of human rights
    418–19, 427
  proportionality test 267–8

regulations 64–5
  binding nature 309–10, 369
  definition 317
  as direct Union law 317–20
  preemptive capacity 368–71
  regulations: the 'legislative' instrument 317–20

  direct application and direct effect 318–20
  general application in all Member States
    317–18
remedies and liabilities 380–408
  conclusion 407–8
  (consistent) interpretation principle *see*
    consistent interpretation principle
  duty of sincere cooperation
    ensuring fulfilment of Treaty obligations
      250–1
    principles of equivalence and of
      effectiveness 382–3
    procedural autonomy of Member States
      253–4, 382–3
  effectiveness principle 382–3, 387–96, 397,
    398, 405
    historical evolution of effectiveness
      standard 388–93
    minimum standards 387–8
    procedural limits to the invocability of
      European law 393–6
  equivalence principle 382–3, 384–7, 398, 405
    national courts raising European law of
      their own motion 394–5
    nature of 384
    non-discrimination: extending national
      remedies to European actions 385
    'similar' actions: the equivalence test
      386–7
  liability principle *see* liability principle
  Member States primarily enforcing
    enforcement of European law 244, 247,
      250–1
    effects of national administrative acts 251–2
    national administrative autonomy and its
      limits 253–5
    procedural autonomy of Member States in
      enforcing European law 381–3
    relative 382–3
residual competence 160–2
review, judicial *see under* judicial powers:
  competences and procedures

sanctions
  economic sanctions 194
  judicial enforcement through financial
    sanctions 286–7
Schengen Agreement /Area 24–5, 33
  incorporated into European Union 35
Schmitt, Carl 56, 58–9
Schuman Plan/ Robert Schuman 12–13
'separation-of-powers' principle 83–7
shared competences 164–7
  see also legislative preemption
Spaak Report/ Paul-Henry Spaak 18
specialised court(s) *see under* Court of Justice of
  the European Union
sovereignty 47–8
  as an emotional question 57
  and the EU 78–9, 152, 213, 220
    constitution 66, 68, 71, 73
    EU's powers remaining enumerated
      powers 64–5, 66, 184

sovereignty (cont.)
  review of 'specific' and 'manifest'
      violations of conferral principle 363
  and State sovereignty 48, 53–4, 66
  see also constitutional nature: a federation of
      States
  and federalism 53–4
    American constitutional tradition:
        federalism as (inter)national law 49–53
    'confederation' versus 'federation' 54–9
    indivisibility of sovereignty 53–4, 57, 66, 68,
        71, 73, 78–9
    divisibility of sovereignty 78–9
    international treaties, interpretation of 154–5
    and Member States see under Member States
    the 'people' and sovereignty 71–2, 73, 75
    sovereign Parliament 152
    and a Union of States 49–53, 213, 217, 220
standing see under judicial powers:
        competences and procedures
States
  federal States see constitutional nature: a
      federation of States
  Member States see Member States
  national law 47–8
    American constitutional tradition:
        federalism as (inter)national law 49–53
    constitutional tradition see constitutional
        nature: a federation of States
  federal treaty 58
  sovereignty see sovereignty
  State liability see liability principle
Stockholm Programme 228–9
subsidiarity principle 177–84, 203
  and administrative powers 248–50
  competition law 248–50
  meaning of 177–8, 248
    definition of executive subsidiarity 249–50
    procedural standard: subsidiarity as political
        safeguard of federalism 178–81
    'reversed' subsidiarity: restrictions on the
        exercise of shared State power
        218–20
    substantive standard: subsidiarity as a
        judicial safeguard 181–4
    tests 178, 181–4
succession doctrine 212–13, 416, 421, 430–1
sui generis theory see under constitutional
        nature: a federation of States
supranationalism 48, 66, 67–8
  see also constitutional history: from Paris to
        Lisbon
supremacy of European law and preemption
        347–79
  European perspective: absolute supremacy
        349–58
    absolute scope of the supremacy principle
        350–4
    'executive' nature of supremacy:
        disapplication not invalidation 355–8

legislative preemption see legislative
        preemption
  meaning of supremacy 364
  national perspective: relative supremacy
        358–63
    competences limits; from 'Maastricht' to
        'Mangold' 361–3
    fundamental rights limits: the 'so-long'
        jurisprudence 359–61
  principles of preemption and supremacy 348
  supremacy over internal law of Member
        States 3, 19–20, 60–1, 64–5, 350–2
  supremacy over international treaties of
        Member States 352–4

Tocqueville, Alexis de 52–3
treaties see international agreements
TREVI mechanism 24–5, 33
trustees doctrine 217–18

United Kingdom
  Charter of Fundamental Rights 441–3
    partial 'opt-out' through the Protocol
        442–3
  courts and judiciary 295, 297
  dual executive 225–6
  legislation 169, 185
  rule of law, definition of 265
  sovereign Parliament 152, 350
United Nations 193
  Charter 71
    fundamental rights 416, 419–22
    United Nations' law: external limits to
        European human rights 419–22
  Security Council Resolutions 194
United States
  administrative powers 243–4
  agencies 125
  American Revolution 72
  Constitution 3, 49–53, 81, 160, 225–6
    Bill of Rights 435–6
    mixed format of the constitutional
        structure 52–3
    'separation-of-powers' principle 83–4
  rule of law, definition of 265
  Supreme Court 136, 259–60, 364–5
    preemption doctrine 367–8

vertical direct effect see under direct and
        indirect effect
voting see under Court of Justice of the
        European Union; European Central
        Bank; European Commission;
        European Council; European
        Parliament; Member States

Werner Report 24
Western European Union 10, 32, 44
World Trade Organization 339–41
  WTO Agreement 339–40, 342–3